PRACTICAL COOKERY

FOR THE LEVEL 2 PROFESSIONAL COOKERY DIPLOMA

3RD EDITION

DAVID FOSKETT
NEIL RIPPINGTON
PATRICIA PASKINS
STEVE THORPE

HODDER
EDUCATION
AN HACHETTE UK COMPANY

Orders: please contact Bookpoint Ltd, 130 Milton Park, Abingdon, Oxon OX14 4SB. Telephone: (44) 01235 827720. Fax: (44) 01235 400454. Lines are open from 9.00 to 5.00, Monday to Saturday, with a 24-hour message answering service. You can also order through our website www.hoddereducation.co.uk

If you have any comments to make about this, or any of our other titles, please send them to educationenquiries@hodder.co.uk

British Library Cataloguing in Publication Data

A catalogue record for this title is available from the British Library

ISBN: 978 1 471 83961 0

This edition published 2015.

Impression number   10 9 8 7 6 5 4 3 2 1

Year   2015, 2016, 2017, 2018

Hachette UK's policy is to use papers that are natural, renewable and recyclable products and made from wood grown in sustainable forests. The logging and manufacturing processes are expected to conform to the environmental regulations of the country of origin.

Typeset by DC Graphic Design Limited, Swanley Village, Kent.

Printed in India for Hodder Education, an Hachette UK Company, 338 Euston Road, London NW1 3BH.

Contents

Foreword

I'm delighted to be asked to write this foreword to *Practical Cookery*.

There's no doubt that training to be a professional chef takes hard work and dedication, but for me nothing beats working with food – experimenting, exploring new techniques and discovering new flavours. I've spent years cooking the same dishes over and over, perfecting the techniques and seeking out the best ways to harness flavour. Practical Cookery will help you as you embark on this process: it provides you with all of the classic recipes, as well the basic skills, techniques and knowledge you'll need when working in the professional kitchen. It will be a point of reference for you to return to time and again throughout your career as you hone your skills.

My approach has also been to question and test culinary ideas, and to combine this with more traditional kitchen skills. While learning the foundations is important, so too is a natural curiosity and a desire to learn about every aspect of gastronomy, including exploring latest principles and techniques. It is this combination of the traditional with the modern that is at the heart of the Practical Cookery approach.

I wish you every success with your course, and with your career in the professional kitchen.

Heston Bluemthal

How to use this book

This book has been written to cover everything you need for the Level 2 Diploma in Professional Cookery. The book is divided into 15 chapters, each covering one unit of your course.

You will find the following features in the book:

Learning objectives at the start of each chapter describe exactly what you need to know and be able to do to complete the course.

Step-by-step photo sequences guide you through important preparation, cooking and finishing techniques.

Take it further boxes include links to other useful sources of information on certain topics in case you want to find out more.

Important **key terms** are defined in each chapter.

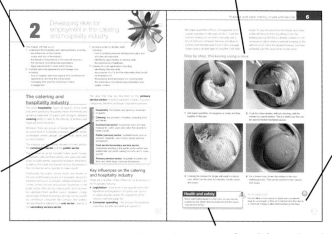

Professional tips give useful tips, information and advice from professional chefs.

Activities, including short questions, group activities and practical tasks, are included throughout each chapter to help you to develop your knowledge and skills.

Important **health and safety points** are highlighted as a feature throughout – make sure you follow these to stay safe in the kitchen.

The following features can be used to help you to prepare for assessment:

- **Assessment recipes** are particularly suitable for practical tests, but always refer to requirements set by your awarding organisation.
- **Test yourself** questions at the end of each chapter help you to test your knowledge and prepare for short-answer and multiple-choice tests.
- **Practice assignment tasks** are included for some units and will help you to prepare for assignments.

Refer to the 'Preparing for assessment' section on page x for more guidance on assessment and how this book can help you to prepare.

In the recipes, the main methods of cookery are shown by icons. So if you want to practise shallow frying for example, look for the relevant icon. They look like this:

Recipes also include the following features:

Ingredients lists are provided for making smaller and larger quantities.

Nutritional data is included for most recipes to help you make informed choices about what to cook and eat.

Healthy eating tips provide suggestions on how recipes can be adapted to make them healthier.

Variation boxes suggest alternative ingredients, cooking methods or presentation, finishing and serving styles that could be used.

Accessing the videos

There are free videos on the website. Look out for the QR codes throughout the book.

To view the videos you will need a QR code reader for your smartphone/tablet. There are many free readers available, depending on the smartphone/tablet you are using.

Once you have downloaded a QR code reader, simply open the reader app and use it to take a photo of the code. The file will then load on your smartphone/tablet.

If you cannot read the QR code or you are using a computer, the weblink next to the code will take you directly to the same place.

Dynamic Learning is an online subscription solution that supports teachers and students with high quality content and unique tools. Dynamic Learning incorporates elements that all work together to give you the ultimate classroom and homework resource.

Teaching and Learning titles include interactive resources, lesson-planning tools, self-marking tests and assessments. Teachers can:
- Use the Lesson Builder to plan and deliver outstanding lessons
- Share lessons and resources with students and colleagues
- Track student progress with Tests and Assessments

Teachers can also combine their own trusted resources alongside those from **Practical Cookery for Level 2 Professional Cookery Diploma**, which has a whole host of informative and interactive resources including:
- Schemes of work providing complete guidance on delivering all VRQ units
- Video demonstrations of key skills and techniques
- Interactive quizzes to practise and consolidate learning
- PowerPoint presentations to explain important concepts and generate discussion

Practical Cookery for Level 2 Professional Cookery Diploma is available as a **Whiteboard eTextbook** an online interactive version of the printed textbook that enable teachers to:
- Display interactive pages to their class
- Add notes and highlight areas
- Add double page spreads into lesson plans

Additionally the **Student eTextbook** of **Practical Cookery for Level 2 Professional Cookery Diploma** is a downloadable version of the printed textbook that teachers can assign to students so they can:
- Download and view on any device or browser
- Add, edit and synchronise notes across two devices
- Access their personal copy on the move

To find out more and sign up for free trials visit: **www.hoddereducation.co.uk/dynamiclearning**

Acknowledgements

We are grateful to Watts Farms for providing much of the fruit and vegetables shown in the photographs. Watts Farms is a family-run fresh product business specialising in the growing, packing and supply of a wide range of produce from spinach, baby leaf salads, herbs and legumes to fruit, chillies, asparagus, brassicas and specialist interest crops.

New nutritional analysis for this book was carried out by Annemarie Aburrow (Expert Dietitian – Nutrition & Dietetic Consultancy) and Jane Krause (JK Health & Nutrition).

Some of the nutritional analysis was created for earlier editions by Joanne Tucker (University of West London), Jenny Arthur, Dr Jenny Poulter, Jane Cliff and Pat Bacon.

Photography

Most of the photos in this book are by Andrew Callaghan of Callaghan Studios/ the photography work could not have been done without the generous help of the authors and their colleagues and students at the University of West London (UWL) and University College Birmingham (UCB). The publishers would particularly like to acknowledge the following for their work.

Gary Farrelly and Ketharanathan Vasanthan organised the cookery at UWL. They were assisted in the kitchen by:
- Tia-Louise Hudson Halsey
- Khloe Best
- Freya Massingham
- Grimaldy Cassidy Dos Santos
- Violeta Saninta
- Amilda Venancio
- Livio Capillera
- James Cher
- Jonathon Bowers
- Rachel Shelly
- Josephine Barone

Neil Rippington organised the photography at UCB. He was assisted in the kitchen by Richard Taylor.

The authors and publishers are grateful to everyone involved for their hard work.

Picture credits

Every effort has been made to trace the copyright holders of material reproduced here. The authors and publishers would like to thank the following for permission to reproduce copyright illustrations:

p. 6 © WavebreakMediaMicro – Fotolia; p. 32 © erwinova – Fotolia; p. 41 © spinetta – Fotolia; p. 42 © karam miri – Fotolia; p. 48 © Stephen Barnes/Technology/Alamy; p. 56 © Medioimages/Photodisc/Getty/Thinkstock; p. 57 © stocksolutions – Fotolia; p. 60 bottom © Africa Studio – Fotolia; p. 61 left © ranplett/ iStockphoto. com; p. 61 right © Gail Philpott/Alamy; p. 62 © alex9500 – Fotolia; p. 64 © legaa – Fotolia; p. 82 © iStockphoto. com; p. 83 © Jason Alden/Rex Feature; p. 176 right © Lilyana Vynogradova – Fotolia; p. 185 © Africa Studio – Fotolia; p. 351 © Alexandra – Fotolia; p. 406 bottom left © Meawpong – Fotolia; p. 406 top right © joanna wnuk – Fotolia; p. 406 centre © ftlaudgirl – Fotolia; p. 406 bottom right © Gray wall studio – Fotolia; p. 408 © Getty Images/iStockphoto/Thinkstock; p. 409 left © B. and E. Dudzinscy – Fotolia; p. 409 right © kuvona – Fotolia; p. 414 © Mara Zemgaliete – Fotolia; p. 415 © matin – Fotolia; p. 452 © baibaz – Fotolia; p. 453 © WavebreakmediaMicro – Fotolia.

The photos on pages 19, 20, 75, 78, 176 (left), 190, 191, 192, 226, 252, 253, 257, 258, 259, 260, 263, 264, 265 (top right), 267, 268, 293, 323, 325, 326, 328, 329, 330, 331, 338, 340, 344, 348, 349, 353, 354, 355, 356, 362, 366, 369, 376, 389, 397, 412, 414, 436, 437, 529 are © Sam Bailey/ Hodder Education

Except where stated above, photographs are by Andrew Callaghan and illustrations by Barking Dog Art and DC Graphic Design Limited. Crown copyright material is licensed under the Open Government Licence v1.0

Preparing for assessment

Chefs are assessed regularly in many different ways: each meal that is served is evaluated by the customer, who will consider many things about their meal experience and often provide feedback.

As part of professional development, through education, training and skills updating, there are many opportunities for an individual chef to gain an indication of how well they are doing, as well as offering opportunities to provide feedback on things that could be improved.

Assessment of the Level 2 Diploma in Professional Cookery

For the Level 2 Diploma in Professional Cookery, assessment takes place at given times through the development of the course and covers a number of different tasks and assessments. These are set by the awarding organisation and the centre offering the programme, and include some of the following examples of assessment and testing.

Knowledge assessment

This includes completion of set exercises and written or oral questioning that enable you to show your individual understanding of a given subject area. This will include the current legislation in relation to providing food for sale, the techniques and methods used to produce dishes to meet customer requirements, product knowledge and an understanding of traditional and contemporary cooking methods. You may be asked to complete a paper-based or online multiple-choice test, answer a series of short-answer questions to test your knowledge, or complete an assignment. Assignments are usually divided into a series of tasks in different formats. You may, for example, be asked to produce a leaflet, information booklet or presentation.

Skills assessment (practical tasks)

A set of practical tasks that are set across all areas of the programme; these normally cover one complete dish. Tutors or mentors use this process to evaluate your progress and are part of a development programme for individual chefs.

Practical assessment (synoptic tests)

Synoptic tests are practical skills tests reflecting a menu concept, with multiple dishes and covering a wide variety of skills. They are often split to show kitchen and pastry skills as separate tests or opportunities. The dishes are expected to be served in order. There is normally an overall mark achieved.

Different awarding organisations have different methods of assessment. The table below summarises the assessment methods for City and Guilds and Pearson EDI for the Level 2 Diploma in Professional Cookery. Assessment methods for other awarding organisations may vary. For up-to-date information on assessment, you should always refer to the guidelines provided by your awarding organisation.

Unit	Assessment methods	
	City and Guilds Level 2 Diploma in Professional Cookery	Pearson Level 2 Diploma in Professional Cookery
Food safety in catering	Multiple-choice test (online or paper based)	Multiple-choice test (online or paper based)
Developing skills for employment in the catering and hospitality industry	Assignment	Assignment
Health and safety in catering and hospitality	Assignment	Assignment
Healthier foods and special diets	Assignment or multiple-choice test	Multiple-choice test (online or paper based)
Catering operations, costs and menu planning	Assignment	Assignment
Prepare and cook stocks, soups and sauces	Short-answer questions / Observation of performance (synoptic practical assessment)	Short-answer questions / Observation of performance
Prepare and cook fruit and vegetables	Short-answer questions / Observation of performance (individual practical task)	Short-answer questions / Observation of performance
Prepare and cook meat and offal	Short-answer questions / Observation of performance (synoptic practical assessment)	Short-answer questions / Observation of performance
Prepare and cook poultry	Short-answer questions / Observation of performance (individual practical task)	Short-answer questions / Observation of performance
Prepare and cook fish and shellfish	Short-answer questions / Observation of performance (synoptic practical assessment)	Short-answer questions / Observation of performance
Prepare and cook rice, pasta, grains and egg dishes	Short-answer questions / Observation of performance (individual practical task and synoptic practical assessment)	Short-answer questions / Observation of performance
Produce hot and cold desserts and puddings	Short-answer questions / Observation of performance (individual practical task and synoptic practical assessment)	Short-answer questions / Observation of performance
Produce paste products	Short-answer questions / Observation of performance (individual practical task and synoptic practical assessment)	Short-answer questions / Observation of performance
Produce biscuit, cake and sponge products	Short-answer questions / Observation of performance (individual practical task and synoptic practical assessment)	Short-answer questions / Observation of performance
Produce fermented dough products	Short-answer questions / Observation of performance (individual practical task and synoptic practical assessment)	Short-answer questions / Observation of performance

Chefs' tips for preparing for assessment

Prior planning and preparation is very important to enable you to achieve the maximum from any assessment – you cannot beat the feeling of receiving the highest mark possible. To do that you will have to work in a methodical manner, be prepared to practise and listen to feedback, as well as personally reflecting on what you have completed.

1 Read the instructions or brief that is given to you; make sure you understand what you have to do. This includes the criteria you will be judged or assessed on, which could include use of equipment, professional standards, use of materials, skills and techniques to be covered, time allowed and any preparations that can be completed before the test starts.

2 Carry out any research, find or develop your recipes, and consider which ingredients and skills you will need to include within the test.

3 Prepare and plan your time; this could be a time plan for the actual assessment, including not only the assessment day, but how you may prepare before the test date.

4 Prepare a list of equipment you will need to complete the task; make sure you have everything that you need available. It may be helpful to check if there is time to set out your work station before the assessment takes place.

On the day of assessment you should ensure you arrive at the assessment centre in plenty of time.

Time planning

Think about how long dishes take to cook and prepare, especially where there are a number of elements in a dish. For example, when preparing loin of lamb with gratin forcemeat, you will need to prepare the forcemeat, which needs to cool before boning out the loin; when preparing glazed lemon sole Véronique, fillet the fish so that the bones can be used for the stock before preparing the garnish.

When writing up the time plan, start from where you wish to finish and work backwards. For example, if you have 3 hours, think of this as 180 minutes – start at 180 minutes and work back to 0:00 on your first draft. Schedule in a break time if it is longer than you need.

Professional practice

This area covers what you do while producing your dishes. The assessor/examiner will be looking at how you conduct yourself in the kitchen area. Consider:

● **Personal hygiene and appearance**: this will cover your dress. It is a good idea to ensure your whites are clean and pressed. Personal hygiene standards will cover things like jewellery, hair and nails. Ensure that you are seen washing hands as required.

● **Craft skills**: use skills that are appropriate for the dish, including knife skills; the ease with which you use the technique and the consistency of skills shown are also important.

● **Correct use of equipment**: use the correct tools or equipment safely and correctly to complete tasks. This will include use of pans and could include energy considerations – do you really need to have the grill on 120 minutes before you glaze a fish dish?

● **Work methods**: ensure you work in a logical and organised manner, using appropriate time and temperature controls for food items. 'Clean as you go' is the mantra used across kitchens, and be aware of cross-contamination threats to your dishes.

Culinary practice and finished dishes

This area covers the selection of ingredients, choice of cooking methods, techniques and application of knowledge and skills to a level appropriate for the assessment. The checking of the finished dish will cover presentation, portioning, flavour, texture, seasoning and of course cooking.

● **Use of food items**: have you selected ingredients that balance in terms of texture, colour and flavours in relation to the overall dish? In some settings you may be asked to consider seasonality as part of the assessment.

● **Techniques or skill**: preparation skills for ingredients should be completed in a logical sequence and with an understanding and awareness of portion sizes or waste from trimming and peeling.

● **Cooking methods**: use the correct method for the dish requirements and ingredients being used. You will need to consider the use of time and temperature to ensure that dishes are cooked correctly and ready for the target service time.

- **Monitoring cooking process**: the tasting and evaluating elements of the dish prior to finishing will cover consistency which will enable you to correct the balance of the dish through the process.
- **Presentation**: the final stage of any practical assessment is how the dish is finished to present to the potential customer. This is an opportunity to show final flair and creativity as a chef – how you garnish and finish the dish. Make sure you don't allow food to go cold while trying to get it on the plate.

Using this book to help you to prepare for assessment

Each chapter of this textbook covers a different unit within the Professional Cookery Diploma. The start of each chapter includes knowledge that can be used to help you prepare for both your knowledge and practical assessments.

Throughout the book you will find a number of opportunities that can support your learning and development and help you to prepare for assessment:

- **Test yourself activities** – these are provided in each chapter and are designed to test your knowledge and help you to prepare for questioning, including short-answer questions and multiple-choice tests.
- **Practice assignment tasks** – these are included in some units and will help you to prepare for assignments.

- **Assessment recipes** – there are a number of recipes which are marked as example assessment dishes. These may form part of your preparation for practical tasks and/or synoptic assessment. They include professional tips and suggestions for alternative ingredients or garnishes that could be used.

Other types of assessment

As well as completing your Professional Cookery Diploma, there are other times which could be considered as an assessment opportunity or a review of knowledge and skills of a chef. These include:

- **Competitions** – many of these are set through each year at local, regional, national and even international levels. These could be based on an individual skill like cutting a chicken for sauté, all the way to a full menu or display product as culinary arts. Sponsorship is often linked to these and some offer quite prestigious development opportunities. There are opportunities to represent your region or country through cookery competitions, both as an individual and as part of a team. The following websites given an insight in to the types of competitions that could be considered: www.worldskillsuk.org; www.nestle-toquedor.co.uk.
- **Skills test (basket of goods)** – as part of employment and application processes, many employers are now using skills assessment. For some this is a simple stage in the kitchen or a complete mystery basket test to assess practical skills as well as working practices prior to offering employment to an individual.

Conversion tables

In this book, metric weights and measures are used. All temperatures are given in degrees Celsius.

Weights and measures

Imperial	Approximate metric equivalent	Imperial	Approximate metric equivalent
¼ oz	5 g	2½ in	6 cm
½ oz	10 g	3 in	8 cm
1 oz	25 g	4 in	10 cm
2 oz	50 g	5 in	12 cm
3 oz	75 g	6 in	15 cm
4 oz	100 g	6½ in	16 cm
5 oz	125 g	7 in	18 cm
6 oz	150 g	12 in	30 cm
7 oz	175 g	18 in	45 cm
8 oz	200 g	Spoons and cups	
9 oz	225 g	1 teaspoon (tsp)	5 ml
10 oz	250 g	1 dessertspoon (dsp)	10 ml
11 oz	275 g	1 tablespoon (tbsp)	15 ml
12 oz	300 g	¼ cup	60 ml
13 oz	325 g	⅓ cup	80 ml
14 oz	350 g	½ cup	125 ml
15 oz	375 g	1 cup	250 ml
16 oz	400 g		
2 lb	1 kg		
¼ pt	125 ml		
½ pt	250 ml		
¾ pt	375 ml		
1 pt	500 ml		
1½ pt	750 ml		
2 pt (1 qt)	1 litre		
2 qt	2 litres		
1 gal	4.5 litres		
¼ in	0.5 cm		
½ in	1 cm		
1 in	2 cm		
1½ in	4 cm		
2 in	5 cm		

Oven temperatures

	°C	Gas regulo	°F
slow (cool)	110	¼	225
	130	½	250
	140	1	275
	150	2	300
	160	3	325
moderate	180	4	350
	190	5	375
	200	6	400
hot	220	7	425
	230	8	450
very hot	250	9	475

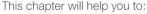

1 Food safety in catering

This chapter will help you to:

1 understand how individuals can take personal responsibility for food safety, including:
   – following food safety procedures, risk assessment and safe food handling
   – reporting food safety hazards
   – legal responsibilities for food handlers and food business operators.
2 understand the importance of keeping yourself clean and hygienic, including:
   – the importance of personal hygiene in food safety
   – effective personal hygiene practices, including those relating to protective clothing, hand washing, personal illness and cuts and wounds.
3 understand the importance of keeping work areas clean and hygienic, including:
   – keeping work areas clean and tidy and cleaning and disinfection methods
   – safe use and storage of cleaning chemicals and materials and waste disposal
   – how work flow, work surfaces and equipment can reduce contamination risks and aid cleaning
   – the importance of pest control.
4 understand the importance of keeping food safe, including:
   – the sources and risks to food safety from contamination and cross-contamination
   – how to deal with food spoilage
   – safe food handling practices and procedures
   – temperature control procedures
   – stock control procedures.

Introduction

Everyone who consumes food that has been prepared and cooked for them expects to be served safe food that will not cause them illness or harm them in any way.

Food safety means putting in place all of the measures needed to make sure that food and drinks are suitable, safe and wholesome throughout all of the processes of food provision – from selecting suppliers and delivery of food, right through to serving the food to the customer.

Food safety and personal responsibility

Why is food safety important?

Eating 'contaminated' food can result in **food poisoning**, causing harm, illness and in some cases even death.

The number of reported cases of food poisoning in the UK each year remains unacceptably high – between 70,000 and 94,000 cases are reported each year. However, as a large number of food poisoning cases are never reported no one really knows the actual number.

Food poisoning is a range of illnesses of the digestive system and is usually caused by eating food that has become contaminated with pathogenic bacteria and/or the toxins they may produce. Other causes of food poisoning are discussed on page 15.

The main symptoms of food poisoning are often similar and typically may include:
- nausea (feeling sick)
- vomiting
- diarrhoea
- dehydration
- abdominal pain
- fever and headache.

Good standards of food safety are essential to comply with the law and avoid legal action, to build a successful business with a good reputation and to provide clean and safe premises for employees and customers.

> **Key term**
>
> **Food poisoning**: a range of illnesses of the digestive system, usually caused by consuming food and drinks that have become contaminated with pathogenic bacteria (bacteria that cause bacterial infection), viruses, chemicals or toxins.

Food safety procedures and safe food handling

Food handlers can help to achieve high standards of food safety by following best practice and by being aware that they can contaminate food and cause food poisoning by their actions and if their personal hygiene is not of the highest standard.

Good food safety standards can be achieved by:
- protecting food from contamination from the time it is delivered right through to when it is served – 'farm to fork'
- putting measures in place to prevent the multiplication of bacteria
- destroying bacteria already present in food, on equipment and surfaces
- always working in a clean, hygienic and organised way
- observing the correct temperatures for storage, preparation, cooking and holding of food
- reporting anything that could contaminate food or prevent good food safety practice, including reporting any unacceptable behaviour
- taking part in food safety training and being part of the **risk assessment** processes (the Hazard Analysis Critical Control Point)
- keeping yourself clean and hygienic and observing correct hand-washing procedures
- reporting any illness before going near food and observing the 48-hour rule.

Reporting food safety hazards

Prompt reporting of food safety hazards is essential to good food safety standards. Most workplaces will have set procedures for reporting any hazards observed and this is usually explained to all employees at their induction or during their initial food safety training. The most usual and fastest way to report hazards is verbally to a supervisor or line manager, but other procedures used include:
- completion of specific hazard reporting forms
- by phone, text or electronic communication devices specific to the workplace
- email
- messages left on whiteboards provided for communication between staff

- kitchen communication diaries, such as the diary pages in 'Safer Food Better Business'
- at staff briefing or handover sessions.

Legal responsibilities

Legal responsibilities of food handlers
- Food handlers must receive food safety training and take part in risk assessment processes relevant to their work, so that they understand the principles of food safety and how to avoid food poisoning.
- They must work in a way that does not endanger or contaminate food and not serve food they know is contaminated.
- They must report to their employer anything that may have an effect on food safety (such as a refrigerator running at the wrong temperature) and cooperate with food safety measures the employer puts in place.
- They must report any illness, especially if stomach related, to a supervisor before starting work. After suffering such an illness, they must not return to work until 48 hours after the last symptom.

Legal responsibilities of food business operators

The latest laws of importance to food businesses took effect from 1 January 2006 – the Food Hygiene Regulations 2006. Almost all of the requirements in these regulations remain the same as the previous Food Safety Act 1990 and the Food Safety (General Food Hygiene) Regulations 1995. These set out the basic food safety requirements for all aspects of a food business – from premises to personal hygiene of staff, with specific attention given to temperatures relating to food.

The main difference in the 2006 laws was to provide a framework for EU legislation to be enforced in England and the requirement to have an approved food safety management procedure in place, with relevant up-to-date records available.

All food businesses must:
- be registered with the local authority
- cooperate with the requirements laid down by the environmental health officer/practitioner
- put proper food safety practices in place, including a food safety management system.

Due diligence

Due diligence can be an important defence under food safety legislation. It means that if there is proof that a business took all reasonable care and did everything it could to prevent food safety problems, legal action may be avoided when something goes wrong. Proof would include accurate written documents such as pest control reports, staff training records or temperature control records.

Training

Food businesses must ensure that all staff who handle food are supervised, instructed and trained in food hygiene appropriate to the work they do. Training can take place in house or with a training provider, but must be recorded, dated and show what was covered in the training. All records of staff training must be kept for possible inspection.

> **Key terms**
>
> **Due diligence**: written and recorded proof that a business took all reasonable precautions to avoid food safety problems and food poisoning.
>
> **Risk assessment**: a careful examination of what could cause harm to people, in order to assess whether adequate precautions have been taken to prevent harm occurring or if more preventative action is needed.

Environmental health officers

Food safety standards and legislation are enforced by environmental health officers (EHOs); they may also be known as environmental health practitioners (EHPs).

They may visit food premises as a matter of routine, after problems have occurred or after a complaint. The frequency of visits depends on the type of business and food being handled and if there have been previous problems.

EHOs/EHPs can enter a food business at any reasonable time, usually when the business is open. The main purpose of inspections is to identify any possible risks from the food business and to assess how well their food safety management systems are working.

The EHO/EHP may make suggestions and offer advice but can also serve notices.

- A **Hygiene Improvement Notice** is served if the EHO/EHP believes that a food business does not comply with regulations. The notice states the

details of the business, what is wrong, why it is wrong, what needs to be put right and the time in which this must be completed (usually not less than 14 days). It is an offence if the work is not carried out during the specified time period.
- A **Hygiene Emergency Prohibition Notice** is served if the EHO/EHP believes that the business poses an imminent risk to people's health. This would include serious issues such as sewage contamination, lack of water supply, rodent infestation and other serious non-compliance with the law. Serving this notice would mean immediate closure of the business for three days during which time the EHO/EHP must apply to the magistrates' court for a Hygiene Emergency Prohibition Order to keep the premises closed.
- A **Hygiene Prohibition Order** prohibits a person, usually the owner/manager, from working in a food business.

Penalties

The magistrates' court can impose fines of up to £5,000, a six-month prison sentence or both. For serious offences, magistrates can impose fines of up to £20,000. In a Crown Court unlimited fines can be imposed and/or two years' imprisonment.

Note: The penalties can apply to all three notices/orders

Hazard analysis and food safety management

In line with legislation across Europe, it is now a legal requirement for all food businesses to have a food safety management system based on **Hazard Analysis Critical Control Point (HACCP)**. When environmental health officers/practitioners inspect a food business they will check that food safety management systems are in place and are working effectively.

Hazard Analysis Critical Control Point (HACCP)

HACCP is an internationally recognised management system that identifies the hazards that could occur at critical points or stages in any process. The system must provide a documented record of the stages all food will go through right up until the time it is eaten.

The stages could be:

- purchase and delivery and receipt of food
- storage
- preparation
- cooking
- cooling
- hot holding
- re-heating
- chilled storage and display
- serving.

Once the hazards have been identified, corrective measures are put in place to control the hazards and keep the food safe.

The HACCP system has seven stages:

1. Identify hazards – what could go wrong.
2. Identify critical control points (CCP) – these are the important stages in production where things could go wrong.
3. Set critical limits for each CCP – for example, the temperature that fresh chicken should be on delivery.
4. Monitor CCPs and put checks in place to prevent problems occurring.
5. Identify and apply corrective action – what will be done if something goes wrong.
6. Verification – check that the HACCP plan is working.
7. Documentation – record all of the above.

The system must be updated regularly, especially when new items are introduced to the menu or systems change (for example the introduction of a new piece of cooking equipment). Specific new controls must be put in place to include them.

> **Key terms**
>
> **Environmental health officer (EHO)**: a person employed by the local authority to advise upon, inspect and enforce food safety legislation in their area. An EHO is now sometimes called an environmental health practitioner (EHP).
>
> **Hazard Analysis Critical Control Point (HACCP)**: a system for identifying the food safety hazards within a business or procedure and putting suitable controls in place to make them safe. Details of the system must be recorded and available for inspection. All food businesses must now have a food safety system based on HACCP.
>
> **Critical control point (CCP)**: a point in a procedure or process where a hazard could occur if controls were not in place.

Keeping records to support the HACCP system is very important for legal reasons and to demonstrate due diligence. Records may include staff training records, refrigeration and freezer temperatures, accident and sickness reporting procedure, lists of suppliers, calibration of temperature probes, personal hygiene policy, pest control policy, visitor policy, cleaning and disinfection procedures, any food safety related complaints, records of new equipment and procedures, equipment maintenance and repair plus any other records relevant to the business.

> **Activity**
>
> You may like to complete this activity in pairs or as a group.
>
> A busy hotel restaurant buys in 40 fresh chickens.
> - The chicken breasts are removed and breadcrumbed; these will be deep fried to order.
> - The drumsticks are roasted and will be served cold on a buffet.
> - The thighs are made into a chicken curry; this will be chilled, reheated the next day and then kept hot on a hot buffet counter.
>
> Identify the possible hazards at each of the following stages and find suitable control measures to ensure that the chicken is safe for the consumers:
> - Purchase, delivery, unloading
> - Storage
> - Preparation
> - Cooking
> - Hot holding
> - Cooling
> - Cold storage
> - Reheating
> - Serving

Safer Food Better Business

The HACCP system may seem complicated for a small or fairly limited business. With this in mind the Food Standards Agency launched the 'Safer Food Better Business' system for England and Wales. It is based on the principles of HACCP but in a format that is easy to understand and use, with pre-printed pages and charts to enter the relevant information such as temperatures of individual dishes. The pack is divided into two main parts:

- The first part covers safe methods such as avoiding cross-contamination, personal hygiene, cleaning, chilling, cooking and cleaning.
- The second part covers opening and closing kitchen checks, proving methods are safe, training records, useful contact details, a cleaning schedule template, lists of suppliers and useful information to help a small business to comply with the law.

The pack contains diary pages for each day that the business is open. Each day the pre-set opening checks and closing checks are completed and the diary page is signed. Nothing else needs to be recorded unless something goes wrong. For example, a piece of equipment not working would be recorded along with the action that was taken.

A copy of Safer Food Better Business is available to download from the Food Standards Agency website, www.food.gov.uk.

A similar system called 'CookSafe' has been developed by the Food Standards Agency (Scotland) and details of this can also be found at www.food.gov.uk.

Other food safety systems that enable businesses to comply with legislation are:
- Assured Safe Catering
- Safe Catering – Your Guide to HACCP (Northern Ireland).

Activity

For a kitchen you are familiar with, suggest some opening checks and closing checks that could be completed each day to make sure the business is following good food safety procedures. For example, an opening check may be to make sure all hand washing basins are clean/disinfected and there is a good supply of liquid soap and paper towels. A closing check may be that all waste bins are empty, cleaned and have new liners.

Food Standards Agency

The Food Standards Agency was set up in 2000 'to protect public health and to protect the interest of customers in relation to food'. The Food Standards Agency website has a wealth of information on food safety matters including up-to-date topical information.

Scores on Doors

This strategy was introduced by the Food Standards Agency to raise food safety standards and reduce the incidence of food poisoning. It is a star rating scheme for England and Wales in which, following inspection, food premises can be awarded up to 5 stars (0 stars being very poor and 5 stars showing excellent food safety).

The intention is that the given star rating certificate will be placed in a prominent position on the door or window of the food premises, but as yet it is not mandatory to do so.

Take it further

For further information about food safety matters, speak to your line manager, your local environmental health department or look at your local authority food safety websites. You may also like to look at:
- The Food Standards Agency – www.food.gov.uk
- Chartered Institute of Environmental Health – www.cieh.org
- Highfield – www.highfield.co.uk
- Food and Drink Federation – www.fdf.org.uk
- Food-Law Reading – www.foodlaw.rdg.ac.uk
- Royal Society for Public Health – www.rsph.org.uk

Keeping yourself clean and hygienic

Why is personal hygiene important?

Because humans are a source of food poisoning bacteria, especially *Staphylococcus aureus*, it is very important that all food handlers take care with personal hygiene and adopt good practices when working with food. Good personal hygiene practices can prevent the transmission of bacteria and other items from entering the food chain.

High standards of personal hygiene, especially frequent and efficient hand washing, are very important in controlling cross-contamination and will avoid the significant amounts of contamination caused by faecal/oral routes (when pathogens normally found in faeces are transferred to ready-to-eat foods, resulting in cross-contamination and possible illness). An obvious way that this may happen is when food handlers visit the toilet, do not wash their hands thoroughly and then handle food.

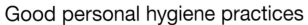

Good personal hygiene practices

Personal hygiene practices for food handlers include the following:

- Arrive at work clean (daily bath or shower) and with clean hair.
- Wear clean kitchen clothing used only in the kitchen. This should completely cover any personal clothing. (For more information on protective clothing, see below.)
- Keep hair well contained in a suitable hat/net.
- Keep nails short and clean, not bitten – do not wear nail varnish or false nails.
- Do not wear jewellery or a watch when handling food. A plain wedding band is allowed, but could still trap bacteria. Jewellery can also fall into food.
- Avoid wearing cosmetics and strong perfumes.
- Smoking must not be allowed in food preparation areas (bacteria from touching the mouth area could get into food, as could ash or smoke, and smoking can cause coughing). At break times food handlers must not smoke while wearing kitchen clothing.
- Do not eat food, sweets or chew gum when handling food. Avoid scratching the skin and spitting should never occur in a food area. All of these practices may transfer bacteria to food.
- Wash, dry and then cover any cuts, burns or grazes with a blue waterproof dressing, then wash hands. For more information on cuts and wounds, see page 7.
- Report any illness to the supervisor as soon as possible and before going near any food. For more information on reporting illness, see below.

Protective clothing

Protective clothing is worn in the kitchen to protect food from contamination, as well as shielding the wearer from heat, burns and splashes and to provide protection for those suffering from **contact dermatitis**.

All items of clothing should be durable (hard wearing), light in colour, in good repair, fit well, suitable for the tasks being completed and any pockets should be on the inside. Fastenings should be press studs or Velcro because buttons can become detached and fall into food.

Kitchen clothing itself could contaminate food. If it gets dirty or stained it should be exchanged for clean clothing. Clothing needs to be comfortable to wear and allow laundering at high temperatures; materials such as cotton are the most widely used. Kitchen protective clothing usually consists of a chef's jacket, trousers, apron, hat/hair net and safety shoes.

> **Key term**
>
> **Contact dermatitis:** a skin reaction suffered by people who are allergic to certain food items, chemicals, plastics or cleaning materials.

▲ Protective clothing helps to protect food from contamination

Hand washing

Hands are constantly in use in the kitchen, touching numerous materials, foods, surfaces and equipment.

You should always wash your hands:

- when you enter the kitchen, before starting work and handling any food
- after a break (particularly after using the toilet)
- after smoking or eating
- between different tasks, but especially after handling raw and before handling cooked/high risk food
- if you touch your hair, nose or mouth/face or use a tissue for a sneeze or cough
- after you apply or change a dressing on a cut or burn

- after using cleaning materials, cleaning preparation areas, equipment or contaminated surfaces
- after handling kitchen waste, external food packaging, money or flowers.

Contamination from hands can happen very easily and great care must be taken with hand washing to avoid this. A basin with hot and cold water and preferably mixer taps must be provided just for hand washing; make sure you use this rather than food preparation sinks.

The correct hand washing technique is described below.
- Wet your hands under warm running water.
- Apply liquid soap (preferably anti-bacterial soap).
- Rub your hands together and rub one hand with the fingers and thumb of the other.
- Remember to wash your fingertips, nails and wrists (if a nailbrush is used make sure it is clean and disinfected).
- Rinse off the soap under warm running water.
- Dry your hands on a paper towel and use the paper towel to turn off the tap before disposing of it into a foot-operated waste bin.

▲ Wash hands correctly to reduce the risk of contamination

Personal illnesses

It is a legal requirement that any illness should be reported to the supervisor as soon as possible and before going near any food. The types of illness include:
- diarrhoea and/or vomiting, nausea and stomach pain; you may not handle food until 48 hours after the last symptom has passed
- infected (septic) cuts, burns or spots
- eye or ear infections
- cold or flu symptoms including sore throat
- cuts, burns, spots or other injuries, especially where they have become septic
- skin problems such as dermatitis.

You must also report any illness you had when on holiday and contact you have had with family members or friends who have the above symptoms, especially where they are stomach related.

Some employers require a fitness to work certificate or other medical clearance before the employee returns to working with food.

Cuts and wounds

Cuts and wounds, especially those that have become **septic**, should be reported to the supervisor.

A waterproof dressing needs to be applied to any cut, burn or skin abrasion. The standard bright blue plasters used in kitchen areas are easily visible if they fall into food, and each one contains a small metal strip which is identified by metal detectors in food manufacturing plants. As well as protecting the wearer, it provides a barrier between the wearer and the food, reducing the risk of bacterial contamination.

Disposable plastic gloves may also be worn to reduce contamination and to demonstrate good practice, but make sure these are changed regularly, especially between tasks.

> **Key term**
>
> **Septic**: a cut or other wound that has become infected with bacteria. It is often wet with a white or yellow appearance.

Keeping work areas clean and hygienic

Cross-contamination

Cross-contamination is when bacteria or other contaminants are transferred from contaminated food (usually raw food), equipment or surfaces to ready-to-eat food. It is the cause of significant amounts of food poisoning and care must be taken to avoid it. Cross-contamination could be caused by:

- foods such as raw meat and cooked meat touching
- raw meat or poultry dripping onto high risk foods
- soil from dirty vegetables coming into contact with high risk foods
- dirty cloths or dirty equipment
- equipment such as chopping boards and knives used for raw then cooked food without proper cleaning/disinfection
- hands touching raw then cooked food without being washed between tasks
- pests spreading bacteria from their own bodies, urine and droppings around the kitchen.

Cross-contamination can be avoided by following hygienic working practices and storing, preparing and cooking food safely.

In the same way that you can limit cross-contamination, you can help to prevent the spread and multiplication of bacteria by having good working practices. Protecting food from contamination by bacteria which could then multiply involves keeping food clean, covered and stored properly.

Cross-contamination can quickly spread bacteria. For example, if a chef leaves a cooked chicken uncovered to cool in a kitchen and then uses a dirty cloth to put the chicken on a plate, bacteria from the cloth are transferred to the chicken and begin to multiply. From one careless action with a dirty cloth, 6,000 pathogens multiply to 3 million in 2 hours 40 minutes. One million pathogens per gram of food are enough to cause food poisoning.

Cleaning and disinfection

As a food handler it is your responsibility, together with those working with you, to keep food areas clean and hygienic at all times. Clean as you go and do not allow waste to build up; clean up any spills straight away.

Kitchen areas such as floors and walls will need planned and thorough **cleaning** but some items, especially in areas where high risk foods are handled, need cleaning and **disinfection**. These are:

- all food contact surfaces, such as chopping boards, bowls, spoons, whisks, etc.
- all hand contact surfaces, such as fridge handles and door handles
- cleaning materials and equipment, such as mops, buckets, cloths and hand wash basins.

Clean food areas play an essential part in the production of safe food and it is a requirement to plan, record and check all cleaning in the form of a planned **cleaning schedule** which will form part of the food safety management system. Clean premises, work areas and equipment are important to:

- control the bacteria that cause food poisoning
- reduce the possibility of physical and chemical contamination
- reduce accidents such as slips, trips and falls
- create a positive image for customers, visitors and employees
- comply with the law
- avoid attracting pests to the kitchen.

Cleaning needs to be planned, checked and recorded on a cleaning schedule. The cleaning schedule must include the following information:

- What is to be cleaned.
- Who should do it (name if possible).
- When it is to be done, for example the time of day.
- Materials to be used including chemicals and their correct dilution, cleaning equipment and the protective clothing/equipment (PPE) to be used.
- Safety precautions that must be taken , for example use of wet floor signs.
- Signatures of the cleaner and the supervisor checking the work, together with the date and time.

Key term

Cross-contamination: contaminants such as pathogenic bacteria transferred from one place to another. This is frequently from raw food to cooked/high risk food.

Cleaning: the removal of dirt and grease, usually with the assistance of hot water and detergent.

Disinfection: action to bring micro-organisms to a safe level. This can be done with chemical disinfectants or heat.

Cleaning schedule: planned and recorded cleaning of all areas and equipment.

Activity

Tick the items below that you think should be both *cleaned* and *disinfected*.

Item	Clean only	Clean/disinfect	Item	Clean only	Clean/disinfect
Cutlery			Staff lockers		
Milk cartons for recycling			Red chopping boards		
Delivery area floor			Fridge door handle		
Grater			Inside of deep fryer		
Food containers from a hot counter			Dishcloths		
Nailbrushes			Door frames		

Cleaning products

Different cleaning products are used for different tasks.

- **Detergent** is designed to remove grease and dirt and hold them in suspension in water. It may be in the form of a liquid, powder, gel or foam and usually needs to be diluted by adding to water. Detergent does not kill bacteria (pathogens), though if mixed with very hot water – which is how detergents work best – it may help to do so. It will clean and degrease surfaces so disinfectant can work properly.
- **Disinfectant** is designed to destroy bacteria when used properly. Make sure that you only use a disinfectant intended for kitchen use. Disinfectant must be left on a cleaned grease-free surface for the required amount of time (contact time) to be effective and works best with cool water.
  Heat may also be used to disinfect, for example, by using steam cleaners or the hot rinse cycle of a dishwasher.
- **Sanitiser** cleans and disinfects and usually comes in spray form. Sanitiser is very useful for frequently used work surfaces and equipment, especially between tasks and also for hand-contact surfaces such as refrigerator handles. Like disinfectant, this may also need contact time.
- **Steriliser** can be used after cleaning to make a surface or piece of equipment bacteria free.

Take great care with kitchen cloths as they are a perfect growing environment for bacteria. Different cloths for different areas will help to reduce cross-contamination and it is especially important to use different cloths for raw food and cooked food preparation. Some kitchens use different colour-coded cloths for the various preparation and cooking areas so it is obvious if the wrong cloth is being used. Even just having one colour for raw preparation areas and a different colour for cooked/high-risk food areas will help to reduce the risk of cross-contamination. One-use disposable cloths or kitchen towel are the most hygienic way to clean food areas.

Take care where tea towels are used. Remember that they can easily spread bacteria so don't use them as an 'all purpose' cloth. Do not keep a tea towel on the shoulder (the cloth touches neck and hair and these are sources of bacteria).

Key terms

Detergent: removes grease and dirt and holds them in suspension in water. It may be in the form of liquid, powder, gel or foam. Detergent will not kill pathogens.

Disinfectant: destroys pathogenic bacteria, bringing it to a safe level.

Sanitiser: cleans and disinfects and usually comes in spray form.

Steriliser: can be chemical or through the action of extreme heat. It will kill all living micro-organisms.

Health and safety

Make sure that items such as cloths, paper towels and fibres from mops do not get into food (physical contamination). To avoid bacterial contamination do not use the same cleaning cloth and equipment in raw food areas and high risk areas.

Cleaning surfaces

Clean and sanitise worktops and chopping boards before working on them and do this again after use, paying particular attention when they have been used for raw foods. Chopping boards can be disinfected after use by putting them through a dishwasher with a high rinse temperature of 82 °C.

For kitchen surfaces one of the cleaning methods shown in Table 1.1 is recommended.

Dishwashing

Using a dishwashing machine

The most efficient and hygienic method of cleaning dishes and crockery is to use a dishwasher, as this will clean and disinfect items that will then air dry, removing the need for cloths. The dishwasher can also be used to clean/disinfect small equipment such as chopping boards.

The stages in machine dishwashing:
- Remove waste food.
- Pre-rinse or spray.
- Load onto the appropriate racks with a space between each item.
- The wash cycle runs at approximately 50–60 °C using a detergent. The rinse cycle runs at 82 °C or above which disinfects items ready for air drying.

Dishwashing by hand

If items need to be washed by hand:
- Scrape/rinse off residual food.
- Wash items in a sink in hot water; the temperature should be 50–60 °C which means rubber gloves will need to be worn. Use a dishwashing brush rather than a cloth, as the brush will help to loosen food particles and is not such a good breeding ground for bacteria as a cloth.

- Rinse in very hot water. If rinsing can be done close to 82 °C this will disinfect the dishes.
- Allow to air dry – do not use tea towels.

Before dishwashers became popular a **double sink method** was often used. With this method, items are rinsed then washed thoroughly in one sink with detergent and hot water. They are then loaded into racks and rinsed in a second sink in very hot water and allowed to air dry.

Cleaning equipment

Small equipment

Small equipment such as knives, bowls, spoons and tongs can cause cross-contamination. It is important to clean these items thoroughly and once again the dishwasher does this well. This is especially important when the equipment is used for a variety of foods and for raw food.

Large equipment

Large equipment such as mixing machines and ovens cannot be moved, so need to be cleaned where they are. This is called **clean in place** and each item will have a specific method outlined on the cleaning schedule. Sometimes steam cleaning methods are used and this also disinfects the items.

Key terms

Double sink method: items are washed in one sink with detergent and hot water; they are then placed in racks and rinsed in very hot water in a second sink and allowed to air dry.

Clean in place: cleaning items where they are rather than moving them to a sink. This is used for large equipment such as mixing machines.

Table 1.1 Cleaning methods

Four-stage cleaning	Six-stage cleaning
Remove debris and loose particles	Remove debris and loose particles
Main clean using hot water (plus detergent if very soiled or greasy) and sanitiser	Main clean to remove soiling grease
Rinse using clean hot water and cloth if recommended on instructions	Rinse using clean hot water and cloth to remove detergent
Allow to air dry or use kitchen paper	Apply disinfectant. Leave for recommended contact time
	Rinse off the disinfectant (if recommended)
	Allow to air dry or use kitchen paper

Safe use and storage of cleaning chemicals and materials

The 2002 Control of Substances Hazardous to Health (COSHH) Regulations state that employees must be kept safe from chemical harm by appropriate training, risk assessment, planning and provision of PPE (personal protective equipment) where it is needed.

- When using any cleaning or disinfection chemicals it is important to use them with care. Always follow the instructions for their use such as how they should be diluted or mixed and how they should be disposed of.
- Most chemicals such as detergent or disinfectant only stay active for an hour or two so long soaking of cloths and mops is not recommended. Wash/disinfect these items, squeeze out, then allow them to air dry.
- Do not store cleaning chemicals in food preparation and cooking areas. Use separate, lockable storage and restrict who has access to this. All chemicals must be stored in their original containers with the instruction label visible.
- Make sure that items such as cloths and paper towels and fibres from mops do not get into uncovered food.
- When using sprays such as sanitiser spray, take care not to spray on the skin or eyes and do not spray over uncovered food.
- Kitchen areas must display safety data sheets with information on chemicals, how they are to be used and how to deal with spillages and accidents. Make sure you are familiar with this information.
- If cleaning materials or chemicals are spilled, warn others in the area and put up a wet floor sign. Wear rubber gloves and a mask if needed, soak up the excess with kitchen paper then clean the area thoroughly.
- If cleaning materials are spilled onto the skin, wash off with cold water and dry. If there is a skin reaction seek first aid immediately and report the incident.

Health and safety ⚠

Cleaning is essential to prevent health hazards but if it is not managed properly it can become a hazard in itself. Do not store chemicals in food preparation and cooking areas and take care with their use to avoid chemical contamination.

Waste disposal

Kitchen waste should be placed in waste bins with lids (preferably foot operated and lined with a strong bin liner). Waste bins should be strong, easy to clean, pest proof and kept in good, sound condition, away from direct sunlight. They need to be emptied regularly to avoid cross-contamination and odour and must never be left un-emptied in the kitchen overnight as this could result in the multiplication of bacteria and attract pests. An over-full heavy bin is also much more difficult to handle than a regularly emptied bin.

Recycling is now everyday practice in kitchens and staff need to become familiar with the separation of different waste items ready for collection. These may be bottles, cans, waste food, paper and plastic items.

Work flow, work surfaces and equipment: reducing contamination and aiding cleaning

Suitable buildings with well-planned fittings, layout and equipment are essential for all food areas. It is a legal requirement that food premises are designed with good food safety in mind and there is the correct equipment to keep food at the required temperatures. Certain essentials must be in place if a building is to be used for food production. There must be:

- supply of electricity and preferably gas
- drinking water and good drainage
- suitable road access for deliveries and refuse collection
- no risk of contamination from surrounding areas and buildings, for example, chemicals, smoke, odours or dust.

Other requirements for food premises are:

- there must be adequate storage areas; proper and sufficient refrigerated storage is especially important
- suitably positioned hand washing and drying facilities which are only used for this purpose
- clean and dirty (raw and cooked) processes should be kept apart. Cleaning and disinfection should be planned with separate storage for cleaning materials and chemicals
- all areas must be designed to allow for thorough cleaning, disinfection and pest control

- personal hygiene facilities must be provided for staff, as well as changing facilities and storage for personal clothing and belongings
- first aid equipment must be provided for staff and any accidents must be recorded (see Chapter 3: Health and safety in catering and hospitality for more details).

Work flow

When planning food premises a linear workflow should be in place. For example:

Delivery → Storage → Preparation → Cooking → Hot holding → Serving

This means there will be no crossover of activities that could result in cross-contamination.

When planning food premises, separating areas for different foods, storage, processes and service areas will help to reduce the risk of contamination and ensure efficient working and effective cleaning. 'Dirty areas' that involve preparation or storage of raw foods or washing of dirty vegetables must be kept separate from the 'clean areas' where cold preparations, finishing and serving takes place. If separate areas for raw and high risk foods are not possible keep them well away from each other, making sure that working areas are thoroughly cleaned and disinfected between tasks.

For more information on features of food preparation areas that ensure safe working practice, please see Chapter 3: Health and safety in catering and hospitality.

Work surfaces and equipment

Kitchen surfaces and equipment should be installed to allow for efficient cleaning and disinfection of the equipment itself and the surrounding areas. Equipment and surfaces need to be smooth, impervious (not absorb liquids) and must of course be non-corrosive, non-toxic and must not crack, chip or flake. Many kitchens have a 'no glass policy' to prevent the possibility of broken glass getting into food.

All food premises, fittings and equipment must be kept in good repair to ensure food safety. For example, cracked surfaces or chipped equipment can support the multiplication of bacteria and a refrigerator running at the wrong temperature may also allow bacteria to multiply in food. If you notice anything is damaged,

broken or faulty, report it to a supervisor immediately. You may have specific reporting forms to do this.

Colour-coded equipment

Colour-coded chopping boards are a good way to keep different types of food separate. Worktops and chopping boards come into contact with the food being prepared so need special attention. Make sure that chopping boards are in good condition as cracks and splits can hold onto bacteria and this could be transferred to food.

▲ Colour-coded chopping boards help to keep different types of food separate

As well as colour-coded chopping boards, some kitchens also provide colour-coded knives, cloths, cleaning equipment, storage trays, bowls and even colour-coded uniforms for different areas to help prevent cross-contamination.

Activity

Which colour-coded chopping board would you select to prepare each of these foods?
a) Potatoes (peeling and cutting)
b) Choux pastries (cutting open)
c) Raw beef (cutting for stewing)
d) Cooked savoury flans (cutting)
e) Bread (removing crusts)
f) Raw chicken (cutting; trimming)
g) Onions (chopping)
h) Raw haddock (skinning; trimming)
i) Fruit (preparing for fruit salad)
j) Cooked smoked mackerel (trimming)

Pest control

When there are reports of food premises forcibly being closed down, an infestation of pests is often the reason. As pests can be a serious cause of contamination and disease, having them near food cannot be allowed and is against the law.

Pests can carry food poisoning pathogens into food premises in their fur, feathers, feet, saliva, urine and droppings. Other problems caused by pests include damage to food stocks and packaging, damage to buildings, equipment and wiring, blockages in equipment and piping. Pests in a food business can also result in legal action, loss of reputation and profit, poor staff morale and closure of the business.

Pests can be attracted to food premises by food, warmth, shelter, water and possible nesting materials such as cardboard boxes, paper towels and packaging materials. Everything possible must be done to keep them out and this is a legal requirement. Any suspicion that pests may be present must be reported to the supervisor or manager immediately.

Common pests that may cause problems in food areas are rats, mice, cockroaches, wasps, flies, ants, pharaoh ants, birds and domestic pets.

Signs of pest infestation

Signs that pests are present include:
- hearing or seeing them (either dead or alive)
- sightings of droppings
- an unpleasant smell
- sightings of pupae/egg cases or larvae
- gnawed wires and/or packaging
- food spillages and damaged food stock
- greasy marks on lower walls
- holes in window and door frames, skirting boards, etc.

Measures to keep pests out

These need to be planned as part of food safety management and include:
- good environmental design blocking entry for pests – for example, no holes around pipe work, avoiding any gaps and cavities where pests could get in and using sealed drain covers and appropriate proofing
- repairing any damage to the building or fixtures and fittings quickly

- using screening or netting on windows and doors. Doors should be self-closing with metal kick plates and bristle strips along the bottom
- checking deliveries and packaging for pests
- placing physical or chemical baits and traps in relevant places; a pest control contractor will do this
- using electronic fly killers. These use ultraviolet light to attract insects that are then electrocuted on charged wires and fall into catch trays. Do not position these directly above food preparation areas and make sure that catch trays are emptied regularly
- keeping food in sealed containers and ensuring no open food is left out uncovered
- checking food stores regularly for signs of pests
- not allowing waste to build up in the kitchen
- not keeping outside waste too close to the kitchen; containers need to be emptied regularly and the area kept clean and tidy
- arranging for professional and organised pest management control, surveys and reports.

Pest control contractors will offer advice on keeping pests out and organise eradication systems for those that do get in. A good pest control contractor can also complete formal audits and supply certificates to prove that pest control management is in place.

Health and safety

Pest control measures can also introduce safety hazards. The bodies of dead insects or even rodents may remain in the kitchen, causing physical and bacterial contamination as well as being very unpleasant. Pesticides, insecticides and baits may cause chemical contamination if not managed properly. Pest control is therefore best undertaken by professionals.

Keeping food safe

Sources and risks to food safety

Food poisoning is an unpleasant illness for anyone but for some groups of people who, are referred to as 'high risk', it can be very serious or even fatal.

These high risk groups include:
- babies and the very young
- elderly people
- pregnant women

- those who are already unwell or recovering from an illness and who may have weakened resistance to food poisoning
- people with a supressed immune system.

It is therefore essential to take great care to prevent food poisoning, and the Food Standards Agency has committed to reducing the numbers of reported cases of food poisoning cases significantly in the UK.

> **Key term**
>
> **Immune system**: a system of structures and processes in the human body which defend against harmful substances and maintain good health. Occasionally the immune system in some people recognises ordinary food as harmful and a reaction occurs.

How is food contaminated?

There are four main ways that food can become contaminated and all must be avoided. However contamination from bacteria (biological) is the most dangerous of all.

- **Biological (microbial) contamination** may occur from **pathogenic bacteria** and the toxins they may produce; it can also occur from **viruses**, yeasts, moulds, **spoilage bacteria** and **enzymes**. These are all around us – in the environment, on raw food, on humans, animals, birds and insects. Of most concern are pathogenic bacteria, as these may be present in food and multiply to dangerous levels but are not visible except with a microscope. When pathogenic bacteria multiply in food or use food to get into the human body, illness can result.
- **Chemical contamination** can occur when chemical items get into food accidentally; these can then make the consumer suffer discomfort or become ill. The kinds of chemical that can get into food include cleaning fluids, disinfectants, machine oil, degreasers and pesticides. Problems can also occur because of chemical reactions between metal containers and acidic foods.
- **Physical contamination** is caused when something gets into foods that should not be there, for example, glass, nuts, bolts and oil from machinery, mercury from thermometers, flaking paint, pen tops, threads from worn clothing, buttons, blue plasters, hair or insects.

- **Allergenic**. Allergens are substances in the environment that can cause a range of reactions (an allergy) by the body when eaten or inhaled. An allergy is when a person's immune system reacts to certain food, causing swelling, itching, rashes, breathlessness and even anaphylactic shock (a severe reaction causing swelling of the throat and mouth that prevents breathing). Foods usually associated with allergies and intolerances are nuts, dairy products, wheat-based products and gluten, eggs and shellfish. Some people may have an allergy to some fruits, vegetables, plants and mushrooms.

> ## Health and safety !
>
> From December 2014 provision of certain food allergy information became mandatory and now all businesses offering food to customers need to provide this information. Under EU regulation FIR 1169/2011 specific information on 14 allergens/ingredients must be available irrespective of whether the food is packaged or chosen from a menu. Statements such as 'may contain nuts' are no longer adequate. For more information and advice, go to the Food Standards Agency website – www.food.gov.uk

> **Key terms**
>
> **Biological contamination**: by living organisms.
>
> **Chemical contamination**: by chemical compounds used for a variety of purposes such as cleaning and disinfection.
>
> **Physical contamination**: by an object which can be of any shape, size or type.
>
> **Allergenic**: a reaction by the immune system to certain foods or ingredients.
>
> **Pathogenic bacteria**: bacteria that can cause illness either by infection or by the toxins they may produce.
>
> **Virus**: micro-organism even smaller than bacteria. It does not multiply in food but can enter the body via food where it then invades living cells.
>
> **Spoilage bacteria**: cause food to change and spoil, for example, develop a bad smell or go slimy.
>
> **Enzyme**: proteins that speed up the rate of a chemical reaction, causing food to ripen, deteriorate and spoil.

Bacteria and contamination: pathogens

Not all bacteria are harmful; some are very useful and are used in the manufacture of foods and medicines such as yoghurt and salami. Harmful bacteria are called pathogenic bacteria or pathogens and can cause food poisoning.

Bacteria are so small that you would need to use a microscope to see them and you cannot taste or smell bacteria on food. This is why pathogens are so dangerous. If they have the required conditions of food, warmth, moisture and time, they will multiply every 10–20 minutes by dividing in half; this is called **binary fission**.

Different types of pathogenic bacteria act in different ways to cause food poisoning. Some multiply in food which, if it is not cooked to high temperatures, can infect the person eating the food. Some just use food to get into the body where they then start to multiply. Others produce toxins (poisons) as they multiply or die, while yet others produce protective spores. Table 1.2 shows some common food poisoning bacteria.

> **Key terms**
>
> **Binary fission**: process by which bacteria divide in half and multiply.
>
> **Human carrier**: someone carrying bacteria (usually salmonella) in their intestines but not showing any signs of illness. They may pass on the salmonella bacteria to food they work with and this could then cause food poisoning in others.
>
> **Convalescent carrier**: someone recovering from a salmonella-related illness who still carries the organism.
>
> **Healthy carrier**: someone carrying salmonella in their intestine without showing any signs of illness.

Food-borne illness

Some organisms cause what is known as food-borne illness. They do not multiply in food but instead use the food to get into the human gut where they then multiply and cause a range of illnesses, some of which can be serious. Symptoms include severe abdominal pain, diarrhoea, vomiting, headaches, blurred vision, flu symptoms, septicaemia, kidney failure and miscarriage. These organisms may be transmitted from person to person, in water and be airborne, as well as through food. Table 1.3 shows examples of these organisms.

> **Key terms**
>
> **Cook/chill meals**: pre-cooked foods that are rapidly chilled and packaged then held at chiller temperatures before being reheated for use.
>
> **Septicaemia**: blood poisoning. It occurs when an infection in the bloodstream causes the body's immune system to begin attacking the body itself.

Toxins

As they multiply, some bacteria produce toxins that can survive boiling temperatures for half an hour or more, so are not killed by many cooking processes. They remain in the food and cause illness when the food is eaten.

Other types of bacteria produce toxins as they die, usually in the intestines of the person who has eaten the infected food.

Spores

Some bacteria produce spores. This is a protective measure to help them survive when conditions surrounding them become hostile, for example, rising temperatures or the presence of chemicals such as disinfectant. The spore forms a protective 'shell' inside the bacteria protecting the essential parts from the high temperatures of normal cooking, disinfection or dehydration. Once spores are formed the cells cannot divide and multiply as before, but simply survive until conditions improve, for example, when high temperatures drop to a level where the spore 'shell' can be discarded and multiplication can start again. Normal cooking temperatures will not kill spores.

Time is crucial in preventing the formation of spores. If food is brought to cooking temperature slowly it allows time for spores to form and when food is cooled too slowly the bacteria can re-form and multiply again. To avoid this, heat food to cooking temperatures quickly and cool food quickly.

Poisoning from fish and vegetable items

Food poisoning can also be caused by poisons produced by some oily fish or shellfish, undercooked red or black kidney beans and items such as poisonous mushrooms, rhubarb leaves and daffodil bulbs. Some moulds produce dangerous toxins so never risk using mouldy food. However, controlled, safe moulds such as those found in blue cheeses are not dangerous.

Table 1.2 Common food poisoning bacteria

Bacteria	Description	Source	Onset time (time between eating contaminated food and showing signs of illness)	Symptoms
Salmonella	This used to be the most common cause of food poisoning in the UK. Modern farming methods have reduced salmonella in chickens and eggs. Food poisoning from this source has reduced, but has not been eliminated.	Raw meat and poultry, eggs and shellfish, pests (e.g. rodents, insects and birds) and human or animal intestines (and excreta). Salmonella poisoning can be passed on through human carriers.	12–36 hours	Diarrhoea, nausea, vomiting, abdominal pain and fever
Staphyococcus aureus	When *Staphyloccus aureus* multiplies in food a toxin (poison) is produced which can be very difficult to kill even at boiling temperatures. To avoid food poisoning, food handlers need to maintain very high standards of personal hygiene.	Human body – present on skin, hands, hair and scalp, nose and throat. Cuts, spots, burns and boils can also be a source.	1–7 hours	Abdominal pain and vomiting; flu-like symptoms
Clostridium perfringens	A number of food poisoning incidents from this organism have occurred when large quantities of meat are brought up to cooking temperatures slowly then allowed to cool slowly for later use or re-heating. *Clostridium perfringens* can produce spores during this heating/cooling phase which are very resistant to any further cooking and allow bacteria to survive in conditions that would usually kill them.	Human and animal faeces (it may be passed on by humans if they do not wash their hands properly after going to the toilet), raw meat, poultry and vegetables (also insects, soil, dust and sewage).	12–18 hours	Mainly severe abdominal pain and diarrhoea
Bacillus cereus	Can produce spores; it can also produce toxins so is a dangerous pathogen.	Often associated with cooking rice in large quantities, cooling it too slowly and then reheating. Reheating temperatures are insufficient to destroy spores and toxins. It has also been linked with other cereal crops, spices, soil and vegetables.	1–16 hours	Vomiting, abdominal pain, diarrhoea
Clostridium botulinum	Fortunately problems with this organism are rare in the UK.	Intestines of some fish, soil and vegetables.	2 hours–8 days	Difficulty with speech, vision, breathing and swallowing. Symptoms can be very serious and even fatal.

Table 1.3 Organisms that cause food-borne illness

Bacteria	Description	Source	Onset time (time between eating contaminated food and showing signs of illness	Symptoms
E. coli (Escherichia coli) 0157	Poisoning from this source can be very dangerous and may lead to kidney failure and death.	Present in the intestines and faeces of animals and humans, raw meat, in the soil on raw vegetables.	12–24 hours	Abdominal pain, fever, diarrhoea, kidney failure
Campylobacter	Causes more food-related illness than any other organism.	Raw poultry and meat, sewage, animals, insects and birds.	18–36 hours	Headache, fever, bloody diarrhoea, severe abdominal pain
Listeria	Listeria is of particular concern because it can multiply slowly at fridge temperatures, i.e. below 5 °C.	Chilled products such as unpasteurised cheeses, paté and prepared salads and cook/chill meals.	Variable but between one day, weeks or even months	Fever, diarrhoea, flu-like symptoms, septicaemia and stillbirth
Typhoid/ paratyphoid	A type of salmonella which causes serious illness which is sometimes fatal.	Often linked with poor drainage and sewage systems, untreated water and carriers	8–14 days	Fever, nausea, red spots on abdomen and severe diarrhoea
Bacillary dysentery	Caused by an organism called *Shigella*.	Sewage, manure, infected people and contaminated food and water.	1–3 days	Abdominal pain, severe diarrhoea, vomiting
Norovirus	Like all viruses will not multiply in food, but may live for a short time on surfaces, utensils and food which it uses to get into the body.	Usually spread by airborne means, person-to-person contact, in water and sewage.	1–2 days	Severe vomiting, diarrhoea, abdominal pain and dehydration

Activity

Place a tick in the appropriate column to decide if these questions about bacteria are true or false.

	True	False
Some bacteria are harmless and can be useful		
A pathogen is a bacterium which causes illness		
All toxins are killed by heating food to 63 °C		
Salmonella can be found in the human intestines		
Bacillus cereus can cause food poisoning through cooked rice		
Stapylococcus areus can be transferred to food by not covering a cut on your hand		
You can tell if a food has pathogens on it because it smells 'off'		
Under ideal conditions bacteria can multiply every 20 hours		
Bacteria can move around from one area of the kitchen to another on their own		
In the UK there are more reported cases of food poisoning from *Campylobacter* than any other pathogen		

Food spoilage

Food spoilage describes food that has spoiled or 'gone off'. Unlike contamination with pathogens, it can usually be detected by sight, smell, taste or texture. Evidence of food spoilage includes:

- mould
- slimy, over-wet or over-dry food
- sour smell or taste
- discoloured and wrinkled food or other texture changes.

Food spoilage is caused by natural breakdown of the food by organisms such as spoilage bacteria, enzymes, moulds and yeasts, which in some cases may not be harmful themselves but can cause the food to deteriorate. Spoilage may also be caused by poor storage, poor handling or by contamination of the food.

Food spoilage can account for a significant amount of unnecessary waste in a business and if food stock is being managed and stored properly it should not happen.

Any food that has spoiled or is out of date must be reported to the supervisor or line manager then disposed of appropriately.

Key terms

Toxin: a poison produced by some bacteria as they multiply in food or as they die in the human body.

Spore: a resistant, resting phase for some bacteria when they form protection around the essential part of the cell that can then survive boiling, freezing and disinfection.

Food spoilage: foods spoiled by the action of bacteria, moulds, yeasts or enzymes. The food may smell or taste unpleasant, be sticky, slimy, dry, wrinkled or discoloured. Food spoilage is usually detectable by sight, smell or touch.

Food preservation

Numerous ways have been sought and used to make food that perishes and spoils naturally last longer. Some very old methods are still in use and new methods are also being developed. Some of the main methods used to preserve food are use of heat and cooking (see page 19); chilling and freezing; salting; smoking; pickling and curing; sugar preservation such as preserves; canning; dehydration (drying); sealing in jars and vacuum packs; chemical preservatives added to food; and **modified atmosphere packaging**.

Often more than one method is used for a particular food, for example, salted, cured and vacuum-packed smoked salmon is still stored at refrigerated temperatures.

Stock rotation is also used to reduce food spoilage (see page 21).

> **Key term**
>
> **Modified atmosphere packaging**: food is placed in a package then surrounded with a gas mixture that helps to slow down its deterioration (often the oxygen has been removed). The package is sealed to keep the food in its own atmosphere. This method is used for a variety of foods including salads, prepared fruit and meat.

Temperature controls

An important way of controlling bacteria is to ensure that food is kept at controlled temperatures as much as possible.

The range of temperatures between 5 °C and 63 °C are called the **danger zone** because these are the temperatures at which bacteria are most likely to multiply, with most rapid activity at around 37 °C.

The following steps should be taken to avoid the danger zone:

- Keep food being held for service above 63 °C or cool it quickly and keep it below 5 °C.
- When cooking food take it through the danger zone quickly.
- When cooling food, cool it quickly (within 90 minutes) so it is not in the danger zone longer than necessary.

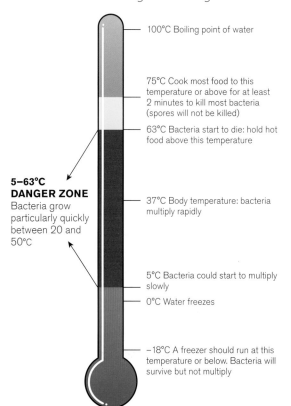

100°C Boiling point of water

75°C Cook most food to this temperature or above for at least 2 minutes to kill most bacteria (spores will not be killed)

63°C Bacteria start to die: hold hot food above this temperature

5–63°C DANGER ZONE Bacteria grow particularly quickly between 20 and 50°C

37°C Body temperature: bacteria multiply rapidly

5°C Bacteria could start to multiply slowly

0°C Water freezes

−18°C A freezer should run at this temperature or below. Bacteria will survive but not multiply

▲ Bacteria can be controlled by ensuring food is kept at controlled temperatures

Temperature recording

Electronic temperature probes are very useful to measure the temperature in the centre of both hot and cold food. They are also good for recording the temperature of deliveries and checking food temperatures in refrigerators.

Make sure the probe is clean and disinfected before use (disposable disinfectant wipes are useful for this). Place the probe into the centre of the food, making sure it is not touching bone or the cooking container.

▲ Electronic temperature probes can be used to measure the temperature of both hot and cold foods

Check regularly that probes are working correctly (calibration). A simple and low cost check is to place the probe in icy water – the reading should be within the range -1 °C to +1 °C. To check accuracy at high temperatures place the probe in boiling water – the temperature reading should be in the range 99 °C to 101 °C. If the probe reads outside of these temperatures it should be repaired or replaced.

> **Key term**
>
> **Danger zone**: the temperature range at which bacteria are most likely to multiply. Danger zone temperature range is between 5 °C and 63 °C with most rapid activity around 37 °C.

Safe food handling practices and procedures

Preparation

Monitor the time that food spends at kitchen (room) temperature and keep this to a minimum. When preparing large amounts, do so in batches, keeping the majority of the food refrigerated until it is needed. High risk food which is out of refrigeration for two hours or more must be thrown away.

If you need to defrost frozen food, place it in a deep tray, cover with film and label it with what the item is and the date when defrosting was started. This is best done in a specific thawing cabinet. Alternatively, place at the bottom of the refrigerator where thawing liquid cannot drip onto other foods. Defrost food completely (i.e. no ice crystals on any part). Once thawed the item should remain at refrigerator temperatures then cooked thoroughly within 12 hours. Make sure that you allow enough time for the thawing process – it may take longer than you think (a 2 kg chicken will take about 24 hours to defrost at 3 °C, for example).

Cooking

Cooking food to a core (centre) temperature of 75 °C for two minutes will kill most bacteria and this temperature is especially important where large amounts of food are being cooked or the consumers are in a high risk category.

Some popular dishes on hotel and restaurant menus may be cooked to a lower temperature than this, depending on the individual dish and customer requirements. Lower temperatures can be used when a whole piece of meat such as a steak or a whole piece of fish is cooked. However, always cook to the higher recommended temperature where meat has been boned/rolled or minced or where food is part of a made up dish such as a fish pie.

Reheating

When reheating previously cooked food, reheat to 75 °C or above (the recommendation in Scotland is 82 °C). The temperature in the centre of the food must be maintained for at least two minutes and re-heating must only be done once.

Holding for service

Cooked food being held for service must be kept above 63 °C (or below 5 °C for cold food).

These temperatures also apply when serving or transporting food.

Chilling

If food is being cooled/chilled to serve cold or for reheating at a later time, it must be protected from contamination and cooled quickly to 8 °C within 90 minutes. This will help prevent any bacteria that may be present from multiplying and avoids the possibility of spores forming. The best way to cool food is in a blast chiller but if this is not available, place in the coolest part of the kitchen, making sure the food is protected from contamination while it is cooling.

The running temperature of refrigerators, freezers and chill cabinets should be checked and recorded at least once a day. Refrigerators and chill cabinets should be below 5 °C and freezers below -18 °C.

▲ Food should be cooled quickly to 8 °C within 90 minutes; the best method is to use a blast chiller

Systems are now available to automatically log the temperatures of all fridges, freezers and display cabinets in a business. Temperatures are recorded and sent to a central computer several times a day. These can then be printed or stored electronically as part of due diligence record keeping. Units not running at correct temperatures will be highlighted by the system.

Stock control procedures

Food deliveries

For food to remain in best condition and be safe to eat, correct storage is essential. This should be planned and the procedures fully understood by kitchen staff. Only approved suppliers who can assure that food is delivered in the best condition should be used. Food must be delivered in suitable packaging, within the required use-by or best before dates and at the correct temperature. Also check that the right quantities have been delivered.

As part of the food safety management system, a record must be kept of all food suppliers used by a business. This is part of **traceability**, which is a requirement under food safety law.

- All deliveries should be checked then moved to the appropriate storage area as soon as possible. Chilled/frozen food must be checked and stored within 15 minutes of delivery to prevent spoilage organisms and pathogenic bacteria from multiplying.
- Use a food probe to check the temperature of food deliveries. Chilled food should be below 5°C (reject if above 8°C); frozen foods should be at or below -18°C (reject if above -16°C). Many suppliers will now provide a print out of temperatures at which each food item was delivered. Keep these temperature records.
- Dry goods should be in undamaged packaging, well within best before dates, be completely dry and in perfect condition on delivery.

Food storage

To store food, remove food items from outer boxes before placing the products in a refrigerator, freezer or dry store. Remove outer packaging carefully, especially from fruit and vegetables, looking out for any possible pests that may have found their way in. The method of storage will depend on the food type. Table 1.4 below shows storage instructions for different food types.

Multi-use refrigerators

When storing food in a multi-use refrigerator:
- Keep the refrigerator running between 1°C and 4°C.
- All food must be covered and labelled with the name of the item and the date.
- Always store raw food at the bottom of the refrigerator with other items above.
- Keep high risk foods well away from raw foods.
- Never overload the refrigerator; to operate properly, cold air must be allowed to circulate between items.
- Wrap strong smelling foods very well as the smell (and taste) can transfer to other foods such as milk.
- Record the temperature at which the refrigerator is operating. Do this at least once a day; keep the refrigerator temperatures with other kitchen records.

Any food that is to be chilled or frozen must be well wrapped or placed in a suitable container with a lid (items may also be vacuum packed). Make sure that all food is labelled and dated before chilling or freezing. Using colour-coded date labels or 'day dots' makes it easier to recognise how long particular items have been stored and which items need to be discarded.

Refrigerators should be cleaned regularly.

Activity

You have been asked to put away a chilled food delivery in a multi-use fridge. Indicate below on which shelf you would position the different foods delivered. The items in the delivery are: raw chicken; cooked ham; cream; salmon fillets; cooked vegetable quiche; eggs; cheese, sponge cakes filled with cream; pate; raw prawns; fresh pasta; rump steak; yoghurt; milk; sausages; butter; and frozen chicken drumsticks that need to be defrosted for use tomorrow.

Shelf 1	
Shelf 1	
Shelf 2	
Shelf 3	
Shelf 4	

Date marking

- **'Use-by'** dates appear on perishable foods with a short life and must be refrigerated. Legally the food must be used by or before the date shown and not stored or offered for sale after the date. It is also an offence to change the date on the food.
- **'Best before'** dates apply to foods that are expected to have a longer life, for example, dry products or canned food. A best before date advises that food should be at its best before this date; using after the date is legal but not advised.

Stock rotation – 'First in–first out'

This term is used to describe stock rotation and is applied to all categories of food. It simply means that foods already in storage are used before new deliveries (providing the food is still within recommended dates and in sound condition). Non-perishable food deliveries should be labelled with the delivery date; use this information along with food labelling codes. Written stock records should be in place and rotation policies should form a part of the food safety management system along with records of procedures for cooking and cooling.

Table 1.4 Storage instructions for different food types

Food type	Storage temperature	Storage instructions
Raw meat and poultry	Refrigerator running at between 0 °C and 2 °C (multi-use refrigerators should be running at below 5 °C).	Store in a refrigerator used just for meat and poultry to avoid drip contamination. If not already packaged, place in trays, cover well with cling film and label. If storing in a multi-use refrigerator, cover, label and place at the bottom of the refrigerator well away from other items.
Fish	Refrigerator running at 1–2 °C (multi-use refrigerators should be running at below 5 °C).	A specific fish refrigerator is preferable. Remove fresh fish from ice containers and place on trays, cover well with cling film and label. If it is necessary to store fish in a multi-use refrigerator, make sure it is well covered, labelled and placed at the bottom of the refrigerator well away from other items. Remember that odours from fish can get into other items such as milk or eggs.
Dairy products/ eggs	Pasteurised milk and cream, eggs and cheese should be stored below 5 °C. Sterilised or UHT milk can be kept in the dry store. After delivery, eggs should be stored at a constant temperature (a fridge is the best place to store them).	Pasteurised milk and cream, eggs and cheese should be stored in their original containers. For sterilised or UHT milk follow the storage instructions on the label. To avoid cross-contamination, prevent eggs from touching other items in the refrigerator.
Frozen foods	In a freezer running at -18 °C or below.	Separate raw foods from ready-to-eat foods and never allow food to be re-frozen once it has de-frosted.
Fruit, vegetables and salad items	Dependent on type; refrigerated items should be stored at around 8 °C to avoid chill damage.	Will vary according to type, e.g. sacks of potatoes, root vegetables and some fruit can be stored in a cool, well-ventilated store room, but salad items, green vegetables, soft fruit and tropical fruit should ideally be kept in refrigerated storage.
Dry goods	A cool, well-ventilated dry store area.	Items such as rice, dried pasta, sugar, flour and grains should be kept in clean, covered containers on wheels or in smaller sealed containers on shelves to stop pests getting into them. Well-managed stock rotation is essential. Retain packaging information as this may include essential allergy advice.
Canned products	Ambient (room) temperature	Stock rotation is essential. Canned food will carry best before dates and it is not advisable to use after this date. 'Blown' (swollen) cans must never be used and do not use badly dented or rusty cans. Once opened transfer any unused canned food to a clean bowl, cover and label it and store in the refrigerator for up to two days.
Cooked foods	Below 5 °C	For example, pies, paté, cream cakes, desserts and savoury flans. They will usually be high risk foods so correct storage is essential. For specific storage instructions, see the labelling on the individual items, but generally, keep items below 5 °C. Store carefully wrapped and labelled and well away from and above raw foods to avoid any cross-contamination.

Key terms

Traceability: the use of records to track food from its source through production and distribution to help control hazards.

Use-by date: date coding that appears on packaged perishable foods that need to be stored in the refrigerator. Use of the food within this date is a legal requirement.

Best before date: date coding that appears on packaged foods that are stored at room temperature and are an indication of quality. Use of the food within the date is not legally binding but it is bad practice to use foods that have exceeded this date.

Stock rotation: managing stock by using older items before newer items, provided the older items are in sound condition and are still within use by or best before dates.

Test yourself

1   List the groups of people considered to be 'high risk' if they contract food poisoning.

2   Give four examples of foods that could cause an allergic reaction in some people.

3   Describe what happens when some bacteria produce spores.

4   There are certain illnesses that a food handler must report to their supervisor before being involved with food. What are they?

5   Give four examples of how you can avoid cross-contamination in a kitchen.

6   It is essential to keep food above 63°C or below 5°C when holding food for service.
   a) Why is this important?
   b) What is the name given to this range of temperatures?

7   What are the recommended temperatures for storing:
   a) dairy foods
   b) frozen fish
   c) fresh meat
   d) soft fruit
   e) flour?

8   What does each of the following types of cleaner do?
   a) detergent
   b) sanitiser
   c) disinfectant.

9   Pest control is important.
   a) Why must pests be kept out of food premises?
   b) Suggest three ways they can be kept out.
   c) How can flying insects be dealt with in a food area?

10 Environmental health officers/practitioners have the power to serve a Hygiene Improvement Notice.
   a) What is a Hygiene Improvement Notice and when would it be served?
   b) What are the essential pieces of information that need to be included in the notice?

2 Developing skills for employment in the catering and hospitality industry

This chapter will help you to:

1 understand the hospitality and catering industry, including:
 – key influences on the industry
 – scope and size of the industry
 – the industry's importance to the national economy
 – the functions of professional associations
 – legal requirements to work within the law.
2 maintain personal appearance and manage time, including:
 – how to maintain personal hygiene and a professional appearance, and why this is important
 – managing time and the importance of time management.
3 produce a plan to develop skills, including:
 – how to produce personal development plans and why they are important
 – identifying opportunities to develop skills
 – the importance of feedback.
4 prepare for a job application, including:
 – identifying interview skills
 – the purpose of a CV and the information that should be included on it
 – the purpose and importance of a covering letter
 – the importance of professional presentation and quality content.

The catering and hospitality industry

The word **hospitality** covers all aspects of the hotel and catering industry. Hospitality means the friendly and generous treatment of guests and strangers, whereas **catering** tends to refer to the offering of facilities, and especially food and drinks.

Wherever there are groups of people there is likely to be some kind of hospitality provision, in other words, somewhere where people can get food, drink and accommodation.

The industry can be roughly divided into two sectors: the **commercial sector** and the **public sector**.

The commercial sector includes hotels, guest houses, restaurants, cafés, fast food outlets, bars, pubs and clubs. It also includes events, visitor and recreation attractions, as well as the travel and tourism sectors. Businesses in the commercial sector operate to make a profit.

Traditionally the public service sector was known as the non-profit making sector, as it provided catering for establishments such as schools, colleges, hospitals, care homes, armed services and prisons. Businesses in the public sector often do not make a profit and may even be subsidised from another source. However, a large percentage of these businesses are now run for a profit by commercial companies like Compass and Sodexo, and are therefore referred to as **cost sector** catering or the **secondary service sector**.

The area that may be described as the **primary service sector** includes hospitality in banks, insurance companies, law firms and large corporate businesses.

Key influences on the catering and hospitality industry

There are a number of key influences on businesses in the hospitality industry.

- **Legislation** – businesses must operate within the legislation and regulations of a particular country or region and also within the regulations of the industry itself (see page 30).
- **Consumer spending** – the amount that potential customers are able and willing to spend on

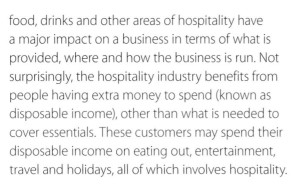

food, drinks and other areas of hospitality have a major impact on a business in terms of what is provided, where and how the business is run. Not surprisingly, the hospitality industry benefits from people having extra money to spend (known as disposable income), other than what is needed to cover essentials. These customers may spend their disposable income on eating out, entertainment, travel and holidays, all of which involves hospitality.

- **Social trends** – people are eating out and staying away from home more than ever before. Trends and fashions for food, restaurants and styles of service are constantly changing and, while there will always be a place for traditional establishments and styles, the industry has to respond to changing tastes and demands for something new and different.
- **Cultural influences** – the hospitality industry must also consider cultural, religious and food preferences. As immigration and global travel have increased they have become even more important and may apply locally, nationally, internationally and even globally.
- **Inflation** – this is the rate at which the level of prices for goods and services rises and therefore spending power falls.
- **Tourism** – the tourism industry continues to increase in size and hospitality will always form part of this. However, tourism also impacts on hospitality in other ways such as increased demand for different styles of food and restaurants experienced when travelling.
- **Culinary achievers and the media** – never before has there been so much coverage of culinary/hospitality high achievers and celebrities

in the media. There are numerous TV programmes featuring well-known celebrity chefs and food companies, and outlets often use their high-profile status in advertising and promotions. There is also wide coverage of well-known chefs on radio, social media, in newspapers and magazines; many have produced books and DVDs. Some have their own restaurants or enhance the profile of other restaurants; they may be the name attracting custom into hotel restaurants. This exposure has a considerable impact on the industry as a whole, highlighting and promoting the image of culinary excellence.

Size, scope and importance of the industry

UK hospitality industry

The UK hospitality industry employs over two million people and continues to grow, providing excellent opportunities for training, employment and career progression.

Around seven per cent of all jobs in the UK are in the hospitality sector, so it accounts for about 1 in every 14 UK jobs, and is predicted to grow even more.

There are approximately 181,500 hospitality, leisure, travel and tourism businesses in the UK. The restaurant industry is the largest within the sector, both in terms of the number of outlets and size of the workforce, followed by pubs, bars and nightclubs and the hotel industry (see Table 2.1).

Table 2.1 Number of businesses (enterprises) by industry

Industry	Number of businesses	%
Restaurants	63,600	45
Pubs, bars and nightclubs	49,150	35
Hotels	10,050	7
Travel and tourist services	6,750	5
Food and service management (contract catering)	6,350	4
Holiday centres and self-catering accommodation	3,650	3
Gambling	1,850	1
Visitor attractions	450	*
Youth and backpacker hostels	150	*
Hospitality, leisure, travel and tourism total	142,050	100

* Negligible

The UK leisure industry (tourism and hospitality) is estimated to be worth around £90 billion. It is estimated that UK accommodation alone contributes £7.5 billion to the total leisure market (this excludes categories such as camp sites and youth hostels). It has been described as one of the biggest and fastest growing industries in the UK.

Take it further

The information above is taken from the People 1st State of the Nation Report 2013. For more information and to access the report, visit the People 1st website: http://people1st.co.uk.

The hospitality industry consists of businesses providing any combination of the three core services of food, drink and accommodation. While there is a clear overlap with tourism, there are a number of sectors within the hospitality industry that are separate from tourism, for example, industrial catering and those aspects of hospitality that attract only the local community.

Restaurants in the UK have approximately 40 per cent of the commercial hospitality market and small establishments employing fewer than ten staff make up the majority of the industry. The south-east of England has the highest concentration of catering and hospitality outlets.

Despite its complexity, hospitality and catering represents one of the largest sectors of the UK economy – it is fifth in size behind retail food, cars, insurance and clothing. It is also an essential support to tourism, another major part of the economy, and one of the largest employers in the country. As well as providing income and profit for company owners and groups of companies, the industry makes very significant contributions to the national economy through taxation.

International hospitality industry

Hospitality is a very large industry, spanning the entire world. Modern businesses find themselves competing in a world economy for survival, growth and profitability. Managers working in the industry have to learn to adjust and change in line with market demands for quality and value for money.

The globalisation of the hospitality and tourism industries has advanced under the pressures of:
- increased technology
- faster communication
- efficient transportation
- deregulation (the removal of regulations and government controls, allowing businesses to operate with more freedom)
- elimination of political barriers
- **socio-cultural changes**
- **global** economic development
- worldwide competition.

An **international** hospitality company must perform successfully in the world's business environment. However, although the whole hospitality industry can be described as global, international or **multinational**, it can also be more localised. Some parts of the industry are **national**, **regional** or even **local**.

Key terms

Socio-cultural: the customs, beliefs, values and language which may shape a person's identity, lifestyle and expectations.

Global: worldwide or universal, applying to the whole world. For example, we talk about the global economy to signify the economy of the whole world.

International: when two or more countries are involved in an industry or business.

Multinational: a term to describe a company that operates in several countries.

National: available in one country, for example, a chain of fish and chip restaurants only operating in the UK.

Regional: applies to a specific region or area, for example, small hotel businesses operating only in Wales or the Lake District.

Local: specific to a local area such as a small family-run restaurant or local cheeses.

Travel, tourism and hospitality together make up the world's largest industry. According to the World Travel and Tourism Council (WTTC), the annual gross output of the industry is greater than the gross national product (GNP) of all countries except the United States and Japan. Worldwide, the industry employs over 112 million people. In many countries, especially in emerging tourist destinations, the hospitality and tourism industry plays a very important role in the national economy, being the major foreign currency earner.

As the world's economies continue to become more dependent on each other, there will be even more international business and leisure travel. The global economy plays an important role in the worldwide opportunities for hospitality and tourism businesses and the industry as a whole.

Types of business

Most hospitality businesses can be divided into three main types: SMEs, public limited companies and private companies. However, many smaller operations in the catering and hospitality industry can be divided into sole traders, self-employed, partnerships and limited liability companies. These are usually private or independent companies.

Small- to medium-sized enterprises (SMEs)

These have up to 250 employees. In the UK as a whole, SMEs account for over half of all employment (58.7 per cent). These are usually private companies that may become public limited companies if they become very large.

Public limited companies (PLC) and private companies

The key difference between public and private companies is that a public company can sell its shares to the public, while private companies cannot. A share is a certificate representing one unit of ownership in a company, so the more shares a person has, the more of the company they own.

Before it can start in business or borrow money, a public company must prove to Companies House (the department where all companies in the UK must be registered) that at least £50,000 worth of shares have been issued and that each share has been paid up to at least a quarter of its nominal value (so 25 per cent of £50,000). It will then receive authorisation to start business and borrow money.

Sole trader (or independent)

A sole trader is the simplest form of a business and is suited to the smallest of operations. The sole trader owns the business, takes all the risks, is liable for any losses and keeps any profits. The advantage of operating a business as a sole trader is that very little formality is needed. The only official records required are those for HM Revenue and Customs (HMRC – the government department responsible for collecting tax), National Insurance and VAT. The accounts are not available to the public.

Self-employed

There is no precise definition of self-employment, although guidance is offered by HMRC. In order to determine whether an individual is truly self-employed, the circumstances of the individual's work need to be considered, including whether the person:

- is in control of their own time, the amount of work they take on and the decision making
- has no guarantee of regular work
- receives no pay for periods of holiday or sickness
- is responsible for all the risks of the business
- attends the premises of the person providing the work
- generally uses their own equipment and materials
- has the right to send someone else to do the work.

Partnership

A partnership consists of two or more people working together as the owners of a business. Unlike limited liability companies (see below), there are no legal requirements in setting up as a partnership.

The partnership is similar to a sole trader in law, in that the partners own the business, take all the risks, stand any losses and keep any profits. Each partner individually is responsible for all the debts of the partnership. So, if the business fails, each partner's personal assets (for example, their personal bank account, stocks, shares, car, house, etc.) are fully at risk. It is possible to have partners with limited liability. In this case the partner with limited liability must not play any active part in the management or conduct of the business. In effect, he or she has simply invested a sum of money in the partnership.

The advantages of operating a business as a partnership can be very similar to those of the sole trader. Very little formality is needed, although anyone contemplating entering into a partnership should consider taking legal advice and having a partnership agreement drawn up.

The main official records that are required are records for the Inland Revenue, National Insurance and VAT. The accounts are not available to the public. There may be important tax advantages, too, when compared with a limited company. For example, the partners might be able pay the tax they owe at a later date or treat deductible expenses more generously.

Limited liability companies

These are companies that are incorporated under the Companies Acts. This means that the liability of their owners (the amount they will have to pay to cover the business's debts if it fails or if it is sued) is limited to the value of the shares each shareholder (owner) owns.

Limited liability companies are much more complex than sole traders and partnerships. This is because the owners can limit their liability. As a consequence it is vital that people either investing in them or doing business with them know the financial standing of the company. Company documents are open to inspection by the public.

Franchises

A franchise is an agreement where a person or group of people pay a fee and some set up costs to use an established name or brand which is well known and is therefore likely to attract more customers than an unknown or start-up brand.

> **Key terms**
>
> **Small- to medium-sized enterprise (SME)**: businesses with up to 250 employees.
>
> **Public limited company (PLC)**: a company that can sell shares to the public.
>
> **Sole trader**: the simplest form of a business; the sole trader owns the business, takes all the risks, is liable for any losses and keeps any profits.
>
> **Partnership**: consists of two or more people working together as the owners of a business; the partners take all the risks, stand any losses and keep any profits.
>
> **Limited liability company**: a business in which the amount the owners will have to pay to cover the business's debts if it fails or if it is sued is limited to the value of the shares each shareholder (owner) owns.
>
> **Franchise**: when a company grants permission for someone to open and run a branch of their company and sell their products.

Professional associations

There are a number of professional bodies relating to the hospitality industry which offer support, training and legal advice. Some provide professional membership for suitable candidates, some award their own qualifications and some have a restricted membership. They may provide information, set standards of excellence, provide awards, or organise training, master classes, demonstrations and competitions.

Associations can be regional, national or international.

People 1st is a skills and workforce development charity for employers in the hospitality, tourism, travel and retail industries. They focus on developing skills in the sector through effective recruitment, training, professional development and talent management, to be able to compete in a rapidly changing global market.

Other organisations include:
- Institute of Hospitality (www.instituteofhospitality.org)
- Royal Academy of Culinary Arts (www.royalacademyofculinaryarts.org.uk)
- Craft Guild of Chefs (www.craftguildofchefs.org)
- Master Chefs of Great Britain (www.masterchefs.co.uk)
- Hospital Caterers Association (www.hospitalcaterers.org)
- Wine and Spirit Education Trust (www.wsetglobal.com)
- Academy of Food and Wine Service (www.afws.co.uk)
- Association of Catering Excellence (www.acegb.org)
- University Caterers Association (www.tuco.org)
- Local Authority Caterers Association (www.laca.co.uk)

> **Take it further**
>
> For more information on the functions of the different professional associations listed above, visit their websites.

Case study - an example of a franchise agreement

The contract caterer, Compass Group, buys a franchise in the Burger King brand from its owners. Compass Group pays Burger King a fee and a proportion of the takings. The franchisor (the branded company franchise provider – in this case Burger King) will normally lay down strict guidelines or 'brand standards' that must be met. These may include: which ingredients and raw materials are used and where they come from; portion sizes; the general product packaging and service. The franchisor will check on the brand standards regularly to ensure that the brand reputation is not being put at risk. The franchisor will normally also provide advertising and marketing support, accounting services, help with staff training and development, as well as designs for merchandising and display materials.

Legal requirements: employment rights and responsibilities

There is a considerable amount of legislation that regulates both the industry itself and employment within the industry. Employers who break the law or attempt to undermine the statutory (legal) rights of their workers – for example, paying less than the national minimum wage or denying them their right to paid annual holidays – are not only liable to prosecution and fines, but could be ordered by tribunals and courts to pay substantial amounts of compensation.

Job descriptions and contracts of employment

Employers must provide the employee with:

- a detailed job description
- a contract of employment with details of the job itself, working hours, rates of pay, the annual holiday the employee will have and the notice period.

An essential feature of a contract of employment is the 'mutuality of obligation'. This means that the employer will provide the employee with work on specified days of the week for specified hours and, if employed under a limited-term contract, for an agreed number of weeks or months. In return, the employee agrees to carry out the work for an agreed wage or salary.

In recent years 'zero hours contracts' have been offered in parts of the hospitality and other industries. These allow employers to employ staff with no guarantee of work, which means employees work only for the hours they are needed by employers, often at short notice. Their pay depends on how much they work. Sick pay is often not included, although holiday pay should be, to comply with working time regulations.

Employers must follow the relevant laws of a particular country relating to issues such as employment law, health and safety law and food safety law.

An employee is a person employed directly by a company under a contract of employment or service. He or she must work in the way that has been agreed to in the contract and job description and follow all the organisation's policies and practices.

A worker or contractor is someone who works for another company (a sub-contractor) that has won a contract to carry out work or provide services at a business. They are not actually an employee of the company itself, but are still protected by the following laws:

- Health and Safety at Work Act 1974
- Working Time Regulations 1998
- Equality Act 2010
- Public Interest Disclosure Act 1998
- National Minimum Wage Act 1998
- Part-time Workers (Prevention of Less Favourable Treatment) Regulations 2000

Age restrictions on employment

Sometimes age restrictions may also apply as part of the terms of employment. For example, many employers will not employ anyone under the age of 18, especially where potentially dangerous equipment is used or they will be involved in serving alcohol.

Recruitment and selection

When advertising for new staff a business must be aware of the following legislation:

- Children and Young Persons Act 1933
- Licensing Act 1964
- Rehabilitation of Offenders Act 1974
- Data Protection Act 1988
- Asylum and Immigration Act 1996
- National Minimum Wage Act 1998
- Working Time Regulations 1998
- Equality Act 2010
- Human Rights Act 1998.

It is unlawful to discriminate against job applicants on grounds of marital status or gender, colour, race, nationality, national or ethnic origins, disability, sexual orientation, religion or beliefs, or trades union membership or non-membership.

Job application forms must be designed with care. If sensitive personal information is needed, such as a health record or disability disclosure, the reason for this should be explained and the candidate reassured that the data will remain confidential and will be used and stored in keeping with the provisions of the Data Protection Act 1998.

Under the terms of the Human Rights Act, candidates must be informed at application stage and at interview if they have to wear a uniform or protective clothing on duty. Any surveillance monitoring the company is likely to carry out must also be disclosed to applicants.

It is an offence under the Asylum and Immigration Act 1996 to employ a foreign national who is subject to immigration control. For example, those needing a visa or work permit, who do not have the right to enter or remain in the UK, or to take up employment while in the UK. Job application forms should caution applicants that they will be required to produce documents confirming their right to be in, and to take up employment in, the UK.

If an applicant resigned or was dismissed from previous employment, the interviewer may need to know why. Any health problems, injuries and disabilities the candidate has disclosed may also need to be discussed in order to determine the applicant's suitability for employment. All employees may be subject to a medical health check before formally being offered employment.

Employers may lawfully ask an applicant if he or she has been convicted of any criminal offence, but must be aware of the right of applicants, under the Rehabilitation of Offenders Act 1974, not to disclose details of any criminal convictions that have since become 'spent'. All cautions and convictions become spent after a specified period of time (although this varies according to the sentence passed) so that eventually, with the exception of prison sentences of over 30 months, they no longer count.

The interviewer should not ask questions about an applicant's sexuality or religion. However, questions on religion may be asked if, for example, aspects of the job may directly affect the beliefs of an individual – an example would be the handling of alcoholic drinks or meat such as pork.

An offer of employment should be made or confirmed in writing, and is often conditional on the receipt of satisfactory references from former employers. Withdrawing an offer of employment once it has been accepted could result in a civil action for damages by the prospective employee.

Statutory sick pay

Employers in Great Britain are liable to pay up to 28 weeks' statutory sick pay to any eligible employee who is unable to work because of illness of injury. Employers who operate their own occupational sick pay schemes may opt out of the statutory sick pay scheme, as long as the payments available to their employees under such schemes are equal to or greater than payments they would be entitled to under statutory sick pay and so long as employees are not required to contribute towards the cost of funding such a scheme. Payments made under statutory sick pay may be offset against contractual sick pay and vice versa.

Working Time Regulations

The Working Time Regulations apply not only to employees but also to every worker (part-time, temporary, seasonal or casual) who undertakes to do work or carry out a service for an employer.

The 1998 Regulations are policed and enforced by employment tribunals (in relation to a worker's statutory rights to rest periods and paid annual holidays) and by local authority environmental health officers.

Personal appearance and managing time
Presenting a professional image

Presenting a professional image is important for your own personal pride and confidence, to promote yourself, your employer and your job role. A positive image gives you status, earns respect and helps to make you a good role model for others. Image can also be used to enhance branding – for example, the company branding on chefs' jackets and smart, distinctive receptionist uniforms. The clothing provided for you at work identifies you as a professional, representing the establishment and the wider industry.

Wearing a uniform can also be essential for health and safety and food safety reasons, helping to protect yourself and others working with you, as well as protecting the food you work with. Clean, hygienic kitchen clothing and good hygienic practices when handling food are part of the requirements of food safety legislation.

▲ Good personal hygiene and smart presentation is important for a professional image, to protect yourself and others, and to comply with legislation

The way you carry out your job and are able to use appropriate skills is part of your personal presentation. Good presentation, both front and back of house, helps increase customer confidence and satisfaction, improves business and improves staff morale and job satisfaction. This leads to happy customers, increased profits and a lower staff turnover. These, in turn, enhance the reputation of the establishment.

Personal hygiene and professional appearance

- Clothing must be smart, clean and in good repair. Wear the correct uniform in the kitchen, freshly laundered at the start of each day and change if it gets stained or dirty. You should never wear kitchen uniform outside the working premises as this is unhygienic. Bacteria from outside can be carried on the uniform into the kitchen and may result in contamination (see Chapter 1). Correct kitchen clothing for chefs consists of a cotton, double-breasted chef's jacket (preferably with long sleeves), loose-fitting, cotton chef's trousers, chef's hat, cotton apron, safety shoes and a cotton neck tie (this is now seen as optional).

- Hair must be clean and well cared for, short or tied back neatly (and in a net or hat); men should be clean shaven.
- No jewellery or watches should be worn in the kitchen.
- Cosmetics and perfume/aftershave should be kept to the absolute minimum.
- Nails must be clean and short (but never bite them). Hands are of absolute importance as they will be in direct contact with food and equipment.
- Wash hands thoroughly on entering the kitchen, between tasks, after breaks or visiting the toilet and after emptying bins or handling chemicals (see Chapter 1).
- Care for your teeth and visit the dentist for regular check-ups.
- Working in a kitchen involves being on your feet all day, so take care of your feet and keep toe nails trimmed and wear clean, well-fitting socks and shoes.

There are some bad and unhygienic practices that must never be allowed in food areas. These include smoking, chewing gum, irregular or poor hand washing and eating or drinking in the work area.

Time management

Employers want to employ people with the right attitude, who are able to show initiative, be punctual, flexible and dependable. They want people who can organise themselves, communicate well and manage their time effectively.

Time management and the prioritising and organisation of work is very important when working in a kitchen, as this is an area where time is crucial to the business. For example, if you work in a data-entry job and you are running an hour behind schedule, it may not be too important and time can be made up later. However, a lunch or dinner served an hour late is a significant problem that will lead to complaints and possible loss of future business.

To manage your time well involves thought and planning. You may have a task list for the day or the week given to you by your supervisor or section head. Before you start to work on the tasks consider them carefully. Which are essential, which are less important and which could be left until the others have been completed? There are a number of things to consider when prioritising and managing your time such as how long will an item take to prepare or cook? Does it need your full attention (such as a stir fry) or can it be left to cook with very little attention (like a stewed meat dish)? Those items that do not need your full attention while they cook allow you to complete other tasks at the same time. Generally give attention to the things that take longest first.

Formulate the tasks you need to complete into a written plan or list you can work from and maybe tick them off on completion. Time management may also involve how you work. Keeping your area clean, tidy and well organised will allow you to work more efficiently. Assemble the tools, equipment and non-refrigerated ingredients before starting the job; this will avoid unnecessary walking between areas. When working with someone else plan the work between you before starting.

Producing a plan to develop skills

It is necessary to evaluate and check your progress from time to time. Feedback from your peers and managers is a useful way of evaluating your performance, but evaluating your own performance and achievement is very important too.

Evaluating current skills

When producing a personal development plan you should identify which skills you need to develop further and ways you could do this.

Table 2.2 provides a useful template to help you to evaluate your current skills. Skills you may need to develop could include:
- communication
- teamwork
- problem solving
- technical
- planning and organisation
- time management
- numeracy and literacy.

Personal development plans

A personal development plan helps you identify targets and set timescales to improve your skills. These targets could be short or longer term. Tables 2.3 and 2.4 could be used to help you set personal targets and make an action plan for personal development.

A personal development plan can be used to record feedback from your mentor, manager or tutor, and help you to improve performance. Keeping a record of your skills and your personal development plans will help you to refer back to your targets and check your progress towards achieving your goals and enabling you to achieve success.

> **Key term**
>
> **Personal development plan**: a statement outlining a person's career aspirations and work-related goals, and a description of the steps to be taken to ensure the plan is achieved.

Table 2.2 Skills for success: an example of a useful template for recording skills acquisition

Knowledge, skills, qualities and experience	Already experienced	Want to know more	Want to develop further	Order of importance
Craft skills				
Knife skills				
Kitchen skills				
Pastry skills				
Larder skills				
Restaurant skills				
Managing your time				
Identifying barriers to personal success				
Being able to reflect positively				
Knowing what kind of career you want				
Preparing a job application				
Writing a covering letter				
Writing an attractive CV				
Understanding what is required to be successful				
Teamwork skills				
Developing professional relationships				
Being assertive				
Dealing with difficult people				
Developing confidence				
Dealing with basic problem solving				
Being self-motivated				
Evaluating personal competitiveness				
Knowing effective interview techniques				
Preparing for an interview				
Developing personal records				
Recording evidence				

Table 2.3 Personal targets

	Target 1	Target 2	Target 3
The importance of the skill and why you need it			
How you will achieve this skill and what support and guidance you will need			
Evidence that you have achieved your aim			

Table 2.4 Action plan for personal development

Target	Steps to take in milestones	Indicators of successful completion	Start date	Target completion date	Done
1	a)				
	b)				
	c)				
2	a)				
	b)				
	c)				

Applying for a job

When applying for a job you will usually be asked to supply information about yourself, such as:

- your personal details
- qualifications you already have and those you are working towards
- experience or work experience
- membership of associations
- personal achievements such as awards or winning competitions
- details of people who will give you a reference.

If the first stage of your application is successful, you will be asked to go for an interview.

Preparing a curriculum vitae (CV)

You will probably be asked to send in a current CV (curriculum vitae). This requires you to list all your educational qualifications and work history, your interests and any other relevant activities you participate in. Employers will usually want to know how you have demonstrated certain skills, how you have dealt with situations in the workplace and what your outside interests are.

When preparing a CV, you should also bear in mind the following points:

- Details of all work experience and work placements should be included, as well as the name of past or present employers and the dates of such employment.
- Include details of progression as well as personal achievements such as employee awards and competitions you have entered.
- Include examples of your personal strengths such as time management, communication or problem-solving skills, but be prepared to elaborate on these at interview.
- Always check spelling, vocabulary, layout and punctuation. You may find it helpful to get a friend or colleague to check your CV.
- Explain what inspires you and how you use your existing skills.
- Specify what your long-term goals are, as well as your immediate goals and targets.

Producing a covering letter

A covering letter introduces you to the company and provides them with their first impression of you. It explains why you are suitable for the job and the skills and qualities you can bring to it. The coving letter also provides you with an opportunity to say how you would be able to contribute positively to the establishment and the organisation as a whole. The letter usually accompanies a copy of your CV.

Interview techniques

First impressions are important so always prepare thoroughly for an interview. Good preparation will help to ensure that you are confident and present yourself to best advantage in the interview.

Curriculum vitae

Name

Current position:

Home address:

Telephone:

Home email:

Date of birth:

General career overview:

[*Include bullet point list of key features and achievements of career, including key experience and skills*]

- X years' industry experience in food and beverage operations, including X years at craft and supervisory level.
- Experienced in [*give details*].
- Proven record of achievement recognised through promotion and career advancement.
- Hard working and a good team member.
- Commitment to continuing professional development through undertaking various in-company training programmes [*give details*].

Professional experience:

- Dates [*write as month and year in full and include job title and name of place, name of specific place and indication of level of operation, e.g. 5**]
- Reporting to [*give details*].
- Give some descriptive information, such as services provided, for how many people and how many staff responsible for. [*For example, á la carte and table d'hôte all-day dining for up to 000 people, function catering for up to 000 people, with a staffing of 000 people.*]
- List key responsibilities.
- List other job features and unique experience.

[*Then repeat this format for all employment going back in time. Write in the third person as it is easier to write in that format and much easier for other people to read.*]

Professional activities:

- [*Bullet point list of any professional memberships and any contributions to industry activities.*]

Competitions and awards:

Education, training and qualifications:

Hobbies and interests:

Nationality: [*Include visa status if appropriate.*]

▲ Your CV should list your qualifications, work history, skills and interests

When preparing for an interview, you should bear in mind the following points:

- Learn something about the company and the job role so you can ask appropriate questions and answer questions the interviewer may ask you.
- Prepare any questions you may have in advance.
- Consider how you are going to introduce yourself at the start of the interview.
- Make sure you are well groomed, smart and look professional.
- Practise the interview with a friend beforehand – this is known as role play.
- Before the interview, plan your journey and work out the travelling time – allow plenty of time to get there so you do not feel rushed.

At the interview follow the points below to create a good impression:

- Maintain eye contact with the interviewer and smile occasionally.
- Speak clearly; be confident, interested and polite.
- Demonstrate good communication skills – use the correct vocabulary.
- Think about the questions you are asked before you answer them. Give clear and concise answers. If you do not understand a question, ask for it to be clarified.

When the interview is over, reflect on your performance. If you are unsuccessful, ask for feedback and learn from the experience. Think about how you might improve in the future.

4 Maynard Avenue
Compton
Sturbridge
B20 1SB
Telephone: 0123 456 789
Email:william.johns@xxx.com

Mr James Bryant
Human Resources Manager
Hambury Hotels Ltd
Hertford Road
Birmingham
XXX XX

23 May 2014

Dear Mr Bryant

Re: 55/001: Commis Chef Trainee programme

I am writing to you to apply for the Commis Chef trainee programme, currently advertised on the Hambury Hotels' website. My current CV is enclosed for your consideration.

Having always been interested in cooking, I applied to study a GNVQ Chef and Restaurant Diploma course after my GCSEs. My interest in becoming a chef started when my school attended an openday at University College Birmingham, my local catering college.

Hambury Hotels has an excellent reputation, focusing on high standards and the opportunity to study for higher qualifications while training and contributing to the work of the hotel. At the college's open day in February, I met with current graduate trainees and I was impressed by the friendliness of your employees and the very positive descriptions of working life at the hotel.

As well as completing my current course in May, my practical experience has included working on a three-month chef placement at the Weigh Bridge Hotel, Sturbridge.

I am available for an interview from 1 June onwards. In the meantime, I look forward to taking the opportunity to talk with you further about my application.

Yours sincerely

William Johns

▲ A covering letter is your opportunity to tell an employer why you are suitable for the job on offer

Professional tip

Places where opportunities for employment and job vacancy advertisements can be found include:
- industry magazines such as *The Caterer*
- local and national newspapers and local radio
- employment websites and employer's own websites
- social media
- personal recommendation and word of mouth
- local job centres, tourist information centres and libraries
- local guides and information books
- staff recruitment agencies
- college careers and recruitment departments
- individual employers.

Test yourself

1   How many people are employed in the UK hospitality industry?

2   For a business to be an SME, what is the maximum number of employees it can have?

3   Which type of business makes up approximately 40 per cent of the commercial hospitality market?

4   There are a number of professional associations related to the hospitality industry.
   a) What is the purpose of professional hospitality industry organisations?
   b) State the advantages to be gained from belonging to a professional organisation.
   c) As a chef, name **two** of the organisations you could apply to for membership.

5   There are many legal requirements that those working in the catering and hospitality industry must follow.
   a) Name **four** items of UK legislation that may affect employees in the hospitality industry.
   b) For each item of legislation, state two main points that the legislation covers.

6   List **six** rules chefs should follow in relation to smart and hygienic kitchen uniform.

7   Setting personal targets is a good way to monitor progress and achievement.
   a) Suggest three targets you may set for yourself.
   b) How would you know when each of these targets had been achieved?

8   When applying for a job you may be asked to provide a copy of your CV.
   a) What is a CV?
   b) What is the main information that should appear on a CV?

9   Suggest **four** ways that you can prepare for a job interview.

10 How could a personal development plan help you to progress in your career?

Practice assignment tasks

Task 1
Look at the hospitality and catering press (such as *The Caterer*) or a recruitment website and find two advertised chef positions that appeal to you.

1   What is it about the advertised jobs that you like?

2   What are the qualifications and previous experience needed for the jobs?

3   From where you are now, what more would you need to do to make you eligible for each of the jobs?

4   Produce a covering letter to send with your CV to apply for one of the jobs.

Task 2
The size and complexity of the UK hospitality industry is surprising to those who do not know much about it.

Produce a large poster or series of PowerPoint slides to use at a school careers fair to inform students, parents and teachers of the significance of the industry. Include:

● the size of the hospitality industry and how much income it contributes to the economy
● the number of hospitality businesses
● the number of jobs the industry provides
● what the main influences on the industry are
● the professional associations linked with hospitality, and the advantages they offer.

Task 3
Like all industries, the hospitality industry is governed by a wide range of legislation.

Make a list of the legal Acts that would affect you when working as a chef and briefly state how each would affect chefs working in the kitchen. Start your list with:

● Health and Safety at Work Act 1974
● Food Safety Act 1990.

This chapter will help you to:

1 understand the importance of health and safety in the catering and hospitality industry, including:
   – who has responsibilities in current legislation, and the legal responsibilities of employers and employees and the power of enforcement officers
   – regulations covering safety issues
   – common causes of ill health and accidents, the benefits of good health and safety practice and costs of poor health and safety practice.
2 identify hazards in the catering and hospitality workplace, including:
   – the causes of and steps to minimise slips, trips and falls, and injuries from manual handling, machinery/equipment, hazardous substances, fire and explosions, and electrical dangers.

3 control hazards in the workplace, including:
   – the risk assessment process
   – control measures to reduce risk
   – accident reporting, PPE and safety signs.
4 maintain a healthy and safe workplace, including:
   – sources of health and safety information
   – features required in the food preparation area and welfare facilities needed for staff to ensure safe working practices
   – incident reporting and emergency procedures.

Introduction

Every day people are injured at work. Some may be permanently disabled and some may even die. Kitchens and other hospitality areas can be dangerous places. For this reason, it is important to work in a safe and systematic way in order to avoid accidents or injury to yourself or anyone else.

The average number of days taken as sick leave each year in the UK is approximately 131 million, and absence due to sickness costs the UK economy approximately £28.8 billion each year. Over 200 people die in accidents at work each year; accidents and injury can happen in any workplace. Stress and accidents are currently the two biggest causes of absence from work.

Health and safety in the catering and hospitality industry

Who is responsible for health and safety?

- Employers/employees
- People in control of work premises
- Self-employed people
- Building and workplace designers

- Manufacturers and suppliers
- Local authorities (environmental health officers)
- Health and Safety Executive (enforcement officers).

Legal responsibilities

All chefs and kitchen workers as well as their employers need to know the laws on health and safety. The Health and Safety at Work Act 1974 gives employees and employers certain responsibilities while working.

Employees must:
- take reasonable care of their own safety and the safety of others working with them
- inform their supervisor or line manager if they see anything they think is unsafe and could cause an accident
- cooperate with anything their employer has put in place to ensure health and safety.

Employers must:
- provide a safe and healthy workplace, with safe equipment, including PPE
- provide methods to deal with chemical substances safely
- conduct risk assessments and provide a health and safety policy statement
- provide necessary training and supervision to keep employees safe.

Under the Health and Safety at Work Act, an employer must do everything possible to ensure the safety of people at work. This means they must:

- provide safe work areas, equipment and utensils
- train staff in safe practices and record this training
- provide first aid equipment
- keep accident records in a file or electronic system
- produce a policy document explaining safe working procedures.

Enforcement officers and their powers

The **Health and Safety Executive (HSE)** and local authorities (councils) are responsible for enforcing health and safety standards and legislation in the workplace.

In general, local authorities are responsible for enforcing health and safety legislation in wholesale and retail outlets, offices, restaurants, hotels, residential homes, entertainment and recreational venues.

The Health and Safety Executive (HSE) is responsible for other premises such as manufacturing, construction sites, local government property, transport, schools and universities, hospitals and nursing homes.

HSE inspectors and **environmental health officers (EHOs)** from the local authority have the power to:

- enter premises for inspection without prior notice at any reasonable time. They will inspect the health and safety standards of the premises and compliance with the law
- check, dismantle and remove equipment and food, inspect records, ask questions, take photographs and seize and destroy items where they consider such action necessary.

> **Key terms**
>
> **Health and Safety Executive (HSE)**: the national independent authority for work-related health, safety and illness. It acts to reduce work-related death and serious injury across Great Britain's workplaces.
>
> **Environmental health officer (EHO)**: a person employed by the local authority to enforce health and safety standards, and to offer help, advice and training. An EHO is now sometimes called an environmental health practitioner (EHP).

Enforcement officers can give verbal or written advice, but may also issue formal notices if they inspect premises and find non-compliance with health and safety law that is more serious and needs further action than an informal warning. One of the following may be issued:

- **Improvement notice** – the inspector will first discuss the problems with the business owner or duty holder before serving the notice. The notice will say what needs to be done, why, and by when. The time allowed to complete the improvements will be at least 21 days to allow for the work to take place or for appeals. The inspector can take further legal action if the notice is not complied with within the specified time period.
- **Prohibition notice** – where the inspector considers the business or a procedure could involve a risk of serious personal injury, the inspector may serve a prohibition notice prohibiting the activity immediately or after a specified time. Business or the activity cannot be resumed until the specified action has been taken. The notice will explain why the action is necessary.

An enforcement notice may instigate prosecution of owners of a business, which can result in unlimited fines, imprisonment for up to two years, or both.

> **Key terms**
>
> **Improvement notice**: a business is given a set amount of time to improve health and safety issues highlighted by an enforcement officer.
>
> **Prohibition notice**: issued when a business or business procedure is deemed to be unsafe by an enforcement officer and the activity must stop immediately.

Activity

If your premises were inspected by an environmental health officer or HSE inspector and they found that you were not complying with regulations, what are the actions that could be taken?

Regulations

There are a number of regulations covering safety issues within the workplace. These include:

- Manual Handling Operations Regulations 1992
- Personal Protective Equipment (PPE) at Work Regulations 1992
- Regulatory Fire Safety Order 2005
- Provision and Use of Work Equipment Regulations 1998 (PUWER)
- Control of Substances Hazardous to Health (COSHH).

More information on each of these regulations can be found below.

Common causes of ill health and accidents

Accidents in the workplace may be due to **occupational**, **environmental** or **human causes**.

Occupational causes include:

- being exposed to hot items or dangerous substances such as steam or oven cleaning chemicals
- being injured by machines such as vegetable cutting machines, liquidisers and mincing machines
- electric shocks from equipment
- being hurt by moving objects, such as falling stacked boxes, or being cut by a knife when chopping
- lifting objects in the wrong way and lifting heavy or awkward objects.

▲ Hot items are a common cause of accidents in the catering and hospitality industry

Environmental causes include:

- badly designed buildings and work areas
- inadequate lighting and ventilation
- slipping on a wet or greasy floor
- walking into, tripping or falling over objects.

Human causes can include:

- dangerous or careless working; becoming distracted and lack of attention
- being under too much pressure and trying to work too quickly
- employees not following the rules for safe working practice
- employees not wearing the correct personal protective equipment (PPE)
- individuals arriving at work not having had enough sleep, or not in a good mental or physical state
- inexperience or lack of training.

> **Key terms**
>
> **Occupational cause**: accidents that are work- or activity-related.
>
> **Environmental cause**: accidents due to a person's surroundings or location.
>
> **Human cause**: accidents due to your own or another person's actions.

Activity

1 List six possible ways that accidents could be avoided in a busy kitchen.
2 How could you inform and warn other staff about staying safe?

Health and safety standards in the workplace

Good standards of health and safety means:

- employees are likely to experience fewer accidents and instances of ill health
- employees are more likely to be healthy, happy and well-motivated
- the workplace will have a good reputation as an organised and safe place to work
- increased productivity which means the business is likely to be more profitable and successful
- the business will comply with the law.

Poor standards of health and safety may result in:
- an increased risk of accidents, illness and stress
- the workplace will have a poor reputation
- more employees will need time off work due to sickness
- higher staff turnover
- compensation claims
- fines and legal costs for non-compliance with the law.

Identifying hazards in the catering and hospitality workplace

Slips, trips and falls

The majority of accidents in catering premises are caused by falling, slipping or tripping. Slips, trips and falls can be caused by:
- badly designed buildings and work areas
- inadequate lighting and ventilation
- poor housekeeping and cleaning standards
- poor or inadequate signage
- dangerous or careless working; becoming distracted and lack of attention
- being under too much pressure and trying to work too quickly
- employees not following the rules for safe working practice
- employees not wearing the correct PPE
- individuals arriving at work not having had enough sleep, or not in a good mental or physical state.

A major reason for the high frequency of this kind of accident is from water and grease spilt onto the floor, making the floor surface slippery. For this reason, any spillage must be cleaned immediately, verbal warnings given and warning notices put in place, where appropriate. Ideally, a member of staff should stand guard until the hazard is cleared.

Another cause of falls is items left on the floor in corridors, passageways or between stoves and tables. People carrying trays and containers may have a restricted view, may not see items on the floor and so may trip over them. This could be made worse if the person falls on to a hot stove, or if the item they are carrying is hot. These falls can have severe consequences. Nothing must be left on the floor where it may cause an obstruction and be a hazard.

▲ The majority of accidents in catering premises are caused by falling, slipping or tripping

Avoiding accidents

There are many precautions that can be taken to avoid slips, trips and falls in catering premises.
- Building and work areas should be well designed for the tasks being completed and must be well maintained.
- Good standards of housekeeping and cleaning must be in place.
- There should be clear, visible signage as appropriate.
- Staff must all be trained in safe working practices and this must be enforced, including the correct use of the necessary PPE.
- Staff must arrive at work having had enough sleep and be ready physically and mentally for the work ahead.
- Floors should be even, with no unexpected steps or gradients. Floor coverings should have an anti-slip finish and be kept clean and grease free.
- Corridors and walkways should be kept clear so that people do not trip over objects that are in the way.
- Appropriate lighting should be provided so employees can see clearly where they are going.
- Adequate ventilation is needed to avoid condensation and to allow excess heat and fumes to escape.
- Kitchens should not be overcrowded. There should be enough space for people to move between areas freely.

- Employees must follow the rules and working practices put in place for the working area and work in an organised way, cleaning as they go.
- Employees must move around the kitchen, through the preparation areas to the service areas without backtracking or crossing over to avoid collisions with others.

Manual handling

Picking up and carrying heavy or difficult loads can lead to accidents if it is not done properly. Handling loads wrongly is the main cause of back/spinal problems in the workplace. Other injuries from manual handling may include muscular injury, fractures, sprains, cuts and bruises.

Lifting and carrying safely

When items need to be moved, lifted or carried, assess the task first and if you are unsure about how to complete the task safely, speak to a supervisor. Many employers provide safe manual handling training.

When assessing the load, consider:

- the size and weight of the item and whether it is an awkward shape
- the temperature of the item, for example, hot pans of food, frozen food, slippery items
- getting help from other people and/or using lifting equipment or trolleys
- reducing the load, for example, unpacking large boxes and moving the contents separately
- the environment, for example, the type of flooring, lighting and temperatures
- using correct PPE, for example, a padded jacket for moving large amounts of frozen food.

When lifting:

- assess the load as above
- keep the back straight, feet apart and bend at the knees
- grip the load evenly according to shape and size
- straighten the back and hold the object close to the body
- move the object, having checked the route ahead is visible, clear and safe
- lower the load carefully.

Using trolleys, trucks and wheeled vehicles

- Load them carefully and do not overload.
- Load them in a way that allows you to see where you are going.
- Stack heavier items at the bottom.
- Plan the route: where there are slopes and gradients the loaded trolley may be more difficult to handle and you could lose control on uneven or bumpy surfaces. Items may fall if not loaded properly.

Other considerations

- If steps are needed to reach higher items, use them with care. Ladder training may be given.
- Take particular care when moving large pots of liquid, especially if the liquid is hot. Do not fill them to the brim.
- Use a warning sign to let people know if equipment might be hot. This is traditionally done by sprinkling a small amount of flour on hot parts such as pan handles but even better is to wrap a thick oven cloth around the handle.
- Take extra care when lifting or carrying any hot equipment such as hot trays from the oven to avoid burning yourself or someone else.

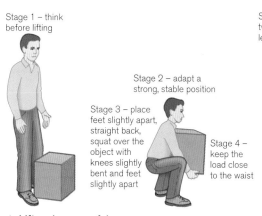

Stage 1 – think before lifting

Stage 2 – adapt a strong, stable position

Stage 3 – place feet slightly apart, straight back, squat over the object with knees slightly bent and feet slightly apart

Stage 4 – keep the load close to the waist

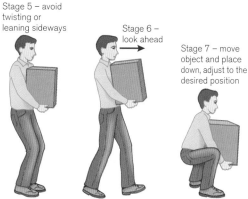

Stage 5 – avoid twisting or leaning sideways

Stage 6 – look ahead

Stage 7 – move object and place down, adjust to the desired position

▲ Lift and carry safely

Kitchen machinery and equipment

Kitchen equipment can cause accidents or injury if misused. Table 3.1 provides examples of ways in which machinery and equipment can cause injuries.

All staff must be trained in the correct use of equipment and machinery, especially young or inexperienced staff. Worn or faulty equipment must not be used and electrical equipment must be regularly maintained and checked, with records kept of this. Kitchen staff must receive training in safe working procedures, reporting any faults with equipment and use of specified PPE. These procedures must be regularly updated and enforced.

Hazardous substances

In hospitality and catering establishments there are many chemicals and substances used for cleaning that can be harmful if not used correctly (see Table 3.2).

Substances that are dangerous to health are labelled as very toxic, toxic, harmful, irritant or corrosive.

Anyone using these chemical substances must be trained in their use. Hazardous substances may enter the body through the skin, eyes, nose (by inhaling) and mouth (by swallowing), so appropriate protective clothing such as goggles, gloves and face masks should always be worn.

Control of Substances Hazardous to Health (COSHH)

The **Control of Substances Hazardous to Health (COSHH) Regulations** state that an employer must not carry on any work that might expose employees to any substances that are hazardous to health, unless the employer has assessed the risks of this work to employees and has put the relevant controls in place. The employer should make sure that measures are in place to control the use of chemical substances and monitor their use. If chemical substances are used you should:

- be trained in their use and safety procedures
- always follow the manufacturer's instructions; read all the labels carefully
- always store them in their original containers, away from heat
- keep the lids tightly closed
- not expose them to heat or to naked flames
- never mix chemicals
- know the first aid procedure in the event of accidental contact with chemicals
- dispose of empty containers immediately
- dispose of waste chemical solutions safely
- wear the appropriate safety equipment and clothing.

Table 3.1 Ways equipment can cause injury

Cause	Examples
Entanglement or entrapment	Hands, fingers, hair or clothing caught in machinery, equipment, closed areas or doors
Impact	Being hit by falling equipment from shelves or falling stacked boxes
Contact	Being in contact with heat, steam or sharp objects
Ejection	Being hit by loose pieces of machinery becoming detached
Faulty equipment	Electrical, mechanical, worn or unsuitable equipment
Inappropriate use of equipment	Using the wrong equipment for a task, using it wrongly or without appropriate training

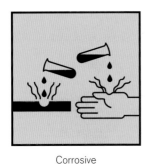

Corrosive

Flammable

Harmful

Toxic

▲ Hazard symbols used on the packaging of chemical products

In order to comply with legal obligations under the COSHH Regulations, all work areas should be checked to find out which chemicals and substances are used. Table 3.2 lists the different work areas and the chemicals and substances likely to be found in them.

The management should keep a COSHH register of all substances used in the establishment. Safety data sheets should be attached to the completed COSSH assessment sheets, as well as being displayed in the working area for members of staff who handle the chemicals to see. Safety data sheets give information on chemicals that help users of those chemicals to stay safe. They describe the possible hazards from the chemical and give information on handling, storage and emergency measures in case of accidents. By law, suppliers of chemicals must provide up-to-date safety data sheets for substances that pose possible hazards to the user.

Fire and explosions

The main causes of fire and explosion in kitchen areas are:

- electricity – misuse and faulty or damaged equipment
- gas leaks or gas appliances left switched on
- smoking in prohibited areas
- hot liquids, oils and other substances
- equipment and tools with a naked flame.

The fire triangle

For a fire to start, three things are needed:

1 A source of heat (ignition)
2 Fuel
3 Oxygen.

Key terms

COSHH Regulations: legal requirement for employers to control substances that are hazardous to health to prevent any possible injury to those using the substances.

Descaler: a substance to remove the hard deposit formed by chemicals in some water supplies. A descaler is often used in kettles, coffee machine pipes and water boilers.

Detergent: a substance that is soluble in water and breaks down grease and holds dirty particles in suspension.

Insecticide: a chemical substance that is used to kill insects.

Liquefied Petroleum Gas (LPG): also referred to as propane or butane; it is used to fuel some cooking appliances.

Rodenticide: a chemical substance that is used to kill rodents such as rats and mice.

Sanitiser: a chemical with detergent and disinfecting properties; it breaks down dirt and grease and controls bacteria.

Solvent: a liquid that is able to dissolve other substances.

If any one of these three things is missing a fire cannot start. Taking care to avoid the three coming together will reduce the chances of a fire starting.

Table 3.2 Work areas and the chemicals and substances likely to be found in them

Area	Chemicals and substances
Kitchen	Cleaning chemicals, including alkalis and acids, detergents, sanitisers, descalers; chemicals associated with burnishing; oils associated with machines; pest-control chemicals – insecticides and rodenticides
Restaurant	Cleaning chemicals, polishes, fuel for flame lamps, including methylated spirits, liquefied petroleum gas (LPG)
Bar	Beer-line cleaner, glass-washing detergent and sanitisers
Housekeeping	Cleaning chemicals, including detergents, sanitisers, descalants, polishes, carpet-cleaning products, floor-care products
Maintenance	Cleaning chemicals, adhesives, solvents, paint, LPG, salts for water softening etc., paint stripper, varnishes, etc.
Offices	Correction fluid, thinners, solvents, methylated spirits, toner for photocopier, duplicating fluids and chemicals, polishes

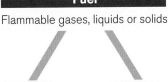

Fuel
Flammable gases, liquids or solids

Ignition source	Oxygen
Smoking or naked flames Hot surfaces Electrical equipment Static electricity	Always present in the air Also comes from oxidising substances

▲ The fire triangle

Methods of extinguishing fires concentrate on cooling (as in a water extinguisher or fire hose) or depriving the fire of oxygen (as in an extinguisher which uses foam or powder to smother the fire).

Regulatory Fire Safety Order 2005

Every employer has a duty for the safety of employees in the event of a fire. The Regulatory Fire Safety Order 2005 states that fires should be prevented and it is the responsibility of the occupant of premises (usually the employer) and the people who might be affected by fire (the employees).

The responsible person must:
- make sure that the fire precautions ensure the safety of all employees and others that may be in the building
- assess the risk of and from fire in the establishment; special consideration must be given to dangerous chemicals or substances, and the risks that these pose if a fire occurs
- review the preventative and protective measures.

Fire safety requires constant vigilance to reduce the risk of a fire, using detection and alarm systems, and well-practised emergency and evacuation procedures in the event of a fire.

Fire precautions

Guidelines for good practice in fire prevention:
- Remove all fire hazards such as large quantities of paper and cardboard or reduce their presence as much as possible.
- Make sure that everyone is protected at work from the risk of fire and the likelihood of a fire spreading.

- Make sure that all escape routes are safe and clearly signposted. They must be easy to access, have no blockages such as boxes stored in front of them, and all staff must know where they are.
- Ways of fighting fires, such as fire extinguishers or fire blankets, must be available on the premises.
- There must be a way of detecting a fire on the premises, for example, smoke detectors and fire alarms, and instructions of what to do in case of fire.
- Pre-arranged plans must be in place describing what to do in case of fire and employees must be trained in the correct procedure.
- Fire-fighting equipment must not be tampered with or moved to another place.
- All fire-fighting equipment provided must be installed and maintained by a competent person.

Fire risk assessments

A fire risk assessment will find out how likely it is that a fire might happen and highlight the dangers from fire in the workplace.

A fire risk assessment must be carried out in all premises where there are five or more people working; this is a legal requirement. Setting up a fire risk assessment follows exactly the same principles as the health and safety risk assessment (see page 49).

Fire detection and fire warning

There must be an effective way of detecting fire and warning people about it quickly enough to allow them to escape before it spreads too far.

In small workplaces, such as small cafés or restaurants, a fire will be detected easily and quickly and is unlikely to cut off the escape routes. In this case, if people can see the exits clearly, a verbal shout of 'Fire!' may be all that is necessary.

In larger establishments, fire warning systems are needed. Manually operated call points are likely to be the very least that is needed. These are the type of fire alarm where you break glass to set off the alarm (as seen on the wall in public buildings).

Fire-fighting equipment

Portable fire extinguishers enable people to tackle fire in its early stages. Staff should be trained to use extinguishers properly and effectively and only use them if they can do so without putting themselves and others in danger.

Fires are classified in accordance with British Standard EN2 as follows:

- Class A – fires involving solid materials where combustion (burning) normally forms glowing embers, as with wood.
- Class B – fires involving liquids (e.g. methylated spirits) or liquefiable solids (such as flammable gels used under a burner).
- Class C – fires involving gases.
- Class D – fires involving metals.
- Class F – fires involving cooking oils or fats.
- Electrical fires – fires caused by electrical equipment where electric current may still be present.

Different types of fire extinguishers are suitable for different types of fire. Portable extinguishers all contain a substance that will put out a fire. The substance will vary, but whatever it is it will be forced out of the extinguisher under pressure. Generally, portable fire extinguishers contain one of the following substances (extinguishing mediums):

- water (used for Class A fires)
- foam (used for Class A and B fires)
- dry powder (used for Class A, B and C fires)
- powder (used for Class D fires)
- carbon dioxide (used for Class B fires and electrical fires)
- wet chemical (used for Class A and Class F fires).

KNOW YOUR FIRE EXTINGUISHER COLOUR CODE

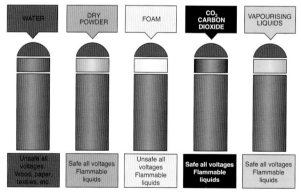

WATER	DRY POWDER	FOAM	CO₂ CARBON DIOXIDE	VAPOURISING LIQUIDS
Unsafe all voltages. Wood, paper, textiles, etc.	Safe all voltages Flammable liquids	Unsafe all voltages Flammable liquids	Safe all voltages Flammable liquids	Safe all voltages Flammable liquids

▲ Types of fire extinguisher

The most useful form of general purpose fire-fighting equipment is the water-type extinguisher or hose reel. These should be located where they are clearly

visible and accessible, such as in corridors. However, fire hose reels use water and therefore must not be used in areas of special risk, such as kitchens where oil, fats and electrical equipment are used. These will need other types of extinguisher such as carbon dioxide, dry powder or wet chemical. Your local fire authority will be able to advise you on fire safety in your premises.

In smaller workplaces, portable fire extinguishers will probably be sufficient to tackle small fires. However, in more complex buildings, or where it is necessary to protect the means of escape for people and the property or contents of the building, it may be necessary to consider a sprinkler system. Sprinkler systems are an efficient means of protecting buildings against extensive damage from fire by spreading water over a large area quickly. They are acknowledged as an effective way of reducing the risk to life from fire.

Electricity

Great care must be taken when dealing with electricity. If someone comes into direct contact with electricity the consequences can be very serious and sometimes fatal. Faulty equipment or incorrect use could lead to electric shock, burns, fires, explosion and death.

If an electric shock occurs, switch off the electrical current. If this is not possible, free the person using something that is dry and will insulate you from the electricity, such as something made of wood or rubber. Do not use your bare hands otherwise the electric shock may be transmitted to you. If the person has stopped breathing, call for help and send for medical assistance. Make sure the accident/incident is reported and recorded.

To avoid accidents from electrical equipment:

- ensure all electrical equipment is maintained and tested regularly by a qualified electrician (this is called Portable Appliance Testing (**PAT testing**)); keep a record of this testing
- check cables and flexes regularly and do not use the equipment if these are damaged
- do not use faulty equipment. Remove or label it so no one else uses it and report the fault to the appropriate person
- the correct fuses and circuit breakers should be in place on all electrical equipment.

▲ All electrical equipment must be tested regularly by a qualified electrician

Key term

PAT testing: portable appliance testing of electrical appliances and equipment by a qualified electrician to make sure they are safe to use. A record is kept of this and a label or sticker is placed on the appliance to show that it has been tested.

Gas

Gas is also potentially hazardous and a build-up of gas can lead to explosion which could cause injury and possibly fatalities. If a gas leak is suspected warn others, turn off all the gas at the mains, leave the kitchen and inform management so that the appropriate authorities can be contacted. It is important to report any gas leaks or smell of gas.

Controlling hazards in the workplace

What is a hazard?

When we assess health and safety we consider hazards. A **hazard** is anything that can cause harm, such as:

- extremes of cold and heat
- uneven floors
- excessive noise
- chemicals
- electricity
- working at height and using ladders
- lifting and carrying heavy items
- moving parts and machinery
- dust and fumes.

The following aspects of the kitchen environment have the potential for hazards:

- **Equipment** – knives, liquidisers, food processors, mixers, mincers and a range of other kitchen equipment.
- **Substances** – cleaning chemicals, detergents, sanitisers, disinfectants, degreasers and other substances.
- **Work methods** – carrying knives and equipment incorrectly, not using equipment properly and not following workplace safety rules.
- **Work areas** – spillages not cleaned up, overcrowded work areas, insufficient work space, uncomfortable work conditions due to extreme heat, cold or insufficient ventilation.

What is a risk?

Risk is the chance of somebody being harmed by a hazard present in the working area. There may be a high risk, medium risk or a low risk of harm occurring.

For example, using a stick blender is a hazard but what is the likelihood of it causing harm?

If it is not used properly and the hands are placed near the moving blades there could be a serious injury. If the blender is not kept well below the surface of hot soup it will splash out and could burn the hands and face. However, with proper training and supervision the blender can be used safely and no injury will occur.

This risk is medium.

Activity

1 Give examples of three more risks there may be in using different pieces of kitchen equipment.
2 Describe the injuries that could possibly occur in using each piece of equipment.
3 Decide whether each of your examples is a low, medium or high risk.

Table 3.3 Common risks and hazards and ways to minimise them

Common risks and hazards	Ways to minimise risks
Poor design and structure of building	Improved and safe design of the building
Poor signage	Correct and visible/clear signage
Poor housekeeping standards	Good housekeeping
Poor lighting and ventilation	Well-lit and well-ventilated areas
Dangerous working practices	Well-trained staff (for example, providing COSHH and manual handling training)
Distraction and lack of attention and working too quickly	Concentrating on the work
Ignoring the rules	Strict enforcement of rules
Not wearing protective clothing	Wearing correct protective clothing

Risk assessment

Employers must have appropriate arrangements in place for maintaining a safe workplace and working areas and these must be recorded in a formal **risk assessment**. This applies to all workplaces where there are five or more employees and is part of the management functions of planning, organisation and control.

Employers must examine the risks in the workplace, record what they are and what should be done about them. Risk in the workplace means anything that could cause harm to employees or other people (including customers, guests, visitors and anyone else on the premises). Table 3.3 (above) describes some common risks and hazards.

These are the five required steps to assessing risk:

1 Look for hazards – the things that can cause harm.
2 Identify who could be harmed by the hazard and how.
3 Work out the risks and decide if the existing precautions are good enough or whether more should be done to prevent harm being caused.
4 Write down what the hazard is and what the risk is and keep this as a record.
5 Re-check the hazard and the risk at regular intervals and go back and change the risk assessment (the written record) if necessary.

After examining a risk carefully, you can estimate the size of the risk and then decide whether it is acceptable or if you need to take more precautions (**control measures**) to prevent harm. Table 3.4 (on the next page) shows one method of recording the risk assessment process.

When the risk assessment has been completed, employers are required to make any improvements that are identified as necessary. The aim is to make sure that no one gets hurt or suffers illness. However, it is important to remember that employers only need to consider risks and hazards which are created by work activities. They do not need to consider every minor hazard or risk that we accept as part of our lives.

Activity

Suggest five potential health and safety hazards there may be in a busy kitchen and for each hazard suggest the controls that could be put in place to keep employees safe.

Key terms

Hazard: something that can cause harm.

Risk: the chance of somebody being harmed by a hazard.

Risk assessment: the process of identifying and evaluating hazards and risks and putting measures in place to control them. This process should be recorded and reviewed.

Control measure: measures put in place to minimise risk.

Table 3.4 Risk assessment record

Hazard	Risk level before control measures	Current control measures	Risk level with controls	Additional control required (action, person responsible and date)	Date of staff training and any actions taken
Electricity	Medium	Use and maintain electrical equipment according to manufacturer's instructions Switch off from supply when not in use Do not operate electrical switches with wet hands Report electrical faults immediately Kitchen signs in appropriate places	Low	Supervision at all times of employees under 18 years old Initial training on equipment use for all staff and additional training if under 18 Refresher training every six months Testing of new equipment Yearly testing of existing equipment	
Hot liquids (e.g. water, oil)	High	All staff to be made aware of the danger of hot containers Do not overfill pans with water When lifting the lid, always use the handle and stand to the side to allow steam to escape. Avoid drips, especially of oil Avoid condensation settling on the floor which would then become wet Warning signs in kitchen	Medium	Supervision at all times of employees under 18 years old Initial training and induction covering hot liquids and their dangers for all staff and additional training if under 18	
Hot surfaces	Medium	If a surface becomes hot during use, precautions must be taken to prevent burns Place pans in a position that minimises the risk of contact Do not reach over them Warning signs in kitchen	Low	Initial staff training and induction as for hot liquids Additional training if under 18	
Knives	Medium	Ensure that knives are kept sharp and have secure handles Keep handles dry and free from grease Ensure that the correct size and type of knife is used Do not leave knives lying on work surfaces or tables When carrying knives, always do so with the point downwards	Low	Initial staff training and induction Additional training if under 18 Knife safety awareness training for all staff First aid training for key staff	

All staff must receive training in the use of the equipment they use. This should be recorded and updated regularly. Table 3.5 shows an example of the type of log that could be used.

Incident/accident reporting

Health and safety must be monitored regularly in the workplace, ideally by a designated health and safety representative. Any incidents or near misses must be recorded, even if no one is injured. All accidents should be reported to your line manager, head chef or a supervisor.

It is a legal requirement to report accidents, so that they can be investigated to assess the risks and analysed to determine why the accident happened. Measures can then be put in place to reduce the risk and prevent future accidents.

Table 3.5 Equipment training log

Equipment name	Areas of safety covered in training	Authorised person/ trainer	Staff signature
Large stick blender	Assembly	Sous chef	
	Correct use of power points (positioning)	Chef de partie	
	Suitable foods for use with blender	Supervisor	
	Using correctly and safely		
	Safe cleaning and storage		
Robo-chef food processor	Assembling various parts and attachments	Sous chef	
	Correct use of safety cut-outs and guards	Chef de partie	
	Suitable foods for use with various attachments	Supervisor	
	Using correctly and safely		
	Safe dismantling cleaning and storage		
Deep fryer	Various parts of deep fryer including draining tap position	Sous chef	
	Temperatures and thermostat	Chef de partie	
	Safety with hot oils	Supervisor	
	Safe use with various foods		
	Avoiding overfilling with oils or food to be cooked		
	Cooling, draining and filtering oil		
	Cleaning and re-filling		
Griddle	Various parts of griddle	Sous chef	
	Care and safety with hot surfaces	Grill chef	
	Suitable foods for cooking on griddle	Supervisor	
	Cleaning and maintenance		

Each accident is recorded in an accident file or electronic system, which must be provided in every business. An example of an incident report form is shown below.

Activity

1 Suggest four health and safety-related concerns you would report to your head chef or supervisor.
2 For each of the concerns listed, what could happen if they were not reported?

RIDDOR (Reporting Injuries, Diseases and Dangerous Occurrences) Act 1996

The law states that all serious work-related accidents, diseases and dangerous occurrences must be recorded and reported to the Health and Safety Executive (HSE). This can now be done online via the HSE website (www.hse.gov.uk). Very serious incidents and fatalities must be reported by telephone directly to the HSE Incident Contact Centre (0845 300 9923).

Full name of injured person:			
Occupation:		Supervisor:	
Time of accident:	Date of accident:	Time of report:	Date of report:
Name of injury or condition:			
Details of hospitalisation:			
Extent of injury (after medical attention):			
Place of accident or dangerous occurrence:			
Injured person's evidence of what happened (include equipment/items and/or other persons):			
Witness evidence (1):		Witness evidence (2):	
Supervisor's recommendations:			
Date:		Supervisor's signature:	

▲ An incident/accident report form – this may be stored electronically

The following injuries must be reported if they occur in the workplace:

- bone fractures (except fingers, thumbs or toes)
- amputation (cutting off) of limbs
- dislocation of a hip, knee or spine
- temporary or permanent loss of sight (blindness)
- eye injuries from chemicals getting into the eye, a hot metal burn to the eye or any penetration of the eye
- any injury from electric shock or burning that leads to unconsciousness or the need to resuscitate the person or send them to hospital for more than 24 hours
- any injury resulting in hypothermia (when someone gets too cold), or illness due to heat, that leads to unconsciousness or the need to resuscitate the person or send them to hospital for more than 24 hours (such as an electric shock or a gas flame blown back and causing burns)
- unconsciousness caused by exposure to a harmful substance or biological agents (such as cleaning products and solvents)
- unconsciousness or illness requiring medical treatment caused by inhaling a harmful substance or absorbing it through the skin (such as breathing in poisonous carbon monoxide leaking from a gas appliance)
- illness requiring medical treatment caused by a biological agent or its toxins or infected material (such as harmful bacteria used in laboratories).

Examples of reportable diseases include:

- dermatitis
- skin cancer
- asthma
- hepatitis
- tuberculosis
- tetanus
- anthrax.

> **Key term**
>
> **RIDDOR**: Reporting Injuries, Diseases and Dangerous Occurrences Act 1996. All injuries, diseases and dangerous occurrences happening in the workplace or because of work carried out on behalf of the employer must be reported to the Health and Safety Executive. This is a legal requirement and it is the employer's responsibility to make any such reports.

Personal protective equipment

The Personal Protective Equipment (PPE) at Work Regulations 1992 require employees to wear personal protective clothing and equipment such as safety shoes, eye protection and gloves when the task requires them. For example, chefs must wear chefs' whites. It is an employee's responsibility to look after any PPE provided to them and to report any defects to their employer.

Employers are responsible for providing PPE to their employees where required, for example, providing masks or goggles for employees to use when cleaning ovens and stoves or when using hazardous substances. Employers are also responsible for ensuring that PPE is in good, clean condition and is replaced as necessary. Employers must provide changing facilities for staff and storage facilities (for example, a locker) in which employees can store their PPE.

Clothing

It is important that people working in the kitchen should wear suitable clothing and footwear. Clothing must be:

- protective
- washable at high temperatures
- lightweight and comfortable
- strong
- absorbent.

Clothes worn in the kitchen must shield the body from excessive heat and also protect the food being worked with.

- **Chefs' jackets** are double-breasted and have long sleeves to protect the chest and arms from the heat of the stove and prevent hot foods or liquids burning or scalding the body.
- **Aprons** are designed to safeguard the body from being scalded or burned and particularly to protect the legs from any liquids that may be spilled; for this reason the apron should be of sufficient length to protect the legs.
- **Trousers** are usually made from lightweight cotton or coated cotton. They are loose fitting for comfort and to protect better from spilled liquids.

● **Chefs' hats** are designed to enable air to circulate on top of the head and thus keep the head cool. The main purpose of the hat is to prevent loose hairs from dropping into food and to absorb perspiration on the forehead. The use of lightweight disposable hats is both acceptable and suitable.

● **Shoes** should be comfortable, non-slip, cover the whole foot and have reinforced toe-caps.

Activity

State the necessary items of PPE that should be made available for a kitchen porter who is:
● carrying out general cleaning tasks
● cleaning large items such as stoves, deep fat fryers, salamanders and walk-in refrigerators and freezers.

Safety signs

We use safety signs to help control hazards. They should not replace other methods of controlling risks.

Yellow warning signs

Yellow signs are warning signs to alert people to various dangers, such as slippery floors, hot oil or hot water. They also warn about hazards such as **corrosive** material.

▲ Yellow warning signs

Blue mandatory signs

Blue **mandatory** signs inform people about precautions they must take. They tell people how to progress safely through a certain area. They must be used whenever special precautions need to be taken, such as wearing protective clothing.

▲ Blue mandatory signs

Red prohibition/fire-fighting signs

Red **prohibition** signs tell people that they should not do something. They are used to stop anyone from doing certain tasks in a hazardous area. Red signs are also used for fire-fighting equipment.

▲ Red prohibition and fire-fighting signs

Green safety signs

These are route signs designed to show where fire exits and emergency exits are. Green is also used for first aid equipment.

▲ Green safety signs

Key terms

Corrosive: something which can eat away or destroy solid materials.

Mandatory: something that must be done, for example, rubber gloves must be worn when handling certain chemicals.

Prohibition: something that is not allowed and must not be done, for example, smoking in certain outside areas.

Take it further

You can find out more about health and safety and how it affects you at work from the sources listed below.

- Acts of Parliament (statutory regulations and European directives) (www.hse.gov.uk/legislation/)
- Mandatory and informative signage within the workplace
- Health and Safety Executive (health and safety inspectors) (www.hse.gov.uk)
- Local authorities (environmental health officers/ practitioners) – search for contact details for your area online.
- Line managers and Human Resource departments
- Trade unions.

Maintaining a healthy and safe workplace

Design of food preparation areas

When planning food premises, good design, layout and efficient use of space can have a significant impact on the staff who work there, both in terms of their productivity and health and safety. Careful consideration should be given to the structure of the premises as well as the floors, stairs, ventilation, heating, air conditioning and lighting. Planned maintenance and housekeeping of the areas will help to keep the workplace safe.

Workflow

We have already seen in Chapter 1 how the use of a linear workflow reduces the risk of contamination. Such a workflow also means there will be no cross-over of activities that could result in accidents. An example of a linear workflow is:

Delivery → Storage → Preparation → Cooking → Hot holding/cooling and chilling → Serving

- Food should flow through the preparation area to the service area. Ideally, raw food should never go into the area where there is cooked food. If this

is unavoidable, make sure the raw food is safely wrapped/covered.
- Equipment should flow through the preparation area to the service area. Dirty equipment should not come into contact with or get mixed up with clean equipment.
- Clean and dirty (raw and cooked) processes should be kept apart.
- Cleaning and disinfection should be planned with separate storage for cleaning materials and chemicals.
- In the kitchen there must be staff hand-washing and drying facilities, which are used only for this purpose.
- All areas must be designed to allow for thorough cleaning, disinfection and pest control.

Services

Lighting and ventilation (natural and artificial) must be sufficient, correctly placed for the tasks being carried out and allow for safe working conditions. Good ventilation is needed to prevent excessive heat, condensation, circulation of airborne contaminants, grease vapours and odours. It will also help to provide a more comfortable working environment.

Drainage must be adequate for the work being carried out, as flooding could result in slippery floors and accidents.

Structure

- Floors should be durable and in good condition; they must be impervious, non-slip, and easy to keep clean.
- Walls should be non-porous, smooth, easy to clean and preferably light in colour.
- Ceiling finishes must resist build-up of condensation which could encourage mould and drip down to cause wet floors. The ceiling should be of a non-flaking material and be washable.
- Windows/doors should be of a good design. Consideration should be given to how easy they are to open and close without strain and the likelihood of trapping fingers. Doors need to allow for equipment such as trolleys being pushed through – automatic doors are good for this. Self-closing doors should allow enough time for the user to pass through and, where appropriate doors, should have vision panels to see who or what may be at the other side.

Staff welfare

Personal hygiene and welfare facilities must be provided for staff, including:

- toilets (some employers also provide showers)
- hand-washing facilities
- changing facilities and storage (lockers) for PPE as well as personal clothing and belongings
- a rest area
- drinking water
- first aid facilities.

▲ Hand-washing facilities must be provided

Reporting abuse

Abuse can take many forms, including **bullying**, **harassment**, verbal abuse, threats and assault, all of which can lead to a serious, hazardous situation. Bullying, harassment and verbal abuse may occur at home, college and at work. It may be carried out by peer groups, neighbours or work colleagues working at the same level as you or at different levels to you. Examples of abuse include:

- refusal to acknowledge you and your achievements
- undermining you, your position and your potential
- ignoring you; making you feel isolated and separated from your colleagues
- deliberately excluding you from what is going on at work
- humiliating, shouting at and threatening you, often in front of others
- setting you unrealistic tasks, which keep changing
- physical attack.

People who are being bullied or harassed can feel scared, vulnerable and isolated. If you are aware of bullying, to yourself or someone else, you must report it immediately to a supervisor, manager or to someone in **Human Resources** so that the correct procedures can be put in place and it can be stopped.

Emergencies in the workplace

Emergencies that might happen in the workplace include:

- serious accidents involving personal injury to, or even death of, one or more persons
- outbreak of fire or an explosion
- security alert or bomb scare
- failure of a major system, such as water or electricity.

Emergency procedures

All organisations must have systems in place to deal with emergencies. Key staff are usually trained to take charge in the event of an emergency. These staff will include fire marshals and first aiders and they will attend regular training, briefings and update meetings.

Fire evacuation procedures must also be in place, which employees need to practise on a regular basis; fire alarms should be tested regularly. Make sure you know the evacuation procedures in your establishment. If you have to leave the premises, the following must be adhered to:

- Turn off the power supplies, gas and electricity. Usually this means hitting the red button in the kitchen or turning off all appliances individually.
- Close all windows and doors.

- Leave the building by the nearest emergency exit. Do not use the lifts.
- Assist anyone who may need help to leave the building such as a disabled person or a child.
- Assemble in the designated area, away from the building.
- Those responsible will check the roll-call of names if possible to establish whether everyone has left the building safely.

First aid

The arrangements for providing first aid in the workplace are set out in the Health and Safety (First Aid) Regulations 1981. The Regulations state that employers must provide adequate and appropriate equipment, facilities and personnel to ensure their employees receive immediate attention if they are injured or taken ill at work. The Regulations apply to all workplaces as well as the self-employed and those businesses with fewer than five employees.

A first aider must always be available to give immediate assistance to those with minor injuries or illness. If the injury is serious, the injured person should be treated by a healthcare professional as a matter of urgency.

Where someone has been injured in an emergency situation such as a fire or explosion, they should only be moved if they are still in danger. Immediate medical attention should be sought.

The first aid box must be kept in an easily accessible place and staff should now where to find it. The recommended contents of a first aid box are fairly basic. Medication or items such as antiseptic creams must not be in the first aid box because they could be misused or cause a reaction in some people.

The usual recommended items are:

- a guidance card
- individually wrapped waterproof dressings (blue) – different sizes
- sterile eye pads
- individually wrapped triangular bandages
- safety pins
- medium-sized, sterile, individually wrapped bandage dressings
- large, sterile, individually wrapped dressings.

It is the responsibility of a named person to check the contents of the first aid box regularly and keep it topped up as necessary.

Activity

Explain to a friend or colleague:
- what to do if there is a fire in the kitchen
- how to raise the alarm
- what the alarm sounds like
- where the fire exits are
- where the assembly point is
- how soon you can go back in the building.

You should know all of the above. If you do not then you must find out.

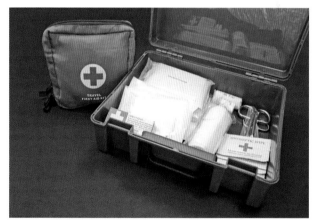

⚠ If a person at work suffers injuries or falls ill, seek help from a first aider

Test yourself

1 Under the Health and Safety at Work Act 1974, what must an employer do to ensure that staff are safe at work?

2 List four common causes of accidents in a kitchen.

3 COSSH regulations cover safety issues in the workplace.
   a) What do the letters COSHH stand for?
   b) What are COSHH regulations in place to protect?

4 In relation to health and safety at work, who has the power to enter premises, check or dismantle equipment, inspect records, ask questions and seize/destroy dangerous articles?

5 Employers must complete a risk assessment to identify risk. What are the five steps in a risk assessment?

6 Using correct PPE can help to reduce the risk of accidents in the workplace.
   a) What is meant by PPE?
   b) Give three examples of PPE used in a kitchen.

7 Health and safety signs are grouped into different colours.
   a) What are red signs used for?
   b) Give two examples of red signs.

8 Fire is a potential hazard in the workplace.
   a) For a fire to start there are three requirements – what are they?
   b) Name two different types of fire extinguisher and state the kind of fire each should be used for.

9 If you have been asked to move a heavy or awkward load, what are the rules for safe lifting and carrying you should follow?

10 Workflow is important in kitchen design.
   a) What is meant by a linear workflow in the kitchen?
   b) What are the advantages of a linear workflow being in place?

Practice assignment tasks

Task 1

You have been asked to produce health and safety guidelines for the staff in your kitchen. Produce a booklet or PowerPoint presentation outlining:
- the benefits of good health and safety practices, and what can happen if these are not in place
- the main hazards and risks in a kitchen area and risk assessment
- the benefits of good workplace design
- common causes of accidents and ill health at work.

Task 2

In your booklet or PowerPoint presentation give details of:
- the main UK health and safety regulations and who is responsible for enforcing them
- the role of environmental enforcement officers – who employs them and when they can come into premises
- further sources of information about health and safety at work.

Task 3

Create a section in your booklet or presentation that covers:
- the procedure for reporting an accident at work
- how to report a serious accident or injury
- how to report a gas leak and an electrical accident
- the procedure to be followed if a fire starts in the kitchen.

Task 4

Select a kitchen in your college or workplace and produce a risk assessment (you may like to copy Table 3.4 in this chapter). Refer to the five stages of risk assessment and record any actions you propose.

4 Healthier foods and special diets

This chapter will help you to:

1 understand the principle of balanced diets, including:
   – current government nutritional guidelines for a healthy diet
   – the sources of essential nutrients
   – the impact of diet on health
   – how to maintain the nutritional value of food.

2 understand how to plan and provide special diets, including:
   – the main features of special diets
   – the impact of special diets on health
   – how to plan and provide meals for those on special diets.

Introduction

With more and more people eating outside the home, caterers are in a strong position to influence customers in the food choices they make. It is important that caterers are aware of the different nutrients and their importance when preparing, cooking and serving dishes as part of a balanced diet, and to make sure that nutritional value is maximised.

Many different groups of people follow special diets and caterers must be aware of the causes, effects and main features of these diets. Caterers should understand best practice when preparing, cooking and serving food for those following special diets.

Principles of a balanced diet

Foods are not 'good' or 'bad'; it is the overall balance of the diet that matters. There is no perfect food that gives you everything you need. No single food provides all of the nutrients essential to keep us healthy and different foods have different nutritional content. In other words, they are good for us in different ways. So we need to eat a variety of foods to give us all the nutrients we need for a healthy diet. A **balanced diet** also makes our meal times more interesting.

Government nutritional guidelines for a healthy diet

A nutritionally balanced diet includes all the nutrients necessary for good health (from all the food groups), without too much or too little of any of the nutrients an individual needs. The Eatwell plate is a guide to the proportion of food which should be eaten from each food group. However, it is important to remember that different people have different nutritional requirements, depending on their age and occupation.

The best way to stay fit and healthy is to eat a diet high in fruit, vegetables, wholegrains and plant-based foods like beans and lentils, but low in fat, sugar and salt.

There have been a number of scientific papers published on the subject of health and nutrition and their findings can be used to help caterers and carers to provide balanced and nutritious dishes. Some suggestions for improving the nutritional value of the food we serve are given below.

- Trim off fat and skin from meat and fish, or use lean meat.
- Include fish in the diet at least twice per week.
- Aim to eat at least five portions of fruit and vegetables a day (a portion could be 1 apple, 1 banana, 2 plums, a heaped tablespoon of dried fruit like raisins (15 g) or three broccoli or cauliflower florets). Fruit and vegetables contain valuable vitamins, minerals, fibre and folic acid, which help to protect us from illness.
- Adjust cooking techniques – grill, bake, poach, boil or steam instead of frying and roasting.
- Reduce the amount of sugar in dishes and in the overall diet.
- Reduce the use of salt and discourage adding salt to cooked food at the table; be aware of the amount of salt in prepared foods. It is recommended that we do not eat more than 6 g of salt per day (our bodies only need 4.1 g).
- Try to drink at least two litres of water each day.

The eatwell plate

FOOD STANDARDS AGENCY
food.gov.uk

Use the eatwell plate to help you get the balance right. It shows how much of what you eat should come from each food group.

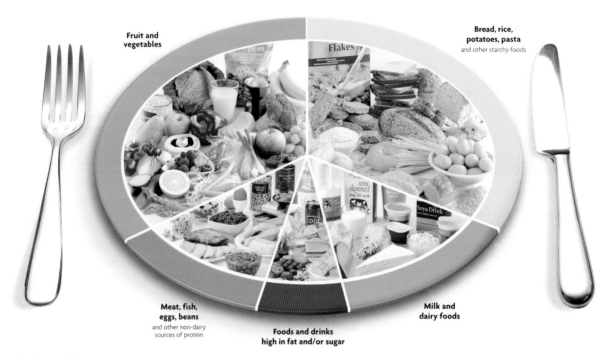

Fruit and vegetables

Bread, rice, potatoes, pasta and other starchy foods

Meat, fish, eggs, beans and other non-dairy sources of protein

Foods and drinks high in fat and/or sugar

Milk and dairy foods

▲ The Eatwell Plate

▲ Aim to eat at least five portions of fruit and vegetable each day

Take it further

For further information and current guidance look at the following websites:
● The Food Standards Agency (www.food.gov.uk)
● The British Nutrition Foundation (www.nutrition.org.uk)
● Department of Health (www.gov.uk/government/organisations/department-of-health)
● Department for Environment, Food and Rural Affairs (www.gov.uk/government/organisations/department-for-environment-food-rural-affairs)

Key term

Balanced diet: a diet which includes all the nutrients necessary for good health (from all the food groups), without too much or too little of any of the nutrients an individual needs.

Sources of essential nutrients

Nutrients in foods help our bodies to do essential everyday activities and to heal themselves if they are injured. A balanced diet can also help to prevent illness and disease.

The main nutrients are:
● carbohydrates
● proteins
● fats
● vitamins
● minerals
● water.

We will now look at each of the nutrients in more detail to find out what they do and which foods they are in.

Carbohydrates

We need carbohydrates for energy. Carbohydrates are made by plants and then either used by the plants as energy or eaten by animals and humans for energy or as dietary fibre. The three main types of carbohydrate are sugars, starches and fibre.

Sugars

Sugars are the simplest form of carbohydrates. When carbohydrates are digested they turn into sugars.

There are several types of sugar:

- glucose – found in the blood of animals and in fruit and honey
- fructose – found in fruit, honey and cane sugar
- sucrose – found in beet and cane sugar
- lactose – found in milk
- maltose – found in cereal grains and used in beer-making.

Starches

Starches break down into sugars. Starches are present in many foods, such as:

- pasta
- cereals
- cakes, biscuits, bread (cooked starch)
- whole grains, e.g. rice, barley, tapioca
- powdered grains, e.g. flour, cornflour, ground rice, arrowroot
- vegetables, e.g. potatoes, parsnips, peas, beans
- unripe fruit, e.g. bananas, apples, cooking pears.

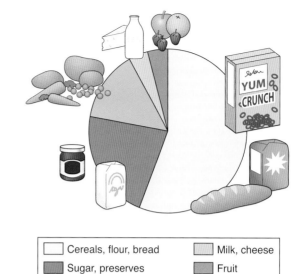

Cereals, flour, bread	Milk, cheese
Sugar, preserves	Fruit
Potatoes, vegetables	

▲ Sources of carbohydrates in the average diet

Fibre

Dietary fibre is a very important form of starch. Unlike other carbohydrates, dietary fibre cannot be digested and does not provide energy to the body.

▲ Fruit and vegetables are a source of fibre

▲ Foods high in carbohydrates

However, dietary fibre is essential for a balanced diet because it:

- helps to remove waste and toxins from the body and maintain bowel action
- helps to control the digestion and processing of nutrients
- adds bulk to the diet, helping us to stop feeling hungry; it is used in many weight reduction foods.

Fibre is found in:

- fruits and vegetables
- wholemeal and granary bread
- wholegrain cereals
- wholemeal pasta
- wholegrain rice
- pulses (peas and beans) and lentils.

The fibre found in fruit and vegetables plays an important role in preventing strokes. It also helps to lower cholesterol and maintain a healthy digestive system.

> **Professional tip**
> Consider using wholemeal breadcrumbs for coatings or stuffings.

Protein

Protein is an essential part of all living things. Every day our bodies carry out millions of tasks (bodily functions) to stay alive. We need protein so that our bodies can grow and repair themselves.

There are two kinds of protein:

- animal protein (found in meat, game, poultry, fish, eggs, milk and cheese)
- vegetable protein (found in vegetables, seeds, pulses, peas, beans, nuts and wheat).

Protein is made up of chemicals known as amino acids and ideally our bodies need to obtain **amino acids** from both animal and vegetable protein. The protein in cheese is different from the protein in meat because the amino acids are different. Some amino acids are essential to the body, so they must be included in a balanced diet. Table 4.1 shows the proportion of protein in different animal and plant foods.

The lifespan of the cells in our bodies varies from a week to a few months. As cells die they need to be replaced. We need protein for our cells to repair and for new ones to grow.

We also use protein for energy. Any protein that is not used up in repairing and growing cells is converted into carbohydrate or fat.

▲ Foods high in protein

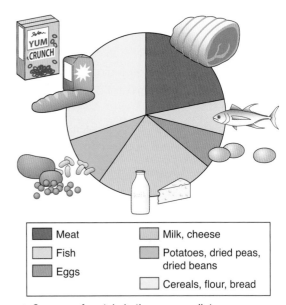

Meat	Milk, cheese
Fish	Potatoes, dried peas, dried beans
Eggs	Cereals, flour, bread

▲ Sources of protein in the average diet

> **Key term**
>
> **Amino acid**: structural units of protein.

Table 4.1 Proportion of protein in some common foods

Animal foods	Protein (%)	Plant foods	Protein (%)
Cheddar cheese	25	Soya flour (low fat)	45
Bacon (lean)	20	Soya flour (full fat)	37
Beef (lean)	20	Peanuts	24
Cod	17	Wholemeal bread	9
Herring	17	White bread	8
Eggs	12	Rice	7
Beef (fat)	8	Peas (fresh)	6
Milk	3	Potatoes (old)	2
Cream cheese	3	Bananas	1
Butter	< 1	Apples	< 1

Fats

Fats are naturally present in many foods and are an essential part of our diet. The main functions of fat are to protect the body, keep it warm and provide energy. Fats form an insulating layer under the skin and this helps to protect the vital organs and to keep the body warm. Fat is also needed to build cell membranes in the body.

Some fats are solid at room temperature and others are liquid at room temperature. Hard fats are mainly animal fats.
- Animal fats include butter, dripping (beef), suet, lard (pork), cheese, cream, bacon, meat fat, oily fish.
- Vegetable fats include margarine, cooking oils, nut oils, soya bean oils.

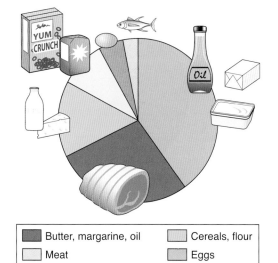

Key:
- Butter, margarine, oil
- Meat
- Milk, cheese
- Cereals, flour
- Eggs
- Fish

▲ Sources of fat in the average diet

Too much fat is bad for us and can lead to:
- being overweight (obesity)
- high levels of cholesterol, which can clog the blood vessels (arteries) in the heart
- heart disease
- bad breath (halitosis)
- Type 2 diabetes (Type 1 diabetes is not diet-related and is not caused by eating too much fat).

There are two types of fats: saturated fats and unsaturated fats. A diet high in saturated fat is thought to increase the risk of heart disease. Table 4.2 shows the percentage of saturated fat in the different types of food in an average diet.

Table 4.2 Percentage of saturated fat in food in an average diet

Type of food	Saturated fat (%)
Milk, cheese, cream	16.0
Meat and meat products	25.2
This splits down into:	
Beef	4.1
Lamb	3.5
Pork, bacon and ham	5.8
Sausage	2.7
Other meat products (e.g. burgers, faggots, pate)	9.1
Other oils and fats (e.g. olive oil, margarine, sunflower oil)	30.0
Other sources, including eggs, fish and poultry	7.4
Biscuits and cakes	11.4

Vitamins

Vitamins are chemicals which are vital for life and are found in small amounts in many foods. If your diet is lacking in a particular vitamin, you may become unhealthy or ill. Vitamins help with many of our bodily functions, such as growth and protection from disease. Table 4.3 describes some vitamins and their functions and sources.

▲ Many fruits are high in vitamins

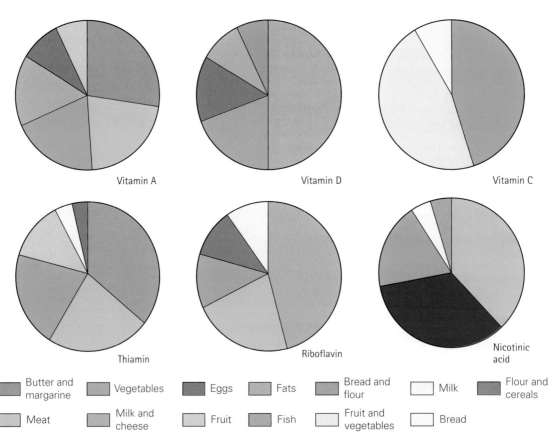

▲ Main sources of vitamins A, C and D, thiamin, riboflavin and nicotinic acid in the average diet

Table 4.3 Vitamins, their functions and sources

Vitamin	Functions	Foods in which they are found
A	Helps children to grow Helps the body to resist infection Helps to prevent night blindness	Fatty foods, dark green vegetables, halibut and cod liver oil, butter and margarine, watercress, herrings, carrots, liver and kidneys, spinach, tomatoes, apricots Fish liver oils are the best source
B (all types)	Helps to keep the nervous system in good condition Enables the body to obtain energy from carbohydrates Encourages the body to grow	
B1 (Thiamin)	Helps the body to produce energy Necessary for the brain, heart and nervous system to function properly	Yeast, bacon, oatmeal, peas, wholemeal bread
B2 (Riboflavin)	Helps with growth Necessary for healthy skin, nails and hair	Yeast, liver, meat extract, cheese, egg
B (Niacin or Nicotinic acid)	Vital for normal brain function Improves the health of the skin, the circulation and the digestive system	Meat extract, brewer's yeast, liver, kidney, beef
C (ascorbic acid)	Needed for children to grow Helps cuts and broken bones to heal Prevents gum and mouth infections	Potatoes, blackcurrants, green vegetables, lemons, grapefruit, bananas, strawberries, oranges, tomatoes, fruit juices
D	Controls the way our bodies use calcium Necessary for healthy bones and teeth	Sunlight helps the body to produce vitamin D Fish liver oils, oily fish, egg yolk, margarine and dairy produce.
E	An antioxidant Helps the body control toxins Helps the body against infection	Nuts, seeds, vegetables, oils, wheat germ and whole grains

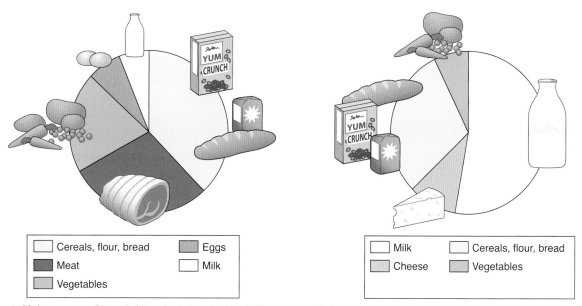

▲ Main sources of iron (left) and calcium (rightr) in the average diet

Minerals

There are 19 minerals in total, most of which our bodies need in very small quantities in order to function properly. Minerals are needed to build bones and teeth, carry out bodily functions and control the levels of fluids in the body. Table 4.4 shows the most common minerals needed by the body.

Table 4.4 Minerals, their functions and sources

Mineral	Functions	Foods in which they are found
Calcium	Builds bones and teeth Helps blood to clot Helps muscles to work (Vitamin D is also needed in order for the bodies to use calcium effectively)	Milk and milk products, green vegetables, the bones of tinned oily fish (e.g. sardines), drinking water, wholemeal bread and white bread (if calcium has been added)
Iron	To build haemoglobin (a substance in the blood that transports oxygen and carbon dioxide around the body) (Iron is better absorbed if vitamin C is also present)	Lean meat, wholemeal flour, offal, green vegetables, egg yolk, fish (Our bodies absorb iron more easily from meat and offal.)
Folic acid	Helps protect against stroke	Dark green vegetables such as broccoli and spinach
Phosphorous	Builds bones and teeth (together with calcium and vitamin D) Controls the structure of brain cells	Liver, bread, cheese, eggs, kidney, fish
Sodium	Regulates the amount of water in the body Helps muscles and nerves to function If too much salt is eaten some of it is excreted in urine. The kidneys control how much salt is lost in urine. We also lose sodium when we sweat (but our bodies cannot control how much salt we lose in this way).	Many foods are cooked with salt (sodium chloride), have salt added to them (e.g. bacon and cheese) or already contain salt (e.g. meat, eggs, fish)
Iodine	Enables the thyroid gland to function properly (produces hormones that control our growth). If the thyroid is not working properly it can make us underweight or overweight.	Sea food, iodised salt, drinking water obtained near the sea, vegetables grown near the sea
Potassium	Balances the fluids in our bodies Helps to maintain a normal heart rate Helps nerves and muscles to function	Bananas, avocados, citrus fruits and green leafy vegetables

Water

Water is vital to life – our organs require it to function properly. Without it we cannot survive for very long. We lose water from our bodies through urine and sweat and we need to replace it regularly to prevent dehydration. It is recommended that we drink eight glasses of water a day.

Water:
- regulates body temperature – when we sweat water evaporates from our skin and cools us down
- helps to remove waste products from the body. If these waste products are not removed they can release poisons, which can make us ill and damage our organs
- helps the body absorb nutrients, vitamins and minerals and helps the digestive system
- acts as a lubricant, helping our eyes and joints to work and stay healthy.

Sources of water include:
- drinks of all kinds
- foods such as fruits, vegetables, meat, eggs
- fibre.

As mentioned above, fibre cannot be digested, but we need it to remove waste from our bodies.

Impact of diet on health

Nearly 24 million adults in the UK today are classed as overweight or obese. Levels of obesity have trebled in the UK over the past 20 years and are still increasing. However, healthy eating is not just about reducing obesity. Medical research suggests that a third of all cancers are caused by poor diet. Diet can be linked to bowel cancer, stomach and lung cancer, as well as to high blood pressure, diabetes, **osteoporosis** and tooth decay.

Eating a balanced nutritional diet, combined with regular exercise, can help to protect us from diseases like stroke, coronary heart disease, diabetes and some cancers, as well as lowering cholesterol and reducing obesity. It is therefore important that caterers understand about healthy eating so that they can provide a range of menu options to help people to make the right choices about food and drink. Table 4.5 shows how a lack of nutrients affects the body and Table 4.6 shows how an excess of nutrients affects the body.

> **Key terms**
>
> **Osteoporosis**: a disease in which the density or thickness of the bones breaks down, putting them at greater risk of fracture. Exercise and good nutrition can reduce the risk of developing osteoporosis.
>
> **Water retention**: when the body does not get rid of enough water.
>
> **Muscle wastage**: when muscles wither away.
>
> **Scurvy**: a disease that can cause bleeding gums and other symptoms.
>
> **Rickets**: a disease of the bones.

Maintaining the nutritional value of food – the chef's role

Although scientists largely agree on what makes a healthy diet, the information presented in the media may seem confusing, and there are still many myths about healthy eating. Contrary to popular opinion, it is not just a case

Table 4.5 Effects of a diet lacking in different nutrients

Nutrient	Effect of having too little or none in your diet
Carbohydrate	Lack of energy; weight loss; low immune system
Fat	Lack of energy; weight loss; low immune system
Protein	**Water retention**; **muscle wastage**; hair loss
Fibre	Bowel disorders; bowel cancer; constipation
Vitamin A	Sight problems; hydration problems
Vitamin B1	Nervous disorders
Vitamin B2	Growth disorders; skin disorders
Vitamin B6	Anaemia; blood disorders
Vitamin B12	Anaemia; blood disorders; possible mental problems
Vitamin C	**Scurvy**; tiredness; blood loss if injured (as blood does not clot properly); bruising
Vitamin D	Rickets
Vitamin E	Mal-absorption and low immune system
Niacin	Possible mental problems; depression; diarrhoea
Iron	Tiredness; lack of energy and strength
Calcium	**Rickets**
Potassium	High blood pressure
Magnesium	Slower recovery from injury or illness
Folic acid	Blood disorders

Table 4.6 Effects of having too much of some nutrients in your diet

Nutrient	Effect of having too much in your diet
Fat	Obesity; heart disease and heart attacks; high blood pressure
Carbohydrate	Obesity; tooth decay; diabetes (caused by too much sugar)
Salt	High blood pressure; stroke

of taking chips off the menu or sticking to salad. We do need to eat lots of fruit and vegetables and less high-fat and sugary foods, but if we eat bulky, filling foods, we can still feel satisfied. Some of the greatest dishes and most exciting cuisines in the world are based on these principles (e.g. paella, biryani, Chinese vegetables stir-fried with noodles, sushi and rice, couscous, and cannelloni stuffed with ricotta and spinach).

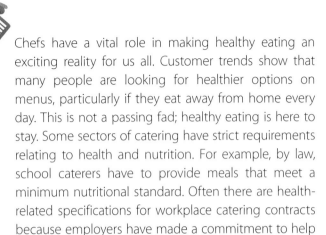

Chefs have a vital role in making healthy eating an exciting reality for us all. Customer trends show that many people are looking for healthier options on menus, particularly if they eat away from home every day. This is not a passing fad; healthy eating is here to stay. Some sectors of catering have strict requirements relating to health and nutrition. For example, by law, school caterers have to provide meals that meet a minimum nutritional standard. Often there are health-related specifications for workplace catering contracts because employers have made a commitment to help maintain the health of their staff.

Chefs can be highly influential in the area of healthy eating. The amounts and types of ingredients used, together with the way they are cooked and served, can make an enormous difference to the nutritional content of a dish or meal. Research has shown that the most effective approach to healthy catering is to make small changes to popular dishes. The following measures give examples of such changes.

- Substituting healthier ingredients (for example, using low fat yoghurt or crème fraiche instead of cream).
- Adding extra vegetables (for example adding a vegetable garnish to a dish; this could increase fibre, vitamins and minerals).
- Reducing added fat (for example, using olive oil or sunflower oil in place of butter or animal fats; trimming fat from meats).
- Changing cooking method – grilling instead of frying; steaming vegetables instead of boiling to preserve vitamins.
- Reducing use of sugar.
- Reducing salt – using herbs or spices in place of salt.

Chefs play a vital role in developing healthier recipes that work. The skill is in deciding when and where dishes can be modified without losing quality and taste. Although some highly traditional dishes are best left alone, subtle changes can be made to others without losing their texture, appearance or flavour. The 'Healthy eating tips' throughout the recipes in this book can help you to make some of these changes.

Activity

What changes could you make to the traditional crumbed escalope of pork with a mushroom sauce to offer a healthier dish?

Planning and providing for special diets

Special diets

People may follow a particular type of diet for a number of reasons and there are certain groups of people who have special nutritional needs.

Different life stages

People have different nutritional needs at different points in life, for example, due to a change in lifestyle or occupation and as a result of growing and aging.

- Pregnant and breastfeeding women should avoid soft mould-ripened cheese, paté, raw eggs, undercooked meat, poultry, fish, liver and alcohol.
- As children grow their nutritional requirements change. Children need a varied and balanced diet that is rich in protein.
- Teenagers need to have a good, nutritionally balanced diet. Girls need to make sure they get enough iron in their diet to help with the effects of puberty.
- The elderly – as we get older our bodies start to slow down and our appetite reduces. However, elderly people still need a nutritionally balanced diet to stay healthy.

Vegetarians and vegans

Vegetarians generally do not eat meat, fish or any food products made from meat or fish. Some vegetarians do not eat eggs. Vegetarians have a lower risk of heart disease, stroke, diabetes, gallstones, kidney stones and colon cancer than people who eat meat. They are also less likely to be overweight or have raised cholesterol levels.

Vegans are vegetarians who also do not eat eggs or milk, or anything containing eggs or milk. They may also not consume animal products such as honey, and may refuse to use products made from leather.

A vegetarian or vegan diet may be followed for ethical reasons, certain religions (such as Hindus) usually follow a vegetarian diet, or it may be followed for health reasons.

Medically-related diets

People who are ill, at home or in hospital, need balanced meals with plenty of nutrients to help them recover. Good nutritional food is part of the healing process.

Activity

Produce a chart listing the foods that you can use when preparing meals for special diets.

Allergies and intolerances

Some people may be intolerant of or allergic to some types of food, so caterers must be able to provide information for customers about what is in all of the dishes on the menu. **Food intolerance** causes a reaction in affected people, often in the form of stomach cramps or diarrhoea, but is not linked to the immune system.

A food **allergy** is a type of intolerance where the body's immune system reacts to certain foods as harmful, causing an allergic reaction. Allergy can cause skin reactions, nausea, vomiting and unconsciousness. A severe food allergy can lead to a potentially life-threatening condition called **anaphylactic shock**, which makes the throat and mouth swell, making it difficult to swallow or breathe. Immediate medical attention should be sought if someone experiences a severe allergic reaction, as some reactions can be fatal.

Key terms

Vegan: a vegetarian who also does not eat eggs or milk, or anything containing eggs or milk.

Food intolerance: does not involve the immune system, but it does cause a reaction to some foods.

Allergy: when the immune system reacts to or rejects certain foods or ingredients.

Anaphylactic shock: anaphylaxis is a severe, potentially life-threatening allergic reaction that can develop rapidly.

There are 14 major allergens that should be highlighted on food labels within an ingredients list or in information that is available for customers within a restaurant or catering setting. They are:

- cereals containing gluten
- crustaceans, for example, prawns, crabs, lobster and crayfish
- eggs
- fish
- peanuts
- soybeans
- milk
- nuts, such as almonds, hazelnuts, walnuts, pecan nuts, Brazil nuts, pistachio, cashew and macadamia (Queensland) nuts
- celery (and celeriac)
- mustard
- sesame
- sulphur dioxide, which is a preservative found in some dried fruit (sulphites)
- lupin
- molluscs, for example clams, mussels, whelks, oysters, snails and squid.

Although the presence of one or more of these allergens in a dish or product should be indicated, food businesses can choose how they do so. For example, this could be done by listing them in bold, contrasting colours or underlining. Some may use an allergy advice statement on their products, for example:

'Allergy Advice: for allergens including cereals containing gluten, see ingredients in bold'; or 'Allergy Advice: for allergens, see ingredients in bold'.

For restaurants this could be:

'Allergy Advice: please inform staff who can then provide a full list of allergens in our dishes'.

Disease-related diets

Gluten-free diet (coeliac)

A gluten-free diet is essential for people who have coeliac disease, a condition where gluten causes the immune system to produce antibodies that attack the lining of the intestines. Gluten is a mixture of proteins found in some cereals, particularly wheat, rye, barley and can include oats. A gluten-free diet is not the same as a wheat-free diet and some gluten-free foods are not wheat free.

Diabetes

Everything we eat is broken down into sugars in our body, but different foods break down at different speeds. People with Type 1 diabetes do not produce any insulin to control their blood sugar levels; people with Type 2 diabetes do not produce enough insulin, or their body does not react to it.

People with diabetes must pay attention to what they eat and when, in order to control their blood sugar levels. The ideal diabetic meal is balanced and contains a variety of nutrients, in an appropriate portion size, but will vary depending on the person, their level of physical activity and the type of diabetes that they have.

> **Key term**
>
> **Diabetes**: a disease in which the body produces no insulin (Type 1) or insufficient insulin (Type 2) and is therefore unable to regulate the amount of sugar in the blood. If left untreated, it causes thirst, frequent urination, tiredness and other symptoms. There are different kinds of diabetes, not all of which need to be treated with insulin. Type 1 diabetes tends to occur in people under 40 and in children; Type 2 diabetes is more common in overweight and older people and can sometimes be controlled by diet alone.

Take it further

You can find out more about catering for a diabetic by looking at the detailed suggestions for meals at: www.diabeticdietfordiabetes.com.

Religious/cultural diets

Some people may not eat certain types of food because of their religious or cultural beliefs. For example:

- **Jewish**: do not eat pork or pork products, shellfish or eels. Meat and milk are not eaten together. Meat must be kosher (killed according to Jewish custom and rules).
- **Muslim**: animals for meat must be slaughtered according to custom (halal). No shellfish or alcohol is consumed.
- **Hindu**: strict Hindus will not eat meat, fish or eggs. Those following a less strict regime may eat meat but not beef.
- **Rastafarian**: often vegetarian; will not eat processed food, eels, tea, coffee or alcohol.

Moral beliefs

Some people choose special diets based on their moral beliefs. For example, some people do not eat meat because they do not believe in killing animals. Some who do eat meat will only buy meat from certain sources, which state that the animals have been ethically reared, free to roam and humanely killed.

Impact of special diets on health

Providing a balanced diet for customers has wider benefits than simply supporting a healthy lifestyle. As discussed earlier in this chapter, a balanced diet can help the natural reduction of cholesterol and obesity, reducing the risk of heart disease. Making healthy catering a real option on menus means more chance of success in helping customers to make an informed choice.

When developing dishes for those following special diets, chefs need to be aware of the nutritional value of the ingredients used, since reducing some nutrients for health reasons can lead to other health risks. For example reducing milk and dairy products in a dish to make it low fat means reducing calcium which helps develop strong bones and prevents rickets. Meat and offal are a source of iron, so those following a vegetarian diet will need to find alternative sources of iron to reduce their risk of anaemia.

The chef's role when planning and providing meals for those on special diets

Food preparation staff need to be especially careful to avoid cross-contamination when preparing food for those on special diets, as even tiny traces of allergenic foods can trigger reactions in some people. Make sure that you are aware of the ingredients in any products that you are using within dishes and are able to provide a recipe to customers to enable them to make informed decisions.

As a caterer you can:

- be receptive to people with a food allergy and encourage them to ask questions about the food on offer
- let the allergic person or their carer check food labels and speak to the chef themselves
- refuse to cater for the person if you are unable to do so safely
- train serving staff in relevant food allergy issues
- avoid the indiscriminate use of nuts (e.g. powdered nuts as a garnish), unless this is an essential part of the recipe
- make sure ingredients are reflected in the names of dishes (for example, if a dish contains nuts, why not call it a nut and carrot salad?)

Practical tips: consider the 5 Cs

The '5 Cs' are a list of safeguards that can be put in place when providing dishes to meet specific dietary requirements:

1 **Content** – read the ingredients lists for potential allergens (for example, malt vinegar contains barley and therefore should not be in dishes for coeliac diets).

2 **Contact** – even small traces of ingredients can cause a reaction; wear gloves and wash hands after handling nuts. Segregate foods containing major allergens from other foods. If possible, keep some preparation areas nut-free.

3 **Contamination** – assess work practices to avoid cross-contamination of products (for example, if making dairy-free ice cream, make first and then store separately; avoid frying with oils that have been used to cook other foods such as fish or nut cutlets).

4 **Cleaning** – ensure that equipment to be used is cleaned thoroughly; even better, use separate equipment. Soap and hot water followed by thorough rinsing have been shown to be effective in removing allergen traces.

5 **Communication** – both within and outside of the kitchen, so that customers can be confident the organisation can meet their requirements.

Finally, there could also be a sixth 'C' – common sense. If you are not clear about the ingredients or dishes being offered, then say so.

Test yourself

1 What are the six main nutrient groups of food?
2 Dietary fibre cannot be digested, so why is it needed in the diet?
3 What are amino acids and why are they important?
4 It is considered that there is too much fat in the average UK diet. Give **three** reasons why too much fat should be avoided.
5 Vitamin A in the diet is essential for good health. Name **five** foods that are a source of vitamin A.
6 Why is vitamin C (ascorbic acid) needed in the diet?
7 How many portions of fruit/vegetables is it recommended that we eat each day? Suggest what these could be, including portion sizes.
8 What is meant by an 'allergy?'
9 Which religious/cultural diets forbid the eating of pork and pork products?
10 Suggest **three** ways that chefs can make the food they cook healthier.

Practice assignment task

Task 1
Produce a leaflet for a local catering establishment on the importance of maintaining a healthy diet.

Task 2
Choose two special diets and design a three-course meal to meet the needs of each.

5 Catering operations, costs and menu planning

This chapter will help you to:

1 understand the organisation of kitchens, including:
   - current trends in food production operations
   - the importance of kitchen layout and correct workflow
   - job roles and responsibilities, the staffing hierarchy and the 'partie system'
   - reasons for good working relationships.
2 be able to plan and prepare menus, including:
   - menus for different types of meal occasion
   - interpreting menus
   - the importance of the menu
   - the factors to be considered when menu planning
   - technical terminology used.
3 understand basic costs and apply basic calculations, including:
   - basic numeracy skills using calculator and manual methods
   - understanding the terms gross and net profit
   - the importance of food costs and how to calculate the food cost of dishes and determine the food cost per portion
   - elements of cost within catering operations
   - factors which must be monitored to control food costs and profit and to ensure net profit is achieved
   - how to determine selling prices at specific percentages of gross and net profit.

Introduction

As a professional chef, it is important that you have an understanding of the customers and market you serve. You need to understand what items on the menu will appeal to customers and how to make menus attractive so that people want to dine in your establishment. To run a successful business it is essential that you have an understanding of costs, including how to cost menus, how to reduce costs in line with budgets and how to work within cost boundaries to deliver a good product and make a profit. Understanding basic costings, operations and menu planning are fundamental to becoming a professional chef and working in a commercial kitchen.

Organisation of the kitchen

Effective organisation will help a kitchen to run professionally. An efficiently run kitchen will prepare and cook the right amount of high quality food for the required number of people, on time, making the most effective use of staff, ingredients and equipment. Regardless of the size of the organisation, the most important factors in its success will be the menu and the systems used to prepare and present the food.

Current trends

Trends in food production operations are affected by:
- changes in technology
- social changes in eating habits
- lifestyle changes
- developments in food technology.

Some current trends that affect the design of kitchens for different types of food production operations are listed below.
- Restaurants and hotels: there is greater use of buffet and **self-assisted service** units; there is less emphasis on luxury, five-star experience.
- Banqueting: there is a move towards plated service, rather than traditional silver service.
- Fast food: new concepts are coming onto the market, with more specialised chicken and seafood concepts and more choices in ethnic food.
- Roadside provision: there are an increasing number of operations and partnerships with service station companies. Basic grill menus are now enhanced by factory-produced à la carte items.
- Food courts: development has slowed down; most food courts offer an 'all day' menu. Restaurant Associates (Compass) are introducing food courts into hotels.
- Theme restaurants: will continue to improve and multiply.

- Hospitals: there is greater emphasis on bought-in freezer and chilled foods, meaning less on-site preparation and cooking. Some hospitals operate their own cook–chill or cook–freeze systems. Many hospitals now have food courts occupied by well-known high street names as franchises, such as Pizza Hut or Burger King.
- Industrial: there are more zero-subsidy staff restaurants (staff pay the full cost of the food they buy) and increased **self-service** for all items. The introduction of cashless systems will enable multi-tenant office buildings to offer varying subsidy levels.
- Prisons and other institutions: little if any change; may follow hospitals by buying in more pre-prepared food; may receive foods from multi-outlet central production units, tied in with schools, meals-on-wheels provision, etc.
- Universities/colleges: greater move towards providing food courts; more snack bars and coffee shops. There is evidence of an increase in small 'satellite' outlets around buildings rather than large refectories or cafeterias.

In most cases companies are trying to reduce labour costs while maintaining or enhancing the meal experience for the customer.

The trend towards providing more attractive eating places (which can be seen in particular in many of the chain and franchise operators) has also had an effect on kitchen planning and design. One trend has been to bring the kitchen area totally or partially into view with back-bar equipment – for example, grills or griddles may be in full public view and food prepared on them to order.

While there will be a continuing demand for the traditional heavy-duty type of equipment found in larger hotels and restaurant kitchens, the constant need to change and update the design and décor of modern restaurants means that the equipment's life is generally shorter – reduced perhaps from ten years to seven or five or even less – in order to cope with the rate of change and redevelopment. This has resulted in the design of catering equipment generally being improved.

Because space is at a premium (property is expensive and the best use possible needs to be made of the space), kitchens are generally becoming smaller. Equipment is therefore being designed to cater for this

trend, becoming more modular and streamlined and generally able to fit into a smaller space. Equipment is also being designed to be easy to use, maintain and clean, because labour is a significant cost and the best use needs to be made of people's time.

> **Key terms**
>
> **Self-service**: customers serve themselves from a self-service counter or buffet.
>
> **Self-assisted service**: someone is on duty to help the customer choose; in some cases there will be a section on a buffet where a chef will be cooking fresh items such as stir fry, omelettes, waffles and pancakes. Here the guest is helped to choose and will take the finished item to their table. This is also known as 'theatre cookery'.

Kitchen layout

Properly planned layouts with adequate equipment, tools and materials to do the job are essential if practical work is to be carried out efficiently. If people and equipment are in the right place then work will proceed smoothly and in the proper sequence, without back-tracking or crossover.

Considerable time, thought and planning must be given to the organisation and layout of a kitchen system. The requirements of the kitchen have to be clearly identified with regard to the type of food that is to be prepared, cooked and served. The working areas and the different types of equipment available must be thought through carefully and the organisation of the kitchen staff must be planned.

When planning a kitchen, it is important to consider the following:

- What type of customers do you want to attract?
- What type of food do you want to serve?
- Will your menu be à la carte, table d'hôte, a combination of both, or self-service?
- Will you organise the kitchen based on the traditional *partie* system (see below)?
- Does the design comply with food safety law and health and safety regulations?

Size and extent of the menu

The owners or management of a food business must know what market they are aiming for (e.g. fine dining, gastro pub), what style of operation they are going to run (e.g. traditional, modern contemporary, silver service, plate service) and what type of food and prices the customers will expect. They also need to know the number of customers they intend to cater for at each service.

A kitchen with a large brigade of chefs can offer an extensive menu as long as the majority of the *mise en place* is carried out during the day. The food can be kept refrigerated until it is needed at service time. If an establishment has a finishing kitchen, the final preparation and presentation of many foods (fish, meat, vegetables, potatoes, pasta and eggs) can be completed quickly and efficiently (by sautéing, grilling, deep frying and so on) just before they are served, so the dishes are served to the customer quickly and freshly cooked. The design of the finishing kitchen is important and needs to include refrigerated cabinets for holding perishable foods, adequate cooking facilities and bain-marie space for holding sauces, etc.

Restaurants that provide a limited menu, such as steak houses, can employ fewer staff to cope with large numbers of customers, if they are organised well. The required standard can still be reached because fewer skills are needed. Nevertheless, whether producing grilled steaks or pancakes, the staff must be organised and work in a systematic way so that the flow of work is smooth.

Other types of establishment, such as schools, hospitals, airlines and department stores, also have to produce large amounts of food to be served at the same time. In order to achieve this, catering staff need to be well organised, supplied with large-scale preparation and production equipment and the means to finish dishes quickly. There has to be a good system in place for the preparation–production–freezing or chilling–reheat cycle, so that staff can simply reheat or finish the foods just before service.

Budget

Most kitchen designs will have a detailed budget. The money available will very often determine the overall design.

Services

The designer must know where the services (gas, electricity, water) are located and make sure that the layout of the kitchen uses the services in the most efficient way.

Labour and skill level

The number and type of people a company intends to employ will have an effect on the technology and equipment that is installed (for example, fewer, unspecialised staff and a lot of pre-prepared food or more skilled people and a traditional *partie* system to make dishes with entirely fresh ingredients).

Use of prepared convenience foods

A kitchen preparing a fast-food menu using prepared convenience food will be planned and equipped very differently from an à la carte or cook–chill kitchen. Certain factors must be taken into consideration, for example will sweets and pastries be made? Will there be a need for a larder or a butcher? Will fresh or frozen food be used, or a combination of both?

Types of equipment available

The type, amount and size of the equipment will depend on the type of menu being provided. The equipment must be located in the right place. Hand-washing facilities and storage of cleaning equipment should also be included.

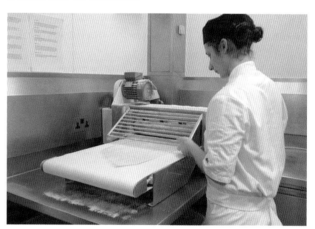

▲ The type and location of equipment should be considered when planning a kitchen

Multi-usage requirements

The need for round-the-clock catering, such as in hospitals, factories where shift work takes place, the police and armed forces, has forced kitchen planners to consider how kitchens can be used efficiently outside peak times. As a result, equipment is being made more adaptable and flexible, so that whole sections of the kitchen can be closed down when not in use, meaning that savings can be made on heating, lighting and maintenance.

Food safety and health and safety legislation

The design and construction of the kitchen must also comply with the Food Safety Act 1990/91/95 and Food Hygiene Regulations 2006. The basic layout and construction should allow enough space for all food handling areas and associated areas for equipment. There should be enough room for the work to be carried out safely and for frequent cleaning of the different areas and equipment.

Food production systems

The menu that will be offered will determine the amount of space and type of equipment needed to produce the food the customers will buy. Whatever system is chosen, good communication between all departments in the kitchen and restaurant is important in order to maintain and improve efficiency.

Partie system

In the late nineteenth century, when labour was relatively cheap, skilled and plentiful, the public wanted elaborate and extensive menus. In response to this, Auguste Escoffier, one of the most respected chefs of his era, devised what is known as the **partie system**, in which different sections of the kitchen were delegated to carry out specific jobs, such as preparing or cooking the fish, meat or vegetables. This system is still used in many establishments today.

The number of *parties* (different areas) required, and the number of staff in each, will depend on the size of the establishment. Obviously the organisation of a kitchen with 100 chefs preparing banquets for up to 1,000 people and a lunch and dinner service for 300 customers with an à la carte menu and floor service, will be quite different from that of a small restaurant serving 30 table d'hôte lunches or a full-view coffee shop, a speciality restaurant with a busy turnover or a hospital kitchen.

Even with two similar kitchens, the internal organisation is likely to vary, as each person in charge will have their own way of running their kitchen. However, everyone working in the system should know what he or she has to do, and how and when to do it.

À la carte menu system

For the à la carte menu, dishes are individually priced. The production system to deliver this menu is normally based on the partie system. A slimmed-down version of this system is normally used to achieve efficiency and productivity, as labour costs are high and therefore the operation has to be affordable.

Self-service counter system

The system used for self-service counters varies considerably in large establishments. The system adopts the process approach: the whole system is focused on process and equipment is sited together based on a particular process, for example, wet processes (boiling and steaming) are separate from dry processes (grilling, frying and baking). The partie system is sometimes used in this production system, but it is very often modified to suit the operation.

Fast food production system

Many fast food production systems focus on the process (i.e. what the main cooking process is – deep frying, grilling etc.). Banks of similar equipment are sited together for ease of operation and the flow is all in one direction.

> **Key terms**
>
> **Mise-en-place**: a French term meaning 'preparation prior to service'.
>
> **Partie system**: a food production system devised by French chef, August Escoffier, in which different sections of the kitchen are delegated to carry out specific jobs.

Work flow

The flow of work through the kitchen and serving areas is essential to the smooth running of any operation. Effective workflow will:

- help to establish good communication between departments
- improve efficiency
- improve the quality of the finished product
- reduce the risk of accidents
- promote good health and safety and food safety.

All of the above will provide a better service to customers.

Where possible, the layout of the kitchen should focus on a **linear workflow**. Back-tracking or crossover of materials and products must be avoided. Food preparation rooms should be planned so that the flow of work to process the food allows it to be moved through the premises, from the point of delivery to the point of sale or service, with the minimum of obstruction.

The overall sequence of receiving, storing, preparing, holding, serving and clearing should involve:
- minimum movement
- minimal back-tracking
- maximum use of space
- maximum use of equipment with minimum time and effort.

Staff time is valuable, so a design that reduces wasteful journeys is efficient and cost effective.

> **Key term**
>
> **Linear workflow**: a flow of work that allows the processing of food to be moved smoothly in one direction through the premises from the point of delivery to the point of sale or service.

Separate areas for different processes

For reasons of efficiency and hygiene, large kitchens should have different working areas for different processes, and food intended for sale should not cross paths with waste food or refuse.

For example, a kitchen may be divided as follows:
- dry areas – for storage
- wet areas – for fish preparation, vegetable preparation, butchery, cold preparation
- hot wet areas – for boiling, poaching, steaming
- hot dry areas – for frying, roasting, grilling
- dirty areas – for refuse, pot wash areas, plate wash.

Adequate workspace must be provided for each process and every effort must be made to separate dirty and clean processes.

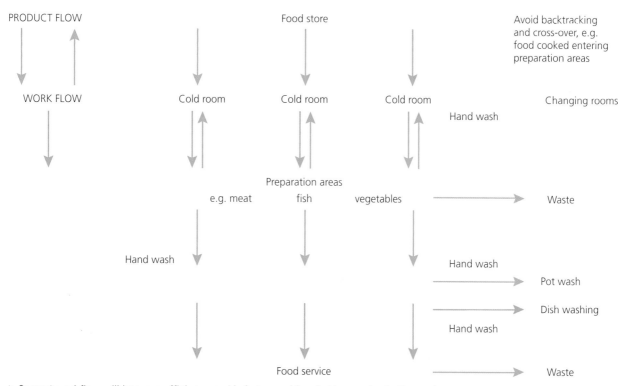

▲ Correct workflow will improve efficiency and help to provide a better service to the customer

Each section should be subdivided into high risk and contaminated sections:

- High risk food which may be contaminated easily while it is being prepared, such as ready-to-eat foods (soups and sauces), cooked meat and desserts.
- Food that may be already be contaminated when it arrives, before processing, for example, unprepared vegetables and raw meat.

The size and style of the menu and the ability of the staff will determine the number of preparation and production areas necessary and their layout; for example, a straight-line layout would be suitable for a snack bar, while an island layout would be more suitable for a hotel restaurant.

Food deliveries and storage

- The receiving area needs to be designed for easy delivery of supplies.
- Food deliveries should have a separate entrance because of the risk of contamination.
- Storage facilities should be located nearby, in a suitable position for the food to be distributed to preparation and production areas.
- Still room facilities (e.g. for storing preserves and cakes) may be required.
- Raw food should be prepared and stored in different areas from cooked food.

Preparation areas

In large catering establishments the preparation areas will be zoned to assist with the workflow. The various preparation processes will have different areas depending on what food is involved. In a vegetable preparation area, water from the sinks and dirt from the vegetables will accumulate, so adequate facilities for drainage should be provided. Pastry preparation, however, involves mainly dry processes.

Whatever the process, there are certain basic rules that can be applied to make working conditions easier and to help ensure that food hygiene regulations are complied with. Proper design and layout of the preparation area is a major contribution to good food safety.

- Vegetable preparation and wash-up areas should be separate from the actual food preparation and service areas.

- The layout must ensure a continuous workflow in one direction in order to avoid crossover of foods and cross-contamination. Staff should not get in each other's way by having to cross each other's paths more than is absolutely necessary.
- Worktop areas should be large enough for the preparation processes to be carried out and should be designed so that the food handler has all the necessary equipment and utensils close to hand.
- Work surfaces, sinks, stores and refrigerators should be within easy reach to avoid unnecessary walking.

Cooking area

'Raw materials' enter the cooking section from the main preparation areas (vegetables, meat and fish, dry goods) so this section must be designed so that the flow continues through to the servery. For example, roasting ovens are best located close to the meat preparation area and steamers next to the vegetable preparation area.

Obviously the cooking area should not be used by other staff to cross to another section of the kitchen or to get to the service area. The layout should be planned so that raw foodstuffs arrive at one point, are processed in the cooking section and then sent to the servery. There should be a clear progression in one direction. Staff working in dirty areas (areas of contamination) should not enter areas of finished product or where blast-chilling is taking place.

▲ Good kitchen design will consider the flow of food through the preparation and service areas

Containers/equipment/utensils

Where possible, equipment should be separated out into specific process areas, for example, pastry equipment should not leave the pastry area, equipment and containers used for preparing and storing raw food should be washed and stored in the raw food area, chopping boards and other small equipment used for raw preparation should not be allowed to enter the cooking areas.

Refuse and washing

There should be sufficient space to access all kitchen equipment so that it can be cleaned thoroughly and for all used equipment from the dining area to be cleared, cleaned and stored. Refuse must be kept in an appropriate area and should not pass through other areas on its way to the storage area.

Staff facilities

It is a good idea to have a separate staff entrance to the kitchen and, for food safety reasons, it is essential to have separate changing facilities for employees wherever possible – they should not have to use customer facilities. Sufficient hand washing facilities for staff must be provided. Good working conditions are likely to mean that staff will take pride in themselves, their work and their working environment.

Staffing hierarchy, job roles and responsibilities

Staffing hierarchy in a traditional kitchen

The organisation of the staffing hierarchy depends on the establishment. A large hotel or restaurant will have a **head chef** or **executive head chef**, with one or two **sous chefs** who deputise for the head chef. The head chefs may also run a department – for example, the pastry chef may also be the sectional chef, chef de partie or sous chef.

The **chef de partie** is in charge of a section such as sauces or vegetables. There may also be a demi chef de partie, who works on the opposite shift to the chef de partie.

Head chef

↓

Sous chef

↓

Chef de partie (sectional chefs)

↓

Commis chefs

↓

Apprentices

▲ Staffing hierarchy in a traditional kitchen

There will also be a number of assistant chefs (e.g. **commis chefs**) and there could be **apprentices** and trainees. Apprentices and trainees will move from section to section to complete their training.

Kitchen porters will also be employed, and in large establishments a kitchen clerk or personal assistant to the chef will be employed to assist with paperwork.

In some establishments, such as hospitals and centralised kitchens, a kitchen manager will take charge of the kitchen and have a number of cooks and kitchen assistants working under them. A centralised kitchen is one that serves a number of different outlets; the food is transported to these outlets usually chilled or frozen. Each outlet will have a satellite or finishing kitchen where the food is finished and made ready to serve to the customer.

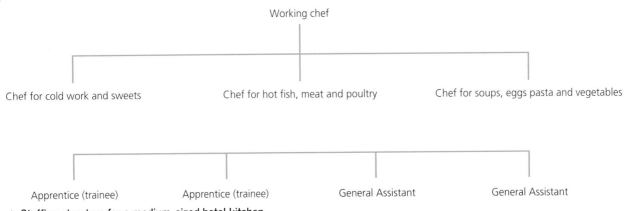

▲ Staffing structure for a medium-sized hotel kitchen

Responsibilities of specific job roles

Modern kitchens are organised in many different ways, but in each case a senior member of staff will be responsible for the smooth operation of the kitchen. This person must have leadership skills, human resource management skills and detailed product knowledge.

- **Head chef** – has overall responsibility for the organisation and management of the kitchen, including staffing, training, menus, budget control and sourcing of food. The head chef is also responsible for implementing food safety and health and safety legislation and practices.
- **Sous chef** – the deputy to the head chef, he or she will take overall responsibility in the head chef's absence. The sous chef may also have specific areas of responsibility, such as food safety, health and safety, quality control or staff training.
- **Chef de partie** – in charge of a specific section within the kitchen, such as meat, vegetables or fish and is responsible for setting tasks within their section. There may be a demi chef de partie working on an opposite shift covering the chef de partie's days off. Commis chefs and apprentices usually work with these chefs in different sections.
- **Commis chef** – the junior chef in the kitchen and works under overall supervision of the sous chef. A commis chef will work around the various kitchen sections.
- **Apprentice** – is similar to a commis chef and will complete similar tasks but is usually on a planned programme of learning, often managed by a college or training provider.

Importance of good working relationships within the kitchen

In order to achieve an efficient and effective system that satisfies customers' needs, it is important to work as a team, developing good working relationships in the kitchen and with the food service staff. This will also contribute to high staff morale and will improve the productivity of staff, ensuring a consistently high quality of food and ultimately offering a better service to customers.

Activity

1 Suggest how the layout of the kitchen you work in could be improved.
2 Think of a successful team. Say why you think it is successful and what you could learn from this team's success.

Planning and preparing menus for catering operations

Planning the menu is one of the essential elements in designing and costing the operations of a catering establishment.

Types of menu

Table d'hôte or set-price menus

A menu forming a meal (usually of two or three courses) at a set price. A choice of dishes may be offered at all courses.

À la carte menus

A menu with all of the dishes individually priced. Customers can therefore compile their own menu, which may be one, two or more courses. A true à la carte dish should be cooked to order and the customer should be prepared to wait.

First courses

Salad of endive with Roquefort, chives and walnuts

Oak smoked salmon with lime and horseradish dressing, served with blini

Half dozen Fines de Claire oysters

Ham hock ravioli with white wine beans, trompettes and parsley

Main courses

Pot roast free-range chicken, tagliatelle of asparagus and morels

Dover sole pan fried with brown butter and capers

John Dory with chives and chinger crust, aromatic broth

Roast rib of Aberdeen Angus beef with Yorkshire pudding and roast potatoes

Saffron risotto cake stuffed with tomato, grilled vegetables and Parmesan

Desserts

Aniseed parfait with ginger bread and spiced port figs

Crisp apple tart with clotted cream and Calvados

Honey roast pear with caramel sauce and cardamom custard

Apricot and chocolate soufflé

£22.50 per person

▲ Table d'hôte menus offer a meal at a set price

Dessert menus

These are often separate from the main menu items and are usually presented to the customer after they have finished their main course.

Function menus

Banquet menu

The banquet menu is often a set menu of three or more courses served to a large number of people. The food must be dressed in such a way that it can be served fairly quickly. Heavily garnished dishes should be avoided. If a large number of dishes have to be dressed at the same time, certain foods deteriorate quickly and will not tolerate storage in a hot place, even for a short time. It is not usual to serve farinaceous (i.e. pasta, noodles, rice) dishes, eggs, stews or savouries. A luncheon menu would usually consist of three courses. Dinner menus, depending on the occasion, generally consist of three to five courses and may be drawn from the following:

- **First course** – soup, cocktail (fruit or shellfish), hors d'oeuvres (assorted or single item), a small salad.
- **Second course** – fish, usually poached, steamed, roasted or grilled fillets with a sauce.
- **Third course** – meat, poultry or game, hot or cold, but not a stew or made-up dish; vegetables and potatoes or a salad would be served.
- **Fourth course** – sweet, hot or cold.
- **Fifth course** – cheese course.

Light buffet (including cocktail parties)

Examples of foods served at this type of event include:

- hot savoury pastry patties of, for example, lobster, chicken, crab, salmon, mushroom, ham
- hot chipolatas; chicken livers, wrapped in bacon and skewered
- bite-sized items – quiche and pizza; hamburgers; meatballs with savoury sauce or dip; scampi or fried fish goujons with tartare sauce
- savoury finger toast to include any of the cold canapes; these may also be prepared on biscuits or shaped pieces of pastry
- game chips, gaufrette potatoes, fried fish balls, celery stalks spread with cheese
- sandwiches; bridge rolls, open or closed but always small

- fresh dates stuffed with cream cheese; crudités with mayonnaise and cardamom dip; tuna and chive Catherine wheels; crab claws with garlic dip; smoked salmon pin wheels; choux puffs with Camembert
- sweets, such as trifles, charlottes, bavarois, fruit salad, gateaux).

For fork buffets, all food must be prepared in a way that enables it to be eaten with a fork or spoon.

▲ A buffet is a popular choice when catering for large numbers

Ethnic or speciality menus

These can be set-price menus or dishes may be individually priced. They may specialise in the food of a particular country (or religion) or in a specialised food itself. Examples of ethnic menus include Chinese, Indian, kosher, African-Caribbean and Greek menus; examples of speciality menus include steak, fish, pasta, vegetarian and pancakes.

Breakfast menus

Breakfast menus can be compiled from the following foods:

- **Fruit, fruit juices, stewed fruit, yoghurts, cereals** (porridge, etc.)
- **Eggs** – fried, boiled, poached, scrambled; omelettes with bacon or tomatoes, mushrooms or sauté potatoes.
- **Fish** – kippers, smoked haddock, kedgeree.
- **Meats (hot)** – fried or grilled bacon, sausages, kidneys, with tomatoes, mushrooms or sauté potatoes, potato cakes.
- **Meats (cold)** – ham, bacon, pressed beef with sauté potatoes.

- **Preserves** – marmalade (orange, lemon, grapefruit, ginger), jams, honey.
- **Beverages** – tea, coffee, chocolate.
- **Bread** – rolls, croissants, brioche, toast, pancakes, waffles.

It is usual to offer three courses from the above options.

As large a choice as possible should be offered, depending on the size of the establishment. However, it is better to offer a smaller number of well-prepared dishes than a large number of hurriedly prepared ones. A choice of plain foods, such as boiled eggs or poached haddock, should be available for people who may not require a fried breakfast.

Breakfast menus can be offered as continental, table d'hôte, à la carte or buffet. For buffet service customers can self-serve the main items they require with assistance from counter hands. It can be planned on a part self-service and assisted service basis, with hot drinks and eggs freshly cooked to order.

Luncheon and dinner menus

Lunch and dinner menus can be table d'hôte (set-price) menus of one, two or three courses, with a choice at each course; or individually priced à la carte menus so that the customer can choose their own menu of whatever number of dishes they require.

The lunch or dinner may also include a buffet, which may be all cold or hot dishes, or a combination of both, either served or organised on a self-service basis. Depending on the time of year and location, barbecue dishes can be considered.

Lunch and dinner menus can also be special party menus, which may be either a set menu with no choice or a set menu with a limited choice, such as soup or melon, main course, choice of two sweets. A special party menu may be served or a self-service buffet.

Afternoon tea menus

These vary considerably, depending on the type of establishment, and may include, for example: assorted sandwiches, bread and butter (white, brown, fruit loaf), assorted jams, scones with clotted cream, pastries, gateaux and tea (Indian, China, iced, fruit, herb).

▲ Afternoon tea menus may include sandwiches, scones, pastries, gateaux and tea

Commercial hotels, tea rooms, public restaurants and staff dining rooms may offer simple snacks, cooked meals and high teas. These may include:

- assorted sandwiches
- buttered buns, scones, cakes, Scotch pancakes, waffles, sausage rolls, assorted bread and butter, various jams, toasted teacakes, scones, crumpets, buns
- eggs (boiled, poached, fried, omelettes)
- fried fish, grilled meats, roast poultry
- cold meats and salads
- assorted pastries, gateaux
- various ices, coupes, sundaes
- tea, coffee, fruit juices and other soft drinks.

Take it further

For more information on nutritional standards in schools, visit the Children's Food Trust website: www.childrensfoodtrust.org.uk.

Also refer to the School Food Plan: www.schoolfoodplan.com

Importance of the menu

Method of communication

The menu is an essential method of communication which informs the customer of what is on offer. It must be clear and easy to follow and must not be misleading or ambiguous. Menus must now state what items contain the EU top 14 allergens within the dishes on the menu (see Chapter 4 Healthier foods and special diets for more information on this).

Planning tool

The menu is also a very useful planning tool because it informs the chef what must be ordered and it is also possible to assess which items are the most popular and the most profitable. The menu is linked to the purchasing of specific items, which in turn are linked to the recipe specifications that aid the costing and budgetary process.

Legal requirement

There is a whole range of laws concerned with consumer protection that are important when planning menus:

- **Trade Descriptions Act 1968** – this states that, 'Any person who in the course of a trade or business applies a false trade description to any goods or supplies or offers to supply any goods to which a false trade description is applied shall be guilty of an offence.' The description of the food on the menu should match the food that arrives on the plate. For example, if the menu states that the soup is homemade, serving readymade soup would constitute a breach of the Act in criminal law and may be reported to the local trading standards department.
- **Sale of Goods and Services Act 1982** – under this Act the goods (items on the menu) described must be of satisfactory quality and fit for purpose. A customer ordering hot food should therefore expect it to be hot. If it is not then the customer is entitled to a full or partial refund.
- **Price Marking Order 2004** – this requires that restaurateurs clearly display prices on the menu and indicate VAT.
- **VAT and service charges** – by law, Value Added Tax (VAT) must be included in meal prices and displayed outside or inside a restaurant, but does not have to be included on the menu. When the bill is presented to the customer, it may show a breakdown of how much VAT is being charged. A service charge may be included in the menu. However, if the customer is not satisfied with the service they are within their rights to have the service charge removed and the bill reduced.

Factors to consider when planning menus

Types of customers

People have varying likes and dislikes. Analyse the type of people you are planning to cater for (e.g. office workers in the city requiring quick service, or holidaymakers in a seaside resort). Study the area in which your establishment is situated and your potential target market of customers.

Make sure the menu is presented in a sensible and welcoming way for the type of customer it is aimed at. Use menu language that customers understand.

Consider any special dietary requirements customers may have – for example, kosher or halal diets, or allergies and intolerances.

Pricing

This is a crucial consideration if an establishment is to be profitable. Costing is essential for the success of any menu. Modern computer techniques can analyse costs swiftly and on a daily basis. Working out estimated customer spend per head is important when catering, for example, for hospital staff and patients, school children and industry workers. Whatever the type of menu, you should charge a fair price and ensure the customer is receiving good value for money. Achieving customer satisfaction can lead to recommendation and repeat business.

Decide what you are going to offer and at what price. Will you price each dish separately or offer set two- or three-course menus or a combination of the two? Be aware of any competition in the locality, including prices and quality.

Staff availability

Staff need to be available and have the skills to produce and serve the menu. Overstretched or under-skilled staff can easily reduce the standard of production envisaged and the quality of individual dishes.

Space and equipment in the kitchen

The available space and equipment in the kitchen will influence the composition of the menu. For example, you may need to avoid overloading the deep fryer, salamanders or steamers. Also consider storage space.

Type of organisation

Different types and sizes of establishment may require different types of menu. For example, a school menu will be regulated by government guidelines and focus on offering a healthy, balanced diet; a gastropub menu may include modern brasserie dishes and popular, traditional pub dishes such as fish and chips.

Seasonality and availability of food

Consider issues such as seasonal foods and reliability of suppliers. Certain dishes acceptable in summer may not be so in winter. Some foods may not be available at certain times of year. Using ingredients that are in season means that they are usually in good supply and reasonable in price.

Important terms used in menu planning

- **Table d'hôte** – a set price menu, usually consisting of two or three courses. A choice of dishes may be offered at all courses.
- **À la carte** – a menu with all the dishes individually priced.
- **Hors d'oeuvres** – starters.
- **Potage** – soup
- **Entrée** – small cuts of meat or poultry usually served with a sauce.
- **Releve** – large cuts of meat which may be carved in the dining room from a trolley. (This is a very old fashioned word and is not normally used today.)
- **Fromage** – cheese course.
- **Farinaceous** – flour or starch-based dishes, for example, pasta, noodle and rice dishes.

Costs and calculations used in the catering industry

Why are food costs important?

It is important to know the exact cost of each process and every item produced because:

- it tells you the net profit made by each section of the organisation and shows the cost of each meal produced
- it will reveal possible ways to economise and can result in a more effective use of stores, labour and materials

- costing provides the information necessary to develop a good pricing policy
- cost records help to provide speedy quotations for all special functions, such as parties and wedding receptions
- it enables the caterer to keep to a budget.

If food costing is controlled accurately, the cost of particular items on the menu and the total expenditure on food over a given period can be worked out. Understanding food costs helps to control costs, prices and profits.

An efficient food cost system will show up any bad buying and inefficient storage and should help to prevent waste and pilfering. This can help the caterer to run an efficient business and give the customer value for money.

Factors in controlling food costs and profit

Sourcing and purchasing of food commodities

The menu dictates what a food operation needs to purchase and based on this the buyer searches for a market that can supply these requirements. Once the right market is found, the buyer must investigate the various products available. The buyer makes decisions regarding quality, amounts, price and what will satisfy the customers but also make a profit. A buyer must have knowledge of the internal organisation of the company and be able to obtain the products needed at a competitive price. They must understand how these items are going to be used in the production operations (i.e. how they are going to be prepared and cooked), to make sure that the right item is purchased. For example, sometimes the item required may not have to be of prime quality – tomatoes for use in soups and sauces, for instance.

Buyers need be able to make good use of market conditions. For example, if there is a lot of fresh salmon at low cost, has the organisation the facility to make use of extra salmon purchases? Is there sufficient freezer space? Can the chef make use of salmon by creating a demand on the menu?

Buying methods

The type of buying method will have an impact on cost. For example, with **informal buying** (talking directly to sales people, which is more suitable for casual buying of small amounts) prices and supply tend to fluctuate more than with formal methods. **Formal buying** involves giving suppliers written specifications and quantities needed. Formal contracts are best for large quantities purchased over a long period of time and prices do not vary much during a year once the basic price has been established.

Types of product

The main products that an establishment purchases can be divided into three types:

1 **Perishable** – products that do not stay fresh for very long, such as fresh fruit and vegetables, dairy products, meat and fish; prices and suppliers may vary; informal methods of buying are frequently used; perishables should be purchased to meet menu needs for a short period only.
2 **Staple** – supplies that are canned, bottled, dehydrated or frozen; formal or informal purchasing may be used; because items are staple and can be stored easily, bid buying is frequently used to take advantage of the favourable prices available when purchasing large quantities.
3 **Daily use needs** – daily use or contract items are delivered frequently to match usage; stocks are kept up to the particular level and supply is automatic; supplies may arrive daily, several times a week, weekly or less often; most items are perishable, therefore supplies must not be excessive but only sufficient to get through to the next delivery.

Selecting suppliers

Selecting suppliers is an important part of the purchasing process. You need to think about how a supplier will be able to meet the needs of your operation and consider price, delivery and quality/standards. Information on suppliers can be obtained from other purchasers, visits to suppliers' establishments and interviews with prospective suppliers. Always question how reliable and competitive a supplier will be under varying market conditions.

▲ Monitoring how food is sourced and bought can help to control food costs

Buying tips

- Keep your knowledge of commodities to be purchased up to date.
- Be aware of the different types and qualities of each commodity.
- When buying fresh commodities, be aware of part-prepared and ready-prepared items available on the market.
- Keep a sharp eye on price variations. Buy at the best price that will ensure the required quality and also make a profit. The cheapest item may prove to be the most expensive if lots of it ends up being wasted. When possible, order by number and weight. For example, 20 kg plaice could be 80 × 250 g plaice, 40 × 500 g plaice or 20 × 1 kg plaice. It could also be 20 kg total weight of various sizes, which makes it difficult to control portion sizes. Some suppliers (e.g. butchers, fishmongers) may offer a portion-control service by selling the required number of a given weight of certain cuts, for example, 100 × 150 g sirloin steaks, 25 kg prepared stewing beef, 200 × 100 g pieces of turbot fillet, 500 × 100 g plaice fillets.
- Organise an efficient system of ordering, keeping copies of all orders for cross-checking, whether orders are given in writing, in person or by telephone.
- Compare purchasing by retail, wholesale and contract procedures to ensure the best method is selected for your particular organisation.

- Explore all possible suppliers: local or markets, town or country, small or large.
- Keep the number of suppliers to a minimum, but have at least two suppliers for every group of commodities. This should help to keep the suppliers' prices and terms competitive.
- Issue all orders to suppliers fairly, allowing enough time for the order to be delivered on time.
- Compare prices continually to make sure that you buy at a good market price.
- Buy perishable goods when they are in full season as this gives the best value at the cheapest price. To help with purchasing the correct quantities, it is useful to compile a purchasing chart for 100 covers from which items can be divided or multiplied according to requirement. An indication of quality standards can also be incorporated in a chart of this kind.
- Deliveries must all be checked against the orders given, for quantity, quality and price. If any goods delivered are below an acceptable standard they must be returned, either for replacement or credit.
- Containers can account for large sums of money. Ensure that all containers are correctly stored, returned to the suppliers where possible and the proper credit given.
- All invoices must be checked for quantities and prices.
- All statements must be checked against invoices and passed swiftly to the office so that payment can be made on time, to ensure maximum discount on purchases.
- Develop good relations with trade representatives (sales people) because much useful up-to-date information can be gained from them.
- Keep up-to-date trade catalogues, visit trade exhibitions, survey new equipment and continually review the space, services and systems in use. Always be on the lookout for ways to increase efficiency.
- Organise a testing panel occasionally to keep up to date with new commodities and new products coming on to the market.
- Consider how computer applications might help the operation.
- Study weekly fresh food price lists.

Controlling quality of food commodities

Standard purchasing specifications

Standard purchasing specifications are drawn up for every item to be purchased, describing exactly what is required. The specification includes criteria related to quality, grade, weight, size and method of preparation if required (such as washed and selected potatoes for baking). Other information might include variety, maturity, age, colour, shape and so on.

Once an accurate specification is approved, it will be referred to every time the item is delivered. A copy is often given to the supplier and the storekeeper. These purchasing specifications (known as primary specifications) will help with the formulation of standardised recipes and assist in the costing and control procedures.

- **Commodity:** round tomatoes.
- **Size:** 50 g (2 oz) 47–57 mm diameter.
- **Quality:** firm, well formed, good red colour, with stalk attached.
- **Origin:** Dutch, available March–November.
- **Class/grade:** super class A.
- **Weight:** 6 kg (13 lb) net per box.
- **Count:** 90–100 per box.
- **Quote:** per box/tray.
- **Packaging:** loose in wooden tray, covered in plastic.
- **Delivery:** day following order.
- **Storage:** temperature 10–13 °C (50–55 °F) at a relative humidity of 75–80%.

Note: avoid storage with cucumbers and aubergines.

▲ Example of a standard purchasing specification for tomatoes

Standard recipes

The standard recipe is a written formula for producing a food item of a specified quality and quantity for use in a particular establishment. It should show the precise quantities and qualities of the ingredients, together with the sequence of preparation and service. It enables the establishment to have greater control over cost and quantity, as it is able to pre-determine the quantities and qualities of ingredients to be used and the amount (number of portions) a recipe should make.

Accurate weighing and measuring

When designing standardised recipes it is important to ensure the correct weights and measures are recorded to achieve consistency. This means that no matter who prepares the dish, the same standard portion size and quality are achieved. Accurate weighing and measuring are essential procedures needed to control food costs and to work within targets and budgets.

Preparation and cooking losses and waste control

It is important to control wastage in the kitchen. Much wastage occurs during preparation and cooking. Wastage occurs because of poor purchasing, incorrect storage and poor preparation skills through lack of training. Wastage must be controlled to ensure that yields and portion control are achieved and the desired number of portions are also achieved from the costed recipe. Excessive food wastage means that the chef is throwing money in the bin.

Elements of cost

Costing dishes is a very important process for a chef and allows the selling price to be established. To calculate the total cost of any one item or meal provided, it is necessary to analyse the total expenditure under several headings. The total cost of each item consists of the following three main elements: food and materials; labour costs; and overheads.

Food and materials costs

These are known as **variable costs** because the level will vary according to the volume of business. Variable costs include food costs, which may vary on a daily or weekly basis. It is important not to have excess stock in storage as it ties up money and over-stocking can result in food wastage. **Fixed costs** include labour and overheads – these are charges that do not change according to the volume of business.

Labour costs

In an operation that uses part-time or extra staff for special occasions, the money paid to these staff also comes under variable costs; by comparison, salaries and wages paid regularly to permanent staff are fixed costs.

Labour costs in the majority of operations fall into two categories:

1 Direct labour costs – the salaries and wages paid to staff such as chefs, waiters, bar staff, housekeepers and chambermaids, which can be allocated to income from food, drink and accommodation sales.

2 Indirect labour costs – includes salaries and wages paid, for example, to managers, office staff and maintenance staff who work for all departments in the establishment (so their labour cost should be charged to all departments).

Overheads

Overheads consist of rent, rates, heating, lighting and equipment, maintenance, gas, electricity and sundry expenses, including cleaning materials.

> **Key terms**
>
> **Variable costs**: costs that vary according to the volume of business; includes food and materials costs.
>
> **Fixed costs**: regular charges, such as labour and overheads, that do not vary according to the volume of business.
>
> **Overheads**: expenses associated with operating the business, such as rent, rates, heating, lighting, electricity, gas, maintenance and equipment.

Gross profit

Gross profit (or kitchen profit) is the difference between the cost of an item and the price it is sold at.

Gross profit = selling price – food cost

For example, if food costs are £2 and the selling price is £4:

Gross profit = £4 – £2 = £2

Net profit

Net profit is the difference between the selling price of the food (sales) and total cost of the product (this includes food, labour and overheads).

Net profit = selling price – total cost

For example, if the selling price is £5 and the total cost is £4:

Net profit = £5 – £4 = £1

Worked example

Food sales for 1 week	= £25,000
Food costs for 1 week	= £12,000
Labour and overheads for 1 week	= £9,000

Total costs for 1 week = food costs + labour and overheads = £12,000 + £9,000 = £21,000

To work out the gross profit:

Gross profit = Food sales – Food cost = £25,000 – £12,000 = **£13,000**

To work out the net profit:

Net profit = Food sales – Total costs = £25,000 – £21,000 = **£4,000**

Activity

Food costs for one week at the restaurant you work in are £15,000. For the same week, the restaurant spends £12,000 on labour and overheads. Food sales for the week total £30,000.

1 Calculate the **gross** profit the restaurant makes for the week.

2 Calculate the **net** profit the restaurant makes for the week.

Profit is always expressed as a percentage:

$$\% \text{ net profit} = \frac{\text{net profit}}{\text{sales}} \times 100$$

Worked example

Using the same example as above, the percentage net profit for the week is:

$$\frac{\text{net profit}}{\text{sales}} \times 100$$

$$= \frac{4,000}{25,000} \times 100$$

$$= 16\%$$

> **Key terms**
>
> **Gross profit**: the difference between the cost of an item and the price at which it is sold.
>
> **Net profit**: the difference between the selling price of an item and the total cost of the product (this includes food, labour and overheads).

It is usual to express each element of cost as a percentage of the selling price. This enables the caterer to control profits.

Worked example

The table shows how each element of cost can be shown as a percentage of the sales.

	Costs	Percentage of sales
Food cost	£12,000	$\frac{12,000}{25,000} \times \mathbf{100} = 48\%$
Labour	£6,000	$\frac{6,000}{25,000} \times \mathbf{100} = 24\%$
Overheads	£3,000	$\frac{3,000}{25,000} \times \mathbf{100} = 12\%$
Total costs	£21,000	$\frac{21,000}{25,000} \times \mathbf{100} = 84\%$
Sales	£25,000	
Net profit (sales – total costs)	£4,000	$\frac{4,000}{25,000} \times \mathbf{100} = 16\%$

Calculating the selling price

If the selling price of a dish is expressed as 100% (the total amount received from its sale), it can be broken down into the amount of money spent on food items and the gross profit. This can be expressed in percentages.

Often, caterers need to ensure that an agreed gross profit is achieved. The selling price needed to achieve a specific gross profit percentage can be calculated by dividing the total food cost by the food cost as a percentage of the sale and multiplying by 100.

Food costs as a percentage of the sale = 100 – gross profit %.

Worked example

If food costs come to £3.50, to calculate the selling price and make sure a 65% gross profit is achieved, the following calculations can be used.

First, calculate food costs as a percentage of the sale:

Food costs as a percentage of the sale = 100 – gross profit % = 100 – 65 = 35%

This is shown in the pie chart below.

The selling price of the dish is 100%: therefore, if gross profit is 65%, the food cost as a percentage of the sale is 35%.

To calculate the selling price:

This can also be presented in monetary terms, as shown in the following diagram:

Here, the total food cost is £3.50 and the selling price is £10; the gross profit is therefore £6.50.

Activity

Food costs for a dish are £10.50. What should be the selling price of the dish to ensure you achieve 65% gross profit?

Raising the required gross profit reduces the food cost as a percentage of the selling price. For example, if the gross profit requirement was raised to 75%, this would reduce the food cost as a percentage of the selling price to 25% (100% – 75%), as shown in the diagram below.

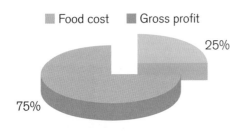

Worked example

If the food cost is £3.50 and the required gross profit is 75%:

To achieve a 75% gross profit, with a £3.50 food cost, the selling price would need to be £14.00.

The percentages still add up to 100%, but the proportion spent on food is now smaller in terms of the selling price (food costs are now 25% of the selling price) because the percentage gross profit is higher. The diagram below illustrates this.

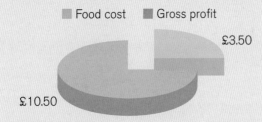

To check that this is correct, the following calculation can be applied:

(brings up to 25%)

... and

(brings up to 75%)

£10.50 (75%) + £3.50 (25%) = £14.00 (100%)

Activity

If a dish costs £3.00 to produce, what should the selling price be to achieve a 70 per cent profit on sales?

Average spend per customer

The average amount spent by each customer is determined by dividing the total sales by the number of customers.

Worked example

If total sales are £25,000 and the restaurant serves 1,000 meals, then the average amount spent by each customer is:

If the percentage composition of sales for a month is known, the average price of a meal for that period can be further analysed.

Worked example

Average price of a meal = £25.00 = 100%

£0.25 = 1%

Remember, the costs as a percentage of sales were as follows:

	Costs	Percentage of sales
Sales	£25,000	
Food cost	£12,000	48%
Labour	£6,000	24%
Overheads	£3,000	12%
Net profit (sales – total costs)	£4,000	16%

This means that the customer's contribution towards:

Food cost = £0.25 × 48 (food cost as a percentage of sales) = £12.00

Labour = £0.25 × 24 (labour as a percentage of sales) = £6.00

Overheads = £0.25 × 12 (overheads as a percentage of sales) = £3.00

Net profit (net profit as a percentage of sales) = £0.25 × 16 = £4.00

Cost price of a dish

A rule that can be applied to calculate the food cost price of a dish is as follows:

Let the cost price of the dish equal 40 per cent and fix the selling price at 100 per cent.

Worked example

If the dish was sold at £10:

Selling price (100%) = £10

Cost of dish (40%) = $\frac{10}{100} \times 40 = £4$

Selling the dish at £10 and making 60 per cent gross profit above the cost price, would be known as 40 per cent food cost.

Worked example

If entrecote steak costs £10.00 per kg, what would be the selling price at 40 per cent food cost of a 250 g sirloin steak?

First, you need to work out how much 250 g would cost.

There are 1000 g in 1 kg, so 250 g = 0.25 kg (250 ÷ 1000).

$$\frac{1\,kg}{4} = 0.25\,kg$$

So, if 1 kg costs £10, the cost of 0.25 kg (or 250 g)

$$\frac{£10}{4} = £2.50$$

250 g entrecote steak at £10.00 per kg = £2.50

If the selling price is fixed at 40% food cost:

$$\text{Selling price} = \frac{2.50\ (\textit{food cost}) \times 100\ (\textit{fixed selling price \%})}{40\ (\textit{fixed food cost \%})} = £6.25$$

The selling price of 250 g of sirloin steak at 40 per cent food cost is £6.25.

Test yourself

1 Describe the system of kitchen organisation referred to as the 'partie' system.
2 What is the usual role of a chef de partie? Give examples.
3 Suggest **three** considerations you would need to make when planning a kitchen.
4 Why is good kitchen workflow considered to be important?
5 Suggest **four** considerations that need to be made when planning a menu for a new city centre restaurant.
6 When a menu is described as table d'hôte what does this mean?
7 Describe **one** factor that should be monitored to control food costs.
8 Describe what is meant by 'portion control' and give **three** examples of how this may be done.
9 Give **one** example of overheads in a hospitality business.
10 What is the name given to the profit made by a business after all the costs such as food, labour and overheads have been taken out?

Practice assignment task

You have been asked to design and plan a kitchen for a new restaurant. As part of your plan, you need to include information about each of the following, stating the reasons for your choices:

- **Equipment and work flow** – choose the most appropriate equipment; remember to consider the flow from goods in to goods out (the movement should be in one direction).
- **Latest trends** – for example, kitchen on view, theatre style, brasserie or bistro, café, gastro pub – factor these into your design.
- **Staffing requirements** – think about how the kitchen will be managed, include details of the numbers of chefs and kitchen assistants you will need.

- **Type of production and service** – consider the process (e.g. traditional, fast food, plated service, take away).
- **Type of menu** – what type of meal occasion is your menu for? Remember to use simple, easily understood language. Refer to the text in this chapter when taking into account the planning of the menu.
- **Selling price of dishes** – think about the customers and how much they are prepared to pay, as well as the location of the restaurant. Calculate the selling price of dishes on your menu. Remember to consider all of the elements of cost.

6 Prepare and cook stocks, soups and sauces

This chapter will help you to:

1 prepare and cook stocks, soups and sauces, including:
- using equipment correctly
- demonstrating safe and hygienic practices
- preparing ingredients
- cooking different types of stocks, soups and sauces
- applying quality points
- finishing soups and sauces
- evaluating the finished product.

2 understand how to:
- identify different types, uses and purposes of stock, soup and sauces
- explain quality points
- prepare and cook products correctly
- chill and store products correctly
- state and explain the cooking times for different stocks
- identify finishing methods and accompaniments for soup
- identify sauce and dish combinations
- demonstrate the skills needed to check and finish sauces.

Recipes included in this chapter

Stock

Stock is the basis of all meat sauces, soups and purées. It is really just the juice of meat extracted by long and gentle simmering, or the infusion/transfer of flavour from an ingredient such as bones, vegetables or shellfish.

When making stock, remember that the object is to draw the goodness out of the materials and into the liquor, giving it the right flavour and nutrients for the end product, whether it is a soup, sauce or a reduction. The type and quality of ingredients you use are important.

Stock can be used for a variety of recipes and preparations in the kitchen. It can be used for soups, sauces, cooking vegetables, braising and stewing both vegetables and meat and fish recipes.

▲ Stock

Types of stock

White stock

A basic preparation where vegetables and bones are **blanched** but not browned to give a clear white stock.

Brown stock

A basic preparation where vegetables and bones are browned, usually in the oven. Once browned, they are covered with water, boiled and simmered to give a rich brown colour.

Nage

A nage is a well-seasoned stock (i.e. mushroom nage is a well-seasoned mushroom stock) usually used for cooking seafood and to enhance flavours.

Convenience stocks

Many establishments use prepared stocks to save time and labour, but also to reduce the food safety risks associated with the preparation, production and storage of stocks. These stocks are purchased as a chilled stock, frozen or in a paste or a dry powder. Many of the fresh chilled products are of a very high quality.

> **Key terms**
>
> **White stock**: a stock produced by blanching but not browning vegetables and bones, to give a clear stock.
>
> **Blanch**: plunging food into boiling water for a brief time before plunging into cold water to halt the cooking process. The purpose of blanching is to soften and/or partly cook the food without colouring it.
>
> **Brown stock**: stock produced by browning vegetables and bones before covering in water, boiling and simmering.

Preparing stock

- Choose high quality ingredients, bones, carcasses and vegetables.
- Do not use ingredients that are past their best, as this will affect both the colour and flavour.
- Unsound meat or bones and decaying vegetables will give stock an unpleasant flavour and cause it to deteriorate quickly.

- Fat should also be skimmed off; if it is not the stock will taste greasy.
- When making chicken stock, the bones should first be soaked to remove the blood that is in the cavity.

> **Health and safety** ⚠
>
> Stocks can easily become contaminated and a risk to health, so be sure to use good ingredients and hygienic methods of preparation.
>
> For information on maintaining a safe and secure working environment, a professional and hygienic appearance, clean food production areas, equipment and utensils, and food hygiene, refer to Chapters 1 and 3.

Cooking stock

- Scum should be removed from the top of the stock as it cooks. If it is not removed it will boil into the stock and spoil the colour and flavour.
- Stock should always simmer gently; if it is allowed to boil quickly, it will evaporate and go cloudy/milky.
- Salt should not be added to stock. Stock is very often reduced and evaporated to give a stronger flavour; if salt is added it would be concentrated and the result would be far too salty.
- If stock is going to be kept, strain it and cool quickly, then place it in the refrigerator.

Reducing stocks: glazes

A **glaze** is a reduced stock. To achieve a glaze the stock is evaporated on the stove until it is of a consistency similar to treacle or a thick jelly. This thicker consistency is caused by collagen – which is found in the bones, tendons and connective tissue of meat – breaking down into gelatine as the stock reduces. This results in a more concentrated flavour. However, care must be taken not to over-reduce the stock otherwise it will become too concentrated and may burn.

Glazes are used to enhance the flavour of soups and sauces. They are also a method of preservation.

> **Key term**
>
> **Glaze**: a reduced stock with a concentrated flavour. Often used to enhance the flavour of soups and sauces.

Cooking times

Cooking times differ for different types of stocks, due to the type of bones used and how much flavour concentration is required. For example, beef bones require a great deal longer than chicken bones – generally 4–6 hours; for chicken bones only 1–2 hours may be needed for the flavour to be extracted. Fish bones are traditionally cooked for 20 minutes; however the stock may be infused with the bones at a lower temperature than boiling point for longer.

Chilling stock

If stock is not going to be used immediately, it must be chilled. The best way to chill stock is to strain it and then blast chill it to 5°C within 90 minutes. Alternatively, if no blast chiller is available, strain the stock into a clean container and place the container in ice water, stirring continuously until 5°C is reached. Store immediately in a refrigerator.

Storing stock

- Chilled stock should be stored in a refrigerator at a temperature below 5°C.
- If it is to be deep-frozen it should be labelled and dated and stored below a temperature between –20°C and –18°C.
- When taken from storage it must be boiled for at least two minutes before being used.
- It must not be reheated more than once.
- Ideally, stock should be made fresh daily and discarded at the end of the day.

Health and safety ⚠

Never store a stock, sauce, gravy or soup above eye level as someone could accidentally spill the contents over themselves if they don't see it.

Soup

Our modern word 'soup' derives from the old French words *sope* and *soupe*.

When cooks in the Middle Ages spoke of 'soup', they were referring to a piece of bread or toast soaked in a liquid, or over which a liquid had been poured. The bread or toast was a vital part of this dish; it was a means by which the liquid could be consumed efficiently by sopping it up (an alternative to using a spoon).

Originally soup was basic sustenance and in most houses it would be a one-pot meal consisting of scrag ends of meat, vegetables, pulses and roots, which would be left cooking for a while to extract lots of flavour. Soup was a meal in itself, served with a generous chunk of bread. These hearty soups are still used today – for example, Scotch broth, minestrone, bouillabaisse, pea and ham, chowder and many more.

More recently, sophisticated dining concepts have altered the role of soups. Fifteen or twenty years ago most soups were thickened either by purée or by roux (roux seemed to be used most frequently); today, more restaurant chefs offer a lighter approach, reducing flour and fat.

Table 6.1 provides some examples of soups their preparation and presentation.

▲ Soup

Table 6.1 Soups, their preparation and presentation

Soup classification	Base	Passed or Unpassed	Finish	Example
Clear	Stock	Strained	Usually garnished	Consommé
Broth	Stock; cut vegetables	Unpassed	Chopped parsley	Scotch broth; minestrone
Purée	Stock; fresh vegetables; pulses	Passed	Croutons	Lentil soup; potato soup
Velouté	Blond roux; vegetables; stock	Passed	Liaison of yolk and cream	Velouté of chicken
Cream	Stock and vegetables; vegetable purée; béchamel; velouté	Passed	Cream, milk or yoghurt	Cream of vegetable; cream of fresh pea; cream of tomato
Bisque	Shellfish stock	Passed	Cream	Lobster soup
Potage	Stock with vegetables	Unpassed; may be passed	Milk (optional)	Bonne Femme (leek and potato)
Chilled	Stock; potato and leek	Passed	Cream	Vichyssoise

Types of soup

Soups can be classified into the following categories.

Roux-based soups

A roux-based soup is a soup which is thickened with a traditional roux (fat and flour). Examples of roux-based soups include:

- Velouté – a velvety French sauce made with white stock and thickened with a **liaison** (see 'Preparing and cooking sauces: thickening' on page 102).
- Cream soup – a roux-based soup finished with cream before it is served.

Potage soups

A French term referring to a thick soup. Examples of potage soups include:

- **Minestrone** – an Italian vegetable-based soup
- **Potage St germain** – green pea soup
- **Potage bonne femme** – an **unpassed** potage and leek soup
- **Potage parmentier** – potato soup (**passed**)
- **Potage Crécy** – carrot soup (passed).

Fish/shellfish soups

Examples of fish/shellfish soups include:

- **Bisque** – a very rich soup with a creamy consistency; usually made of lobster or shellfish (crab, shrimp, etc.).

- **Bouillabaisse** – a Mediterranean fish soup/stew, made of multiple types of seafood, olive oil, water and seasonings including garlic, onions, tomato and parsley.
- **Chowder**: a hearty North American soup, usually with a seafood base.

Chilled soups

Examples of chilled soups include:

- **Gazpacho** – a Spanish tomato–vegetable soup served ice cold
- **Vichyssoise** – a simple, flavourful puréed potato and leek soup, thickened with the potato itself and served cold.

Professional tip

No fat is added to Vichyssoise when it is served cold, because if it were, the dish would leave a fatty residue on the palate and offer a less-than-clear mouth feel.

Key terms

Liaison: a mixture of egg yolks and cream that is used to thicken a sauce.

Passed: a thin soup such as a consommé, served by passing through a fine muslin cloth to remove the solid particles.

Unpassed: a thin soup such as a broth which is served along with all the ingredients used.

Purée soups

A soup with a vegetable base that has been puréed in a food mill or blender. It is often altered after milling with the addition of broth, cream, butter, sour cream or coconut milk. These soups are named after the main puréed vegetable. They are soups which are passed and may be garnished. Examples include:

- **Purée Dubarty (cauliflower)** – garnished with small florets of cauliflower
- **Purée St germain (also known as Potage St germain)** – green pea
- **Purée of vegetables** – mixed vegetables such as potatoes, leeks, carrots and celery
- **Lentil soup**.

Broths

A soup in which bones, meat, fish, grains, or vegetables have been simmered in water or stock. Examples of broths include:

- **consommé** – a completely clear double or triple broth (broth added to another broth) with a meat, rather than bone base; consommé is painstakingly strained to make it clear
- **dashi** – the Japanese equivalent of consommé; made of giant seaweed or *konbu*, dried bonito and water.

> **Key terms**
>
> **Roux**: a soup thickened with a traditional roux of fat and flour.
>
> **Potage**: a thick soup.
>
> **Broth**: a soup consisting of a stock or water in which meat or fish and/or vegetables have been simmered.
>
> **Purée**: a soup with a vegetable base that has been puréed.
>
> **Consommé**: a completely clear broth.

> **Healthy eating tip**
>
> Look for clear soups containing vegetables, beans and lean protein like chicken, fish or lean beef. Italian minestrone, bouillabaisse and gazpacho are excellent choices; cream-based soups can often be adapted to fit a healthier menu.

Preparing and cooking soup

Most soup-making begins by preparing a stock (see above), made by slowly simmering vegetables with seasonings and then straining the liquid.

The underlying flavours of these foundation ingredients are enhanced by adding herbs and seasonings. In many cases, this flavour base begins by preparing a mixture of flavouring elements cooked in a little fat or oil. Because of their aromatic properties and flavours, most soups begin this phase with a combination of onion, garlic, leeks and carrots (this is called a **mirepoix**) or **aromats**. The result is the foundation of all soups.

To this foundation meat, fish, vegetables, fruits, seasonings, fats like butter or cream and vegetables or dried pulses are added in countless variations to create the wealth of soups available.

> **Healthy eating tip**
>
> Soup offers a very good, healthy option. For healthier soup, butter can be replaced with vegetable oil, reducing the cholesterol intake. Cream can be replaced with fromage frais or yogurt. Broths and vegetable soups are healthy options as they are both light and filling.

> **Key terms**
>
> **Mirepoix**: approximately 1 cm diced carrot, onion and celery cooked in fat or oil and used as a flavour base for soups.
>
> **Aromats**: herbs such as parsley, chervil and basil used as a flavour base; may also include vegetables such as onions and celery.

Quality points

- Use fresh, quality ingredients.
- Peel, prepare and weigh ingredients as part of the mise-en-place. Make sure you have the correct ratio of ingredients for the required number of portions.

Weighing and measuring

It is important to weigh every ingredient to determine the exact flavour and consistency of the soup, but more importantly to determine the exact nutritional content per portion. Measuring the ingredients accurately will also result in the correct yield and less wastage.

Cuts of vegetables

Soups which require small cuts of vegetables (such as paysanne for minestrone and gros brunoise for Scotch broth), are either cut by hand or by using a machines which cuts vegetables to the required size. (Refer to Chapter 7 for more information on cuts of vegetables.)

Refer to Chapter 7 for more information on cuts of vegetables.

Professional tip

Always use strong, thick-bottomed pans to cook soup to avoid scalding and browning.

Step by step: passing and straining soups

Conical strainers are used to pass the soup to obtain a fine consistency. Conical strainers come in a range of sizes from fine (chinois) to medium.

1 Slowly simmer vegetables and seasonings with stock to develop flavours.

2 Purée using a stick blender, liquidiser or food processor.

3 To ensure a smooth consistency, pass the soup through the conical strainer. Use a ladle to carefully pump the soup through.

Professional tip

Preparing soups using stick blenders, liquidisers and food processors produces excellent purée soups with a smooth consistency.

Finishing methods: garnishes and accompaniments for soup

Examples of garnishes that can be served with soup include:

- **Croutons** – slices of white or brown bread cut into 1 cm dice, carefully shallow fried in vegetable oil or clarified butter.
- **Sippets** – corners of bread cut from a flat tin loaf, finely sliced and toasted in the oven. Both croutons and sippets may be flavoured by rubbing chopped garlic into the bread.
- **Toasted flutes (croutes de flute)** – very small thin baguette slices, toasted or sprinkled with olive oil or melted butter and baked in the oven until crisp.

Accompaniments that can be served with soup include:

- brunoise, julienne or paysanne of vegetables
- concassé
- fine noodles
- rice
- chopped herbs
- finely diced cooked chicken.

Most soups in the recipe section are ungarnished so choose from the above suggestions to finish your soup or devise a garnish of your own.

Serving soup

- Serve hot soups at 63 °C or above to control the growth of pathogenic organisms. Discard soup if not sold after two hours.
- Cold soups should be served at 5 °C or below. Chill the soup in a blast chiller below 8 °C within 90 minutes to slow down bacterial growth.
- Depending on the function and purpose, soups are usually served in portions of 250 ml maximum. Sometimes, for example, if speciality soup is served as an *amuse bouche*, the portion size is reduced to approximately 50 ml.

Sauces

A sauce is a liquid that has been thickened (see below for more information on thickening sauces). Sauces add flavour and moisture to dishes; they also contribute to the overall texture of the dish. They provide a contrast to, or compliment the dish with which they are being served. They can also be used to enhance the nutritional value of a dish.

Quality points

A sauce should:

- be smooth
- look glossy
- have a definite flavour
- be of a light texture and free flowing
- use a thickening medium in moderation.

Types of sauces

Sauces can be categorised as follows.

Béchamel sauces

Béchamel is a basic white sauce made using butter, flour and milk. Many sauces are derived from a basic béchamel sauce by the addition of additional ingredients or garnishes. Table 6.2 provides some examples of béchamel sauces and dishes with which they are often served.

Velouté sauces

A basic velouté sauce is a blond roux, to which a white stock and chicken, veal, fish etc., are added.

Sauces derived from velouté and dishes with which they are often served are shown in Table 6.3.

Video: Blond roux and velouté http://bit.ly/1viPHtG

Table 6.2 Béchamel sauce derivatives

Sauce	Additions to basic béchamel	Served with
Egg	Hard-boiled eggs, diced	Poached or boiled fish
Cheese (mornay)	Grated cheese, egg yolk and cream	Fish or vegetables
Cream	Cream, milk, natural yoghurt or fromage frais	Poached fish and boiled vegetables
Onion	Chopped or diced, cooked onions; cream	Roast lamb or mutton
Soubise	As for onion sauce, but passed through a strainer	Roast lamb or mutton
Parsley	Chopped parsley	Poached or boiled fish and vegetables
Mustard	English or continental mustard	Grilled herrings
Anchovy	Anchovy essence	Poached, boiled or fried fish

Table 6.3 Velouté sauce derivatives

Sauce	Additions to basic velouté	Served with
Caper	Capers and single cream	Boiled leg of mutton
Aurore	Mushroom trimmings, cream, egg yolk, lemon juice, tomato purée	Poached or boiled chicken, poached eggs, chaud-froid sauce
Mushroom	Sliced button mushrooms, egg yolk and cream	Poached or boiled chicken, sweetbreads
Ivory	Meat glaze and cream	Poached or boiled chicken
Suprême	Cream and lemon juice	

Jus lié and brown sauces (demi-glace)

Today, **demi-glace** is often replaced with **jus lié**, or a good reduced stock. A jus lié is a lightly thickened brown stock – traditionally veal – which is flavour-enhanced with tomato and mushroom trimmings and thickened with arrowroot. In some cases a ham bone is added; this is optional.

A good brown stock is reduced in some recipes with red wine and lightly thickened with arrowroot, similar to jus lié. A glaze is a reduced stock (usually brown).

There are many variations of brown sauce. Some of these are shown in Table 6.4.

Table 6.4 Brown sauce derivatives

Sauce	Additions to basic brown sauce	Served with
Chasseur	Mushrooms, tomato concassé, white wine, tarragon	Sauté of chicken or shallow-fried steaks
Devilled	Cayenne pepper, white wine, mignonette pepper	Grilled chicken, sautéed kidneys
Bordelaise	Red wine, shallots, bone marrow	Shallow-fried steaks, grilled steaks
Charcutiere	White wine, gherkins	Grilled pork chops
Robert	White wine, mustard	Veal steaks, chops
Piquant	Gherkins, capers and herbs	Grilled chicken, shallow-fried steaks
Sherry	Sherry	Veal escalopes, veal chops, chicken suprêmes (shallow fried)
Madeira	Madeira	Veal and pork escalopes, fried calves' liver
Brown onion	Sliced brown onions, white wine	Burgers, sausages (shallow fried and grilled)
Lyonnaise	Sliced brown onions, white wine	Burgers, sausages (shallow fried and grilled)
Italian	Mushrooms, tomatoes and ham	Sautéed calves' and lambs' liver
Pepper	Crushed peppercorns	Grilled and shallow-fried steaks

Purée-based sauces

Purée-based sauces can be fruit based (for example apple sauce or cranberry sauce); vegetable based (for example, tomato sauce); or herb based. A herb-based sauce is one where the herbs are puréed with the base and constitute the main flavour; an example is green sauce (a mayonnaise with herbs). green sauce is served with cold poached salmon.

Gravies

Examples of gravies include:
- beef, lamb or roast chicken jus
- red wine
- roast gravy – jus de roti
- thickened gravy – jus lié.

Other sauces and dressings

Other sauces include:
- horseradish
- sweet and sour
- bread

- salsas (for example, salsa verde, yoghurt and cucumber salsa, tomato and cucumber salsa, avocado and coriander salsa)
- chutneys (for example, pear chutney)
- pickles (for example, mixed pickle)
- dressings (for example, pesto, tapenade, cranberry and orange dressing for duck).

Emulsions

Many sauces are **emulsions**. Foods which are called emulsions include cream, butter, mayonnaise and margarine. The oil and water in the food products are held together with an emulsifying agent which stops them from separating. Mayonnaise and hollandaise are examples of emulsions; the emulsifying agent is lecithin found in the egg yolk.

> **Key terms**
>
> **Béchamel:** white sauce
>
> **Jus lié:** thickened gravy
>
> **Demi-glace:** brown refined sauce
>
> **Emulsion:** a dispersion of oil and water

Butter sauces

There are a number of butter sauces and these are shown in Table 6.5.

Table 6.5 Butter sauces

Sauce	Description	Served with
Clarified butter	Butter that has been melted and skimmed; the butter is carefully poured off to leave the milky residue behind, giving a clear fat that can reach higher temperatures than normal butter without burning.	Steamed vegetables, or poached or grilled fish
Beurre noisette	This translates to 'nut butter'; its flavour comes from the caramelisation of the milk in the butter solids. It is achieved by placing diced hard butter into a moderately hot pan and bringing to a foam. The milk cooking in the fat creates a popping/cracking sound, which stops when it is caramelised.	Poached or steamed vegetables and fish; popularly used with shallow fried fish
Beurre noir (black butter)	Beurre noisette taken a little further (almost to burn the sediment), with vinegar added	Skate
Beurre fondu/ emulsion	An emulsion between fat and liquid; melted butter emulsified with any nage will give a slightly thicker sauce.	Used to coat vegetables or fish
Compound butter sauces	Made by mixing the flavouring ingredients into softened butter, which can then be shaped into a roll 2 cm in diameter, placed in wet greaseproof paper or foil, hardened in a refrigerator and cut into ½ cm slices when required. Examples include parsley butter, herb butter, chive butter, garlic butter, anchovy butter, shrimp butter, mustard and liver paté.	Grilled and some fried fish; grilled meats

Preparing and cooking sauces: thickening

A sauce is a liquid that has been thickened. There are a number of methods of thickening sauces.

Beurre manié

A paste made from equal quantities of soft butter and flour. It is mainly used for fish sauces. It is added to a simmering liquid, which should be whisked continuously to prevent it becoming lumpy.

Egg yolks and cream (liaison)

Using egg yolks for thickening is commonly known as a liaison, and is traditionally used to thicken a classic velouté. Egg yolks and cream are mixed together and added to the sauce off the boil. It is essential to keep stirring the sauce once you have added the eggs, otherwise they will curdle. Once the sauce is thickened it must be removed and served immediately. Do not allow the liquid to boil or simmer. Egg yolks are used in mayonnaise, hollandaise and custard sauces, although in a different way for each sauce.

Roux

A roux is a combination of fat and flour, which are cooked together. Liquid is then added to the cooked mixture to make the sauce. There are three degrees to which a roux may be cooked:

- **White** – used for white (béchamel) sauces and soups. Cook equal quantities of margarine or butter and flour together for a few minutes, without colouring, until the mixture is a sandy texture. Polyunsaturated vegetable margarine or vegetable oil can be used as an alternative; using oil gives a slack roux but means the liquid can be incorporated easily.
- **Blond** – used for veloutés, tomato sauce and soups. Cook equal quantities of margarine, butter or vegetable oil and flour for longer than a white roux, without colouring, until it is a sandy texture.
- **Brown** – traditionally used for brown (espagnole) sauce and soups. It is slightly browned in the roux-making process by cooking the fat and flour mixture for a bit longer than in the other methods.
- **Continental** – a very easy and straightforward thickening agent that can be frozen and used as a quick thickener during service or at the last minute.

Mix equal quantities of flour and vegetable oil to a paste and place in the oven at 140°C. Cook the mixture, mixing it in on itself continually until a biscuit texture is achieved. Remove and allow to cool to room temperature. Form it into a sausage shape using a double layer of cling film. Chill, then freeze. To use, remove it from the freezer and shave a little off the end of the log. Whisk it into the boiling sauce (as the flour is already cooked it is not necessary to add it slowly to prevent lumping as this will not occur). Once the desired thickness has been achieved, pass the sauce (strain it) and serve.

Step by step: thickening using a roux

1 Add equal quantities of margarine or butter and flour together to the pan.

2 Cook for a few minutes, without colouring, until the mixture is a sandy texture. This is a white roux that can be used to thicken béchamel sauces.

3 Cooking the mixture for longer will result in a blond roux, which can be used for veloutés, tomato sauce and soups.

4 For a brown roux, brown the mixture in the roux-making process. This can be used for brown sauces and soups.

Health and safety ⚠

Never add boiling liquid to a hot roux, as you may be scalded by the steam that is produced and the sauce may become lumpy.

Professional tip

Do not allow a roux sauce to stand over a moderate heat for any length of time as it may become thin due to a chemical change (called dextrinisation) in the flour.

Cornflour, arrowroot or starch

Cornflour, arrowroot or starch are used for thickening gravy and sauces. These are diluted with water, stock or milk and then stirred into the boiling liquid, which is allowed to re-boil for a few minutes and is then strained. For large-scale cooking and economy, flour may be used.

Sauce flour

Sauce flour is a specially milled flour that does not need to have any fat added to it to prevent it from going lumpy. Sauces may be thickened using this flour. It is useful when making low-fat sauces.

Blood

Traditionally used in recipes such as jugged hare, but is used rarely today.

Cooking liquor

Liquor from certain dishes and/or stock can be reduced to give a light sauce.

Rice

Rice is used to thicken some shellfish bisques.

Butter (*monter au beurre*) and olive oil

Monter au beurre means 'mounting' the sauce with small pieces of butter or oil to thicken and give the sauce a shine.

Checking and finishing sauces

When you have finished preparing a sauce, always check the:

- consistency – the sauce should be light and free flowing. It should lightly coat the back of a metal spoon
- flavour – it should be seasoned but not over seasoned.

Professional tip

It is important to develop your palate to recognise correct tastes and flavours.

Storing sauces

- Cool rapidly and store in a refrigerator at a temperature below 5 °C.
- If the sauce is to be deep-frozen, label and date and store between −20 °C and −18 °C.
- If sauces are to be deep-frozen, any flour has to be replaced with a modified starch to prevent curdling on thawing and reheating.
- When taken from storage, boil the sauce for at least two minutes before using. Do not reheat the sauce more than once.

Test yourself

1 List the ingredients and describe the cooking principles for brown beef stock.
2 State **four** quality points you should look for in a white vegetable stock.
3 Give **two** examples of each of the following:
   a) purée soups
   b) potage soups
   c) chilled soups
   d) broths
4 Name **two** alternatives to cream when finishing a soup.
5 At what temperature should hot soup be served?
6 Describe how you would cook lobster bisque.
7 Name **two** derivatives of béchamel.
8 Give an example of a dish with which chasseur sauce is traditionally served.
9 Describe how you should store stocks and sauces.

1 White stock

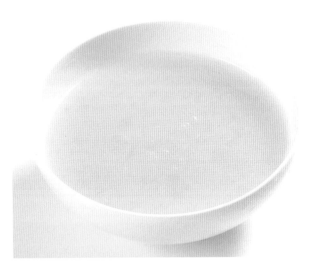

	4.5 litres	10 litres
Raw, meaty bones	1 kg	2.5 kg
Water	5 litres	10.5 litres
Onion, carrot, celery, leek	400 g	1.5 kg
Bouquet garni	½	1 ½
Peppercorns	8	16

1 Chop the bones into small pieces, and remove any fat or marrow.
2 Place the bones in a large stock pot, cover with cold water and bring to the boil.
3 Wash off the bones under cold water, then clean the pot.
4 Return the bones to the cleaned pot, add the water and reboil.
5 Skim as and when required, wipe round inside the pot and simmer gently.
6 After 2 hours, add the washed, peeled whole vegetables, bouquet garni and peppercorns.
7 Simmer for 6–8 hours. Skim, strain and, if to be kept, cool quickly and refrigerate.

Energy	Cals	Fat	Sat fat	Carb	Sugar	Protein	Fibre	Sodium
105 kJ	25 kcal	0.3 g	0.1 g	4.9 g	4 g	1 g	2.4 g	0.022 g

2 White vegetable stock

	4 portions	10 portions
Onions	100 g	250 g
Carrots	100 g	250 g
Celery	100 g	250 g
Leeks	100 g	250 g
Water	1.5 litres	3.75 litres

1 Roughly chop all the vegetables.
2 Place all the ingredients into a saucepan, add the water, bring to the boil.
3 Allow to simmer for approximately 1 hour.
4 Skim if necessary. Strain and use.

Variation

White fungi stock: add 200–400 g white mushrooms, stalks and trimmings (all well washed) to the recipe.

3 Fish stock

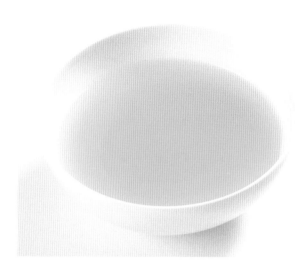

	2 litres
Fish bones, no heads, gills or roe (turbot, sole or brill bones are best)	5 kg
Olive oil	100 ml
Onions, finely chopped	3
Leeks, finely chopped	3
Celery sticks, finely chopped	3
Fennel bulb, finely chopped	1
Dry white wine	350 ml
Parsley stalks	10
Thyme	3 sprigs
White peppercorns	15
Lemons, finely sliced	2

1 Wash off the bones in cold water for 1 hour.

2 Heat the olive oil in a pan that will hold all the ingredients and still have a 1 cm gap at the top for skimming. Add all the vegetables and sweat without colour for 3 minutes.

3 Add the fish bones and sweat for a further 3 minutes.

4 Add the white wine and enough water to cover. Bring to a simmer, skim off the impurities and add the herbs, peppercorns and lemon. Turn off the heat.

5 Infuse for 25 minutes, then pass into another pan and reduce by half. The stock is now ready for use.

4 Crab stock

	2 litres
Crab shells, smashed	2 kg
Prawns, wish shells still on	1.5 kg
Corn oil	50 ml
Brandy (optional)	200 ml
Pernod (optional)	100 ml
Carrots, peeled and chopped for mirepoix	250 g
Leeks, prepared and chopped for mirepoix	250 g
Celery, chopped for mirepoix	150 g
Garlic cloves, smashed	2
Shallot, peeled	180 g
Tomato paste	150 ml
Fish stock	2.5 litres
Small sprig of thyme	
Bay leaf	1

1 Roast the shells in the oil and deglaze with the brandy and Pernod (or, if not using these, some of the stock).

2 In a separate pan, roast the vegetables, then add the tomato paste, stock and herbs, add the roasted shells and the prawns, and simmer for 20 minutes.

3 Turn off the heat and allow to infuse for 30 minutes. Pass, and reduce by half. The stock is now ready for use.

5 Brown stock

	4.5 litres	10 litres
Raw, meaty bones	1 kg	2.5 kg
Water	5 litres	10.5 litres
Onion, carrot, celery, leek	400 g	1.5 kg
Bouquet garni	½	1 ½
Peppercorns	8	16

Professional tip

A few squashed tomatoes and washed mushroom trimmings can also be added to brown stocks to improve flavour, as can a calf's foot and/or a knuckle of bacon. If bacon is used, dishes made with the stock will not be suitable for some religious diets.

Video: Making brown stock http://bit.ly/ 1viP8zV

1 Chop the beef bones and brown well on all sides either by placing in a roasting tin in the oven, or carefully browning in a little fat in a frying pan.

2 Drain off any fat and place the bones in a stock pot.

3 Brown any sediment that may be in the bottom of the tray, deglaze (swill out) with ½ litre of boiling water, simmer for a few minutes and add to the bones.

4 Add the cold water, bring to the boil and skim. Simmer for 2 hours.

5 Wash, peel and roughly cut the vegetables, fry in a little fat until brown, strain and add to the bones.

6 Add the bouquet garni and peppercorns.

7 Simmer for 6–8 hours. Skim and strain.

6   Brown vegetable stock

	4 litres approximately
Onions	300 g
Carrots	300 g
Celery	300 g
Leeks	300 g
Sunflower oil	180 ml
Tomatoes	150 g
Mushroom trimmings	150 g
Peppercorns	18
Water	4 litres
Yeast extract	15 g

1 Cut the vegetables into mirepoix. Fry the mirepoix in the oil until golden brown.

2 Drain and place in a suitable saucepan. Add all the other ingredients except the yeast extract and water.

3 Cover with the water and bring to the boil.

4 Add the yeast extract and simmer gently for approximately 1 hour. Then skim if necessary and use.

Variation

Brown fungi stock: add 200–400 g open or field mushrooms, stalks and trimmings (all well washed) to the recipe.

7   Reduced veal stock for sauce

No flour is used in the thickening process and consequently a lighter textured sauce is produced. Care needs to be taken when reducing this type of sauce so that the end product is not too strong or bitter.

	4 litres
Veal bones, chopped	4 kg
Water	4 litres
Calves' feet, split lengthways (optional)	2
Carrots, roughly chopped	400 g
Onions, roughly chopped	200 g
Celery, roughly chopped	100 g
Tomatoes, blanched, skinned, quartered	1 kg
Mushrooms, chopped	200 g
Large bouquet garni	1
Unpeeled cloves of garlic (optional)	4

1 Brown the bones and calves' feet in a roasting tray in the oven.

2 Place the browned bones in a stock pot, cover with cold water and bring to simmering point.

3 Using the same roasting tray and the fat from the bones, brown off the carrots, onions and celery.

4 Drain off the fat, add the vegetables to the stock and deglaze the tray.

5 Add the remainder of the ingredients; simmer gently for 4–5 hours. Skim frequently.

6 Strain the stock into a clean pan and reduce until a light consistency is achieved.

8 Pumpkin velouté

	4 portions	10 portions
Shallots, sliced	1	3
Butter	320 g	800 g
Clove of garlic, sliced (optional)	½	1
Large squash or pumpkin (300 g), flesh diced	1	2
Parmesan, grated	30 g	70 g
Truffle oil	1 tbsp	2 tbsp
Salt, pepper		
Chicken stock	400–600 ml	1–1.5 litres

Energy	Cals	Fat	Sat fat	Carb	Sugar	Protein	Fibre
2883 kJ	689 kcal	71.4 g	43.9 g	6.7 g	1.5 g	5.3 g	1.5 g

1 Sweat the shallots in the butter, without colour, until cooked and soft.

2 Add the garlic, pumpkin (or squash), Parmesan and truffle oil. Correct the seasoning and cook for 5 minutes.

3 Add the chicken stock, bring to the boil, simmer for 5 minutes.

4 Liquidise, pass, correct the seasoning and serve hot. Blast chill if to be stored.

9 Carrot and butterbean soup

	4 portions	10 portions
Onions, peeled and chopped	1	2
Cloves of garlic, chopped	2	5
Sunflower oil	15 ml	35 ml
Large to medium carrots, brunoise	250 g	750 g
Vegetable stock	500 ml	1.25 litres
Butter beans, cooked	400 g	1 kg
Seasoning		

Energy	Cals	Fat	Sat fat	Carb	Sugar	Protein	Fibre	Sodium
638 kJ	152 kcal	4.6 g	0.6 g	21.9 g	8.5 g	7 g	9.4 g	0.492 g

1 Cook the onion and garlic in the oil for a few minutes, without colour, then add the carrots and stir well.

2 Add the vegetable stock. Bring to the boil, turn down to a simmer and cook for about 15 minutes until the carrot is cooked through.

3 Add the beans and cook for a further 5 minutes or so until they are heated through.

4 Liquidise in a food processor until smooth; check seasoning.

Professional tip

With any soup recipe, it is important to simmer the soup gently. Do not let it boil vigorously, because too much water will evaporate. If the soup has boiled, add more stock or water to make up for this.

10 Chicken soup (*crème de volaille* or *crème reine*)

1 Gently cook the sliced onions, leek and celery in a thick-bottomed pan, in the butter or oil, without colouring.

2 Mix in the flour; cook over a gentle heat to a sandy texture without colouring.

3 Cool slightly; gradually mix in the hot stock. Stir to the boil.

4 Add the bouquet garni and season.

5 Simmer for 30–45 minutes; skim when necessary. Remove the bouquet garni.

6 Liquidise or pass firmly through a fine strainer.

7 Return to a clean pan, reboil and finish with milk or cream; correct the seasoning.

8 Add the chicken garnish and serve.

	4 portions	10 portions
Onion, leek and celery, sliced	100 g	250 g
Butter or oil	50 g	125 g
Flour	50 g	125 g
Chicken stock	1 l	2.5 l
Bouquet garni	1	2
Salt, pepper		
Milk or cream	250 ml or 125 ml	625 ml or 300 ml
Cooked dice of chicken (garnish)	25 g	60 g

Energy	Cals	Fat	Sat fat	Carb	Sugar	Protein	Fibre	Sodium *
900 kJ	217 kcal	16.7 g	10.4 g	12.6 g	2.6 g	4.8 g	1.6 g	0.097 g

* Using butter and cream

Variation

Natural yoghurt, skimmed milk or non-dairy cream may be used in place of dairy cream.

Add cooked small pasta or sliced mushrooms.

Healthy eating tips
- Use soft margarine or sunflower/vegetable oil in place of the butter.
- Use the minimum amount of salt.
- The least fatty option is to use a combination of semi-skimmed milk and yoghurt or fromage frais – not cream.

11 Mushroom soup (*crème de champignons*)

	4 portions	10 portions
Onion, leek and celery, sliced	100 g	250 g
Butter or oil	50 g	125 g
Flour	50 g	125 g
White stock (preferably chicken)	1 litre	2.5 litres
White mushrooms, washed and chopped	200 g	500 g
Bouquet garni		
Salt, pepper		
Milk (or cream)	125 ml (or 60 ml)	300 ml (or 150 ml)

Energy	Cals	Fat	Sat fat	Carb	Sugar	Protein	Fibre	*
712 kJ	170 kcal	11.8 g	5.2 g	12.6 g	3.0 g	3.8 g	1.6 g	

* Using hard margarine

1 Gently cook the sliced onions, leek and celery in the butter or oil in a thick-bottomed pan, without colouring.

2 Mix in the flour and cook over a gentle heat to a sandy texture without colouring.

3 Remove from the heat and cool slightly.

4 Gradually mix in the hot stock. Stir to the boil.

5 Add the well-washed, chopped mushrooms, the bouquet garni and season.

6 Simmer for 30–45 minutes. Skim when needed.

7 Remove the bouquet garni. Pass through a sieve or liquidise.

8 Pass through a medium strainer. Return to a clean saucepan.

9 Reboil, correct the seasoning and consistency; add the milk or cream.

Variation

Natural yoghurt, skimmed milk or non-dairy cream may be used in place of dairy cream.

A garnish of thinly sliced mushrooms may be added. Wild mushrooms may also be used.

Healthy eating tips
● Use soft margarine or sunflower/vegetable oil in place of the butter.
● Use the minimum amount of salt.
● The least fatty option is to use a combination of semi-skimmed milk and yoghurt or fromage frais – not cream.

12 Asparagus soup (*crème d'asperges*)

	4 portions	10 portions
Onion, sliced	50 g	125 g
Celery, sliced	50 g	125 g
Butter or oil	50 g	125 g
Flour	50 g	125 g
White stock (preferably chicken)	1 litre	2.5 litres
Asparagus stalk trimmings	200 g	500 g
or		
Tin of asparagus	150 g	325 g
Bouquet garni		
Salt, pepper		
Milk or cream	250 ml or 125 ml	625 ml or 300 ml

Energy	Cals	Fat	Sat fat	Carb	Sugar	Protein	Fibre
919 kJ	223 kcal	13.1 g	8.0 g	18.9 g	8.8 g	8.4 g	2.5 g

1 Gently sweat the onions and celery, without colouring, in the butter or oil.

2 Remove from the heat, mix in the flour, return to a low heat and cook out, without colouring, for a few minutes. Cool.

3 Gradually add the hot stock. Stir to the boil.

4 Add the well-washed asparagus trimmings, or the tin of asparagus, and bouquet garni. Season.

5 Simmer for 30–40 minutes, then remove bouquet garni.

6 Liquidise and pass through a strainer.

7 Return to a clean pan, reboil, correct seasoning and consistency. (Milk with a little cornflour can be added to adjust the consistency.)

8 Add the milk or cream and serve.

Healthy eating tips
- Use an unsaturated oil (sunflower/vegetable) to lightly oil the pan. Drain off any excess after the frying is complete and skim the fat from the finished dish.
- Season with the minimum amount of salt.

13 Cream of tomato soup (crème de tomates fraiche)

9 Simmer for approximately 1 hour. Skim when required.

10 Remove the bouquet garni and mirepoix.

11 Liquidise or pass firmly through a sieve, then through a conical strainer.

12 Return to a clean pan, correct the seasoning and consistency. Bring to the boil.

13 Serve fried or toasted croutons separately.

Professional tip

- Flour may be omitted from the recipe if a thinner soup is required.
- A slightly sweet/sharp flavour can be added to the soup by preparing what is known as a gastric (gastrique). In a thick-bottomed pan, reduce 100 ml of malt vinegar and 35 g caster sugar until it is a light caramel colour. Mix this into the completed soup.
- Some tomato purée can be stronger than others, so you may have to add a little more or less when making this soup.

	4 portions	10 portions
Butter or oil	50 g	125 g
Bacon trimmings, optional	25 g	60 g
Onion, diced	100 g	250 g
Carrot, diced	100 g	250 g
Flour	50 g	125 g
Fresh, fully ripe tomatoes	1 kg	2.5 kg
Stock	1 litre	2.5 litres
Bouquet garni		
Salt, pepper		
Croutons		
Sliced stale bread	1	3
Butter	50 g	125 g

Energy	Cals	Fat	Sat fat	Carb	Sugar	Protein	Fibre	Sodium
1159 kJ	277 kcal	16.2 g	4.8 g	28.5 g	13.6 g	6.3 g	6.6 g	0.321 g

Healthy eating tips

- Use soft margarine or sunflower/vegetable oil in place of the butter.
- Toast the croutons rather than frying them.
- Use the minimum amount of salt – there is plenty in the bacon.

Variation

Without fresh tomatoes: substitute 150 g of tomato purée for the fresh tomatoes (375 g for 10 portions). When reboiling the soup (step 12), add 500 ml of milk or 125 ml of cream, yoghurt or fromage frais.

Try adding the juice and lightly grated peel of 1–2 oranges or cooked rice or a chopped fresh herb, such as chives.

1 Melt the butter or heat the oil in a thick-bottomed pan.

2 Add the bacon, onion and carrot (mirepoix) and brown lightly.

3 Mix in the flour and cook to a sandy texture.

4 Gradually add the hot stock.

5 Stir to the boil.

6 Remove the eyes from the tomatoes, wash them well, and squeeze them into the soup after it has come to the boil.

7 If colour is lacking, add a little tomato purée soon after the soup comes to the boil.

8 Add the bouquet garni and season lightly.

Activity

1 Prepare, cook and taste the recipe for tomato soup with and without a gastric. Discuss and assess the two versions.

2 Name and prepare a variation of your own.

3 Review the basic recipe for tomato soup and adjust to meet dietary requirements for a customer who requires a low fat vegetarian version.

14 Cream of spinach and celery soup

	4 portions	10 portions
Shallots, peeled and chopped (small mirepoix)	2	5
Leeks, washed and chopped (small mirepoix)	1	2
Cloves of garlic, peeled and chopped	2	5
Corn oil	2 tbsp	5 tbsp
Celery sticks, washed and chopped (small mirepoix)	4	10
Flour	15 g	35 g
Fresh spinach, well washed	500 g	1.25 kg
Milk	600 ml	1.5 litres
Vegetable stock (see recipe 2)	600 ml	1.5 litres
Salt, to taste		

1 Cook the shallots, leeks and garlic in the oil for a few minutes, without colour.

2 Add the celery and cook for another few minutes until starting to soften.

3 Add the flour and mix well, then throw in the spinach and mix around. Add the milk and vegetable stock slowly, ensuring there are no lumps.

4 Stir continuously, bring to a simmer, then switch off and remove from heat. Cover and leave for a few minutes.

5 Blend until smooth in a food processor. Check seasoning and serve.

Energy	Cals	Fat	Sat fat	Carb	Sugar	Protein	Fibre	Sodium *
886 kJ	214 kcal	12.7 g	4.7 g	15.1 g	11.3 g	10.1 g	6.1 g	0.316 g

* Using whole milk

15 Minestrone

	4 portions	10 portions
Mixed vegetables (onion, leek, celery, carrot, turnip, cabbage), peeled	300 g	750 g
Butter or oil	50 g	125 g
White stock or water	0.5 litres	1.5 litres
Bouquet garni		
Salt, pepper		
Peas	25 g	60 g
French beans	25 g	60 g
Spaghetti	25 g	60 g
Potatoes, peeled	50 g	125 g
Tomato purée	1 tsp	3 tsp
Tomatoes, skinned, deseeded, diced	100 g	250 g
Fat bacon	50 g	125 g
Parsley } optional		
Clove of garlic	1	2½

Energy	Cals	Fat	Sat fat	Carb	Sugar	Protein	Fibre *
1115 kJ	22.9 kcal	22.9 g	5.8 g	11.9 g	4.2 g	3.8 g	4.1 g

* Using sunflower oil

1 Cut the peeled and washed mixed vegetables into paysanne.
2 Cook slowly without colour in the oil or butter in the pan with a lid on.
3 Add the stock, bouquet garni and seasoning; simmer for approximately 20 minutes.
4 Add the peas and the beans cut into diamonds and simmer for 10 minutes.
5 Add the spaghetti in 2 cm lengths, the potatoes cut into paysanne, the tomato purée and the tomatoes, and simmer gently until all the vegetables are cooked.
6 Meanwhile finely chop the fat bacon, parsley and garlic, and form into a paste.
7 Mould the paste into pellets the size of a pea and drop into the boiling soup.
8 Remove the bouquet garni, correct the seasoning.
9 Serve grated Parmesan cheese topped with croutons of bread or slices of French bread (flutes) separately.

1 Vegetables chopped into paysanne

2 Fry or sweat the vegetables

3 Simmer the ingredients in the stock

4 Add the pellets of paste to the soup

Healthy eating tips

- Use an unsaturated oil (sunflower or vegetable) to lightly oil the pan. Drain off any excess after the frying is complete and skim the fat from the finished dish.
- Season with the minimum amount of salt as the bacon and cheese are high in salt.

16 Paysanne soup (*potage*)

	4 portions	10 portions
Chicken or vegetable stock	1 litre	2.5 litres
Diced streaky bacon (optional)	50 g	125 g
Celery sticks	50 g	125 g
Onion	100 g	250 g
Carrots	100 g	250 g
Turnips	50 g	125 g
Leeks	50 g	125 g
cabbage (optional)	50 g	125 g
Potatoes	100 g	250 g
Butter, margarine or oil	50 g	125 g
Chopped parsley, chopped basil		

Energy	Cals	Fat	Sat fat	Carb	Sugar	Protein	Fibre	Sodium *
772 kJ	186 kcal	14 g	7.8 g	10.8 g	5.7 g	4.8 g	3.4 g	0.310 g

*Using butter

1 Cut the celery, onion, carrots, leeks, cabbage and potatoes into paysanne.

2 In a suitable saucepan, add the butter, margarine or oil. Fry the streaky bacon until lightly cooked.

3 Add the onion, leeks and celery and sweat for 2–3 minutes.

4 Add the rest of the vegetables.

5 Add the stock. Bring to the boil. Simmer until all the vegetables are cooked.

6 The soup may be finished with 125 ml boiled milk (300 ml for 10 portions).

7 Sprinkle on the chopped parsley and basil.

Note

Diced tomato concassé may also be added: 50 g for 4 portions, 125 g for 10.

17 Prawn bisque

	4 portions	10 portions
Oil	50 ml	125 ml
Butter	30 g	75 g
Unshelled prawns	250 g	625 g
Flour	20 g	50 g
Tomato purée	1 tbsp	2 tbsp
Shellfish nage (4 portions)	1 litre	2.5 litres
Fish stock	150 ml	375 ml
Whipping cream	120 ml	300 ml
Dry sherry	75 ml	180 ml
Paprika, pinch	¼ tsp	½ tsp
Seasoning		
Chives, chopped		

Energy	Cals	Fat	Sat fat	Carb	Sugar	Protein	Fibre
1578 kJ	381 kcal	31.2 g	13.0 g	8.2 g	4.0 g	12.9 g	0.8 g

1 Heat the oil and the butter. Add the prawns and cook for 3–4 minutes on a moderately high heat.

2 Sprinkle in the flour and cook for a further 2–3 minutes.

3 Add the tomato purée and cook for a further 2 minutes.

4 Meanwhile, bring the nage up to a simmer and, once the tomato purée has been cooked in, slowly add to the prawn mix, being mindful that you have formed a roux; stir in the fish stock to prevent lumping.

5 Once all the stock has been added, bring to the boil and simmer for 3–4 minutes.

6 Pass through a fine sieve, return the shells to the pan and pound to extract more flavour and more colour.

7 Pour over the fish stock, bring to the boil, then pass this back onto the already passed soup.

8 Bring to the boil, add the cream and sherry, correct the seasoning and served with chopped chives.

18 New England clam chowder

	4 portions	10 portions
Salt pork or bacon, cut into 0.5 cm dice	50 g	125 g
Onion, finely chopped	50 g	125 g
Cold water	300 ml	750 ml
Potatoes, cut into 0.5 cm dice	500 g	1.25 kg
Fresh trimmed clams, or tinned clams, and their juices	200 g	500 g
Cream	180 ml	450 ml
Thyme, crushed or chopped	1 g	2 g
Salt, white pepper		
Butter, softened	20 g	50 g
Paprika		

Energy	Cals	Fat	Sat fat	Carb	Sugar	Protein	Fibre *
1109 kJ	269 kcal	14.9 g	7.7 g	24.5 g	2.5 g	14.9 g	1.8 g

* Using bacon or salt pork

1 Dry-fry the pork in a thick-bottomed saucepan for about 3 minutes, stirring constantly until a thin film of fat covers the bottom of the pan.

2 Stir in the chopped onion and cook gently until a light golden brown.

3 Add the water and potatoes, bring to the boil and simmer gently until the potatoes are cooked but not mushy.

4 Add the chopped clams and their juice, the cream and thyme, and heat until almost boiling. Season with salt and pepper.

5 Correct the seasoning, stir in the softened butter and serve, dusting each soup bowl with a little paprika.

Note

The traditional accompaniment is salted cracker biscuits. An obvious variation would be to use scallops in place of clams.

19 Leek and potato soup (vichyssoise)

Ingredient	4 portions	10 portions
Onions, finely sliced	160 g	400 g
Leeks, finely sliced	175 g	430 g
Butter	125 g	300 g
Potatoes, diced small	750 g	1.8 kg
Water/vegetable stock	1.8 litres	4.5 litres
Salt	15 g	30 g
Pepper to taste		
Garnish		
Whipped cream		
Chives, chopped		

Energy	Cals	Fat	Sat fat	Carb	Sugar	Protein	Fibre
1653 kJ	397 kcal	26.4 g	16.3 g	36.9 g	4.5 g	5.3 g	4.0 g

1 Sweat the sliced onion and leek without colour in the butter. Cook until very tender.

2 Add the potatoes and bring quickly to the boil with the water or vegetable stock.

3 Liquidise in food processor and allow to cool.

4 Check seasoning. Note that seasoning needs to reflect the serving temperature.

5 Serve cold with whipped cream and chopped chives.

20 Chilled tomato and cucumber soup (gazpacho)

Ingredient	4 portions	10 portions
Tomato juice	500 ml	1.25 litres
Tomatoes, skinned, de-seeded and diced	100 g	250 g
Cucumber, peeled and diced	100 g	250 g
Green pepper, diced	50 g	125 g
Onion, chopped	50 g	125 g
Mayonnaise	1 tbsp	2–3 tbsp
Vinegar	1 tbsp	2–3 tbsp
Seasoning		
Clove garlic	1	2–3

Energy	Cals	Fat	Sat fat	Carb	Sugar	Protein	Fibre
382 kJ	91 kcals	6.71 g	1 g	6.2 g	g	1.83 g	1.56 g

This soup has many regional variations. It is served chilled and has a predominant flavour of cucumber, tomato and garlic.

1 Mix all the ingredients together.

2 Season and add crushed chopped garlic to taste.

3 Stand in a cool place for an hour.

4 Correct the consistency with iced water and serve chilled.

Variation

The soup can be liquidised (as in the photo) and garnished with chopped tomato, cucumber and pepper.

The soup may also be finished with chopped herbs.

A tray of garnishes may accompany the soup, e.g. chopped red and green pepper, chopped onion, tomato, cucumber and croutons.

---

21 Potato and watercress soup (*purée cressonnière*)

	4 portions	10 portions
Butter or oil	25 g	60 g
Onion, peeled and sliced	50 g	125 g
White of leek, sliced	50 g	125 g
White stock or water	1 litre	2.5 litres
Potatoes, peeled and sliced	400 g	1.5 kg
Watercress	small bunch	small bunch
Bouquet garni		
Salt, pepper		
Parsley, chopped		
Croutons		
Stale bread	1 slice	3 slices
Butter, margarine or oil	50 g	125 g

Energy	Cals	Fat	Sat fat	Carb	Sugar	Protein	Fibre	Sodium *
583kJ	139kcal	5.5g	3.3g	21g	3.8g	2.7g	3.4g	0.057g

* Using butter

1 Pick off 12 neat leaves of watercress and plunge into a small pan of boiling water for 1–2 seconds. Refresh under cold water immediately; these leaves are to garnish the finished soup.

2 Melt the butter or heat the oil in a thick-bottomed pan.

3 Add the peeled and washed sliced onion and leek, cook for a few minutes without colour with the lid on.

4 Add the stock, the peeled, washed and sliced potatoes, the rest of the watercress, including the stalks, and the bouquet garni. Season.

5 Simmer for approximately 30 minutes. Remove the bouquet garni, skim off all fat.

6 Liquidise or pass the soup firmly through a sieve then pass through a medium conical strainer.

7 Return to a clean pan, reboil, correct the seasoning and consistency, and serve.

8 Garnish with watercress.

9 Serve fried or toasted croutons separately.

22 Red lentil soup

	4 portions	10 portions
Ham hock	320 g	800 g
Onion, peeled	25 g	60 g
Whole carrot, peeled	½	1
Baby shallots	1	3
Leeks	50 g	125 g
Celery	50 g	125 g
Oil	40 ml	100 ml
Red lentils	200 g	500 g
Cooking liquid from the hock	1 litre	2.5 litres
Milk, cream or crème fraiche	120 ml	300 ml

Energy	Cals	Fat	Sat fat	Carb	Sugar	Protein	Fibre
1807 kJ	432 kcal	71.4 g	43.9 g	6.7 g	1.5 g	5.3 g	1.5 g

1 Place the ham hock, onion and carrot in a pan and cover with about 3 litres of water.

2 Bring to the boil and then turn down to a slow simmer. (When the hock is cooked, the centre bone will slide out in one smooth motion.)

3 Slice the shallots, leek and celery into 1 cm dice.

4 Heat a pan with the oil, add the vegetables and cook until they are slightly coloured; add the lentils and cover them with the ham stock.

5 Bring to the boil, then turn the heat down to a very slow simmer.

6 Cook until all the lentils have broken down.

7 Allow to cool for 10 minutes and then purée until smooth.

8 Correct the consistency as necessary, and finish with boiled milk, cream or crème fraiche.

Variation

Meat-free version: omit the ham hock and use a vegetable stock or water instead of the cooking liquid.

23 Roasted red pepper and tomato soup

	4 portions	10 portions
Red peppers	4	10
Plum tomatoes	400 g	1.25 kg
Butter or oil	50 g	125 g
Onion, chopped	100 g	250 g
Carrot, chopped	100 g	250 g
Stock	500 ml	1.5 litres
Crème fraiche	2 tbsp	5 tbsp
Basil	25 g	75 g
Croutons		
Slice stale bread	1	3
Butter	50 g	125 g

1 Core and deseed the peppers and halve the tomatoes.

2 Lightly sprinkle with oil and place on a tray into a hot oven or under a grill until the pepper skins are blackened.

3 Allow the peppers to cool in a plastic bag.

4 Remove the skins and slice the flesh.

5 Place the butter or oil in a pan, add the onions and carrots and fry gently for 5 minutes.

6 Add the stock, peppers and tomatoes and bring to the boil.

7 Simmer for 30 minutes, correct the seasoning and blend in a food processor until smooth.

Note

To serve, add crème fraiche and basil leaves torn into pieces, and serve with croutons.

Energy	Cals	Fat	Sat fat	Carb	Sugar	Protein	Fibre
983 kJ	235 kcal	16.8 g	7.1 g	18.3 g	16.4 g	3.6 g	4.5 g

24 Vegetable purée soup

	4 portions	10 portions
Onions, leek and celery, sliced	100 g	250 g
Other suitable vegetables**, sliced	200 g	500 g
Butter or oil	50 g	125 g
Flour	50 g	125 g
White stock or water	1 litre	2.5 litres
Bouquet garni		
Salt, pepper		

** Suitable vegetables include Jerusalem artichokes, cauliflower, celery, leeks, onions, parsnips, turnips and fennel.

Energy	Cals	Fat	Sat fat	Carb	Sugar	Protein	Fibre	*
601 kJ	143 kcal	10.3 g	4.4 g	11.4 g	1.8 g	1.9 g	1.9 g	

* Using hard margarine

1 Gently cook all the sliced vegetables in the fat under a lid, without colour.

2 Mix in the flour and cook slowly for a few minutes without colour. Cool slightly.

3 Gradually mix in the hot stock. Stir to the boil.

4 Add the bouquet garni and season.

5 Simmer for approximately 45 minutes; skim when necessary.

6 Remove the bouquet garni; liquidise or pass firmly through a sieve and then through a medium strainer.

7 Return to a clean pan, reboil, and correct the seasoning and consistency.

Variation

Add a little spice, sufficient to give a subtle background flavour, e.g. garam masala with parsnip soup.

Just before serving add a little freshly chopped herb(s), e.g. parsley, chervil, tarragon, coriander.

Healthy eating tips
- Use an unsaturated oil (sunflower or vegetable) to lightly oil the pan. Drain off any excess after the frying is complete and skim the fat from the finished dish.
- Season with the minimum amount of salt.
- Try using more vegetables to thicken the soup in place of the flour.

Video: Making a purée soup http://bit.ly/ 17qT0U8

25 Vegetable and barley soup

	4 portions	10 portions
Corn oil	50 ml	125 ml
Onions, finely diced	1	2
Leeks, cut into rounds	1	2
Carrots, peeled and roughly chopped	2	3
Celery sticks, cut into ½cm dice	2	3
Cloves of garlic, crushed	2	4
Large potatoes, peeled and cut into ½ cm dice	3	7
Pearl barley (cooked)	150 g	375 g
Vegetable stock	1.5 litres	3.75 litres
Head of Swiss chard, washed and shredded (including stalks)	1	2
Seasoning		

Energy	Cals	Fat	Sat fat	Carb	Sugar	Protein	Fibre	Sodium
905 kJ	217 kcal	13.3 g	1.9 g	21.7 g	7.9 g	4.1 g	2.5 g	0.235 g

1 Heat the oil in a pan large enough to hold all the ingredients.
2 Place the onions, leeks, carrots and celery in the oil and cook until slightly golden.
3 Add the garlic and cook for a further 2 minutes. Add the potato and cook for a further 2 minutes.

4 Add the barley and vegetable stock. Bring to the boil, then simmer for 15 minutes, until the potatoes are just soft.
5 Stir in the Swiss chard and cook for a further 2 minutes.
6 Check the seasoning, correct if necessary then serve.

ASSESSMENT

26 Scotch broth

	4 portions	10 portions
Lean beef (skirt)	200 g	500 g
Beef stock	1 litre	2.5 litres
Barley	25 g	60 g
Vegetables (carrot, turnip, leek, celery, onion), cut into paysanne	200 g	500 g
Bouquet garni		
Salt, pepper		
Chopped parsley		

Energy	Cals	Fat	Sat fat	Carb	Sugar	Protein	Fibre	Sodium
655 kJ	157 kcal	7.8 g	3.1 g	4.9 g	2.7 g	16.6 g	1.6 g	0.201 g

1 Place the beef, free from fat, in a saucepan and cover with cold water.

2 Bring to the boil, then immediately wash off under running water.

3 Clean the pan, replace the meat, cover with cold water, bring to the boil and skim.

4 Add the washed barley, simmer for 1 hour.

5 Add the vegetables, bouquet garni and seasoning.

6 Skim when necessary; simmer for approximately 30 minutes, until tender.

7 Remove the meat, allow to cool and cut from the bone, remove all fat and cut the meat into neat dice the same size as the vegetables; return to the broth.

8 Correct the seasoning, skim off all the fat, add the chopped parsley and serve.

Healthy eating tips
- Remove all fat from the meat.
- Use only a small amount of salt.
- There are lots of healthy vegetables in this dish and the addition of a large bread roll will increase the starchy carbohydrate.

27 Clear soup (consommé)

	4 portions	10 portions
Chopped or minced beef	200 g	500 g
Salt, to taste		
Egg whites	1–2	3–5
Cold white or brown beef stock	1 litre	2.5 litres
Mixed vegetables (onion, carrot, celery, leek)	100 g	250 g
Bouquet garni		
Peppercorns	3–4	8–10

Energy	Cals	Fat	Sat fat	Carb	Sugar	Protein	Fibre
126 kJ	30 kcal	0.0 g	0.0 g	1.8 g	0.0 g	5.6 g	0.0 g

1 Thoroughly mix the beef, salt, egg white and a quarter of the cold stock in a thick-bottomed pan.

2 Peel, wash and finely chop the vegetables.

3 Add to the beef with the remainder of the stock, the bouquet garni and the peppercorns.

4 Place over a gentle heat and bring slowly to the boil, stirring occasionally.

5 Allow to boil rapidly for 5–10 seconds. give a final stir.

6 Lower the heat so that the consommé is simmering very gently.

7 Cook for 1 ½–2 hours without stirring.

8 Strain carefully through a double muslin.

9 Remove all fat, using both sides of 8 cm square pieces of kitchen paper.

10 Correct the seasoning and colour, which should be a delicate amber.

11 Degrease again, if necessary. Bring to the boil and serve.

1 Mix one quarter of the stock with the beef, salt and egg white.

2 Once the remaining stock and the vegetables have been added, bring slowly to the boil.

3 After the soup has simmered for at least 1 ½ hours, strain it carefully.

Professional tip

A consommé should be crystal clear. The clarification process is caused by the albumen of the egg white and meat coagulating, rising to the top of the liquid and carrying other solid ingredients. The remaining liquid beneath the coagulated surface should be gently simmering. Cloudiness is due to some or all of the following:

- poor quality stock
- greasy stock
- unstrained stock
- imperfect coagulation of the clearing agent
- whisking after boiling point is reached, whereby the impurities mix with the liquid
- not allowing the soup to settle before straining
- lack of cleanliness of the pan or cloth
- any trace of grease or starch.

Healthy eating tips

- This soup is fat free!
- Keep the salt to a minimum and serve as a low-calorie starter for anyone wishing to reduce the fat in their diet.

Variation

Consommés are varied in many ways by altering the flavour of the stock (chicken, chicken and beef, game, etc.), also by the addition of numerous garnishes (julienne or brunoise of vegetables, shredded savoury pancakes or pea-sized profiteroles) added at the last moment before serving, or small pasta.

Cold, lightly jellied consommés, served in cups, with or without garnish (diced tomato), may be served in hot weather.

28 Lamb jus

	Makes 2 litres
Thyme	bunch
Bay leaves, fresh	4
Garlic	2 bulbs
Red wine	1 litre
Lamb bones	2 kg
Veal bones	1 kg
White onions, peeled	6
Large carrots, peeled	8
Celery sticks	7
Leeks, chopped	4
Tomato purée	6 tbsp

1 Pre-heat the oven to 175°C. Place the herbs, garlic and wine in a large, deep container. Place all the bones on to a roasting rack on top of the container of herbs and wine, and roast in the oven for 50–60 minutes. When the bones are completely roasted and have taken on a dark golden-brown appearance, remove from oven.

2 Place all the ingredients in a large pot and cover with cold water. Put the pot onto the heat and bring to the simmer; immediately skim all fat that rises to the surface.

3 Turn the heat off and allow the bones and vegetables to sink. Once this has happened, turn the heat back on and bring to just under a simmer, making as little movement as possible to create more of an infusion than a stock.

4 Skim continuously. Leave to infuse for 12 hours, then pass through a fine sieve, place in the blast chiller until cold and then in the refrigerator overnight. Next day, reduce down rapidly, until you have about 2 litres remaining.

---

29 Beef jus

	Makes 1 litre
Mushrooms, finely sliced	750 g
Butter	100 g
Shallots, finely sliced	350 g
Beef trim diced	350 g
Sherry vinegar	100 ml
Red wine	700 ml
Chicken stock	500 ml
Beef stock	1 litre

1 Caramelise the mushrooms in foaming butter, strain, then put aside in pan.

2 Caramelise the shallots in foaming butter, strain, then put aside in pan.

3 In another pan, caramelise the beef trim until golden brown.

4 Place the mushrooms, shallots and beef trim in one of the pans. Deglaze the other two pans with the vinegar, then add to the pan with the beef, shallots and mushrooms in it.

5 In a separate pan, reduce the wine by half and add to the main pan.

6 Add the stock, then reduce to sauce consistency.

7 Pass through a sieve, then chill and store until needed.

30 Chicken jus

	Makes 1 litre
Chicken stock	600 ml
Lamb jus	600 ml
Chicken wings, chopped small	300 g
Vegetable oil	60 ml
Shallots, sliced	100 g
Butter	50 g
Tomatoes, chopped	200 g
White wine vinegar	40 ml
Red wine vinegar	75 ml
Tarragon	1 tsp
Chervil	1 tsp

1 Put the jus and stock in a pan and reduce to 1 litre.
2 Roast the chicken wings in oil until slightly golden.
3 Add the shallots and butter, and cook until lightly browned (do not allow the butter to burn).
4 Strain off the butter and return the bones to the pan; deglaze with the vinegar and add tomatoes.
5 Ensure the bottom of the pan is clean. Add the reduced stock/jus and simmer for 15 minutes.
6 Pass through a sieve, then reduce to sauce consistency.
7 Remove from the heat and infuse with the aromats for 5 minutes.
8 Pass through a chinois and then muslin cloth.

31 Red wine jus

	Makes 1 litre
Shallots, sliced	150 g
Butter	50 g
Garlic, halved	10 g
Red wine vinegar	100 ml
Red wine	250 ml
Chicken stock	350 ml
Lamb or beef jus	250 ml
Bay leaves	2
Sprig of thyme	1

1 Caramelise the shallots in foaming butter until golden, adding the garlic at the end.

2 Strain through a colander and then put back into the pan and deglaze with the vinegar.

3 Reduce the red wine by half along with the stock and jus, at the same time as colouring the shallots.

4 When everything is done, combine and simmer for 20 minutes.

5 Pass through a sieve and reduce to sauce consistency.

6 Infuse the aromats for 5 minutes.

7 Pass through muslin cloth and store until needed.

32 Roast gravy (*jus rôti*)

1 Chop the bones and brown in the oven, or brown in a little oil on top of the stove in a frying pan. Drain off all the fat.

2 Place the bones in a saucepan with the stock or water.

3 Bring to the boil, skim and allow to simmer.

4 Add the lightly browned vegetables, which may be fried in a little fat in a frying pan or added to the bones when partly browned.

5 Simmer for 1 ½–2 hours.

6 Remove the joint from the roasting tin when cooked.

7 Return the tray to a low heat to allow the sediment to settle.

8 Carefully strain off the fat, leaving the sediment in the tin.

9 Return the joint to the stove and brown carefully; deglaze with the brown stock.

10 Allow to simmer for a few minutes.

11 Correct the colour and seasoning. Strain and skim off all fat.

	Serves 4	Serves 10
Raw veal bones or beef and veal trimmings	200 g	500 g
Stock or water	500 ml	1.25 litres
Onions, chopped	50 g	125 g
Celery, chopped	25 g	60 g
Carrots, chopped	50 g	125 g

Energy	Cals	Fat	Sat fat	Carb	Sugar	Protein	Fibre	Sodium
309 kJ	74 kcal	3.9 g	1.5 g	3.3 g	2.7 g	6.2 g	1.3 g	0.086 g

Professional tip

For preference, use beef bones for roast beef gravy and the appropriate bones for lamb, veal, mutton and pork.

Healthy eating tips
- Use an unsaturated oil (sunflower or vegetable). Lightly oil the pan.
- Season with the minimum amount of salt.

33 Thickened gravy (*jus lié*)

1 Start with roast gravy (recipe 32) or reduced veal stock (recipe 7). Add a little tomato purée, a few mushroom trimmings and a pinch of thyme and simmer for 10–15 minutes.

2 Stir some arrowroot diluted in cold water into the simmering gravy.

3 Reboil, simmer for 5–10 minutes and pass through a strainer.

Energy	Cals	Fat	Sat fat	Carb	Sugar	Protein	Fibre	Sodium
247 kJ	59 kcal	2.6 g	1 g	4.7	1.4 g	4.1 g	0.7 g	0.062 g

Variation

Add a little rosemary, thyme or lavender.

34 Béchamel sauce (white sauce)

1 Melt the butter or heat the oil in a thick-bottomed pan.

2 Mix in the flour with a heat-proof plastic or wooden spoon.

3 Cook for a few minutes, stirring frequently. As you are making a white roux, do not allow the mixture to colour.

4 Remove the pan from the heat and allow the roux to cool.

5 Return the pan to the stove and, over a low heat, gradually mix the milk into the roux.

6 Add the studded onion.

7 Allow the mixture to simmer gently for 30 minutes, stirring frequently to make sure the sauce does not burn on the bottom.

8 Remove the onion and pass the sauce through a conical strainer.

	1 litre	4.5 litres
Butter or oil	100 g	400 g
Plain white flour	100 g	400 g
Milk, warmed	1 litre	4.5 litres
Onion, studded with cloves	1	2–3

Professional tip

To prevent a skin from forming, brush the surface of the sauce with melted butter. When ready to use, stir this into the sauce. Alternatively, cover the sauce with greaseproof paper.

The following three recipes (Mornay sauce, Soubise sauce and Parsley sauce) use sauce flour to thicken the sauce rather than a traditional roux base. This produces a lower fat sauce and a simpler method of production.

35 Mornay sauce

	500 ml
Milk	500 ml
Grated cheese	50 g
Egg yolk	1
Sauce flour	40 g

1 The milk may be first infused with a studded onion clouté, carrot and a bouquet garni. Allow to cool.

2 Place the milk in a suitable saucepan, gradually whisk in the sauce flour. Bring slowly to the boil until the sauce has thickened.

3 Mix in the cheese and egg yolk when the sauce is boiling.

4 Remove from the heat. Strain if necessary.

5 Do not allow the sauce to reboil at any time.

Professional tip

Add a little cornflour prior to heating to stabilise the sauce.

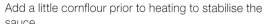

36 Soubise sauce

	500 ml
Onion, chopped or diced	100 g
Milk	500 ml
Sauce flour	40 g
Seasoning	

1 Cook the onions without colouring them, either by boiling or sweating in butter.

2 The milk may be first infused with a studded onion clouté, carrot and a bouquet garni. Allow to cool.

3 Place the milk in a suitable saucepan, gradually whisk in the sauce flour. Bring slowly to the boil until the sauce has thickened.

4 Add the onions, season, simmer for approximately 5–10 minutes.

5 Blitz well. Pass through a strainer.

37 Parsley sauce

	500 ml
Milk	500 ml
Sauce flour	40 g
Parsley, chopped	1 tbsp
Seasoning	

1 The milk may be first infused with a studded onion clouté, carrot and a bouquet garni. Allow to cool.

2 Place the milk in a suitable saucepan, gradually whisk in the sauce flour. Bring slowly to the boil until the sauce has thickened.

3 Season, simmer for approximately 5–10 minutes. Use as required.

38 Velouté (chicken, veal, mutton)

1 Melt the butter or heat the oil in a thick-bottomed pan.

2 Add the flour and mix in.

3 Cook out to a sandy texture over gentle heat without colouring.

4 Allow the roux to cool.

5 Gradually add the boiling stock.

6 Stir until smooth and boiling.

7 Allow to simmer for approximately 1 hour.

8 Pass it through a fine conical strainer.

Note

This is a basic white sauce made from white stock and a blond roux.

A velouté sauce for chicken or veal dishes is usually finished with cream and, in some cases, egg yolks. The finished sauce should be of a light consistency, barely coating the back of a spoon.

	4 portions	10 portions
Butter or oil	100 g	400 g
Flour	100 g	400 g
Stock (chicken, veal, mutton) as required	1 litre	4.5 litres

Energy	Kcal	Fat	Sat fat	Carb	Sugar	Protein	Fibre	*
4594 kJ	1094 kcal	82.6 g	35.4 g	79.0 g	1.6 g	13.3 g	3.6 g	

* Using hard margarine, for 1 litre. Using sunflower oil instead, this recipe provides, for 1 litre: 5304 kJ/1263 kcal Energy; 101.5 g Fat; 13.3 g Sat Fat; 78.9 g Carb; 1.5 g Sugar; 13.2 g Protein; 3.6 g Fibre

Healthy eating tip
● Make sure all the fat has been skimmed from the stock before adding it to the roux.

39 Aurore sauce

	4 portions	10 portions
Chicken or veal velouté	250 ml	625 ml
Mushroom trimmings, washed and dried	50 g	125 g
Fresh cream, double or single	50 ml	125 ml
Egg yolks	1	3
Lemon juice	½ lemon	1 ½ lemons
Tomato purée	1 tbsp	1 ½ tbsp
Seasoning		

1 Place the velouté in a suitable saucepan and bring to the boil.
2 Add the mushroom trimmings. Allow to simmer for 10 minutes.
3 Add the tomato purée; mix well.
4 Strain through a fine chinois.
5 In a basin mix the egg yolks and cream.
6 Add a little of the hot sauce to this mix; whisk well.
7 Return to the main sauce and stir. Do NOT allow to re-boil.
8 Finish with lemon juice.

Note

Serve with poached chicken or poached eggs. If serving with poached or steamed fish, use fish velouté.

40 Ivory sauce

	4 portions	10 portions
Chicken or veal velouté	250 ml	625 ml
Mushroom trimmings, washed and dried	50 g	125 g
Cream, single or double	50 ml	125 ml
Lemon juice	½ lemon	1 ½ lemons
Chicken or beef meat glaze	1 tbsp	1 ½ tbsp
Seasoning		

Energy	Cals	Fat	Sat fat	Carb	Sugar	Protein	Fibre	Sodium *
351 kJ	85 kcal	6.8 g	4.3 g	4.9 g	0.8 g	1.3 g	0.6 g	0.037 g

* Using butter and single cream

Note

Serve with grilled veal or pork chops, grilled or poached chicken.

1 Place the velouté into a suitable saucepan and bring to the boil.

2 Add the mushroom trimmings; simmer for 10 minutes.

3 Pass the sauce through a fine chinois.

4 Add the meat glaze; stir well to achieve an ivory colour.

5 Add the lemon juice and finish with cream. Correct the seasoning.

41 Mushroom sauce

	1 litre	4.5 litres
Butter or oil	100g	400g
Flour	100g	400g
Stock (chicken, veal, fish, mutton) as required	1 litre	4.5 litres
Mushroom trimmings	50g	225g
White button mushrooms, well-washed, sliced, sweated	200g	900g
Cream	120ml	540ml
Egg yolk	2	9
Lemon, juice of	½	1

1 Melt the butter or heat the oil in a thick-bottomed pan.

2 Add the flour and mix in.

3 Cook out to a sandy texture over gentle heat without colouring.

4 Allow the roux to cool.

5 Gradually add the boiling stock.

6 Stir until smooth and boiling.

7 Add the mushrooms and trimmings. Allow to simmer for approximately 1 hour.

8 Pass it through a fine conical strainer.

9 Simmer for 10 minutes, then add the egg yolk, cream and lemon juice.

42 Suprême sauce

	4 portions	10 portions
Margarine, butter or oil	100g	400g
Flour	100g	400g
Stock (chicken, veal, fish or mutton)	1 litre	4.5 litres
Mushroom trimmings	25g	60g
Egg yolk	1	2
Cream	60ml	150ml
Lemon juice	2–3 drops	5–6 drops

1 Melt the fat or oil in a thick-bottomed pan.

2 Add the flour and mix in. Cook to a sandy texture over a gentle heat, without colouring.

3 Allow the roux to cool, then gradually add the boiling stock. Stir until smooth and boiling.

4 Add the mushroom trimmings. Simmer for approximately 1 hour.

5 Pass through a final conical strainer.

6 Finish with a liaison of the egg yolk, cream and lemon juice. Serve immediately.

Energy	Cals	Fat	Sat fat	Carb	Sugar	Protein	Fibre	Sodium
1339kJ	322kcal	25.2g	15.3g	21.1g	1.8g	4.1g	1.6g	0.162g

Professional tip

Once the liaison has been added, do not re-boil this sauce.

Note

This sauce can be served hot with boiled chicken, vol-au-vonts, etc., and can also be used for white chaud-froid sauce. The traditional stock base is a good chicken stock.

43 Fish velouté

	1 litre	2.5 litres
Butter	100g	250g
Flour	100g	250g
Fish stock	1 litre	2.5 litres

Energy	Cals	Fat	Sat fat	Carb	Sugar	Protein	Fibre
4805kJ	1144kcal	90.4g	39.0g	77.8g	1.6g	9.5g	3.6g

1 Prepare a blond roux using the butter and flour.

2 Gradually add the stock, stirring continuously until boiling point is reached.

3 Simmer for approximately 1 hour.

4 Pass through a fine conical strainer.

Note

This will give a thick sauce that can be thinned down with the cooking liquor from the fish for which the sauce is intended. For white wine sauce add to 1 litre of velouté, 250ml of white wine reduced by half by boiling. Finish with 125ml of single cream

Healthy eating tip

● Make sure all the fat has been skimmed from the stock before adding it to the roux.

44 Chasseur sauce (*sauce chasseur*)

	4 portions	10 portions
Butter or oil	25 g	60 g
Shallots, chopped	10 g	25 g
Garlic clove, chopped (optional)	1	1
Button mushrooms, sliced	50 g	125 g
White wine, dry	60 ml	150 ml
Tomatoes, skinned, deseeded, diced	100 g	250 g
Demi-glace, jus lié or reduced stock	250 ml	625 ml
Parsley and tarragon, chopped		

Energy	Cals	Fat	Sat fat	Carb	Sugar	Protein	Fibre
227 kJ	55 kcal	5.3 g	2.5 g	1.4 g	1.2 g	0.5 g	0.5 g

1 Melt the butter or heat the oil in a small sautéuse.
2 Add the shallots and cook gently for 2–3 minutes without colour.
3 Add the garlic and the mushrooms, cover and cook gently for 2–3 minutes.
4 Strain off the fat.
5 Add the wine and reduce by half. Add the tomatoes.
6 Add the demi-glace; simmer for 5–10 minutes.
7 Correct the seasoning. Add the tarragon and parsley.

Healthy eating tip
- Use an unsaturated oil (sunflower or vegetable). Lightly oil the pan.
- Skim the fat from the finished dish.
- Season with the minimum amount of salt.

Note

May be served with fried steaks, chops, chicken, etc.

45 Piquant sauce (*sauce piquante*)

	4 portions	10 portions
Vinegar	60 ml	150 ml
Shallots, chopped	50 g	125 g
Demi-glace, jus lié or reduced stock	250 ml	625 ml
Gherkins, chopped	25 g	60 g
Capers, chopped	10 g	25 g
Chervil, tarragon and parsley, chopped	½ tbsp	1 ½ tbsp

Energy	Cals	Fat	Sat fat	Carb	Sugar	Protein	Fibre	Sodium
151 kJ	36 kcal	1.3 g	0.5 g	3 g	1.3 g	2.4 g	0.7 g	0.034 g

1 Place the vinegar and shallots in a small sautéuse and reduce by half.

2 Add the demi-glace; simmer for 15–20 minutes.

3 Add the rest of the ingredients.

4 Skim and correct the seasoning.

Note

May be served with made up dishes, sausages and grilled meats.

46 Robert sauce (*sauce Robert*)

	4 portions	10 portions
Oil or butter	20 g	50 g
Onions, finely chipped	10 g	25 g
Vinegar	60 ml	150 g
Demi-glace, jus lié or reduced stock	250 ml	625 ml
English or continental mustard	1 level tsp	2 ½ level tsp
Caster sugar	1 level tbsp	2 ½ level tbsp

Energy	Cals	Fat	Sat fat	Carb	Sugar	Protein	Fibre	Sodium *
401 kJ	96 kcal	5.7 g	3.1 g	8.3 g	6.5 g	2.5 g	0.4 g	0.180 g

* Using butter

1 Melt the fat or oil in a small sautéuse.

2 Add the onions. Cook gently without colour.

3 Add the vinegar and reduce completely.

4 Add the demi-glace; simmer for 5–10 minutes.

5 Remove from the heat and add the mustard, diluted with a little water and the sugar; do not boil.

6 Skim and correct the seasoning.

Healthy eating tip

● Use unsaturated oil (sunflower or olive). Lightly oil the pan and drain off any excess after the frying is complete. Skim the fat from the finished dish.

● Season with the minimum amount of salt.

Note

May be served with fried sausages and burgers or grilled pork chops.

47 Madeira sauce (*sauce Madère*)

	4 portions	10 portions
Demi-glace, jus lié or reduced stock	250 ml	625 ml
Madeira wine	2 tbsp	5 tbsp
Butter	25 g	60 g

1 Boil the demi-glace in a small sautéuse.

2 Add the Madeira and re-boil.

3 Correct the seasoning.

4 Pass through a fine conical strainer.

5 Gradually mix in the butter.

Note

May be served with braised ox tongue or ham.

Variation

Dry sherry or port wine may be substituted for Madeira and the sauce renamed accordingly.

Energy	Cals	Fat	Sat fat	Carb	Sugar	Protein	Fibre	Sodium
365 kJ	88 kcal	6.4 g	3.7 g	3.5 g	1.4 g	2.1 g	0.3 g	0.069 g

48 Brown onion sauce (*sauce Lyonnaise*)

	4 portions	10 portions
Margarine, oil or butter	25 g	60 g
Onions, sliced	100 g	250 g
Vinegar	2 tbsp	5 tbsp
Demi-glace, jus lié or reduced stock	250 ml	625 ml

Energy	Cals	Fat	Sat fat	Carb	Sugar	Protein	Fibre	Sodium *
374 kJ	90 kcal	6.8 g	3.9 g	3.5 g	1.8 g	3.7 g	1 g	0.147 g

* Using butter

1 Melt the fat or oil in a sautéuse.

2 Add the onions; cover with a lid and cook gently until tender and golden in colour.

3 Remove the lid and colour lightly.

4 Add the vinegar and completely reduce.

5 Add the demi-glace; simmer for 5–10 minutes.

6 Skim and correct the seasoning.

Note

May be served with burgers, fried liver or sausages.

Healthy eating tip

● Use unsaturated oil (sunflower or olive). Lightly oil the pan and drain off any excess after the frying is complete. Skim the fat from the finished dish.

● Season with the minimum amount of salt.

49 Italian sauce (*sauce Italienne*)

	4 portions	10 portions
Margarine, oil or butter	25 g	60 g
Shallots, chopped	10 g	25 g
Mushrooms, chopped	50 g	125 g
Demi-glaze, jus-lié or reduced stock	250 ml	625 ml
Lean ham, chopped	25 g	60 g
Tomatoes, skinned, de-seeded	100 g	250 g
Diced parsley, chervil and tarragon, chopped		

Healthy eating tip

- Use unsaturated oil (sunflower or olive). Lightly oil the pan and drain off any excess after the frying is complete.
- Trim as much fat as possible from the ham.
- The ham is salty, so do not add more salt; flavour will come from the herbs.
- Skim all fat from the finished sauce.

Energy	Cals	Fat	Sat fat	Carb	Sugar	Protein	Fibre	Sodium *
359 kJ	86 kcal	6.5 g	3.7 g	4.4 g	2.2 g	2.4 g	0.8 g	0.070 g

* Using butter

1 Melt the fat or oil in a small sautéuse.

2 To make a duxelle, add the shallots and cook gently for 2–3 minutes.

3 Add the mushrooms and cook gently for a further 2–3 minutes.

4 Add the demi-glace, ham and tomatoes. Simmer for 5–10 minutes.

5 Correct the seasoning; add the chopped herbs.

50 Pepper sauce (*sauce poivrade*)

	4 portions	10 portions
Margarine, oil or butter	25 g	60 g
Onions	50 g	125 g
Carrots	50 g	125 g
Celery	50 g	125 g
Bay leaf	1	1
Sprig of thyme		
Vinegar	2 tbsp	5 tbsp
Mignonette pepper	5 g	12 g
Demi-glace, jus lié or reduced stock	250 ml	625 ml

1 Melt the fat or oil in a small sautéuse.

2 Add the vegetables and herbs (mirepoix) and allow to brown.

3 Add the wine, vinegar and pepper. Reduce by half.

4 Add the demi-glace and simmer for 20–30 minutes.

5 Pass through a fine conical strainer.

6 Correct the seasoning.

Healthy eating tips
- Use unsaturated oil (sunflower or olive). Lightly oil the pan and drain off any excess after the frying is complete. Skim the fat from the finished dish.
- Season with the minimum amount of salt.

Note

Usually served with joints or cuts of venison.

51 Apple sauce

	8 portions
Cooking apples	400g
Sugar	50g
Butter or margarine	25g

Energy	Cals	Fat	Sat fat	Carb	Sugar	Protein	Fibre	Sodium
276kJ	65kcal	2.6g	1.6g	11g	11g	0.2g	1.1g	0.020g

1 Peel, core and wash the apples.

2 Place with other ingredients in a covered pan and cook to a purée.

3 Pass through a sieve or liquidise.

52 Cranberry and orange dressing

	4 portions	10 portions
Cranberries	400g	1kg
Granulated sugar	50g	125g
Red wine	125ml	250ml
Red wine vinegar	2 tbsp	5 tbsp
Orange zest and juice	2	4

Energy	Cals	Fat	Sat fat	Carb	Sugar	Protein	Fibre
398kJ	93kcal	0.2g	0.0g	22.7g	22.7g	1.3g	4.2g

1 Place the cranberries in a suitable saucepan with the rest of the ingredients.

2 Bring to the boil and simmer gently for approximately 1 hour, stirring from time to time.

3 Remove from the heat and leave to cool. Use as required.

Professional tip

The dressing may also be liquidised if a smooth texture is required.

53 Green or herb sauce

	4 portions	10 portions
Spinach, tarragon, chervil, chives, watercress	50 g	125 g
Mayonnaise	150 ml	375 ml

1 Pick, wash, blanch and refresh the green leaves.

2 Squeeze dry.

3 Pass through a very fine sieve.

4 Mix with the mayonnaise.

Note

May be served with cold salmon or trout.

Energy	Cals	Fat	Sat fat	Carb	Sugar	Protein	Fibre	Sodium
1082 kJ	263 kcal	28 g	4.3 g	0.9 g	0.6 g	0.8 g	0.2 g	0.18 g

54 Reduction of stock (glaze)

A glaze is a stock, fond or nage that has been reduced: that is, much of the water content is removed by gently simmering. The solid content, and all the flavour, stays in the glaze.

Any kind of stock can be used, but it is important to be careful if using meat stock. Meat stock contains collagen; if the stock is cooked at boiling temperature, there will be a lot of collagen in the glaze. This means the sauce will become thick more quickly than non-meat glazes. It will then be impossible to reduce it any more without burning it.

Glazes have a strong flavour and contain a lot of salt, so only use small amounts.

55 Reduction of wine, stock and cream

	approx. 250 ml
White stock	500 ml
White wine	125 ml
Double or whipping cream	125 ml

1 Place the stock and white wine in a suitable saucepan.

2 Reduce by at least two-thirds to a slightly syrup consistency and finish with cream.

Measure out all the ingredients

Reduce the wine and stock

Add the cream

56 Hollandaise sauce

	Makes 500 g
Peppercorns, crushed	12
White wine vinegar	3 tbsp
Egg yolks	6
Melted butter	325 g
Salt and cayenne pepper	

1 Place the peppercorns and vinegar in a small pan and reduce to one-third.

2 Add 1 tablespoon of cold water and allow to cool. Add the egg yolks.

3 Put on a bain marie and whisk continuously to a sabayon consistency.

4 Remove from the heat and gradually whisk in the melted butter.

5 Add seasoning and pass through muslin or a fine chinois.

6 Store in an appropriate container.

Health and safety !

Egg-based sauces should not be kept warm for more than 2 hours. After this time, they should be thrown away, but are best made fresh to order.

Faults

If you add oil or butter when making hollandaise or mayonnaise, the sauce may curdle because the lecithin has had insufficient time to coat the droplets. This can be rectified by adding the broken sauce to more egg yolks.

Variation

Mousseline sauce: hollandaise base with lightly whipped cream.

Maltaise sauce: hollandaise base with lightly grated zest and juice of one blood orange.

57 Béarnaise sauce

1 Place the shallots, tarragon, peppercorns and vinegar in a small pan and reduce to one-third.
2 Add 1 tablespoon of cold water and allow to cool.
3 Add the egg yolks.
4 Put on a bain-marie and whisk continuously to a sabayon consistency.
5 Remove from the heat and gradually whisk in the melted butter. Add seasoning.
6 Pass through muslin or a fine chinois.
7 To finish, add the chopped chervil and tarragon.
8 Store in an appropriate container.

	500 ml
Shallots, chopped	50 g
Tarragon	10 g
Peppercorns, crushed	12
White wine vinegar	3 tbsp
Egg yolks	6
Melted butter	325 g
Salt and cayenne pepper, chervil and tarragon to finish, chopped	

Health and safety

Egg-based sauces should not be kept warm for more than two hours and should be thrown away after this time. They are best made fresh to order.

Variation

Choron sauce: 200 g tomato concassé, well dried. Do not add the chopped tarragon and chervil to finish.

Foyot or valois sauce: 25 g warm meat glaze.

Paloise sauce: made as for béarnaise sauce, using chopped mint stalks in place of the tarragon in the reduction. To finish, add chopped mint instead of the chervil and tarragon.

58 Sauce diable

	Makes 250 g
Butter	25 g
Shallots, finely chopped	25 g
Dry white wine	150 ml
Reduced brown stock or jus lié	250 ml
Cayenne pepper	2 g

1 In a suitable pan, add the butter and gently sweat the shallots without colour.

2 Add the white wine; reduce by half.

3 Add the brown stock or jus lié; bring to the boil and simmer for two minutes.

4 Season with cayenne pepper. Correct the seasoning and consistency.

Note

Serve with grilled chicken and steaks.

59 Tomato sauce (*sauce tomate*)

1 Melt the fat or oil in a small sautéuse.

2 Add the vegetables, herbs (mirepoix) and bacon scraps and brown slightly.

3 Mix in the flour and cook to a sandy texture. Allow to colour slightly.

4 Mix in the tomato purée; allow to cool.

5 Gradually add the boiling stock; stir to the boil.

6 Add the garlic and season then simmer for one hour.

7 Correct the seasoning and cool.

8 Pass through a fine conical strainer.

Note

This sauce has many uses; it is served with pasta, eggs, fish and meats.

	4 portions	10 portions
Margarine, butter or oil	10 g	25 g
Onions (for mirepoix)	50 g	125 g
Carrots (for mirepoix)	50 g	125 g
Celery (for mirepoix)	25 g	60 g
Bay leaf (for mirepoix)	1	3
Bacon scraps (optional)	10 g	25 g
Flour	10 g	25 g
Tomato purée	50 g	125 g
Stock	375 ml	1 litre
Clove of garlic	½	2
Salt and pepper		

Variation

The amount of tomato purée used may need to vary according to its strength.

The sauce can also be made without using flour, by adding 400 g of fresh, fully ripe tomatoes or an equivalent tin of tomatoes for four portions.

60 Sweet and sour sauce

	4 portions	10 portions
White vinegar	375 ml	1 litre
Brown sugar	150 g	375 g
Tomato ketchup	125 ml	300 ml
Light soy sauce	1 tbsp	2 ½ tbsp
Seasoning		

1 Boil the vinegar and sugar in a suitable pan.
2 Add the tomato ketchup, Worcester sauce and seasoning.
3 Simmer for a few minutes then use as required. This sauce may also be lightly thickened with cornflour or another thickening agent.

61 Mayonnaise

	8 portions
Egg yolks, very fresh or pasteurised	3
Vinegar or lemon juice	2 tsp
Small pinch of salt	
English or continental mustard	½ tsp
A mild-flavoured oil such as corn oil or the lightest olive oil	250 ml
Water, boiling	1 tsp

Energy	Cals	Fat	Sat fat	Carb	Sugar	Protein	Fibre	Sodium
1248 kJ	303 kcal	33 g	5.1 g	0.1 g	0.1 g	1.1 g	0 g	0.07 g

Health and safety !

Because of the risk of salmonella food poisoning, it is strongly recommended that pasteurised egg yolks are used.

1 Place yolks, vinegar, salt and mustard in the bowl of a food mixer.

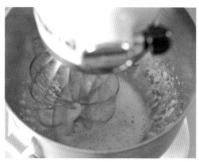

2 Whisk until thoroughly mixed.

3 Continue to whisk vigorously and start to add the oil – this needs to be done slowly.

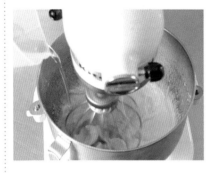

4 Keep whisking until all the oil has been added.

5 Whisk in the boiling water.

6 Taste and correct seasoning if necessary.

Variation

Add:
- fresh chopped herbs
- garlic juice – peel a clove garlic and press it using a garlic press
- thick tomato juice.

Professional tip

If the mayonnaise becomes too thick while you are making it, whisk in a little of water or vinegar.

Faults

Mayonnaise may separate, turn or curdle for several reasons:
- you have added the oil too quickly
- the oil is too cold
- you have not whisked enough
- the egg yolks were stale and weak.

To reconstitute (bring it back together):
- Take a clean basin, pour 1 teaspoon of boiling water and gradually but vigorously whisk in the curdled sauce a little at a time.
- Alternatively, in a clean basin, whisk a fresh egg yolk with ½ teaspoon of cold water then gradually whisk in the curdled sauce.

62 Tartare sauce (*sauce tartare*)

	8 portions
Mayonnaise	250 ml
Capers, chopped	25 g
Gherkins, chopped	50 g
Sprig of parsley, chopped	

1 Combine all the ingredients.

Note

This sauce is usually served with deep-fried fish.

Professional tip

Finely chop the gherkins and capers and use a blender to give the desired texture and consistency, but do not purée completely.

Healthy eating tip

Proportionally reduce the fat by adding some low-fat yoghurt instead of some of the mayonnaise.

Energy	Cals	Fat	Sat fat	Carb	Sugar	Protein	Fibre	Sodium
911 kJ	221 kcal	24 g	3.6 g	0.8 g	0.6 g	0.6 g	0.1 g	0.24 g

63 Remoulade sauce (*sauce remoulade*)

1 Prepare as for tartare sauce (recipe 62), adding 1 teaspoon of anchovy essence and mixing thoroughly. Makes 8 portions.

Note

This sauce may be served with fried fish. It can also be mixed with a fine julienne of celeriac to make an accompaniment to cold meats, terrines, etc.

Energy	Cals	Fat	Sat fat	Carb	Sugar	Protein	Fibre	Sodium
907 kJ	220 kcal	24 g	3.6 g	0.8 g	0.6 g	0.7 g	0.1 g	0.25 g

64 Andalusian sauce (*sauce Andalouse*)

1 Take 250 ml of mayonnaise and add 2 tbsp tomato juice or ketchup and 1 tbsp red pepper cut into julienne. Makes 250 ml.

Note

May be served with cold salads.

Professional tip

For Andalusian sauce, Thousand Island dressing, green sauce and other similar recipes, use a blender to achieve the desired texture and flavour, but do not purée completely.

65 Thousand Island dressing

	4–6 portions
Mayonnaise	250 mls
Tomato ketchup	30 mls
White wine vinegar	1 tbsp
Caster sugar	1 tsp
Finely chopped onion	15 g
Finely chopped clove of garlic	1
Tabasco sauce	2 drops
Worcester sauce	½ tsp
Gherkins finely chopped	2

Energy	Cals	Fat	Sat fat	Carb	Sugar	Protein	Fibre	Sodium
928 kJ	225 kcal	24 g	3.6 g	2.6 g	2.3 g	0.5 g	0.1 g	0.25 g

1 Mix all ingredients together.

2 Use as a dressing for fish cocktails and salads. Thousand Island dressing is an example of a dressing which has become a standard condiment.

66 Tomato vinaigrette

	4 portions	10 portions
Tomatoes	200 g	500 g
Caster sugar	½ tsp	1 ¼ tbsp
White wine vinegar	1 tbsp	2 ½ tsp
Extra virgin olive oil	3 tbsp	8 tbsp
Seasoning		

1 Blanch and deseed the tomatoes; purée in a food processor.
2 Add the sugar, vinegar, olive oil and seasoning; whisk well to emulsify.
3 The vinaigrette should be smooth.

Energy	Cals	Fat	Sat fat	Carb	Sugar	Protein	Fibre	Sodium
26 kJ	6 kcal	0g	0g	0.7g	0.6g	0.1g	0g	Trace

67 Mint sauce

	8 portions
Mint	2–3 tbsp
Caster sugar	1 tsp
Vinegar	125 ml

1 Chop the washed, picked mint and mix with the sugar.
2 Place in a china basin and add the vinegar.
3 If the vinegar is too sharp, dilute it with a little water.

Serve with roast lamb.

Energy	Cals	Fat	Sat fat	Carb	Sugar	Protein	Fibre	Sodium
382 kJ	93 kcal	9.6g	1.4g	1.4g	1.3g	0.2g	0.3g	0.25g

Professional tip

A less acid sauce can be produced by dissolving the sugar in 125 ml boiling water and, when cold, adding the chopped mint and 1–2 tablespoon vinegar to taste.

68 Yoghurt and cucumber raita

	4 portions
Cucumbers	2
Salt	
Spring onions, chopped	2 tbsp
Yoghurt	500 ml
Cumin seeds	1 ½ tsp
Lemon juice	1
Fresh coriander or mint, chopped	

Energy	Cals	Fat	Sat fat	Carb	Sugar	Protein	Fibre	Sodium
366 kJ	87 kcal	1.4 g	0.8 g	11.9 g	11.7 g	7.2 g	1.3 g	0.133 g

1 Peel the cucumbers, halve them lengthways and remove the seeds. Cut into small dice.

2 Sprinkle the dice with salt and leave for 15 minutes, then drain away the liquid and rinse the cucumbers quickly in cold water. Drain well.

3 Combine the onion, yoghurt and lemon juice; taste to see if more salt is required.

4 Roast the cumin seeds in a dry pan, shaking the pan or stirring constantly until brown.

5 Bruise or crush the seeds and sprinkle over the yoghurt mixture.

6 Serve chilled, garnished with mint and coriander.

Note

This is a dish from Punjab, northern India. Serve as an accompaniment to curry.

Professional tip

Sprinkling the cucumber with salt removes the juices, which are hard to digest. Remember to wash off the salt before use.

69 Balsamic vinegar and olive oil dressing

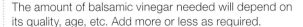

	8 portions
Water	62 ml
Olive oil	250 ml
Balsamic vinegar	62 ml
Sherry vinegar	2 tbsp
Caster sugar	½ tsp
Seasoning	

1 Whisk all ingredients together and correct the seasoning.

Professional tip

The amount of balsamic vinegar needed will depend on its quality, age, etc. Add more or less as required.

This dressing works well because it is not an emulsion. The oil and vinegar provide a stark contrast and can be stirred just before serving.

70 Horseradish sauce (*sauce raifort*)

	8 portions
Horseradish	25 g
Vinegar or lemon juice	1 tbsp
Salt, pepper	
Cream or crème fraiche, lightly whipped	125 ml

1 Wash, peel and rewash the horseradish. grate finely.
2 Mix all the ingredients together.

Note

Serve with roast beef, smoked trout, eel or halibut.

Professional tip

It is essential to blend the ingredients without over-mixing them, in order to get a good flavour.

Energy	Cals	Fat	Sat fat	Carb	Sugar	Protein	Fibre	Sodium *
135kJ	33kcal	3g	1.9g	0.7g	0.6g	0.7g	0.3g	0.029g

* Using cream

71 Tomato and cucumber salsa

	8 portions
Ripe tomatoes, skinned, deseeded, chopped	400 g
Cucumber, peeled, chopped	½
Spring onions, chopped	6
Fresh basil, chopped	1 tbsp
Fresh parsley, chopped	1 tbsp
Olive oil	3 tbsp
Lemon or lime (juice of)	1
Salt and pepper	

1 In a large bowl, mix all the ingredients together.
2 Correct seasoning and serve.

Energy	Cals	Fat	Sat fat	Carb	Sugar	Protein	Fibre
202kJ	49kcal	4.3g	0.7g	2.0g	2.0g	0.6g	0.7g

Healthy eating tip

Rely on the herbs for flavour, with the minimum amount of salt.

Variation

This recipe may be varied by using any chopped salad ingredients and fresh herbs (e.g. tarragon, chervil). Do not be afraid to experiment.

Extra vegetables can be added and the salsa used liberally with grilled fish or chicken. Rice could be served with this, or the salsa used to fill a tortilla.

72 Salsa verde

	8 portions
Mint, coarsely chopped	1 tbsp
Parsley, coarsely chopped	3 tbsp
Capers, coarsely chopped	3
Garlic clove (optional)	1
Dijon mustard	1 tsp
Lemon, juice of	½
Extra virgin olive oil	120 ml
Salt	

1 In a large bowl, mix all the ingredients together and check the seasoning.

Note

Serve with grilled fish.

Energy	Cals	Fat	Sat fat	Carb	Sugar	Protein	Fibre *
281 kJ	69 kcal	7.5 g	1.1 g	0.2 g	0.1 g	0.1 g	0.0 g

* Per tablespoon

73 Avocado and coriander salsa

	8 portions
Ripe avocado, peeled and diced	1
Ripe tomatoes, peeled, deseeded and diced	3
Shallot, peeled and cut into rings	1
Fresh coriander, chopped	1 tsp
Pine kernels, toasted	10 g
Cucumber, diced	25 g
Lemon or lime (juice)	1
Virgin olive oil	3 tbsp
Salt and pepper to taste	

Energy	Cals	Fat	Sat fat	Carb	Sugar	Protein	Fibre
361 kJ	87 kcal	8.6 g	1.4 g	1.8 g	1.4 g	0.8 g	1.0 g

1 In a large bowl, mix all the ingredients together, check seasoning and serve.

Note

Use with cold dishes such as salads or terrinnes.

Healthy eating tip

Although avocado is rich in fat, it is unsaturated fat and therefore healthier.

Try using the salsa to fill a tortilla, and add grilled fish or chicken to make a healthy meal.

74 Pear chutney

	1 litre	5 kg (approx.)
White wine vinegar	180 g	900 g
Demerara sugar	180 g	900 g
Ginger, brunoise	25 g	125 g
Onion, diced	75 g	375 g
Nutmeg	Pinch	5 g
Saffron	Pinch	0.25 g
Cinnamon	Pinch	5 g
Golden sultanas	25 g	375 g
Tomato concassé	150 g	750 g
Pears, diced	400 g	2 kg

1 Make a thick syrup with the white wine vinegar and the sugar.

2 Add the ginger, onion, nutmeg, saffron, cinnamon, sultanas and concassé, and reduce to a thick syrup.

3 Add the diced pears and reduce again to a sticky consistency.

4 Cool the chutney and then store in a Kilner jar.

Note

Serve with cheese, cold meats, pâtés or terrines.

75 Tomato chutney

	1 litre
Tomatoes, peeled	1.5 kg
Onions, finely chopped	450 g
Brown sugar	300 g
Malt vinegar	375 ml
Mustard powder	1 ½ tsp
Cayenne pepper	½ tsp
Coarse salt	2 tsp
Mild curry powder	1 tbsp

1 Peel and coarsely chop the tomatoes, then combine with the remaining ingredients in a large heavy-duty saucepan.

2 Stir over heat without boiling until the sugar dissolves. Simmer uncovered, stirring occasionally until the mixture thickens (about 1 ½ hours).

3 Place in hot, sterilised jars. Seal while hot.

Note

Serve with cheese, cold meats or terrines.

76 Pesto sauce

	Makes 250 ml
Fresh basil leaves	100 ml
Pine nuts (lightly toasted)	1 tbsp
Garlic (picked and crumbled)	2 cloves
Parmesan cheese (grated)	40 g
Pecorino cheese (grated)	40 g
Olive oil	5 tbsp
Salt and pepper	

1 Place all ingredients into a food processor and mix to a rough-textured sauce.

2 Transfer to a bowl and leave for at least 1 hour to enable the flavours to develop.

Note

Pesto is traditionally served with large flat pasta called Trenetta.

Pesto is also used as a cordon in various fish and meat-plated dishes, e.g. grilled fish, medallions of veal.

Variation

Use flat-leaved parsley in place of basil and walnuts in place of pine nuts.

77 Tapenade

1 Mix all the ingredients together, adding the olive oil to make a paste.

2 For a smoother texture, place garlic, lemon juice, capers and anchovies into a food processor and process until a smooth texture. Add the olives and parsley, and sufficient oil to form a smooth paste.

3 Season, if required.

4 Garnish with a sprinkle of roast cumin and chopped red chilli.

5 Serve chilled.

	4 portions	10 portions
Capers	45 g	110 g
Lemon juice	1 tbsp	2 tbsp
Anchovy fillets, chopped	6	15
Black olives, copped	250 g	625 g
Parsley, chopped	1 tsp	2 tsp
Salt and pepper	Pinch	Pinch
Virgin olive oil	4 tbsp	10 tbsp
Garlic cloves crushed/chopped	1	3
Roast cumin		
Chopped red chilli		

Energy	Cals	Fat	Sat fat	Carb	Sugar	Protein	Fibre	Sodium
773 kJ	188 kcal	19.8 g	2.9 g	0.3 g	0.1 g	2 g	2.7 g	2.03 g

Note

Tapenade is a Provencale dish consisting of puréed or finely chopped black olives, capers, anchovies and olive oil. It may also contain garlic, herbs, tuna, lemon juice or brandy. Its name comes from the Provencale word for capers: *tapeno*. It is popular in the South of France, where it is generally eaten as an hors d'oeuvre, spread on toast.

78 Mixed pickle

Cauliflower, cucumber, green tomatoes, onions and marrow	
For the spiced vinegar	
Vinegar	1 litre
Blade mace	5 g
Allspice	5 g
Cloves	5 g
Stick cinnamon	5 g
Peppercorns	6
Root ginger (for hot pickle)	5 g

1 To make the spiced vinegar, tie the spices in muslin, place them in a covered pan with the vinegar and heat slowly to boiling point.

2 Remove from the heat and stand for 2 hours, then remove the bag.

3 Prepare the vegetables, with the exception of the marrow, and soak them in brine for 24 hours.

4 Peel the marrow, remove the seeds and cut into small squares, sprinkle and salt, and let it stand for 12 hours.

5 Drain the vegetables, pack them into jars, and cover with cold spiced vinegar.

6 Cover the jars and allow the pickle to mature for at least a month before use.

79 Gribiche sauce

	Makes 500 g
Sieved hard boiled eggs	2
Vegetable oil	325 ml
French mustard	1 tsp
White wine vinegar	100 ml
Chopped capers	30 g
Chopped gherkins	30 g
Chopped parsley	½ tsp
Chopped chives	½ tsp
Chopped basil	½ tsp
Seasoning	

This is an emulsified sauce. The mustard is a natural emulsifying agent.

1 Place the sieved egg yolks in a basin and add the mustard and vinegar.

2 Whisk together with a balloon whisk.

3 Slowly add the oil, whisking continuously.

4 When the emulsion is formed, add the remainder of the ingredients and season.

Note

Serve with steamed fish, fried fish, cold meats, chicken and gammon.

80 Butter sauce (*beurre blanc*)

	4 portions	10 portions
Water	125 ml	300 ml
Wine vinegar	125 ml	300 ml
Shallot, finely chopped	50 g	125 g
Unsalted butter	200 g	500 g
Lemon juice	1 tsp	2 ½ tsp
Salt and pepper		

1 Reduce the water, vinegar and shallots in a thick-bottomed pan to approximately 2 tablespoons.

2 Allow to cool slightly.

3 Gradually whisk in the butter in small amounts, whisking continually until the mixture becomes creamy.

4 Whisk in the lemon juice, season lightly and keep warm in a bain marie.

Variation

The sauce may be strained if desired. It can be varied by adding, for example, freshly shredded sorrel or spinach, or blanched fine julienne of lemon or lime. It is suitable for serving with fish dishes.

Energy	Cals	Fat	Sat fat	Carb	Sugar	Protein	Fibre	Sodium
1568 kJ	381 kcal	41.1 g	26 g	0.9 g	0.9 g	0.6 g	0.2 g	0.355 g

81 Melted butter (*beurre fondu*)

	4 portions	10 portions
Butter	200 g	500 g
Water or white wine	2 tbsp	5 tbsp

Method 1: boil the butter and water together gently until combined, then pass through a fine strainer.

Method 2: melt the butter in the water and carefully strain off the fat, leaving the water and sediment in the pan.

Note

Usually served with poached fish and certain vegetables, for example, blue trout, salmon; asparagus, sea kale.

Energy	Cals	Fat	Sat fat	Carb	Sugar	Protein	Fibre
388 kJ	94 kcal	10.3 g	6.5 g	0.1 g	0.1 g	0.1 g	0.0 g

82 Compound butter

Compound butters are made by mixing the flavouring ingredients into softened butter, which can then be shaped into a roll 2 cm in diameter, placed in wet greaseproof paper or foil, hardened in a refrigerator and cut into slices when required.

Herb butter

Parsley butter: chopped parsley and lemon juice.
Herb butter: mixed herbs (chives, tarragon, fennel, dill) and lemon juice.
Chive butter: chopped chives and lemon juice.
Garlic butter: garlic juice and chopped parsley or herbs.
Anchovy butter: few drops anchovy essence.
Shrimp butter: finely chopped or pounded shrimps.
Garlic: mashed to a paste.
Mustard: continental-type mustard.
Liver pâté: mashed to a paste.

Note

Compound butters are served with grilled and some fried fish, and with grilled meats.

83 Herb oil

	Makes 200 ml
Picked flat leaf parsley	25 g
Chives	10 g
Picked basil leaves	10 g
Picked spinach	100 g
Corn oil	250 ml

1 Blanch all the herbs and spinach for 1 ½ minutes.
2 Drain well, place with the oil in a liquidiser and blitz for 2 ½ minutes. Pass and decant when rested.

Note

Uses include salads, salmon mi cuit and other fish dishes.

84 Lemon oil

	Makes 250 ml
Lemons, rind (with no pith – the whitish layer between skin and fruit)	3
Lemongrass stick, cut lengthways and chopped into 2 cm strips	1
Grapeseed oil	250 ml
Olive oil	2 tbsp

1 Place all the ingredients into a food processor and pulse the mix until the lemon peel and lemongrass are approximately 3 mm thick.

2 Allow to stand for 2 days. Decant and store in the fridge until ready for use (or freeze for longer if you wish).

85 Mint oil

	Makes 150 ml
Mint	100 g
Oil	150 ml
Salt	3 tbsp

1 Blanch the mint for 30 seconds.

2 Refresh and squeeze the water out.

3 Place in a blender and slowly add the oil.

4 Allow to settle overnight and decant into bottles.

Note

Uses include lamb dishes, salads and fish dishes.

86 Vanilla oil

	Makes 200 ml
Vegetable oil	200 ml
Vanilla pods, whole	6
Vanilla extract	50 ml

1 Warm the oil to around 60 °C; add the vanilla in its various forms and infuse, scraping all the seeds into the oil.

2 Store in a plastic bottle.

Note

Uses include salads, salmon mi cuit and other fish dishes.

87 Basil oil

	Makes 200 ml
Fresh basil	25 g
Oil	200 ml
Salt, to taste	
Mill pepper	

1 Blanch and refresh the basil; purée with the oil.

2 Allow to settle overnight and decant.

3 Store in bottles with a sprig of blanched basil.

Variation

Basil extract can be used in place of fresh basil; 50 g of grated Parmesan or gorgonzola cheese may also be added to the basil oil.

88 Walnut oil

	Makes 500 ml
Olive or walnut oil	500 ml
Walnuts, finely crushed	75 g
Parmesan cheese	75 g
Salt, to taste	50 ml
Mill pepper	

1 Mix all the ingredients together and bottle until required.

89 Parsley oil

	Makes 200 ml
Picked flat leaf parsley	75 g
Picked spinach	50 g
Corn oil	250 ml

1 Blanch the parsley and spinach for 1 ½ minutes, drain well and place with the oil in a liquidiser.

2 Liquidise for 2 ½ minutes, place in the fridge and allow the sediment to settle overnight.

3 The next day, decant when rested and use.

Note

Uses include fish and meat dishes.

90 Roasted pepper oil

Infusing the ingredients

	Makes 500 ml
Virgin olive oil	500 ml
Mirepoix of vegetables	200 g
Red pepper (cleaned and roasted)	2
Yellow pepper (cleaned and roasted)	2
Green pepper (cleaned and roasted)	2
Bay leaves	2
Black peppercorns	8
Garlic cloves, roasted	2
Sea salt	½ tsp
Olive oil	1 tsp
White wine vinegar	1 tsp

1 Heat 1 teaspoon of olive oil in a pan.

2 Sweat the mirepoix and one of each of the peppers until golden brown.

3 Add 1 bay leaf, the black peppercorns, one clove of garlic and the sea salt, and cook for a further 3–4 minutes.

4 Add half the olive oil and bring to simmering point.

5 Take off the heat and allow to cool.

6 When completely cool, pass through a chinois into a clean Kilner jar.

7 Add the white wine vinegar and the remaining olive oil, roasted garlic, roasted peppers and remaining bay leaf.

8 For full flavour, leave for at least one month before use. To use, strain the oil, discarding the ingredients.

Recipe supplied by Mark McCann.

7 Prepare and cook fruit and vegetables

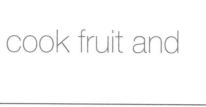

This chapter will help you to:

1 prepare and cook fruits and vegetables:
- using equipment correctly to peel, wash and trim fruits and vegetables
- cooking, assembling, holding and serving fruit and vegetable dishes in a safe and hygienic way
- storing prepared vegetables before or after cooking, if appropriate.

2 understand how to:
- identify commonly used fruits and vegetables, their classifications and seasons
- identify the quality points of fruits and vegetables
- identify correct methods for storing, preparing, cooking, preserving and holding fruits and vegetables for service
- identify additions, coatings, preparations, cooking liquids, sauces, finishes and garnishes.

Recipes included in this chapter

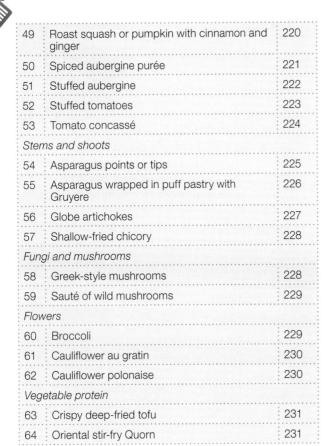

Introduction

Fresh vegetables and fruits are important foods, both from an economic and nutritional point of view. On average, each person consumes 125–150 kg per year of fruit and vegetables.

Buying fruits and vegetables is difficult because the products are highly perishable and will lose quality quickly if not properly stored and handled. Availability of fruits and vegetables also varies as a result of seasonal fluctuations and supply and demand. Automation in harvesting and packaging speeds up the handling process; this along with use of preservation methods helps to retain quality.

Fruit and vegetables are an excellent source of antioxidants, which can lower the risk of heart disease, cancer and diabetes-related damage, and even slow down the body's natural ageing process.

Video: vegetable quality and buying points http://bit.ly/17qTnOH

Vegetables

Vegetable is a culinary term that generally refers to the edible part of a plant. All parts of herbaceous plants (plants that have leaves and stems that die down at the end of the growing season) eaten as food by humans are normally considered to be vegetables. Although mushrooms actually belong to the biological family of fungi, they are also commonly considered to be vegetables.

In general, vegetables are thought of as being savoury, rather than sweet, although there are many exceptions (e.g. parsnips, sweet potatoes, pumpkin). Some vegetables are scientifically classed as fruits (e.g. tomatoes and avocados), but are commonly used as vegetables because they are not sweet.

Vegetables are eaten in a variety of ways – as part of main meals (served with poultry, meat or fish), as an ingredient and as snacks.

The nutritional content of different types of vegetables varies considerably. With the exception of pulses, vegetables do not contain much protein or fat. They contain water-soluble vitamins like vitamin B and vitamin C, fat-soluble vitamins including vitamin A and vitamin D, as well as carbohydrates and minerals. Root vegetables contain starch or sugar for energy, a small but valuable amount of protein, some mineral salts and vitamins. They are also useful sources of cellulose (fibre) and water. Green vegetables are rich in mineral salts and vitamins, particularly vitamin C and carotene. The greener the leaf, the larger the quantity of vitamins it contains. The chief mineral salts are calcium and iron.

Fresh vegetables are an important part of our diet, so it is essential to pay attention to quality, purchasing, storage and efficient preparation and cooking if their nutritional content is to be conserved.

Take it further

The EU has a quality grading system for vegetables:
- **Extra class:** produce of the highest quality
- **Class 1:** produce of good quality
- **Class 2:** produce of reasonably good quality
- **Class 3:** produce of low market quality.

Classifications, uses, quality points and cooking methods for commonly used vegetables

Vegetables can include tubers (potatoes), leaves and brassicas (lettuce), stems (asparagus), roots (carrots), flowers (broccoli), bulbs (garlic), pods and seeds (peas and beans) and botanical fruits such as cucumbers, squash, pumpkins and capsicums.

Other vegetable classifications include vegetable fruits, fungi and mushrooms, vegetable protein, nuts and seaweed/sea vegetables.

Roots

A root is the part of the plant growing down into the soil to support the plant and take up water and nutrients.

Quality points for root vegetables will vary depending on type, but in general root vegetables must be clean and free from soil; firm and not soft or spongy; sound and free from blemishes; and of an even size and shape.

Tubers

A tuber is an underground stem, used for storing food also able to produce new plants.

Potato varieties

All potatoes should be sold by name (for example, King Edward, Désirée, Maris Piper); this is important as the caterer needs to know which varieties are best suited for specific cooking purposes.

Cooked potatoes may have different textures, depending on whether they are waxy or floury varieties. This is due to changes that happen to the potato cells during cooking. Waxy potatoes are translucent and may feel moist and pasty. Floury potatoes are brighter, look grainier and feel drier. These differences affect the performance of the potato when cooked in different ways (e.g. boiling versus roasting).

- **Floury potatoes** are especially popular in the UK. They are suitable for baking, mashing and chipping as they have a soft, dry texture when cooked. They are not suitable for boiling, however, because they tend to disintegrate. Popular varieties of floury potato include King Edward and Maris Piper.
- **Waxy potatoes** are more solid than floury potatoes and hold their shape when boiled, but do not mash well. They are particularly suitable for baked and layered potato dishes such as boulangère potatoes. Popular varieties include Cara and Charlotte.

POTATO VARIETIES
GROWING IN GREAT BRITAIN

General

Baking

CARA
Firm moist texture. Short oval to round shape, white skin with pink eyes, cream flesh.
③

MARFONA
Firm moist texture. Short oval shape, light yellow skin, light yellow flesh.
③

ESTIMA
Firm moist texture. Oval shape, light yellow skin, light yellow flesh.
④

MARIS PIPER
Pleasant floury texture Short oval shape, cream skin, cream flesh.
⑤

KING EDWARD
Soft floury texture. Oval to long oval shape, white skin with pink colouration, cream flesh.
⑥

DESIREE
Firm slightly waxy texture. Oval shape, red skin, light yellow flesh.
⑤

Chipping

MARIS PIPER
Pleasant floury texture. Short oval shape, cream skin, cream flesh.
⑤

KING EDWARD
Soft floury texture. Oval to long oval shape, white skin with pink colouration, cream flesh.
⑥

SANTE
Dry firm texture. Short oval shape, light yellow skin, light yellow flesh.
⑥

Boiling/Mashing

SAXON
Firm moist texture. Short oval shape, white skin cream flesh.
④

NADINE
Firm waxy texture. Oval shape, cream skin, cream flesh.
②

ESTIMA
Firm moist texture. Oval shape, light yellow skin, light yellow flesh.
④

Salads

NICOLA
Firm cooked texture. Long oval shape, yellow skin, light yellow flesh.
④

CHARLOTTE
Firm waxy texture. Oval to long oval shape, light yellow skin, yellow flesh.
④

MARIS PEER
Firm cooked texture. Short oval shape, white skin, cream flesh.
⑤

waxy texture							floury texture	
①	②	③	④	⑤	⑥	⑦	⑧	⑨

Waxy potatoes are firmer and hold their shape. Floury potatoes are softer and break up more easily.

Please note these potato varieties are suggestions and there are many more available. Ask your greengrocer, farm shop or supermarket for more advice or log onto our website www.potato.org.uk

For further information, please contact: British Potato Council, 4300 Nash Court, John Smith Drive, Oxford Business Park South, Oxford, OX4 2RT. Tel: 01865 714455 Fax: 01865 782200

Roasting

WILJA
Moderately firm waxy texture. Long oval shape, yellow skin, light yellow flesh.
④

ROMANO
Soft, dry texture. Short oval shape, red skin, cream flesh.
⑤

KING EDWARD
Soft floury texture. Oval to long oval shape, white skin with pink colouration, cream flesh.
⑥

▲ Varieties of potato (Source: British Potato Council)

Ready prepared potatoes

Potatoes can be bought in many convenience forms: peeled, turned, cut into various shapes for frying, scooped into balls (Parisienne) or an olive shape. Chips are available fresh, frozen, chilled or vacuum packed. Frozen potatoes are available as croquettes, hash browns, sauté and roast. Mashed potato powder is also available. The advantages of using ready prepared potatoes are that they are labour saving and reduce wastage. However, they cost more than fresh potatoes and may not taste as good.

Professional tip

Potato yields:
- 0.5 kg of old potatoes will yield approximately 3 portions.
- 0.5 kg of new potatoes will yield approximately 4 portions.
- 1.5 kg of old potatoes will yield approximately 10 portions.
- 1.25 kg of new potatoes will yield approximately 10 portions.

Table 6.1 Root vegetables

Vegetable	Description	Uses	Quality points	Cooking methods
Beetroot	Two main types: round and long	Soups, salads and as a vegetable. The tops of the beetroot can be eaten like spring greens	Good colour without blemishes (when raw)	Steam, boil, roast, purée
Carrot	Grown in numerous varieties and sizes	Soups, sauces, stocks, stews, salads and as a vegetable	Firm, without blemishes or any discolouration	Boil, steam, roast
Celeriac	Large, light brown celery-flavoured root	Soups, salads and as a vegetable	Firm, small to medium bulbs without any discoloration or blemishes	Boil, steam, roast
Horseradish	Long, light brown, narrow root	Grated and used for horseradish sauce. Becoming more widely used in culinary work, in creams, foams and chutneys	Fresh, firm roots without blemishes and discolouration	Sauces, steaming
Mooli	Long, white, thick member of radish family	Soups, salads, or as a vegetable	Firm roots without any discolouration or blemishes	Boil, steam, braise
Parsnip	Long, white root, tapering to a point. It has a unique nut-like flavour	Soups added to casseroles and as a vegetable (roasted, puréed etc.)	Roots firm to touch, without any blemishes; creamy white in colour	Boil, steam, roast
Radish	Small summer variety; round or oval	Served with dips, in salads or as a vegetable in white or cheese sauce	Good red colour, firm to touch	Salads, stir-fry
Salsify and scorzonera (black salsify)	Also called oyster plant because of similarity of taste; long, narrow, white, or black-skinned root (scorzonera), slightly astringent in flavour	Soups, salads and as a vegetable	Firm to touch; good brownish colour	Braise, boil
Swede	Large root with yellow flesh	As a vegetable mashed or parboiled and roasted; may be added to stews	Unblemished without discoloration	Boil, steam, roast
Turnip	Two main varieties: long and round	Soups, stews and as a vegetable	Firm without blemishes	Boil, steam, roast

Table 6.2 Tubers

Vegetable	Description	Uses	Quality points	Cooking methods
Artichokes, Jerusalem	Potato-like tuber with a bittersweet flavour	Soups, salads and as a vegetable	Firm without discolouration	Roast, boil, steam
Potatoes	Several named varieties of potato are grown and these will be available according to the season. The various varieties fall into four categories: floury, firm, waxy, or salad. The different varieties have differing characteristics (see below)	Varies depending on variety	Firm, smooth, not excessively wrinkled, withered or cracked. Do not to buy those with a lot of sprouts or green areas	Some varieties are more suitable for certain methods of cooking than others (see below).
Sweet potatoes	Long tubers with purple or sand coloured skins and orange or cream flesh; flavour is sweet and aromatic	As a vegetable (fried, puréed, creamed, candied) or made into a sweet pudding	Firm with no discolouration	Boil, steam, roast, purée
Yams	Similar to sweet potatoes; usually cylindrical, often knobbly in shape; popular in Caribbean cookery	As for sweet potatoes	Large and firm	Boil, steam, roast, purée

Table 6.3 Potato varieties and recommended cooking methods

Potato variety	Cooking methods
Cara	Boil, bake, chip, wedge
Charlotte	Boil, salad use
Desiree	Boil, roast, bake, chip, mash, wedge
Golden Wonder	Boil, roast, crisps
King Edward	Boil, bake, roast, mash, chip
Maris Piper	Boil, roast, bake, chip
Pink Fir Apple	Boiled, salad use
Premiere	Boil
Record	Crisps
Romano	Boil, bake, roast, mash
Saxon	Boil, bake, chip
Wilja	Boil, bake, chip, mash

Bulbs

Bulbs are an organ in some plants which consist of an underground axis with many thick overlapping leaves.

Table 6.4 Bulbs

Vegetable	Description	Uses	Quality points	Cooking methods
Fennel	The bulb is the swollen leaf base and has a pronounced flavour	Raw in salads and cooked	Firm bulbs without any discolouration	Boil, steam, braise, stir fry, roast, and grill
Garlic	An onion-like bulb with a papery skin, inside of which are small individually wrapped cloves. Garlic has a pungent distinctive flavour and should be used sparingly	Used extensively in many forms of cookery; may be roasted and served as a garnish		Roast, sauté
Leeks	Summer leeks have long white stems, bright green leaves and a milder flavour than winter leeks, which have a stockier stem and a stronger flavour	Stocks, soups, sauces, stews, hors d'oeuvre and as a vegetable	Fresh, no signs of woodiness (lignin)	Boil, steam, braise, stir fry
Onions	There are numerous varieties with different coloured skins and varying strengths	After salt, the onion is probably the most frequently used flavouring in cookery, can be used in almost every type of food except sweet dishes	Firm to touch	Boil, steam, roast, purée, grill
Shallot	Has a similar but more refined flavour than the onion and is therefore more often used in a wide range of culinary work	May be roasted, used with grated vegetables and stir fries	Firm to the touch	Sauté, braise
Spring onions	Slim and tiny, like miniature leeks. Ramp looks like a spring onion but is stronger	Soups, salads and Chinese and Japanese cookery	Tops must be a bright green colour, bulbs firm to touch	Stir fry; with grilled and roasted vegetables

Leaves

A leaf is part of the plant that lives off water and makes food by photosynthesis.

Table 6.5 Leaves

Vegetable	Description	Uses	Quality points
Chicory	A lettuce with course, crisp leaves and a sharp, bitter taste in the outside leaves, inner leave are milder	Braise or roast	A good white yellowish colour
Chinese leaves	Long white, densely packed leaves with a mild flavour, resembling celery	Makes a good substitute for lettuce; boiled, braised or stir fried as a vegetable	Purchase fresh firm leaves without blemishes
Cress	There are 15 varieties of cress with different flavours	Suitable for a large range of foods	Leaves must be firm and bright in colour
Lettuce	Many varieties including cabbage, cos, little gem, iceberg, oak leaf, Webb's	Chiefly for salads, or used as a wrapping for other foods, e.g. fish fillets	Leaves must be bright in colour and firm
Nettles	Once cooked, the sting disappears	Soups	Should be picked young
Rocket	A type of cress with larger leaves and a peppery taste	Salads, garnishes	Leaves must be firm, not withered or bruised
Sorrel	Bright green sour leaves, which can be overpowering if used on their own	Salad and soups	Best when tender and young. Leaves should be bright green, not withered or bruised
Spinach	Tender, dark green leaves with a mild musky flavour	Soups, garnishing egg and fish dishes, as a vegetable and raw in salads. May also be used in stir fries	Leaves must be bright green, not withered or bruised
Swiss chard	Large, ribbed, slightly curly leaves with a flavour similar to but milder than spinach	As for spinach. May also be used in stir fries	Leaves must be bright green, not withered or bruised
Vine leaves	All leaves from grape vines can be eaten when young	To wrap food such as meat or fish before further cooking	Must be a good smooth dark green colour
Watercress	Long stems with round, dark, tender green leaves and a pungent peppery flavour	Soups, salads, and for garnishing roasts and grills of meat and poultry.	Leaves must be bright green colour, not withered or bruised

Flowers

A flower is the reproductive part of the plant. It is often brightly coloured to attract insects.

Table 6.6 Flowers

Vegetable	Description	Uses	Quality points	Cooking method
Broccoli	Various types including calabrese, white, green, purple sprouting, delicate vegetable with a gentle flavour	Soups, salads, stir fry dishes and cooked and served in many ways as a vegetable	Flower must be bright in colour, green without any discolouration	Steam or boil
Cauliflower	Heads of creamy white florets with a distinctive flavour	Soup, and cooked and served in various ways as a vegetable	Flowers must be firm without any discolouration	Various. May also be puréed

Brassicas

Brassicas are plants that are part of the mustard family.

Table 6.7 Brassicas

Vegetable	Description	Uses	Quality points	Cooking method
Brussels sprouts	Small green buds growing on thick stems	Can be used for soup but are mainly used as a vegetable, and can be cooked and served in a variety of ways	Small sprouts are better, fresh clean flavour not overpowering. Bright green colour, no discoloration, blemishes or bruising	Boil, steam, shred and shallow fry
Cabbage	Three main types including green, white and red, many varieties of green cabbage available at different seasons of the year; early green cabbage is deep green and loosely formed; later in the season they firm up, with a solid heart; Savoy is considered the best of the winter green cabbage	Green and red as a vegetable; white cabbage is used for coleslaw	Good colour, no discolouration or withering	Boiled, braised or stir fried
Kale and curly kale	Thick green leaves. The curly variety is the most popular	Stir fries	Leaves must be firm, without any discoloration or withering	Boiled, steamed or braised
Pak choi	Chinese cabbage with many varieties	Stir fries	Leaves must be crisp and firm, good colour without any withering	Boiled, steamed or braised

Pods and seeds

A pod is a fruit or seed case that usually splits along two seams to release its seeds when mature. A seed is the reproductive part of flowering plants.

Table 6.8 Pods and seeds

Vegetable	Description	Uses	Quality points	Cooking method
Broad beans	Pale green, oval-shaped beans contained in a thick fleshy pod	Young broad beans can be removed from the pods, cooked in their shells and served as a vegetable in various ways; old broad beans will toughen when removed from the pods and will have to be shelled before being served. Used as a vegetable, garnish, stir fries and stews	Must be firm to touch, good colour	Boil, steam
Butter or lima beans	Butter beans are white, large, and flattish and oval shaped, lima beans are smaller	As a vegetable or salad, stew or casserole ingredient	Good colour, firm	Boil, steam
Mangetout	Also called snow peas or sugar peas; flat pea pod with immature seeds that, after topping, tailing and stringing, may be eaten in their entirety	As a vegetable, in salads and for stir fry dishes	Must be bright green in colour, firm without any discoloration	Boil, steam, shallow fry, stir fry
Okra	Curved and pointed seed pods with a flavour similar to aubergines	Cooked as a vegetable or in creole type stews	Must be green in colour and firm	Boil, steam, shallow fry or braise
Peas	Garden peas are normal size, petit pois are a dwarf variety, marrowfat peas are dried	Popular as a vegetable. Peas are also used for soups, salads, stews and stir fry dishes	Must be a good green colour	Usually boiled
Runner beans	Popular vegetable that must be used when young		Bright green colour and a pliable velvety feel; if coarse, wilted or older beans are used they will be stringy and tough. Must be bright green colour and firm	Boil, steam, also used in stir fries
Sweetcorn	Also known as maize or Sudan corn; available 'on the cob', fresh or frozen or in kernels, canned or frozen	A versatile commodity and used as a first course, in soups, salads, casseroles and as a vegetable	Bright yellow in colour, no discoloration	Boil, steam, also used in stir fries

Stems and shoots

A stem is the part of the plant usually above the ground which bears the buds, leaves, flowers and fruit. It can be underground. A shoot is a young stem.

Table 6.9 Stems and shoots

Vegetable	Description	Uses	Quality points	Cooking method
Asparagus	Three main types are white, with creamy white stems and a mild flavour; French, with violet or bluish tips and a stronger more astringent flavour, and green, with what is considered a delicious aromatic flavour	Used on every course of the menu, except the sweet course	Firm, crisp with no discoloration	Boil, steam or stir fry
Bean sprouts	Slender young sprouts of the germinating soya or mung bean	As a vegetable accompaniment, in stir fry dishes and salads	Crisp	Stir fry, salads
Cardoon	Longish plant with root and fleshy ribbed stalks, white to light green in colour	Soups, stocks, sauces, cooked as a vegetable and raw in salads and dips	Firm to touch without discoloration	Boil, steam or braise
Celery	Long-stemmed bundles of fleshy, ribbed stalks, white to light green in colour	Soups, stocks, sauces, cooked as a vegetable and raw in salads and dips	Crisp and firm	Boil, steam or braise
Chicory	Also known as Belgian endive; conical heads of crisp white, faintly bitter leaves	Cooked as a vegetable and raw in salads and dips	No discoloration or withered leaves	Steam or braise
Globe artichokes	Resemble fat pine cones with overlapping fleshy, green, inedible leaves, all connected to an edible fleshy base or bottom	Used as a first course, hot or cold, stuffed, as a vegetable and in casseroles. The fronds may be used in casseroles, stews and as a garnish	Good bright green colour; leaves must be firm and crisp	Boil, baked, fry, or in casseroles
Kohlrabi	Stem that swells to turnip shape above the ground, those about the size of a large egg are best for cookery purposes (other than soup or purées)	May be cooked as a vegetable, stuffed and baked and added to stews and casseroles	Firm to touch with no discoloration	Boil, steam, braise
Palm hearts	The buds of cabbage palm trees. Firm ivory colour	Salads, pasta dishes, stews, casseroles	Good colour, tightly closed	Boil, steam, braise, salads

Vegetable	Description	Uses	Quality points	Cooking method
Samphire	The two types are marsh samphire, which grows in estuaries and salt marshes, and white rock samphire (sometimes called sea fennel), which grows on rocky shores. Marsh samphire is also known as glass wort and sometimes sea asparagus	As a garnish and in stir fries	Good colour, firm to touch	Boil or steam
Water chestnuts	Common name for a number of aquatic herbs and their nut-like fruit; best known type is the Chinese water chestnut, sometimes known as the Chinese sedge	Popular in Chinese and Thai dishes	Firm, without discoloration	Boil, steam and stir fry

Vegetable fruits

These are fruits of plants that are used as a vegetable.

Table 6.10 Vegetable fruits

Vegetable	Description	Uses	Quality points	Cooking method
Aubergine	Firm, elongated, varying in size with smooth shiny skins, ranging in colour from purple red to purple black; inner flesh is white with tiny soft seeds, almost without flavour, it requires other seasonings, e.g. garlic, lemon juice, herbs, to enhance its taste. Varieties include baby, Japanese, white, striped, Thai	Popular sliced in layered dishes such as moussaka. Also in pastes and dips	No discoloration or blemishes	Sliced and fried or baked, steamed or stuffed
Avocado	Fruit that is mainly used as a vegetable because of its bland, mild, nutty flavour. Two main types are the summer variety, which is green when unripe and purple black when ripe, with golden yellow flesh, and the winter variety, which is more pear-shaped with smooth green skin and pale green to yellow flesh	Eaten as first courses and used in soups, salads, dips and as garnishes to other dishes, hot and cold	Purchase when slightly unripe, without bruises	Salads
Courgettes	Baby marrow, light to dark green in colour, with a delicate flavour becoming stronger when cooked with other ingredients, e.g. herbs, garlic, spices	As a vegetable or ingredient in other dishes. Grated in salads	Smooth shiny skins, firm	Boil, steam, fry, bake, stuff and stir fry
Cucumber	A long, smooth-skinned fruiting vegetable, ridged and dark green in colour	Salads, soups, sandwiches, garnishes and as a vegetable. May also be, puréed with fromage frais, yoghurt or cream and used as a dip	Green, firm and crisp	Braise, purée

Vegetable	Description	Uses	Quality points	Cooking method
Marrow	Long, oval-shaped edible gourds with ridged green skins and a bland flavour		No discoloration or bruising	As for courgettes
Pepper	Available in three colours. Green peppers are unripened and they turn yellow to orange and then red (they must remain on the plant to do this)	Used raw and cooked in salads, vegetable dishes, stuffed and baked, casseroles and stir-fry dishes	Bright colour, firm and crisp	Sauté, braise, stir fry
Pumpkin	Vary in size and can weigh up to 50 kg; associated with Halloween as a decoration	Soups or pumpkin pie	Firm to touch, no discoloration	Steam, boil, braise
Squash	Many varieties, e.g., acorn, butternut, summer crookneck, delicate, hubbond, kuboche, onion	Soups, salads, vegetable dishes	Flesh firm and glowing. All types must have a good colour without bruising or discoloration.	Boil, bake, steam or purée
Tomatoes	Along with onions, probably the most frequently used 'vegetable' in cookery; several varieties, including cherry, yellow, globe, large ridged (beef) and plum. Vine-ripened tomatoes are allowed to ripen on the vine before being picked. Commercial tomatoes are picked when green, so that they are easier to handle. They don't bruise or break; en route to the suppliers they will turn red	Soups, sauces stews, salads, sandwiches and as a vegetable. Sundried for use when fresh tomatoes lack flavour	Firm, even colour, no bruising or discoloration	Grill, roast, fry, salads

Mushrooms and fungi

All mushrooms, both wild and cultivated, have a great many uses in cookery, in soups, stocks, salads, vegetables, savouries and garnishes. Wild mushrooms are also available in dried form. All mushrooms must be firm to touch, with no presence of slime or discolouration or unpleasant smell. They should have a good colour.

- **Mushrooms** – field mushrooms are found in meadows from late summer to autumn; they have a creamy white cap and stalk and a strong earthy flavour. Used in a variety of dishes; can be grilled or shallow fried.
- **Cultivated mushrooms** –available in three types: button (small, succulent, weak in flavour), cap and open or flat mushrooms. Used in a variety of dishes; can be grilled or shallow fried.
- **Ceps** – wild mushrooms with short, stout stalks with slightly raised veins and tubes underneath the cap in which the brown spores are produced. Grill or shallow fry.
- **Chanterelles or girolles** – wild, funnel-shaped, yellow-capped mushrooms with a slightly ribbed stalk that runs up under the edge of the cap. Grill or shallow fry.
- **Horns of plenty** – trumpet-shaped, shaggy, almost black wild mushrooms. Grill or shallow fry.
- **Morels** – delicate, wild mushrooms varying in colour from pale beige to dark brown–black with a flavour that suggests meat. Grill, shallow fry, often used as a garnish.

- **Oyster** – creamy gills and firm flesh; delicate with shorter storage life than regular mushrooms. Grill or shallow fry.
- **Shiitake** – solid texture with a strong, slightly meaty flavour. Grill or shallow fry.
- **Truffles** – black (French) and white (Italian) are rare, expensive but highly esteemed for the unique flavour they can give to so many dishes. Black truffles from France are sold fresh, canned or bottles; white truffles from Italy are never cooked, but grated or finely sliced over certain foods (e.g. pasta, risotto).

▲ Clockwise from top left: girolles, chestnut mushrooms, hedgehog mushrooms, large cup (Portobello) mushroom, button mushrooms, brown chanterelles and shiitake mushrooms

Vegetable protein

- **Soya products** – these are high in protein and produced from leguminous seeds. They contain important essential amino acids that cannot be made in the body. The soya bean is an important world product from which many products are made. Soya flour is used to boost the protein in a variety of dishes.
- **Tofu** – this is produced from soya beans. The beans are boiled, puréed and pressed through a sieve to produce soya milk. The milk is then processed in a similar way to soft cheese. Always keep tofu in a refrigerator and follow the instructions on the packet. Tofu is also known as bean curd. Silken tofu is a Japanese-style tofu with a softer consistency than regular tofu. It is used in soups, sauces and desserts, and is seen as a healthier option to cream.
- **Tempeh** – this is a fermented soya bean product that is cooked and pressed. It is similar to tofu, but has a firmer texture and is purchased chilled.

- **Seitan** – this is produced from wheat; it has a high gluten content and is used as a vegetarian alternative.
- **Textured vegetable protein (TVP) –** this is a meat substitute manufactured from protein derived from wheat, oats, cottonseed, soybeans and other sources. The main source of TVP is the soybean, because of its high protein content. TVP is used mainly as a meat extender, to make meat go further. The TVP content can vary from 10 to 60 per cent replacement of fresh meat. Some caterers on very tight budgets use it, but it is mainly used in food manufacturing. By partially replacing the meat in certain dishes – such as casseroles, stews, pies, pasties, sausage rolls, hamburgers, meat loaf and paté – it is possible to reduce costs, meet nutritional targets and serve food that looks acceptable.

▲ Vegetable proteins

Mycoprotein

Mycoprotein is a meat substitute produced from a plant that is a distant relative of the mushroom. It contains protein and fibre, and is the result of a fermentation process similar to the way yoghurt is made. It may be used as an alternative to chicken or beef or in vegetarian dishes.

Quorn is a mycoprotein. It is a low-fat food that can be used in a variety of dishes (e.g. oriental stir-fry). Quorn does not shrink during preparation and cooking. Quorn mince or pieces can be substituted for chicken or minced meats. Its mild savoury flavour means that it complements the herbs and spices in a recipe and it is able to absorb flavour. Frozen Quorn may be cooked straight from the freezer, or may be defrosted overnight in the refrigerator. Once thawed, it must be stored in the refrigerator and used within 24 hours.

Seaweed/sea vegetables

Seaweed is commonly used as a food in Japan, but less so in Europe and America. Some examples of edible seaweed include:

- **Nori** or **purple laver** – a purplish–black seaweed often seen wrapped round sushi rice in sushi. Nori grows as a very thin, flat reddish–black seaweed and is found in most temperate zones around the world.
- **Honori** or **green laver** – occurs naturally in the bays and gulfs of southern areas of Japan.
- **Kombu** or **huidai** –the Japanese name for the dried seaweed that is derived from a mixture of luminaria species.
- **Wakame, quandai-cai** – this is a brown seaweed that occurs on rocky shores and bays in the temperate zones of Japan, the Republic of Korea and China. Wakame has a high dietary fibre content, higher than nori or kombu.
- **Hiziki (hizikia fusiforme)** – a brown seaweed collected from the wild in Japan.
- **Mozuku** – a brown seaweed that is harvested from natural populations in the more tropical climate of the southern islands of Japan.
- **Dulse** – a red algae with leathery fronds (leaves). It is also found in Eastern Canada and is especially abundant around Grand Manan Island. In Nova Scotia and Maine, dried dulse is often served as a salty cocktail snack.
- **Irish moss** or **carrageenan** – used in Irish foods and as a setting agent.
- **Sea moss (ogo)** – collected and sold as a salad vegetable in Hawaii.
- **Wakame** – a thin, stringy seaweed, deep green in colour and common in Japan and other Asian countries. It is used in miso soup.
- **Arame** – a seaweed that comes in small, flaky strips. It is used in soups, salads and stir fries. It goes well with sushi and tofu.

Nuts

There are many varieties of nuts available, including:
- almonds
- Brazil nuts
- cashew nuts
- coconuts
- hazelnuts
- macadamia nuts
- peanuts
- pecans
- pine nuts
- pistachios
- sweet chestnuts
- walnuts.

Nuts in the shell have longer storage potential than shelled nuts. Broken pieces are more perishable than halves or whole kernels. A rancid nut has a flat, metallic taste and a lingering aftertaste. Because of their high fat content, nuts can easily absorb odours from external sources and therefore should not be stored around other foods that have strong odours, unless they are stored in tightly sealed containers.

Seasons for commonly used vegetables

With the advancement and development of transportation and refrigeration, vegetables and fruit can be purchased from all over the world. In many cases seasons no longer exist: for example, we can enjoy strawberries all year round.

However, knowing where fruit and vegetables come from (**provenance**) has become increasingly important; today's consumer is concerned about the environment, carbon omissions and restricting the amount of food travelling around the world using aircraft cargo. Many consumers now prefer to purchase from local suppliers and therefore knowledge of when fruits and vegetables are in season is important. Table 6.11 shows the UK seasons for commonly used vegetables.

Key term

Provenance: where food comes from, for example, where it is grown, reared, produced or finished.

Table 6.11 UK seasons for commonly used vegetables

	Spring (March, April, May)	Summer (June, July, August)	Autumn (September, October, November)	Winter (December, January, February)
Asparagus	x			
Aubergine		x		
Beetroot		x	x	x
Broad beans		x		
Brussels sprouts				x
Cabbage				x
Carrots		x	x	
Cauliflower	x			x
Celeriac			x	x
Chicory				x
Courgettes		x		
Cucumber	x	x		
Field mushrooms			x	
Fennel		x	x	x
Fresh peas		x		
Garlic		x		
Green beans		x		
Jersey royal new potatoes	x			
Jerusalem artichoke				x
Kale			x	x
Leeks			x	x
Lettuce and salad leaves		x	x	
Marrow			x	
New potatoes		x		
Parsnips				x
Potatoes			x	x
Pumpkin			x	
Purple sprouting broccoli	x			
Radishes	x	x		
Red cabbage				x
Rocket		x	x	
Runner beans		x		
Salad onions		x		
Savoy cabbage	x			
Sorrel	x	x	x	
Spring greens	x			
Spring onion	x			

	Spring (March, April, May)	Summer (June, July, August)	Autumn (September, October, November)	Winter (December, January, February)
Squashes			x	
Swede				x
Sweetcorn			x	
Tomatoes		x	x	
Turnips				x
Watercress	x	x	x	

Storage

The fact that vegetables do not stay fresh for very long causes particular problems. Fresh vegetables are living organisms and will lose quality quickly if they are not properly stored and handled. The fresher the vegetables, the better their flavour, so ideally they should not be stored at all. However, as storage is often necessary it should be for the shortest time possible.

Many root and non-root vegetables that grow underground can be stored over winter in a root cellar or other similarly cool, dark and dry place, to prevent the growth of mould, greening and sprouting. It is important to understand the properties and weaknesses of the particular roots to be stored (i.e. what will help them to last longer and what will damage them quickly). These vegetables can last through to early spring and be almost as nutritious as when they were fresh.

Potatoes can be stored for several months without affecting their quality, but they should be stored at a constant temperature of 3 °C. If this is not possible, buying fresh potatoes regularly is best practice. There are three essential rules to bear in mind when storing potatoes: 'dry, dark and cool'. You should avoid light as this will cause sprouting and eventually the greening effect that contains mild toxins.

> **Professional tip**
>
> If you have inadvertently purchased potatoes with this green tinge, remove the green bits and the rest of the potato is then fine to use.

Health and safety

If vegetables are stored at the incorrect temperature micro-organisms may develop. If vegetables are stored in damp conditions, moulds may develop.

During storage, leafy vegetables lose moisture and vitamin C. They should be stored for as short a time as possible in a cool place in a container, such as a plastic bag or a sealed plastic container.

- Store all vegetables in a cool, dry, well-ventilated room at an even temperature of 4–8 °C, which will help to minimise spoilage. Check vegetables daily and discard any that are unsound.
- Remove root vegetables from their sacks and store in bins or racks.
- Store green vegetables on well-ventilated racks.
- Store salad vegetables in a cool place and leave in their containers.
- Store frozen vegetables at –18 °C or below.
- Check for use-by dates, damaged packaging and any signs of freezer burn.

Preservation methods

- **Canning** – certain vegetables are preserved in tins, for example, artichokes, asparagus, carrots, celery, beans, peas (fine, garden, processed), tomatoes (whole, purée), mushrooms, truffles.
- **Dehydration** – onions, carrots, potatoes and cabbage are shredded and quickly dried until they contain only 5 per cent water.
- **Drying** – the seeds of legumes (peas and beans) have their moisture content reduced to 10 per cent.
- **Pickling** – onions and red cabbage are examples of vegetables preserved in spiced vinegar.
- **Salting** – French and runner beans may be sliced and preserved in dry salt.
- **Freezing** – many vegetables, such as peas, beans, sprouts, spinach and cauliflower, are deep frozen.

- **Blanching** – this is a technique which is used to partly cook and preserve the colour of green vegetables by plunging them in boiling water and then running them under cold water. It is also used to remove skin from tomatoes. Blanching is also used to cook potato chips without colour; they can then be stored and as they are required are plunged into hot oil to make crisp.
- **Vacuum packing** – this involves placing perishable food in a plastic film package and removing the air from inside and sealing the package.

Preparing vegetables
Cuts of vegetables
The size to which vegetables are cut may vary according to their use; however, the shape does not change unless overcooked.

Step by step: Julienne (strips)

1 Cut the vegetables into 2 cm lengths (short julienne).

2 Cut the lengths into thin slices.

3 Cut the slices into thin strips.

4 Double the length gives a long julienne, used for garnishing (e.g. salads, meats, fish and poultry dishes).

Step by step: Brunoise (small dice)

1 Cut the vegetables into convenient-sized lengths.

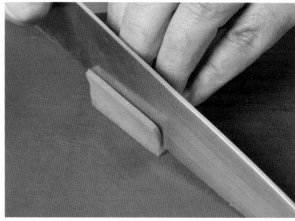

2 Cut the lengths into 2 mm slices.

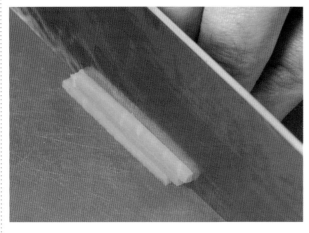

3 Cut the slices into 2 mm strips.

4 Cut the strips into 2 mm squares.

Step by step: Jardinière (batons)

1 Cut the vegetables into 1.5 cm lengths.

2 Cut the lengths into 3 mm slices.

3 Cut the slices into batons (3 × 3 × 18 mm).

Step by step: Macédoine (0.5 cm dice)

1 Cut the vegetables into convenient lengths.

2 Cut the lengths into 0.5 cm slices.

3 Cut the slices into 0.5 cm strips.

4 Cut the strips into 0.5 cm squares.

Paysanne

There are at least four accepted methods of cutting paysanne. In order to cut economically, the shape of the vegetables should dictate which method to choose. All are cut thinly. Options include:

- 1 cm sided triangles
- 1 cm sided squares
- 1 cm diameter rounds
- 1 cm diameter rough-sided rounds.

▲ Paysanne vegetables

Concassé

This means roughly chopped (e.g. skinned and deseeded tomatoes are roughly chopped for many food preparations).

▲ Tomato concassé

Additions and coatings

There are various ways of cooking vegetables with a coating. The most common is in a light batter (tempura) and deep fried. Some vegetables like cauliflower may be dipped in milk and flour and deep fried. The flour used can be white, wholemeal or gramflour. Other vegetables may be cooked coated in flour, egg and breadcrumbs and shallow or deep fried. Examples of coatings include:

- tempura batter – used with a range of vegetables, peppers, mushrooms, celery, French beans, cauliflower, onions etc.
- breadcrumbs (*pané à l'Anglais*) – used with mushrooms, potatoes, butternut squash
- milk and flour (*pané à la Française*) – used with broccoli and cauliflower.

Mushroom duxelle, which is used to stuff tomatoes, may be used to coat vegetables such as braised celery and sprinkled with breadcrumbs, toasted and served.

Breadcrumbs with additions (chopped nuts, herbs and spices) may be used to coat vegetables before they are served, or brushed with melted butter or vegetable oil and toasted and served.

Cooking vegetable dishes

Approximate times only are given in the recipes in this chapter for cooking vegetables – quality, age, freshness and size all affect the length of cooking time required. Young, freshly picked vegetables will need to be cooked for a shorter time than vegetables that have been allowed to grow older and that may have been stored after picking.

Most vegetables are cooked **al dente**. This means the vegetables are cooked until they are firm, crisp and with a bite. This retains some of the vital vitamins such as vitamin C.

Vegetables that contain high levels of starch (e.g. potatoes) need to be cooked through completely, to soften the starch.

Key term

Al dente: cooked until firm, crisp and with a bite.

Boiling and blanching

As a general rule, all root vegetables (except new potatoes) are put in cold salted water, which is then heated until boiling. Vegetables that grow above the ground are put directly into boiling salted water, so they are cooked for the minimum amount of time. Cooking them as quickly as possible helps them to keep their flavour, food value and colour.

Delicate vegetables – particularly green vegetables – must be blanched in salted boiling water and then refreshed in ice-cold water to stop the cooking process. The main reason for this is because, between the temperatures of 66 °C and 77 °C, chlorophyll (the pigment in green plants) is unstable. To retain the colour of the vegetables it is important to get through this temperature zone as quickly as possible.

Steaming and stir-frying

All vegetables cooked by boiling may also be cooked by steaming. The vegetables are prepared in exactly the same way as for boiling, then placed into steamer trays, lightly seasoned with salt and steamed under pressure. As with boiling, they should be cooked for the minimum period of time in order to conserve maximum food value and retain colour. High-speed steam cookers are ideal for this purpose and, because they cook so quickly, can be used for batch cooking (cooking in small quantities throughout the service) so that large quantities do not have to be cooked prior to service, then refreshed and reheated.

Many vegetables can be cooked from raw by stir-frying, which is a quick and nutritious method of cooking.

Professional tip

Test whether fat or oil is hot enough by dropping in a small piece of vegetable: if it starts to sizzle and fry, the fat or oil is hot enough.

Health and safety

Make sure all the vegetables are dry before placing into the hot oil. Always have a spider and basket at hand when you are deep frying in order to remove the food quickly and safety if there is a problem. Wear protective clothing (a chef's jacket with long sleeves) and make sure every chef is confident of the procedures and systems for frying and knows the fire drill.

Roasting

The vegetables are washed, peeled and cut to regular size, placed into a roasting tray with a little vegetable oil and seasoning (for example salt, pepper; sprinkled with chopped herbs, crushed garlic; spices such as all spice, cinnamon and nutmeg may also be added). The oven should be at approximately 200 °C.

Roast potatoes are cut into chunks and parboiled slowly until just cooked on the inside before draining, tossing in a liberal amount of olive oil or other vegetable oil and seasoning and roasting. They are roasted in a hot oven (220 °C) for 15 minutes. Then the temperature is turned down to 180 °C and the potatoes are basted every 5 minutes to ensure a crisp coat all over. Once cooked, serve immediately, as keeping them warm for too long will cause the inside to steam, making the outside soft and leathery.

Grilling

This is a healthy way of cooking vegetables as little or no fat is used. Some vegetables are better parboiled before grilling (for example, potatoes, carrots, fennel, yams and butternut squash). The vegetables may also be sprinkled with fresh chopped herbs or spices. Vegetables may be grilled under the salamander or on grill plates or on a barbeque.

Professional tip

When grilling, roasting or stir frying vegetables, the oil or fat chosen will add to the flavour and give a distinctive background taste to the vegetables. Fats and oils carry important flavour components.

Stewing

Stewing vegetables is a traditional method of cooking vegetables. The vegetables are cut into even pieces, gently sweated on the stove in a little oil, then a stock or tomato juice is added and allowed to simmer on the stove or in an oven. The stewed vegetables may be flavoured with chopped herbs and/or spices. A classical stewed vegetable dish is ratatouille (this consists of aubergines, peppers, courgettes, onions, tomatoes in their juices).

Braising

These vegetables are most suitable for braising: potatoes, onions, cabbage, fennel and celery. Braising requires most vegetables to be blanched (with the exception of potatoes) and placed in a shallow pan with stock (this should come two-thirds of the way up the pan, so as not to cover the vegetables).

Cooking liquids

Appropriate cooking liquids for vegetables include:

- boiling water
- boiling stock – vegetable, meat or fish
- wine – white or red
- some fruit juices – for example, elderflower, orange, cranberry, pomegranate
- mineral water – Vichy is the classical mineral water used to cook carrots.

Holding for service

The professional way to hold vegetables for service is to cook them in advance, normally *al dente*, chill them quickly either in ice water or cold running water, or more appropriately in a blast chiller. Hold them chilled until required for service, when they are reheated, depending on the type of vegetable and the recipe. Reheat either in a chauffent, a saucepan of boiling water, or quickly reheating in a little oil or butter. The recommended method of reheating is in a combination oven, with an injection of steam, or quickly in a microwave.

When holding vegetables for service it is important not to leave vegetables hot for too long in deep containers as they will lose some of their nutritional value and colour.

Storing vegetables after cooking

It is important to store vegetables not for immediate use in a refrigerator at 5°C.

> **Health and safety** !
>
> To prevent bacteria from raw vegetables passing on to cooked vegetables, store them in separate areas. Thaw out frozen vegetables correctly and *never* refreeze them once they have thawed out.

Fruit

Types of fruit

Fruits are usually classified into the following categories:
- **Soft fruits** – for example, strawberries, raspberries, blackcurrants, blueberries, cranberries, blackberries and gooseberries.
- **Hard fruits** – for example, apples, pears and coconuts.
- **Stone fruits** – for example, apricots, plums, peaches, cherries and avocados.
- **Citrus fruits** – examples include lemons, limes, oranges, grapefruit, kumquats and mandarins.
- **Tropical fruits** – for example, bananas, breadfruit, passion fruit, mangoes, custard apples, cape gooseberries, dates, dragon fruit, lychee, pineapples, melons and paw paw (papaya).

> **Professional tip**
>
> Care must be taken when buying melons to ensure they are not over- or underripe. This can be assessed by carefully pressing the top or bottom of the fruit and smelling the outside skin for sweetness. There should be a slight degree of softness to the cantaloupe and charentais melons. The stalk should be attached, otherwise the melon deteriorates quickly.

Quality points for fruit

Fresh fruit should be:
- whole and fresh looking (for maximum flavour the fruit must be ripe but not overripe)
- firm, according to type and variety
- clean and free from traces of pesticides and fungicides
- free from external moisture
- free from any unpleasant foreign smell or taste
- free from pests or disease
- sufficiently mature; it must be capable of being handled and travelling without being damaged
- free from any defects characteristic of the variety in shape, size and colour
- free of bruising and any other damage due to weather conditions.

Soft fruits deteriorate quickly, especially if they are not sound. Take care to see that they are not damaged or overripe when purchased. Soft fruits should look fresh; there should be no signs of wilting, shrinking or mould. The colour of certain soft fruits is an indication of their ripeness (e.g. strawberries or dessert gooseberries).

Seasons for commonly used fruits

Table 7.12 Seasons for commonly used fruits

	Spring (March, April and May)	Summer (June, July and August)	Autumn (September, October and November)	Winter (December, January and February)
Apples			X	X
Blackberries			X	
Blueberries		X		
Currants (white, red and black)		X		
Damsons			X	
Elderberries			X	
Pears			X	X
Plums		X	X	
Quince			X	
Raspberries		X		
Rhubarb	X			
Sloes			X	
Strawberries		X		

Storage

- Hard fruits, such as apples, should be left in boxes and kept in a cool store.
- Soft fruits, such as raspberries and strawberries, should be left in their punnets or baskets in a cold room.
- Stone fruits, such as apricots and plums, are best placed in trays so that any damaged fruit can be seen and discarded.

- Peaches and citrus fruits are left in their delivery trays or boxes.
- Bananas should not be stored in too cold a place because their skins will turn black.

Fruit recipes also appear in other chapters, for example in chutneys and sauces (in Chapter 6), desserts (Chapter 12) and cakes (Chapter 14).

Preparation and cooking of fruits

Step by step: segmenting (grapefruit)

1 Using a sharp knife, use a straight cut to remove the top.

2 Repeat to remove the other end of the grapefruit.

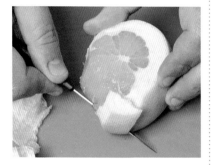

3 Cut around the flesh, keeping very close to the skin to remove both the pith and the skin.

4 Remove all of the pith and skin to reveal the pink fruit.

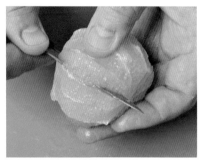

5 Cut down one side of the vein in the fruit and then down the other side of the vein to remove the segment.

6 Repeat the process to remove all segments. Some segments will be larger than others.

Poaching/stewing

Traditionally fruit is poached in a light syrup of sugar and water. The density of the syrup (the amount of sugar to water) will depend on the ripeness of the fruit – the riper the fruit, the denser the syrup needs to be to hold the fruit in shape.

Traditionally this method is known as stewing fruit due to the gentle slow method of cooking. The finished product is known as a compote of fruit, which is traditionally served at breakfast as a mixture of poached fruit such as prunes, pears, apples, etc. Poached fruit is also served as a dessert, usually as a garnish or accompaniment.

Apart from water and sugar, fruit juice (for example, orange, cranberry, apple and mango) is often used to poach fruit. Various wines are also used (white, red, sparkling, rosé and Marsala).

Baking

Fruit may be baked in the oven (for example baked pineapple, apple and pear). The fruit is usually sprinkled with sugar (white or brown) and spices such as cinnamon or mixed spice. Often thin slices of apple, pineapple or pear are baked in the oven until crisp and used as a garnish for desserts.

Grilling or barbequing

Fruit such as pineapple may also be marinated in wine or spirits such as rum and grilled on an oiled barbeque or under the salamander.

Test yourself

1. Name **six** varieties of potato suitable for roasting and boiling.
2. State **two** quality points to look for when buying leeks.
3. Describe the following cuts of vegetables:
   a) macedoine
   b) jardinière
   c) julienne
   d) paysanne
4. Describe the preparation and cooking of braised red cabbage.
5. How should fresh green vegetables be stored?
6. What is meant by 'blanching' of vegetables?
7. Explain what is meant by 'textured vegetable protein'.
8. Which fruit or vegetable classification does each of the following belong to?
   a) carrot
   b) sweet potato
   c) cauliflower
   d) peach
   e) grapefruit
9. Describe how fresh strawberries should be stored to help retain their quality.
10. State **three** advantages of canning as a preservation method for vegetables.

1 Grapefruit (*pamplemousse*)

Energy	Cals	Fat	Sat fat	Carb	Sugar	Protein	Fibre	Sodium *
101 kJ	24 kcal	0.1 g	0 g	5.4 g	5.4 g	0.6 g	1.4 g	0.002 g

* Per ½ grapefruit

Professional tip

Make sure all the pith is removed from the grapefruit: it tastes very bitter.

Healthy eating tip

This, and the other fruit dishes in this chapter, contribute to the recommended five portions of fruit and vegetables per day. Include them as often as possible on the menu.

Variation

Grapefruit may also be served hot, sprinkled with rum and demerara sugar.

Grapefruit and orange cocktail: allow half an orange and half a grapefruit per head.

Orange cocktail: use oranges in place of grapefruit.

Florida cocktail: a mixture of grapefruit, orange and pineapple segments.

The fruit should be peeled with a sharp knife in order to remove all the white pith and yellow skin. Cut into segments and remove all the pips. The segments and the juice should then be dressed in a cocktail glass or grapefruit coupe and chilled. A cherry may be added. Allow ½–1 grapefruit per head. The common practice of sprinkling with caster sugar is incorrect, as some customers prefer their grapefruit without sugar.

2 Avocado pear (*l'avocat*)

The pears must be ripe (test by pressing gently – the pear should give slightly). Allow half an avocado per portion.

1 Cut in half length-wise. Remove the stone.
2 Serve garnished with lettuce accompanied by vinaigrette or variations on vinaigrette.

Energy	Cals	Fat	Sat fat	Carb	Sugar	Protein	Fibre	Sodium
568 kJ	138 kcal	14.1 g	3 g	1.4 g	0.4 g	1.4 g	3.3 g	0.004 g

Variation

Avocado pears are sometimes filled with shrimps or crabmeat bound with a shellfish cocktail sauce or other similar fillings, and may be served hot or cold using a variety of fillings and sauces.

Avocados may also be halved lengthwise, the stone removed, the skin peeled and the flesh sliced and fanned on a plate. Garnish with a simple or composite salad.

Healthy eating tip
Serve with plenty of salad vegetables and bread or toast (optional butter or spread).

1 Cut the avocado in half

2 Remove the stone

3 Peel the skin before slicing the avocado (if required)

4 Slice the avocado

3 Fresh fruit salad

	4 portions	10 portions
Orange	1	2–3
Dessert apple	1	2–3
Dessert pear	1	2–3
Cherries	50 g	125 g
Grapes	50 g	125 g
Banana	1	2–3
Stock syrup		
Caster sugar	50 g	125 g
Water	125 ml	375 ml
Lemon, juice of	½	1

Energy	Cals	Fat	Sat fat	Carb	Sugar	Protein	Fibre
493 kJ	117 kcal	0.0 g	0.0 g	30.3 g	29.5 g	0.9 g	3.0 g

1 For the syrup, boil the sugar with the water and place in a bowl.

2 Allow to cool, add the lemon juice.

3 Peel and cut the orange into segments.

4 Quarter the apple and pear, remove the core, peel and cut each quarter into two or three slices, place in the bowl and mix with the orange.

5 Stone the cherries, leave whole.

6 Cut the grapes in half, peel if required, and remove the pips.

7 Mix carefully and place in a glass bowl in the refrigerator to chill.

8 Just before serving, peel and slice the banana and mix in.

Variation

All the following fruits may be used: dessert apples, pears, pineapple, oranges, grapes, melon, strawberries, peaches, raspberries, apricots, bananas, cherries, Kiwi fruit, plums, mangoes (see recipe 4), pawpaws and lychees. Allow about 150 g unprepared fruit per portion.

Kirsch, Cointreau or Grand Marnier may be added to the syrup. All fruit must be ripe.

A fruit juice (e.g. apple, orange, grape or passion fruit) can be used instead of syrup.

4 Tropical fruit plate

An assortment of fully ripe fruits, for example pineapple, papaya, mango (see photos), peeled, deseeded, cut into pieces and neatly dressed on a plate. An optional accompaniment could be yoghurt, vanilla ice cream, creme fraiche, fresh or clotted cream.

Healthy eating tip
This colourful dessert helps to meet the recommended target of five portions of fruit and vegetables per day.

Peeling a mango

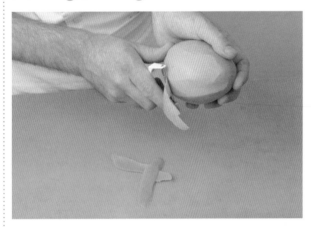

1 Peeling a mango

2 To dice a mango, first slice through it, keeping lateral to the stone

3 Next, score the flesh

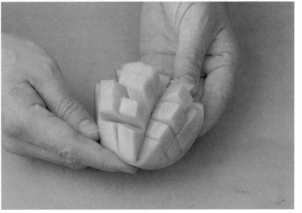

4 Bend out the cubes

5 Caribbean fruit curry

	4 portions	10 portions
Pineapple	1 small	1 large
Dessert apples	2	5
Small dessert pears	2	5
Mangoes	2	5
Bananas	2	5
Guava	1	2–3
Pawpaw	1	2–3
Rind and juice of lime	1	2–3
Onion, chopped	50 g	125 g
Sunflower margarine or butter	25 g	60 g
Sunflower oil	60 ml	150 ml
Madras curry powder	50 g	125 g
Wholemeal flour	25 g	60 g
Ginger, freshly grated	10 g	25 g
Desiccated coconut	50 g	125 g
Tomato, skinned, deseeded and diced	100 g	250 g
Tomato purée	25 g	60 g
Yeast extract	5 g	12 g
Sultanas	50 g	125 g
Fruit juice	0.5 litre	1.25 litres
Cashew nuts	50 g	125 g
Single cream or smetana	60 ml	150 ml

1 Skin and cut the pineapple in half, remove the tough centre. Cut into 1 cm chunks. Peel the apples and pears, remove the cores, cut into 1 cm pieces. Peel and slice the mangoes. Skin and cut the bananas into 1 cm pieces. Cut the guavas and pawpaws in half, remove the seeds, peel, dice into 1 cm pieces. Marinate the fruit in the lime juice.

2 Fry the onion in the sunflower margarine and oil until lightly brown, add the curry powder, sweat together, add the wholemeal flour and cook for 2 minutes.

3 Add the ginger, coconut, tomato concassé, tomato purée and sultanas.

4 Gradually add sufficient boiling fruit juice to make a light sauce.

5 Add yeast extract, stir well. Simmer for 10 minutes.

6 Add the sultanas, fruit juice and cashew nuts, stir carefully, allow to heat through.

7 Finish with cream or smetana.

8 Serve in a suitable dish; separately serve poppadoms, wholegrain pilaff rice and a green salad.

Energy	Cals	Fat	Sat fat	Carb	Sugar	Protein	Fibre	Sodium *
2856 kJ	682 kcal	39.1 g	14.9 g	78.7 g	68.3 g	8.7 g	13.2 g	0.161 g

* Using butter and single cream

Healthy eating tips
- Lightly oil a well-seasoned pan with the sunflower oil to fry the onion.
- No added salt is needed.
- Try finishing the dish with low-fat yoghurt in place of the cream.
- Serve with plenty of starchy carbohydrate and salad.

6 Buttered celeriac, turnips or swedes

	4 portions	10 portions
Celeriac, turnips or swedes	400g	1kg
Salt, sugar		
Butter	25g	60g
Parsley, chopped		

Energy	Cals	Fat	Sat fat	Carb	Sugar	Protein	Fibre
253kJ	60kcal	5.4g	3.3g	2.5g	2.5g	0.7g	1.9g

1 Peel and wash the vegetables.

2 Cut into neat pieces or turn barrel shaped.

3 Place in a pan with a little salt, a pinch of sugar and the butter. Barely cover with water.

4 Cover with a buttered paper and allow to boil steadily in order to evaporate all the water.

5 When the water has completely evaporated, check that the vegetables are cooked; if not, add a little more water and continue cooking. Do not overcook.

6 Toss the vegetables over a fierce heat for 1–2 minutes to glaze.

7 Drain well, and serve sprinkled with chopped parsley.

7 Goats' cheese and beetroot tarts, with salad of watercress

	4 portions	10 portions
Puff pastry	400g	1kg
Shallots	150g	375g
Beetroot, cooked	200g	500g
Goats' cheese	200g	500g
Watercress, bunch	1	2

Energy	Cals	Fat	Sat fat	Carb	Sugar	Protein	Fibre
2377kJ	568kcal	37.7g	9.0g	43.6g	7.5g	18.6g	1.8g

1 Roll the puff pastry to a thickness of 3 mm.

2 Chill the rolled puff pastry for 10 minutes.

3 Finely slice the shallots and sweat down without colour.

4 Cut the puff pastry into 4 discs approximately 150 mm in diameter.

5 Chill the pastry discs for 10 minutes.

6 Dice the cooked beetroot into pieces 10 × 10 mm.

7 To make the tarts, place the shallots on the pastry discs.

8 Cook at 180 °C for 12 minutes.

9 Once cooked, remove from the oven and top with the diced beetroot and crumbled goats' cheese.

10 To finish the dish, place the tarts on plates and finish with picked watercress and vinaigrette.

8 Golden beetroot with Parmesan

	4 portions	10 portions
Golden beetroot	400 g	1 kg
Parmesan, freshly grated	50 g	125 g
Seasoning		

Energy	Cals	Fat	Sat fat	Carb	Sugar	Protein	Fibre	Sodium
370 kJ	88 kcal	2.8 g	2.4 g	7.7	7.1 g	6.2 g	2.5 g	0.210 g

1 Peel the golden beetroot and cut into 5 mm slices. Either steam or plain boil until tender.

2 Drain well and place in a suitable serving dish. Sprinkle with Parmesan and grill under the salamander or in the oven.

9 Parsnips (*panais*)

1 Wash well. Peel the parsnips and re-wash well.

2 Cut into quarters lengthwise, remove the centre root if tough.

3 Cut into neat pieces and cook in lightly salted water until tender, or steam.

4 Drain and serve with melted butter or in a cream sauce.

Variation

Parsnips may be roasted in the oven in a little fat (as shown here) or in with a joint, and can be cooked and prepared as a purée.

Energy	Cals	Fat	Sat fat	Carb	Sugar	Protein	Fibre
235 kJ	56 kcal	0.0 g	0.0 g	13.5 g	2.7 g	1.3 g	2.5 g

Professional tip

For great roast parsnips, blanch them for 2 minutes, drain, then roast in hot olive oil.

10 Salsify (*salsifi*)

Half a kilogram will yield 2–3 portions.

1 Wash, peel and rewash the salsify.
2 Cut into 5 cm lengths.
3 Cook in a blanc (see below). Do not overcook.

Salsify may then be served brushed with melted butter, or coated in mornay sauce (see page 131), sprinkled with grated cheese and browned under a salamander. It may also be passed through batter and deep-fried.

To make the blanc:

	4 portions	10 portions
Flour	10 g	20 g
Cold water	0.5 litres	1 litre
Salt, to taste		
Lemon, juice of	½	1

Energy	Cals	Fat	Sat fat	Carb	Sugar	Protein	Fibre
76 kJ	18 kcal	0.0 g	0.0 g	2.8 g	2.8 g	1.9 g	0.0 g

1 Mix the flour and water together.
2 Add the salt and lemon juice. Pass through a strainer.
3 Place in a pan, bring to the boil, stirring continuously.

11 Vichy carrots (*carottes Vichy*)

	4 portions	10 portions
Carrots	400 g	1 kg
Salt, pepper		
Sugar		
Butter	25 g	60 g
Vichy water (optional)		
Parsley, chopped		

Energy	Cals	Fat	Sat fat	Carb	Sugar	Protein	Fibre *
338 kJ	82 kcal	5.4 g	3.4 g	8.0 g	7.5 g	0.7 g	2.4 g

1 Peel and wash the carrots (which should not be larger than 2 cm in diameter).
2 Cut into 2 mm-thin slices on the mandolin.
3 Place in a pan with a little salt, a pinch of sugar and butter. Barely cover with Vichy water.
4 Cover with a buttered paper and allow to boil steadily in order to evaporate all the water.
5 When the water has completely evaporated, check that the carrots are cooked; if not, add a little more water and continue cooking. Do not overcook.
6 Toss the carrots over a fierce heat for 1–2 minutes in order to give them a glaze.
7 Serve sprinkled with chopped parsley.

Vichy water is water from the French town of Vichy. This dish is characterised by the glaze produced by reducing the butter and sugar.

Healthy eating tip
Use the minimum amount of salt.

* Using water only

12 Baked jacket potatoes *(pommes au four)*

Lightly scoring the potatoes will help to make sure that they cook evenly.

The potatoes can also be cooked in the microwave on full power. Prick the skins first. Cook for 5 minutes for each potato. Wrap in foil to rest for 3 minutes.

Healthy eating tips
- Potatoes can be baked without sea salt.
- Fillings based on vegetables with little or no cheese or meat make a healthy snack meal.

Energy	Cals	Fat	Sat fat	Carb	Sugar	Protein	Fibre	*
401 kJ	94 kcal	0.2 g	0.0 g	21.8 g	0.9 g	2.7 g	1.6 g	

* Using medium potato, 180 g analysis given per potato

1 Select good-sized potatoes; allow 1 potato per portion.

2 Scrub well and make a 2 mm-deep incision round the potato.

3 Place the potato, on a small mound of ground (sea) salt to help keep the base dry, on a tray in a hot oven at 230–250 °C for about 1 hour. Turn the potatoes over after 30 minutes.

4 Test by holding the potato in a cloth and squeezing gently; if cooked it should feel soft.

Variation

Split and filled with any of the following: grated cheese, minced beef or chicken, baked beans, chilli con carne, cream cheese and chives, mushrooms, bacon, ratatouille, prawns in mayonnaise, coleslaw, and so on.

The cooked potatoes can also be cut in halves lengthwise, the potato spooned out from the skins, seasoned, mashed with butter, returned to the skins, sprinkled with grated cheese and reheated in an oven or under the grill.

13 Château potatoes *(pommes château)*

1 Select small, even-sized potatoes and wash them.

2 Turn the potatoes into barrel-shaped pieces about the same size as fondant potatoes (recipe 17).

3 Place in a saucepan of boiling water for 2–3 minutes, then refresh immediately. Drain in a colander.

4 Finish as for roast potatoes. Use a non-stick tray, lightly oiled greaseproof paper or non-stick mat for the roasting.

Energy	Cals	Fat	Sat fat	Carb	Sugar	Protein	Fibre	Sodium
839 kJ	200 kcal	2.9 g	0.7 g	34.4 g	1.2 g	4.2 g	3.5 g	0.0 g

14 Croquette potatoes (*pommes croquettes*)

1 Use a duchess mixture (see recipe 16) moulded into cylinder shapes 5 × 2 cm.

2 Pass through flour, eggwash and breadcrumbs. Chill.

3 Reshape with a palette knife and chill. Deep-fry in hot deep oil (185 °C) in a frying basket.

4 When the potatoes are a golden colour, drain well and serve.

Healthy eating tips
- Add the minimum amount of salt.
- Use peanut or sunflower oil to fry the croquettes, and drain on kitchen paper.

Energy	Cals	Fat	Sat fat	Carb	Sugar	Protein	Fibre *
1699kJ	405kcal	25.4g	6.6g	40.8g	1.1g	6.0g	2.2g

15 Delmonico potatoes (*pommes Delmonico*)

1 Wash, peel and rewash the potatoes.

2 Cut into 6 mm dice.

3 Barely cover with milk, season lightly with salt and pepper and allow to cook for 30–40 minutes.

4 Place in an earthenware dish, sprinkle with breadcrumbs and melted butter, brown in the oven or under the salamander and serve.

Energy	Cals	Fat	Sat fat	Carb	Sugar	Protein	Fibre *
900kJ	214kcal	6.3g	3.7g	37.5g	2.7g	4.4g	2.0g

* Using old potatoes and whole milk

1 Dice the potatoes

2 Place in a dish, barely covered with milk, to cook

3 After baking, sprinkle with breadcrumbs and gratinate

16 Duchess potatoes (*pommes duchesse*)

	4 portions	10 portions
floury potatoes	600 g	1.5 kg
Egg yolks	1	3
Butter	25 g	60 g
Salt, pepper		

Energy	Cals	Fat	Sat fat	Carb	Sugar	Protein	Fibre	*
819 kJ	195 kcal	8.2 g	3.3 g	28.6 g	0.6 g	3.5 g	1.5 g	

* Using old potatoes, whole milk, hard margarine

1 Wash, peel and rewash the potatoes. Cut to an even size.
2 Cook in lightly salted water.
3 Drain off the water, cover and return to a low heat to dry out the potatoes.
4 Pass through a medium sieve or a ricer or mouli.
5 Place the potatoes in a clean pan.
6 Add the egg yolks and stir in vigorously with a kitchen spoon.
7 Mix in the butter. Correct the seasoning.
8 Place in a piping bag with a large star tube and pipe out into neat spirals, about 2 cm in diameter and 5 cm tall, on to a lightly greased baking sheet.
9 Place in a hot oven at 230 °C for 2–3 minutes in order to firm the edges slightly.
10 Remove from the oven and brush with eggwash.
11 Brown lightly in a hot oven or under the salamander.

Add egg yolks to the mashed potato

Pipe the potato into neat spirals, ready for baking

Note

At step 3, it is important to return the drained potatoes to the heat, so that they are as dry as possible.

17 Fondant potatoes (*pommes fondantes*)

Energy	Cals	Fat	Sat fat	Carb	Sugar	Protein	Fibre	*
956kJ	228kcal	7.0g	2.1g	39.6g	0.9g	4.1g	1.5g	

* Using old potatoes and hard margarine for 1 portion (125g raw potato)

1 Select small or even-sized medium potatoes.

2 Wash, peel and rewash.

3 Turn into 8-sided barrel shapes, allowing 2–3 per portion, about 5cm long, end diameter 1.5cm, centre diameter 2.5cm.

4 Brush with melted butter or oil.

5 Place in a pan suitable for the oven.

6 Half cover with white stock, season lightly with salt and pepper.

7 Cook in a hot oven at 230–250°C, brushing the potatoes frequently with melted butter or oil.

8 When cooked, the stock should be completely absorbed by the potatoes.

9 Brush with melted butter or oil and serve.

Turn the potatoes into barrel shapes

Place in a pan, half covered with stock, to cook

Professional tip

To give the potatoes a good glaze, use a high-quality stock and baste during cooking.

Healthy eating tips

● Use a little unsaturated oil to brush over the potatoes before and after cooking.
● No added salt is needed; rely on the stock for flavour.

Variation

Fondant potatoes can be lightly sprinkled with:
● thyme, rosemary or oregano (or this can be added to the stock), as shown in the photo above
● grated cheese (Gruyère and Parmesan or Cheddar)
● chicken stock in place of white stock.

Video: Making fondant potatoes http://bit.ly/ 1ASKJEX

18 Fried or chipped potatoes (*pommes frites*)

Energy	Cals	Fat	Sat fat	Carb	Sugar	Protein	Fibre	*
1541 kJ	367 kcal	15.8g	2.8g	54.1g	0.0g	5.5g	1.5g	

* Using old potatoes and peanut oil

1 Prepare and wash the potatoes.

2 Cut into slices 1 cm thick and 5 cm long.

3 Cut the slices into strips 5 × 1 × 1 cm.

4 Wash well and dry in a cloth.

5 Cook in a frying basket without colour in moderately hot oil (165 °C).

6 Drain and place on kitchen paper on trays until required.

7 When required, place in a frying basket and cook in hot oil (185 °C) until crisp and golden.

8 Drain well, season lightly with salt and serve.

Because chips are so popular, the following advice from the Potato Marketing Board is useful.

● Cook chips in small quantities; this will allow the oil to regain its temperature more quickly; chips will then cook faster and absorb less fat.

● Do not let the temperature of the oil exceed 199 °C as this will accelerate the fat breakdown.

● Use oils high in polyunsaturates for a healthier chip.

● Ideally use a separate fryer for chips and ensure that it has the capacity to raise the fat temperature rapidly to the correct degree when frying chilled or frozen chips.

● Although the majority of chipped potatoes are purchased frozen, the Potato Marketing Board recommends the following potatoes for those who prefer to make their own chips: Maris Piper, Cara, Désirée. King Edward and Santé are also good choices.

Healthy eating tips

● Chipped potatoes may be blanched twice, first at 140 °C, followed by a re-blanch at 160 °C until lightly coloured.

● Blanch in a steamer until just cooked, drain and dry well – final temperature 165 °C.

19 Hash brown potatoes

1 Wash, peel and rewash the potatoes.

2 Coarsely grate the potatoes, rewash quickly and then drain well.

3 Melt the fat in a suitable frying pan. Add the lardons of bacon, fry until crisp and brown, remove from the pan and drain.

4 Pour the fat back into the frying pan, add the grated potato and season.

5 Press down well, allow 2 cm thickness, and cook over a heat for 10–15 minutes or in a moderate oven at 190 °C, until a brown crust forms on the bottom.

6 Turn out into a suitable serving dish and sprinkle with the lardons of bacon and chopped parsley.

	4 portions	10 portions
Potatoes	600 g	2 kg
Butter or margarine	25 g	60 g
Lardons of bacon	100 g	250 g
Seasoning		

Energy	Cals	Fat	Sat fat	Carb	Sugar	Protein	Fibre
954 kJ	228 kcal	11.3 g	5.3 g	25.8 g	0.9 g	7.1 g	2.0 g

Healthy eating tips
- Dry-fry the lardons in a well-seasoned pan.
- Brush a little oil over the potatoes and cook in a hot oven. Use the minimum amount of salt.

20 Macaire potatoes (potato cakes) (*pommes Macaire*)

Half a kilogram will yield 2–3 portions.

1 Prepare and cook as for baked jacket potatoes (recipe 12).

2 Cut in halves, remove the centre with a spoon, and place in a basin.

3 Add 25 g butter per 0.5 kg, a little salt and milled pepper.

4 Mash and mix as lightly as possible with a fork.

5 Using a little flour, mould into a roll, then divide into pieces, allowing one or two per portion.

6 Mould into 2 cm round cakes. Quadrille with the back of a palette knife. Flour lightly.

7 Shallow-fry on both sides in very hot oil and serve.

Energy	Cals	Fat	Sat fat	Carb	Sugar	Protein	Fibre	*
4392 kJ	1047 kcal	65.7 g	14.7 g	109.8 g	2.7 g	11.4 g	10.8 g	

* Using hard margarine and sunflower oil

Place the potatoes on a baking tray with salt

Once baked, cut in half and scoop out the centre

Mould the potato into cakes

Professional tip

Make sure the potato mixture is firm enough to be shaped, and fry the cakes in very hot oil, or they will lose their shape.

Variation

Additions to potato cakes can include:
- chopped parsley, fresh herbs or chives, or duxelle
- cooked chopped onion
- grated cheese.

21 Mashed potatoes (*pommes purées*)

	4 portions	10 portions
Floury potatoes	0.5 kg	1.25 kg
Butter	25 g	60 g
Milk, warm	30 ml	80 ml

1 Wash, peel and rewash the potatoes. Cut to an even size.
2 Cook in lightly salted water, or steam.
3 Drain off the water, cover and return to a low heat to dry out the potatoes.
4 Pass through a medium sieve or a ricer.
5 Return the potatoes to a clean pan.
6 Add the butter and mix in with a wooden spoon.
7 Gradually add warm milk, stirring continuously until a smooth creamy consistency is reached.
8 Correct the seasoning and serve.

Energy	Cals	Fat	Sat fat	Carb	Sugar	Protein	Fibre *
763 kJ	182 kcal	7.1 g	4.4 g	29.0 g	1.1 g	2.4 g	1.5 g

* Using old potatoes, butter and whole milk

Pass the cooked potato through a sieve

Add milk to the potatoes and combine

Professional tip

Drain the potatoes as soon as they are cooked. If they are left standing in water, they will become too wet and spoil the texture of the dish.

Healthy eating tips
- Add a minimum amount of salt.
- Add a little olive oil in place of the butter, and use semi-skimmed milk.

Variation

Try:
- dressing in a serving dish and surrounding with a cordon of fresh cream
- placing in a serving dish, sprinkling with grated cheese and melted butter, and browning under a salamander
- adding 50g diced cooked lean ham, 25g diced red pepper and chopped parsley
- adding lightly sweated chopped spring onions
- using a good-quality olive oil in place of butter
- adding a little garlic juice (use a garlic press)
- adding a little fresh chopped rosemary or chives
- mixing with equal quantities of parsnip
- adding a little freshly grated horseradish or horseradish cream.

22 Parmentier potatoes (*pommes parmentier*)

0.5 kg will yield 2–3 portions

1 Select medium to large potatoes.
2 Wash, peel and rewash.
3 Trim on 3 sides and cut into 1 cm slices.
4 Cut the slices into 1 cm strips.
5 Cut the strips into 1 cm dice.
6 Wash well and dry in a cloth.
7 Cook in hot shallow oil in a frying pan until golden brown.
8 Drain, season lightly and serve sprinkled with chopped parsley.

Energy	Cals	Fat	Sat fat	Carb	Sugar	Protein	Fibre	*
1819kJ	433kcal	33.5g	6.3g	32.8g	0.7g	2.3g	1.7g	

* Using peanut oil

23 Potatoes cooked in milk with cheese

	4 portions	10 portions
Potatoes	500g	1.25kg
Milk	250ml	600ml
Salt and pepper		
Grated cheese	50g	125g

1 Slice the peeled potatoes to ½cm thick.

2 Place in an ovenproof dish and just cover with milk.

3 Season, sprinkle with grated cheese and cook in a moderate oven (190°C) until the potatoes are cooked and golden brown.

Energy	Cals	Fat	Sat fat	Carb	Sugar	Protein	Fibre
747kJ	178kcal	5.4g	3.4g	5.4g	4.0g	8.0g	1.8g

24 Potatoes with bacon and onions (*pommes au lard*)

	4 portions	10 portions
Potatoes, peeled	400g	1.25kg
Streaky bacon (lardons)	100g	250g
Button onions	100g	250g
White stock	250ml	600ml
Salt, pepper		
Parsley, chopped		

1 Cut the potatoes into 1cm dice.

2 Cut the bacon into 0.5cm lardons; lightly fry in a little fat together with the onions and brown lightly.

3 Add the potatoes, half cover with stock, season lightly with salt and pepper. Cover with a lid and cook steadily in the oven at 230–250°C for approximately 30 minutes.

4 Correct the seasoning, serve in a vegetable dish, sprinkled with chopped parsley.

Energy	Cals	Fat	Sat fat	Carb	Sugar	Protein	Fibre
836kJ	199kcal	10.1g	3.8g	22.2g	1.8g	6.4g	2.5g

* Using old potatoes

Healthy eating tips
- Dry-fry the bacon in a well-seasoned pan and drain off any excess fat.
- Add little or no salt.

25 Roast potatoes (*pommes rôties*)

1 Wash, peel and rewash the potatoes.

2 Cut into even-sized pieces (allow 3–4 pieces per portion).

3 Heat a good measure of oil or dripping in a roasting tray.

4 Add the well-dried potatoes and lightly brown on all sides.

5 Season lightly with salt and cook for about 1 hour in a hot oven at 230–250 °C.

6 Turn the potatoes over after 30 minutes.

7 Cook to a golden brown. Drain and serve.

Energy	Cals	Fat	Sat fat	Carb	Sugar	Protein	Fibre	*
956 kJ	228 kcal	7.0 g	1.1 g	39.6 g	0.9 g	4.1 g	1.5 g	

* Using old potatoes and peanut oil for 1 portion (125 g raw potato)

Healthy eating tips
● Brush the potatoes with peanut or sunflower oil, with only a little in the roasting tray.
● Drain off all the fat when cooked.

Professional tip

Roast potatoes can be parboiled for 10 minutes, refreshed and well dried before roasting. This will cut down on the cooking time and can also give a crisper potato.

26 Sauté potatoes (*pommes sautées*)

1 Select medium, even-sized potatoes. Scrub well.

2 Plain boil or cook in the steamer. Cool slightly and peel.

3 Cut into 3 mm slices.

4 Toss in hot shallow oil in a frying pan until lightly coloured; season lightly with salt.

5 Serve sprinkled with chopped parsley.

Note

Maris piper or Cara potatoes are good varieties for this dish.

Energy	Cals	Fat	Sat fat	Carb	Sugar	Protein	Fibre	*
1249 kJ	297 kcal	11.4 g	1.3 g	46.8 g	0.4 g	4.9 g	1.7 g	

* Using old potatoes and sunflower oil

Healthy eating tips
● Use a little hot sunflower oil to fry the potatoes.
● Add little or no salt; the customer can add more if required.

1 Cut the potatoes into 3mm slices

2 Toss the slices in hot oil to cook (sauté)

27 Sauté potatoes with onions (*pommes lyonnaise*)

Allow 0.25kg onion to 0.5kg potatoes.

1 Shallow-fry the onions slowly in 25–50g oil, turning frequently, until tender and nicely browned; season lightly with salt.

2 Prepare sauté potatoes as for recipe 26.

3 Combine the two and toss together.

4 Serve as for sauté potatoes.

Energy	Cals	Fat	Sat fat	Carb	Sugar	Protein	Fibre	Sodium
1098kJ	261kcal	9.4g	1.1g	41.5g	6.4g	4.5g	5.3g	300mg

Finely slice the onions

Sauté the potatoes and onions together

28 Swiss potato cakes *(rösti)*

	4 portions	10 portions
Potatoes, unpeeled	400 g	1 kg
Oil or butter	50 g	125 g
Salt, pepper		

1 Parboil in salted water (or steam) for approximately 5 minutes.

2 Cool, then shred into large flakes on a grater.

3 Heat the oil or butter in a frying pan.

4 Add the potatoes, and season lightly with salt and pepper.

5 Press the potato together and cook on both sides until brown and crisp.

Energy	Cals	Fat	Sat fat	Carb	Sugar	Protein	Fibre	*
700kJ	168kcal	10.5g	6.5g	17.3g	0.7g	2.2g	1.3g	

* Using butter

1 Shred the parboiled potatoes on a grater

2 Press into shape in the frying pan

3 Turn out carefully after cooking

The potato can be made in a 4-portion cake or in individual rounds.

Healthy eating tips
- Lightly oil a well-seasoned pan with sunflower oil to fry the rösti.
- Use the minimum amount of salt.

Variation
- The potato cakes may also be made from raw potatoes.
- Add sweated chopped onion.
- Add sweated lardons of bacon.
- Use 2 parts of grated potato to 1 part grated apple.

29 Purée of Jerusalem artichokes (topinambours en purée)

	4 portions	10 portions
Jerusalem artichokes	600 g	1.5 kg
Salt, pepper		
Butter	25 g	60 g

Energy	Cals	Fat	Sat fat	Carb	Sugar	Protein	Fibre
502 kJ	108 kcal	5.3 g	3.3 g	16.0 g	2.5 g	2.5 g	7.0 g

1　Wash, peel and rewash the artichokes.

2　Cut in pieces if necessary. Barely cover with water; add a little salt.

3　Simmer gently until tender. Drain well.

4　Pass through a sieve or mouli or liquidise.

5　Return to the pan, reheat and mix in the butter; correct the seasoning and serve.

Healthy eating tip
Use the minimum amount of salt.

Variation

125 ml (300 ml for 10 portions) cream or natural yoghurt may be mixed in before serving.

30 Braised onions (oignons braisés)

1　Select medium even-sized onions; allow ½ kg per 2–3 portions.

2　Peel, wash and cook in lightly salted boiling water for 30 minutes, or steam.

3　Drain and place in a pan or casserole suitable for use in the oven.

4　Add bouquet garni, half cover with stock; put on the lid and braise gently in the oven at 180–200 °C until tender.

5　Drain well and dress neatly in a vegetable dish.

6　Reduce the cooking liquor with an equal amount of jus-lie, reduced stock or demi-glace. Correct the seasoning and consistency and pass. Mask the onions and sprinkle with chopped parsley.

Energy	Cals	Fat	Sat fat	Carb	Sugar	Protein	Fibre	Sodium
245 kJ	58 kcal	0.4 g	0.1 g	10.9	10.4 g	3.4 g	2.8 g	0.233 g

31 Caramelised button onions

Butter or vegetable oil	50 g
Button onions	250 g
Water or brown stock	
Sugar	50 g

Energy	Cals	Fat	Sat fat	Carb	Sugar	Protein	Fibre	Sodium
713 kJ	171 kcal	10.8 g	6.5 g	18.4 g	16.7 g	1.2 g	1.2 g	0.5 g

1 Place the butter or oil in a shallow pan.
2 Fry the button onions quickly to a light golden brown colour.
3 Barely cover with water or brown stock. Add the sugar. Cook the button onions until they are tender and the liquid has reduced with the sugar to a light caramel glaze. Carefully coat the onions with the glaze.

Professional tip

The important thing is to reduce the stock and sugar until they form a light caramel syrup.

32 Onion bhajias

	4 portions	10 portions
Bessan or gram flour	45 g	112 g
Hot curry powder	1 tsp	2½ tsp
Salt		
Water	75 ml	187 ml
Onion, finely shredded	100 g	250 g

Energy	Cals	Fat	Sat fat	Carb	Sugar	Protein	Fibre
630 kJ	152 kcal	12.1 g	1.3 g	8.5 g	1.7 g	2.9 g	2.4 g

1 Mix together the flour, curry powder and salt.
2 Blend in the water carefully to form a smooth, thick batter.
3 Stir in the onion, stir well.
4 Drop the mixture off a tablespoon into deep oil at 200 °C. Fry for 5–10 minutes until golden brown.
5 Drain well and serve as a snack with mango chutney as a dip.

Professional tip

The oil must be at the correct temperature before the bhajias are fried.

Healthy eating tip
● Use the minimum amount of salt.
● Make sure the oil is hot so that less is absorbed into the surface. Drain on kitchen paper.

33 Poached fennel

1 Trim the fennel heads and remove any blemishes.
2 Gently place in a suitable pan of boiling stock or water.
3 Remove to the side of the stove and gently poach until tender.

Energy	Cals	Fat	Sat fat	Carb	Sugar	Protein	Fibre	Sodium *
47 kJ	11 kcal	0.2g	0g	1.5	1.4g	0.9g	3.1g	0.056g

* Per half bulb

Note

Poached fennel may be served as an accompanying vegetable or used as a garnish.

34 Roast garlic

1 Peel the garlic.
2 Divide it into natural segments and place in a suitable roasting tray.
3 Sprinkle with olive oil and roast in the oven until golden brown and tender.

Energy	Cals	Fat	Sat fat	Carb	Sugar	Protein	Fibre	Sodium *
255 kJ	61 kcal	3.2g	0.4g	5.7	0.6g	2.8g	1.9g	0.001g

* Per bulb

35 Braised red cabbage (*choux à la flamande*)

	4 portions	10 portions
Red cabbage	300 g	1 kg
Salt, pepper		
Butter	50 g	125 g
Cooking apples	100 g	250 g
Caster sugar	10 g	25 g
Vinegar or red wine	125 ml	300 ml
Bacon trimmings (optional)	50 g	125 g

Energy	Cals	Fat	Sat fat	Carb	Sugar	Protein	Fibre
754 kJ	180 kcal	15.2 g	8.4 g	7.8 g	7.7 g	3.4 g	3.2 g

Variation

Other flavourings include 50 g sultanas, grated zest of one orange, pinch of ground cinnamon.

1 Quarter, trim and shred the cabbage. Wash well and drain.

2 Season lightly with salt and pepper.

3 Place in a well-buttered casserole or pan suitable for placing in the oven (not aluminium or iron, because these metals will cause a chemical reaction that will discolour the cabbage).

4 Add the peeled and cored apples. Cut into 1 cm dice and sugar.

5 Add the vinegar and bacon (if using), cover with a buttered paper and lid.

6 Cook in a moderate oven at 150–200 °C for 1 ½ hours.

7 Remove the bacon (if used) and serve.

Strain off most of the liquid after braising

Healthy eating tip
The fat and salt content will be reduced by omitting the bacon.

36 Pickled red cabbage

1 Remove the outer leaves of the cabbage and shred the rest finely.

2 Place in a deep bowl, sprinkle each layer with dry salt and leave for 24 hours.

3 Rinse and drain, cover with spiced vinegar (see recipe for mixed pickle, page 156) and leave for a further 24 hours, mixing occasionally. Pack and cover.

37 Spinach purée (épinards en purée)

3 Wilt for 2–3 minutes, taking care not to overcook.

4 Place on a tray and allow to cool.

5 Pass through a sieve or mouli, or use a food processor.

6 Reheat in 25–50 g butter, mix with a kitchen spoon, correct the seasoning and serve.

Variation

Creamed spinach purée can be made by mixing in 30 ml cream and 60 ml béchamel or natural yoghurt before serving. Serve with a border of cream.

An addition would be 1 cm triangle-shaped croutons fried in butter.

Spinach may also be served with toasted pine kernels or finely chopped garlic.

Energy	Cals	Fat	Sat fat	Carb	Sugar	Protein	Fibre	Sodium *
713kJ	171kcal	10.8g	6.5g	18.4g	16.7g	1.2g	1.2g	0.5g

* Using 25 g butter per 0.5 kg

Half a kilogram of spinach will yield 2 portions.

1 Remove the stems and discard them.

2 Wash the leaves very carefully in plenty of water, several times if necessary.

38 Stir-fried cabbage with mushrooms and beansprouts

Healthy eating tips
- Reduce the oil by half when cooking the cabbage.
- No added salt is needed as soy sauce is used.

1 Heat the oil in a suitable pan (e.g. a wok).
2 Add the cabbage and stir for 2 minutes.
3 Add the soy sauce, stir well. Cook for a further minute.
4 Add the mushrooms and cook for a further 2 minutes.
5 Stir in the beansprouts and cook for 1–2 minutes.
6 Stir well. Season with freshly ground pepper and serve.

Professional tip

The cabbage must be shredded evenly and the mushrooms cut evenly, so that they will cook at the same rate.

	4 portions	10 portions
Sunflower oil	2 tbsp	5 tbsp
Spring cabbage or pak choi, shredded	400 g	1 kg
Soy sauce	2 tbsp	5 tbsp
Mushrooms, sliced	200 g	500 g
Beansprouts	100 g	250 g
Freshly ground pepper		

Energy	Cals	Fat	Sat fat	Carb	Sugar	Protein	Fibre	Sodium
413 kJ	100 kcal	6.9 g	0.8 g	4.9	3.9 g	4.8 g	5.8 g	0.558 g

39 Broad beans *(fèves)*

Half a kilogram will yield about 2 portions.

1 Shell the beans and cook in boiling, salted water for 10–15 minutes until tender. Do not overcook.

2 If the inner shells are tough, remove before serving.

Energy	Cals	Fat	Sat fat	Carb	Sugar	Protein	Fibre *
344 kJ	81 kcal	0.6g	0.1g	5.0g	0.4g	7.9g	6.5g

* 100 g portion

Removing the inner shells of broad beans

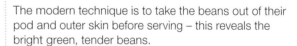

Professional tip

The modern technique is to take the beans out of their pod and outer skin before serving – this reveals the bright green, tender beans.

Variation

Try:
- brushing with butter
- brushing with butter then sprinkling with chopped parsley
- binding with ½ litre cream sauce or fresh cream.

40 Corn on the cob *(maïs)*

Allow 1 cob per portion.

1 Trim the stem.

2 Cook in lightly salted boiling water for 10–20 minutes or until the corn is tender. Do not overcook.

3 Remove the outer leaves and fibres.

4 Serve with a sauceboat of melted butter.

Note

Creamed sweetcorn can be made by removing the corn from the cooked cobs, draining well and binding lightly with cream (fresh or non-dairy), béchamel sauce or yoghurt.

Energy	Cals	Fat	Sat fat	Carb	Sugar	Protein	Fibre
646 kJ	154 kcal	209g	0.5g	28.5g	2.1g	5.1g	5.9g

41 Haricot bean salad (*salade de haricots blancs*)

	4 portions	10 portions
Haricot beans, cooked	200 g	500 g
Vinaigrette	1 tbsp	2 ½ tbsp
Parsley, chopped		
Onion, chopped and blanched if necessary	¼	½
Chives (optional)	15 g	40 g
Salt, pepper		

Healthy eating tips
- Lightly dress with vinaigrette.
- Add salt sparingly.

Energy	Cals	Fat	Sat fat	Carb	Sugar	Protein	Fibre
278 kJ	66 kcal	2.1 g	0.4 g	9.0 g	0.7 g	3.3 g	3.1 g

1 Combine all the ingredients.

This recipe can be used for any type of dried bean.

42 Ladies' fingers (okra) in cream sauce (*okra à la crème*)

1 Top and tail the ladies' fingers.

2 Blanch in lightly salted boiling water, or steam; drain.

3 Sweat in the margarine or butter for 5–10 minutes, or until tender.

4 Carefully add the cream sauce.

5 Bring to the boil, correct the seasoning and serve in a suitable dish.

Okra may also be served brushed with butter or sprinkled with chopped parsley.

Professional tip

Okra can become glutinous (slimy) when it is cooked in a sauce. To avoid this, wash the okra and let it dry before cooking.

	4 portions	10 portions
Ladies' fingers (okra)	400 g	1.25 kg
Butter or margarine	50 g	125 g
Cream sauce	250 ml	625 ml

Healthy eating tips
- Use a little unsaturated oil to sweat the okra.
- Try using half cream sauce and half yoghurt, adding very little salt.

Energy	Cals	Fat	Sat fat	Carb	Sugar	Protein	Fibre	*
928 kJ	221 kcal	20.2 g	9.8 g	5.7 g	5.7 g	4.4 g	3.2 g	

* Using hard margarine

43 Mangetout

Half a kilogram of mangetout will yield 4–6 portions.

1 Top and tail, wash and drain.

2 Cook in boiling salted water for 2–3 minutes, until slightly crisp.

3 Serve whole, brushed with butter.

Energy	Cals	Fat	Sat fat	Carb	Sugar	Protein	Fibre	Sodium
94kJ	22kcal	0.1g	0g	2.8g	2.4g	3.1g	0g	0.03g

Video: Boiling vegetables http://bit.ly/1E6f57O

44 Peas French-style *(petit pois à la française)*

	4 portions	10 portions
Peas (in the pod)	1 kg	2.5 kg
Spring or button onions	12	40
Lettuce, small	1	2–3
Butter	25 g	60 g
Salt		
Caster sugar	½ tsp	1 tsp
Flour	5 g	12 g

Energy	Cals	Fat	Sat fat	Carb	Sugar	Protein	Fibre
515kJ	123kcal	5.6g	3.4g	12.9g	5.8g	5.9g	5.7g

1 Shell and wash the peas and place in a sautéuse.

2 Peel and wash the onions, shred the lettuce and add to the peas with half the butter, a little salt and the sugar.

3 Barely cover with water. Cover with a lid and cook steadily, preferably in the oven, until tender.

4 Correct the seasoning.

5 Mix the remaining butter with the flour, making a *beurre manié*, and place it into the boiling peas in small pieces until thoroughly mixed; serve.

Note

When using frozen peas, allow the onions to almost cook before adding the peas.

1 Shell the peas and discard the pods

2 Place the prepared ingredients into the sautéuse

3 Add a *beurre manié* at the end of the cooking time

45 Courgette and potato cakes with mint and feta cheese

	6 portions
Courgettes	3 large
Potatoes	350g
Fresh mint, chopped	2 tbsp
Spring onions, finely chopped	2
Feta cheese	200g
Eggs	1
Plain flour	25g
Butter	25g
Olive oil	1 tbsp
Salt, pepper	

Energy	Cals	Fat	Sat fat	Carb	Sugar	Protein	Fibre	Sodium
930kJ	223kcal	14.2g	7.5g	15.2	2.3g	9.4g	2.1g	0.556g

1 Lightly scrape the courgettes to remove the outside skin. Purée in a food processor. Remove, sprinkle with salt to remove the excess moisture, leave for 1 hour. Rinse under cold water, squeeze out all excess moisture, dry on a clean cloth.

2 Steam or parboil the potatoes for 8–10 minutes. Cool and peel.

3 Carefully grate the potatoes, place in a bowl, then season.

4 Add the courgettes, mint, spring onion, chopped feta cheese and the beaten egg. Mix well.

5 Divide the mixture into 6 and shape into cakes approximately 1 cm thick.

6 Dust with flour.

7 Brush the cakes with melted butter and oil, place on a baking sheet, cook in an oven at 200 °C for 15 minutes; turn over and continue to cook for a further 15 minutes.

8 Serve on suitable plates garnished with fresh blanched mint leaves and salsa verde (see page 153).

Professional tip

Make sure that all excess moisture is removed from the courgettes at step 1. If they are too moist, the mixture will be difficult to handle.

Healthy eating tips
- Make sure the puréed courgettes are rinsed well to remove the added salt.
- Use a little sunflower oil to brush the cakes before cooking.

46 Deep-fried courgettes (*courgettes frites*)

1 Wash. Top and tail, and cut into round slices 3–6 mm thick.

2 Pass through flour, or milk and flour, or batter, and deep-fry in hot oil at 185 °C. Drain well and serve.

> **Professional tip**
> Make sure the oil is very hot before adding the courgette. Fry it quickly and drain it before serving.

Energy	Cals	Fat	Sat fat	Carb	Sugar	Protein	Fibre *
481 kJ	111 kcal	11.4 g	1.4 g	1.8 g	1.7 g	1.8 g	0.9 g

* Using vegetable oil

47 Fettuccini of courgette with chopped basil and balsamic vinegar

	4 portions	10 portions
Courgettes, large	2	5
Olive oil	50 ml	125 ml
Olive oil, to finish	20 ml	125 ml
Balsamic vinegar, to finish	20 ml	50 ml
Basil leaves, shredded	2	5

Energy	Cals	Fat	Sat fat	Carb	Sugar	Protein	Fibre	Sodium
745 kJ	181 kcal	17.9 g	2.6 g	1.9 g	1.8 g	1.8 g	1.2 g	0.0 g

1 Slice the courgettes finely lengthwise, using a mandolin (Japanese slicer).

2 Heat the olive oil in a suitable pan. Sauté the courgette slices quickly without colour for 35 seconds.

3 Place on suitable plates. Drizzle with olive oil and balsamic vinegar, and top with shredded basil leaves.

> **Note**
> This may be served as a vegetarian starter or as a garnish for fish and meat dishes.

48 Shallow-fried courgettes (*courgettes sautées*)

1 Wash. Top and tail, and cut into round slices 3–6 mm thick.

2 Gently fry in hot oil or butter for 2 or 3 minutes, drain and serve.

Energy	Cals	Fat	Sat fat	Carb	Sugar	Protein	Fibre *
456 kJ	111 kcal	10.7 g	6.6 g	1.9 g	1.8 g	1.9 g	0.9 g

* Using butter

49 Roast butternut squash or pumpkin with cinnamon and ginger

	4 portions	10 portions
Butternut squash or pumpkin	500 g	1.25 kg
Butter or margarine	25 g	60 g
Olive oil	2 tbsp	5 tbsp
Ground cinnamon	½ tsp	1 tsp
Ginger, peeled and freshly chopped	½ tsp	1 tsp
Caster sugar	10 g	25 g
Lemon, juice of	½	1

Energy	Cals	Fat	Sat fat	Carb	Sugar	Protein	Fibre	Sodium
342 kJ	81 kcal	4.1 g	0.5 g	10.4 g	5.6 g	1.4 g	2.5 g	trace

1 Peel the squash, cut it in half and remove the seeds.

2 Cut the squash into 1.5 cm dice or into small wedges.

3 Place the butter into a suitable roasting pan and heat gently. Add the olive oil, ginger and cinnamon.

4 Add the squash gently and stir until the squash is coated in the spice mixture. Season and add the sugar.

5 Place in an oven at 200 °C until tender and golden brown.

6 When cooked, sprinkle with lemon juice.

Variation

Garlic may be added to the spice mixture, and mixed spice may be used in place of cinnamon.

1 Peel and halve the squash, then remove the seeds

2 Cut the squash into even pieces

3 Stir the squash pieces into the warm butter and spices before roasting

50 Spiced aubergine purée

	4–6 portions
Diced aubergine	1 kg
Salt	20 g
Cumin	5 g
Tomato purée	45 g
Water	200 ml
Harissa paste	15 g
Vegetable nage	200 ml

1 Dice the aubergine and mix with the salt and cumin in a suitable bowl.

2 Allow to stand for 30 minutes.

3 Dry in a cloth and deep-fry for 10 minutes.

4 Purée with the rest of the ingredients and pass.

Variation

This purée can be added to rice or couscous, or used as a filling for stuffed vegetables. It can also be used as a garnish for meat dishes.

Energy	Cals	Fat	Sat fat	Carb	Sugar	Protein	Fibre	Sodium
176 kJ	41 kcal	1 g	0.2 g	6.5	6 g	2.7 g	6 g	1.608 g

51 Stuffed aubergine (*aubergine farcie*)

	4 portions	10 portions
Aubergines	2	5
Shallots, chopped	10 g	25 g
Oil or fat, to fry		
Mushrooms	100 g	250 g
Parsley, chopped		
Tomato concassé	100 g	250 g
Salt, pepper		
Demi-glace or jus lié	125 ml	300 ml

Energy	Cals	Fat	Sat fat	Carb	Sugar	Protein	Fibre	Salt
557 kJ	134 kcal	12.2 g	1.5 g	4.3 g	3.8 g	2.4 g	4.5 g	0.7 g

1 Cut the aubergines in two lengthwise.

2 With the point of a small knife, make a cut round the halves approximately 0.5 cm from the edge, then make several cuts 0.5 cm deep in the centre.

3 Deep-fry in hot fat at 185 °C for 2–3 minutes; drain well.

4 Scoop out the centre pulp and chop it finely.

5 Cook the shallots in a little oil or fat without colouring.

6 Add the well-washed mushrooms. Cook gently for a few minutes.

7 Mix in the pulp, parsley and tomato; season. Replace in the aubergine skins.

8 Sprinkle with breadcrumbs and melted butter. Brown under the salamander.

9 Serve with a cordon of demi-glace or jus lié.

52 Stuffed tomatoes (*tomates farcies*)

	4 portions	10 portions
Tomatoes, medium-sized	8	20
Duxelle		
Shallots, chopped	10 g	25 g
Butter or oil	25 g	60 g
Mushrooms	150 g	375 g
Salt, pepper		
Clove of garlic, crushed (optional)	1	2–3
Breadcrumbs (white or wholemeal)	25 g	60 g
Parsley, chopped		

Energy	Cals	Fat	Sat fat	Carb	Sugar	Protein	Fibre
430 kJ	102 kcal	5.9 g	3.5 g	10.6 g	5.7 g	2.5 g	2.2 g

1 Wash the tomatoes, remove the eyes.

2 Remove the top quarter of each tomato with a sharp knife.

3 Carefully empty out the seeds without damaging the flesh.

4 Place on a greased baking tray.

5 Cook the shallots in a little butter or oil without colour.

6 Add the washed chopped mushrooms; season with salt and pepper; add the garlic if using. Cook for 2–3 minutes.

7 Add a little of the strained tomato juice, the breadcrumbs and the parsley; mix to a piping consistency. Correct the seasoning. At this stage, several additions may be made (e.g. chopped ham, cooked rice).

8 Place the mixture in a piping bag with a large plain tube and pipe into the tomato shells. Replace the tops.

9 Brush with oil, season lightly with salt and pepper.

10 Cook in a moderate oven at 180–200 °C for 4–5 minutes.

11 Serve garnished with picked parsley or fresh basil or rosemary.

Healthy eating tips

- Use a small amount of an unsaturated oil to cook the shallots and brush over the stuffed tomatoes.
- Add the minimum amount of salt.
- Adding cooked rice to the stuffing will increase the amount of starchy carbohydrate.

1 Slice off the top and cut out the eye of the tomato

2 Remove the seeds from inside

3 Pipe in the filling and then replace the top

53 Tomato concassé (*tomate concassé*)

1 Plunge the tomatoes into boiling water for 5–10 seconds – the riper the tomatoes, the less time is required. Refresh immediately.
2 Remove the skins, cut in quarters and remove all the seeds.
3 Roughly chop the flesh of the tomatoes.
4 Meanwhile, cook the chopped onion or shallots without colour in the butter or oil.
5 Add the tomatoes and season lightly.
6 Simmer gently on the side of the stove until the moisture is evaporated.

	4 portions	10 portions
Tomatoes	400 g	1.25 kg
Shallots or onions, chopped	25 g	60 g
Butter or oil	25 g	60 g
Salt, pepper		

Note

This is a cooked preparation that is usually included in the normal *mise-en-place* of a kitchen as it is used in a great number of dishes.

Uncooked tomato concassée is often used for *mise en place*.

1 Blanch the tomatoes and then peel them

2 Cut each tomato into quarters

3 Remove the seeds from each petal

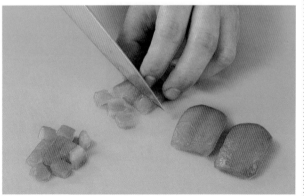

4 Roughly chop the tomatoes

54 Asparagus points or tips *(pointes d'asperges)*

Energy	Cals	Fat	Sat fat	Carb	Sugar	Protein	Fibre	Sodium
124kJ	29kcal	0.9g	0.1g	1.6g	1.6g	3.5g	1.6g	0.07g

1 Using the back of a small knife, carefully remove the tips of the leaves.

2 Scrape the stem, either with the blade of a small knife or a peeler.

3 Wash well. Tie into bundles of about 12 heads.

4 Cut off the excess stem.

5 Cook in lightly salted boiling water for approximately 5–8 minutes.

6 Test if cooked by gently pressing the green part of the stem, which should be tender; do not overcook.

7 Lift carefully out of the water. Remove the string, drain well and serve.

Note

Young thin asparagus, 50 pieces to the bundle, is known as sprew or sprue. It is prepared in the same way as asparagus except that, when it is very thin, the removal of the leaf tips is dispensed with. It may be served as a vegetable, perhaps brushed with butter.

Asparagus tips are also used in numerous garnishes for soups, egg dishes, fish, meat and poultry dishes, cold dishes, salad, and so on.

Professional tip

As the flavour of asparagus is mild and can be leached out very easily through the cooking medium, a method of cookery that ensures that no flavour is lost in the cooking process is microwaving.

1 To microwave, place a piece of cling film over a plate that will fit in the microwave and, more importantly, is microwave safe.

2 Spread the cling film with a little oil and salt, evenly place the asparagus on the plate in a single layer.

3 Cover the plate and asparagus with another piece of cling film, and microwave for 30-second stints until the asparagus is tender; serve immediately.

The benefit of this method is that it retains flavour and colour, and it can be cooked in minutes, as opposed to batch cooking, which will, invariably, cause the asparagus to lose flavour and colour the longer it is stored.

If larger-scale cooking is required, the more traditional method, boiling in lightly salted water, should be used: cooking, say, 100 portions of asparagus in the microwave should be avoided for obvious reasons!

55 Asparagus wrapped in puff pastry with Gruyère

	4 portions	10 portions
Gruyère cheese	175 g	400 g
Parmesan, freshly grated	3 tbsp	7 tbsp
Crème fraiche	250 ml	625 ml
Puff pastry (page 519)	350 g	875 g
Eggwash or milk, for brushing		
Asparagus, freshly cooked	350 g	875 g
Salt, pepper		
Watercress, for garnish		

Energy	Cals	Fat	Sat fat	Carb	Sugar	Protein	Fibre
2017 kJ	485 kcal	37.7 g	15.0 g	23.4 g	2.5 g	15.9 g	0.8 g

1 Cut the Gruyère cheese into 1 cm dice. In a suitable bowl, mix the Parmesan cheese and crème fraiche; season.

2 Roll out the puff pastry to approximately 0.25 cm thick and cut into squares approximately 18 × 18 cm.

3 Brush the edges with eggwash or milk.

4 Divide the crème fraiche, putting equal amounts onto the centre of each square. Lay the asparagus on top. Place the diced Gruyère cheese firmly between the asparagus.

5 Fold the opposite corners of each square to meet in the centre, like an envelope. Firmly pinch the seams together to seal them. Make a small hole in the centre of each one to allow the steam to escape. Place on a lightly greased baking sheet.

6 Allow to relax for 20 minutes in the refrigerator. Brush with eggwash or milk, sprinkle with Parmesan.

7 Bake in a hot oven at 200 °C for approximately 20–25 minutes until golden brown.

8 Serve garnished with watercress.

Professional tip

Make sure the pastry parcels are well sealed so that the mixture does not escape during cooking.

Healthy eating tip
The puff pastry and cheese make this dish high in fat. Serve with plenty of starchy carbohydrate to dilute it.

56 Globe artichokes (*artichauts en branche*)

Energy	Cals	Fat	Sat fat	Carb	Sugar	Protein	Fibre	*
32 kJ	8 kcal	0.0 g	0.0 g	1.4 g	1.4 g	0.6 g	0.0 g	

* Not including sauce

1 Allow 1 artichoke per portion.

2 Cut off the stems close to the leaves.

3 Cut off about 2 cm across the tops of the leaves.

4 Trim the remainder of the leaves with scissors or a small knife.

5 Place a slice of lemon at the bottom of each artichoke.

6 Secure with string.

7 Simmer in gently boiling, lightly salted water (to which a little ascorbic acid – one vitamin C tablet – may be added) until the bottom is tender (20–30 minutes).

8 Refresh under running water until cold.

9 Remove the centre of the artichoke carefully.

10 Scrape away all the furry inside (the choke) and leave clean.

11 Replace the centre, upside down.

12 Reheat by placing in a pan of boiling salted water for 3–4 minutes.

13 Drain and serve accompanied by a suitable sauce.

Note

Artichokes may also be served cold with vinaigrette sauce.

Professional tip

Do not cook artichokes in an iron or aluminium pan because these metals cause a chemical reaction that will discolour them.

57 Shallow-fried chicory (*endive meunière*)

	4 portions	10 portions
Fish or chicken stock	200 ml	500 ml
Chicory heads	8	20
Fresh lemon juice	3 tbsp	8 tbsp
Caster sugar	3 tbsp	8 tbsp
Sea salt, black pepper		
Butter	25 g	60 g

Energy	Cals	Fat	Sat fat	Carb	Sugar	Protein	Fibre	*
484 kJ	118 kcal	12.0 g	7.3 g	4.8 g	1.3 g	0.9 g	1.5 g	

* Using 37.5 g butter

1 Trim the stem, remove any discoloured leaves, wash.

2 Bring a pan of water to the boil and add the lemon juice, 1 tbsp of the sugar, and salt to taste. Blanch the chicory for 8–10 minutes and drain well.

3 Drain all of the liquid from the chicory. In a large frying pan, heat the butter and brown the chicory on all sides. Deglaze with a little stock and simmer for a few minutes, basting the chicory at all times.

4 Serve with 10 g per portion nut-brown butter, lemon juice and chopped parsley.

58 Greek-style mushrooms (*champignons à la grecque*)

	4 portions	10 portions
Water	250 ml	625 ml
Olive oil	60 ml	150 ml
Lemon, juice of	1	1 ½
Bay leaf	½	1
Sprig of thyme		
Peppercorns	6	18
Coriander seeds	6	18
Salt		
Small white button mushrooms, cleaned	200 g	500 g

Energy	Cals	Fat	Sat fat	Carb	Sugar	Protein	Fibre	Salt	*
587 kJ	142 kcal	15.2 g	2.2 g	0.4 g	0.3 g	1.0 g	0.6 g		

1 Combine all the ingredients except the mushrooms, to create a Greek-style cooking liquor.

2 Cook the mushrooms gently in the cooking liquor for 3 to 4 minutes.

3 Serve cold with the unstrained liquor.

Professional tip

Simmer the vegetables carefully so that they are correctly cooked and absorb the flavours.

Variation

Other vegetables such as artichokes and cauliflower can also be cooked in this style, using the same liquor.

- For artichokes, peel and trim 6 artichokes for 4 portions (or 15 for 10); cut the leaves short and remove the chokes. Blanch the artichokes in water with a little lemon juice for 10 minutes, refresh, then simmer in the Greek-style liquor for 15–20 minutes.
- For cauliflower, trim and wash one medium cauliflower for 4 portions (2 for 10); break it into small sprigs about the size of cherries. Blanch the sprigs for about 5 minutes, refresh, then simmer in the Greek-style liquor for 5–10 minutes. Keep the cauliflower slightly undercooked and crisp.

59 Sauté of wild mushrooms

1 Allow 50 g of mixed wild mushrooms per portion.

2 Shallow fry in butter or oil.

Energy	Cals	Fat	Sat fat	Carb	Sugar	Protein	Fibre	Sodium
322 kJ	78 kcal	8.1 g	5.3 g	0.1	0.1 g	1.2 g	1 g	0.002 g

60 Broccoli

1 Cook in lightly salted water, or steam.

Note

Because of their size, green and purple broccoli need less cooking time than cauliflower. Broccoli is usually broken down into florets and, as such, requires very little cooking: once brought to the boil, 1–2 minutes should be sufficient. This leaves the broccoli slightly crisp.

Tenderstem broccoli is increasingly popular. It has long, slim, evenly sized stems and small flower heads, so it cooks quickly. The distinctive flavour is similar to asparagus. Green and purple varieties are available, and, because of the uniform shape, they can be presented very attractively.

Energy	Cals	Fat	Sat fat	Carb	Sugar	Protein	Fibre	Sodium
125 kJ	30 kcal	1 g	0.3 g	1.4 g	1.1 g	3.9 g	4.6 g	0.2 g

61 Cauliflower au gratin (*chou-fleur mornay*)

1 Cut the cooked cauliflower into four.
2 Reheat in a pan of hot salted water (*chauffant*), or reheat in butter in a suitable pan.
3 Place in vegetable dish or on a greased tray.
4 Coat with 250 ml of mornay sauce (see page 131).
5 Sprinkle with grated cheese.
6 Brown under the salamander and serve.

Healthy eating tip
No additional salt is needed as cheese is added.

Energy	Cals	Fat	Sat fat	Carb	Sugar	Protein	Fibre
632 kJ	150 kcal	10.4 g	3.9 g	8.6 g	3.8 g	6.3 g	2.0 g

62 Cauliflower polonaise (*chou-fleur polonaise*)

1 Cut the cooked cauliflower into four. Reheat in a chauffant or in butter in a suitable pan.
2 Heat 50 g butter, add 10 g fresh breadcrumbs in a frying pan and lightly brown. Sprinkle over the cauliflower, sprinkle with sieved hardboiled egg and chopped parsley.

Energy	Cals	Fat	Sat fat	Carb	Sugar	Protein	Fibre
575 kJ	139 kcal	11.9 g	6.9 g	4.1 g	1.9 g	4.0 g	1.7 g

63 Crispy deep-fried tofu

	4 portions	10 portions
Firm tofu, cut into cubes	200 g	500 g

1 Coat the tofu cubes with any of the following: flour, egg and breadcrumbs; milk and flour; cornstarch; arrowroot.

2 Deep-fry the tofu at 180 °C, until golden brown. Drain.

3 Serve garnished with freshly grated ginger and julienne of herbs or serve with a tomato sauce flavoured with coriander.

Healthy eating tips
● Use an unsaturated oil to fry the tofu.
● Make sure the oil is hot so that less is absorbed.
● Alternatively, try dry-frying the tofu.

Energy	Cals	Fat	Sat fat	Carb	Sugar	Protein	Fibre	*
543kJ	131kcal	8.9g	0.0g	1.0g	0.5g	11.8g	0.0g	

* For a 50 g portion

64 Oriental stir-fry Quorn

	4 portions	10 portions
Soy sauce	62 ml	156 ml
Ginger, freshly grated	12 g	30 g
Black pepper, to taste		
Quorn pieces, defrosted	200 g	500 g
Vegetable oil	1 tbsp	3 tbsp
Spring onions	8	20
Red pepper, halved, deseeded and finely sliced	1	3
Yellow pepper, halved, deseeded and finely sliced	1	3
Green pepper, halved, deseeded and finely sliced	1	3
Dry sherry	1 tbsp	3 tbsp
Vegetable stock	62 ml	156 ml
Sugar	¼ tsp	1 tsp
Cornflour	6 g	15 g
Blanched almonds or cashews	50 g	100 g

Energy	Cals	Fat	Sat fat	Carb	Sugar	Protein	Fibre
836kJ	200kcal	11.8g	1.3g	11.6g	7.3g	12.7g	5.6g

1 Prepare a marinade by mixing the soy sauce with the ginger, and season with black pepper.

2 Add the Quorn pieces, mix well and chill for 1 hour.

3 Strain the Quorn from the marinade. In a wok, add half the vegetable oil and stir-fry the Quorn quickly for approximately 4 minutes. Remove from the wok.

4 Add the remaining oil, and fry the spring onion and peppers for another 1–2 minutes.

5 Return the Quorn to the wok.

6 Add the strained marinade, sherry, stock and sugar. Bring to the boil.

7 Thicken lightly with the cornflour. Add the blanched almonds or cashews and stir gently to enable the ingredients to be covered with the sauce.

8 Serve with noodles or rice.

Healthy eating tips
● Use a little unsaturated oil to fry the Quorn, onions and peppers.
● No added salt is needed; there is plenty of flavour from the soy sauce, ginger and stock.

65 Deep-fried seaweed

1 Carefully pick over the seaweed. Wash and thoroughly drain and dry on a cloth.

2 Quickly fry in hot, deep fat (approximately 175–190 °C).

3 Remove and drain on absorbent kitchen paper.

Energy	Cals	Fat	Sat fat	Carb	Sugar	Protein	Fibre	Sodium *
686 kJ	166 kcal	15.9g	0g	4.2	0g	1.9g	0g	0.003g

* Per 28 g serving

Professional tip

The seaweed must be cooked quickly in hot oil, until it is crisp.

66 Japanese sea vegetable and noodle salad

	4 portions	10 portions
Dried arame	125 g	320 g
Shredded green cabbage	500 g	1.25 kg
Coarsely chopped parsley	2 tbsp	5 tbsp
Julienne of carrots	125 g	320 g
Finely chopped celery	50 g	125 g
Chopped chives	50 g	125 g
Cooked udon noodles	400 g	1 kg
Sesame oil	2 tbsp	5 tbsp
Rice vinegar	3 tbsp	7 tbsp
Smoked tofu, diced in 1 cm	75 g	180 g

1 In a large bowl, cover the arame with water and soak for 10 minutes. Drain well.

2 Place the arame back in the bowl, add the cabbage, parsley, carrots, celery, chives and mix well.

3 Add the cooked noodles, oil and vinegar; season and mix well.

4 Serve garnished with diced tofu.

Energy	Cals	Fat	Sat fat	Carb	Sugar	Protein	Fibre	Sodium
1138 kJ	271 kcal	9.4g	1.3g	39g	8.3g	10.2g	7.5g	0.4g

67 Sea kale (*chou de mer*)

Half a kilogram of sea kale will yield about 3 portions.

1 Trim the roots and remove any discoloured leaves.
2 Wash well and tie into a neat bundle.
3 Cook in boiling lightly salted water for 15–20 minutes. Do not overcook.
4 Drain well, serve accompanied with a suitable sauce (e.g. melted butter, hollandaise).

Energy	Cals	Fat	Sat fat	Carb	Sugar	Protein	Fibre
33 kJ	8 kcal	0.0 g	0.0 g	0.6 g	0.6 g	1.4 g	0.0 g

68 Alu-chole (vegetarian curry)

1 Heat the ghee in a suitable pan.
2 Add the cinnamon, bay leaves and cumin seeds; fry for 1 minute.
3 Add the onion and garlic. Fry until golden brown.
4 Add the chopped tomatoes, curry paste and salt, and fry for a further 2–3 minutes.
5 Stir in the potatoes and water. Bring to the boil. Cover and simmer until the potatoes are cooked.
6 Add the chickpeas; allow to heat through.
7 Stir in the coriander leaves and tamarind sauce or lemon juice; serve.

Note

This is a dish from northern India. It can be served as a vegetarian dish with rice, or to accompany meat and chicken dishes.

Professional tip

Fry the spices well to extract the maximum flavour from them.

	4 portions	10 portions
Vegetable ghee or oil	3 tsp	7 ½ tsp
Small cinnamon sticks	4	10
Bay leaves	4	10
Cumin seeds	1 tsp	2 ½ tsp
Onion, finely chopped	100 g	250 g
Cloves garlic, finely chopped and crushed	2	5
Plum tomatoes, canned, chopped	400 g	1 kg
Hot curry paste	3 tsp	7 ½ tsp
Salt, to taste		
Potatoes in 1 cm dice	100 g	250 g
Water	125 ml	312 ml
Chickpeas, canned, drained	400 g	1 kg
Coriander leaves, chopped	50 g	125 g
Tamarind sauce or lemon juice	2 tbsp	3 tbsp

Healthy eating tips
● Use a small amount of unsaturated oil to fry the spices and onion.
● Skim the fat from the finished dish.
● No added salt is necessary.

Energy	Cals	Fat	Sat fat	Carb	Sugar	Protein	Fibre [*]
1214 kJ	290 kcal	17.5 g	1.6 g	26.6 g	5.3 g	10.6 g	5.5 g

* Using lemon juice and vegetable oil

69 Chinese vegetables and noodles

	4 portions	10 portions
Chinese noodles	400 g	1.250 kg
Oil	60 ml	150 ml
Celery	100 g	250 g
Carrots, cut in paysanne	100 g	250 g
Bamboo shoots	50 g	125 g
Mushrooms, finely sliced	75 g	180 g
Chinese cabbage, shredded	75 g	180 g
Beansprouts	100 g	250 g
Soy sauce	30 ml	75 ml

Garnish (spring onions, sliced lengthways and quickly stir-fried)

1 Cook the noodles in boiling salted water for about 5–6 minutes until *al dente*. Refresh and drain.

2 Heat the oil in a wok and stir-fry all the vegetables, except the beansprouts, for 1 minute. Then add the beansprouts and cook for a further minute.

3 Add the drained noodles, stirring well; allow to reheat through.

4 Correct the seasoning.

5 Serve in a suitable dish, garnished with the spring onions.

Healthy eating tips
● Keep added salt to a minimum.
● Use an unsaturated oil (olive or sunflower) and reduce the quantity used.

Energy	Cals	Fat	Sat fat	Carb	Sugar	Protein	Fibre *
2332 kJ	554 kcal	21.6 g	1.8 g	80.6 g	5.7 g	14.3 g	1.9 g

* Using canned bamboo shoots

70 Coleslaw

	4 portions	10 portions
White or Chinese cabbage	200 g	500 g
Carrots	50 g	125 g
Onion (optional)	25 g	60 g
Mayonnaise, natural yoghurt or fromage frais	125 ml	300 ml

Energy	Cals	Fat	Sat fat	Carb	Sugar	Protein	Fibre *
2514 kJ	599 kcal	59.0 g	8.8 g	11.7 g	11.4 g	5.9 g	7.2 g

* Using mayonnaise, for 4 portions

1 Trim off the outside leaves of the cabbage.

2 Cut into quarters. Remove the centre stalk.

3 Wash the cabbage, shred finely and drain well.

4 Mix with a fine julienne of raw carrot and shredded raw onion. To lessen the harshness of raw onion, blanch and refresh.

5 Bind with mayonnaise, natural yoghurt or vinaigrette.

Professional tip

Cut the cabbage into fine julienne to give the coleslaw a good, even texture.

Healthy eating tip

Replace some or all of the mayonnaise with natural yoghurt and/or fromage frais.

71 Mixed vegetables (*macédoine* or *jardinière de légumes*)

1 Peel and wash the carrots and turnips; cut into 0.5 cm dice (macédoine) or batons (jardinière); cook separately in lightly salted water, do not overcook. Refresh.

2 Top and tail the beans; cut into 0.5 cm dice, cook and refresh, do not overcook.

3 Cook the peas and refresh.

4 Mix the vegetables and, when required, reheat in hot salted water.

5 Drain well, serve brushed with melted butter.

	4 portions	10 portions
Carrots	100 g	250 g
Turnips	50 g	125 g
Salt		
French beans	50 g	125 g
Peas	50 g	125 g

Video: Cutting vegetables into macédoine http://bit.ly/ 1znW8rU

Energy	Cals	Fat	Sat fat	Carb	Sugar	Protein	Fibre
58 kJ	14 kcal	0.1 g	0.0 g	2.5 g	1.7 g	1.0 g	2.1 g

72 Ratatouille

	4 portions	10 portions
Baby marrow (courgette)	200 g	500 g
Aubergines	200 g	500 g
Tomatoes	200 g	500 g
Oil	50 ml	125 ml
Onions, finely sliced	50 g	125 g
Clove of garlic, peeled and chopped	1	2
Red peppers, diced	50 g	125 g
Green peppers, diced	50 g	125 g
Salt, pepper		
Parsley, chopped	1 tsp	2–3 tsp

Energy	Cals	Fat	Sat fat	Carb	Sugar	Protein	Fibre
579 kJ	138 kcal	12.6 g	1.7 g	5.2 g	4.6 g	1.3 g	2.4 g

1 Trim off both ends of the marrow and aubergines.

2 Remove the skin using a peeler.

3 Cut into 3 mm slices.

4 Concassé the tomatoes (peel, remove seeds, roughly chop).

5 Place the oil in a thick-bottomed pan and add the onions.

6 Cover with a lid and allow to cook gently for 5–7 minutes without colour.

7 Add the garlic, marrow and aubergine slices, and the peppers.

8 Season lightly with salt and mill pepper.

9 Allow to cook gently for 4–5 minutes, toss occasionally and keep covered.

10 Add the tomato and continue cooking for 20–30 minutes or until tender.

11 Mix in the parsley, correct the seasoning and serve.

The vegetables need to be cut evenly so that they will cook evenly; it also improves the texture of the dish.

Healthy eating tips
- Use a little unsaturated oil to cook the onions.
- Use the minimum amount of salt.

Ingredients for ratatouille

Adding the tomato to the vegetables during cooking (step 10)

73 Tempura

	4 portions
Vegetable oil	500 ml
Courgettes, sliced	2
Sweet potato, scrubbed and sliced	1
Green pepper, seeds removed and cut into strips	1
Shiitake mushroom, stalks removed and halved if large	4
Onion, sliced as half moons	1
Parsley sprigs, to garnish	4
Batter (NB all ingredients must be stored in the fridge until just before mixing)	
Egg yolk	1
Ice-cold sparkling water	200 ml
Plain flour, sifted	100 g
Tentsuyu dipping sauce (optional)	
Dashi stock	200 ml
Mirin	3 tbsp
Soy sauce	3 tbsp
Ginger, grated	½ tsp

Energy	Cals	Fat	Sat fat	Carb	Sugar	Protein	Fibre
3397 kJ	815 kcal	55.9 g	7.4 g	67.4 g	5.3 g	14.8 g	5.0 g

1 To prevent splattering during the frying, make sure to dry all deep-fry ingredients thoroughly first with a kitchen towel.

2 For the batter, beat the egg yolk lightly and mix with the ice-cold water.

3 Add half the flour to the egg and water mixture. Give the mixture a few strokes. Add the rest of the flour all at once. Stroke the mixture a few times with chopsticks or a fork until the ingredients are loosely combined. The batter should be very lumpy. If over-mixed, tempura will be oily and heavy.

4 Heat the oil to 160 °C.

5 Dip the vegetables into plain flour and then into the batter, a few pieces at a time. Fry until just crisp and golden (about 1 ½ minutes).

6 Drain the cooked vegetables on a kitchen towel.

7 Serve immediately with a pinch of salt, garnished with parsley sprigs and lemon wedges, dry-roasted salt or with Tentsuyu dipping sauce in a small bowl with grated ginger. This dish can also be served with an accompaniment of grated white radish.

8 To make the Tentsuyu sauce (if required), combine the ingredients in a small saucepan; heat it through and leave to one side.

Note

Any vegetables with a firm texture may be used for tempura.

1 Use sparkling water to make tempura batter

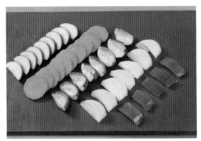

2 Cut a variety of vegetables into even pieces

3 Dip each piece into the batter and then deep-fry it

Professional tip

The water and other batter ingredients must be ice cold.

The batter should be lumpy to give it texture. Do not over-mix it; this will make it oily and heavy.

Only fry a few pieces at once.

Healthy eating tip

Use sunflower or groundnut oil for frying.

74 Vegetarian strudel

Energy	Cals	Fat	Sat fat	Carb	Sugar	Protein	Fibre
2117 kJ	504 kcal	27.6 g	4.0 g	54.1 g	10.5 g	14.3 g	9.7 g

Note

Wholemeal breadcrumbs can be substituted with white breadcrumbs.

	4 portions	10 portions
Strudel dough		
Strong flour	200 g	500 g
Pinch of salt		
Sunflower oil	25 g	60 g
Egg	1	2–3
Water at 37 °C	83 ml	125 ml
Filling		
Large cabbage leaves	200 g	500 g
Sunflower oil	4 tbsp	10 tbsp
Onion, finely chopped	50 g	125 g
Cloves garlic, chopped	2	5
Courgettes	400 g	1 kg
Carrots	200 g	500 g
Turnips	100 g	250 g
Tomato, skinned, deseeded and diced	300 g	750 g
Tomato purée	25 g	60 g
Toasted sesame seeds	25 g	60 g
Wholemeal breadcrumbs	50 g	125 g
Fresh chopped basil	3 g	9 g
Seasoning		
Eggwash		

1 To make the strudel dough, sieve the flour with the salt and make a well.

2 Add the oil, egg and water, and gradually incorporate the flour to make a smooth dough; knead well.

3 Place in a basin, cover with a damp cloth; allow to relax for 3 minutes.

4 Meanwhile, prepare the filling: take the large cabbage leaves, wash and discard the tough centre stalks, blanch in boiling salted water for 2 minutes, until limp. Refresh and drain well in a clean cloth.

5 Heat the oil in a sauté pan, gently fry the onion and garlic until soft.

6 Peel and chop the courgettes into ½ cm dice, blanch and refresh. Peel and dice the carrots and turnips, blanch and refresh.

7 Place the well-drained courgettes, carrots and turnips into a basin, add the tomato concassé, tomato purée, sesame seeds, breadcrumbs and chopped basil, and mix well. Season.

8 Roll out the strudel dough to a thin rectangle, place on a clean cloth and stretch until extremely thin.

9 Lay the drained cabbage leaves on the stretched strudel dough, leaving approximately a 1 cm gap from the edge.

10 Place the filling in the centre. Eggwash the edges.

11 Fold in the longer side edges to meet in the middle. Roll up.

12 Transfer to a lightly oiled baking sheet. Brush with the sunflower oil.

13 Bake for 40 minutes in a preheated oven at 180–200 °C.

14 When cooked, serve hot, sliced on individual plates with a cordon of tomato sauce made with vegetable stock.

Professional tip

It is essential to roll out and stretch the strudel dough so that it is very thin, but without breaking it.

Healthy eating tips
- Use the minimum amount of salt.
- Use a little unsaturated oil to cook the onion and garlic.

75 Crisp polenta and roasted Mediterranean vegetables

Energy	Cals	Fat	Sat fat	Carb	Sugar	Protein	Fibre	Sodium
3267 kJ	790 kcal	71.4 g	18.9 g	28.6 g	14.0 g	10.1 g	6.6 g	0.1 g

	4 portions	10 portions
Polenta		
Water	200 ml	500 ml
Butter	30 g	75 g
Polenta flour	65 g	160 g
Parmesan, grated	25 g	60 g
Egg yolks	1	2
Crème fraiche	110 g	275 g
Seasoning		
Roasted vegetables		
Red peppers	2	5
Yellow peppers	2	5
Courgettes	2	5
Red onions	2	5
Vegetable oil	200 ml	500 ml
Seasoning		
Clove of garlic	1	3
Thyme, sprigs	2	5

To make the polenta:

1 Bring the water and the butter to the boil.

2 Season the water well and whisk in the polenta flour.

3 Continue to whisk until very thick.

4 Remove from the heat and add the Parmesan, egg yolk and crème fraiche.

5 Whisk until all incorporated; check the seasoning.

6 Set in a lined tray.

7 Once set, cut using a round cutter or cut into squares.

8 Reserve until required.

To make the roasted vegetables:

1 Roughly chop the vegetables into large chunks. Ensure the seeds are removed from the peppers.

2 Toss the cut vegetables in the oil and season well.

3 Place the vegetables in an oven with the aromats for 30 minutes at 180 °C.

4 Remove from the oven and drain. Reserve until required.

To serve:

1 To serve the dish, shallow-fry the polenta in a non-stick pan until golden on both sides.

2 Warm the roasted vegetables and place them in the middle of the plate. Place the polenta on top.

3 Finish with rocket salad and balsamic dressing.

> **Professional tip**
>
> Line the tray with cling film and silicone paper before pouring in the polenta – this will stop it from sticking to the tray when it sets.

76 Niçoise salad

	4 portions	10 portions
Tomatoes	100 g	250 g
French beans, cooked	200 g	500 g
Diced potatoes, cooked	100 g	250 g
Salt, pepper		
Vinaigrette	1 tbsp	2 ½ tbsp
Anchovy fillets	10 g	25 g
Capers	5 g	12 g
Stoned olives	10 g	25 g

1 Peel the tomatoes, deseed and cut into neat segments.

2 Dress the beans, tomatoes and potatoes neatly.

3 Season with salt and pepper. Add the vinaigrette.

4 Decorate with anchovies, capers and olives.

Healthy eating tips
- Lightly dress with vinaigrette.
- The anchovies are high in salt, so no added salt is necessary.

Energy	Cals	Fat	Sat fat	Carb	Sugar	Protein	Fibre	*
867 kJ	207 kcal	9.6 g	1.5 g	25.0 g	4.9 g	6.9 g	9.9 g	

* For 4 portions

77 Potato salad (*salade de pommes de terre*)

1 Cut the potatoes into ½–1 cm dice; sprinkle with vinaigrette.

2 Mix with the onion or chive, add the mayonnaise and correct the seasoning. (The onion may be blanched to reduce its harshness.)

3 Dress neatly and sprinkle with chopped parsley or herbs.

Note

This is not usually served as a single hors d'oeuvre or main course.

Professional tip

Mixing the potato, onion and mayonnaise gives a good flavour and texture, but be careful not to mix them too much or the potatoes will break up.

Variation

Potato salad can also be made by dicing raw peeled or unpeeled potato, cooking them – preferably by steaming (to retain shape) – and mixing with vinaigrette while warm.

Try adding two chopped hard-boiled eggs or 100 g of peeled dessert apple mixed with lemon juice, or a small bunch of picked watercress leaves.

Potatoes may be cooked with mint and allowed to cool with the mint.

Cooked small new potatoes can be tossed in vinaigrette with chopped fresh herbs (e.g. mint, parsley, chives).

	4 portions	10 portions
Potatoes, cooked	200 g	500 g
Vinaigrette	1 tbsp	2 ½ tbsp
Onion or chive (optional), chopped	10 g	25 g
Mayonnaise or natural yoghurt	125 ml	300 ml
Salt, pepper		
Parsley or mixed fresh herbs, chopped		

Energy	Cals	Fat	Sat fat	Carb	Sugar	Protein	Fibre	*
2013 kJ	479 kcal	34.9 g	5.1 g	40.0 g	1.3 g	4.0 g	2.6 g	

* Using mayonnaise, for 4 portions

78 Vegetable salad/Russian salad (salade de légumes/salade russe)

1. Peel and wash the carrots and turnips, cut into 0.5 cm dice or batons.
2. Cook separately in salted water, refresh and drain well.
3. Top and tail the beans, and cut into 0.5 cm dice; cook, refresh and drain well.
4. Cook the peas, refresh and drain well.
5. Mix all the well-drained vegetables with vinaigrette and then mayonnaise.
6. Correct the seasoning. Dress neatly.

Note

Do not overcook the vegetables, and drain them well before adding the dressing – otherwise the salad will be too wet.

Healthy eating tips
- Try half mayonnaise and half natural yoghurt.
- Season with the minimum amount of salt.

	4 portions	10 portions
Carrots	100 g	250 g
Turnips	50 g	125 g
French beans	50 g	125 g
Peas	50 g	125 g
Vinaigrette	1 tbsp	2–3 tbsp
Mayonnaise or natural yoghurt	125 ml	300 ml
Salt, pepper		

Energy	Cals	Fat	Sat fat	Carb	Sugar	Protein	Fibre *
1566 kJ	373 kcal	35.0 g	5.2 g	10.1 g	8.2 g	5.0 g	11.9 g

* Using mayonnaise, for 4 portions

79 Waldorf salad

1. Dice celery or celeriac and crisp russet apples.
2. Mix with shelled and peeled walnuts and bind with mayonnaise.
3. Dress on quarters or leaves of lettuce (may also be served in hollowed-out apples).

Note

When mixing in the mayonnaise, add just enough to give the right texture and flavour.

Healthy eating tip
Try using some yoghurt in place of the mayonnaise, which will proportionally reduce the fat.

Energy	Cals	Fat	Sat fat	Carb	Sugar	Protein	Fibre	Sodium
657 kJ	159 kcal	14 g	1.8 g	7 g	6.9 g	1.6 g	2.2 g	0.08 g

80 Caesar salad

1 Separate the lettuce leaves, wash, dry thoroughly and refrigerate.

2 Lightly grill or fry (in good fresh oil) the croutons on all sides.

3 Plunge the eggs into boiling water for 1 minute, remove and set aside.

4 Break the lettuce into serving-sized pieces and place into a salad bowl.

5 Mix the dressing, break the eggs, spoon out the contents, mix with a fork, add to the dressing and mix into the salad.

6 Mix in the cheese, scatter the croutons on top and serve.

Professional tip

Because the eggs are only lightly cooked, they must be perfectly fresh, and the salad must be prepared and served immediately. In the interests of food safety, the eggs are sometimes hard boiled.

Alternatively, the salad may be garnished with hard-boiled gull's eggs.

	4 portions	10 portions
Cos lettuce (medium size)	2	4
Croutons, 2 cm square	16	40
Eggs, fresh	2	4
Dressing		
Garlic, finely chopped	1 tsp	2 tsp
Anchovy fillets, mashed	4	8
Lemon juice	1	2
Virgin olive oil	6 tbsp	15 tbsp
White wine vinegar	1 tbsp	2 tbsp
Salt, black mill pepper		
To serve		
Parmesan, freshly grated	75 g	150 g

Healthy eating tips
- No added salt is needed; anchovies and cheese are high in salt.
- Oven bake the croutons.
- Serve with fresh bread or rolls.

Energy	Cals	Fat	Sat fat	Carb	Sugar	Protein	Fibre	*
1494 kJ	361 kcal	32.2 g	7.9 g	5.1 g	2.0 g	12.9 g	1.2 g	

* Using toast for croutons

8 Prepare and cook meat and offal

This chapter will help you to:

1 prepare and cook meat and offal, including:
- selecting correct tools and equipment
- demonstrating safe and hygienic practices
- preparing and cooking dishes using the correct preparation skills, cooking methods and principles, and the correct portions
- using moulds/basins or shaping pastes according to the recipe
- applying flavourings and coatings
- using correct storage procedures
- making sauces, coulis, gravies and jus; flavoured butters/oils; and preparing dressings, garnishes and accompaniments
- applying finishing skills and assembling dishes correctly
- evaluating the finished dish.

2 understand how to:
- identify types of meat and offal and state the most commonly used joints and cuts
- explain the quality points of meat and offal
- identify tools and equipment used
- explain portion sizes and weights
- state the correct storage temperature for meat and offal
- explain suitable cooking methods and why cooking principles should be applied
- know when meat and offal are cooked
- describe preservation methods and their advantages and disadvantages
- describe how to check and finish the dish.

Recipes included in this chapter

Meat

Meat is the flesh of an animal considered to be edible; it is normally called butchers' meat by caterers and usually comes from cattle, sheep and pigs. Meat is a product of selective breeding and feeding techniques, which means that animals are produced to a high standard in terms of welfare, shape and yield, to produce tender flesh.

Structure of meat

To cook meat properly it is important to understand its structure.

- Meat is made of fibres bound together by **connective tissue**.
- Connective tissue is made up of **elastin** (yellow) and **collagen** (white). Yellow tissue needs to be removed.
- Small fibres are present in tender cuts and young animals.
- Coarser fibres are present in tougher cuts and older animals.
- Fat helps to provide flavour, and moistens meat in roasting and grilling.
- Tenderness, flavour and moistness are increased if meat is hung after slaughter and before being used.

Meat varies considerably in its fat content. The fat is found around the outside of meat, in **marbling** and inside the meat fibres. The visible fat (saturated) should be trimmed off as much as possible before cooking.

Take it further

Lots of useful information about meat can be obtained at www.qmscotland.co.uk.

Key terms

Connective tissue: animal tissue that binds together the fibres of meat.

Elastin: yellow protein found in connective tissue. This needs to be removed.

Collagen: white protein found in connective tissue.

Marbling: white flecks of fat within meat.

Quality points

Meat is a natural product and is therefore not a uniform product, varying in quality from carcass to carcass. Flavour, texture and appearance are determined by the type of animal and the way it has been fed.

Fat gives a characteristic flavour to meat and helps to keep it moist during roasting, but meat does not have to be fatty to be good quality and flavoursome.

The colour of meat a not a guide to quality. Consumers tend to choose light-coloured meat – bright red beef, for example – because they think it will be fresher than a dark red piece. Freshly butchered beef is bright red because the pigment (**myoglobin**) in the tissues has been chemically affected by the oxygen in the air, not because the meat itself is fresh. After several hours, the colour changes to dark red or brown as the pigment reacts further with oxygen in the air (is oxidised) to become **metamyoglobin**; darker meat can therefore still be fresh.

The colour of fat can vary from almost pure white in lamb, to bright yellow in beef. Colour depends on the feed, the breed and, to a certain extent, on the time of year.

> **Key terms**
>
> **Myoglobin**: pigment in the tissues which gives meat its bright red colour.
>
> **Metamyoglobin**: created when myoglobin is oxidised (reacts with oxygen in the air). This changes the colour of meat to dark red or brown.

The most useful guide to tenderness and quality is knowledge of the cuts of meat and their location on the carcass. The various cuts for each type of meat are described below, but a few principles can be followed.

- The leanest and most tender cuts – the '**prime**' cuts – come from the **hindquarters**.
- The parts of the animal that have had plenty of muscular exercise and where fibres have become hardened – the '**coarse**' cuts – come from the neck, legs and **forequarters**. These provide meat for braising and stewing, and many consider them to have more flavour, although they require slow cooking to make them tender.
- The meat from young animals is generally more tender. Tenderness is a prime factor, so sometimes animals are injected with an **enzyme** such as **papin** before slaughter, which softens the fibres and muscles. This simply speeds up the natural process, as meat contains its own enzymes that gradually break down the protein cell walls as the carcass ages.
- It is for this tenderisation process that meat is hung for 10 to 20 days in controlled conditions (temperature and humidity) before it is sold. The longer meat is aged, the more expensive it becomes, as the cost of refrigeration is high and the meat itself shrinks because of evaporation and the trimming of the outside hardened edges.

> **Key terms**
>
> **Prime cut**: the leanest and most tender cuts of meat; these come from the hindquarters
>
> **Coarse cut**: cuts from the neck, legs and forequarters; these are tougher cuts and therefore often cooked using slower methods such as braising and stewing.
>
> **Hindquarter**: the back part of the side of meat.
>
> **Forequarter**: the front section of the side of meat.
>
> **Enzyme**: a biological catalyst.
>
> **Papin**: an enzyme that is sometimes injected into animals before slaughter to speed up the softening of fibres and muscles.

Preservation methods

In order to preserve meat and offal it is important to reduce the micro-organisms that can cause food spoilage. The following methods are used to preserve meat:

- **Salting** – meat can be pickled in brine. The salt draws out moisture and creates an environment inhospitable to bacteria. This method of preservation may be applied to silverside, brisket and ox tongues. Salting is used in the production of bacon, before the sides of pork are smoked, and for hams.
- **Smoking** – mainly used to enhance flavour and colour of the product; as a preservation method its effect is limited to the surface of the product. There are two main types of smoking used: hot smoking, which cooks the meat during the process; cold smoking, which is part of a preservation method. Substitutes are used in some kitchens, which add flavour and the characteristics of smoked food to dishes. These add the flavour without the carcinogenic substances associated with smoke.
- **Pickling** – using acidic foods such as yoghurt, vinegar or wine raises the acidity levels and helps reduce the potential for food spoilage. This is used in Tandoori dishes.
- **Chilling** – this means that meat is kept at a temperature just above freezing point in a controlled atmosphere. Chilled meat cannot be kept in the usual type of cold room for more than a few days, although sufficient time must be allowed for the meat to hang, enabling it to become tender.
- **Vacuum packing** – small cuts of meat can be vacuum-packed prior to chilling. This removes contact with air and therefore may extend the shelf life.
- **Freezing** – small carcasses, such as lamb and mutton, can be frozen; their quality is not normally affected by freezing. They can be kept frozen until required and then thawed out before being used. Some beef is frozen, but it is not such good quality as chilled beef as it takes on ice crystals which, when thawed, affect the quality of the meat.
- **Canning** – large quantities of meat are canned. Corned beef, for example, has a very high protein content. Pork is used for tinned luncheon meat.

Advantages of preserving meat are that foods are ready prepared, saving time and labour. It is also easier to apply

portion control and manage costs and the preservation process will help to extend seasons or availability for some meat, as well as making storage easier while maintaining quality.

Disadvantages of preservation include the loss of some of the nutrients and a reduction in skills required, especially where meat and offal are bought in already prepared and preserved.

Portion sizes and weights

Portion control is about the size and quantity of food served to an individual customer. This is based on the type of customer or establishment, quality of products and cost in relation to the selling price of the dish or commodity; the type of menu or number of courses offered will also influence portion size. A chef's knowledge should enable them to work out the number of portions that can be expected from a specific commodity. For example, steaks are often bought and sold by weight per cut, for example, sirloin steaks at 200 g or fillet steaks at 150 g per serving/steak. For roast joints or prepared meats, this is around 6–8 portions per boneless kilo, therefore 125–200 g per portion.

> ### Health and safety !
>
> When using boning knives, wear a safety apron as protection; if a lot of boning is being done then it is also a good idea to wear protective gloves.

Storage

Hang and store meat between 0° C and 2° C.

Meat and offal should be stored covered with cling film, labelled with appropriate information about the product and the use by date.

Store uncooked meat on trays to prevent dripping, covered in separate refrigerators at a temperature of 3–5 °C, preferably at the lower temperature. When separate refrigerators are not available, store raw meat separately at the bottom of the refrigerator to prevent cross-contamination and away from cooked meats to prevent cross-contamination.

- Beef can be stored for up to 3 weeks.
- Veal can be stored for 1–3 weeks.
- Lamb can be stored for 10–15 days.
- Pork can be stored for 7–14 days.

Preparation

Meat from specific parts of an animal may be cut and cooked according to local custom (for more information on preparation methods, see the sections for each type of meat below). Some religions specify how meat should be butchered – especially in Jewish kosher and Islamic halal butchery, which stipulates the animal must be killed by an authorised person of the religion, all of the blood must be removed by draining, the meat must be soaked and salted, and consumed within 72 hours. Kosher dietary laws also state that only the forequarters of permitted animals – goats, sheep, deer and cattle – may be used.

> ### Health and safety !
>
> When preparing uncooked meat or poultry followed by cooked food, or changing from one type of meat or poultry to another, all equipment, working areas and utensils must be thoroughly cleaned or changed. Wash all work surfaces with a bactericidal detergent to kill bacteria. This is particularly important when handling poultry and pork. If colour-coded boards are used, it is essential to always use the correct colour-coded boards for the preparation of foods and different ones for cooked foods.

Cooking

Meat is an extremely versatile product that can be cooked in many ways and matched with practically any vegetable, fruit or herb. The cut (e.g. shin, steak, brisket), the method of heating (e.g. roasting, braising, grilling) and the time and temperature all affect the way the meat will taste.

Raw meat is difficult to chew because the muscle fibres contain collagen (see 'Structure of meat' above), which is softened only by mincing – as in steak tartare – or by cooking. When you cook meat, the protein gradually **coagulates** as the internal temperature increases. At 77 °C, coagulation is complete and the protein begins to harden, so any further cooking makes the meat tougher.

Since tenderness combined with flavour is the aim in meat cookery, time and temperature are the key concerns. In principle, slow cooking retains the juices and produces a more tender result than fast cooking at high temperatures. There are, of course, occasions when high temperatures are essential: for instance, you need to grill a steak under a hot flame for a very short time in order to get a crisp, brown surface and a pink, juicy interior – using a low temperature would not give you the desired result. In potentially tough cuts (e.g. breast of lamb), or where there is a lot of connective tissue (e.g. in neck of lamb), slower cooking converts the tissues to **gelatine** and helps to make the meat more tender. Meat containing bone will take longer to cook because bone is a poor conductor of heat.

> **Key terms**
>
> **Coagulate**: the transformation of liquids or moisture in meat to a solid form.
>
> **Gelatine**: a nearly transparent, glutinous substance, obtained by boiling the bones, ligaments, etc., of animals, and used in making jellies.

- Tough or coarse cuts of meat should be cooked by braising, pot roasting or stewing. These longer, slower methods of cooking dissolve the collagen, forming gelatine and making the meat more tender and tasty.
- Prime cuts, such as beef fillets, contain little collagen and do not require long cooking to tenderise the meat. Although most chefs would start the prime cuts at a high temperature for a short period, this does not always give a perfect result.
- **Searing** meat in hot fat or in a hot oven before roasting or stewing helps to produce a crisp exterior by coagulating the protein. However, it does not seal in the juices. Also, if the temperature is too high and the meat is cooked for too long, rapid evaporation of the juices and contraction of the meat will cause much of the juices and fat to be lost, making the meat tougher, drier and less tasty. This is particularly true for prime cuts, as they do not contain much fat or collagen to start with. A lower temperature and longer in the oven will produce a better result.
- Sprinkling salt on meat before cooking will also speed up the loss of moisture because salt absorbs water.
- Marinating in a suitable marinade, such as wine and wine vinegar, helps to tenderise the meat and adds flavour.

> **Professional tip**
>
> Meat bones are useful for giving flavour to soups and stocks, especially beef bones with plenty of marrow. Veal bones are gelatinous and help to enrich and thicken soups and sauces. Fat can be rendered down for frying, or used as an ingredient (suet or lard).

Slow cooking meat

When cooking meats at low temperatures, there is one obvious flaw: the meat will not be exposed to the high cooking temperatures that develop that beautiful roasted flavour. This chemical reaction of browning is called the **Maillard reaction**. This occurs at 140 °C and above, when the wonderful roasted meat flavours begin to be released.

When slow cooking meats at lower temperatures they need to be started very quickly on a hot pan on the stove to start the Maillard reaction. In some cases you will need to return the meat quickly to the pan to re-caramelise the outside; alternatively, if the joint is dense and large, remove it from the low oven and increase the temperature to 190–200 °C. When the oven is up to temperature, put the joint back in for a short while to crisp the outside. The density of the meat and size of the joint will ensure that there is very little secondary cooking or residual heat left to cook through to the core.

> **Key term**
>
> **Maillard reaction**: the chemical reaction that occurs when heat is applied to meat, causing browning.

As already mentioned, the collagen that makes up connective tissue requires long cooking at a moderate temperature to convert it into gelatine. This provides a form of secondary or internal basting. When **basting** the outside of the meat, take care not to raise the internal temperature of the meat too much as this will destroy the secondary basting properties of the collagen – at temperatures above 88 °C the collagen will dissolve rapidly into the braising medium, making the meat less tender and moist. Therefore, the traditional braising method of bringing a casserole to a simmer and placing it in the oven at 140 °C could, in theory, make the meat dry. The more modern approach to braising is to have the cooking medium at between 80 °C and 85 °C, and this can be controlled best on the top of the stove. Alternatively, set your oven at approximately 90 °C and check the cooking medium once in a while.

> **Key term**
>
> **Basting**: moistening meat periodically, especially while cooking, using a liquid such as melted butter, or a sauce.

When slow cooking prime joints, generally the temperature of cooking is reduced as, in some cases, shrinkage can occur from 59°C, up to 65°C for sirloin of beef. A steak of sirloin beef has more collagen than a fillet and is generally cooked on a high heat, either roasted or pan fried. This will make the sirloin extremely tender and moist, with a roasted outer and the flavoursome roasted meat taste that people enjoy. An average sirloin joint for roasting can weigh 2–5 kg whole off the bone. The method for cooking this is to seal the meat on the outside and then place it into a pre-heated oven at 180°C, cook at 180°C for 10 minutes, then reduce the temperature to 64°C (the oven door will need to be open at this stage). Once the oven has come down to 64°C, close the door and cook for a further 1 hour 50 minutes. This will give you an extremely tender piece of sirloin.

Checking and finishing

During the cooking process a chef will check that meat is cooking correctly, without losing too much moisture, and is reaching the required colour or glaze before allowing the meat to rest before carving or serving.

To maintain the quality and safety of meat and poultry dishes once cooked, it is advisable to check internal temperatures using a probe. The recommended temperatures are shown in Table 8.1.

Table 8.1 Recommended internal temperatures*

Meat	Recommended internal temperatures
Beef	Rare: 45–47°C; medium: 50–52°C; well done: 64–70°C
Lamb	Pink: 55°C; well done: 62°C
Pork	60–65°C
Veal	60°C

* These temperatures only apply to complete pieces of meat. If they have been boned, rolled, layered or minced, higher temperatures may be required

The finishing or assembly of dishes is where the chef ensures sauces and accompaniments are of the correct consistency, size and balance for the dish. For example, if turned vegetables or croutons are part of the dish, the chef will ensure there are sufficient for each portion

served. A sauce should be of the correct consistency for the dish. Service temperature needs to be correct for the dish being served – hot, warm or cold as per the dish specification.

Further guidance on checking and finishing dishes is provided in 'Preparing for assessment' on page x.

Beef

Joints and cuts

Cuts of beef vary considerably, from very tender fillet steak to tough brisket or shin, and there is a greater variety of cuts in beef than for any other type of meat. While their names may vary, there are 14 primary cuts from a side of beef, each one composed of muscle, fat, bone and connective tissue. The least developed muscles, usually from the inner areas, can be roasted or grilled, while leaner and more sinewy meat is cut from the more highly developed external muscles. Exceptions are rib and loin cuts, which come from external but basically immobile muscles.

Knowing where the cuts come from (the hindquarter or the forequarter) helps to decide which method of cooking to use.

A whole side weighs approximately 180 kg and is divided into the wing ribs and the fore ribs.

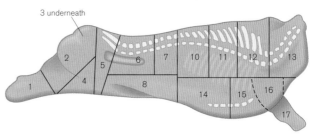

▲ Side of beef

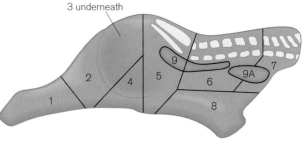

▲ Hindquarter of beef

Table 8.2 Joints, uses and weights of the hindquarter (numbers in left-hand column refer to the picture of the side of beef above)

Joint	Description	Uses	Preparation	Approximate weight
(1) Shin	Firm, lower leg muscle	Consommé, beef tea, stewing	Bone out, remove excess sinew; cut or chop as required	7 kg
(2) Topside	A lean, tender cut	Braising, stewing, second-class roasting	Roasting and braising: remove excess fat, cut into joints and tie with string Stewing: cut into dice or steaks	10 kg
(3) Silverside	A coarse joint	Pickled in brine then boiled	Remove thigh bone; this joint is usually kept whole	14 kg
(4) Thick flank	A boneless, coarse joint	Braising and stewing	As for topside	12 kg
(5) Rump	A good quality cut, though less tender than fillet or sirloin	Grilling and frying as steaks, braised in the piece	Bone out; cut off the first outside slice for pies and puddings. Cut into approximately 1.5 cm slices for steaks. The point steak – considered the most tender – is cut from the pointed end of the slice	10 kg
(6) Sirloin	A boneless cut; more tender than rump, but not as tender as fillet	Roasting, grilling and frying in steaks	Roasting whole on the bone: cut back the covering fat in one piece for approximately 10 cm. Trim off the sinew, replace the covering fat and tie with string if necessary. Ensure that the fillet has been removed Roasting boned out: remove fillet and bone out; remove sinew as before. Remove the excess fat and sinew from the boned side. Roast open, or rolled and tied with string Grilling and frying: as for roasting and cut into steaks as required (see below)	9 kg
(7) Wing ribs	Usually consists of the last three rib bones which, because of their curved shape, act as a natural trivet. A prime quality, first-class roasting joint	Roasting, grilling and frying in steaks	Cut seven-eighths of the way through the spine or chine bone, remove the nerve, saw through the rib bones on the underside 5–10 cm from the end. Tie firmly with string. When the joint is cooked, remove the chine bone to make the meat easier to carve	5 kg
(8) Thin flank	Also known as the skirt. A boneless, gristly cut	Stewing, boiling, sausages	Trim off excessive fat and cut or roll as required	10 kg
(9) Fillet	The leanest, most tender cut; from the centre of the sirloin	Roasting, grilling and frying in steaks	Roasting and pot roasting: remove head and tail of the fillet, leaving an even centre piece from which all the nerve and fat should be removed. This may be larded by using a larding needle to insert pieces of fatty bacon cut into long strips Grilling and frying: Varies depending on weight and the number of steaks obtained from it. See below for more detail	3 kg

▲ Shin

▲ Topside

▲ Silverside

Step by step: preparing a wing rib

1 Remove the chine bone from the joint.

2 Cut away the chine.

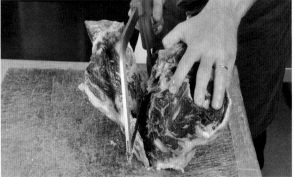

3 Use a saw to finish removing the chine.

4 Trim and clean the top bone.

5 Remove the elastin.

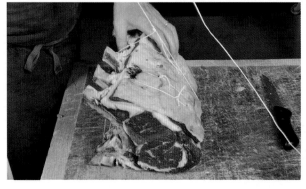

6 Tie the bone back – it will act as a trivet.

Sirloin steaks

- **Minute steaks**: cut into 1 cm slices, flatten with a cutlet bat dipped in water, making it as thin as possible, then trim.
- **Sirloin steaks (entrecôte)**: cut into 1 cm slices and trim (approximate weight 150 g).
- **Double sirloin steaks**: cut into 2 cm-thick slices and trim (approximate weight 250–300 g).
- **Porterhouse and T-bone steak**: porterhouse steaks are cut including the bone from the rib end of the sirloin; T-bone steaks are cut from the rump end of the sirloin, including the bone and fillet.

▲ Sirloin steaks

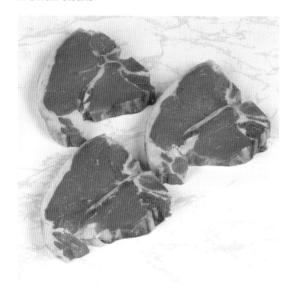

▲ T-bone steaks

Video: Beef hindquarter joints http://bit.ly/ 1G36Ecv

Fillet

A typical breakdown of a 3 kg fillet would be:

- **Chateaubriand**: double fillet steak 3–10 cm thick, 2–4 portions. Average weight 300 g–1 kg. Cut from the head of the fillet, trim off all the nerve and leave a little fat on the steak.
- **Fillet steaks:** approximately 4 steaks of 100–150 g each, 1.5–2 cm thick. These are cut as shown in the diagram above and trimmed as for chateaubriand.
- **Tournedos:** approximately 6–8 at 100 g each, 2–4 cm thick. Continue cutting down the fillet. Remove all the nerve and all the fat, and tie each tournedos with string.
- **Tail of fillet:** approximately 0.5 kg. Remove all fat and sinew, and slice or mince as required.

▲ Fillet steaks

Forequarter of beef

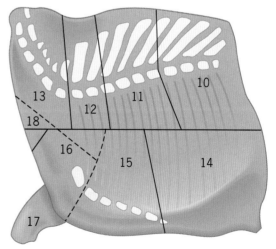

▲ Forequarter of beef

Table 8.3 Joints, uses and weights of the forequarter (numbers in left-hand column refer to the diagram above)

Joint	Description	Uses	Preparation	Approximate weight
(10) Fore rib	First class roasting joint	Roasting and braising	As for wing ribs	8 kg
(11) Middle rib				10 kg
(12) Chuck rib		Stewing and braising	Bone out, remove excess fat and sinew, and use as required.	15 kg
(13) Sticking piece	Lean and high in flavour	Stewing and sausages		9 kg
(14) Plate	Belly			10 kg
(15) Brisket	Quite a fatty joint; sold on or off the bone, or salted	Pickled in brine and boiled, pressed beef, slow roasting		19 kg
(16) Leg of mutton cut	Lower neck and upper belly	Braising and stewing		11 kg
(17) Shank	Lower front leg	Consommé, beef tea		6 kg

Quality points of beef

- The lean meat should be bright red, with small flecks of white fat (marbled).
- The fat should be firm, brittle in texture, creamy white in colour and odourless. Older animals and dairy breeds usually have fat that is a deeper-yellow colour.

Activity

1 Name two joints from a hindquarter of beef and two from a forequarter.
2 List joints from a beef carcass that are traditionally roasted.
3 What is meant by marbling?
4 A sirloin of beef may be cut into steaks. Name these steaks.
5 What is a chateaubriand?

Veal

Veal is obtained from good-quality carcasses weighing around 100 kg. This quality of veal is required for first-class cookery and is produced from calves slaughtered at between 12 and 24 weeks.

The average weight of English or Dutch milk-fed veal calves is 18 kg.

Joints and cuts

The joints of veal are shown in Table 8.4.

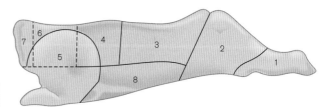

▲ Side of veal

Quality points of veal

- Veal is available all year round.
- The flesh should be pale pink in colour and firm in texture – not soft or flabby.
- Cut surfaces should be slightly moist, not dry.
- Bones, as in all young animals, should be pinkish white and porous, with some blood in their structure.
- The fat should be firm and pinkish white.
- The kidney should be firm and well covered with fat.

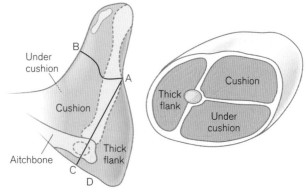

▲ Dissection of veal

Table 8.4 Joints, uses and weights of veal (numbers in left-hand column refer to those used in the diagram)

Joint	Uses	Preparation	Approximate weight
(1) Knuckle	Osso buco, sauté, stock	Stewing (on the bone) (osso buco): cut and saw into 2–4 cm thick slices through the knuckle.	2 kg
		Sauté: bone out and trim, then cut into even 25 g pieces.	
(2) Leg	Roasting, braising, escalopes, sauté	Braising or roasting whole: remove the aitch bone, clean and trim 4 cm off the knuckle bone. Trim off the excess sinew.	5 kg
		Braising or roasting the nut: remove all the sinew; if there is insufficient fat on the joint then bard thinly (cover with bacon fat) and secure with string.	
		Escalopes: remove all the sinew, cut against the grain into large 50–75 g slices and bat out thinly.	
		Sauté: remove all the sinew and cut into 25 g pieces.	
(3) Loin	Roasting, frying, grilling	Roasting: bone out and trim the flap, roll out and secure with string. This joint may be stuffed before rolling.	3.5 kg
(4) Best end			3 kg
		Frying: trim and cut into cutlets.	
(5) Shoulder	Braising, stewing	Braising: bone out as for lamb; usually stuffed.	2 kg
		Stewing: bone out, remove all the sinew and cut into 25 g pieces.	
(6) Neck end	Stewing, sauté	Stewing and sautéing: bone out and remove all the sinew; cut into approximately 25 g pieces.	2.5 kg
(7) Scrag	Stewing, stock		1.5 kg
(8) Breast	Stewing, roasting	Stewing: as for neck end.	2.5 kg
		Roasting: bone out, season, stuff and roll up, then tie with string.	

Table 8.5 Joints of the leg (see the diagram above)

Cut	Corresponding beef joint	Weight	Proportion	Uses
Cushion or nut	Topside	2.75 kg	15%	Escalopes, roasting, braising, sauté
Under cushion or under nut	Silverside	3 kg	17%	
Thick flank	Thick flank	2.5 kg	14%	
Knuckle (whole)	-	2.5 kg	14%	Osso buco, sauté
Bones (thigh and aitch)	-	2.5 kg	14%	Stock, jus lié, sauces
Useable trimmings	-	2 kg	11%	Pies, stewing

(The letters refer to those in the diagram on page 254)

1 Remove the knuckle by dividing the knee joint (A) and cut through the meat away from the cushion line (A–B).
2 Remove the aitch bone (C) at thick end of the leg, separating it at the ball and socket joint.
3 Remove all the outside skin and fat, exposing the natural seams. It will now be seen that the thigh bone divides the meat into two-thirds and one-third (thick flank).
4 Stand the leg on the thick flank with point D uppermost. Divide the cushion from the under cushion, following the natural seam, using the hand and the point of a knife. Having reached the thigh bone, remove it completely.

5 When the boned leg falls open, the three joints can easily be seen joined only by membrane. Separate and trim the cushion, removing the loose flap of meat.
6 Trim the under cushion, removing the layer of thick gristle. Separate into three small joints through the natural seams. It will be seen that one of these will correspond with the round in silverside of beef.
7 Trim the thick flank by laying it on its round side and making a cut along the length about 2 cm deep. A seam is reached and the two trimmings can be removed.
8 The anticipated yield of escalopes from this size of leg would be 62 kg – that is, 55 kg × 100 g or 73 kg × 80 g.

Step by step: boning a loin of veal

1 The loin of veal.

2 Using a boning knife, carefully remove the fillet.

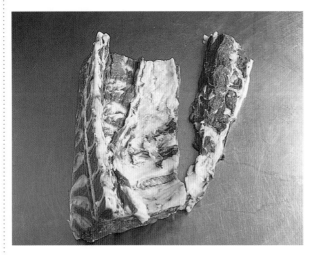

3 The joint and the fillet.

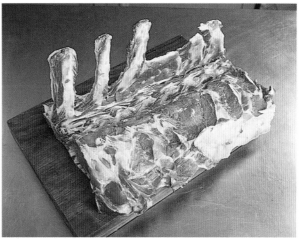

4 Bring the loin down from the rib to the backbone, and trim the rib bones.

5 Trim the excess fat and sinew from the meat.

6 The fillet, boned loin and bones (which can be used for stock).

Activity

1 From which joints of veal are escalopes usually cut?
2 What is the basic difference between a blanquette of veal and a fricassée of veal?
3 What is the traditional dish produced from a knuckle of veal?

Lamb and mutton

Lamb is the meat from a sheep under a year old; above that age the animal is called a **hogget** and its meat becomes **mutton**.

> **Key terms**
>
> **Lamb**: a sheep under a year old
>
> **Hogget**: a sheep over a year old.
>
> **Mutton**: meat from a mature sheep.

There is greater demand for lamb than mutton as the lamb carcass provides smaller cuts of more tender meat. Mutton needs to be well ripened by long hanging before cooking and, as it is usually fatty, needs a good deal of trimming. The flesh of a younger lamb is usually more tender.

A good way to judge age is through weight, especially with legs of lamb: the highest quality weighs about 2.3 kg and never more than 4 kg. Smaller chops are also more tender and therefore more expensive. Mutton is rarely available to buy; when it is, it is much less expensive than lamb.

As a guide, when ordering lamb allow approximately 100 g meat off the bone per portion and 150 g on the bone per portion. However, these weights are only approximate and will vary according to the quality of the meat and what it will be used for. For example, a chef will often cut up a carcass differently from a shop butcher because a chef needs to consider the presentation of the particular joint, while the butcher is more often concerned with being economical.

In general, bones only need to be removed when preparing joints, to make carving easier. The bones are used for stock and the excess fat can be rendered down for second-class dripping.

Cuts, joints, uses and weights

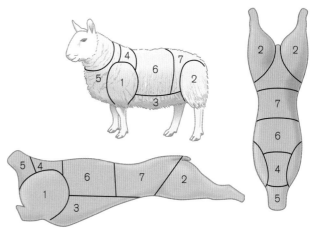

▲ Joints of lamb

Chops
Loin chops

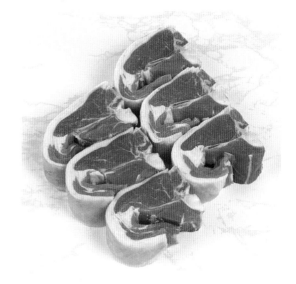

▲ Lamb loin chops

Skin the loin, remove the excess fat and sinew, then cut into chops approximately 100–150 g in weight.

A first-class loin chop should have a piece of kidney skewered in the centre.

Table 8.6 Joints, uses and weights (numbers in left-hand column refer to the diagram above)

Joint	Uses	Preparation	Approximate weight lamb	Approximate weight mutton
Whole carcass			16 kg	25 kg
(1) Shoulder (two)	Roasting, stewing	Boning: remove the blade bone and upper arm bone, then tie with string; the shoulder may be stuffed before tying. Cutting for stews: bone out the meat and cut into even 25–50 g pieces.	3 kg	4.5 kg
(2) Leg (two)	Roasting (mutton boiled)	Boning: remove the pelvic or aitchbone; trim the knuckle, cleaning 3 cm of bone; trim off excess fat and tie with string if necessary.	3.5 kg	5.5 kg
(3) Breast (two)	Roasting, stewing	Remove excess fat and skin. Roasting: bone; stuff and roll; tie with string. Stewing: bone and then cut into even 25–50 g pieces.	1.5 kg	2.5 kg
(4) Middle neck	Stewing	Remove excess fat, excess bone and gristle; cut into even 50 g pieces. When butchered correctly, this joint can give good uncovered second-class cutlets.	2 kg	3 kg
(5) Scrag end	Stewing, broth	Chop down the centre, remove the excess bone, fat and gristle, and cut into even 50 g pieces, or bone out and cut into pieces.	0.5 kg	1 kg
(6) Best end rack (two)	Roasting, grilling, frying	Remove the skin from head to tail and from breast to back. Remove the sinew and the tip of the blade bone. Clean the sinew from between the rib bones and trim the bones. Score the fat neatly to approximately 2 mm deep. Trim the overall length of the rib bones to two and a half times the length of the nut of meat.	2 kg	3 kg
(7) Saddle	Roasting, grilling, frying	For large banquets it is sometimes better to remove the chumps and use short saddles: remove the skin, starting from head to tail and from breast to back. Split down the centre of the backbone to produce two loins. Each loin can be roasted whole. Roasting: skin and remove the kidney. Trim the excess fat and sinew. Cut off the flaps, leaving about 15 cm each side so that they meet in the middle under the saddle. Remove the aitch or pelvic bone. Score neatly and tie with string. For presentation the tail may be left on, protected with foil and tied back. The saddle can also be completely boned, stuffed and tied. Grilling and frying: cut into loin and chump chops (see below).	3.5 kg	5.5 kg

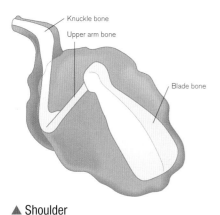

▲ Shoulder

▲ Best ends of lamb (racks, french trimmed)

▲ Saddle of lamb

Double loin chop (also known as a Barnsley chop)

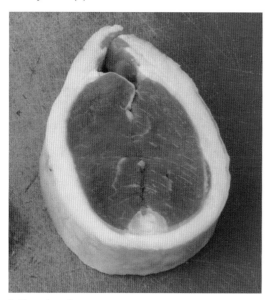

▲ Barnsley chops

These are cut approximately 2 cm across a saddle on the bone.

When trimmed they are secured with a skewer and may include a piece of kidney in the centre of each chop.

Chump chops

These are cut from the chump end of the loin.

Cut into approximately 150 g chops and trim where necessary.

Noisette

This is a cut from a boned-out loin.

Cut slantwise into approximately 2 cm thick slices, bat out slightly and trim into a cutlet shape.

Rosette

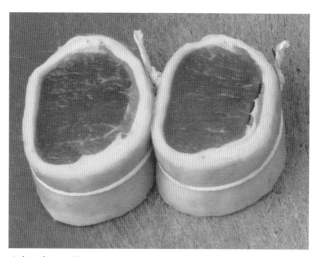

▲ Lamb rosettes

This is a cut from a boned-out loin approximately 2 cm thick. It is shaped round and tied with string.

Cutlets

▲ Lamb cutlets

Step by step: preparing a best end of lamb (skinning, scoring, trimming and tying)

1 Remove the bark/skin, leaving as much fat as possible on the joint.

2 Mark/score 2 cm from the end of the bone.

3 Score down the middle of the back of the bone, scoring the cartilage.

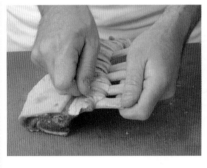

4 Pull the skin fat and meat from the bone (to bring out the bone ends – this is an alternative to scraping them).

5 Remove the elastin.

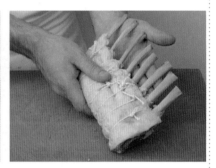

6 Tie the joint.

Prepare as for roasting, excluding the scoring, and divide evenly between the bones. Alternatively, the cutlets can be cut from the best end and prepared separately. A double cutlet consists of two bones, so a six-bone best end yields six single or three double cutlets.

Quality points of lamb and mutton

- A good-quality animal should be compact and evenly fleshed.
- The lean flesh should be firm and a pleasing dull-red colour with a fine texture or grain.
- There should be an even distribution of surface fat, which should be a hard, brittle, flaky texture and a clear white colour.
- In a young animal the bones should be pink and porous, so that when they are cut a little blood can

be seen inside them. As animals grow older, their bones become hard, dense and white, and are more likely to splinter when chopped.

- Good-quality lamb should have fine, white fat, with pink flesh when freshly cut.
- In mutton the flesh is a deeper colour.
- Lamb has a very thin, parchment-like covering on the carcass, known as the 'fell', which is usually left on roasts to help them maintain their shape during cooking. It should, however, be removed from chops.

Activity

1 Name two joints from a carcass of lamb that are usually roasted.
2 What cut of lamb is traditionally used for Irish stew?
3 List the quality points you would look for in lamb.

Pork

The keeping quality of pork is less than that of other meat; therefore it must be handled, prepared and cooked with great care. Pork should always be well cooked.

At 5–6 weeks old, a piglet is known as a sucking or suckling pig. Its weight is then between 5 kg and 10 kg.

Joints and cuts of pork

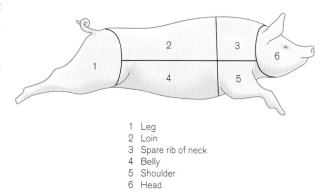

1 Leg
2 Loin
3 Spare rib of neck
4 Belly
5 Shoulder
6 Head

▲ Pig carcass

Table 8.7 Cuts, uses and weights of pork (numbers in left-hand column refer to the diagram above)

Joint	Uses	Preparation	Approximate weight
(1) Leg	Roasting and boiling	Roasting: remove the pelvic or aitch bone, trim and score the rind neatly – that is, with a sharp-pointed knife, make a series of 3 mm deep incisions approximately 2 cm apart all over the skin of the joint; trim and clean the knuckle bone. Boiling: it is usual to pickle the joint either by rubbing dry salt and saltpetre into the meat, or by soaking in a brine solution; then remove the pelvic bone, trim and secure with string if necessary.	5 kg
(2) Loin	Roasting, frying and grilling	Roasting (on the bone): saw down the chine bone in order to facilitate carving; trim the excess fat and sinew and score the rind in the direction that the joint will be carved; season and secure with string. Roasting (boned out): remove the fillets and bone out carefully; trim off the excess fat and sinew, score the rind and neaten the flap, season, replace the filet mignon, roll up and secure the string; this joint is sometimes stuffed. Grilling or frying chops: remove the skin, excess fat and sinew, then cut and saw or chop through the loin in approximately 1 cm slices; remove the excess bone and trim neatly.	6 kg
(3) Spare rib	Roasting, pies	Roasting: remove the excess fat, bone and sinew, and trim neatly. Pies: remove the excess fat and sinew, bone out and cut as required.	1.5 kg
(4) Belly	Pickling, boiling, stuffed, rolled and roasted	Remove all the small rib bones, season with salt, pepper and chopped sage, roll and secure with string. This joint may be stuffed.	2 kg
(5) Shoulder	Roasting, sausages, pies	Roasting: the shoulder is usually boned out, the excess fat and sinew removed, seasoned, scored and rolled with string; it may be stuffed and can also be divided into two smaller joints. Sausages and pies: skin, bone out and remove the excess fat and sinew; cut into even pieces or mince.	3 kg
(6) Head (whole)	Brawn		4 kg

▲ Leg of pork

▲ Loin of pork

Quality points of pork

- Lean flesh should be pale pink, firm and of a fine texture.
- Fat should be white, firm, smooth and not excessive.
- Bones should be small, fine and pinkish.
- Skin or rind should be smooth.

Activity

1 Which joint of pork is suitable for escalopes of pork?
2 Which joint of pork is suitable for roasting?

Bacon

Bacon is the cured flesh of a bacon-weight pig (60-75 kg) that is specifically reared for bacon because its shape and size yield economic bacon joints.

Bacon is cured either by dry salting and then smoking or by soaking in brine followed by smoking. Green bacon is brine-cured but not smoked; it has a milder flavour but does not keep for as long as smoked bacon. Depending on the degree of salting during the curing process, bacon joints may need to be soaked in cold water for a few hours before being cooked.

Step by step: preparing pork belly for roasting

1 Pork belly before it has been prepared

2 Remove all the small rib bones

3 Cut the fat

4 Score the fat

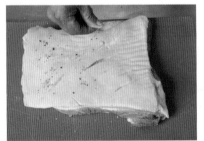

5 Season with salt, pepper and chopped sage

6 Ready for roasting

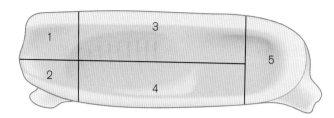

1 Collar
2 Hock
3 Back
4 Streaky
5 Gammon

Grilling cuts

Gammon

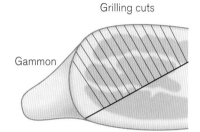

▲ Side of bacon

Quality points of bacon

- There should be no sign of stickiness.
- There should be a pleasant smell.
- Rind should be thin, smooth and free from wrinkles.
- Fat should be white, smooth and not excessive in proportion to the lean.
- The lean should be a deep-pink colour and firm.

Activity

1 What is the difference between a ham and a gammon?
2 Which part of the pig does streaky bacon come from?

Table 8.8 Cuts, uses and weights of bacon (numbers in left-hand column refer to the diagram above)

Joint	Uses	Preparation	Approximate weight
(1) Collar	Boiling, grilling	Boiling: remove bone (if any) and tie with string. Grilling: remove the rind, trim off the outside surface and cut into thin slices (rashers), across the joint.	4.5 kg
(2) Hock	Boiling, grilling	Boiling: leave whole or bone out and secure with string.	4.5 kg
(3) Back	Grilling, frying	Grilling: remove all bones and rind, and cut into thin rashers.	9 kg
(4) Streaky		Frying: remove the rind, trim off the outside surface, and cut into rashers or chops of the required thickness.	4.5 kg
(5) Gammon	Boiling, grilling, frying	Frying and grilling: fairly thick slices are cut from the middle of the gammon; they are then trimmed and the rind removed.	7.5 kg

▲ Back bacon

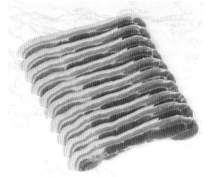

▲ Streaky bacon

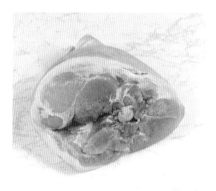

▲ Gammon

Offal and other edible parts of the carcass

Offal is the edible parts taken from the inside of a carcass of meat. It includes liver, kidneys, heart and sweetbreads. Tripe, brains, tongue, head and oxtail are also sometimes included under this term.

Storing offal

Fresh offal (unfrozen) should be purchased as required and can be refrigerated under hygienic conditions at a temperature of –1 °C, at a relative humidity of 90 per cent, for up to seven days.

Frozen offal must be kept in a deep freeze and defrosted in a refrigerator as required. Liver and kidney dishes may traditionally have been served undercooked or lightly cooked, but it is now advised that they are cooked thoroughly all the way through to avoid possible food poisoning risks.

Liver

Liver is a good source of protein and iron. It contains vitamins A and D, and is low in fat.

- **Calf's liver**: considered to be the most tender and tasty. It is also the most expensive.
- **Lamb's liver**: mild in flavour, light in colour and tender.

- **Sheep's liver**: from an older animal, so is firmer, deeper in colour and has a stronger flavour.
- **Ox** or **beef liver**: the cheapest type and, if taken from an older animal, can be coarse and have a strong flavour. It is usually braised.
- **Pig's liver**: has a strong, full flavour and is used mainly for paté recipes.

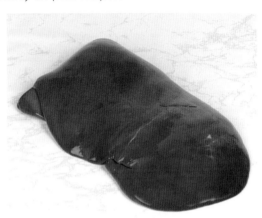

▲ Calves' liver

Quality points

- Liver should look fresh, moist and smooth, with a pleasant colour and no unpleasant smell.
- Liver should not be dry or contain an excessive number of tubes.

Step by step: preparation of liver

1 Remove skin, gristle and tubes.

2 Cut into thin slices on the slant. Ox liver may be marinated in milk to tenderise.

Kidneys

- **Lamb's kidneys**: light in colour, delicate in flavour and ideal for grilling and frying.
- **Sheep's kidneys**: darker in colour and stronger in flavour.
- **Calf's kidneys**: light in colour, delicate in flavour and used in a variety of dishes.
- **Ox kidney**: dark in colour, strong in flavour, and is either braised or used in pies and puddings (mixed with beef).
- **Pig's kidneys**: smooth, long and flat and have a strong flavour.

Step by step: preparing kidneys

1 Whole kidneys

2 Slice into kidney to open it up

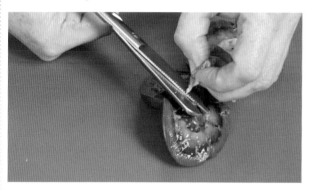

3 Lift up and cut out the white sinew from the centre

4 Before, during and after preparation

Quality points

- Suet – the saturated fat in which kidneys are encased – should be left on until they are used, otherwise the kidneys will dry out. The suet should be removed when kidneys are being prepared for cooking.
- Both suet and kidneys should be moist and have no unpleasant smell. The food value is similar to that of liver.

Hearts

Hearts are a good source of protein. Most need slow braising to tenderise them.

- **Lambs' hearts**: small and light; they are normally served whole.
- **Sheeps' hearts**: dark and solid; they can be dry and tough unless cooked carefully.
- **Ox** or **beef hearts**: dark coloured and solid and tend to be dry and tough.
- **Calves' hearts**: coming from a younger animal, they are lighter in colour and more tender.

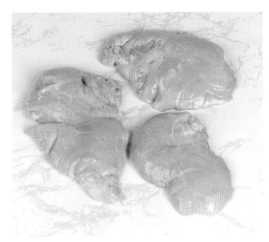

▲ Veal sweetbreads

▲ Lambs' hearts

Quality points

- Hearts should not be too fatty and should not contain too many tubes.
- When cut they should be moist, not sticky, and with no unpleasant smell.

Preparation

- Remove the tubes and excess fat.
- Hearts are often stuffed prior to braising

Sweetbreads

These are the pancreas and thymus glands, known as heart breads and neck. The heart bread is round, plump and a better quality than the neck bread, which is long and uneven. Sweetbreads are an easily digested source of protein, which makes them valuable for use in special diets for people who are ill.

Calf's heart bread, considered the best, weighs up to 600 g; lamb's heart bread weighs up to 100 g.

Quality points

- Heart and neck breads should be fleshy and a good size.
- They should be creamy white and have no unpleasant smell.

Preparation

1 Soak in several changes of cold salted water to remove blood, which will darken the sweetbreads during cooking (over 2–3 hours).
2 Blanch and refresh.
3 Peel off the membrane and connective tissues.
4 The sweetbreads can then be pressed between two trays with a weight on top and refrigerated.

Tripe

Tripe is the stomach lining or white muscle of the ox, consisting of the rumen or paunch and the honeycomb tripe (considered the best); sheep tripe, darker in colour, is available in some areas. Tripe contains protein, is low in fat and high in calcium.

Quality points

- Tripe should be fresh, with no signs of stickiness or unpleasant smell.

Preparation

1 Wash well and soak in cold water.
2 Cut into even pieces.

Brains

Calves' brains are normally used. They are a good source of protein, with other trace elements.

Quality points

- They must be fresh and have no unpleasant smell.

Preparation

1 Using a chopper or saw, remove the top of the skull, making certain that the opening is large enough to remove the brain undamaged.
2 Soak the brain in running cold water, then remove the membrane or skin and wash well to remove all blood.
3 Keep in cold salted water until required.

Tongues

Ox, lamb and sheep tongues are those most used in cooking. Ox tongues are usually salted then soaked before being cooked. Lamb tongues are cooked fresh.

Quality points

- Tongues must be fresh and have no unpleasant smell.
- There should not be too much waste at the root end.

Preparation

1 Remove the bone and gristle from the throat end.
2 Soak in cold water for 2–4 hours.
3 If salted, soak for 3–4 hours.

Head

Sheep's head can be used for stock, pigs' head for brawn (a cold meat preparation) and calves' head for speciality dishes (e.g. calf's head vinaigrette).

Quality points

- Heads should have plenty of flesh on them.
- They should be fresh.
- They should not be sticky or have any unpleasant smell.

Preparation

1 Bone out by making a deep incision down the middle of the head to the nostrils.
2 Follow the bone carefully and remove all the flesh in one piece.
3 Remove the tongue.

4 Wash the flesh well and keep covered in acidulated water (e.g. water containing lemon juice) to keep it fresh.
5 Wash off, blanch and refresh.
6 Cut into 2–5 cm squares.
7 Cut off the ears and trim the inside of the cheek.

Oxtail

Oxtails usually weigh 1–2 kg.

Quality points

- Oxtail should be lean, without much fat.
- There should be no sign of stickiness.
- There should be no unpleasant smell.

Preparation

1 Cut between the natural joints, trim off excess fat
2 The large pieces may be split in two.

Trotters

Pig's trotters are used as a garnish or in stocks to add flavour.

▲ Pig's trotters

Quality points

- Check they are clean and undamaged prior to use.

Preparation

1 Boil in water for a few minutes
2 Scrape with the back of a knife to remove the hairs,
3 Wash off in cold water and split in half.

Suet

Beef suet should be creamy-white, brittle and dry. Other meat fat should be fresh, not sticky, and with no unpleasant smell.

Marrow

Marrow comes from the bones of the leg of beef. It should be a good size, firm, creamy-white and odourless. Sliced, poached marrow may be used as a garnish for some meat dishes and savouries.

Bones

Bones must be fresh, not sticky, with no unpleasant smell, and preferably meaty as they are used for stock – the foundation for so many preparations.

Activity

1 Name the nutritional benefits from two types of offal.
2 List the quality points you would look for when purchasing offal.

Test yourself

1 Give **three** examples of joints of beef from:
   a) the hindquarter
   b) the forequarter
2 List **two** quality points to look for when buying beef.
3 Explain **three** reasons why portion control should be considered when preparing meat and offal.
4 Where are cutlets of lamb cut from?
5 Describe the stages in the preparation of a best end of lamb.
6 Describe **two** advantages of freezing as a preservation method for lamb.
7 Which part of the veal carcass are escalopes cut from?
8 Give **two** reasons why braising is a suitable cooking method for neck of veal.
9 State the difference between pickling and salting as a preservation method for meat.
10 Describe the stages in the preparation and cooking of a leg of pork.
11 List **four** quality points to look for when buying pork.
12 Why is braising the most appropriate cooking method for hearts?
13 What are the **two** types of sweetbread?
14 List the offal that would be used from a whole carcass of pork.
15 Which preservation methods could be used for offal?

1   Chateaubriand with Roquefort butter

	2–3 portions
Olive oil	
1 chateaubriand	500 g
Salt, pepper	
Roquefort cheese	25 g
Unsalted butter	40 g
Ground black pepper	½ tsp

Energy	Cals	Fat	Sat fat	Carb	Sugar	Protein	Fibre
2368 kJ	566 kcal	43.3 g	19.9 g	0.0 g	0.0 g	44.0 g	0.0 g

1 Heat the olive oil in a hot frying pan and brown the chateaubriand all over.

2 Season the chateaubriand and place in the oven at 190 °C; the timing depends on the degree of cooking required.

3 Remove from oven, allow to rest, then carve into thick slices.

4 Mash together the Roquefort cheese, butter and black pepper. Form into a roll using aluminium foil or cling film. Refrigerate.

5 Place a slice of Roquefort and butter on each slice of chateaubriand. Serve with deep-fried potatoes and a tossed green salad.

Professional tip

For the best texture and flavour, brown the chateaubriand all over before roasting, and leave it slightly underdone.

2   Roast wing rib of beef

	10 portions
Wing rib of beef	1 × 2 kg
Beef dripping	25 g
Gravy	
Carrots (for the mirepoix)	50 g
Onion (for the mirepoix)	50 g
Red wine	200 ml
Plain flour	30 g
Beef stock	300 ml

Yorkshire puddings (see recipe 3), prepared English mustard or horseradish sauce, to serve

Energy	Cals	Fat	Sat fat	Carb	Sugar	Protein	Fibre
3185 kJ	758 kcal	31.04 g	13.0 g	31.6 g	4.5 g	90.0 g	1.6 g

1 Preheat the oven to 195 °C.

2 Place the dripping in a heavy roasting tray and heat on the stove top.

3 Place the beef in the tray and brown well on all sides.

4 Place in the oven on 195 °C for 15 minutes then turn down to 75 °C for 2 hours.

5 Remove and allow to rest before carving.

For the gravy:

1 Remove the beef. Place the tray with the fat, sediment and the juice back on the stove.

2 Add the mirepoix and brown well.

3 Add the red wine and reduce by two-thirds.

4 Mix the flour and a little stock together to form a viscous batter-like mix.

5 Add the stock to the roasting tray and bring to the boil.

6 Pour in the flour mix and whisk into the liquid in the tray.

7 Bring to the boil, simmer and correct the seasoning.

8 Pass through a sieve and retain for service

To complete:
Slice the beef and warm the Yorkshire puddings, serve with the gravy, horseradish and mustard.

> **Professional tip**
>
> This dish would work well with most vegetables or potatoes. As an alternative, why not add slightly blanched root vegetables to the roasting tray at the start of the beef cooking, remove and reheat for service? They will obtain maximum flavour from the beef and juices.

3 Yorkshire puddings

	4 portions	10 portions
Flour	85 g	215 g
Eggs	2	5
Milk	85 ml	215 ml
Water	40 ml	100 ml
Dripping or oil	20 g	50 g

Energy	Cals	Fat	Sat fat	Carb	Sugar	Protein	Fibre	Sodium *
730 kJ	174 kcal	9.3 g	2.1 g	17.5	1.3 g	6.3 g	0.9 g	0.050 g

* Using whole milk

1 Place the flour and eggs into a mixing bowl and mix to a smooth paste.

2 Gradually whisk in the milk and water and place in the refrigerator for 1 hour. Pre-heat the oven to 190 °C.

3 Heat the pudding trays in the oven with a little dripping or oil in each well.

4 Carefully ladle the mixture in, up to about two-thirds full.

5 Place in the oven and slowly close the door (if you have a glass-fronted door it will be easy to monitor progress; if not, after about 30 minutes check the puddings). The myth about opening the door during cooking has an element of truth in it – however, it is slamming and the speed at which the door is opened that have most effect, so have just a small, careful peek to check and see if they are ready.

6 For the last 10 minutes of cooking, invert the puddings (take out and turn upside down in the tray) to dry out the base.

7 Serve immediately.

> **Professional tip**
>
> The oven, and the oil, must be very hot before the mixture is placed into the pudding tray; if they are not hot enough, the puddings will not rise.

4 Sirloin steak with red wine jus (entrecôte bordelaise)

	4 portions	10 portions
Butter or oil	50 g	125 g
Sirloin steaks (approximately 150–200 g each)	4	10
Red wine	60 ml	150 ml
Red wine jus (see page 128)	¼ litre	½ litre
Parsley, chopped		

Energy	Cals	Fat	Sat fat	Carb	Sugar	Protein	Fibre *
3013 KJ	717 kcal	62.2 g	21.6 g	6.0 g	3.0 g	26.1 g	1.4 g

* Using sunflower oil and 150 g raw steak per portion. Using sunflower oil and 200 g raw steak per portion provides: 3584 kJ/853 kcal Energy; 73.6 g Fat; 26.2 g Sat Fat; 6.0 g Carb; 3.0 g Sugar; 34.4 g Protein; 1.4 g Fibre

1 Heat the butter or oil in a sauté pan.

2 Lightly season the steaks on both sides with salt and pepper.

3 Fry the steaks quickly on both sides, keeping them underdone.

4 Dress the steaks on a serving dish.

5 Pour off the fat from the pan.

6 Deglaze with the red wine. Reduce by half and strain.

7 Add the red wine sauce, reboil and correct the seasoning.

8 Coat the steaks with the sauce.

9 Sprinkle with chopped parsley and serve.

Note

Traditionally, two slices of beef bone marrow, poached in stock for 2–3 minutes, would be placed on each steak.

Professional tip

Cook the steaks to order (and make the sauce by deglazing the pan and reducing), not in advance.

Healthy eating tip

● Use little or no salt to season the steaks.
● Fry in a small amount of an unsaturated oil and drain off all excess fat after frying.
● Serve with plenty of boiled new potatoes or a jacket potato and a selection of vegetables.

5 Boiled silverside, carrots and dumplings

1 Soak the meat in cold water for 1–2 hours to remove excess brine.

2 Place in a saucepan and cover with cold water, bring to the boil, skim and simmer for 45 minutes.

3 Add the whole prepared onions and carrots and simmer until cooked.

4 Divide the suet paste into even pieces and lightly mould into balls (dumplings).

5 Add the dumplings and simmer for a further 15–20 minutes.

6 Serve by carving the meat across the grain, garnish with carrots, onions and dumplings, and moisten with a little of the cooking liquor.

	4 portions	10 portions
Silverside, pre-soaked in brine	400 g	1.25 kg
Onions	200 g	500 g
Carrots	200 g	500 g
Suet paste	100 g	250 g

Energy	Cals	Fat	Sat fat	Carb	Sugar	Protein	Fibre
1068 kJ	254 kcal	10.17 g	4.6 g	15.5 g	5.5 g	26.3 g	2.6 g

Note

A large joint of silverside is approximately 6 kg; for this size of joint, soak it overnight and allow 25 minutes cooking time per 0.5 kg plus 25 minutes.

The beef is salted because this gives the desired flavour. The meat is usually salted before it is delivered to the kitchen.

Variation

Herbs can be added to the dumplings.

Boiled brisket and tongue can be served with the silverside.

French-style boiled beef is prepared using unsalted thin flank or brisket with onions, carrots, leeks, celery, cabbage and a bouquet garni, all cooked and served together, accompanied with pickled gherkins and coarse salt.

Healthy eating tip

Adding carrots, onions, boiled potatoes and a green vegetable will give a healthy balance.

6 Boeuf bourguignonne

	4 portions	10 portions
Beef		
Beef shin pre-soaked in red wine (see below) for 12 hours	600 g	1.5 kg
Olive oil	50 ml	125 ml
Bottle of inexpensive red Bordeaux wine	1	2
Onion	100 g	250 g
Carrot	100 g	250 g
Celery sticks	75 g	180 g
Leek	100 g	250 g
Cloves of garlic	2	5
Sprig fresh thyme	1	2
Bay leaf	1	2
Seasoning		
Veal/brown stock to cover		
Garnish		
Button onions, cooked	150 g	300 g
Cooked bacon lardons	150 g	300 g
Button mushrooms, cooked	150 g	300 g
Parsley, chopped	2 tsp	5 tsp
To finish		
Mashed potato	300 g	750 g
Washed, picked spinach	300 g	750 g
Cooked green beans	250 g	625 g

1 Pre-heat the oven to 180 °C.

2 Trim the beef shin of all fat and sinew, and cut into 2½ cm-thick rondelles.

3 Heat a little oil in a thick-bottomed pan and seal/brown the skin. Place in a large ovenproof dish.

4 Meanwhile, reduce the red wine by half.

5 Peel and trim the vegetables as appropriate, then add them to the pan that the beef has just come out of and gently brown the edges. Then place this, along with the garlic and herbs, in the ovenproof dish with the meat.

6 Add the reduced red wine to the casserole, then pour in enough stock to cover the meat and vegetables. Bring to the boil, then cook in the oven pre-heated to 180 °C for 40 minutes; after that, turn the oven down to 90–95 °C and cook for a further 4 hours until tender.

7 Remove from the oven and allow the meat to cool in the liquor. When cold, remove any fat. Reheat gently at the same temperature to serve.

8 Heat the garnish elements separately and sprinkle over each portion. Serve with a mound of mashed potato, wilted spinach and buttered green beans. Finish the whole dish with chopped parsley.

Variation

Other joints of beef can be used here; beef or veal cheek can be used, reducing the time for the veal, or modernise the dish by using the slow-cooked fillet preparation and serving the same garnish.

Professional tip

Shallow fry the beef in hot oil to brown it all over, but do not let it boil in the oil. Then allow it to stew gently in the red wine.

Energy	Cals	Fat	Sat fat	Carb	Sugar	Protein	Fibre	Sodium
2838 kJ	681 kcal	33.3 g	9.1 g	20.1 g	7.2 g	44.9 g	8.0 g	900 mg

1 Marinate the beef

2 Brown the meat

3 Gently brown the vegetables then add to the meat in a large ovenproof dish

4 Pour in stock to cover the meat and vegetables

7 Beef olives (paupiettes de boeuf)

	4 portions	10 portions
Stuffing		
White or wholemeal breadcrumbs	50 g	125 g
Parsley, chopped	1 tbsp	3 tbsp
Thyme, small pinch		
Suet, prepared and chopped	5 g	25 g
Onion, finely chopped and lightly sweated in oil	25 g	60 g
Salt		
Egg	½	1
Olives		
Lean beef (topside)	400 g	1.25 kg
Salt, pepper		
Dripping or oil	35 g	100 g
Carrot	100 g	250 g
Onion	100 g	250 g
Flour, browned in the oven	25 g	60 g
Tomato purée	25 g	60 g
Brown stock	500–750 ml	1.25–1.5 litres
Bouquet garni		

Energy	Cals	Fat	Sat fat	Carb	Sugar	Protein	Fibre	*
1134 KJ	271 kcal	13.1 g	2.6 g	13.6 g	5.0 g	25.4 g	1.5 g	

* Using 625 ml stock

1 Combine all the stuffing ingredients and mix thoroughly.

2 Cut the meat into thin slices across the grain and bat out.

3 Trim to approximately 10 × 8 cm, chop the trimmings finely and add to the stuffing.

4 Season the slices of meat lightly with salt and pepper, and spread a quarter of the stuffing down the centre of each slice.

5 Roll up neatly and secure with string.

6 Fry off the meat to a light-brown colour, add the vegetables and continue cooking to a golden colour.

7 Drain off the fat into a clean pan and make up to 25 g fat if there is not enough (increase the amount for 10 portions). Mix in the flour.

8 Mix in the tomato purée, cool and then mix in the boiling stock.

9 Bring to the boil, skim, season and pour on to the meat.

10 Add the bouquet garni.

11 Cover and simmer gently, preferably in the oven, for approximately 1 ½–2 hours.

12 Remove the string from the meat.

13 Skim, correct the sauce and pass on to the meat.

Professional tip

When you have stuffed and shaped the olives, tie them with string so that they will keep their shape during cooking.

Healthy eating tips

● Use little or no salt to season the steaks.
● Fry in a small amount of an unsaturated oil and drain off all excess fat after frying.
● Serve with a large portion of potatoes and vegetables

1 Roll the meat around the stuffing and tie the roll securely

2 Fry the rolls to a light golden brown

3 Pour the cooking liquid over the rolls

8 Beef stroganoff *(sauté de boeuf stroganoff)*

	4 portions	10 portions
Fillet of beef (tail end)	400 g	1.5 kg
Butter or oil	50 g	125 g
Salt, pepper		
Shallots, finely chopped	25 g	60 g
Dry white wine	125 ml	300 ml
Cream	125 ml	300 ml
Lemon, juice of	¼	½
Parsley, chopped		

Energy	Cals	Fat	Sat fat	Carb	Sugar	Protein	Fibre	*
1364 kJ	325 kcal	23.7 g	7.9 g	1.7 g	1.7 g	21.2 g	0.3 g	

* Using sunflower oil

1 Cut the meat into strips approximately 1 × 5 cm.

2 Place the butter or oil in a sautéuse over a fierce heat.

3 Add the beef strips, lightly season with salt and pepper, and allow to cook rapidly for a few seconds. The beef should be brown but underdone.

4 Drain the beef into a colander. Pour the butter back into the pan.

5 Add the shallots, cover with a lid and allow to cook gently until tender.

6 Drain off the fat, add the wine and reduce to one-third.

7 Add the cream and reduce by a quarter.

8 Add the lemon juice and the beef strips; do not reboil. Correct the seasoning.

9 Serve lightly sprinkled with chopped parsley. Accompany with rice pilaff (see page 421).

Healthy eating tips
- Use little or no salt to season the meat.
- Fry in a small amount of an unsaturated oil.
- Serve with a large portion of rice and a salad.

9 Steak pudding

1 Line a greased ½ litre basin with three-quarters of the suet paste and retain one-quarter for the top.

2 Mix all the other ingredients, except the water, together.

3 Place in the basin with the water to within 1 cm of the top.

4 Moisten the edge of the suet paste, cover with the top and seal firmly.

5 Cover with greased greaseproof paper and also, if possible, foil or a pudding cloth tied securely with string.

6 Cook in a steamer for at least 3 ½ hours for 4 portions. For individual puddings, cook for 1 ½ hours approximately.

7 Serve with the paper and cloth removed, clean the basin, place on a round flat dish and fasten a napkin round the basin.

Note

Extra gravy should be served separately. If the gravy in the pudding is to be thickened, the meat can be lightly floured.

	4 portions	10 portions
Suet paste (see page 522)	200 g	500 g
Prepared stewing beef (chuck steak)	400 g	1.5 kg
Worcester sauce	1 tsp	3 tsp
Parsley, chopped	1 tsp	2 ½ tsp
Salt, pepper		
Onion, chopped (optional)	50–100 g	200 g
Water	125 ml approximately	300 ml approximately.

Energy	Cals	Fat	Sat fat	Carb	Sugar	Protein	Fibre
1369 kJ	326 kcal	17.3 g	7.8 g	20.6 g	1.0 g	23.0 g	1.1 g

Healthy eating tips

● Use little or no salt as the Worcester sauce contains salt.
● Trim off as much fat as possible from the raw stewing beef.
● Serve with plenty of potatoes and vegetables.

1 Line the basin with suet paste

2 Fill the basin, then cover the top with paste

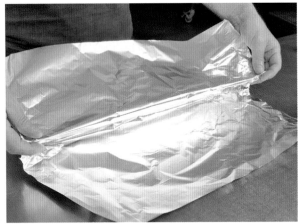

3 Make a foil cover for the basin, with a fold to allow it to expand

4 Tie the cover over the basin securely

10 Steak pie

	4 portions	10 portions
Prepared stewing beef (chuck steak)	400 g	1.5 kg
Oil or dripping	50 ml	125 ml
Onion, chopped (optional)	100 g	250 g
Worcester sauce, few drops		
Parsley, chopped	1 tsp	3 tsp
Water, stock, red wine or dark beer	125 ml	300 ml
Salt, pepper		
Cornflour	10 g	25 g
Short, puff or rough puff paste (see pages 518 and 519)	100 g	250 g

Energy	Cals	Fat	Sat fat	Carb	Sugar	Protein	Fibre	*
1442 KJ	346 kcal	22.2 g	2.9 g	13.6 g	1.8 g	24.3 g	0.4 g	

* Using puff pastry (McCance data)

1. Cut the meat into 2 cm strips then cut into squares.
2. Heat the oil in a frying pan until smoking, add the meat and quickly brown on all sides.
3. Drain the meat off in a colander.
4. Lightly fry the onion.
5. Place the meat, onion, Worcester sauce, parsley and the liquid in a pan, season lightly with salt and pepper.
6. Bring to the boil, skim, then allow to simmer gently until the meat is tender.
7. Dilute the cornflour with a little water, stir into the simmering mixture, reboil and correct seasoning.
8. Place the mixture into a pie dish and allow to cool.
9. Cover with the paste, eggwash and bake at 200 °C for approximately 30–45 minutes.

Healthy eating tips

- Use little or no salt as the Worcester sauce contains salt.
- Fry in a small amount of an unsaturated oil and drain off all excess fat after frying.
- There will be less fat in the dish if short paste is used.
- Serve with boiled potatoes and plenty of vegetables.

Variation

Try:

- adding 50–100 g ox or sheep's kidneys with skin and gristle removed and cut into neat pieces
- adding 50–100 g sliced or quartered mushrooms
- adding 1 heaped teaspoon of tomato purée and some mixed herbs.

In place of cornflour, the meat can be tossed in flour before frying off.

In place of plain flour, 25–50 per cent wholemeal flour may be used in the pastry.

1 Dice the steak evenly

2 Coat the meat in cornflour before frying it

3 Cover the top with paste and trim off the excess

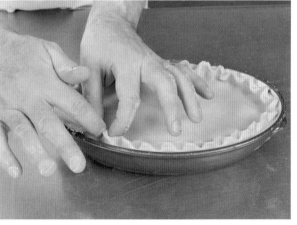

4 Press gently to ensure a seal between the paste and the dish

11 Carbonnade of beef (*carbonnade de boeuf*)

	4 portions	10 portions
Lean beef (topside)	400 g	1.25 kg
Salt, pepper		
Flour (white or wholemeal)	25 g	60 g
Dripping or oil	25 g	60 g
Onions, sliced	200 g	500 g
Beer	250 ml	625 ml
Caster sugar	10 g	25 g
Tomato purée	25 g	60 g
Brown stock		

Energy	Cals	Fat	Sat fat	Carb	Sugar	Protein	Fibre
1037 KJ	247 kcal	9.1 g	1.8 g	14.0 g	8.1 g	24.7 g	1.1 g

1 Cut the meat into thin slices.

2 Season with salt and pepper and pass through the flour.

3 Quickly colour on both sides in hot fat and place in a casserole.

4 Fry the onions to a light brown colour. Add to the meat.

5 Add the beer, sugar and tomato purée and sufficient brown stock to cover the meat.

6 Cover with a tight-fitting lid and simmer gently in a moderate oven at 150–200 °C until the meat is tender (approximately 2 hours).

7 Skim, correct the seasoning and serve.

Note

Carbonnade of beef is usually served with braised red cabbage, separately.

Healthy eating tips

- Trim off as much fat as possible before frying and drain off all surplus fat after frying.
- Use the minimum amount of salt to season the meat.
- Skim all fat from the finished sauce.
- Serve with plenty of potatoes and vegetables.

1 Slice the meat thinly

2 Pass each slice through the flour

3 Pour the liquid over the browned meat and onions

12 Hamburg or Vienna steak *(bitok)*

	4 portions	10 portions
Onion, finely chopped	25 g	60 g
Butter or oil	10 g	25 g
Lean minced beef	200 g	500 g
Small egg	1	2–3
Breadcrumbs	100 g	250 g
Cold water or milk	2 tbsp (approximately)	60 ml (approximately)

Energy	Cals	Fat	Sat fat	Carb	Sugar	Protein	Fibre
681 KJ	162 kcal	6.7 g	1.9 g	12.7 g	1.0 g	13.8 g	1.0 g

1 Cook the onion in the fat without colour, then allow to cool.

2 Add to the rest of the ingredients and mix in well.

3 Divide into even pieces and, using a little flour, make into balls, flatten and shape round.

4 Shallow-fry in hot fat on both sides, reducing the heat after the first few minutes, making certain they are cooked right through.

5 Serve with a light sauce, such as piquant sauce (see page 136).

Note

The 'steaks' may be garnished with French-fried onions and sometimes with a fried egg.

Healthy eating tips

- Use a small amount of an unsaturated oil to cook the onion and to shallow-fry the meat.
- The minced beef will produce more fat, which should be drained off.
- Serve with plenty of starchy carbohydrate and vegetables.

13 Goulash *(goulash de boeuf)*

	4 portions	10 portions
Prepared stewing beef	400 g	1.25 kg
Lard or oil	35 g	100 g
Onions, chopped	100 g	250 g
Flour	25 g	60 g
Paprika	10–25 g	25–60 g
Tomato purée	25 g	60 g
Stock or water	750 ml (approximately)	2 litres (approximately)
Turned potatoes or small new potatoes	8	20
Choux paste (see page 520)	125 ml	300 ml

Energy	Cals	Fat	Sat fat	Carb	Sugar	Protein	Fibre
1625 KJ	389 kcal	20.4 g	6.0 g	26.1 g	3.9 g	26.9 g	1.7 g

1   Remove excess fat from the beef. Cut into 2 cm square pieces.

2   Season and fry in the hot fat until slightly coloured. Add the chopped onion.

3   Cover with a lid and sweat gently for 3–4 minutes.

4   Add the flour and paprika and mix in with a wooden spoon.

5   Cook out in the oven or on top of the stove. Add the tomato purée, mix in.

6   Gradually add the stock, stir to the boil, skim, season and cover.

7   Allow to simmer, preferably in the oven, for approximately 1 ½–2 hours until the meat is tender.

8   Add the potatoes and check that they are covered with the sauce. (Add more stock if required.)

9   Re-cover with the lid and cook gently until the potatoes are cooked.

10 Skim and correct the seasoning and consistency. A little cream or yoghurt may be added at the last moment.

11 Serve garnished with turned potatoes, or alternatively sprinkled with a few gnocchis made from choux paste (see page 438), reheated in hot salted water or lightly tossed in butter or margarine.

Healthy eating tips
- Trim off as much fat as possible before frying and drain all surplus fat after frying.
- Use the minimum amount of salt to season the meat.
- Serve with a large side salad.

14 Best end or rack of lamb with breadcrumbs and parsley

Best end lamb, french trimmed	1
Fresh white breadcrumbs	25–50 g
Chopped parsley	1 tbsp
Egg	1
Melted butter or margarine	25–50 g

Energy	Cals	Fat	Sat fat	Carb	Sugar	Protein	Fibre	Sodium *
2530 kJ	612 kcal	51.3 g	24.2 g	6.6	0.5 g	31.2 g	0.2 g	0.233 g

* Using butter

1   Roast the best end at 220 °C for 15 minutes.

2   Ten minutes before cooking is completed cover the fat surface of the meat with a mixture of 25–50 g of fresh white breadcrumbs mixed with plenty of chopped parsley, an egg and 25–50 g melted butter or margarine.

3   Return to the oven for approximately 10 minutes to complete the cooking, browning carefully.

Professional tip
Cook the lamb until it is pink. Carefully bind the breadcrumbs with herbs and beaten egg, so that they will hold together during cooking.

Variation
Try:
- mixed fresh herbs used in addition to parsley
- adding finely chopped garlic
- chopped fresh herbs, shallots and mustard.

15 Roast leg of lamb with mint, lemon and cumin

	4 portions	10 portions
Mint	25 g	62.5 g
Lemons, juice of	2	5
Cumin	2 tsp	5 tsp
Olive oil	4 tbsp	10 tbsp
Leg of lamb	3.5 kg	2 × 3.5 kg

Energy	Cals	Fat	Sat fat	Carb	Sugar	Protein	Fibre
2192 KJ	524 kcal	39.1 g	13.7 g	0.3 g	0.3 g	29.7 g	0.0 g

* Using a 225 g portion of lamb

1 Place the mint, lemon juice, cumin and olive oil in a food processor. Carefully blend the mint, lemon juice, cumin and olive oil to give maximum flavour.

2 Rub the mixture into the lamb and place in a suitable roasting tray.

3 Roast the lamb in the normal way at 200 °C.

Note

Serve on a bed of boulangère potatoes or dauphinoise potatoes and a suitable green vegetable, e.g. leaf spinach with toasted pine nuts, or with a couscous salad.

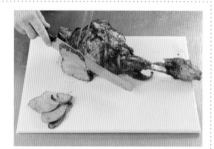

1 Ingredients for roast leg of lamb with mint, lemon and cumin

2 Place the leg of lamb in a roasting tray and rub with the mint and lemon mixture

3 Carving a leg of lamb

16 Slow-cooked shoulder of lamb with potatoes *boulangère*

	4 portions	10 portions
Boned shoulder of lamb, rolled and tied	1	3
Olive oil	1 tbsp	3 tbsp
Salt, pepper		
Rosemary	6 sprigs	18 sprigs
Thyme	6 sprigs	18 sprigs
Garlic	4 cloves	10 cloves
Mirepoix	400 g	1 kg
Bay leaves	1	3
Red wine or dry cider	250 ml	625 ml
Brown stock	300 ml	750 ml
Redcurrant jelly	1 tbsp	2 tbsp
Potatoes *boulangère*		
Potatoes	400 g	1.25 kg
Onions	100 g	250 g
Salt, pepper		
White stock	125 ml	350 ml
Butter or oil	25–50 g	60–100 g
Parsley, chopped		

Energy	Cals	Fat	Sat fat	Carb	Sugar	Protein	Fibre	Sodium
1815 kJ	437 kcal	30.8 g	14.5 g	2.2 g	0.3 g	27.6 g	0.4 g	600 mg

1 Rub the lamb with oil, and season with salt and pepper. Place in a suitable roasting tray and cook in an oven at 200 °C for 15 minutes.

2 Remove from the oven and reduce the temperature to 140 °C.

3 Add the remaining ingredients to the roasting tray.

4 Cook for 2 hours, basting every 20 minutes.

5 Remove the lamb from the roasting tray and return it to the oven on a rack. Place the potatoes *boulangère* directly below the lamb. Cook for ½ –1 hour, until the lamb is tender and sticky.

6 To finish the sauce, once the lamb is removed from the roasting tray, reduce the cooking liquor to the required consistency. Add the strained redcurrant jelly, mix well, correct seasoning, then strain.

For potatoes *boulangère*:

1 Cut the potatoes into 2 mm slices on a mandolin. Set aside the best slices to use for the top.

2 Peel, halve and finely slice the onions.

3 Mix the onions and potatoes together and season lightly with pepper and salt.

4 Place in a well-buttered shallow earthenware dish or roasting tin.

5 Barely cover with stock.

6 Neatly arrange overlapping slices of potato on top.

7 Brush lightly with oil.

8 Place in a hot oven at 230–250 °C for 20 minutes until lightly coloured.

9 Reduce the heat and allow to cook steadily, pressing down firmly from time to time with a flat-bottomed pan.

10 When ready all the stock should be cooked into the potato. Allow 1½ hours cooking time in all.

11 Serve sprinkled with chopped parsley. If cooked in an earthenware dish, clean the edges of the dish with a cloth dipped in salt, and serve in the dish.

17 Pot roast shoulder of lamb

	10 portions
Lamb shoulder (boned)	3 kg
Gratin forcemeat (see page 312)	300 g
Salt	1 tsp
Pepper	½ tsp
Wholewheat flour	3 tbsp
Oil	3 tbsp
Brown stock	500 mls
Potatoes (turned)	10
Carrots (turned)	10
Button onions	10
Worcestershire sauce	1 tsp

Energy	Cals	Fat	Sat fat	Carb	Sugar	Protein	Fibre	Sodium
3636 kJ	874 kcal	64 g	29 g	16.6	4.5 g	58.8 g	3.6 g	0.453 g

1 Preheat the oven to 160 °C.

2 Stuff shoulder with forcemeat and tie.

3 Dredge the lamb with seasoned flour.

4 Heat oil in a large roast pot over medium high heat.

5 Add the floured lamb to hot pan and brown evenly on all sides.

6 Pour stock to cover lamb.

7 Cover the pot and place in the preheated oven. Slow cook the lamb for 2 ½ to 3 hours.

8 During the last 45 minutes, add the vegetables to the pot. Cover and continue to cook until meat and vegetables are tender.

9 Remove the cooked lamb and vegetables from the pot to a serving platter.

10 Strain the cooking liquor and adjust the consistency; this can be thickened if desired.

11 Finish with Worcestershire sauce and season to taste.

18 Grilled lamb cutlets (*côtelettes d'agneau grillées*)

1. Season the cutlets lightly with salt and mill pepper.
2. Brush with oil or fat.
3. If the grill is heated from below, place the prepared cutlet on the greased, preheated bars. Cook for approximately 5 minutes, turn and complete the cooking.
4. If using a salamander, place the cutlets on a greased tray, cook for approximately 5 minutes, turn and complete the cooking.
5. Serve dressed, garnished with a deep-fried potato and watercress. A compound butter (e.g. parsley, herb or garlic) may also be served.
6. Each cutlet bone may be capped with a cutlet frill.

Healthy eating tip

When served with boiled new potatoes and boiled or steamed vegetables, the dish becomes more 'balanced'.

Energy	Cals	Fat	Sat fat	Carb	Sugar	Protein	Fibre	Sodium
1493kJ	357kcal	20.7g	9.8g	0.0g	0.0g	42.8g	0.0g	0.1g

19 Grilled loin or chump chops, or noisettes of lamb

1. Season the chops or noisettes lightly with salt and mill pepper.
2. Brush with oil and place on hot greased grill bars or place on a greased baking tray.
3. Cook quickly for the first 2–3 minutes on each side, in order to seal the pores of the meat.
4. Continue cooking steadily, allowing approximately 12–15 minutes in all.

Note

A compound butter may also be served, together with deep-fried potatoes.

Variation

Sprigs of rosemary or other herbs may be laid on the chops during the last few minutes of grilling to impart flavour.

Energy	Cals	Fat	Sat fat	Carb	Sugar	Protein	Fibre	Sodium
1338kJ	320kcal	16.1g	7.4g	0.0g	0.0g	43.8g	0.1g	0.1g

20 Lamb kebabs (*shish kebab*)

Energy	Cals	Fat	Sat fat	Carb	Sugar	Protein	Fibre	Sodium
1544kJ	378kcal	25.1g	9.9g	7.2g	5.9g	29.6g	20.6g	0.1g

1 Cut the meat into cubes and place on skewers with squares of green pepper, tomato, onion and bay leaves in between. The pieces of lamb and vegetables must be cut evenly so that they will cook evenly

2 Sprinkle with chopped thyme and cook over a hot grill.

Note

Kebabs, a dish of Turkish origin, are pieces of food impaled and cooked on skewers over a grill or barbecue. There are many variations and different flavours can be added by marinating the kebabs in oil, wine, vinegar or lemon juice with spices and herbs for 1–2 hours before cooking.

Kebabs can be made using tender cuts, or mince of lamb and beef, pork, liver, kidney, bacon, ham, sausage and chicken, using either the meats individually or combining two or three. Vegetables and fruit can also be added (e.g. onion, apple, pineapple, peppers, tomatoes, aubergine). Kebabs can be made using vegetables exclusively (e.g. peppers, onion, aubergine, tomatoes). Kebabs are usually served with a pilaff rice (see page 421) or chickpeas and finely sliced raw onion.

The ideal cuts of lamb are the nut of the lean meat of the loin, best end or boned-out meat from a young shoulder of lamb.

Variation

Miniature kebabs (one mouthful) can be made, impaled on cocktail sticks, grilled and served as a hot snack at receptions.

Fish kebabs can be made using a firm fish, such as monkfish or tuna, and marinating in olive oil, lemon or lime juice, chopped fennel or dill, garlic and a dash of Tabasco or Worcester sauce.

21 Irish stew

Energy	Cals	Fat	Sat fat	Carb	Sugar	Protein	Fibre
1339KJ	319kcal	11.2g	5.2g	26.1g	5.7g	30.2g	5.0g

	4 portions	10 portions
Stewing lamb (scrag, middle neck or shoulder)	500g	1.5kg
Salt, pepper		
Bouquet garni		
Potatoes	400g	1kg
Onions	100g	250g
Celery	100g	250g
Savoy cabbage	100g	250g
Leeks	100g	250g
Button onions	100g	250g
Parsley, chopped		

1 Trim the meat and cut into even pieces. Blanch and refresh.

2 Place in a shallow saucepan, cover with water, bring to the boil, season with salt and skim. If tough meat is being used, allow ½–1 hour stewing time before adding any vegetables.

3 Add the bouquet garni. Turn the potatoes into barrel shapes.

4 Cut the potato trimmings, onions, celery, cabbage and leeks into small neat pieces and add to the meat; simmer for 30 minutes.

5 Add the button onions and simmer for a further 30 minutes.

6 Add the potatoes and simmer gently with a lid on the pan until cooked.

7 Correct the seasoning and skim off all fat.

8 Serve sprinkled with chopped parsley.

Keep the meat and vegetables covered with liquid during cooking, to keep the dish consistent and tasty.

Variations

Alternatively, a more modern approach is to cook the meat for 1½–2 hours until almost tender, then add the vegetables and cook until all are tender. Optional accompaniments include Worcester sauce and/or pickled red cabbage (see page 213).

Healthy eating tips
● Trim as much fat as possible from the stewing lamb.
● Use the minimum amount of salt.
● Serve with colourful seasonal vegetables to create a 'healthy' dish.

Ingredients for Irish stew

Boil the meat

Add the vegetables

22 White lamb stew (blanquette d'agneau)

	4 portions	10 portions
Stewing lamb	500 g	1.5 kg
White stock	750 ml	1.5 litres
Onion, studded	50 g	125 g
Carrot	50 g	125 g
Bouquet garni		
Salt, pepper		
Butter, margarine or oil	25 g	60 g
Flour	25 g	60 g
Cream, yoghurt or quark	2–3 tbsp	5 tbsp
Parsley, chopped		

Energy	Cals	Fat	Sat fat	Carb	Sugar	Protein	Fibre *
1181 KJ	283 kcal	15.5 g	7.8 g	9.2 g	3.9 g	27.3 g	0.0 g

* Using butter and 2 tbsp low-fat yoghurt

1 Trim the meat and cut into even pieces. Blanch and refresh.

2 Place in a saucepan and cover with cold water.

3 Bring to the boil then place under running cold water until all the scum has been washed away.

4 Drain and place in a clean saucepan and cover with stock, bring to the boil and skim.

5 Add whole onion and carrot, and bouquet garni, season lightly with salt and simmer until tender, approximately 1–1 ½ hours.

6 Meanwhile prepare a blond roux with the butter and flour and make into a velouté with the cooking liquor. Cook out for approximately 20 minutes.

7 Correct the seasoning and consistency, and pass through a fine strainer on to the meat, which has been placed in a clean pan.

8 Reheat, mix in the cream and serve, finished with chopped parsley.

9 To enrich this dish a liaison of yolks and cream is sometimes added at the last moment to the boiling sauce, which must not be allowed to reboil, otherwise the eggs will scramble and the sauce will curdle.

Healthy eating tips

● Trim as much fat as possible from the lamb before cooking.
● Use the minimum amount of salt.
● Reduce the fat content by using low-fat yoghurt in place of the cream when reheating.
● Serve with mashed potato with spring onion and colourful vegetables.

Professional tip

Be very careful when adding the liaison of yolks and cream; make sure the sauce does not come back to the boil or it will curdle.

1 Ingredients for blanquette of lamb

2 Cook the meat on the stove

3 Make a roux

4 Make a velouté by combining the roux with the liquid

23 Lamb fillets with beans and tomatoes

Energy	Cals	Fat	Sat fat	Carb	Sugar	Protein	Fibre	Sodium
4767 kJ	1137 kcal	37.9 g	13.3 g	23.5	7.5 g	76.5 g	10.7 g	0.197 g

	4 portions	10 portions
Olive oil	Approximately 50 ml	Approximately 125 ml
Onions, finely chopped	50 g	125 g
Garlic, crushed and chopped	2	5
Dried cannellini beans, soaked	500 g	1.25 kg
Lamb stock	1 litre	2.5 litres
Bay leaves	2	5
Salt, pepper		
Cherry tomatoes	750 g	1 kg
Lamb fillets	900 g	2.25 kg

1 Heat the olive oil in a suitable pan, and gently fry the onion and garlic. Rinse the beans, drain and add to the pan.

2 Add the stock and bay leaves. Bring to the boil. Simmer for approximately 1 hour until the beans are tender. Season.

3 Cook the cherry tomatoes in a hot oven at 190 °C with a drizzle of oil.

4 Rub a little olive oil into the lamb fillets. Leave for approximately 20 minutes at room temperature.

5 Season the lamb and shallow-fry. Serve with the tomatoes and the beans nearly arranged on a plate.

Professional tip

Lamb fillets only need a little cooking. Cook them at the last minute so that they will look and taste as good as possible.

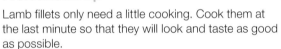

24 Braised lamb shanks

Energy	Cals	Fat	Sat fat	Carb	Sugar	Protein	Fibre	Sodium
3098 kJ	742 kcal	24.2 g	7.4 g	10.5	8.1 g	98.3 g	4 g	0.280 g

	4 portions	10 portions
Lamb shanks	4	10
Olive oil for braising (to fill casserole about 1 cm deep)		
Leeks, roughly chopped	1	2
Celery sticks, roughly chopped	2	5
Carrots, roughly chopped	2	5
Onions, roughly chopped	2	5
Garlic head, broken into cloves (unpeeled)	1	2
Bay leaf	1	3
Thyme sprig	1	2
Rosemary sprig	1	2
Red wine	375 ml	1 litre
Chicken stock	600 ml	1.5 litres

1 Take a casserole (or oven-proof dish) and place on the hob over a high heat. Pour in the olive oil and, when hot, add the lamb shanks, turning occasionally until brown.

2 Once browned, remove the lamb from the pot and tip in the leek, celery, carrot, onion and garlic cloves. Stir them all together and add the bay leaf, thyme and rosemary. These ingredients will all add flavour to the dish but won't be served at the end.

3 Once the vegetables are lightly browned, place the lamb back into the pot, allowing it to rest on top of the vegetables.

4 Pour in the red wine and chicken stock and bring to the boil.

5 Cover the pot with a lid or kitchen foil and place in the oven at 150°C to braise for 2 hours 30 minutes, or up to 5 hours depending on the amount of lamb being used. When the meat is cooked, the bone can easily be turned out of the meat (if you would like to present the bone, only give it a small turn to check if the lamb is ready, as it will be difficult to re-insert the bone once removed).

6 Pass the cooking stock through a fine sieve and reduce to the correct consistency (coats the back of a spoon).

7 Serve the lamb shanks with the cooking juices poured over the top.

Note

The lamb can be served with mashed potato and roast vegetables.

---

25 Roast saddle of lamb with rosemary mash

	4 portions	10 portions
Saddle of lamb, boned		
Milk	250 ml	625 ml
Rosemary	2 sprigs	5 sprigs
Potatoes, mashed	1.3 kg	3.2 kg

1 Bone the saddle of lamb and roast in the normal way (see page 258).

2 Bring the milk to the boil with the rosemary. Remove from the heat, cover and leave to infuse for 10–15 minutes.

3 To make the rosemary mash, prepare a potato purée using the milk infused with rosemary.

Energy	Cals	Fat	Sat fat	Carb	Sugar	Protein	Fibre	Salt
3215 kJ	770 kcal	45.7 g	22.1 g	58.9 g	4.7 g	34.4 g	5.6 g	0.2 g

26 Mixed grill

	4 portions	10 portions
Sausages	4	10
Cutlets	4	10
Kidneys	4	10
Tomatoes	4	10
Mushrooms	4	10
Streaky bacon, rashers	4	10
Deep-fried potato, to serve		
Watercress, to serve		
Parsley butter, to serve		

Energy	Cals	Fat	Sat fat	Carb	Sugar	Protein	Fibre *
2050KJ	488kcal	40.8g	19.3g	0.0g	0.0g	30.4g	0.0g

* 1 portion (2 cutlets). With deep-fried potatoes, parsley and watercress, 1 portion provides: 3050kJ/726kcal energy; 59.2g fat; 26.6g sat fat; 20.2g carb; 2.5g sugar; 29.5g protein; 4.9g fibre

Note

Garnish with deep-fried potato, watercress and a slice of compound butter on each kidney or offered separately.

These are the usually accepted items for a mixed grill, but it will be found that there are many variations to this list (e.g. steaks, liver, a Welsh rarebit and fried egg).

1 Grill in the order listed above.

2 Dress neatly on an oval flat dish or plates.

Professional tip

The items must be cooked in the order listed above, so that they are all fully and evenly cooked at the end.

Healthy eating tip

Add only a small amount of compound butter and serve with plenty of potatoes and vegetables.

27 Brown lamb or mutton stew (*navarin d'agneau*)

	4 portions	10 portions
Stewing lamb	500g	1.5kg
Oil	2 tbsp	5 tbsp
Salt, pepper		
Carrot, chopped	100g	250g
Onion, chopped	100g	250g
Clove of garlic (if desired)	1	3
Flour (white or wholemeal)	25g	60g
Tomato purée	1 level tbsp	2¼ level tbsp
Brown stock (mutton stock or water)	500g	1.25 litre
Bouquet garni		
Parsley, chopped, to serve		

Energy	Cals	Fat	Sat fat	Carb	Sugar	Protein	Fibre *
1320kJ	314kcal	18.7g	6.2g	9.4g	3.2g	27.9g	1.3g

* Using sunflower oil

1 Trim the meat and cut into even pieces.

2 Partly fry off the seasoned meat in the oil, then add the carrot, onion and garlic, and continue frying.

3 Drain off the surplus fat, add the flour and mix.

4 Singe in the oven or brown on top of the stove for a few minutes, or add previously browned flour.

5 Add the tomato purée and stir with a wooden spoon.

6 Add the stock and season.

7 Add the bouquet garni, bring to the boil, skim and cover with a lid.

8 Simmer gently until cooked (preferably in the oven) for approximately 1–2 hours, until the lamb is tender.

9 When cooked, place the meat in a clean pan.

10 Correct the sauce and pass it on to the meat.

11 Serve sprinkled with chopped parsley.

Video: Making brown lamb stew http://bit.ly/1CIMkfD

Healthy eating tips
● Trim off as much fat as possible before frying.
● Use the minimum amount of salt to season the meat.
● Serve with plenty of potatoes and vegetables.

Professional tip

● Make sure the oil is hot before placing the meat in the pan to brown quickly all over.
● Do not allow the meat to boil in the oil, because this will spoil the flavour and texture.

Variations

Garnish with vegetables (glazed carrots and turnips, glazed button onions, potatoes, peas and diamonds of French beans, which may be cooked separately or in the stew).

1 Fry the lamb, onions and carrots

2 Mix in the flour

3 Add the stock and bring to the boil

28 Hot pot of lamb or mutton

	4 portions	10 portions
Stewing lamb	500 g	1.25 kg
Salt, pepper		
Onions, thinly sliced	100 g	250 g
Potatoes, thinly sliced	400 g	1.25 kg
Brown stock	1 litre	2.5 litres
Oil (optional)	25 g	60 g
Parsley, chopped		

Energy	Cals	Fat	Sat fat	Carb	Sugar	Protein	Fibre	*
1505 KJ	360 kcal	17.0 g	6.4 g	22.0 g	1.8 g	29.0 g	2.5 g	

* Using sunflower oil

1 Trim the meat and cut into even pieces.

2 Place in a deep earthenware dish. Season with salt and pepper.

3 Lightly sauté the onions in the oil, if desired. Mix the onion and approximately three-quarters of the potatoes together.

4 Season and place on top of the meat; cover three parts with stock.

5 Neatly arrange an overlapping layer of the remaining potatoes on top, sliced about 2 mm thick.

6 Thoroughly clean the edges of the dish and place to cook in a hot oven at 230–250 °C until lightly coloured.

7 Reduce the heat and continue cooking for approximately 1 ½–2 hours.

8 Press the potatoes down occasionally during cooking.

9 Serve with the potatoes brushed with butter or margarine and sprinkle with the chopped parsley.

Note

Neck chops or neck fillet make a succulent dish.

When the dish is ready, the top layer of potatoes should be golden brown.

Variations

Try:
- using leek in place of onion
- adding 200 g lambs' kidneys
- quickly frying off the meat and sweating the onions before putting in the pot
- adding 100–200 g sliced mushrooms
- adding a small tin of baked beans or a layer of thickly sliced tomatoes before adding the potatoes
- using sausages in place of lamb.

1 Chop the lamb into even-sized pieces

2 Layer the potatoes over the lamb

3 Pour over the stock

29 Shepherd's pie (cottage pie)

	4 portions	10 portions
Onions, chopped	100 g	250 g
Oil	35 ml	100 ml
Lamb or mutton (minced), cooked	400 g	1.25 kg
Salt, pepper		
Worcester sauce	2–3 drops	5 drops
Potatoes, cooked	400 g	1.25 kg
Butter or margarine	25 g	60 g
Milk or eggwash		
Jus lié or demi-glace	125–250 ml	300–600 ml

Energy	Cals	Fat	Sat fat	Carb	Sugar	Protein	Fibre	*
1744 KJ	415 kcal	25.3 g	9.1 g	22.1 g	2.5 g	26.3 g	1.6 g	

* Using sunflower oil, with hard margarine in topping

1 Cook the onion in the oil without colouring.
2 Add the cooked meat from which all fat and gristle has been removed.
3 Season and add Worcester sauce (sufficient to bind).
4 Bring to the boil; simmer for 10–15 minutes.
5 Place in an earthenware or pie dish.
6 Prepare the potatoes – mix with the butter or margarine, then mash and pipe, or arrange neatly on top.
7 Brush with the milk or eggwash.
8 Colour lightly under a salamander or in a hot oven.
9 Serve accompanied with a sauceboat of jus lié.

Note

This dish prepared with cooked beef is known as cottage pie.

Pipe the potato carefully so that the meat is completely covered.

When using reheated meats, care must be taken to heat thoroughly and quickly.

Healthy eating tips
- Use an oil rich in unsaturates (olive or sunflower) to lightly oil the pan.
- Drain off any excess fat after the lamb has been fried.
- Try replacing some of the meat with baked beans or lentils, and add tomatoes and/or mushrooms to the dish.
- When served with a large portion of green vegetables, a healthy balance is created.

Variation

Try:
- adding 100–200 g sliced mushrooms
- adding a layer of thickly sliced tomatoes, then sprinkling with rosemary
- mixing a tin of baked beans in with the meat
- sprinkling with grated cheese and browning under a salamander
- varying the flavour of the mince by adding herbs or spices
- varying the potato topping by mixing in grated cheese, chopped spring onions or herbs, or by using duchess potato mixture
- serving lightly sprinkled with garam masala and with grilled pitta bread.

30 Samosas

Samosa pastry	16–20 pasties	40–50 pasties
Short pastry made from ghee fat and fairly strong flour (the dough must be fairly elastic)	400 g	1 kg

Energy	Cals	Fat	Sat fat	Carb	Sugar	Protein	Fibre
237 kJ	57 kcal	3.6 g	1.3 g	5.5 g	1.5 g	0.9 g	0.8 g

1 Cut the paste into strips approx. 13 × 7cm. Fold over the end of the pastry.

2 Eggwash the upper side of the pastry, then fold over the top part to form a pocket.

3 Flip over the pocket, ease it open and fill it.

4 Once completely full, eggwash the top edge and the flap of pastry.

5 Fold over the pastry and wrap it round to seal the samosa.

6 Deep fry until golden brown and crisp.

7 Serve on a suitable dish. Samosas can be garnished with coriander leaves and served with chutney.

Note

A portion would be 4 or 5 pasties. Samosas can also be served individually as finger food.

Filling 1: lamb	4 portions	10 portions
Saffron	½ tsp	1¼ tsp
Boiling water	2½ tsp	6¼ tsp
Vegetable oil	3 tsp	7½ tsp
Fresh ginger, finely chopped	12 g	30 g
Cloves of garlic, crushed and chopped	2	5
Onions, finely chopped	50 g	125 g
Salt, to taste		
Lean lamb, minced	400 g	1 kg
Pinch of cayenne pepper		
Garam masala	1 tsp	2½ tsp

1 Infuse the saffron in the boiling water; allow to stand for 10 minutes.

2 Heat the vegetable oil in a suitable pan. Add the ginger, garlic, onions and salt, stirring continuously. Fry for 7–8 minutes, until the onions are soft and golden brown.

3 Stir in the lamb, add the saffron with the water. Cook, stirring the lamb until it is cooked.

4 Add the cayenne and garam masala, reduce the heat and allow to cook gently for a further 10 minutes.

5 The mixture should be fairly tight with very little moisture.

6 Transfer to a bowl and allow to cool before using.

Healthy eating tips
- No added salt is necessary.
- Use a small amount of unsaturated oil to fry the onions and lamb.
- Drain off the excess fat before adding the water.

Filling 2: potato	4 portions	10 portions
Potatoes, peeled	200 g	500 g
Vegetable oil	1½ tsp	3¾ tsp
Black mustard seeds	½ tsp	1¼ tsp
Onions, finely chopped	50 g	125 g
Fresh ginger, finely chopped	12 g	30 g
Fennel seeds	1 tsp	2½ tsp
Cumin seeds	¼ tsp	1 tsp
Turmeric	¼ tsp	1 tsp
Frozen peas	75 g	187 g
Salt, to taste		
Water	1 tbsp	2½ tbsp
Fresh coriander, finely chopped	1 tsp	2½ tsp
Garam masala	½ tsp	2½ tsp
Pinch of cayenne pepper		

1 Cut the potatoes into 0.5 cm dice; cook in water until only just cooked.

2 Heat the oil in a suitable pan, add the mustard seeds and cook until they pop.

3 Add the onions and ginger. Fry for 7–8 minutes, stirring continuously until golden brown.

4 Stir in the fennel, cumin and turmeric, add the potatoes, peas, salt and water.

5 Reduce to a low heat, cover the pan and cook for 5 minutes.

6 Stir in the coriander; cook for a further 5 minutes.

7 Remove from the heat, stir in the garam masala and the cayenne seasoning.

8 Remove from the pan, place into a suitable bowl to cool before using.

Healthy eating tips
- Use the minimum amount of salt.
- Use a small amount of unsaturated oil to fry the mustard seeds and the onion.
- Skim any fat from the finished dish.

1 Cut the paste into strips approx. 13 × 7 cm. Fold over the end of the pastry.

2 Eggwash the upper side of the pastry, then fold over the top part to form a pocket.

3 Flip over the pocket, ease it open and fill it.

4 Once completely full, eggwash the top edge and the flap of pastry.

5 Fold over the pastry and wrap it round to seal the samosa.

6 Deep fry until golden brown and crisp.

31 Fricassée of veal *(fricassée de veau)*

	4 portions	10 portions
Boned stewing veal (shoulder or breast)	400 g	1.25 kg
Butter or oil	35 g	100 g
Flour	25 g	60 g
White veal stock	500 ml	1.25 litres
Salt, pepper		
Egg yolk	1	2–3
Cream	2–3 tbsp	5–7 tbsp
Squeeze of lemon juice		
Parsley, chopped, to finish		

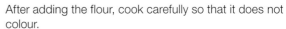

Energy	Cals	Fat	Sat fat	Carb	Sugar	Protein	Fibre
992 KJ	236 kcal	13.6 g	7.5 g	5.3 g	0.4 g	23.3 g	0.2 g

* Using butter

1 Trim the meat. Cut into even 25 g pieces.

2 Sweat the meat gently in the butter without colour in a sauté pan.

3 Mix in the flour and cook out without colour.

4 Allow to cool.

5 Gradually add boiling stock just to cover the meat, stir until smooth.

6 Season, bring to the boil, skim.

7 Cover and simmer gently on the stove until tender (approximately 1½–2 hours).

8 Pick out the meat into a clean pan. Correct the sauce.

9 Pass on to the meat and reboil. Mix the yolk and cream in a basin.

10 Add a little of the boiling sauce, mix in and pour back on to the meat, shaking the pan until thoroughly mixed; do not reboil. Add the lemon juice.

11 Serve, finished with chopped parsley and heart-shaped croutons fried in butter or oil.

Professional tip

After adding the flour, cook carefully so that it does not colour.

Add the liaison of yolks and cream carefully. Do not allow the sauce to boil after this, because it will curdle.

Healthy eating tips

● Add the minimum amount of salt.
● Brush the croutons with olive oil and bake them, or serve with sippets (small, thin pieces of toasted bread).
● A large serving of starchy carbohydrates and vegetables will help to proportionally reduce the fat content.

Variation

Add mushrooms and button onions. Proceed as for this recipe but, after 1 hour's cooking, pick out the meat, strain the sauce back on to the meat and add 2 small button onions per portion. Simmer for 15 minutes, add 2 small white button mushrooms per portion, washed and peeled if necessary, then complete the cooking. Finish and serve as in this recipe. This is known as *fricassée de veau à l'ancienne*.

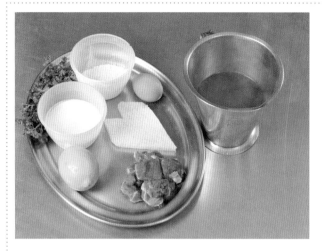

1 Ingredients for fricassée of veal

2 Cook the meat and flour

3 Add the stock and continue to cook

4 Add the liaison of egg yolk and cream

32 White stew or blanquette of veal (*blanquette de veau*)

Proceed as for white lamb stew (recipe 23), using 400 g of prepared stewing veal.

Energy	Cals	Fat	Sat fat	Carb	Sugar	Protein	Fibre	Sodium
3608 kJ	863 kcal	24.9 g	6.9 g	23.5	7.5 g	36.8 g	10.7 g	0.091 g

33 Grilled veal cutlet (*côte de veau grillé*)

1 Lightly season the prepared chop with salt and mill pepper.

2 Brush with oil. Place on previously heated grill bars.

3 Cook on both sides for 8–10 minutes in all.

4 Brush occasionally to prevent the meat from drying.

Note

Serve with watercress, a deep-fried potato and a suitable sauce or butter, such as bearnaise or compound butter, or on a bed of plain or flavoured mashed potato (see page 203). Sprigs of rosemary may be added to the chop before or halfway through cooking.

Healthy eating tips

- Use the minimum amount of salt to season the meat.
- Serve with a small amount of sauce or butter and a large portion of mixed vegetables.

Energy	Cals	Fat	Sat fat	Carb	Sugar	Protein	Fibre
990KJ	236kcal	9.7g	2.6g	0.0g	0.0g	36.9g	0.0g

*

34 Braised shin of veal (*osso buco*)

	4 portions	10 portions
Salt and ground pepper		
Plain flour	45g	112g
Thick slices of veal shin on the bone	4 × 200g	10 × 200g
Butter	50g	125g
Oil	2 tbsp	5 tbsp
White wine	150ml	375ml
Plum tomatoes	450g	1.125kg
Light veal or chicken stock	300ml	750ml
Sprigs of parsley and thyme		
Bay leaf	1	1

Energy	Cals	Fat	Sat fat	Carb	Sugar	Protein	Fibre
1732kJ	413kcal	19.7g	8.5g	12.5g	3.9g	47.3g	1.5g

1 Pre-heat the oven to 180° C.

2 Season the flour and use to coat the meat well on both sides.

3 Heat the butter and oil in a casserole, add the veal and fry, turning once, until browned on both sides. Add the wine and cook, uncovered, for 10 minutes. Blanch, peel and chop the tomatoes, and add along with the stock and herbs.

4 Cover and cook in the centre of the oven until the meat is very tender and falls away from the marrow bone in the middle.

Note

Part of the attraction of this dish is the marrow found in the bones. Although very rich, it is a special treat. Traditionally, osso buco is served with a gremolata, which is a combination of chopped parsley, garlic and lemon zest that is added to the dish at the very end. It has been omitted from this recipe, offering you a simple base.

Delicious served with sauté potatoes or with a risotto alla Milanese.

35 Hot veal and ham pie

	4 portions	10 portions
Bacon rashers	100 g	250 g
Stewing veal without bone	400 g	1.25 kg
Hardboiled egg, chopped or quartered	1	2
Parsley, chopped	1 tsp	2 tsp
Onion, chopped	50 g	125 g
Salt, pepper		
White stock	250 ml	625 ml
Rough puff or puff paste (see page 519)	100 g	250 g

Energy	Cals	Fat	Sat fat	Carb	Sugar	Protein	Fibre
1394 KJ	332 kcal	20.7 g	8.1 g	8.9 g	0.8 g	27.9 g	0.7 g

Healthy eating tips

- Little or no salt is needed – there is plenty in the bacon.
- Serve with plenty of starchy carbohydrate and vegetables to proportionally reduce the fat.

1 Bat out the bacon thinly and use it to line the bottom and sides of a ½ litre pie dish, reserving two or three pieces for the top.

2 Trim the veal, cut it into small pieces and mix with the egg, parsley and onion. Season and place in the pie dish.

3 Just cover with stock. Add the rest of the bacon.

4 Roll out the pastry, eggwash the rim of the pie dish and line with a strip of pastry 1 cm wide. Press this down firmly and eggwash.

5 Without stretching the pastry, cover the pie and seal firmly.

6 Trim off any excess pastry with a sharp knife, notch the edge neatly, eggwash and decorate.

7 Allow to rest in the refrigerator or a cool place.

8 Place on a baking sheet in a hot oven at 200 °C for 10–15 minutes until the paste has set and is lightly coloured.

9 Remove the pie from oven, cover with foil and return to the oven, reducing the heat to 190 °C for 15 minutes, to 160 °C for a further 15 minutes, then to 140 °C.

10 Complete the cooking at this temperature ensuring that the liquid is gently simmering. Cook the pie for approx. 1–1 ½ hours, or less if the pieces of meat are small (e.g. 50 minutes–1 hour if using 1 cm pieces).

Variation

Variations include rabbit, pork, chicken or guinea fowl in place of veal.

36 Escalope of veal (*escalope de veau*)

Veal escalope Holstein

	4 portions	10 portions
Nut or cushion of veal	400 g	1.25 kg
Seasoned flour	25 g	60 g
Egg	1	2
Breadcrumbs	50 g	125 g
Oil, for frying	50 g	125 g
Butter, for frying	50 g	125 g
Beurre noisette (optional)	50 g	125 g
Jus lié (page 130)	60 ml	150 ml

Energy	Cals	Fat	Sat fat	Carb	Sugar	Protein	Fibre
2079 KJ	495 kcal	39.8 g	11.4 g	10.3 g	0.5 g	24.7 g	1.0 g

* Fried in sunflower oil, using butter to finish

1 Trim and remove all sinew from the veal.

2 Cut into four even slices and bat out thinly using a little water.

3 Flour, egg and crumb. Shake off surplus crumbs. Mark with a palette knife.

4 Place the escalopes into shallow hot fat and cook quickly for a few minutes on each side.

5 Dress on a serving dish or plate.

6 An optional finish is to pour over 50 g *beurre noisette* (nut-brown butter) and finish with a cordon of jus lié.

Note

The escalopes need to be batted out thinly. Excess breadcrumbs must be shaken off before the escalopes are placed into the hot fat.

Healthy eating tips

● Use an unsaturated oil to fry the veal.
● Make sure the fat is hot so that less will be absorbed into the crumb.
● Drain the cooked escalope on kitchen paper.
● Use the minimum amount of salt.
● Serve with plenty of starchy carbohydrate and vegetables.

Variation

Escalope of veal Viennoise: as for this recipe, but garnish the dish with chopped yolk and white of egg and chopped parsley; on top of each escalope place a slice of peeled lemon decorated with chopped egg yolk, egg white and parsley, an anchovy fillet and a stoned olive; finish with a little lemon juice and nut-brown butter.

Veal escalope Holstein: prepare and cook the escalopes as for this recipe; add an egg fried in butter or oil, and place two neat fillets of anchovy criss-crossed on each egg; serve.

Escalope of veal with spaghetti and tomato sauce: prepare escalopes as for this recipe, then garnish with spaghetti with tomato sauce (page 145), allowing 10 g spaghetti per portion.

37 Veal escalopes with Parma ham and mozzarella cheese (*involtini di vitello*)

	4 portions	10 portions
Small, thin veal escalopes	400 g (8 in total)	1.25 kg (20 in total)
Flour (for dusting)		
Parma ham, thinly sliced	100 g	250 g
Mozzarella cheese, thinly sliced	200 g	500 g
Fresh sage leaves	8	20
or		
dried sage	1 tsp	2 ½ tsp
Salt, pepper		
Butter or oil	50 g	125 g
Parmesan cheese, grated		

Energy	Cals	Fat	Sat fat	Carb	Sugar	Protein	Fibre
1642 KJ	394 kcal	26.1 g	15.5 g	0.1 g	0.1 g	39.8 g	0.0 g

1 Sprinkle each slice of veal lightly with flour and flatten.

2 Place a slice of Parma ham on each escalope.

3 Add several slices of mozzarella cheese to each.

4 Add a sage leaf or a light sprinkling of dried sage.

5 Season, roll up each escalope and secure with a toothpick or cocktail stick. Make sure the ham and cheese are well sealed within the escalope before cooking.

6 Melt the butter in a sauté pan, add the escalopes and brown on all sides.

7 Transfer the escalopes and butter to a suitably sized ovenproof dish.

8 Sprinkle generously with grated Parmesan cheese and bake in a moderately hot oven at 190 °C for 10 minutes.

9 Clean the edges of the dish and serve.

Healthy eating tips

● Use a small amount of oil to fry the escalopes and drain the cooked escalopes on kitchen paper.
● No added salt is necessary as there is plenty of salt in the cheese.
● Serve with plenty of vegetables.

1 Layer the veal, ham and cheese, then roll them up

2 Transfer the fried escalopes to an ovenproof dish and sprinkle with cheese

38 Roast leg of pork

Energy	Cals	Fat	Sat fat	Carb	Sugar	Protein	Fibre	*
1357 KJ	323 kcal	22.4 g	8.9 g	0.0 g	0.0 g	30.4 g	0.0 g	

* 113 g portion

1 Prepare leg for roasting (see page 621).

2 Moisten with water, oil, cider, wine or butter and lard, then sprinkle with salt, rubbing it well into the cracks of the skin. This will make the crackling crisp.

3 Place on a trivet in a roasting tin with a little oil or dripping on top.

4 Start to cook in a hot oven at 230–250 °C, basting frequently.

5 Gradually reduce the heat to 180–185 °C, allowing approximately 25 minutes per 0.5 kg plus another 25 minutes. Pork must always be well cooked. If using a probe, the minimum temperature should be 75 °C for 2 minutes.

6 When cooked, remove from the pan and prepare a roast gravy from the sediment (see page 129).

7 Remove the crackling and cut into even pieces for serving.

Note

Serve the joint garnished with picked watercress and accompanied by roast gravy, sage and onion dressing and apple sauce. If to be carved, proceed as for roast lamb (see page 621).

Variation

Other joints can also be used for roasting (e.g. loin, shoulder and spare rib).

39 Sage and onion dressing for pork

	4 portions	10 portions
Onion, chopped	50 g	125 g
Pork dripping	50 g	125 g
White breadcrumbs	100 g	250 g
Chopped parsley, pinch		
Powdered sage, good pinch		
Salt, pepper		

Energy	Cals	Fat	Sat fat	Carb	Sugar	Protein	Fibre	Sodium
865 kJ	204 kcal	12.9 g	6.3 g	20.6	1.9 g	2.7 g	0.2 g	0.150 g

1 Cook the onion in the dripping without colour.

2 Combine all the ingredients. Dressing is usually served separately.

Healthy eating tips

● Use a small amount of unsaturated oil instead of dripping.
● Add the minimum amount of salt.

Professional tip

Modern practice is to refer to this as a dressing if served separately to the meat, but as stuffing if used to stuff the meat.

40 Roast pork belly with shallots and champ potatoes

	4 portions	10 portions
Pork belly	1.2 kg	2.5 kg
Salt, pepper		
Olive oil	1 tbsp	3 tbsp
Shallots	20	50
Butter	70 g	175 g
Potatoes, peeled and chopped	1 kg	25 kg
Spring onions, chopped	8	20
Double cream	4 tbsp	10 tbsp

Energy	Cals	Fat	Sat fat	Carb	Sugar	Protein	Fibre	Sodium
2680 kJ	645 kcal	50.5 g	18.3 g	0.0 g	0.0 g	47.8 g	0.0 g	0.2 g

1 Place the pork on a rack in a roasting tray; season and oil. Roast in the oven for 10 minutes at 200 °C and then for 3–3 ½ hours at 140 °C.

2 Peel the shallots, fry gently in half the butter until caramelised. Keep warm.

3 Purée the potatoes.

4 Melt the remaining butter in a pan and sauté the spring onions until soft. Add the spring onion and the butter to the potato purée.

5 Add the cream and mix well.

6 Serve the pork with the caramelised shallots and potato.

7 Serve with a reduced brown stock flavoured with cider; alternatively, a red wine sauce may be served.

41 Spare ribs of pork in barbecue sauce

	4 portions	10 portions
Onion, finely chopped	100 g	250 g
Clove of garlic, chopped	1	2
Oil	60 ml	150 ml
Vinegar	60 ml	150 ml
Tomato purée	150 g	375 g
Honey	60 ml	150 ml
Brown stock	250 ml	625 ml
Worcester sauce	4 tbsp	10 tbsp
Dry mustard	1 tsp	2 tsp
Pinch thyme		
Salt		
Spare ribs of pork	2 kg	5 kg

Energy	Cals	Fat	Sat fat	Carb	Sugar	Protein	Fibre	*
6151 KJ	1465 kcal	12.6 g	37.3 g	20.3 g	17.1 g	63.5 g	0.3 g	

* Using sunflower oil

1 Sweat the onion and garlic in the oil without colour.

2 Mix in the vinegar, tomato purée, honey, stock, Worcester sauce, mustard and thyme, and season with salt.

3 Allow the barbecue sauce to simmer for 10–15 minutes.

4 Place the prepared spare ribs fat side up on a trivet in a roasting tin.

5 Brush the spare ribs liberally with the barbecue sauce.

6 Place in a moderately hot oven: 180–200 °C.

7 Cook for ¾–1 hour.

8 Baste generously with the barbecue sauce every 10–15 minutes.

9 The cooked spare ribs should be brown and crisp.

10 Cut the spare ribs into individual portions and serve.

Professional tip

Apply plenty of barbecue sauce before and during cooking, to give the ribs a good flavour.

Healthy eating tips
- Sweat the onion and garlic in a little unsaturated oil.
- No added salt is necessary as the Worcester sauce is salty.

42 Pork loin chops with pesto and mozzarella

	4 portions	10 portions
Salt, pepper		
Loin chops	4	10
Olive oil (if frying)	2 tbsp	5 tbsp
Pesto	4 tsp	10 tsp
Mozzarella	4 slices	10 slices

1 Season, then shallow-fry or grill the chops until almost cooked.

2 Spread the pesto on top of each chop and top each with a slice of mozzarella.

3 Finish under the grill for approximately 1 minute until the cheese is golden and just cooked through.

Energy	Cals	Fat	Sat fat	Carb	Sugar	Protein	Fibre	*
3531 KJ	844 kcal	66.3g	25.6g	0.5g	0.4g	61.2g	0.0g	

*Using a 225 g portion of pork and 60 g of mozzarella

Note

Serve with a suitable pasta, e.g. butttered noodles and a green vegetable or tossed salad.

43 Pork escalopes with Calvados sauce

	4 portions	10 portions
Crisp eating apples (e.g. russet)	2	5
Cinnamon	¼ tsp	¾ tsp
Lemon juice	1 tbsp	2½ tbsp
Brown sugar	2 tsp	5 tsp
Butter, melted	25 g	70 g
Pork escalopes	4 × 100 g	10 × 100 g
Butter or oil	50 g	125 g
Shallots or onions, finely chopped	50 g	125 g
Calvados	30 ml	75 ml
Double cream or natural yoghurt	125 ml	300 ml
Salt, cayenne pepper		
Basil, sage or rosemary, chopped		

Energy	Cals	Fat	Sat fat	Carb	Sugar	Protein	Fibre
1856 KJ	447 kcal	34.2 g	20.3 g	12.7 g	12.5 g	22.8 g	1.1 g

* Using lean meat only, and double cream

1 Core and peel the apples.

2 Cut into ½-cm-thick rings and sprinkle with a little cinnamon and a few drops of lemon juice.

3 Place on a baking sheet, sprinkle with brown sugar and a little melted butter, and caramelise under the salamander or in the top of a hot oven.

4 Lightly sauté the escalopes on both sides in the butter.

5 Remove from the pan and keep warm.

6 Add the chopped shallots to the same pan, cover with a lid and cook gently without colouring (use a little more butter if necessary).

7 Strain off the fat, leaving the shallots in the pan, and deglaze with the Calvados.

8 Reduce by a half and then add the cream or yoghurt, seasoning and herbs.

9 Reboil, correct the seasoning and consistency, and pass through a fine strainer onto the meat.

10 Garnish with slices of caramelised apple.

Special care must be taken not to overheat if using yoghurt, otherwise the sauce will curdle.

Variation

Calvados can be replaced with twice the amount of cider and reduced by three-quarters as an alternative.

Add a crushed clove of garlic and 1 tablespoon of continental mustard (2–3 cloves and 2½ tablespoons for 10 portions).

Healthy eating tips

1 Use a little unsaturated oil to sauté the escalopes.
2 Add the minimum amount of salt.
3 Try using yoghurt stabilised with a little cornflour, or half cream and half yoghurt.

44 Raised pork pie

Raised pork pie	4 portions	10 portions
Shoulder of pork, without bone	300 g	1 kg
Bacon	100 g	250 g
Allspice (or mixed spice) and chopped sage	½ tsp	1 ½ tsp
Salt, pepper		
Bread, soaked in milk	50 g	125 g
Stock or water	2 tbsp	5 tbsp
Eggwash		
Stock, hot	125 ml	375 ml
Gelatine	5 g	12.5 g
Picked watercress and salad to serve		

1 Cut the pork and bacon into small even pieces and combine with the rest of the main ingredients.

2 Keep one-quarter of the paste warm and covered.

3 Roll out the remaining three-quarters and carefully line a well-greased raised pie mould. Ensure that there is a thick rim of pastry.

4 Add the filling and press down firmly.

5 Roll out the remaining pastry for the lid and eggwash the edges of the pie.

6 Add the lid, seal firmly, neaten the edges, cut off any surplus paste; decorate if desired.

7 Make a hole 1 cm in diameter in the centre of the pie; brush all over with eggwash.

8 Bake in a hot oven (230–250 °C) for approximately 20 minutes.

9 Reduce the heat to moderate (150–200 °C) and cook for 1 ½–2 hours in all.

10 If the pie colours too quickly, cover with greaseproof paper or foil. Remove from the oven and carefully remove tin. Eggwash the pie all over and return to the oven for a few minutes.

11 Remove from the oven and fill with approximately 125 ml of good hot stock in which 5 g of gelatine has been dissolved.

Note

Serve when cold, garnished with picked watercress and offer a suitable salad.

Energy	Cals	Fat	Sat fat	Carb	Sugar	Protein	Fibre	Sodium
3005 kJ	721 kcal	47.7 g	19.3 g	49.2 g	1.7 g	26.7 g	2.7 g	1.2 g

Hot water paste	4 portions	10 portions
Strong plain flour	250 g	500 g
Salt		
Lard or margarine (alternatively use 100 g lard and 25 g butter or margarine)	125 g	300 g
Water	125 ml	300 ml

1 Sift the flour and salt into a basin. Make a well in the centre.

2 Boil the fat with the water and pour immediately into the flour.

3 Mix with a wooden spoon until cool enough to handle.

4 Mix to a smooth paste and use while still warm.

45 Stir-fried pork fillet

	4 portions	10 portions
Shallots, finely chopped	2	6
Clove of garlic (optional), chopped	1	2
Button mushrooms, sliced	200g	400g
Olive oil		
Pork fillet	400g	2kg
Chinese five-spice powder	1 pinch	2 pinches
Soy sauce	1 tbsp	2 tbsp
Clear honey	2 tsp	3 tsp
Dry white wine	2 tbsp	5 tbsp
Salt, pepper		

Energy	Cals	Fat	Sat fat	Carb	Sugar	Protein	Fibre
831kJ	199kcal	9.8g	2.2g	5.1g	4.2g	22.9g	0.8g

1 Gently fry the shallots, garlic and sliced mushrooms in a little oil in a frying pan or wok.

2 Add the pork cut into strips, stir well, increase the heat, season and add the Chinese five-spice powder; cook for 3–4 minutes then reduce the heat.

3 Add the soy sauce, honey and wine, and reduce for 2–3 minutes.

4 Correct the seasoning and serve.

Healthy eating tips
● No extra salt is needed, as soy sauce is added.
● Adding more vegetables and a large portion of rice or noodles can reduce the overall fat content.

46 Sweet and sour pork

	4 portions	10 portions
Loin of pork, boned	250g	600g
Sugar	12g	30g
Dry sherry	70ml	180ml
Soy sauce	70ml	180ml
Cornflour	50g	125g
Vegetable oil, for frying	70ml	180ml
Oil	2 tbsp	5 tbsp
Clove of garlic	1	2
Fresh root ginger	50g	125g
Onion, chopped	75g	180g
Green pepper, in 1cm dice	1	2½
Chillies, chopped	2	5
Sweet and sour sauce (see page 146)	210ml	500ml
Pineapple rings (fresh or canned)	1	3
Spring onions	2	5

Energy	Cals	Fat	Sat fat	Carb	Sugar	Protein	Fibre	Sodium
823kJ	194kcal	0g	0g	47.8	47.4g	1g	0.4g	0.842g

1 Cut the boned loin of pork into 2 cm pieces.

2 Marinate the pork for 30 minutes in the sugar, sherry and soy sauce.

3 Pass the pork through cornflour, pressing the cornflour in well.

4 Deep-fry the pork pieces in oil at 190 °C until golden brown, then drain. Add the tablespoons of oil to a sauté pan.

5 Add the garlic and ginger, and fry until fragrant.

6 Add the onion, pepper and chillies, sauté for a few minutes.

7 Stir in the sweet and sour sauce, bring to the boil.

8 Add the pineapple cut into small chunks, thicken slightly with diluted cornflour. Simmer for 2 minutes.

9 Deep-fry the pork again until crisp. Drain, mix into the vegetables and sauce or serve separately.

10 Serve garnished with rings of spring onions or button onions.

Professional tip

It is important to allow the pork enough time to marinate.

47 Boiled bacon (hock, collar or gammon)

1 Soak the bacon in cold water for 24 hours before cooking. Change the water.

2 Bring to the boil, skim and simmer gently (approximately 25 minutes per 0.5 kg, plus another 25 minutes). Allow to cool in the liquid.

3 Remove the rind and brown skin; carve.

4 Serve with a little of the cooking liquor.

Note

Boiled bacon may be served with pease pudding and a suitable sauce such as parsley (see page 132). It may also be served cold, or used as an ingredient in other dishes. Pease pudding is a purée of yellow split peas. The peas are covered with water and simmered with an onion studded with clove. When cooked, the water is drained and onion removed. The peas are puréed in a food processor and seasoned. A little butter may be added.

Energy	Cals	Fat	Sat fat	Carb	Sugar	Protein	Fibre
1543 KJ	367 kcal	30.5 g	12.2 g	0.0 g	0.0 g	23.1 g	0.0 g

* Using 113 g per portion

48 Griddled gammon with apricot salsa

	4 portions	10 portions
Gammon steaks	4 × 150 g	10 × 150 g
Oil		
Apricot salsa		
Fresh apricots or dried, reconstituted, stoned and chopped	200 g	500 g
Lime, grated rind and juice	1	3
Fresh root ginger, grated	2 tsp	5 tsp
Clear honey	2 tsp	5 tsp
Olive oil	1 tbsp	2½ tsp
Sage, chopped, fresh	1 tbsp	2½ tbsp
Spring onions, chopped	4	10
Salt, pepper		

Energy	Cals	Fat	Sat fat	Carb	Sugar	Protein	Fibre
1112k	266kcal	14.2g	4.2g	8.1g	7.4g	26.9g	1.0g

1 Heat the griddle pan, lightly oil it then cook the gammon steaks.

2 Make the salsa: mix together in a processor the apricots, lime rind and juice, ginger, honey, olive oil and sage.

3 Add the finely chopped spring onions, correct the seasoning then mix well.

Note

The texture should be the consistency of thick cream but coarse. A little extra olive oil or some apricot juice may be required.

Healthy eating tip
- Use more juice and less oil in the salsa to reduce the fat.
- Gammon is a salty meat, so no extra salt is needed.
- Serve with a large portion of potatoes and vegetables or salad.

49 Sautéed forcemeat (gratin forcemeat)

	Makes 300 g
Chicken liver or calves' liver (free from skin and sinews)	150 g
Pork fat, diced	5 g
Mushroom trimmings	50 g
Sautéed shallots	25 g
Butter	50 g
Spice salt	5 g
Pinch thyme and marjoram	
Brandy	10 mls

1 Brown the pork fat in the butter, to set firm. Remove from pan and set to one side.

2 Sauté the liver in the same pan to set

3 Return pork back to the pan.

4 Add mushrooms, sautéed shallot and seasonings.

5 Sauté all together, then flame with brandy.

6 Remove from heat and allow to cool.

7 Place all ingredients in food processor and blend. The forcemeat is then ready to use.

Professional tip

This forcemeat could be used to stuff a loin of lamb or skirt of beef rolled and then pot roasted, or served on croutons to accompany poultry or game dishes.

50 Potted meats

	1 pot
Cooked meat, e.g. beef, salt beef, tongue, venison, chicken or a combination	200 g
Salt, pepper and mace	
Clarified butter	100 g

Energy	Cals	Fat	Sat fat	Carb	Sugar	Protein	Fibre
1160 KJ	280 kcal	23.8 g	14.5 g	0.2 g	0.2 g	16.4 g	0.0 g

* 1 of 4 portions

Professional tip

Carefully purée the meat to give the desired texture.

1 Using an electric blender or chopper, reduce the meat, seasoning and 85 g of the butter to a paste.

2 Pack firmly into an earthenware or china pot and refrigerate until firm.

3 Cover with 1 cm of clarified butter and refrigerate. Serve with a small tossed green salad and hot toast.

Healthy eating tips

Keep added salt to a minimum.

Serve with plenty of salad vegetables and butter or toast (optional butter or spread).

51 Braised oxtail (*ragoût de queue de boeuf*)

	4 portions	10 portions
Oxtail	1 kg	2.5 kg
Dripping or oil	50 g	125 g
Onion	100 g	250 g
Carrot	100 g	250 g
Flour, browned in the oven	35 g	100 g
Tomato purée	25 g	60 g
Brown stock	1 litre	2.5 litres
Bouquet garni		
Clove of garlic	1	2
Salt, pepper		
Parsley, chopped		

Energy	Cals	Fat	Sat fat	Carb	Sugar	Protein	Fibre
2481 KJ	595 kcal	38.0 g	12.0 g	12.3 g	4.7 g	51.6 g	1.4 g

1 Cut the oxtail into sections. Remove the excess fat.

2 Fry on all sides in hot fat.

3 Place in a braising pan or casserole.

4 Roughly cut the onion and carrot. Fry them, then add them to the braising pan.

5 Mix in the flour.

6 Add tomato purée, brown stock, bouquet garni and garlic, and season lightly.

7 Bring to the boil, then skim.

8 Cover with a lid and simmer in the oven until tender (approximately 3 hours).

9 Remove the meat from the sauce, place in a clean pan.

10 Correct the sauce, pass on to the meat and reboil.

11 Serve sprinkled with chopped parsley.

Note

This is usually garnished with glazed turned or neatly cut carrots and turnips, button onions, peas and diamonds of beans. Oxtail must be very well cooked so that the meat comes away from the bone easily.

Variation

Haricot oxtail can be made using the same recipe with the addition of 100 g (250 g for 10 portions) cooked haricot beans, added approximately ½ hour before the oxtail has completed cooking.

Healthy eating tips

- Keep added salt to a minimum.
- Fry in a small amount of an unsaturated oil and drain off all excess fat after frying.
- Serve with mashed potato and additional green vegetables.

Browning the pieces of oxtail

Mixing in the flour

52 Braised lambs' hearts (*coeurs d'agneau braisés*)

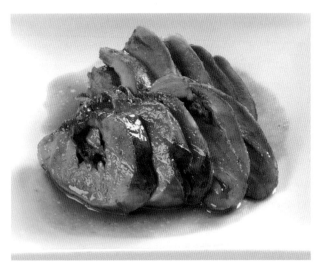

	4 portions	10 portions
Lambs' hearts	4	10
Salt, pepper		
Fat or oil	25 g	60 g
Onions	100 g	250 g
Carrots	100 g	250 g
Brown stock	500 ml	1.25 litre
Bouquet garni		
Tomato purée	10 g	25 g
Demi-glace or jus lié	250 ml	625 ml

Energy	Cals	Fat	Sat fat	Carb	Sugar	Protein	Fibre
614 KJ	147 kcal	10.3 g	5.9 g	0.1 g	0.1 g	13.7 g	0.0 g

* Using sunflower oil

1 Remove tubes and excess fat from the hearts.

2 Season and colour quickly on all sides in hot fat to seal the pores.

3 Place into a small braising pan (any pan with a tight-fitting lid that may be placed in the oven) or in a casserole.

4 Place the hearts on the lightly fried sliced vegetables.

5 Add the stock, which should come two-thirds of the way up the meat; season lightly.

6 Add the bouquet garni and tomato purée and, if available, add a few mushroom trimmings.

7 Bring to the boil, skim, cover with a lid and cook in a moderate oven at 150–200 °C.

8 After 1 ½ hours add the demi-glace or jus lié, reboil, skim and strain.

9 Continue cooking until tender.

10 Remove the hearts and correct the seasoning, colour and consistency of the sauce.

11 Pass the sauce on to the sliced hearts and serve.

Professional tip

Shallow frying the hearts in hot oil before braising gives the finished dish its attractive golden brown colour.

Healthy eating tips

● Lightly oil the pan using an unsaturated oil (olive or sunflower).
● Drain off any excess fat and skim all fat from the finished dish.
● Keep added salt to a minimum.

Variation

The hearts can be prepared and cooked as above and, prior to cooking, the tube cavities can be filled with a firm stuffing (e.g. recipe 16).

53 Grilled lambs' kidneys (*rognons grillés*)

1 Season the prepared skewered kidneys.
2 Brush with melted butter, margarine or oil.
3 Place on preheated greased grill bars or on a greased baking tray.
4 Grill fairly quickly on both sides (approximately 5–10 minutes depending on size).

Note

Serve with parsley butter, picked watercress and straw potatoes.

Energy	Cals	Fat	Sat fat	Carb	Sugar	Protein	Fibre
614kJ	147kcal	10.3g	5.9g	0.1g	0.1g	13.7g	0.0g

Healthy eating tips
● Use the minimum amount of salt.
● Serve with plenty of starchy carbohydrate and vegetables.

Professional tip
Cook kidneys to order so that they are fresh and tasty.

54 Kidney sauté (*rognons sautés*)

4 Place in a colander to drain, then discard the drained liquid.
5 Deglaze pan with demi-glace or jus, correct the seasoning and add the kidneys.
6 Do not reboil before serving as kidneys will toughen.

Healthy eating tips
● Lightly oil the pan using an unsaturated oil (olive or sunflower).
● Drain off any excess fat.
● Add the minimum amount of salt to the demi-glace.
● Serve with plenty of starchy carbohydrates and vegetables.

	4 portions	10 portions
Sheep's kidneys	8	20
Butter, margarine or oil	50g	125g
Demi-glace, lamb jus or jus lié	250ml	625ml

Energy	Cals	Fat	Sat fat	Carb	Sugar	Protein	Fibre
1680KJ	400kcal	28.3g	4.3g	15.5g	3.7g	21.8g	1.8g

* Using sunflower oil

1 Skin and halve the kidneys. Remove the sinews.
2 Cut each half into 3 or 5 pieces and season.
3 Fry quickly in a frying pan using the butter, margarine or oil for approximately 4–5 minutes.

Variation

After draining the kidneys, the pan may be deglazed with white wine, sherry or port. As an alternative, a sauce suprême (see page 135) may be used in place of demi-glace.

An alternative recipe is **kidney sauté Turbigo**. Cook as for kidney sauté, then add 100g small button mushrooms cooked in a little butter, margarine or oil, and 8 small 2cm-long grilled or fried chipolatas. Serve with the kidneys in an entrée dish, garnished with heart-shaped croutons. (Double these amounts for 10 portions.)

55 Lambs' kidneys bouchées

	12 bouchées
Puff pastry (see page 519)	200 g
Lambs' kidneys	8
Vegetable oil	50 ml
Butter	50 g
Sherry vinegar	50 ml
Parsley, chopped	1 tsp

Energy	Cals	Fat	Sat fat	Carb	Sugar	Protein	Fibre	Sodium
673 kJ	162 kcal	12.4 g	4.8 g	6.2 g	0.3 g	6.7 g	0 g	127 mg

1 Roll out the pastry approximately ½ cm thick. Cut out with a round, fluted 5 cm cutter.

2 Place the rounds on a greased, dampened baking sheet; eggwash. Dip a plain 4 cm diameter cutter into hot fat or oil and make an incision 3 mm deep in the centre of each. Allow to rest in a cool place.

3 Bake at 220 °C for about 20 minutes.

4 Remove from the oven and allow to cool. Remove the caps or lids carefully and remove all the raw pastry from inside the cases.

5 Remove the fat from the kidneys and skin them. Cut them into small pieces.

6 Heat the oil in a shallow pan, add the kidneys and sauté for 1–2 minutes. Add the butter and baste the kidneys.

7 Add the sherry vinegar and chopped parsley. (A little jus lié may also be added.) Baste the kidneys in the liquor.

8 Fill each bouchée with the cooked kidneys. Serve immediately.

Note

A filled bouchée may be offered as a canapé or an *amuse bouche*. Alternative fillings include sautéd chicken liver prepared in a similar way.

56 Fried lambs' liver and bacon (*foie d'agneau au lard*)

	4 portions	10 portions
Liver	300 g	1 kg
Butter, margarine or oil, for frying	50 g	125 g
Back bacon	50 g (approximately 4 rashers)	125 g (approximately 10 rashers)
Jus lié, reduced lamb stock or red wine jus	125 ml	300 ml

Energy	Cals	Fat	Sat fat	Carb	Sugar	Protein	Fibre	*
1039 KJ	250 kcal	20.1 g	3.8 g	0.1 g	0.1 g	17.2 g	0.0 g	

* Using oil, jus lié and reduced stock

1 Skin the liver and remove the gristle. Cut into thin slices on the slant.

2 Pass the slices of liver through seasoned flour. Shake off the excess flour.

3 Fry quickly on both sides in hot fat. (Liver is often served still pink in the centre but it is safer to cook it to a higher core temperature.)

4 Remove the rind and bone from the bacon and grill on both sides.

5 Serve the liver and bacon with a cordon and a sauceboat of jus or reduced stock.

Healthy eating tips
● Keep added salt to a minimum.
● Use a small amount of an unsaturated oil to fry the liver.
● Serve with plenty of potatoes and vegetables.

57 Braised veal sweetbreads (white) (ris de veau braisé – à blanc)

1 Wash, blanch, refresh and trim the sweetbreads (see page 266).
2 Season and place in a casserole or sauté pan on a bed of roots smeared with the oil, margarine or butter.
3 Add the bouquet garni and stock.
4 Cover with buttered greaseproof paper and a lid.
5 Cook in a moderate oven at 150–200 °C for approximately 45 minutes.
6 Remove the lid and baste occasionally with cooking liquor to glaze.
7 Serve with some of the cooking liquor, thickened with diluted arrowroot if necessary, and passed on to the sweetbreads.

Sweetbreads are glands, and two types are used for cooking. The thymus glands (throat) are usually long in shape and are of inferior quality. The pancreatic glands (stomach) are heart-shaped and of superior quality.

	4 portions	10 portions
Heart-shaped sweetbreads	8	20
Salt, pepper		
Onion	100 g	250 g
Carrot	100 g	250 g
Oil, margarine or butter	50 g	125 g
Bouquet garni		
Veal stock	250 ml	625 ml

Energy	Cals	Fat	Sat fat	Carb	Sugar	Protein	Fibre
1103 KJ	263 kcal	20.7 g	4.4 g	1.7 g	0.0 g	17.6 g	0.0 g

* Using hard margarine and sunflower oil

Variation

Braised veal sweetbreads (brown): prepare as in this recipe, but place on a lightly browned bed of roots. Barely cover with brown veal stock, or half-brown veal stock and half jus lié. Cook in a moderate oven at 150–200 °C without a lid (for approximately 1 hour), basting frequently. Cover with the corrected, strained sauce to serve. (If veal stock is used, thicken with arrowroot.)

Braised veal sweetbreads with vegetables: braise white with a julienne of vegetables in place of the bed of roots, the julienne served in the sauce.

1 Blanch the sweetbreads.

2 Peel the sweetbreads.

3 Add the stock and braise.

58 Grilled veal sweetbreads

1 Blanch, braise (as in recipe 57, page 317), cool and press the sweetbreads.

2 Cut in halves crosswise, pass through melted butter and grill gently on both sides.

3 Serve with a sauce and garnish as indicated.

Energy	Cals	Fat	Sat fat	Carb	Sugar	Protein	Fibre	Sodium *
444 kJ	106 kcal	2.6 g	0.8 g	0	0 g	19.3 g	0 g	0.042 g

* Per 85 g serving

59 Sweetbread escalope (*escalope de ris de veau*)

1 Braise the sweetbreads white, press slightly between two trays and allow to cool.

2 Cut into slices ½–1 cm thick, dust with flour and shallow-fry.

3 Serve with suitable garnish and sauce (e.g. on a bed of leaf spinach; coat with mornay sauce and glaze).

> **Professional tip**
>
> Pressing the sweetbread escalope between two trays gives it a good shape.

Video:
Sautéing lamb
sweetbreads
http://bit.ly/
17TNKKa

Energy	Cals	Fat	Sat fat	Carb	Sugar	Protein	Fibre	Sodium *
1026 kJ	246 kcal	12.5 g	5.3 g	6.1	3.3 g	26.3 g	2.7 g	0.428 g

* Per 85 g serving with mornay sauce

Prepare and cook poultry

This chapter will help you to:

1 prepare and cook poultry, including:
- using tools and equipment correctly
- working in a safe and hygienic way
- demonstrating correct preparation skills, cooking methods and principles
- demonstrating portion control
- applying flavourings and coatings and preparing sauces, coulis, gravies, jus, dressings, flavoured butters/oils, garnishes and accompaniments
- applying finishing skills, assembling dishes correctly and evaluating finished dishes
- storing poultry correctly.

2 understand how to:
- identify different types of poultry, their quality points, portion sizes/weights and commonly used cuts
- describe preservation methods and their advantages and disadvantages
- store poultry safely at the correct temperatures
- apply cooking principles and suitable methods of cookery
- determine when poultry is cooked
- check and finish a dish.

Recipes included in this chapter

Poultry

The word 'poultry' refers to all domestic fowl (birds) bred for food. It includes chickens, turkeys, ducks, geese and pigeons. Chicken is the type most commonly used in cooking.

The flesh of poultry is more easily digested than that of butchers' meat. It contains protein, so it is useful for building and repairing body tissues and providing heat and energy. The fat content is low and contains a high percentage of unsaturated fat.

Preservation of poultry

Poultry can be preserved or shelf life extended through the use of appropriate preservation methods:

- **Chilling /vacuum packing/freezing** – place the poultry in a bag, use a vacuum to remove air and seal it. This can be completed for small joints or portions that can then be stored at the correct temperature.
- **Smoking** – small cuts or parts of poultry are normally smoked. This enhances the flavour and colour of the flesh. This process is often used in cold dishes, where a hot smoking process has been used once chilled.

● **Canning** – preservation of cooked poultry either as pieces or as a product (for example, goose liver or confit duck legs).

Further information on the advantages and disadvantages of preserving poultry can be found in Chapter 1 on food safety.

Storage

The correct storage of poultry is important for food safety. Uncooked poultry should be stored on trays to prevent dripping, in a separate fridge whenever possible. If a separate refrigerator is not available, store covered, labelled and dated and place in the bottom of a multi-use fridge away from other items.

● Chilled birds should be stored in a refrigerator between 1 °C and 4 °C.
● Oven-ready birds are eviscerated (gutted) and should be stored in a refrigerator.
● Frozen birds must be kept in a deep freeze until required, but must be completely thawed, preferably in a refrigerator, before being cooked. This procedure is essential to reduce the risk of food poisoning: chickens are potential carriers of campylobacter and salmonella and if birds are cooked from frozen there is a risk that the degree of heat required to kill off campylobacter and salmonella may not reach the centre of the bird. When using frozen poultry, check that:
   ● the packaging is undamaged
   ● there are no signs of freezer burns, which are indicated by white patches on the skin.

Preparing and cooking poultry

When preparing uncooked poultry followed by cooked food, or changing from one type of meat or poultry to another, all equipment, working areas and utensils must be thoroughly cleaned or changed. Unhygienic equipment, utensils and preparation areas increase the risk of cross-contamination and danger to health. Wash all work surfaces with a bactericidal detergent to kill bacteria. This is particularly important when handling poultry. If colour-coded boards are used, it is essential to always use the correct boards for the preparation of raw or cooked poultry.

For key preparation techniques, see the sections on the different types of poultry below.

All poultry must be cooked until it reaches a core temperature of 75 °C, even if this is not stated in the recipe.

Video: Buying poultry
http://bit.ly/
1CIMF1V

Chicken

Types of chicken

Originally chickens were classified according to size and cooking method by specific names, as shown in Table 9.1.

There is approximately 15–20 per cent bone in poultry.

Table 9.1 Traditional classification of chicken

	Description	Uses	Weight	Number of portions
Single baby chicken (poussin)	These are spring chickens that are 4–6 weeks old	Roasting or grilling	0.3–0.5 kg	1
Double baby chicken (poussin)			0.5–0.75 kg	2
Small roasting bird (broiler chickens)	3–4 months old	Roasting or grilling	0.75–1 kg	3–4
Medium roasting bird	Fully grown, tender prime birds	Roasting, grilling, sautéing, casseroles, suprêmes and pies	1–2 kg	4–6
Large roasting or boiling chicken		Roasting, boiling and casseroles	2–3 kg	6–8
Capon	Large, specially bred cock birds	Roasting	3–4.5 kg	8–12
Old boiling fowl		Stocks and soups	2.5–4 kg	

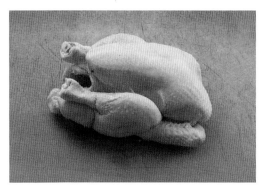

▲ Poussin

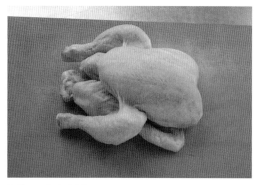

▲ Corn-fed chicken

Quality points

Good-quality chickens have the following features:

- The breast should be plump and firm.
- The wishbone (breastbone) should be easy to bend between fingers and thumb.
- The skin should be white and unbroken. Broiler chickens have a faint bluish tint.
- Corn-fed chickens are yellow. Free range chickens have more colour, a firmer texture and more flavour.
- Bresse chickens are specially bred in France and are highly regarded
- Old birds have coarse scales, large spurs on the legs and long hairs on the skin.

Cuts of chicken

The pieces of cut chicken are as follows (numbers refer to the diagram):

1 wing
2 breast
3 thigh
4 drumstick
5 winglet
6 carcass.

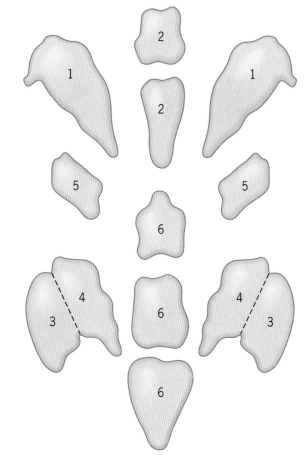

▲ Cuts of chicken

Preparation techniques

Step by step: trussing a chicken for roasting or boiling

1 Place the bird on its back.

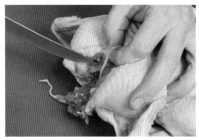

2 To facilitate carving, remove the wishbone.

3 Insert a trussing needle through the bird, midway between the leg joints.

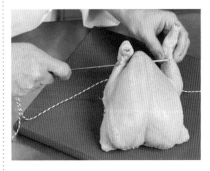

4 Thread the needle through the tendon and breast.

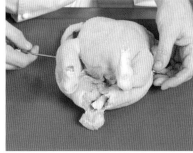

5 The needle comes out by the wing.

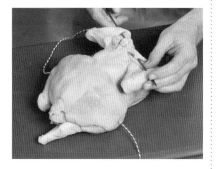

6 Turn over the chicken.
7 Run the needle under the skin through the wing, crown and other wing.

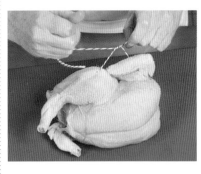

8 The string ends at the same place it started. Tie the ends of the string securely.

9 The trussed bird will hold its shape during roasting.

Step by step: cutting for sauté, fricassee and pies

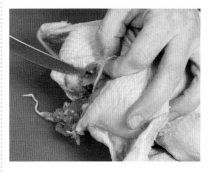

1 Using a large, sharp knife, remove the wishbone.

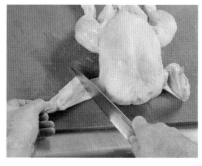

2 Remove the winglets and trim.

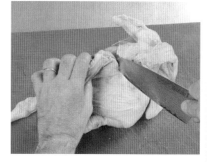

3 Remove the legs from the carcass, cutting around the oyster.

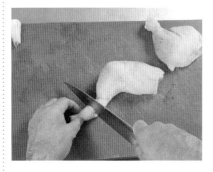

4 Cut off the feet.

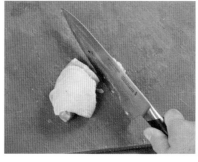

5 Separate the thighs from the drumsticks.

6 Trim the drumsticks neatly.

7 Remove each breast.

8 Separate the wings from the breasts and trim them.

9 Cut each breast in half.

10 Cut the cavity, splitting the carcass (this may be used for stock).

11 Chicken cut for sauté, on the bone, clockwise from top left: thighs, wings, breast pieces, drumsticks and winglets.

Step by step: preparation of a chicken for grilling (spatchcock)

1 Remove the wishbone.
2 Cut off the feet at the first joint.

3 Insert a large knife through the neck end and out of the vent (the gap at the other end, just under the parson's nose). Cut through the backbone and open out the bird.

4 Place the bird on its back, remove the back and rib bones.

5 Chicken spatchcock with the rib bones removed, ready for cooking.

Step by step: preparation for suprêmes

A supreme is the wing and half the breast of a chicken with the trimmed wing bone attached; one chicken yields two suprêmes. Use a chicken weighing 1.25–1.5 kg.

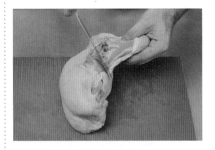

1 Cut off both the legs.
2 Remove the skin from the breasts.

3 Scrape the wing bone bare where it meets the breast and cut off the winglets near the joints, leaving 1.5–2 cm of bare bone attached to the breasts. Then remove the wishbone.

4 Cut the breasts close to the breastbone and follow the bone down to the wing joint.

5 Cut through the joint and pull off the suprêmes, using the knife to help.

6 Lift the fillets (the small, tender part that is slightly separate from the rest of the breast) from the suprêmes and remove the sinew from both. Make an incision lengthways, along the thick side of the suprêmes (do not cut all the way through); open this and place the fillets inside. Close, lightly flatten with a bat moistened with water, and trim if necessary.

Step by step: preparation for ballotines

A ballotine is a boned, stuffed leg of bird.

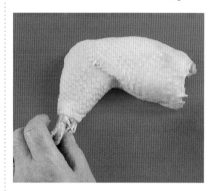

1 Using a small, sharp knife, cut the leg open around the bone

2 Start to separate the knuckle from the meat (scrape the flesh off the bone) of the drumstick towards the claw joint.

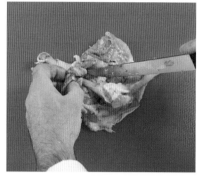

3 Lift the knuckle away (tunnel boning).

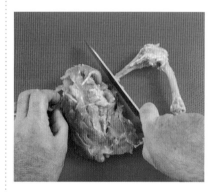

4 Cut off the drumstick bone, leaving approximately 2–3 cm at the claw joint end.

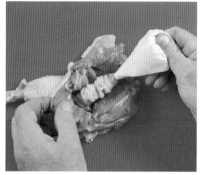

5 Fill the cavities in both the drumstick and thigh with a savoury stuffing.

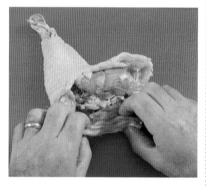

6 Neaten the shape and secure with string using a trussing needle.

Ballotines of chicken may be cooked and served using any of the recipes for sautéed chicken presented in this chapter.

Cutting cooked chicken (roasted or boiled)

1 Remove the legs and cut in two (drumstick and thigh).
2 Remove the wings.
3 Separate the breast from the carcass and divide in two.
4 Serve a drumstick with a wing and a thigh with a breast.

Activity

1 What is another name for suprême of chicken?
2 List the quality points for fresh chicken.
3 Name the food poisoning bacteria associated with fresh chicken.

Turkey

Turkeys can vary in weight from 3.5 to 20 kg. They are trussed in the same way as a chicken. The wishbone should always be removed before trussing, to make carving easier. The sinews should be drawn out of the legs.

Allow 200 g per portion raw weight.

When cooking a large turkey, the legs may be removed, boned, rolled, tied and roasted separately from the remainder of the bird. This will reduce the cooking time, and help the legs and breast to cook more evenly (see recipe 339).

Stuffings may be rolled in foil, steamed or baked and thickly sliced. If a firmer stuffing is required, mix in one or two raw eggs before cooking. If stuffing a whole bird prior to cooking, this should only be in the neck cavity to ensure the stuffing cooks thorough in the roasting process.

Quality points

Good-quality turkeys have the following features:

- Large full breast with undamaged skin and no signs of stickiness
- Smooth legs with supple feet and a short spur. As birds age the legs turn scaly and the feet harden.

Step by step: preparing a turkey for roasting

1 Remove the legs; cooking them separately will reduce the cooking time and enable the legs and breast to cook more evenly.

2 Remove the leg bones.

3 Stuff and roll each leg if required.

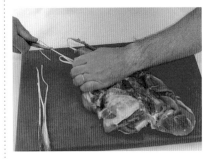

4 Tie the stuffed legs securely.

5 Cut the remainder of the bird in half, again to reduce the cooking time.

6 The two halves, ready for roasting, with one leg left whole and the other boned, stuffed and rolled.

Duck, duckling, goose, gosling

These are water-based fowl with web feet. They tend to have a higher fat content than other poultry, therefore it is normal when roasting whole to roast on a trivet to allow the fat to run from the bird. Goose and duck fat is used in roasting vegetables and frying.

Approximate sizes are as follows:

- duck: 3–4 kg
- goose: 6 kg
- duckling: 1.–2 kg
- gosling: 3 kg

▲ Gressingham duck prepared for cooking

Quality points

Good-quality birds have the following features:
- Plump breasts.
- Webbed feet that tear easily.
- A lower back that bends easily.
- Feet and bill should be yellow.

Roasting

Preparation is the same as for chicken. The only difference is that these birds have a gizzard, which should not be split but should be trimmed off with a knife.

Roast birds can be served whole and carved at the table, or can be carved up before they are served, in which case:
- remove the legs and cut into two (drumstick and thigh)
- remove the wings and divide the breast into two
- serve a drumstick with a wing and a thigh piece with a piece of breast.

Guinea fowl

A grey and white feathered bird that, once plucked, resembles a chicken, although has darker flesh and scales on the lower leg which enables it to be identified. Normally around the size of a medium chicken, the quality points for selecting guinea fowl are as for chicken.

Younger birds are known as squabs, and the quality points described for chicken can be used for buying and using guinea fowl.

Guinea fowl can be prepared and cooked as per chicken recipes.

Test yourself

1   List the **five** birds that are termed as poultry.
2   List **five** quality points for a good quality chicken.
3   Describe each of the following cuts:
   a) a spatchcock chicken.
   b) a suprême
   c) a chicken cut for sauté.
4   State **three** considerations when roasting a chicken.
5   What is the safe internal temperature required for cooked poultry?
6   Describe how vacuum packing is used to preserve poultry.
7   Describe **three** advantages of canning when used to preserve poultry.
8   Explain why shallow frying is an appropriate cooking method for turkey escalopes.
9   Briefly describe how to truss a turkey.
10 State why you would baste a whole duck when roasting.

1 Chicken sauté chasseur (*poulet sauté chasseur*)

	4 portions	10 portions
Butter or oil	50 g	125 g
Salt, pepper		
Chicken, 1.25–1.5 kg, cut for sauté	1	2½
Shallots, chopped	10 g	25 g
Button mushrooms, washed and sliced	100 g	250 g
Dry white wine	3 tbsp	8 tbsp
Jus-lié, demi-glace or reduced brown stock	250 ml	625 ml
Tomato concassé	200 g	500 g
Parsley and tarragon, chopped		

Energy	Cals	Fat	Sat fat	Carb	Sugar	Protein	Fibre *
2430 kJ	579 kcal	45.8 g	20.7 g	2.1 g	1.6 g	37.6 g	1.5 g

* Using butter

1 Place the butter or oil in a sauté pan on a fairly hot stove.

2 Season the pieces of chicken and place in the pan in the following order: drumsticks, thighs, wings and breast.

3 Cook to a golden brown on both sides.

4 Cover with a lid and cook on the stove or in the oven until tender. Dress neatly in a suitable dish.

5 Add the shallots to the sauté pan, rubbing them into the pan sediment to extract the flavour. Cover with a lid and cook on a gentle heat for 1–2 minutes.

6 Add the washed, sliced mushrooms and cover with a lid. Cook gently for 3–4 minutes, without colour. Drain off the fat.

7 Add the white wine and reduce by half. Add the jus lié, demi-glace or reduced stock.

8 Add the tomatoes. Simmer for 5 minutes.

9 Correct the seasoning and pour over the chicken.

10 Sprinkle with chopped parsley and tarragon and serve.

Ballotines of chicken chasseur can be prepared as above or lightly braised (as shown).

Placing the chicken into the hot pan

Cooking the shallots in the pan that was used for the chicken – they will pick up the sediment and flavour

Healthy eating tips
- Use a minimum amount of salt to season the chicken.
- The fat content can be reduced if the skin is removed from the chicken.
- Use a little unsaturated oil to cook the chicken, and drain off all excess fat from the cooked chicken.
- Serve with a large portion of new potatoes and seasonal vegetables.

Professional tip

The leg meat takes longer to cook than the breast meat, which is why the drumsticks and thighs should be added first.

Add the soft herbs and tomatoes just before serving.

2 Fricassée of chicken (fricassée de volaille)

	4 portions	10 portions
Chicken, 1.25–1.5 kg	1	2–3
Salt, pepper		
Butter, margarine or oil	50 g	125 g
Flour	35 g	100 g
Chicken stock	0.5 litre	1.75 litres
Egg yolks	1–2	5
Cream or non-dairy cream	4 tbsp	10 tbsp
Parsley, chopped		

Energy	Cals	Fat	Sat fat	Carb	Sugar	Protein	Fibre
2699 kJ	643 kcal	51.3 g	23.3 g	7.4 g	0.6 g	38.2 g	0.4 g

* Using butter

1 Cut the chicken as for sauté (page 323); season with salt and pepper.

2 Place the butter in a sauté pan. Heat gently.

3 Add the pieces of chicken. Cover with a lid.

4 Cook gently on both sides without colouring. Mix in the flour.

5 Cook out carefully without colouring. Gradually mix in the stock.

6 Bring to the boil and skim. Allow to simmer gently until cooked.

7 Mix the yolks and cream in a basin (liaison).

8 Pick out the chicken into a clean pan.

9 Pour a little boiling sauce on to the yolks and cream and mix well.

10 Pour all back into the sauce, combine thoroughly but do not reboil.

11 Correct the seasoning and pass through a fine strainer.

12 Pour over the chicken, reheat without boiling.

13 Serve sprinkled with chopped parsley and garnish with heart-shaped croutons, fried in butter, if desired.

Variation

Fricassée de volaille à l'ancienne: a fricassée of chicken with button onions and mushrooms can be made in a similar way, with the addition of 50–100 g button onions and 50–100 g button mushrooms. They are peeled and the mushrooms left whole, turned or quartered depending on size and quality. The onions are added to the chicken as soon as it comes to the boil and the mushrooms 15 minutes later. Heart-shaped croutons may be used to garnish. This is a classic dish.

Professional tip

Sauté the chicken lightly. Add the liaison of yolks and cream carefully. Do not allow the sauce to come back to the boil once the liaison has been added, or it will curdle.

Healthy eating tips
- Keep added salt to a minimum throughout the cooking.
- Use a little unsaturated oil to cook the chicken, and drain off all excess fat after cooking.
- Try oven-baking the croutons brushed with olive oil.
- The sauce is high in fat, so serve with plenty of starchy carbohydrate and vegetables.

3 Chicken in red wine (coq au vin)

	4 portions	10 portions
Roasting chicken, 1.5 kg	1	2–3
Lardons	50 g	125 g
Small chipolatas	4	10
Button mushrooms	50 g	125 g
Butter	50 g	125 g
Sunflower oil	3 tbsp	7 tbsp
Small button onions	12	30
Red wine	500 ml	900 ml
Beurre manié		
Butter	25 g	60 g
Flour	10 g	25 g

Energy	Cals	Fat	Sat fat	Carb	Sugar	Protein	Fibre	*
4794 kJ	1141 kcal	95.7 g	32.9 g	16.6 g	2.3 g	49.0 g	1.7 g	

* Using sunflower oil and hard margarine

1 Cut the chicken as for sauté (see page 323). Blanch the lardons.

2 If the chipolatas are large, divide into two.

3 Wash and cut the mushrooms into quarters.

4 Sauté the lardons, mushrooms and chipolatas in a mixture of butter and oil. Remove when cooked.

5 Lightly season the pieces of chicken and place in the pan in the correct order (see recipe 1) with button onions. Sauté until almost cooked.

6 Place in a casserole with the mushrooms and lardons.

7 Drain off the fat from the sauté pan. Deglaze with the red wine and stock; bring to the boil.

8 Transfer the liquid to the casserole (just covering the chicken); cover with a lid and finish cooking.

9 Remove the chicken and onions, place into a clean pan.

10 Lightly thicken the liquor with a *beurre manié* of butter and flour by whisking small pieces of it into the simmering liquid.

11 Pass the sauce over the chicken and onions, add the mushrooms, chipolatas and lardons. Correct the seasoning and reheat.

12 Add the *beurre manié* slowly, mixing well, to create a thick, smooth sauce.

Sauté the other ingredients before the chicken

Sauté the chicken pieces and onion in the same pan

Add a *beurre manié*

4 Chicken spatchcock (*poulet grillé à la crapaudine*)

	4 portions	10 portions
Chicken, 1.25–1.5 kg	1	2 ½

Energy	Cals	Fat	Sat fat	Carb	Sugar	Protein	Fibre
1560 kJ	372 kcal	24.1 g	8.0 g	0.0 g	0.0 g	38.9 g	0.0 g

Healthy eating tips
- Use a minimum amount of salt to season the chicken.
- The fat content can be reduced if the skin is removed from the chicken.
- Use a small amount of an unsaturated oil to brush the chicken.
- Serve with a large portion of potatoes and vegetables.

1 Cut horizontally from below the point of the breast over the top of the legs down to the wing joints, without removing the breasts. Fold back the breasts.

2 Snap and reverse the backbone into the opposite direction so that the point of the breast now extends forward.

3 Flatten slightly. Remove any small bones.

4 Skewer the wings and legs in position.

5 Season with salt and mill pepper.

6 Brush with oil or melted butter.

7 Place on preheated grill bars or on a flat tray under a salamander.

8 Brush frequently with melted fat or oil during cooking and allow approximately 15–20 minutes on each side.

9 Test if cooked by piercing the drumstick with a needle or skewer – there should be no sign of blood.

Note

Serve garnished with picked watercress and offer a suitable sauce separately (e.g. devilled sauce or a compound butter).

5 Grilled chicken (*poulet grillé*)

1 Season the chicken with salt and mill pepper, and prepare as for grilling (see page 324).

2 Brush with oil or melted butter or margarine, and place on preheated greased grill bars or on a barbecue or a flat baking tray under a salamander.

3 Brush frequently with melted fat during cooking; allow approximately 15–20 minutes each side.

4 Test if cooked by piercing the drumstick with a skewer or trussing needle; there should be no sign of blood issuing from the leg.

5 Serve garnished with picked watercress and offer a suitable sauce separately.

Energy	Cals	Fat	Sat fat	Carb	Sugar	Protein	Fibre
975kJ	234kcal	15.7g	4.3g	0.0g	0.0g	23.3g	0.0g

* Based on chicken with bone, wing and leg quarters

Healthy eating tips
● Use a minimum of salt and an unsaturated oil.
● Garnish with grilled tomatoes and mushrooms.
● Serve with Delmonico potatoes and green vegetables.

Variations

Grilled chicken is frequently garnished with streaky bacon, tomatoes and mushrooms.

The chicken may be marinated for 2–3 hours before grilling, in a mixture of oil, lemon juice, spices, herbs, freshly grated ginger, finely chopped garlic, salt and pepper. Chicken or turkey portions can also be grilled and marinated beforehand if wished (breasts or boned-out lightly battened thighs of chicken).

6 Chicken à la king (*emincé de volaille à la king*)

	4 portions	10 portions
Button mushrooms	100g	250g
Butter or oil	25g	60g
Red pepper, skinned	50g	125g
Chicken, boiled or steamed	400g	1.25kg
Sherry	30ml	75ml
Chicken velouté	125ml	150ml
Cream or non-dairy cream	30ml	75ml

Energy	Cals	Fat	Sat fat	Carb	Sugar	Protein	Fibre	*
1226kJ	292kcal	16.7g	7.8g	3.2g	0.8g	30.4g	0.9g	

* Using butter or hard margarine

1 Wash, peel and slice the mushrooms.

2 Cook them without colour in the butter or oil.

3 If using raw pepper, discard the seeds, cut the pepper into dice and cook with the mushrooms.

4 Cut the chicken into small, neat slices.

5 Add the chicken to the mushrooms and pepper.

6 Drain off the fat. Add the sherry.

7 Add the velouté and bring to the boil.

8 Finish with the cream and correct the seasoning.

9 Place in a serving dish and decorate with small strips of cooked pepper.

Note

Use a velouté with a good chicken flavour, to create the best sauce.

Slice the mushrooms and dice the red pepper   Neatly slice the cooked chicken   Add the velouté during cooking

Variations

Try adding 1 or 2 egg yolks to form a liaison with the cream, mixed into the boiling mixture at the last possible moment and immediately removed from the heat.

Chicken à la king may be served in a border of golden-brown duchess potato, or a pilaff of rice (see page 421) may be offered as an accompaniment. It is suitable for a hot buffet dish.

Healthy eating tips
- Use the minimum amount of salt.
- Remove the skin from the cooked chicken.
- Try reducing or omitting the cream used to finish the sauce.
- Serve with plenty of rice and vegetables or salad.

7 Chicken Kiev

	4 portions	10 portions
Suprêmes of chicken	4 × 150 g	10 × 150 g
Butter	100 g	250 g
Seasoned flour	25 g	65 g
Eggs	2	5
Breadcrumbs	100 g	250 g

Energy	Cals	Fat	Sat fat	Carb	Sugar	Protein	Fibre	Sodium
2094 kJ	500 kcal	26.1 g	14.4 g	24.4 g	0.9 g	43.4 g	1.0 g	0.5 g

1 Make an incision along the thick sides of the suprêmes. Insert 25 g cold butter into each. Season.

2 Pass through seasoned flour, eggwash and crumbs, ensuring complete coverage. Eggwash and crumb twice if necessary.

3 Deep-fry until completely cooked. When the chicken is cooked, a probe in the thickest part will read 75 °C+, and the juices will run clear when the chicken is pierced. Drain and serve.

1 Carefully make an incision in the top of the suprême

2 Stuff with softened butter

3 Dip the chicken in egg and then coat with breadcrumbs

Variation

Additional ingredients may be added to the butter before insertion:
- chopped garlic and parsley
- fine herbs such as tarragon or chives
- liver paté.

Professional tip

The butter must be pushed well into the suprême, and the incision must be sealed, or the butter will leak out during cooking.

8 Crumbed breast of chicken with asparagus (suprême de volaille aux pointes d'asperges)

	4 portions	10 portions
Suprêmes of chicken (page 324)	4 × 125 g	10 × 125 g
Egg	1	2
Breadcrumbs (white or wholemeal)	50 g	125 g
Oil	50 g	125 g
Butter or margarine	100 g	250 g
Jus-lié	60 ml	150 ml
Asparagus	200 g	500 g

Energy	Cals	Fat	Sat fat	Carb	Sugar	Protein	Fibre
1831 kJ	439 kcal	26.4 g	8.9 g	15.7 g	1.5 g	35.5 g	1.3 g

1 Pané the suprêmes. Shake off surplus crumbs.

2 Neaten and mark on one side with a palette knife.

3 Heat the oil and 50 g (125 g for 10 portions) of the butter or margarine in a sauté pan.

4 Gently fry the suprêmes to a golden brown on both sides (6–8 minutes). Use a probe to check that the centre has reached 75 °C.

5 Dress the suprêmes on a flat dish and keep warm.

6 Mask the suprêmes with the remaining butter cooked to the nut-brown stage.

7 Surround the suprêmes with a cordon of jus lié.

8 Garnish each suprême with a neat bundle of asparagus points (previously cooked, refreshed and reheated with a little butter).

Healthy eating tips
- Use a minimum amount of salt.
- Remove the skin from the suprêmes and fry in a little unsaturated vegetable oil. Drain on kitchen paper.
- Try omitting the additional cooked butter.
- Serve with boiled new potatoes and vegetables.

9 Deep-fried chicken

1 Cut the chicken as for sauté. It is advisable to remove bones from chicken that will be deep-fried.

2 Coat with flour, egg and crumbs (pané), or pass them through a light batter (see page 376) to which herbs can be added.

3 Deep-fry in hot fat (approx. 170–180 °C) until golden brown and cooked through – about 5 minutes. When the chicken is cooked, a probe in the thickest part will read 75 °C+, and the juices will run clear when the chicken is pierced.

4 For suprêmes, make an incision, stuff with a compound butter, flour, egg and crumb, and deep-fry as in Chicken Kiev (recipe 7).

Healthy eating tip
The fat content can be reduced if the skin is removed from the chicken.

Energy	Cals	Fat	Sat fat	Carb	Sugar	Protein	Fibre
1754 kJ	421 kcal	28.6 g	6.1 g	14.5 g	0.4 g	27.2 g	0.5 g

10 Tandoori chicken

1 Cut slits bone-deep in the chicken pieces.

2 Sprinkle the salt and lemon juice on both sides of the pieces, lightly rubbing into the slits; leave for 20 minutes.

3 Combine the remaining ingredients in a blender or food processor.

4 Brush the chicken pieces on both sides, ensuring the marinade goes into the slits. Cover and refrigerate for 6–24 hours.

5 Preheat the oven to the maximum temperature.

6 Shake off as much of the marinade as possible from the chicken pieces; place on skewers and bake for 15–20 minutes or until cooked.

	4 portions	10 portions
Chicken, cut as for sauté (page 323)	1.25–1.5 kg	3–4 kg
Salt	1 tsp	2½ tsp
Lemon, juice of	1	2½
Natural yoghurt	300 ml	800 ml
Small onion, chopped	1	3
Clove of garlic, peeled	1	3
Ginger, piece of, peeled and quartered	5 cm	12 cm
Fresh hot green chilli, sliced	½	1
Garam masala	2 tsp	5 tsp
Ground cumin	1 tsp	2½ tsp
Red and yellow colouring, few drops each		

Note

Serve with red onion rings and lime or lemon wedges.

Professional tip

If cooking in a tandoori oven, make sure the chicken is secure on the skewer, so that it cannot slip off during cooking.

Healthy eating tips
- Skin the chicken and reduce the salt by half.
- Serve with rice and vegetables.

Energy	Cals	Fat	Sat fat	Carb	Sugar	Protein	Fibre
1436 kJ	342 kcal	14.1 g	4.6 g	10.1 g	8.6 g	44.6 g	0.3 g

* Estimated edible meat used; vegetable oil used

11 Chicken tikka

	4 portions	10 portions
Chicken, cut for sauté	1 × 1.5 kg	2.5 × 1.5 kg
Natural yoghurt	125 ml	250 ml
Grated ginger	1 tsp	2 ½ tsp
Ground coriander	1 tsp	2 ½ tsp
Ground cumin	1 tsp	2 ½ tsp
Chilli powder	1 tsp	2 ½ tsp
Clove garlic, crushed and chopped	1	2–3
Lemon, juice of	½	1
Tomato purée	50 g	125 g
Onion, finely chopped	50 g	125 g
Oil	60 ml	150 ml
Lemon, wedges of	4	10
Seasoning		

Energy	Cals	Fat	Sat fat	Carb	Sugar	Protein	Fibre
1780 kJ	427 kcal	27.1 g	5.2 g	5.5 g	5.1 g	41.3 g	0.6 g

* Estimated edible meat used

1 Place the chicken pieces into a suitable dish.

2 Mix together the yoghurt, seasoning, spices, garlic, lemon juice and tomato purée.

3 Pour this over the chicken, mix well and leave to marinate for at least 3 hours.

4 In a suitable shallow tray, add the chopped onion and half the oil.

5 Lay the chicken pieces on top and grill under the salamander, turning the pieces over once, or gently cook in a moderate oven at 180 °C for 20–30 minutes.

6 Baste with the remaining oil.

7 Serve on a bed of lettuce garnished with wedges of lemon.

Healthy eating tips
● Skin the chicken and keep the added salt to a minimum.
● Use half the amount of unsaturated oil.
● Serve with rice and a vegetable dish.

Note

Baste the chicken during grilling so that it does not become too dry.

Mix together the spices

Mix the chicken pieces into the marinade

Griddle the chicken in a shallow tray

12 Terrine of chicken and vegetables

	8–10 portions
Carrots, turnips and swedes, peeled and cut into 7 mm dice	50 g of each
Broccoli, small florets	50 g
Baby corn, cut into 7 mm rounds	50 g
French beans, cut into 7 mm lengths	50 g
Chicken (white meat only), minced	400 g
Egg whites	2
Double cream	200 ml
Salt, mill pepper	

Energy	Cals	Fat	Sat fat	Carb	Sugar	Protein	Fibre
930 kJ	226 kcal	17.3 g	9.4 g	2.0 g	1.8 g	15.5 g	0.9 g

1 Blanch all the vegetables individually in boiling salted water, ensuring that they remain firm. Refresh in cold water and drain well.

2 Blend the chicken and egg whites in a food processor until smooth. Turn out into a large mixing bowl and gradually beat in the double cream.

3 Season with salt and mill pepper, and fold in the vegetables.

4 Line a lightly greased 1-litre terrine with cling film.

5 Spoon the farce into the mould and overlap the cling film.

6 Cover with foil, put the lid on and cook in a bain-marie in a moderate oven for about 45 minutes. Use a temperature probe to check that the centre has reached 70 °C.

7 When cooked, remove the lid and leave to cool overnight.

Healthy eating tips
- Keep the added salt to a minimum.
- Serve with plenty of salad vegetables and bread or toast (optional butter or spread).

1 Cut the vegetables into neat dice, rounds and florets

2 Line the terrine with cling film and spoon in the mixture

3 Cover the mixture with cling film and press down gently

13 Roast turkey

	4 portions	10 portions
Turkey, with legs on	1 small hen	4–5 kg
Sea salt and freshly ground black pepper		
Unsalted butter, melted	250 g	625 g

Energy	Cals	Fat	Sat fat	Carb	Sugar	Protein	Fibre
1076 kJ	257 kcal	9.6 g	3.2 g	0.0 g	0.0 g	42.0 g	0.0 g

Professional tip

The secret to keeping turkey moist is to baste as much as you can and, when the turkey is cooked, place it on its breast, breast-side down, allowing all the cavity juices to penetrate the meat.

1 Adjust an oven rack to its lowest position and remove the other racks in the oven. Pre-heat to 165 °C.

2 Remove turkey parts from neck and breast cavities and reserve for other uses, if desired. Dry bird well with paper towels, inside and out. Salt and pepper inside the breast cavity.

3 Set the bird on a roasting rack in a roasting pan, breast-side up, brush generously with half the butter and season with salt and pepper. Tent the bird with foil.

4 Roast the turkey for 2 hours. Remove the foil and baste with the remaining butter. Increase the oven temperature to 220 °C and continue to roast until an instant-read thermometer registers 74 °C in the thigh of the bird, about 45 minutes more.

5 Remove turkey from the oven and set aside to rest for 15 minutes before carving. Carve and serve with roast gravy, cranberry sauce, bread sauce, and either or both sausage meat and chestnut dressing and parsley and thyme dressing. Chipolata sausages and rolled rashers of grilled bacon may also be served.

14 Turkey escalopes

1 Cut 100 g slices from boned-out turkey breast and lightly flour. Gently cook on both sides in butter or oil with a minimum of colour; alternatively flour, egg and crumb the slices and shallow fry.

2 Serve with a suitable sauce and/or garnish (e.g. pan-fried turkey escalope cooked with oyster mushrooms and finished with white wine and cream).

Professional tip

The oil or fat must be hot enough before the escalopes are placed in the pan. If it is too cool, the breadcrumbs will absorb the fat and the dish will be greasy.

Energy	Cals	Fat	Sat fat	Carb	Sugar	Protein	Fibre	Sodium
1712 kJ	414 kcal	37.0 g	14.0 g	5.9 g	0.2 g	14.8 g	0.3 g	100 mg

15 Roast duck or duckling (*canard ou caneton rôti*)

	4 portions	10 portions
Duck	1	2–3
Salt		
Oil		
Brown stock	0.25 litres	600 ml
Salt, pepper		
Watercress, bunch	1	2
Apple sauce (page 140)	125 ml	300 ml

Energy	Cals	Fat	Sat fat	Carb	Sugar	Protein	Fibre	*
3083 kJ	734 kcal	60.5 g	16.9 g	8.2 g	7.8 g	40.0 g	1.4 g	

* With apple sauce and watercress

1 Lightly season the duck inside and out with salt.

2 Truss and brush lightly with oil.

3 Place on its side in a roasting tin, with a few drops of water.

4 Place in a hot oven for 20–25 minutes.

5 Turn on to the other side.

6 Cook for a further 20–25 minutes. Baste frequently.

7 To test if cooked, pierce with a fork between the drumstick and thigh and hold over a plate. The juice issuing from the duck should not show any signs of blood. If using a probe, the temperature should be 62 °C. If the duck is required pink, the temperature should be 57 °C.

8 Prepare the roast gravy with the stock and the sediment in the roasting tray. Correct the seasoning, remove the surface fat.

9 Serve garnished with picked watercress. Accompany with a sauceboat of hot apple sauce, a sauceboat of gravy, and game chips. Also serve a sauceboat of sage and onion dressing (recipe 16).

Note

Arrange the duck to cook sitting on one leg, then the other leg and then the breast, so the whole bird cooks evenly.

The temperatures in this recipe reflect industry standards for cooking duck. An environmental health officer may advise higher temperatures.

Video:
Preparing a
duck
http://bit.ly/
1EoOFMD

Healthy eating tips

● Use the minimum amount of salt to season the duck and the roast gravy.
● Take care to remove all the fat from the roasting tray before making the gravy.
● This dish is high in fat and should be served with plenty of boiled new potatoes and a variety of vegetables.

16 Sage and onion dressing for duck

	4 portions	10 portions
Onion, chopped	100 g	250 g
Duck fat or butter	100 g	250 g
Powdered sage	¼ tsp	½ tsp
Parsley, chopped	¼ tsp	½ tsp
Salt, pepper		
White or wholemeal breadcrumbs	100 g	250 g
Duck liver (optional), chopped	50 g	125 g

1 Gently cook the onion in the fat without colour. Add the chopped liver (if required) and fry until cooked.

2 Add the herbs and seasoning. Mix in the crumbs. Form into thick sausage shapes, in foil.

3 Place in a tray and finish in a hot oven at 180 °C for approximately 5–10 minutes. Check with a probe that the centre has reached 75 °C.

Note

Serve separately with roast duck.

17 Duckling with orange sauce *(caneton bigarade)*

Energy	Cals	Fat	Sat fat	Carb	Sugar	Protein	Fibre
3125 kJ	744 kcal	60.1 g	17.1 g	11.8 g	9.3 g	39.9 g	0.1 g

* Using butter

	4 portions	10 portions
Duckling, 2 kg	1	2–3
Butter	50 g	125 g
Carrots	50 g	125 g
Onions	50 g	125 g
Celery	25 g	60 g
Bay leaf	1	2–3
Small sprig thyme	1	2–3
Salt, pepper		
Brown stock	250 ml	625 ml
Arrowroot	10 g	25 g
Oranges	2	5
Lemon	1	2
Vinegar	2 tbsp	5 tbsp
Sugar	25 g	60 g

1 Clean and truss the duck. Use a fifth of the butter to grease a deep pan. Add the mirepoix (vegetables and herbs).

2 Season the duck. Place the duck on the mirepoix.

3 Coat the duck with the remaining butter.

4 Cover the pan with a tight-fitting lid. Place the pan in the oven at 200–230 °C.

5 Baste occasionally; cook for approximately 1 hour.

6 Remove the lid and continue cooking the duck, basting frequently until tender (about a further 30 minutes or until required temperature is reached).

7 Remove the duck, cut out the string and keep the duck in a warm place. Drain off all the fat from the pan.

8 Deglaze with the stock, bring to the boil and allow to simmer for a few minutes. Thicken by adding the arrowroot diluted in a little cold water.

9 Reboil, correct the seasoning, degrease and pass through a fine strainer.

10 Thinly remove the zest from half the oranges and the lemon(s), and cut into fine julienne.

11 Blanch the julienne of zest for 3–4 minutes, then refresh.

12 Place the vinegar and sugar in a small sautéuse and cook to a light caramel stage.

13 Add the juice of the oranges and lemon(s).

14 Add the sauce and bring to the boil.

15 Correct the seasoning and pass through a fine strainer.

16 Add the julienne to the sauce; keep warm.

17 Remove the legs from the duck, bone out and cut into thin slices.

18 Carve the duck breasts into thin slices and dress neatly.

19 Coat with the sauce and serve.

An alternative method of service is to cut the duck into eight pieces, which may then be either left on the bone or the bones removed.

Professional tip

Baste the duck during cooking; the butter will give it flavour. The sauce may be finished with an orange liqueur

Healthy eating tips
- Use the minimum amount of salt to season the duck and the final sauce.
- Take care to remove all the fat from the roasting tray before deglazing with the stock.
- Reduce the fat by removing the skin from the duck, and 'balance' this fatty dish with a large portion of boiled potatoes and vegetables.

18 Confit duck leg with red cabbage and green beans

	4 portions	10 portions
Confit oil	1 litre	2.5 litres
Garlic cloves	4	10
Bay leaf	1	3
Sprig of thyme	1	2
Duck legs	4 × 200 g	10 × 200 g
Butter	50 g	125 g
Green beans, cooked and trimmed	300 g	750 g
Braised red cabbage	250 g	625 g
Seasoning		

Energy	Cals	Fat	Sat fat	Carb	Sugar	Protein	Fibre	Sodium
3859 kJ	932 kcal	83 g	28 g	7.7	6.4 g	39.2 g	4.2 g	257 g

1 Gently heat the confit oil, add the garlic, bay leaf and thyme.

2 Put the duck legs in the oil and place on a medium to low heat, ensuring the legs are covered.

3 Cook gently for 4–4½ hours (if using goose, 5–6½ hours may be needed).

4 To test if the legs are cooked, squeeze the flesh on the thigh bone and it should just fall away.

5 When cooked, remove the legs carefully and place on a draining tray.

6 When drained, put the confit leg on a baking tray and place in a pre-heated oven at 210 °C; remove when the skin is golden brown (approximately 9–10 minutes), taking care as the meat is delicate.

7 Heat the butter in a medium sauté pan and reheat the green beans.

8 Place the braised cabbage in a small pan and reheat slowly.

9 Place the duck leg in a serving dish or plate along with the red cabbage and green beans.

Professional tip

Confit oil is 50/50 olive oil and vegetable oil infused with herbs, garlic, whole spice or any specific flavour you wish to impart into the oil; then, through slow cooking in the oil, the foodstuff picks up the flavour.

Confit duck legs can be prepared up to three or four days in advance. Remove them carefully from the fat they are stored in, clean off any excess fat and place directly into the oven. This is a great timesaver in a busy service.

19 Suprêmes of guineafowl with a pepper and basil coulis

	4 portions	10 portions
Red peppers	3	7
Olive oil	150 ml	375 ml
Fresh basil, chopped	2 tbsp	5 tbsp
Salt, pepper		
Guineafowl suprêmes (approximately 150 g each)	4	10

Energy	Cals	Fat	Sat fat	Carb	Sugar	Protein	Fibre	*
904 kJ	216 kcal	4.7 g	1.3 g	7.8 g	7.3 g	35.8 g	0.5 g	

*Using chicken instead of guineafowl

1 Skin the peppers by brushing with oil and gently scorching in the oven or under the grill. Alternatively, use a blowtorch with great care. Once scorched, peel the skin from the peppers, cut in half and deseed.

2 Place the skinned and deseeded peppers in a food processor, blend with the olive oil and pass through a strainer.

3 Add the chopped basil and season.

4 Season the guineafowl and either shallow-fry or grill.

5 Pour the coulis on to individual plates. Place the guineafowl on top and serve immediately.

10 Prepare and cook fish and shellfish

1 This chapter will help you to:
- prepare and cook fish and shellfish, including:
- using tools and equipment correctly, in a safe and hygienic way
- demonstrating preparation skills, portion control, cooking and finishing skills
- producing sauces, dressings, garnishes and accompaniments.

2 understand how to:
- identify different types of fish and shellfish, their quality points, weights and commonly used cuts
- store fish and shellfish safely
- describe the preservation methods used for fish and shellfish
- apply cooking principles and suitable methods of cookery
- determine when fish and shellfish are cooked and check the finished dish.

Recipes included in this chapter

Fish

Marine and freshwater fish were a crucial part of man's diet long before cultivated vegetables and domestic livestock were used for food; they were relatively easy to catch and eat and predominantly eaten raw. Fish is a good source of essential protein and vitamins.

> **Professional tip**
> Fish is as good a source of protein as meat.

There are more than 20,000 species of fish in the world's seas, yet we use only a fraction of these. This may be because certain types are neither edible nor ethical. Using certain types of fish might be considered wrong if, for example, there was a danger that it could kill off the species or greatly reduce its numbers.

For health reasons, or just as a matter of choice, many people choose to eat fish rather than meat, so fish consumption is steadily increasing. This popularity has resulted in a far greater selection becoming available and, because of swift and efficient transport, well over 200 types of fish are on sale throughout the year. However, demand has also led to overfishing, causing a steep decline in the stocks of some species. To meet increasing demand, some species of fish such as trout, salmon, cod, sea bass and turbot are reared in fish farms to supplement natural resources.

Types of fish

Fish are vertebrates (animals with a backbone) and are split into two main groups: flat and round.

White fish can be round (for example, cod, whiting and hake) or flat (for example, plaice, sole and turbot). White fish are categorised as **demersal** fish and live at or near the bottom of the sea.

> **Professional tip**
> The flesh of white fish does not contain any fat. Vitamins A and D are only present in the liver and used in cod liver or halibut liver oil.

▲ White, round fish: cod

▲ White, flat fish: turbot

Oily fish are round in shape (examples include herring, mackerel, salmon, tuna and sardines). These are categorised as **pelagic** fish and swim mid-water.

▲ Oily fish: salmon

Oily fish contain fat-soluble vitamins A and D in their flesh and omega-3 fatty acids (the unsaturated fatty acids that are essential for good health). It is recommended that we eat more oily fish. However, owing to its fat content, oily fish is not as easily digestible as white fish.

Key terms

Flat fish: have a flatter profile and always have white flesh because the oils are stored in the liver. They include sole, plaice, dabs, turbot, brill, bream, flounder and halibut.

Round fish: can vary greatly in size from small sardines to very large tuna. They can either have white flesh, such as bass, grouper, mullet, haddock and cod, or darker, oily flesh such as tuna, mackerel, herring, trout and salmon.

Oily fish: are always round and, because the fish oils are dispersed through the flesh (rather than stored in the liver as in white fish), the flesh is darker. These include mackerel, salmon, sardines, trout, herrings and tuna.

Demersal fish: live in deep water and feed from the bottom of the sea; they are almost always white fleshed fish and can be round or flat.

Pelagic fish: live in more shallow or mid-depth waters and are usually round, oily fish such as mackerel, herrings and sardines.

Quality points when choosing and buying fish

Whole fish

Whole fish should have:

- clear, bright eyes, which are not sunken
- bright red gills
- no missing scales; scales should also be firmly attached to the skin
- moist skin (fresh fish feels slightly slippery)
- shiny skin with bright, natural colouring
- a stiff tail and fins
- firm flesh
- a fresh sea smell and no odour of ammonia.

Fillets

Fillets should be:

- neatly cut and trimmed with firm flesh
- neatly packed, close together
- a translucent white colour if they are from a white fish, with no discoloration.

Smoked fish

Smoked fish should have:

- a bright, glossy surface
- firm flesh (sticky or soggy flesh means the fish may have been of poor quality or undersmoked)
- a pleasant, smoky smell.

Frozen fish

Frozen fish should:

- be frozen hard with no signs of thawing (defrosting)
- be in packaging that is not damaged
- show no evidence of freezer burn; this shows as dull, white, dry patches.

Cuts of fish

Commonly used cuts of fish:

- **Darnes** – thick slices through the bone of round fish (for example, salmon and cod).
- **Tronçons** – thick slices of large flat fish through the bone (for example, turbot and halibut).
- **Fillets** – cuts that remove the flesh from the backbone/rib bones, leaving fish fillets with no bones. Fillets from a round fish are taken either side of the backbone so there will be two fillets. With a flat fish, two fillets are taken from either side of the backbone on both sides of the fish which gives four fillets.
- **Suprêmes** – prime cuts without bone or skin and cut at an angle from large fillets of fish such as salmon, turbot or halibut.
- **Goujons** – prepared from skinless filleted fish such as sole or plaice, cut into strips approximately 8 × 0.5 cm.
- **Délice** – a neatly folded, skinless, boneless fillet from a flat fish.
- **Paupiettes** – fillets of fish such as sole, plaice or whiting, often spread with a suitable stuffing or filling and rolled before cooking.
- **En tresse** – neatly plaited strips of fish, for example, sole fillets cut into three even pieces lengthwise to within 1 cm of the top, and neatly plaited.

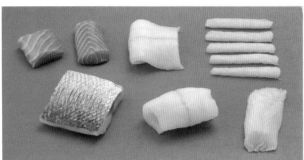

▲ Cuts of fish

Portion sizes and weights

Fresh fish can be bought by the kilogram, by the number of fillets or whole fish of the weight that is required. For example, 30 kg of salmon could be ordered as 2 × 15 kg, 3 × 10 kg or 6 × 5 kg, the number of whole fish, fillets, suprêmes or darnes. Frozen fish can be purchased whole (gutted), filleted, cut or prepared in a wide variety of different ways.

There are a number of ways that can be used to achieve good portion control with fish; for example:

- the specific size and weight of a whole fish such as trout, sea-bass or Dover sole served as a portion
- specified cut sizes of darnes, tronçons and suprêmes used as a portion
- number of fillets from small fish, for example, two fillets from a plaice as a portion
- number of shellfish items such as six king prawns, four scallops or half a lobster making a portion
- number and size of paupiettes or délice offered as a portion
- dividing a fish pie into equal-sized portions
- filling an individual pie dish, serving dish, or pastry case
- using a ladle to measure the portion size of a fish stew or soup.

Unless otherwise stated, as a guide allow 100 g fish off the bone and approximately 300 g on the bone for a portion.

Preservation

Fish deteriorates quickly after it has been caught and over many years ways have been sought to preserve fish for longer. The following are some of the ways that fish is preserved.

Chilling

Chilling fish between 0 °C and 4 °C and preferably below 2 °C will help it to keep a little longer. Remove fish from delivery boxes, place on clean trays and cover with cling film or wet greaseproof paper, date and label. Refrigerate as outlined above. Fish may also be vacuum packed before chilling.

Vacuum packing

The cleaned fish is placed in a plastic pouch and using a vacuum packaging machine all the surrounding air is removed and the pouch is tightly sealed.

Freezing

Fish is either frozen at sea or as soon as possible after reaching port. The freezing process should be fast because the longer it takes to freeze, the larger and more angular the ice crystals become, breaking the protein strands within the fish. This results in liquid leaking out when it is defrosted, leaving an inferior product. When fish is frozen quickly, the ice crystals are small, there is less leakage and less damage.

Most fish should be defrosted before being cooked but some prepared fish products such as frozen, bread crumbed scampi or plaice can be cooked from frozen. Plaice, halibut, turbot, haddock, pollack, sole, cod, trout, salmon, herring, whiting, scampi, smoked haddock and kippers as well as a wide range of prepared products are available frozen.

Frozen fish should be checked to ensure:

- no evidence of freezer burn (very low temperatures damage the fish leaving white patches and a change in texture and flavour. It can be avoided by wrapping or packaging the fish well)
- undamaged packaging
- minimum fluid loss during thawing
- flesh that is still firm after thawing.

Frozen fish should be stored at -18 °C to -23 °C and defrosted overnight in a refrigerator. It should *not* be defrosted in water as this spoils the taste and texture of the fish and valuable water-soluble nutrients are lost. Fish should not be re-frozen as this will impair its taste and texture as well as being a food-safety risk.

Canning

Oily fish such as sardines, salmon, anchovies, pilchards, tuna, herring and herring roe (eggs) are often canned. They can be canned either in their own juice (as with salmon) or in oil, a sauce, brine or spring water. In some countries bottling is popular for fish such as herrings and this is a similar process to canning.

▲ Canned fish

Salting

In the UK, the salting of fish is usually accompanied by a smoking process (see below). Cured herrings are packed in salt. Caviar – the roe (unfertilised eggs) of the sturgeon – is slightly salted then sieved, canned and refrigerated.

In some Caribbean countries, salted dried fish, especially cod, has been popular for many years and this is now available in numerous other countries. It needs to be soaked in plenty of cold water for several hours before use.

Pickling

Herrings pickled in vinegar are filleted, rolled and skewered, and are known as rollmops.

Smoking

Fish that is to be smoked may be gutted or left whole. It is then soaked in a strong salt solution (brine) and in some cases a dye is added to add colour (although use of dyes is becoming less popular). After this, it is drained, hung on racks in a kiln and exposed to smoke for five or six hours.

- **Cold smoking** takes place at no more than 33 °C, to avoid cooking the flesh. Therefore, all cold-smoked fish is actually raw and, with the exception of smoked salmon and trout, is usually cooked before being eaten.
- **Hot-smoked** fish is cured between 70 °C and 80 °C to cook the flesh at the same time, so does not require further cooking.

Smoked fish should be wrapped up well and kept separate from other fish to prevent the smell and dye penetrating other foods.

Table 10.1 Advantages and disadvantages of preservation methods for fish

Method	Advantages	Disadvantages
Chilling	Chilling temperatures slow down deterioration and fish will keep a little longer	Only a short-term method of preservation – fish should still be used as quickly as possible.
Freezing	Very low temperatures completely stop any deterioration and when done properly, quality is not lost	If not done with care, damage such as freezer burn can occur (see freezing above). If not frozen quickly the ice crystals can damage the fish (see above).
Canning	Offers long-term preservation without refrigeration or freezing	The texture and flavour of the fish can be changed in the canning process.
Pickling/ smoking	Adds a different flavour texture and sometimes colour	Only gives short-term preservation on its own – to extend the life other preservation methods may be used too.
Drying	Once completely dry offers long-term preservation without refrigeration or freezing	Fish needs lengthy soaking before use to re-hydrate and to remove some of the salt used in the drying process. The texture, colour and flavour are different to fresh fish.

Storage

Spoilage of fish is mainly caused by the actions of natural enzymes and bacteria. The enzymes in the gut of the living fish help convert its food to tissue and energy. When the fish dies, these enzymes carry on working and, along with bacteria in the digestive system, start breaking down the flesh itself. Bacteria also exist on the skin and in the fish intestine. While the fish is alive, the normal defence mechanisms of the body prevent the bacteria from invading the flesh. Once the fish dies, however, the bacteria invade the flesh and start to break it down; warmer temperatures speed up the deterioration. Although these bacteria are harmless to humans, they reduce the eating quality of the fish and can result in unpleasant odours.

To ensure quality, fish should always be stored correctly:

- Once caught, fish has a shelf life of 10–12 days if properly refrigerated at a temperature between 0°C and 4°C.
- If the fish is delivered whole with the innards still in the fish, it should be gutted and the cavity washed well before it is stored.
- Use the fish as soon as possible after delivery, although it can be stored overnight.
- Remove it from the delivery containers, rinse, pat dry, place on a clean tray (this could be blue), cover with cling film and store in a refrigerator just for fish (running at a temperature of 1–2°C) or at the bottom of a multi-use refrigerator (running between 1–4°C). Make sure the fish is covered or wrapped, labelled and dated.
- For fish products that do not need to be used immediately, use in rotation (use older items before newly delivered items).
- Ready-to-eat cooked fish, such as 'hot' smoked mackerel, cooked prawns and crab, should be stored on shelves above other raw foodstuffs to avoid cross-contamination.
- Frozen fish should be stored in a freezer at -18°C or slightly below. Frozen fish needs to be defrosted in a covered container at the bottom of the refrigerator.
- Smoked fish should be stored and refrigerated as for other fish but very well wrapped in cling film to avoid the strong smell permeating other items in the refrigerator.

Health and safety !

Fish offal and bones present a high risk of contamination and must not be mixed or stored with raw prepared fish.

Tools and equipment for preparing fish

Tools and equipment may vary slightly for each of type of fish preparation. However, the basic equipment that will be needed includes:

- knives – mainly a rigid blade chef's knife and a flexible blade fish filleting knife
- a large chopping knife – for removal of fish heads
- fish tweezers – for removal of pin bones
- scissors – for trimming and removal of fins
- colour-coded boards – blue for raw fish and yellow for cooked fish
- trays – preferably different colours or types for raw and cooked fish
- bowls – for trimmings, debris and additional ingredients
- kitchen paper and colour-coded or single-use disposable cloths

Health and safety !

Unhygienic equipment, utensils and preparation areas increase the risk of cross-contamination and danger to health. Use equipment reserved just for raw fish. If this is not possible, wash and sanitise equipment before and immediately after each use. Clean small equipment and chopping boards thoroughly with colour-coded or single-use cloths, along with detergent/disinfectant or sanitiser, or by putting them through a dishwasher. Clean surfaces and larger equipment with hot water and detergent, then disinfect or use hot water and sanitiser.

Preparing fish

All fish should be washed under running cold water before and after preparation.

Health and safety !

Thorough, regular and effective hand-washing is essential before and after handling fish.

Trimming

Whole fish are trimmed to remove the scales, fins and head using fish scissors and a knife. If the head is to be left on (as in the case of a salmon for a cold buffet), the gills and the eyes are removed.

Gutting and scaling

If the fish needs to be gutted, the following procedure should be used.

1 Cut from the vent (hole) to two-thirds along the fish.
2 Draw out the intestines with the fingers or, in the case of a large fish, use the hook handle of a utensil such as a ladle.
3 Ensure that the blood lying along the main bone is removed, then wash and drain thoroughly.
4 If the fish is to be stuffed then it may be gutted by removing the innards through the gill slits, thus leaving the stomach skin intact, forming a pouch in which to put the stuffing. When this method is used, care must be taken to ensure that the inside of the fish is clear of all traces of blood.

To scale a fish such as salmon, trout, seabass, bream or mackerel, hold the fish at the tail end, scrape the back of the blade of a knife blade against the grain of the scales towards the head until the scales are removed. Wash the fish thoroughly to remove any loose scales.

▲ Gutting a red mullet

Step by step: filleting round fish (salmon)

1 Using a chef's knife with a rigid blade, remove the head and clean thoroughly.

2 Using a fish filleting knife, remove the first fillet by cutting along the backbone from head to tail. Keeping the knife close to the bone, remove the fillet.

3 Reverse the fish and remove the second fillet in the same way, this time cutting from tail to head.

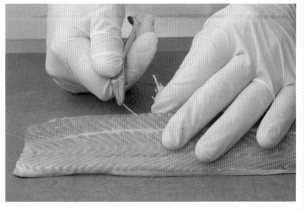

4 Trim the fillets to neaten them and, if required, skin them using the filleting knife.

Step by step: filleting and skinning flat fish (with the exception of Dover sole)

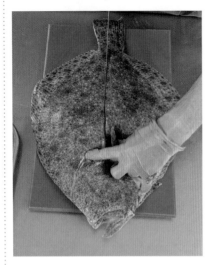

1 Using a filleting knife, make an incision from the head to tail down the line of the backbone.

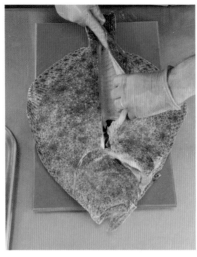

2 Remove the first fillet, holding the knife almost parallel to the work surface and keeping the knife close to the bone.

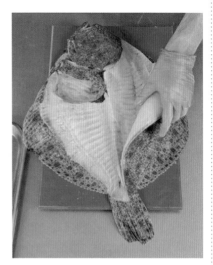

3 Repeat for the second fillet.

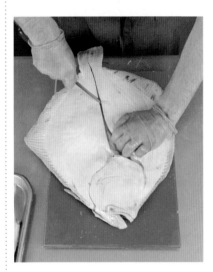

4 Turn the fish over and repeat, removing the last two fillets.

5 Hold the fillet firmly at the tail end. Cut the flesh as close to the tail as possible, as far as the skin. Keep the knife parallel to the work surface, grip the skin firmly and move the knife from side to side to remove the skin.

6 Trim the fillets to neaten them.

Professional tip

If you find it difficult to grip the tail end of a fillet because it is slippery, place a little salt on the fingers and this will help you to hold it firmly. Alternatively, grip using kitchen paper.

Step by step: preparation of whole Dover sole

1 Score the skin just above the tail.

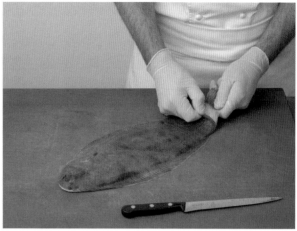

2 Hold the tail of the fish firmly, then cut and scrape the skin until you have lifted enough to grip.

3 Gently pull the skin away from the tail to the head. Both black and white skins may be removed in this way.

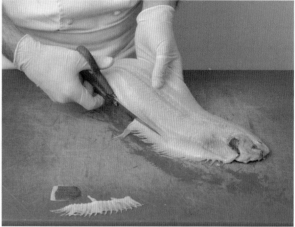

4 Trim the tail and side fins with fish scissors, remove the eyes, and clean and wash the fish thoroughly.

Step by step: stuffing a whole round fish

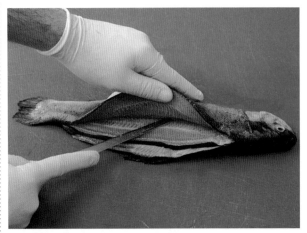

1 Scale, trim and gut the fish.

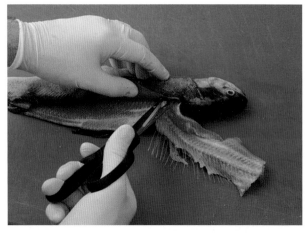

2 Remove the spine, snipping the top with scissors. Clean the cavity.

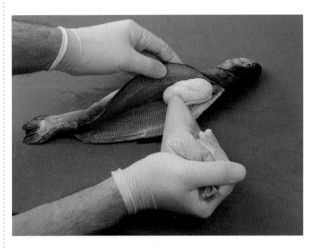

3 Using a piping bag, fill the cavity with the required stuffing.

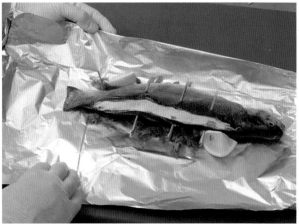

4 Secure the cut edges in place before cooking.

Wrapping

Thick fillets, suprêmes and items such as monkfish tails are sometimes wrapped before cooking. The wrapping may hold another ingredient in place, such as a fish mousse or stuffing, duxelle, julienne of vegetables or shellfish. Suitable wrappings include filo pastry, thinly sliced cured ham or pig's caul (a lacy, fatty membrane surrounding the internal organs of a pig).

Before cooking, fish can be enclosed in a suitable pastry such as shortcrust, puff or a suet pastry for dumplings.

Health and safety

Keep working areas clean and tidy – always clean as you go, not allowing debris to build up.

Flavourings and coatings

Additional flavours may be added by the use of seasonings, herbs, spices or spice pastes and various purées. Marinades can be used with most fish and the ingredients for these will vary, depending on the type of fish, method of cookery and the flavours required. Popular marinade mixture ingredients include: wine, vinegar, oils, herbs, spices, yoghurt, lemon/lime juice and prepared sauces such as soy sauce or teriyaki sauce.

Coatings such as flour, egg and breadcrumbs (pané), milk and flour and batter are often added to fish before cooking (for more information see 'Cooking methods' below).

Seasonality and availability of fish

The quality of fish can vary due to climatic and environmental conditions. generally, all fish spawn (release their eggs) over a period of four to six weeks. During spawning, they use up a lot of their reserves of fat and protein in the production of eggs. This has the effect of making their flesh watery and soft. Fish in this condition are termed 'spent fish'. This takes anything between one and two months, depending on local environmental conditions.

Weather conditions also have an enormous effect on fishing activities. The full range of species may not always be available during stormy weather, for instance. Table 10.2 shows when different types of fish are available.

Cooking fish

When cooked, fish loses its translucent look and becomes opaque. It will also flake easily so should be handled with care because it is delicate and can break up.

Fish can easily become dry and lose its flavour if overcooked, so it is important to consider methods of cookery carefully. Overcooked and dry fish will be far less enjoyable to eat and is less attractive than fish that is cooked properly.

To maintain the quality and food safety of fish dishes it is advisable to check the internal temperature using a temperature probe. It is recommended that all fish should be cooked to a minimum internal temperature of 63°C. This is for whole fish and cuts of fish. Made up fish dishes such as fish pie or fish cakes should be cooked to a minimum of 75°C. Because fish cooks so quickly, an experienced chef will be able to tell when certain types of fish are cooked by touch (touch temperature).

Health and safety !

Environmental Health Officers may require higher temperatures for fish, especially if vulnerable groups of people are being served (see Chapter 1: Food safety).

Cooking methods

The following are the main methods used for cooking fish.

Frying

Frying is probably the most popular method of cooking fish.

- **Shallow frying** – this method is suitable for small whole fish, cuts or fillets cooked in oil or fat in a frying pan. The fish should be seasoned and lightly coated with flour before frying, to protect it and seal in the flavour. The fish can also be lightly coated with semolina, matzo meal, oatmeal or breadcrumbs before frying. If using butter as the frying medium, it must be clarified to reduce the risk of the fish burning. Oil is the best medium, to which a little butter may be added for flavour. Turn the fish only once during cooking, to avoid it breaking up.
- **Deep frying** – this method is suitable for small whole white fish, cuts and fillets, as well as made up items such as fishcakes. All white fish are suitable for deep frying in batter, including cod, pollack, haddock and skate. Depending on size, the fish may be left whole, or may be portioned or filleted. The fish should be seasoned and coated before frying, usually with a batter or an egg and breadcrumb (**pané**) mixture; milk and flour can also be used. This prevents penetration of the cooking fat or oil into the fish. Where possible always use a thermostatically controlled deep fryer only half filled with oil or to the level indicated on the fryer. Heat the oil to 175°C and place the fish into the oil carefully and cook until evenly coloured. Remove carefully and drain the fish on absorbent paper after cooking.
- **Stir-frying** – this is a very fast and popular method of cooking. The fish is cooked along with suitable vegetables and often noodles, bean shoots or rice. Spices, flavourings and suitable sauces may also be added. Use a wok or deep frying pan and a high cooking temperature. Food should be cut into thin strips and all prepared before cooking begins. This method is well suited to cooking firm-fleshed fish cut into strips or shellfish.

Table 10.2 Seasonality of fish

	Jan	Feb	Mar	Apr	May	Jun	Jul	Aug	Sep	Oct	Nov	Dec
Bream	■	■			*	*■	■	■	■	■	■	■
Brill	■	■	*	*	*		■	■	■	■		
Cod			*	*			■	■	■	■	■	
Eel												
Mullet (grey)			*	*								
Gurnard	■	■	■	■					■	■	■	■
Haddock	■	■	■	■		■	■	■	■	■	■	■
Hake	■	■	*■	*■	*■				■	■	■	■
Halibut	■	■	■	*■	*				■	■	■	■
Herring				■	■	■	■	■	■	■	■	■
John Dory				■	■	■	■	■	■			
Marckerel						■	■	■	■	■	■	■
Monkfish												
Plaice			*	*								
Red mullet					■	■	■	■	■			
Salmon (farmed)												
Salmon (wild)				■	■	■	■	■	■			
Sardines	■	■	■			■	■	■	■	■	■	■
Sea bass				*	*	■	■	■	■	■	■	■
Sea trout					■	■	■	*■	*■	*■	*■	■
Skate									■	■	■	■
Squid									■	■	■	
Sole (Dover)	*								■	■	■	■
Sole (lemon)	■	■	■	■	■	■						
Trout							■	■	■	■	■	
Tuna												
Turbot	■	■	■*	*	*					■	■	■
Whiting	■	■								■	■	■

Key:

Available ▢ At best ■

*Spawning and roeing – this can deprive the flesh of nutrients and will decrease the yield.

Grilling

Grilling, or griddling, is a fast and convenient method suitable for fillets or small whole fish. When grilling whole fish, trim and prepare neatly and de-scale. Cut through the flesh at the thickest part of the fish to allow even cooking. Lightly oil and season fish or fillets; to avoid breaking do not turn more than once.

Poaching

Poaching is suitable for whole fish such as salmon, trout or bass; certain cuts on the bone such as salmon, turbot, brill, halibut, cod, skate; and fillets, suprêmes or fish prepared into délice or paupiette.

The prepared fish should be completely immersed in the cooking liquid, which can be water, water and milk, fish stock (for white fish) or a court bouillon (water, vinegar, onion, carrot, thyme, bay leaf, parsley stalks and peppercorns) for oily fish. Most kinds of fish can be cooked in this way and should be poached gently for 5–8 minutes, depending on the thickness of the fish. Whole fish are covered with a cold liquid and brought to the boil then cooked just below simmering point. Cut fish are usually placed in the liquid which is at simmering point then cooked just below simmering point. The resulting liquid is ideal for use in sauces and soups.

When poaching smoked fish, place in cold, unsalted water and bring to a steady simmer. This liquid will be salty and may not be suitable use in stocks and sauces.

En sous vide

This is a method where the fish is sealed in a vacuum pack and cooked, in a water bath and has become a popular way to cook fish. It helps to reduce moisture loss and also allows the fish to cook with a marinade or sauce if required.

Boiling

Boiling is used mainly for shellfish and as many shellfish are sold already cooked this is often done at sea or soon after landing because shellfish can deteriorate quickly. Shellfish are often boiled from live and include lobsters, crabs, oysters, langoustines, crayfish, clams, cockles, mussels, prawns and shrimps.

Roasting

Roast fish now frequently appears on restaurant menus but because fish is much more delicate than meat, only whole fish or larger, firmer cuts are suitable to roast and care must be taken not to overcook. The fish may be brushed with oil or clarified butter before cooking and may be raised a little from the base of the pan using vegetables. More usually the fish is placed skin down in the hot cooking pan to add colour and texture or the skin is seared in hot oil first then cooked skin side up. The fish is usually basted with the pan juices as it cooks.

When the fish is cooked and removed, the tray can be **deglazed** with a suitable wine (usually a dry white) and fish stock to form the base of an accompanying sauce.

Fish can also be coated in a light crust of breadcrumbs mixed with a good oil, butter or margarine, lemon juice, fresh chopped herbs such as parsley, tarragon, chervil, rosemary, a duxelle-based mixture or a light coating of creamed horseradish.

The cooked fish may be served with a sauce or salsa, or placed on a bed of creamed or flavoured mashed potato with a compound butter sauce and quarters of lemon. Examples of this method of cooking include roast cod on garlic mash and roast sea bass flavoured with fennel.

> **Key terms**
>
> **Pané**: coating the fish with a light coating of seasoned flour, beaten egg then breadcrumbs.
>
> **Deglaze**: to add wine stock or water to the pan in which the fish was cooked to use the sediments and flavours left in the pan.

Baking

Many fish (whole, portioned or filleted) may be oven-baked. To retain their natural moisture it is necessary to protect the fish from direct heat and this may be done by coating or wrapping. Prepared fish dishes such as fish pies may also be finished by baking.

Before baking whole, fish need to be scaled, gutted and washed. They may be stuffed with items such as a duxelle-based mixture, flavoured breadcrumbs, fish mousses, herbs or vegetables such as onion or fennel. They can be wrapped in pastry (puff or filo), coated with a crumb mixture or completely covered with a thick coating of dampened sea salt. A prepared dish such as a fish pie may be topped or finished with puff pastry, mashed potato or a sauce.

Whole fish or cuts of fish

- Depending on the size and shape of the fish, 100–150 g thick portions can be cut, leaving the skin on (this helps to retain the natural moisture of the fish).
- Place the prepared portions in a greased ovenproof dish, brush with oil and bake slowly, skin side up (may be seared in hot oil first). Alternatively place skin side down in a hot pan to sear it.
- Add herbs (e.g. parsley, rosemary, thyme) and finely sliced vegetables (e.g. mushrooms, onions, shallots).
- The fish can then be simply served, for example on a bed of creamy or flavoured mashed potato with a suitable sauce, such as compound butter or a salsa.

Steaming

Most fish are suitable for steaming but generally cuts of fish such as darnes, tronçons, fillets and suprêmes are used. Steaming is also a good method for fish fillets made into délice or paupiettes, as they are or with a filling. It is a popular method to cook fish for use in other dishes such as fish cakes or fish pie.

Preparation is usually simple with the fish just seasoned then placed in a steamer tray lined with greaseproof paper or in a small steamer over simmering water covered with a lid. Cook for 10–15 minutes, depending on the thickness of the fish or the fillets. Steaming can also be done by putting the food between two plates and placing the plates over a pan of simmering water.

Fish is prepared as for poaching. Any fish that can be poached or boiled may also be cooked by steaming. This method has a number of advantages: it is an easy method of cooking; because it is quick, it conserves flavour, colour and nutrients; it is suitable for large-scale cookery.

Fish may be steamed then a suitable sauce used to finish the dish or be offered with it. Any cooking liquor from the steamed fish may be strained off, reduced and incorporated into the sauce. Preparation can also include adding finely cut ingredients such as ginger, spring onions, garlic, mushrooms and soft herbs, lemon juice and dry white wine, either to the fish on the steamer dish before cooking or when the fish is served. Fish is sometimes marinaded before steaming to add extra flavour.

Braising and stewing

These tend to be less popular methods for cooking fish but generally whole fish or larger cuts of fish can be braised in a closed container covering or half covering the fish with a suitable liquid such as those used for poaching. Vegetables such as onion, shallot and fennel may be added, along with herbs, spices, lemon or lime.

Stewing of fish may be similar to braising but in many countries there are traditional fish stews using a variety of fish and shellfish, along with onions, shallots, tomatoes, garlic and a variety of other ingredients. Examples of these would be Bouillabaisse from France, Cataplana from Portugal, Cioppino from Italy or Moqueca from Brazil.

Tables 10.3 and 10.4 give examples of fish types that are available and suitable cooking methods.

Sauces and dressings

Cooked fish can be served with a wide variety of flavourings and sauces. The sauces selected will depend on the type of fish, the cooking method and flavourings, coatings, toppings or finishes already used. It is possible that no further sauce or dressing is needed. However, the following may be served with various types of fish:

- flavoured or herb/spice infused oils
- flavoured or herb butter
- fish glazes
- roux-based sauces such as béchamel-, velouté-, or jus lié-based sauces
- emulsified butter sauces such as hollandaise sauce
- reduction sauces with stock, butter or cream
- butter or olive oil monter sauces and sabayon
- mayonnaise-based sauces such as tartare sauce
- cold dressings such as vinaigrette, raita, various chutneys, pickles and jellies
- salsas, tapanade and pesto
- commercially prepared sauces such as ketchups, Worcestershire sauce, sweet chilli sauce.

For more information on sauces see Chapter 6.

Table 10.3 Examples of white fish and suitable cooking methods

	Baking	Boiling	Deep frying	Grilling	Poaching	Roasting	Shallow frying	Steaming	Stir-frying
Cod	✓	✓	✓	✓	✓	✓	✓	✓	
Coley		✓	✓	✓			✓		
Dover sole			✓	✓	✓		✓		
Grouper				✓		✓	✓		
Haddock	✓		✓	✓	✓		✓		
Hake	✓			✓	✓		✓		
Halibut	✓			✓	✓	✓	✓	✓	✓
Huss			✓	✓	✓		✓		
John Dory	✓			✓			✓		
Lemon sole	✓		✓	✓	✓		✓		
Monkfish	✓					✓	✓		✓
Plaice	✓		✓	✓			✓		
Sea bass	✓			✓	✓		✓	✓	
Shark	✓			✓	✓	✓	✓	✓	✓
Skate wings		✓	✓		✓		✓		
Swordfish	✓			✓			✓		✓
Turbot	✓	✓	✓	✓	✓	✓	✓		✓

Table 10.4 Examples of oily fish and suitable cooking methods

	Baking	Boiling	Deep frying	Grilling	Poaching	Roasting	Shallow frying	Steaming	Stir-frying
Barracuda				✓			✓		
Dorade (red sea bream)	✓			✓			✓		✓
Emperor bream	✓			✓			✓		
Herring				✓			✓		
Mackerel	✓			✓	✓				
Marlin	✓			✓	✓		✓		
Red mullet	✓			✓		✓	✓		
Red snapper	✓			✓	✓		✓		
Salmon	✓	✓		✓	✓	✓	✓	✓	✓
Sardines				✓			✓		
Trout	✓			✓			✓		
Tuna				✓	✓		✓		✓
Whitebait			✓				✓		

Assembling fish dishes

As shown in the fish recipe pages, there are numerous ways to serve and present fish using skill and imagination. An essential starting point is to ensure that the fish, accompaniments, garnishes and sauces are at the right temperature – hot, warm or cold. Serving dishes and plates must be clean and at the required temperature. The plate should look well balanced, with the food presented as attractively as possible. Accompaniments should be appropriate in flavour, colour, texture and size and garnishes appropriate – not so large that they overpower the dish.

A number of different effects can be achieved with an accompanying sauce. Popular techniques include:

- flooding – sauce is ladled or spooned across the plate before or after the fish is plated
- masking – carefully spooning a sauce over the fish to thinly coat it
- drizzling – a thin 'drizzle' of sauce is added to the plate or the plated fish
- glazing – usually refers to finishing the fish with a light sauce and finishing under a salamander
- cordon – a line or ribbon of sauce used across the plate before or after plating the fish.

Activity

1 Name three types of flat fish.
2 Name three types of round fish.
3 List the quality points to be considered when purchasing fresh fish.
4 How should raw fresh fish be stored?
5 How much fish should be used for one portion?
6 Suggest four suitable methods that could be used for cooking salmon.

Shellfish

Types of shellfish

Shellfish such as lobsters and crabs are all invertebrates, which means they do not have an internal skeleton. They are split into two main groups: **molluscs** and **crustaceans**.

Molluscs have either:

- an external hinged double shell such as scallops and mussels (these are called **bivalves**)
- a single spiral shell such as winkles or whelks (these are called **univalves**)
- soft bodies with an internal shell such as squid and octopus (these are also called **cephalopods**).

▲ Molluscs (mussel)

Crustaceans have tough outer shells that act like armour and also have flexible joints to allow quick movement, for example, crab and lobster.

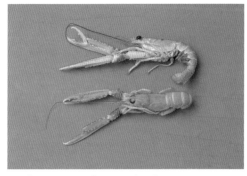

▲ Crustaceans (langoustines)

Key terms

Molluscs: shellfish with either a hinged double shell, such as mussels, or a spiral shell, such as winkles.

Crustaceans: shellfish with tough outer shells and flexible joints to allow quick movement; for example, crab and lobster.

Bivalves: molluscs with a single spiral shell; for example, winkles or whelks.

Univalves: molluscs with an external hinged double shell; for example, scallops and mussels.

Cephalopods: molluscs with a soft body and an internal shell; for example, squid, and octopus.

Video: Buying shellfish
http://bit.ly/ 1DCYHek

Quality points when choosing and buying shellfish

Shellfish are prized for their tender, fine-textured flesh, which can be prepared in a variety of ways, but are prone to rapid spoilage. The reason for this is that they contain quantities of certain amino acids (the 'building blocks' of proteins) which encourage bacterial growth.

To ensure freshness and best flavour, choose live shellfish and cook them yourself. This is possible with the expansion of globalisation and air freight creating a faster, healthy trade in live shellfish with greater availability.

Choosing shellfish

- Shells should not be cracked or broken.
- The shells of mussels and oysters should be tightly shut; open shells that do not close when tapped sharply should be discarded.
- Lobsters, crabs and prawns should have a good colour and feel heavy for their size.
- Lobsters and crabs should have all their limbs.

Storage

All shellfish will start to spoil as soon as they have been removed from their natural environment; therefore, the longer shellfish are stored, the more they will deteriorate due to the bacteria present. Best practice is to cook immediately and store in the same way as cooked fish. Shellfish can be blanched quickly to remove the shell and membrane (especially in lobsters), but they will still need to be stored as a raw product as they will require further cooking.

Bear in mind the following quality, purchasing and storage points:

- When possible, all shellfish should be purchased live so as to ensure freshness.
- Shellfish should be kept in suitable containers, covered with damp cloths or cling film, and stored in a cold room or fish refrigerator.
- Shellfish should be cooked as soon as possible after purchasing.

Preservation

Because shellfish deteriorate so quickly after they are caught, preservation methods similar to those used for fish are frequently used so the shellfish can be kept for longer without causing harm. Shellfish are often boiled soon after they are caught which slows down deterioration and therefore some shellfish on sale are 'ready cooked'. Popular preservation methods are cooking, chilling, freezing, pickling, vacuum packaging, canning and smoking.

Table 10.5 Seasonality of shellfish

	Jan	Feb	Mar	Apr	May	Jun	Jul	Aug	Sep	Oct	Nov	Dec
Crab (brown cock)	■	■	■	■								
Crab (spider)		■	■	■	■	■			■	■		
Crab (brown hen)	■			■	■	■	■					■
Clams	■	■	■									
Cockles	■	■	■									
Crayfish (signal)					■	■	■	■	■			
Lobster							■	■	■	■	■	
Langoustines			■	■	■	■						
Mussels							■		■	■	■	■
Oysters (rock)	■	■	■	■								
Oysters (native)									■	■	■	■
Prawns							■	■	■			■
Scallops							■	■	■	■	■	

Key:

Available		At best ■

Preparation and cooking

The flesh of fish and shellfish is different from meat: the connective tissue is very fragile, the muscle fibres are shorter and the fat content is relatively low. Shellfish should be cooked as little as possible – to the point that the protein in the muscle groups just coagulates. Beyond this point the flesh tends to dry out, making it tougher and drier. Shellfish are known for their dramatic colour change, from blue/grey to a vibrant orange colour. This is because they contain red and yellow pigments called carotenoids, bound to molecules of protein. Once heat is applied, the bonds are broken and the bright colour is revealed.

Shrimps and prawns

Prawns are crustaceans that come in a variety of sizes and have a firm, meaty flesh. Cold water prawns are often cooked and sometimes peeled while still at sea; the tropical warm-water prawns, such as king and tiger prawns, are often reared in fish farms.

Smell is a good guide to freshness. Shrimps and prawns can be used for garnishes, decorating fish dishes, cocktails, sauces, salads, hors d'oeuvres, omelettes and snack and savoury dishes. They can also be used for a variety of hot dishes such as stir-fries, risotto, curries, etc. Potted shrimps remain a popular menu item.

King prawns are a larger variety, which can be used in any of the ways listed above and are an ingredient of many oriental dishes.

Step by step: preparing prawns (removing head, carapace, legs and tail and dark intestinal vein)

1 Remove any loose parts; then, holding the prawn in one hand, remove the head by twisting it off the body.

2 Turn the prawn over and pull the shell open along the length of the belly, starting at the head end and pulling it open so that you can pull the prawn from the shell. Sometimes the very end of the shell is left on for appearance reasons.

3 Once the shell is off, look if there is a black line running down the back (the intestinal tract). It's not harmful to eat, but looks better without it. Using a small, sharp knife, make a shallow cut along the length of the black line.

4 Then lift out the intestinal tract (this is called 'deveining'). Wash before using.

Langoustines, crayfish, scampi, Dublin Bay prawns

Langoustine, crayfish, scampi and Dublin Bay prawns are also known as Norway lobster. They are succulent, white shellfish related to the lobster, though are more the size of a large prawn and are sold fresh, frozen, raw or cooked. Their tails are prepared like prawns and they are used in a variety of ways: salads, rice dishes, stir-fries, deep-fried, poached and served with a number of different sauces. They are also used as garnishes for hot and cold fish dishes, especially on buffets.

Freshwater crayfish are also known as *écrevisse*. These are small freshwater crustaceans with claws, found in lakes and lowland streams. They are prepared and cooked like shrimps and prawns and used in many dishes, including soup. They are often used whole to garnish hot and cold fish dishes.

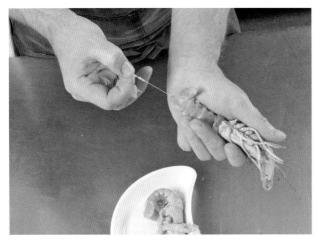

▲ Remove the cord from langoustine before cooking

Lobster

Although there many different lobster varieties around the world, the two main ones are the American lobster, which tends to be the largest, and the European lobster, which is usually smaller. Their preferred habitat is hard surfaces or crevices on the sea bed at depths of around 20–60 m. Lobsters grow very slowly and can live up to 100 years. As they grow they shed their hard shell and form another one. Maturity is reached at about 5 years old and at a length of 18–20 cm. They can weigh up to 9 kg but are usually around 2–3 kg.

Lobsters are served cold in cocktails, lobster mayonnaise, hors d'oeuvres, salads, sandwiches and in halves on cold buffets. Used hot; they are served simply, usually cut and served in half, in the shell with clarified butter or a sauce or as one of the classic hot lobster dishes such as Lobster Thermador. Lobster is also used in soups, sauces, rice dishes, stir-fry dishes and as a filling for ravioli or cannelloni.

Buying lobster

- Purchase alive, with both claws attached, to ensure freshness.
- Lobsters should be heavy in proportion to their size.
- The coral (the roe) of the hen (female) lobster is necessary to give the required colour for certain soups, sauces and lobster dishes.
- Hen lobsters are distinguished from cock lobsters by their broader tails.

To cook lobster:
1 Wash then plunge the lobster into a pan of boiling salted water containing 60 ml of vinegar to 1 litre of water.
2 Cover with a lid, re-boil, then allow to simmer for 15–20 minutes according to size.

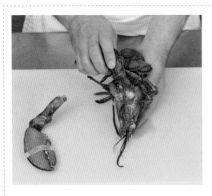

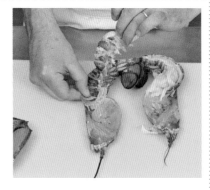

1 Remove lobster claws and legs   **2** Cut lobster in half   **3** Remove meat from a cleaned lobster

3 Overcooking can cause the tail flesh to toughen and the claw meat to become hard and fibrous.

4 Allow to cool in the cooking liquid when possible.

To clean a cooked lobster:

1 Remove the claws and the pincers from the claws.

2 Crack the claws and joints and remove the meat.

3 Cut the lobster in half by inserting the point of a large knife 2 cm above the tail on the natural central line.

4 Cut through the tail firmly.

5 Turn the lobster around and cut through the upper shell (carapace).

6 Remove the halves of the sac (which contains grit). This is situated at the top, near the head.

7 Using a small knife, remove the intestinal tract from the tail and wash if necessary.

Crawfish

These are sometimes referred to as 'spiny lobsters', but unlike lobsters they have no claws and their meat is solely in the tail. Crawfish vary considerably in size from 1 to 3 kg; they are cooked in the same way as lobsters and the tail meat can be used in any of the lobster recipes. Because of their impressive appearance, crawfish dressed whole are sometimes used on cold buffets. They are very expensive and are available fresh or frozen.

Crab

There are large numbers of edible species of crab (estimated at around 4,000). The meat from crab is very different in the claws and the main body. Crab claws have a sweet, dense white meat similar to lobster, while the flesh from under the main body shell is soft, rich and brown. The male crabs tend to have larger claws and more white meat. Whole crab can be served simply in the shell with salad and bread or prepared as dressed crab. Crab meat can be used cold for hors d'oeuvres, cocktails, salads and sandwiches. Served hot, it can be used in a variety of shellfish dishes, covered with a suitable sauce and served with rice, pasta, gnocchi or in Chinese-style dumplings in bouchées or pancakes, or made into crab fish cakes.

- European Brown crab is available all year, reaches 20–25 cm across, has large front claws with dark pincers, a red or brown shell and red legs. This is the most widely available crap across Europe.
- Atlantic Blue crab has a blue/brown shell and tends to be smaller than the European crab at 10–15 cm.

These crabs regularly shed their hard shell and are sometimes caught with their newly forming soft shell. These can be cooked in the shell and eaten whole – soft shell crab. The Blue crab is popular in the east of the United States.

- Dungeness crab can reach up to 20 cm and has plenty of good, white, dense meat in the claws. The meat in the shell tends to be different from other crabs and is pale grey/green in colour. It is popular in the west of the United States.
- Spider crabs are popular in France and Spain and do look like a big spider. The meat has a good flavour but it has no large claws so no white claw meat.

▲ Crab

Buying crab

- Buy alive where possible to ensure freshness.
- Ensure that both claws are attached.
- Crabs should be heavy in relation to size.

Cook crab in the same way as lobsters.

Cockles

Cockles are enclosed in small, attractive, cream-coloured shells. As they live in sand, it is essential to purge them by washing well under running cold water and leaving them in cold salted water (changed frequently) until no traces of sand remain.

Cockles can be cooked either by steaming, boiling in unsalted water, on a preheated griddle or as for any mussel recipe. They should be cooked only until the shells open.

They can be used in soups, sauces, salads, stir-fries and rice dishes and as garnish for fish dishes.

Mussels

Mussels are bivalves. They can be from either the sea or freshwater (rivers and lakes), but the sea varieties are by far the most widely used. Mussels are now extensively 'farmed' – cultivated on wooden frames in the sea, producing tender, delicately flavoured plump flesh. They are produced off British coasts and also imported from France, Holland and Belgium. French mussels are small; Dutch and Belgian mussels are plumper. The production of mussels is considered to be ecologically sound which means the species is not threatened or damaging to the environment.

Mussels can be used for soups, sauces and salads and cooked in a wide variety of hot dishes including the popular and traditional *moules marinière* (mussels with white wine).

▲ Mussels

Buying mussels

- Shells must be tightly closed or close when tapped, indicating that the mussels are alive.
- They should be of a good size and weight with limbs attached.
- There should not be an excessive number of barnacles attached
- They should smell fresh.

Mussels should be kept in containers, covered with cling film or damp cloths, and stored in a cold room or fish refrigerator.

Preparing mussels

1 Discard any mussels with broken shells.
2 Scrape the shells to remove any barnacles.
3 Remove the byssus threads (these are sometimes called the beard).

4 Wash in several changes of cold water to clean and purge the mussels then drain well in a colander.

There are various ways the mussels can be cooked, but the most popular and traditional way is described below.

1 Prepare a cooking liquid of shallots, butter, garlic and herbs along with fish stock
2 Cook the mussels in the liquid in a large pan with a tightly fitting lid until they open which usually takes 4–5 minutes. Remove the mussels and check they have all opened, throw away any that are still closed.
3 Strain the liquid, whisk in cream and serve with the mussels still in their shells.

Alternatively:

1 In a thick-bottomed pan with a tight-fitting lid, place 25 g chopped shallot or onion for each litre of mussels.
2 Add the mussels, cover with a lid and cook on a fierce heat for 4–5 minutes until the shells open completely.
3 Remove the mussels from the shells.
4 Retain the carefully strained liquid to make a sauce to serve with the mussels.

Scallops

Scallops are bivalves with a fan-shaped shell. They vary in size from 15 cm for great scallops, around 8 cm for bay scallops and queen scallops that are the size of cockles. Inside they have round white flesh and the orange coral, which is the roe and is often discarded. Scallops are popular and prices tend to remain high, especially for 'hand-dived' scallops rather than those caught by a dredging trawler. They are prepared by prising the two halves of the shell apart and removing the white flesh and the orange roe if required.

Scallops are found on the seabed and are therefore dirty or sandy, so it is advisable to purchase them ready cleaned. If scallops are bought in their shells, the shells should be tightly shut, which indicates they are alive and fresh. The orange roe should be bright and moist. Scallops in their shells should be covered with damp cloths and kept in a refrigerated cold room or fish refrigerator.

To remove scallops from their shells, insert a sharp knife between the two halves of the shell and prise apart. The flesh can then be removed with a knife. Scallops should then be well washed. Remove the orange roe, leaving only the white scallop.

▲ Scallops

Scallops should be lightly cooked; if overcooked they shrink and toughen.

● Poach gently for 2–3 minutes in dry white wine with a little onion, carrot, thyme, bay leaf and parsley. Serve with a suitable sauce such as white wine or mornay sauce.
● Lightly pan fry on both sides for a few seconds in butter or oil in a very hot pan (if the scallops are very thick they can be cut in half sideways) and serve with a suitable garnish (sliced wild or cultivated mushrooms or a fine brunoise of vegetables and tomato) and a liquid that need not be thickened such as white wine and fish stock, or cream- or butter-thickened sauce). Fried scallops can also be served hot on a base of salad leaves.
● Deep-fry, either coated in egg and crumbs or passed through a light batter, and served with segments of lemon and a suitable sauce such as tartare sauce.
● Wrap in thin streaky bacon or cured ham and place on skewers for grilling or barbecuing.

Whelks

The common whelk is familiar around the coast of Britain. Whelks can often be bought in jars, packed in vinegar and water.

To cook:
1 Place the whelks in a saucepan and add water to cover them by 1 cm.
2 Add a sprig of thyme and a bay leaf.
3 Bring to a boil and cook at a gentle simmer.

Whelks require only a very short cooking time otherwise the flesh has a tendency to become tough.

British winkles

Winkles are small, black shellfish that look like snails and grow up to 3 cm in size.

The main types of British winkle, which can be readily identified on rocky shores, are:
● small periwinkle – approximately 4 mm
● rough periwinkle – at least four different subspecies, with the largest reaching 30 mm
● flat periwinkle.

To remove the winkles easily from their shells they need to be cooked.

To cook:
1 Place the winkles in a saucepan and cover with water. Add salt and a bay leaf.
2 Turn on the heat, wait for the first sign of boiling and allow to boil 2 to 3 minutes longer – no more.
3 Take out one winkle to test if cooked; if uncooked it will resist removal from the shell.
4 When the winkles are cooked, run them quickly under cold water, otherwise they will toughen.
5 Serve simply in melted butter.

Oysters

Oysters are highly regarded salt water bivalves found near the bottom of the sea, with a number of different species available. The upper shell (valve) is flattish and attached by a ligament hinge to the lower, bowl-shaped shell. Those available around British coastlines are native, flat or rock oysters with Colchester and Whitstable in Kent being significant oyster areas.

Professional tip

Native oysters tend to be the most expensive and generally thought of as superior. Pacific or rock oysters tend to have a frillier shell and are smaller, with milder meat.

When buying oysters, the shells should be clean, bright, tightly closed and unbroken.

Traditionally oysters are eaten raw so it is essential they are very fresh and cleaned/purged well. Preparation usually involves prising the two halves of the shell apart with a small, pointed oyster knife. The oysters are then served with lemon and red pepper.

Store oysters in their delivery boxes, in the refrigerator, covered with damp cloths or kitchen paper. The shells should be tightly closed or should do so when tapped. Discard any that do not close. Unopened live oysters can be kept in the fish refrigerator for two to three days. Do not store in an airtight container or under fresh water as this will cause them to die. Shucked oysters (ones that have been removed from their shells) can be kept refrigerated in a sealed container for four to five days.

Squid

Squid was traditionally popular in Mediterranean cuisine but has increased in popularity throughout the rest of Europe. It is available all year round, either fresh or frozen. Squid vary in size, from 5 to 7 cm in length, up to 25 cm. The ink sac and transparent cartilage need to be removed. The main body is usually cut into rings for cooking. Squid needs to be cooked very quickly or by a slow moist method, otherwise it can be tough.

Step by step: preparing squid

1 Pull the head away from the body, together with the innards.

2 Taking care not to break the ink bag, remove the long transparent blade of cartilage (the backbone or quill).

3 Cut the tentacles just below the eye and remove the small round cartilage at the base of the tentacles.

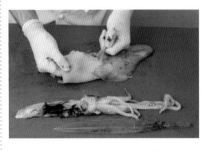

4 Scrape or peel off the reddish membrane that covers the pouch, rub with salt and wash under cold water.

5 Discard the head, innards and pieces of cartilage. Cut up the squid as required.

Activity

1 Explain the difference between molluscs and crustaceans.
2 How should scallops be opened?
3 Name two ways of preparing/cooking oysters.
4 List the food safety precautions that must be taken when preparing and cooking shellfish.
5 Suggest some of the ways that shellfish could be preserved to make them last longer.
6 What are other names for scampi?

Test yourself

1 State **three** types of oily fish.
2 Describe the difference between a tronçon and a suprême.
3 At what temperatures should fresh fish and frozen fish be stored?
4 Describe how you would skin a Dover sole.
5 State **three** types of shellfish that are crustaceans.
6 Describe **three** quality points to look for when purchasing lobsters.
7 How would you store mussels until they are ready to use?
8 State **three** factors in relation to portion control that you should take into consideration when preparing and serving suprêmes of turbot.
9 Describe **four** preservation methods for fish.
10 Explain why steaming is a suitable cooking method for darnes of salmon.

1 Fried egg and breadcrumbed fish fillets

Pané the fish, passing it through flour, egg and breadcrumbs in turn.

Energy	Cals	Fat	Sat fat	Carb	Sugar	Protein	Fibre
1736kJ	415kcal	14.0g	1.8g	41.6g	35g	33.2g	2.1g

1 Pass the fillets through flour, beaten egg and fresh white breadcrumbs. (Pat the surfaces well to avoid loose crumbs falling into the fat, burning and spoiling both the fat and the fish.)

2 Deep fry at 175°C, until the fish turns a golden-brown. Remove and drain well.

Note

Serve with either lemon quarters or tartare sauce.

 Video: Deep-frying fish
http://bit.ly/
1ClMoMm

2 Fried sole (*sole frite*)

For fish courses use 200–250g sole per portion; for main courses 300–400g sole per portion.

1 Remove the black and white skin. Remove the side fins.

2 Remove the head. Clean well.

3 Wash well and drain. Pané and deep-fry at 175°C.

Note

Serve on a dish paper with picked or fried parsley and a quarter of lemon on a flat dish, and with a suitable sauce, such as tartare or anchovy.

Energy	Cals	Fat	Sat fat	Carb	Sugar	Protein	Fibre	Sodium *
1446kJ	345kcal	11.1g	1.3g	0	0g	60.6g	0g	0.330g

* Per 300g portion

3 Goujons of plaice

1 Cut fillets of plaice into strips approximately 8 × 0.5 cm. Wash and dry well.

2 Pass through flour, beaten egg and fresh white breadcrumbs. Pat the surfaces well so that there are no loose crumbs which could fall into the fat and burn.

3 Deep-fry at 175–180 °C, then drain well.

> **Professional tip**
>
> Keep the coating ingredients (flour, egg and breadcrumbs) separate. Shake off any excess flour and egg before dipping the fish into the breadcrumbs.
>
> Other fish, e.g. sole or salmon, may be used instead of plaice.

Energy	Cals	Fat	Sat fat	Carb	Sugar	Protein	Fibre	Salt
994 kJ	261 kcal	13.8 g	0.0 g	13.8 g	0.0 g	21.3 g	0.6 g	0.3 g

Note

Serve with lemon quarters and a suitable sauce (e.g. tartare).

1 Cut the fish fillet into goujons

2 Pané the fish into breadcrumbs

3 Roll the goujons to make sure the coating sticks

4 Fish meunière

	4 portions	10 portions
White fish fillets, skinned	400–600 g	1–1.5 kg
Large lemons	2	5
Clarified butter	100 g	250 g
Chopped parsley	1 tsp	2 tsp

Energy	Cals	Fat	Sat fat	Carb	Sugar	Protein	Fibre
1314 kJ	313 kcal	24.1 g	10.3 g	3.1 g	0.0 g	21.2 g	0.1 g

Healthy eating tips
- Use a small amount of unsaturated oil to fry the fish.
- Use less *beurre noisette* per portion. Some customers will prefer the finished dish without the additional fat.

1 Prepare and clean the fish, wash and drain.

2 Pass through seasoned flour, shake off all surplus.

3 Shallow-fry on both sides, presentation side first, in hot clarified butter or oil.

4 Dress neatly on an oval flat dish or plate/plates.

5 Peel a lemon, removing the peel, white pith and pips.

6 Cut the lemon into slices and place one on each portion.

7 Squeeze some lemon juice on the fish.

8 Allow 10–25 g butter per portion and colour in a clean frying pan to the nut-brown stage (*beurre noisette*).

9 Pour over the fish.

10 Sprinkle with chopped parsley and serve.

Note

Many fish, whole or filleted, may be cooked by this method, for example, sole, sea bass, bream, fillets of plaice, trout, brill, cod, turbot, herring, scampi.

Professional tip
When the butter has browned, try adding a squeeze of lemon juice or a splash of white wine for extra flavour.

Variation

Fish meunière with almonds: as for fish meunière, adding 10 g of almonds cut in short julienne or coarsely chopped into the meunière butter just before it begins to turn brown. This method is usually applied to trout.

Fish belle meunière: as for fish meunière, with the addition of a grilled mushroom, a slice of peeled tomato and a soft herring roe (passed through flour and shallow-fried), all neatly dressed on each portion of fish.

Fish Doria: as for fish meunière, with a sprinkling of small turned pieces of cucumber carefully cooked in 25 g of butter in a small covered pan, or blanched in boiling salted water.

Fish grenobloise: as for fish meunière, the peeled lemon being cut into segments, neatly dressed on the fish, with a few capers sprinkled over.

Fish Bretonne: as for fish meunière, with a few picked shrimps and cooked sliced mushrooms sprinkled over the fish.

For each of these classical dishes, chefs may wish to add some chopped herbs for flavour; for example, add chopped dill to fish Doria.

5 Délice of flat white fish Dugléré

Ingredient	4 portions	10 portions
Fillets of flat white fish (e.g. Sole, plaice)	400–600 g	1–1.5 kg
Fish stock for poaching	approx. 200 ml	approx. 500 ml
For the sauce		
Butter	25 g	60 g
Shallots, finely chopped	20 g	50 g
Fish stock	60 ml	150 ml
Dry white wine	60 ml	150 ml
Whipping cream	200 ml	500 ml
Butter, sliced and kept cold on ice	50 g	125 g
Tomatoes, skinned and neatly diced (concassé)	2	5
Parsley, chopped finely	10 g	20 g

Energy	Cals	Fat	Sat fat	Carb	Sugar	Protein	Fibre	Sodium
1974 kJ	475 kcal	38 g	23 g	3.5 g	3.2 g	28 g	0.7 g	0.58 g

1 Skin the fish, trim and wash.

2 Fold the fillets neatly, ensuring the skinned side is facing inwards (délice).

3 Using a wide, shallow pan, poach the délice gently in fish stock for 4–6 minutes (depending on the thickness of the fillet).

4 To make the sauce, sweat the finely chopped shallots with the butter in a saucepan, until translucent.

5 Add the fish stock and reduce by one-third.

6 Add the dry white wine and reduce again by half.

7 Add the whipping cream and reduce by one-third, until the cream starts to thicken the sauce to a coating consistency.

8 Add the cold, sliced butter and ripple the sauce over the butter until the butter has emulsified into the sauce (monté). Check the seasoning and adjust accordingly. Do not allow the sauce to reboil as the butter will split and the sauce will become greasy.

9 Add the neatly cut tomato concassé and finely chopped parsley to the sauce.

10 To serve, drain the fish well and place neatly on a plate; carefully coat each délice with the sauce and serve.

Folding each fillet into a délice

Sweating the finely chopped shallots

Coating each délice with sauce

6 Fillets of fish Véronique (*filets de poisson Véronique*)

	4 portions	10 portions
Fillets of white fish	4 × 100–150 g	10 × 100–150 g
Butter, for dish and greaseproof paper		
Shallots, finely chopped	10 g	25 g
Fish stock	60 ml	150 ml
Dry white wine	60 ml	150 ml
Lemon, juice of	½	1
Fish velouté	250 ml	625 ml
Egg yolk or spoonful of sabayon	1	2½
Butter	50 g	125 g
Cream, lightly whipped	2 tbsp	5 tbsp
White grapes, blanched, skinned and pipped	50 g	125 g

Energy	Cals	Fat	Sat fat	Carb	Sugar	Protein	Fibre
1077 kJ	256 kcal	19.3 g	10.7 g	6.9 g	2.1 g	11.8 g	0.4 g

1 Skin and fillet the fish, trim and wash.

2 Butter and season an earthenware dish.

3 Sprinkle with the sweated chopped shallots and add the fillets of fish.

4 Season, add the fish stock, wine and lemon juice.

5 Cover with buttered greaseproof paper.

6 Poach in a moderate oven at 150–200 °C for 7–10 minutes.

7 Drain the fish well and retain the cooking liquor. Dress the fish neatly on a flat dish or clean earthenware dish.

8 Bring the cooking liquor to the boil with the velouté and egg yolk or sabayon.

9 Correct the seasoning and consistency, and pass through double muslin or a fine strainer.

10 Mix in the butter then, finally, add the cream.

11 Coat the fillets with the sauce. glaze under the salamander.

12 Arrange the grapes neatly on the dish.

Professional tip

Chill the grapes well before use, so that they provide a real contrast of flavour.

Healthy eating tips
- Keep the added salt to a minimum.
- Reduce the amount of butter and cream added to finish the sauce.
- Less sauce could be added plus a large portion of potatoes and vegetables.

7 Fillets of fish in white wine sauce
(filets de poisson vin blanc)

1. Skin and fillet the fish, trim and wash.
2. Butter and season an earthenware dish.
3. Sprinkle with the sweated chopped shallots and add the fillets of sole.
4. Season, add the fish stock, wine and lemon juice.
5. Cover with buttered greaseproof paper.
6. Poach in a moderate oven at 150–200 °C for 7–10 minutes.
7. Drain the fish well; dress neatly on a flat dish or clean earthenware dish.
8. Bring the cooking liquor to the boil with the velouté.
9. Correct the seasoning and consistency and pass through double muslin or a fine strainer.
10. Mix in the butter then, finally, add the cream.
11. Coat the fillets with the sauce. garnish with flat parsley or *fleurons* (puff paste crescents).

Professional tip

In this recipe, the shallots should be sweated before use; however, if they are very finely chopped, they could be added raw.

	4 portions	10 portions
Fillets of white fish	4 × 100–150 g	10 × 100–150 g
Butter, for dish and greaseproof paper		
Shallots, finely chopped and sweated	10 g	25 g
Fish stock	60 ml	150 ml
Dry white wine	60 ml	150 ml
Lemon, juice of	¼	½
Fish velouté	250 ml	625 ml
Butter	50 g	125 g
Cream, lightly whipped	2 tbsp	5 tbsp

Energy	Cals	Fat	Sat fat	Carb	Sugar	Protein	Fibre
1421 kJ	342 kcal	24.0 g	12.8 g	5.8 g	0.9 g	25.9 g	0.2 g

Variation

Add to the fish before cooking:
- 100 g thinly sliced white button mushrooms and chopped parsley – fish *bonne-femme*
- as for *bonne-femme* plus 100 g diced, peeled and deseeded tomatoes – fish *bréval*.

Healthy eating tips
- Keep the added salt to a minimum.
- Reduce the amount of butter and cream added to finish the sauce.
- Less sauce could be added, plus a large portion of potatoes and vegetables.

Video: Filleting a flat fish
http://bit.ly/ 17grHfz

8 Skate with black butter (*raie au beurre noir*)

	4 portions	10 portions
Skate wings	400–600 g	1 ¼ kg
Court bouillon (see recipe 38)		
Butter	50 g	125 g
Vinegar	1 tsp	2 ½ tsp
Parsley, chopped		
Capers	10 g	25 g

Energy	Cals	Fat	Sat fat	Carb	Sugar	Protein	Fibre
725 kJ	174 kcal	10.8 g	6.5 g	0.1 g	0.1 g	19.0 g	0.0 g

1 Cut the skate into 4 (or 10) even pieces.

2 Simmer in a court bouillon until cooked (approximately 10 minutes).

3 Drain well, place on a serving dish or plates.

4 Heat the butter in a frying pan until well browned, almost black; add the vinegar, pour over the fish, sprinkle with chopped parsley and a few capers and serve.

Variation

Proceed as for steps 1–3, then drain well and serve on a bed of plain or herb-flavoured mashed potato, accompanied by a compound butter sauce (page 158) or a salsa (page 153).

Healthy eating tips
- Pour less black butter over the cooked fish.
- Serve with a large portion of potatoes and vegetables.

9 Grilled fillets of sole, plaice or haddock

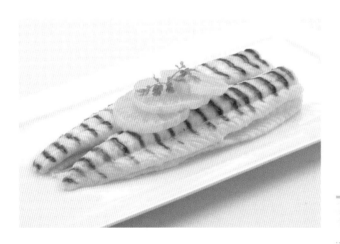

1 Remove the black skin from sole and plaice. Wash the fillets and dry them well.

2 Pass through flour, shake off surplus and brush with oil.

3 Place on hot grill bars, a griddle or a greased baking sheet if grilling under a salamander. Brush occasionally with oil. Turn the fish carefully and grill on both sides. Do not overcook.

Note

Serve with lemon slices with rind removed.

Energy	Cals	Fat	Sat fat	Carb	Sugar	Protein	Fibre	Sodium
802 kJ	191 kcal	7.8 g	1.0 g	3.9 g	0.1 g	26.6 g	0.2 g	100 mg

Professional tip

Oil the grill bars well, so that the fish does not stick.

10 Frying batters *(pâtes à frire)* for fish

Recipe A

Portions	6–8	10
flour	200 g	500 g
salt		
yeast	10 g	25 g
water or milk	250 ml	625 ml

1. Sift the flour and salt into a basin.
2. Dissolve the yeast in a little of the water.
3. Make a well in the flour. Add the yeast and the liquid.
4. Gradually incorporate the flour and beat to a smooth mixture.
5. Allow to rest for at least 1 hour before using.

Recipe B

Portions	6–8	10
flour	200 g	500 g
salt		
egg	1	2–3
water or milk	250 ml	625 ml
oil	2 tbsp	5 tbsp

1. Sift the flour and salt into a basin. Make a well. Add the egg and the liquid.
2. Gradually incorporate the flour and beat to a smooth mixture.
3. Mix in the oil. Allow to rest before using.

Recipe C

Portions	6–8	10
flour	200 g	500 g
salt		
water or milk	250 ml	625 ml
oil	2 tbsp	5 tbsp
egg whites, stiffly beaten	2	5 tbsp

1. As for Recipe B, but fold in the egg whites just before using.

Note

Other ingredients can be added to batter (e.g. chopped fresh herbs, grated ginger, garam masala, beer).

11 Fried fish in batter

Energy	Cals	Fat	Sat fat	Carb	Sugar	Protein	Fibre
736kJ	415kcal	14.0g	1.8g	41.6g	3.5g	33.2g	2.1g

1 Pass the prepared, washed and well-dried fish through flour, shake off the surplus and pass through the batter.

2 Place carefully away from you into the hot deep-fryer at 175°C until the fish turns a golden-brown. Remove and drain well.

Note

Serve with either lemon quarters or tartare sauce.

Professional tip

Remove any excess batter before frying; too much batter will make the dish too heavy.

1 Pass the prepared fish through the batter

2 Shake off any excess and then lower carefully into the fryer

12 Whitebait (*blanchailles*)

1 Pick over the whitebait, wash carefully and drain well.
2 Pass through milk and seasoned flour.
3 Shake off surplus flour in a wide-mesh sieve and place fish into a frying-basket.
4 Plunge into very hot fat, just smoking (195 °C).
5 Cook until brown and crisp (approximately 1 minute).
6 Drain well.
7 Season lightly with salt and cayenne pepper.

Note

Serve garnished with fried or picked parsley and quarters of lemon.

Energy	Cals	Fat	Sat fat	Carb	Sugar	Protein	Fibre
2174kJ	525kcal	47.5g	0.0g	5.3g	0.1g	19.5g	0.2g

Allowing 100g per portion.

Professional tip

It is important to shake off any excess flour before frying; too much flour will cause the fish to stick together.

13 Pan-fried fillets of sea bass with rosemary mash and mushrooms

	4 portions	10 portions
Vegetable oil	10 ml	25 ml
Salt, pepper		
Sea bass portions, skin on	4 × 100 g	10 × 100 g
Wild mushrooms, sliced	200 g	600 g
Extra virgin olive oil	10 ml	25 ml
Rosemary, chopped	pinch	1 tsp
Mashed potato (see page 203)	400 g	1 kg

Healthy eating tips
● Using an unsaturated oil (sunflower or olive), lightly oil the non-stick pan to fry the sole.
● Use a little olive oil to fry the mushrooms.
● Keep added salt to a minimum.
● Serve with plenty of seasonal vegetables and new potatoes.

Energy	Cals	Fat	Sat fat	Carb	Sugar	Protein	Fibre	*
1183kJ	282kcal	11.6g	3.6g	17.3g	0.6g	28.2g	1.3g	

1 Heat the vegetable oil in a non-stick pan, season and then fry the sea bass, skin side first, until it has a golden colour and is crispy.

2 Turn the fish over and gently seal without colouring.

3 Remove from the pan (skin side up) and keep warm.

4 Quickly and lightly fry the mushrooms in extra virgin olive oil.

5 Mix the rosemary into the mashed potato.

6 Arrange the potato in the centre of hot plates.

7 Place the fish on top, skin side down.

8 Garnish with the mushrooms and olive oil and serve.

14 Nage of red mullet with baby leeks

	4 portions	10 portions
Mussels, cooked and removed from shell	16	40
Lemons, juice of	2	5
Baby spinach	200 g	500 g
Baby leeks	12	30
Baby asparagus, spears of	12	30
Green beans, pieces of	2 tbsp	5 tbsp
Red mullet fillets (approximately 120 g each), pin bones and scales removed	4	10
Nage		
Large onion	1	3
Carrots, peeled	2	5
Celery sticks	2	5
Leeks	2	5
Cloves of garlic	1	3
Half white and half pink peppercorns	12	30
Star anise	1	3
White wine	375 ml	950 ml
Noilly Prat	375 ml	950 ml
Chervil	10 g	25 g
Parsley	10 g	25 g
Tarragon	10 g	25 g
Chives, chopped	1 tbsp	3 tbsp

1 In a large pan place the onions, carrots, celery and leeks, which have been cut into 2 cm pieces.

2 Just cover the vegetables with water. Bring to the boil. Simmer for 4–5 minutes. Remove from the heat and add the rest of the ingredients.

3 Cover with cling film and allow to cool to room temperature. Place into a plastic container and store in the fridge overnight to develop flavour.

4 Pass through a fine sieve. Any surplus nage can be frozen for later use.

5 To finish, place 500 ml of the vegetable nage in a pan, add the mussels, a squeeze of lemon, spinach, baby leeks, asparagus and green beans.

6 Bring to the boil, check the seasoning and retain.

7 Heat a non-stick pan with a little vegetable oil. Season the mullet fillets and cook for 1 minute on each side (thickness dependent), starting with the skin side down.

8 Divide the vegetable garnish between the plates. Place the red mullet on top of the vegetable garnish and, returning the pan the mullet was cooked in to the stove, pour in the nage.

9 When the nage has returned to the boil, spoon over the fish and garnish. Serve immediately.

Energy	Cals	Fat	Sat fat	Carb	Sugar	Protein	Fibre	Sodium
2172 kJ	519 kcal	9.2 g	0.9 g	26.8 g	19.7 g	46.2 g	13.1 g	0.6 g

Professional tip

This dish is open to many substitutions of fish and shellfish but one key point to remember is that the nage should not be allowed to overpower the main ingredients.

15 Poached smoked haddock

	4 portions	10 portions
Smoked haddock fillets	400–600 g	1.2 kg
Milk and water, mixed		

Energy	Cals	Fat	Sat fat	Carb	Sugar	Protein	Fibre	Sodium *
702 kJ	168 kcal	7.6 g	4.6 g	1.4	1.4 g	23.4 g	0 g	0.962 g

* 125 g portion

Variation

This is a popular breakfast dish and is also served as a lunch and a snack dish.

When cooked, garnish with slices of peeled tomato or tomato concassé, lightly coat with cream, flash under the salamander and serve.

Top with a poached egg.

When cooked, lightly coat with Welsh rarebit mixture, brown under the salamander and garnish with peeled slices of tomato or tomato concassée.

1 Cut fillets into even portions, place into a shallow pan and just cover with half milk and water.

2 Simmer gently for a few minutes until cooked.

3 Drain well and serve.

16 Steamed fish with garlic, spring onions and ginger

	4 portions	10 portions
White fish fillets, e.g. cod, sole	400 g	1.5 kg
Salt		
Fresh ginger, freshly chopped	1 tbsp	2 ½ tbsp
Spring onions, finely chopped	2 tbsp	5 tbsp
Light soy sauce	1 tbsp	2 ½ tbsp
Cloves of garlic, peeled and thinly sliced	4	10
Oil	1 tbsp	2 ½ tbsp

Energy	Cals	Fat	Sat fat	Carb	Sugar	Protein	Fibre *
468 kJ	112 kcal	3.5 g	0.7 g	1.2 g	0.4 g	18.7 g	0.1 g

* Using 2 cloves of garlic

1 Wash and dry the fish well; rub *lightly* with salt on both sides.

2 Put the fish on to plates, scatter the ginger evenly on top.

3 Put the plates into the steamer, cover tightly and steam gently until just cooked (5–15 minutes, according to the thickness of the fish).

4 Remove the plates, sprinkle on the spring onions and soy sauce.

5 Brown the garlic slices in the hot oil and pour over the dish.

Note

Garlic and ginger have intense flavours, so they must be chopped very finely.

Healthy eating tips
- Steaming is a healthy way of cooking.
- Serve with a large portion of rice or noodles and stir-fried vegetables.

Variation

This is a Chinese recipe that can be adapted in many ways – for example, replace the spring onions and garlic and use thinly sliced mushrooms, diced tomato (skinned and deseeded), finely chopped shallots, lemon juice, white wine, chopped parsley, dill or chervil.

17 Steamed halibut with lime and fennel

	4 portions	10 portions
Halibut fillet, skinned (or use any other white fish such as pollack, cod, haddock)	4 × 100 g	10 × 100 g
Spring onions – thinly sliced	4	10
Salt and black pepper		
Red chilli – deseeded and cut into very thin slices	½	1 ½
Lime juice	3 tbsp	8 tbsp
Olive oil or sunflower oil	3 tbsp	8 tbsp
Limes cut into rounds	1	3
Bay leaves	2	6
Garlic – finely chopped	1 clove	2 ½ cloves
Coriander – chopped	1 tbsp	2 ½ tbsp
Fennel bulb –very thinly sliced	1	2 ½
Thai fish sauce (Nam Pla)	1 tbsp	2 ½ tbsp

Energy	Cals	Fat	Sat fat	Carb	Sugar	Protein	Fibre	Sodium
914 kJ	219 kcal	13.3 g	1.9 g	2.2	1.6 g	22.8 g	2.1 g	0.117 g

1 Mix together the lime juice, oil, garlic and fish sauce and marinate the fish in this for 30 minutes, spooning the mixture over the fish frequently.

2 Remove the fish from the marinade and scatter each piece with spring onion, coriander, chilli and a slice of lime.

3 Season the fennel and place in a steamer tray, small steamer or between two plates over simmering water.

4 Top with the fish, make sure it is well covered and steam gently for 5–10 minutes until the fish is cooked and the fennel tender.

5 Remove the fish and continue to cook the fennel if necessary.

6 Divide the fennel between the plates and top each with fish.

18 Griddled monkfish with leeks and Parmesan

	4 portions	10 portions
Oil		
Leeks, finely sliced	100 g	250 g
Parmesan, grated	100 g	250 g
Salt, pepper		
Prepared monkfish fillets	750 g	1.8 kg
Egg white, lightly beaten	2	5
Lemons	1	3
Mixed salad leaves, to serve		

Energy	Cals	Fat	Sat fat	Carb	Sugar	Protein	Fibre
1009kJ	239kcal	8.3g	5.0g	1.0g	0.8g	40.3g	0.6g

1 Heat the griddle pan and oil lightly.

2 Cut the leeks into fine julienne with the Parmesan, then season.

3 Cut the monkfish into 1.5 cm thick slices. Dry, dip in the beaten egg white, then in the leek and Parmesan.

4 Place the monkfish on the griddle to cook (approximately 3–4 minutes).

Note

Garnish with lemon wedges and mixed leaves.

Healthy eating tips
● There is no need to add salt as there is plenty in the cheese.
● Serve with a large portion of potatoes and vegetables or salad.

19 Grilled round fish (herring, mackerel, bass, mullet)

Energy	Cals	Fat	Sat fat	Carb	Sugar	Protein	Fibre	Sodium *
2238kJ	536kcal	33.2g	8.3g	0	0g	59.5g	0g	0.474g

* Per 300 g portion of herring

1 Descale fish where necessary, using the back of a knife.

2 Remove heads, clean out intestines, trim off all fins and tails using fish scissors. Leave herring roes in the fish.

3 Wash and dry well.

4 Make three light incisions 2 mm deep on either side of the fish. This is known as 'scoring' and helps the heat to penetrate the fish.

5 Pass through flour, shake off surplus and brush with oil.

6 Place on hot grill bars, a griddle or a greased baking sheet if grilling under a salamander. Brush occasionally with oil.

7 Turn the fish carefully and grill on both sides. Do not overcook.

Note

Serve with lemon quarters and a suitable sauce (e.g. compound butter or salsa).

Herrings are traditionally served with a mustard sauce. Mackerel may be butterfly filleted and grilled.

20 Grilled swordfish and somen noodle salad with coriander vinaigrette

	4 portions	10 portions
Swordfish fillets	4 × 75 g	10 × 75 g
Buckwheat somen noodles	200 g	500 g
Romaine lettuce	¼	½
Celery, finely diced	50 g	125 g
Chopped onion (red)	50 g	125 g
Vinaigrette		
Olive oil	70 ml	170 ml
Sesame oil	35 ml	85 ml
Vegetable oil	35 ml	85 ml
Rice wine	2 tbsp	4 ½ tbsp
Lemon, juice of	½	1
Lime, juice of	1	2
Fresh ginger, chopped	2 tbsp	5 tbsp
Garlic, chopped	1 clove	3 cloves
Coriander leaves	1 tbsp	2 ½ tbsp
Sesame seeds (black)	2 tbsp	5 tbsp
Seasoning		

1 Prepare the vinaigrette by placing all the ingredients in a liquidiser, purée until smooth. Season to taste.

2 Season the swordfish fillets, brush with the vinaigrette. grill for 2–3 minutes on each side until cooked. Allow to cool.

3 Cook the noodles in boiling water, refresh and drain. Allow to cool.

4 Shred the lettuce finely, mix with the diced celery and finely chopped red onion. Season with the vinaigrette.

5 Serve by arranging the noodles in the centre of each plate.

6 Place the swordfish fillets on the noodles, season with vinaigrette.

7 Garnish with romaine lettuce. Freshly ground black pepper may be used to finish the dish.

Energy	Cals	Fat	Sat fat	Carb	Sugar	Protein	Fibre [*]
2599 kJ	623 kcal	42.6 g	6.1 g	40.3 g	2.7 g	21.2 g	2.5 g

[*] Using wheat pasta for buckwheat pasta

Healthy eating tips
- Keep added salt to a minimum.
- Adding less vinaigrette to the finished dish can reduce the fat content.

21 Roast fillet of sea bass with vanilla and fennel

	4 portions	10 portions
Sea bass fillets (approximately 160 g each, cut from a 2–3 kg fish) skin on, scaled and pin-boned	4	10
Seasoning		
Vegetable oil	50 ml	125 ml
Fennel		
Bulbs of baby fennel	8	20
Vegetable oil	50 ml	125 ml
Fish stock	500 ml	1 ¼ litres
Clove of garlic	1	3
Vanilla sauce		
Shallots, peeled and sliced	1	3
Fish stock	500 ml	1 ¼ litres
White wine	200 ml	500 ml
Vanilla pods	2	5
Butter	50 g	125 g
Chives, chopped	1 tsp	3 tsp
Tomato concassé	100 g	250 g

Energy	Cals	Fat	Sat fat	Carb	Sugar	Protein	Fibre	Sodium
2322 kJ	559 kcal	40 g	10.1 g	8.5	7.6 g	34 g	9.3 g	0.229 g

For the fennel:

1 Trim the fennel bulbs well, ensuring they are free from blemishes and root.

2 Heat the oil in a pan, place in the fennel and slightly brown.

3 Add the stock and garlic, bring to the boil and cook until tender.

For the sauce:

1 Heat a small amount of vegetable oil in a pan.

2 Add the shallots and cook without colour, add the stock, white wine and split vanilla and reduce by two-thirds.

3 Pass through a chinois and reserve for serving.

4 Add the butter and chopped chives.

To finish:

1 Pre-heat the oven to 180 °C.

2 Heat the oil in a non-stick pan and place the seasoned sea bass fillets in skin side down.

3 Cook for 2 minutes on the stove and then place in the oven for 3 minutes (depending on thickness) still with the skin side down.

4 Meanwhile, reheat the fennel and add the tomato concassé to the sauce.

5 Remove the sea bass from the oven and turn in the pan, finishing the flesh side for 30 seconds to 1 minute.

6 Lay the fennel in the centre of the plate, mask with sauce. Place the sea bass on top.

7 Serve immediately.

Note

This fish can also be steamed.

22 Baked cod with a herb crust

	4 portions	10 portions
Cod fillets, 100–150 g each	4	10
Herb mustard		
Fresh breadcrumbs	100 g	250 g
Butter, margarine or oil	100 g	250 g
Cheddar cheese, grated	100 g	250 g
Parsley, chopped	1 tsp	1 tbsp
Salt, pepper		

Energy	Cals	Fat	Sat fat	Carb	Sugar	Protein	Fibre	*
1882 kJ	452 kcal	30.8 g	18.7 g	12.7 g	0.8 g	31.7 g	0.4 g	

* Using mustard powder (1 tsp) for herb mustard

Professional tip

Add a little bit of beaten egg to the breadcrumb mixture; this will help bind the mixture together.

1 Place the prepared, washed and dried fish on a greased baking tray or ovenproof dish.

2 Combine the ingredients for the herb crust (the mustard, breadcrumbs, butter, margarine or oil, cheese, parsley and seasoning) and press evenly over the fish.

3 Bake in the oven at 180 °C for approximately 15–20 minutes until cooked and the crust is a light golden-brown.

Note

Serve either with lemon quarters or a suitable salsa (see Chapter 6) or sauce, e.g. tomato or egg.

Healthy eating tips
● Use a little sunflower oil when making the herb crust.
● Cheese is salty – no added salt is needed.
● Serve with a large portion of tomato or cucumber salsa and new potatoes.

23 Red mullet ceviche with organic leaves

	4 portions	10 portions
Shallots, finely diced	2	5
Olive oil	1 tbsp	3 tbsp
White wine vinegar	50 ml	125 ml
Fish stock	1 litre	2 ½ litres
Lemons, juice of	1	3
Cucumber, diced	2 tbsp	5 tbsp
Red mullet fillet spined and scaled (approximately 120 g each)	4	10
Organic salad leaf (5 varieties)	300 g	750 g
Vinaigrette	50 ml	125 ml
Caviar (optional)	50 g	125 g
Saffron dressing		
Water	10 ml	25 ml
Saffron	Pinch	Pinch
Vegetable oil	50 ml	125 ml
Vinegar	10 ml	25 ml

Energy	Cals	Fat	Sat fat	Carb	Sugar	Protein	Fibre	Sodium
1245 kJ	299 kcal	20.2 g	1.9 g	5	4.4 g	23.9 g	2.6 g	0.129 g

1 Bring the shallots, olive oil, white wine vinegar and fish stock to the boil. Add the lemon and cucumber and allow to cool at room temperature.

2 Place the red mullet in a container and cover with the liquid. Top with cling film to ensure all the air is kept out, capitalising on maximum curing. This will need to remain in the fridge for a minimum of 6 hours.

Dressing:

1 Add water and a pinch of saffron to a pan and bring to the boil.

2 Whisk in the vegetable oil and vinegar.

3 Season.

To finish:

1 Mix the dressed leaves lightly in vinaigrette.

2 Place the red mullet carefully on a plate with a little of the curing liquor, shallots and cucumber.

3 Top with the organic salad and finish with the saffron dressing and caviar (if using).

Note

A cured dish always tastes of the true ingredients. Using red mullet, as here, the flavours are bold and earthy, and paired with the saffron it makes a perfect summer starter.

24 Poached salmon

	1 portion
Whole or half darne	1
Court Bouillon	
Water	500 ml
Vinegar	2 tbsp
Carrot, sliced	1
Onion, sliced	½
Bay leaf	1
Celery	1
Peppercorns	1

Energy	Cals	Fat	Sat fat	Carb	Sugar	Protein	Fibre	Sodium
1284 kJ	309 kcal	20.6 g	5.5 g	0.3 g	0.3 g	30.4 g	0.1 g	0.1 g

1 Place the prepared and washed darnes of salmon in a court bouillon just below simmering for approximately 5 minutes.

2 Drain well and carefully remove the centre bone and outer skin. Ensure that the fish is cleaned of any cooked blood.

Note

Serve with a suitable sauce (e.g. hollandaise) or melted herb butter, and thinly sliced cucumber.

Depending on the size of the salmon, either a whole or half a darne would be served as a portion.

Video: Cutting fish into darnes http://bit.ly/1zOtrmN

25 Grilled salmon, pea soup and quails' eggs

	4 portions	10 portions
Soup		
Vegetable oil	50 ml	125 ml
Shallots, peeled and sliced	2	5
Garlic cloves, crushed	1	3
Raw potato, chopped	200 g	500 g
Peas	600 g	1.5 kg
Milk	500 ml	1.5 litres
Stem of mint	1	3
Salmon		
Salmon fillet	4 × 150 g	10 × 150 g
Plain flour	25 g	60 g
Olive oil	4 tbsp	9 tbsp
To finish		
Spinach, washed	200 g	500 g
Peas, cooked and crushed	600 g	1.5 kg
Butter	50 g	125 g
Seasoning		
Quails' eggs, lightly poached	8	20
First press olive oil		
Fresh herbs		

Energy	Cals	Fat	Sat fat	Carb	Sugar	Protein	Fibre
5032 kJ	1213 kcal	83.7 g	29.3 g	53.4 g	13.2 g	64.9 g	15.9 g

Soup:

1 Heat the oil and add the shallots and garlic, cook without colour for 2 minutes.

2 Then add the potato and cook for a further 2 minutes.

3 Add the peas and milk, bring to the boil and remove from the heat.

4 Add the mint sprig and allow to infuse for 3-4 minutes. Remove and then blitz the soup in a processor.

5 Pass through a strainer and retain.

Salmon:

1 Heat a lower-heat grill, ensuring the bars are clean.

2 Lightly oil the bars and then dust the salmon fillet in the flour.

3 Carefully place the salmon fillet on the grill and score.

4 Once sealed rotate the fish 45 degrees and mark, creating a diamond shape.

5 After 2–3 minutes turn the salmon over, taking care not to break the flesh.

6 After 2 minutes cooking on the other side check if cooked by gently pushing your index finger into the centre – the fish should still have a little structure.

To finish:

1 Wilt the spinach in a hot pan, add the peas and butter and season.

2 Place the poached eggs in the soup and quickly re-heat.

3 Place a mound of spinach and peas in the centre of a bowl with the salmon on top and 2 quails' eggs per bowl.

4 Finish the dish with a drizzle of fine olive oil and fresh herbs.

Note

This is a suitable summer dish, light and very seasonal. As an alternative, replace the salmon with salt cod.

26 Sardines with tapenade

	4 portions	10 portions
Sardines	8–12	20–30
For the tapenade		
Kalamata olives	20	50
Capers	1 tbsp	2 ½ tbsp
Lemon juice	1 tsp	2 ½ tsp
Olive oil	2 tsp	5 tsp
Anchovy paste (optional)	½ tsp	1¼ tsp
Freshly ground black pepper		

Energy	Cals	Fat	Sat fat	Carb	Sugar	Protein	Fibre	Sodium
3167 kJ	757 kcal	44.0g	12.4g	0.0g	0.0g	90.5g	0.8g	1.0g

1 Finely chop the olives and capers. Add the lemon juice, olive oil, anchovy paste and black pepper. Mix well.

2 Allow 2–3 sardines per portion. Clean the sardines and grill them on both sides, either on an open flame grill or under the salamander.

3 When cooked, smear the tapenade on top. The tapenade can be heated slightly before spreading.

Variations

A little chopped basil and a crushed chopped clove of garlic may also be added to the tapenade.

1 Raw sardines

2 Grilled sardines

3 Smear the sardines with tapenade

27 Fish kebabs

Fish kebabs or brochettes are best made using a firm fish (e.g. salmon, tuna, marlin, turbot). The fish (free from skin and bone) is cut into cubes and can be:

- simply seasoned with salt and pepper; or
- lightly rolled in herbs (e.g. cumin seeds and mustard); or
- placed in a simple marinade (e.g. olive oil, lemon juice and chopped parsley) for 30 minutes.

Other ingredients to be threaded on the skewers can be halves of small, par-boiled new potatoes, cherry tomatoes and mushrooms. The kebabs are lightly brushed with oil and cooked on a fierce grill or barbecue. Scallops are also suitable for kebabs (see page 361).

Energy	Cals	Fat	Sat fat	Carb	Sugar	Protein	Fibre	Sodium *
550kJ	132kcal	7.9g	1.5g	0.5	0.5g	14.6g	0.2g	0.034g

* Per kebab made with salmon and 2 cherry tomatoes

Professional tip

Brushing the kebabs with oil stops them from sticking to the grill.

28 Fish kedgeree (*cadgery de poisson*)

	4 portions	10 portions
Fish (usually smoked haddock or fresh salmon)	400g	1kg
Milk for poaching		
Rice pilaff (see page 421)	200g	500g
Eggs, hard-boiled	2	5
Butter	50g	125g
Salt, pepper		
Chives, chopped	1 tsp	2 tsp
Curry sauce, to serve	250ml	625ml

Energy	Cals	Fat	Sat fat	Carb	Sugar	Protein	Fibre *
1974kJ	472kcal	28.2g	15.3g	29.3g	4.7g	25.7g	1.2g

* Using smoked haddock

1 Poach the fish in milk. Remove all skin and bone. Flake the fish.

2 Cook the rice pilaff. Cut the eggs into dice.

3 Combine the eggs, fish and rice and heat in the butter. Correct the seasoning and add the chives.

Note

Serve hot with a sauceboat of curry sauce.

This dish is traditionally served for breakfast, lunch or supper. The fish used should be named on the menu (e.g. salmon kedgeree).

Healthy eating tips

- Reduce the amount of butter used to heat the rice, fish and eggs.
- Garnish with grilled tomatoes and serve with bread or toast.

Removing the skin from the poached fish   Flaking the fish   Dicing the hard-boiled eggs

29 Fish pie

	4 portions	10 portions
Béchamel (thin) (see page 130)	250 ml	625 ml
Cooked fish (free from skin and bone)	200 g	500 g
Mushrooms, cooked and diced	50 g	125 g
Egg, hard-boiled and chopped	1	3
Parsley, chopped		
Salt, pepper		
Potatoes, mashed or duchess	200 g	500 g
Eggwash or milk, to finish		

Energy	Cals	Fat	Sat fat	Carb	Sugar	Protein	Fibre
879 kJ	209 kcal	12.0 g	5.3 g	11.9 g	3.2 g	14.1 g	0.9 g

1 Bring the béchamel to the boil.

2 Add the fish, mushrooms, egg and parsley. Correct the seasoning.

3 Place in a buttered pie dish.

4 Carefully spread or pipe the potato on top. Brush with eggwash or milk.

5 Brown in a hot oven and use a food probe to check temperature is 75 °C.

Cooking the fish, mushrooms and egg in the béchamel   Piping mashed potato over the top before baking

Healthy eating tips
- Keep the added salt to a minimum.
- This is a healthy main course dish, particularly when served with plenty of vegetables.

Variation

Many variations can be made to this recipe with the addition of:
- prawns or shrimps
- herbs such as dill, tarragon or fennel
- raw fish poached in white wine, the cooking liquor strained off, double cream added in place of béchamel and reduced to a light consistency.

30 Smoked mackerel mousse

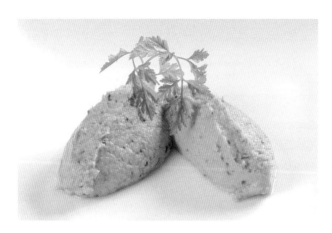

1 Ensure that the mackerel is completely free from skin and bones.
2 Liquidise with the required seasoning.
3 Three-quarter whip the cream.
4 Remove mackerel from liquidiser and fold into the cream. Correct the seasoning.

Note

Serve in individual dishes accompanied with hot toast.

Variation

This recipe can be used with smoked trout or smoked salmon trimmings.

It can also be used for fresh salmon, in which case 50 g of cucumber can be incorporated with the selected seasoning.

Healthy eating tips
- Serve with plenty of salad vegetables and bread or toast (optional butter or spread).
- Use the minimum amount of salt.

	4 portions	10 portions
Smoked mackerel, free from bone and skin	200 g	500 g
Optional seasoning: pepper, chopped parsley, fennel or chervil, 1 tbsp tomato ketchup, two ripe tomatoes free from skin and pips		
Double cream (or non-dairy cream)	90 ml	250 ml

Energy	Cals	Fat	Sat fat	Carb	Sugar	Protein	Fibre	*
1192 kJ	289 kcal	27.5 g	10.7 g	0.4 g	0.4 g	9.8 g	0.0 g	

* Using double cream

31 Soused herring or mackerel

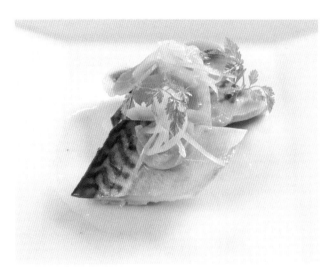

	4 portions	10 portions
Herrings or mackerel	2	5
Salt, pepper		
Button onions	25 g	60 g
Carrots, peeled and fluted	25 g	60 g
Bay leaf	½	1 ½
Peppercorns	6	12
Thyme	1 sprig	2 sprigs
Vinegar	60 ml	150 ml

Energy	Cals	Fat	Sat fat	Carb	Sugar	Protein	Fibre *
2419 kJ	576 kcal	44.5 g	9.4 g	3.0 g	3.0 g	41.0 g	1.1 g

* For 4 portions

1 Clean, scale and fillet the fish.
2 Wash the fillets well and season with salt and pepper.
3 Roll up with the skin outside. Place in an earthenware dish.
4 Peel and wash the onion. Cut the onion and carrots into neat, thin rings.
5 Blanch for 2–3 minutes.
6 Add to the fish with the remainder of the ingredients.

7 Cover with greaseproof paper and cook in a moderate oven for 15–20 minutes.
8 Allow to cool, place in a dish with the onion and carrot.
9 Garnish with picked parsley, dill or chives.

Healthy eating tips
● Serve with plenty of salad vegetables and bread or toast (optional butter or spread).
● Keep added salt to a minimum.

32 Haddock and smoked salmon terrine

	4 portions	10 portions
Smoked salmon	140 g	350 g
Haddock, halibut or Arctic bass fillets, skinned	320 g	800 g
Salt, pepper		
Eggs, lightly beaten	1	2
Crème fraiche	40 ml	105 ml
Capers	3 tbsp	7 tbsp
Green or pink peppercorns	1 tbsp	2 tbsp

Energy	Cals	Fat	Sat fat	Carb	Sugar	Protein	Fibre
563 kJ	133 kcal	3.4 g	0.7 g	0.1 g	0.1 g	25.7 g	0.1 g

1 Grease a 1 litre loaf tin with oil; alternatively, line with cling film.

2 Line the tin with thin slices of smoked salmon. Let the ends overhang the mould. Reserve the remaining salmon until needed.

3 Cut two long slices of haddock the length of the tin and set aside.

4 Cut the rest of the haddock into small pieces. Season all the haddock with salt and pepper.

5 In a suitable basin, combine the eggs, crème fraiche, capers, and green or pink peppercorns. Add the pieces of haddock.

6 Spoon the mixture into the mould until one-third full. Smooth with a spatula.

7 Wrap the long haddock fillets in the reserved smoked salmon. Lay them on top of the layer of the fish mixture in the terrine.

8 Fill with the remainder of the haddock and crème fraiche mixture.

9 Smooth the surface and fold over the overhanging pieces of smoked salmon.

10 Cover with tin foil, secure well.

11 Cook in a water bath (bain-marie) of boiling water. Place in the oven at 200 °C for approximately 45 minutes, until set.

12 Remove from oven and bain-marie. Allow to cool. Do not remove foil cover.

13 Place heavy weights on top and leave in refrigerator for 24 hours.

14 When ready to serve, remove the weights and foil. Remove from mould.

Note

Cut into thick slices, serve on suitable plates with a dill mayonnaise and garnished with salad leaves and fresh dill.

Professional tip

Line the tin carefully so that the finished terrine will look attractive.

Healthy eating tips
- Season with the minimum amount of salt.
- Offer the customer the mayonnaise separately.
- Serve with a warm bread or rolls (butter optional).

33 Salmon fishcakes

Energy	Cals	Fat	Sat fat	Carb	Sugar	Protein	Fibre
1821 kJ	438 kcal	30.2 g	13.6 g	18.0 g	1.5 g	24.5 g	1.6 g

	4 portions	10 portions
Salmon fillet – skinned and boneless	400 g	1 kg
Cooked mashed potato (make sure this is fairly dry)	225 g	560 g
Spring onions	3	8
Flat leaf parsley	10 g	25 g
Dill	Sprig	Sprig
Butter	50 g	125 g
Juice of lemon	1	2
Crème fraiche	1 tbsp	2½ tbsp
Thai fish sauce (*nam pla*) – optional	Few drops	1 tsp
Eggs	1	2
Pané		
Plain flour, seasoned		
Eggs		
Breadcrumbs		

1 Place the salmon in an oiled roasting tin, season with salt and pepper, dot with butter and squeeze the lemon juice over.

2 Bake for approximately 7 minutes at 200 °C.

3 Allow the salmon to cool a little then flake into bite sized pieces.

4 Chop the spring onions and herbs.

5 Add the salmon to the potato, herbs, spring onion, beaten egg and crème fraiche. Add a little *nam pla* if using and season.

6 Form into neat, even-sized cake shapes (a ring mould could be used), place on a tray lined with cling film and chill thoroughly for several hours.

7 Coat with seasoned flour, egg and breadcrumbs (pané), chill well again or the formed cakes can be frozen.

8 Cook in a deep fryer as required, drain on kitchen paper.

Note

Serve with a suitable sauce or salsa and/or mixed salad leaves.

34 Baked salmon salad with sea vegetables

	4 portions	10 portions
Fillet of salmon	4 × 150 g	10 × 150 g
Lime	2	5
Olive oil	2 tbsp	5 tbsp
Chopped basil leaves	1 tbsp	4 tbsp
Mayonnaise	4 tbsp	7 tbsp
Stale bread diced	100 g	250 g
Broad beans	200 g	500 g
Sea kale	100 g	250 g
Samphire	100 g	250 g
Salad leaves, rocket		
Lime wedges	4	10

1 Place the salmon on a suitable tray (on parchment paper or a non-stick tray), season with salt and pepper, sprinkle with olive oil and squeeze the juice of a lime on top.

2 Cover with foil and gently bake in a pre-heated oven at 200 °C for approximately 15 minutes.

3 Place the diced bread in a food processor with 2 tablespoons olive oil. Blitz until the bread becomes breadcrumbs

4 Place on a tray and bake the crumbs until golden brown.

5 Add the basil leaves to the mayonnaise; add a squeeze of lime juice.

6 Blanch the broad beans and sea kale in boiling water for 3–4 minutes.

7 Refresh in cold water and drain.

8 Place in a bowl, sprinkle with olive oil, lime juice and season.

9 Dress the cooked salmon on a suitable plate, mask with the basil mayonnaise and sprinkle with breadcrumbs.

10 Garnish with the broad beans, sea kale and sapphire, finish with the salad leaves and lime wedges.

Variations

As an alternative to breadcrumbs, use roasted flaked almonds.

Energy	Cals	Fat	Sat fat	Carb	Sugar	Protein	Fibre	Sodium *
2548 kJ	613 kcal	45 g	6.9 g	18.3 g	1.8 g	37.5 g	2.8 g	0.77 g

*With breadcrumbs as topping. With almonds values are as follows: energy: 2940 kJ, cals: 709 kcal 58 g, fat: 8.1 g, sat fat: 7.7 g, carb: 2.2 g sugar: 40 g, protein: 5.5 g, fibre: 0.64 g

35 Scallops with caramelised cauliflower

	4 portions	10 portions
Raisins	100 g	250 g
Capers	100 g	250 g
Water	180 ml	450 ml
Sherry vinegar	1 tbsp	2 tbsp
Grated nutmeg		
Salt and cayenne pepper		
Butter	30 g	75 g
Head of cauliflower, sliced into ½ cm-thick pieces	½	1
Large hand-dived scallops (roe removed)	12	30

Energy	Cals	Fat	Sat fat	Carb	Sugar	Protein	Fibre	Sodium
968 kJ	230 kcal	7.9 g	4.3 g	21.2	18.5 g	19.7 g	1.9 g	0.198 g

1 In a small saucepan, cook the raisins and capers in the water until the raisins are plump – about 5 minutes.

2 Pour mixture into blender and add the vinegar, nutmeg, salt and pepper, blend just until smooth.

3 Set sauce aside.

4 In a sauté pan, heat butter and cook the cauliflower until golden on both sides. To prevent cauliflower from burning, if necessary, add about 1 tablespoon of water to pan during cooking. Set cauliflower aside.

5 In a separate pan, sauté the scallops in a little butter, about 1 minute on each side. To serve, place 3 scallops on each plate, top with cauliflower and finish with the caper-raisin emulsion.

Professional tip

When using scallops, always use hand-dived scallops as your first choice, as dredged scallops are sometimes unethically sourced. You will pay a little more for the hand-dived variety but the difference is certainly worth it.

Be careful not to overcook the scallops, as they will become tough.

36 Oysters in their own shell

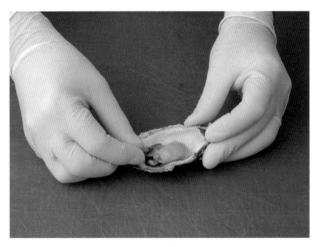

	4 portions
Rock or native oysters	24
Lemon	1
To accompany:	
Brown bread and butter	
Tabasco or chilli sauce	

Energy	Cals	Fat	Sat fat	Carb	Sugar	Protein	Fibre	Sodium
192 kJ	45 kcal	0.9 g	0.2 g	2.7 g	1 g	6.8 g	0.4 g	0.31 g

1 Select only those oysters that are tightly shut and have a fresh smell (category A is best, which means the waters they have grown in are clean).

2 To open an oyster, only the point of the oyster knife is used. Hold the oyster with a thick oven cloth to protect your hand.

3 With the oyster in the palm of your hand, push the point of the knife about 1 cm deep into the 'hinge' between the 'lid' and the body of the oyster.

4 Once the lid has been penetrated, push down. The lid should pop open. Lift up the top shell, cutting the muscle attached to it.

5 Remove any splintered shell from the flesh and solid shell.

6 Return each oyster to its shell and serve on a bed of crushed ice with chilli sauce, brown bread and lemon.

Note

Make sure the oysters have been grown in or fished from clean waters, and take note of the famous rule only to use them when there is an 'r' in the month, although rock oysters are available throughout the year.

37 Oyster tempura

The recipe for tempura batter is on page 237.

1 Open the fresh oysters.

2 Place each oyster on a tray on absorbent kitchen paper.

3 Lightly sprinkle with finely chopped herbs, parsley, basil and chives.

4 Pass each oyster through seasoned flour.

5 Dip in tempura batter and fry in hot deep oil at 180 °C until golden brown.

6 Remove from the oil and drain well.

Note

Serve as a garnish or as a hot hors d'oeuvre with a suitable dip, such as tomato chilli and lemon and garlic mayonnaise.

Energy	Cals	Fat	Sat fat	Carb	Sugar	Protein	Fibre	Sodium *
858kJ	205kcal	12.2g	1.6g	10.8	0.1g	13.7g	0.4g	0.579g

* Per 2 oysters

Professional tip

Make sure the oil is at the right temperature. Cook the oysters quickly until crisp and golden brown.

38 Poached langoustines with aioli dip

	4 portions	10 portions
Raw langoustine tails, large (or king or tiger prawns)	36	90
Court bouillon		
Carrots	2	5
Fennel bulbs	1	3
Garlic cloves	2	5
Water	1.4 litres	3.5 litres
White wine	290 ml	725 ml
A few fresh parsley and chervil stalks		
White peppercorns, crushed	3	7
Aioli		
Sweet potato (about 250 g each), orange flesh	1	2 ½
Mayonnaise	3 tbsp	7 ½ tbsp
Pinches saffron strands, soaked in a little water	2	5
Eggs, boiled and yolks removed and reserved	3	7
Crushed garlic	½ tsp	1 ½ tsp
A little olive oil		
Salt and pepper		
Lemon, juice of	½	1

Energy	Cals	Fat	Sat fat	Carb	Sugar	Protein	Fibre	Sodium
2041 kJ	489 kcal	24.9 g	4.4 g	17.5	7.1 g	38.1 g	4.1 g	0.594 g

Bouillon:

1 Place vegetables in pan and cover with water.

2 Gently bring to the boil and simmer for 5–10 minutes.

3 Add the white wine, parsley, chervil stalks and crushed peppercorns.

4 Cook for a further 10 minutes then leave to stand until cool.

5 Strain out the vegetables and chill the liquid.

Aioli:

1 Pre-heat the oven to 200 °C. Bake the sweet potato for about 35–45 minutes or until tender. Peel off the skin and gently crush the flesh.

2 Place sweet potato flesh in a liquidiser, add the mayonnaise, saffron, egg yolks and garlic and blend.

3 Add olive oil to moisten, season and finish with a squeeze of lemon juice.

4 Remove entrails from langoustines by taking the middle segment or tail shell between thumb and forefinger, then twist it and pull.

5 Plunge the langoustines into the simmering court bouillon for 30–40 seconds. Remove and leave to cool naturally. Serve with the aioli.

Professional tip

Allow the bouillon to simmer gently and bring out the flavours.

Be careful not to overcook the langoustines, as they will become tough.

Note

Langoustines are normally bought 'dipped'. This means they have already been blanched; they are not alive.

39 Crab cakes with rocket salad and lemon dressing

	4 portions	10 portions
Crab cakes		
Shallots, finely chopped	25 g	60 g
Spring onions, finely chopped	4	10
Fish/shellfish glaze	75 ml	185 ml
Crab meat	400 g	1 kg
Mayonnaise	75 g	185 g
Lemons, juice of	1	3
Plum tomatoes skinned, cut into concassé	2	5
Wholegrain mustard	1 tsp	3 tsp
Seasoning		
Fresh white breadcrumbs	200 g	500 g
Eggs, beaten with 100 ml of milk	2	5
Salad and lemon dressing		
Vegetable oil	170 ml	425 ml
White wine vinegar	25 ml	60 ml
Lemons, juice of	1	3
Seasoning		
Rocket, washed and picked	250 g	625 g
Parmesan, shaved	100 g	250 g

Crab cakes:

1 Mix the shallots, spring onions and the fish glaze with the hand-picked crab meat.

2 Add the mayonnaise, lemon juice, tomato concassé and mustard, check and adjust the seasoning.

3 Allow to rest for 30 minutes in the refrigerator.

4 Scale into 80–90 g balls and shape into discs 1½ cm high, place in the freezer for 30 minutes to harden.

5 When firm to the touch, coat in breadcrumbs using the flour, egg and breadcrumbs.

6 Allow to rest for a further 30 minutes.

7 Heat a little oil in a non-stick pan, carefully place the cakes in and cook on each side until golden brown.

For the salad and dressing:

1 Combine the oil, vinegar and lemon juice together, check the seasoning.

2 Place the rocket and Parmesan in a large bowl and add a little dressing, just to coat.

3 Place this in the centre of each plate, top with the crab cakes and serve.

Energy	Cals	Fat	Sat fat	Carb	Sugar	Protein	Fibre
3002 kJ	719 kcal	43.9 g	10.5 g	41.9 g	4.4 g	41.4 g	4.1 g

Professional tip

Any excess crab meat can be used up in this recipe – a quick, classic dish. The crab can be exchanged for salmon or most fresh fish trimmings.

40 Mussels in white wine sauce (*moules marinière*)

	4 portions	10 portions
Shallots, chopped	50 g	125 g
Parsley, chopped	1 tbsp	2 tbsp
White wine	60 ml	150 ml
Strong fish stock	200 ml	500 ml
Mussels	2 kg	5 kg
Butter	25 g	60 g
Flour	25 g	60 g
Seasoning		

Energy	Cals	Fat	Sat fat	Carb	Sugar	Protein	Fibre	Sodium
1900 kJ	452 kcal	14.3 g	5.3 g	18.1 g	0.9 g	61.4 g	0.6 g	1.5 g

1 Take a thick-bottomed pan and add the shallots, parsley, wine, fish stock and the cleaned mussels.

2 Cover with a tight-fitting lid and cook over a high heat until the shells open.

3 Drain off all the cooking liquor in a colander set over a clean bowl to retain the cooking juices.

4 Carefully check the mussels and discard any that have not opened.

5 Place in a dish and cover to keep warm.

6 Make a roux from the flour and butter; pour over the cooking liquor, ensuring it is free from sand and stirring continuously to avoid lumps.

7 Correct the seasoning and garnish with more chopped parsley.

8 Pour over the mussels and serve.

Variation

For an eastern influence, why not add a little red chilli and replace the parsley with coriander?

41 Scallop ceviche with organic leaves

	4 portions	10 portions
Large scallops (roe removed)	12	30
Limes, juice of	2	5
Oranges, juice of	1	3
Lemons, grated rind	1	3
Limes, grated rind	1	3
Orange, grated rind	1	1
Salt and freshly cracked pepper to taste		
Orange liqueur	2 tbsp	5 tbsp
Vinaigrette	50 ml	125 ml
Organic leaves (5 varieties)	500 g	1 ¼ kg

Energy	Cals	Fat	Sat fat	Carb	Sugar	Protein	Fibre	Sodium
631 kJ	149 kcal	4.6 g	0.9 g	7.5	3.6 g	17.6 g	0g	0.343 g

1 Slice the raw scallops thinly (laterally into 3) and lay on a clean non-reactive tray.

2 Mix all the other ingredients (except the organic leaves) and pour evenly over the scallops.

3 Leave covered in the refrigerator overnight. (The acid in the citrus juice will cure the scallops.)

4 To serve, arrange the scallops in a circle form (9 slices), dress the leaves and arrange in the centre of the scallops.

5 Drizzle any excess cure/dressing around the scallops and serve.

Note

Only the freshest scallops can be used for this recipe as the slightest taint of age will dominate and spoil the dish. Some food safety experts discourage the consumption of uncooked shellfish.

Do not serve to vulnerable groups (see page 68).

42 Scallops and bacon

	4 portions	10 portions
Large scallops, shelled, roe and skirt removed, washed	12	30
Pancetta bacon rashers (rind off)	12	30
Olive oil	50 ml	125 ml
Lemon	1	2
Asparagus sticks, peeled, blanched for 1 minute and refreshed	16	40
Seasoning		

Energy	Cals	Fat	Sat fat	Carb	Sugar	Protein	Fibre	Sodium
1705 kJ	410 kcal	26.8 g	6.9 g	5.9 g	28 g	36.4 g	2.3 g	1.3 g

1 Wrap the scallops in the pancetta, pin with a cocktail stick and season (be mindful that the pancetta is salty).

2 Heat the oil in a non-stick pan, place the scallops in and cook until golden-brown. Squeeze the lemon over the scallops and allow the juice to evaporate slightly.

3 Remove from the pan and retain with all the pan juices.

4 Return the pan to the heat and add the asparagus, cooking for a further 2 minutes.

5 To serve, divide the asparagus onto plates. Top with the scallops, pour over the pan juices and serve.

43 Prawns with chilli and garlic

	4 portions	10 portions
Clove of garlic, crushed	1	3
Lime, juice of	1	2
Lemon, juice of	½	1
Mild red chillies, deseeded and finely chopped	2	5
Olive oil	1 tbsp	3 tbsp
Honey	1 tbsp	3 tbsp
Extra-large prawns, raw, shells on, heads removed	32	80
Black pepper		
To serve:		
Salsa verde (see page 153)	100 ml	250 ml
Garlic bread	4 slices	10 slices
Green salad		

Energy	Cals	Fat	Sat fat	Carb	Sugar	Protein	Fibre	Sodium
728 kJ	173 kcal	3.8 g	0.6 g	6.6 g	6.3 g	28.6 g	0.1 g	0.3 g

1 In a shallow dish, mix together the garlic, lime juice, lemon juice, chillies, olive oil and honey.

2 Make an incision (do not cut all the way through – leave the prawn intact) in the back of each prawn and remove the entrails. Wash and dry well.

3 Add the prawns to the oil/chilli mix, season with black pepper and marinate in the fridge for 30 minutes.

4 Meanwhile, prepare the green salad, salsa verde and garlic bread.

5 Remove the prawns from the marinade and heat a small amount of oil in a non-stick frying pan.

6 Place the prawns in the pan and cook until pink and cooked through, basting with any leftover marinade while cooking.

7 To serve, place warm garlic bread on plates and pile up the prawns on top, allowing the cooking juices to run into the bread. Drizzle with salsa verde and serve with a green salad.

44 Seafood stir-fry

	4 portions	10 portions
Small asparagus spears	100 g	250 g
Sunflower or groundnut oil	1 tbsp	2 ½ tbsp
Fresh ginger, grated	1 tsp	2 ½ tbsp
Leeks, cut into julienne	100 g	250 g
Carrots, cut into julienne	100 g	250 g
Baby sweetcorn	100 g	250 g
Light soy sauce	2 tbsp	5 tbsp
Oyster sauce	1 tbsp	2 ½ tbsp
Clear honey	1 tsp	2 ½ tbsp
Cooked assorted shellfish, e.g. prawns, mussels, scallops	400 g	1 kg
Garnish		
Large cooked prawns	4	10
Fresh chives	25 g	62 g

Energy	Cals	Fat	Sat fat	Carb	Sugar	Protein	Fibre
724 kJ	172 kcal	4.9 g	0.8 g	9.1 g	4.9 g	23.2 g	2.1 g

1 Blanch the asparagus for 2 minutes in boiling water, refresh then drain.

2 Heat the oil in a wok, add the ginger, leek, carrots and sweetcorn, stir-fry for 3 minutes without colour.

3 Add the soy sauce, oyster sauce and honey. Stir.

4 Stir in the cooked shellfish and continue to stir-fry for 2–3 minutes until the vegetables are just tender and the shellfish is thoroughly heated through.

5 Add the blanched asparagus and stir-fry for another 1 minute.

6 Serve with fresh cooked noodles garnished with large fresh prawns and chopped chives.

Professional tip

If you blanch the vegetables before stir-frying them, they will keep their colour and flavour and can be fried more quickly.

Healthy eating tips
- No added salt is needed – soy sauce is high in sodium.
- Increasing the ratio of vegetables to seafood will improve the 'balance' of this dish.

1 Ingredients for seafood stir-fry

2 Fry the ginger and vegetables

3 Combine all the ingredients and continue to stir-fry

45 Seafood in puff pastry (*bouchées de fruits de mer*)

	4 portions	10 portions
Button mushrooms	50 g	125 g
butter	25 g	60 g
Lemon, juice of	¼	½
Cooked lobster, prawns, shrimps, mussels, scallops	200 g	500 g
White wine sauce (see page 135)	125 ml	300 ml
Chopped parsley		
Salt, pepper		
Puff pastry *bouchée* cases	4	10
Picked parsley, to garnish		

Energy	Cals	Fat	Sat fat	Carb	Sugar	Protein	Fibre *
1327 kJ	316 kcal	17.6 g	3.1 g	28.9 g	1.1 g	12.2 g	1.2 g

* Fried in peanut oil

1 Peel and wash the mushrooms, cut into neat dice.

2 Cook in butter with the lemon juice.

3 Add the cooked shellfish (mussels, prawns, shrimps left whole, the scallops and lobster cut into dice).

4 Cover the pan with a lid and heat through slowly for 3–4 minutes.

5 Add the white wine sauce and chopped parsley, and correct the seasoning.

6 Meanwhile warm the *bouchées* in the oven or hot plate.

7 Fill the *bouchées* with the mixture and place the lids on top.

8 Serve garnished with picked parsley.

Note

Vol-au-vents can be prepared and cooked in the same way as bouchées.

Healthy eating tips

● The white wine sauce is seasoned, so added salt is not required.
● Serve with a salad garnish.

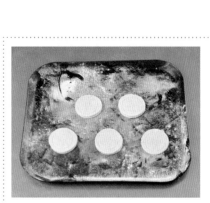

1 Raw puff pastry *bouchées*, before baking

2 Combine the shellfish with the mushrooms

3 Fill the pastry cases

1 This chapter will help you to:
- prepare and cook rice, pasta, grains and eggs, including:
- using tools and equipment correctly, in a safe and hygienic way
- using the correct type and amount of rice, pasta, grains or eggs
- preparing, cooking, assembling, finishing and evaluating the dish.

2 have the knowledge to:
- identify types of rice, pasta, grains and eggs, and their uses
- apply preparation methods, cooking principles and suitable methods of cookery, and identify adjustments needed
- check and finishes dishes
- identify sauces and accompaniments
- hold, cool and store dishes correctly.

Recipes included in this chapter

Rice

Rice is a type of grain. It is one of the world's most important crops, being the main food crop for about half the world's population. A hot, wet atmosphere is required to grow rice, and therefore it is grown mainly in India, the Far East, South America, Italy and the southern states of the USA. In order to grow, rice needs more water than any other cereal crop.

There are around 250 different varieties of rice. Rice is used in a variety of dishes, both starters and main courses. Rice introduces texture, flavour and carbohydrate content to dishes. The resulting texture and flavour depends on the cooking method and temperature.

Types of rice

Long grain

Long-grain rice is a narrow, pointed grain that has had the full bran and most of the germ removed so that it is less fibrous than brown rice. Because of its firm structure (which helps to keep the grains separate when cooked) it is suitable for plain boiling and savoury dishes such as kedgeree and curry.

Short grain

Short-grain rice is a short, rounded grain with a soft texture. It is suitable for sweet dishes and risotto, and is often used in dessert cooking.

Brown rice

This is any rice that has had the outer covering removed, but retains its bran. As a result, it is more nutritious and contains more fibre. It takes longer to cook than long-grain rice. The nutty flavour of brown rice lends itself to some recipes, but does not substitute well in traditional dishes such as paella, risotto or puddings. Brown rice can be used for any other rice recipes, but allow extra cooking time to soften the grain (use one part grain to two parts water for 35–40 minutes).

Arborio rice (risotto rice)

Arborio rice is a medium- to long-grain rice and is used in risottos because it can absorb a good deal of cooking liquid without becoming too soft.

▲ Long-grain rice

▲ Short-grain rice

▲ Brown rice

▲ Arborio rice

Key terms

Long-grain rice: a narrow, pointed grain that has had the full bran and most of the germ removed. Used for plain boiling and in savoury dishes.

Short-grain rice: a short, rounded grain with a soft texture. Suitable for sweet dishes and risotto.

Brown rice: any rice that has had the outer covering removed, retaining its bran.

Other types of rice

Many other types of rice are now available, which can add different colours and textures to dishes. Some of these are described below.

- **Basmati**: a narrow, long-grain rice with a distinctive flavour, suitable for serving with Indian dishes. Basmati rice needs to be soaked before being cooked to remove excess starch.
- **Wholegrain rice**: the whole unprocessed grain of the rice.
- **Wild rice**: this is not, in fact, rice but the seed of an aquatic grass. Difficulty in harvesting makes it expensive, but the colour (a purplish black) and its subtle nutty flavour make it a good base for a special dish or rice salad. It can be economically mixed with other types of rice (but may need pre-cooking as it takes 45–50 minutes to cook).
- **Red rice**: an unmilled, short-grain rice from the Camargue in France, with a brownish-red colour and a nutty flavour. It is slightly sticky when cooked and particularly good in salads.
- **Pre-cooked instant rice**: par-boiled, ready cooked and boil-in-the-bag rice are similar.
- **Ground rice**: used for milk puddings.
- **Easy-cook rice**: traditional rice is milled direct from the field; this rice is steamed under pressure before it is milled. This process hardens the grain and reduces the possibility of overcooking. The raw rice is golden in colour and turns white during cooking. It is used in a variety of dishes the same as other types of rice.
- **Aromatic rice**: speciality rice which has a distinct flavour and aroma. Their quality and flavour can differ from one year to the next, based on the harvest and climate change. Examples include jasmine rice (a soft, sticky rice often used when making sushi) and American aromatic rice such as Japonica.

Other rice products

Rice is used to produce many different rice products.

- **Rice flakes** (brown and white) – can be added to muesli or made into a milk pudding or porridge.
- **Rice flour** – used for thickening cream soups.
- **Rice paper** – edible paper made from milled rice; used in pastry work for nougat and macaroons, etc.
- **Rice wine** – made from fermented wine. Sake is the most famous rice wine and is drunk extensively in

Japan. Other examples include Mirin (a sweet rice wine used in rice dishes) and Shaoxing (a Chinese rice wine).

- **Rice cakes** – best known in Japan and the countries of the Pacific Rim, where rice production is the economic staple and the grain is the basis for many meals and foods.
- **Rice noodles** – made from rice flour, which is blended with water and either rolled out, cut or extruded. They are usually dried and come in a range of shapes and sizes similar to pasta shapes. Fresh noodles are often cut into wide ribbons and used in soups and stir fries. The noodles cook so that they are slightly transparent; they tend to be chewy and slightly resilient. Sometimes ingredients such as mung bean flour may be added to them to change their consistency and appearance. Types of rice noodles include laska noodles, rice fluke noodles, rice sticks and river rice noodles.
- **Rice vermicelli** – a variety of types are available throughout Asia and are used in soups, salads and spring rolls.

Preparing rice

Washing and soaking

Most rice bought today does not require washing. However, the washing and soaking of rice removes any excess starch, which tends to cloud the cooking liquid. Washing impure rice removes debris, dirt and impurities.

Using correct amounts of liquid

Rice absorbs liquid easily. Table 11.1 gives a guide on liquid absorption, to help you to achieve the correct texture and overall result for each type of rice dish.

Table 11.1 Proportions of liquid for cooking different types of rice

Type of rice	Proportion of liquid to rice
Boiling	3–4 times liquid to rice
Pilaff (braised)	2:1 liquid to rice
Risotto	3:1 liquid to rice
Paella	4:1 liquid to rice
Sushi	1:5 liquid to rice
Wild rice	4:1 liquid to rice

As the grains cook, starch is released which naturally thickens the liquid. This is particularly important when making risotto and sushi.

Liquids used for cooking rice include white stock, milk, or a combination of half white stock and half white wine.

Cooking rice

Rice grains are porous and absorb water easily. Rice should be cooked so that it is **al dente** (to the bite), except if the rice is being moulded.

Rice can be cooked using a number of different cooking methods, including:

- boiling
- steaming
- frying
- stewing
- braising
- microwaving.

When boiling rice, cook in a large quantity of water and drain well.

> **Key term**
>
> **Al dente**: cooked firm, to the bite.

Storing and holding rice

Uncooked rice can be stored on the shelf in a tightly sealed container. The shelf life of brown rice is shorter than that of white rice because the bran layers contain oil that can become rancid. Refrigeration is recommended for longer shelf life.

Cooked rice can be refrigerated for up to seven days, or stored in the freezer for six months.

> **Health and safety** ⚠
>
> Often rice is refreshed in running cold water or ice water, then drained and stored in the refrigerator. However, it is not advisable to reheat rice due to the risk of food poisoning caused by *bacillus cereus*.

Once cooked, keep hot (above 65 °C for no longer than two hours), or cool quickly (within 90 minutes) and keep cool (below 5 °C). If this is not done, the spores of *bacillus cereus* (a bacterium found in the soil) may revert to bacteria and multiply.

Pasta

Pasta is the name for a type of food thought to be originally from Italy and consisting of dough made from durum wheat and water. The dough is stretched and flattened into various shapes and either used fresh or dried.

Durum wheat has a 15 per cent protein content, which makes it a good alternative to rice and potatoes for vegetarians. Pasta also contains carbohydrates in the form of starch, which gives the body energy.

Types of pasta

There are basically four types of pasta, each of which may be plain or flavoured with spinach or tomato:

- dried durum wheat pasta
- fresh egg pasta
- semolina pasta
- wholewheat pasta.

Dried pasta

Almost 90 per cent of the pasta eaten in Italy is dried. Dried pasta comes in numerous shapes and sizes; the most common in the UK include spaghetti, fettuccini (long, narrow ribbons), penne (short tubes cut diagonally), farfalle (bow tie or butterfly shaped) and fusilli (short spirals). Sheets of pasta are used for lasagne.

▲ A variety of dried pasta shapes

Quality points

- When purchasing dried pasta, the box or container should be sealed and the pasta unbroken.
- Check the best before date.
- Dried pasta must be dry and not damp, with a good even colour and no signs of infestation.

Fresh pasta

Fresh pasta is produced from wheat (usually from durum wheat flour). It is made into an unleavened dough with water, oil and in some recipes eggs. Fresh pasta has a short shelf life, as the pasta usually contains eggs.

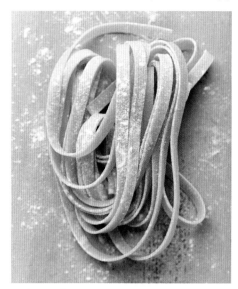

▲ Tagliatelle is a common type of fresh pasta

Quality points

When purchasing fresh pasta it must be within 5 °C, evenly coloured, intact and not torn or damaged. The pasta must easily separate. Fresh pasta will carry a use-by date.

Stuffed pasta

Stuffed pasta is pasta shapes stuffed with a variety of fillings. Shapes include cannelloni (tubes), ravioli and tortellini.

Examples of fillings include:

- mushroom duxelle
- minced beef or lamb flavoured with herbs
- ricotta cheese with basil
- fish forcemeat
- couscous with chopped cooked vegetables
- minced lamb, beef or pork with spinach purée
- minced chicken with fine herbs (parsley, chervil and tarragon)

▲ Tortellini is a type of stuffed pasta

Sauces and additions used with pasta

Examples of sauces to accompany pasta include:

- tomato sauce
- cream, butter or béchamel-based sauces
- rich meat sauce
- olive oil and garlic
- soft white or blue cheese
- pesto.

Examples of cheeses used in pasta cooking:

- **Parmesan** – the most popular hard cheese used with pasta, ideal for grating. The flavour is best when it is freshly grated. If it is bought ready grated, or if it is grated and stored, the flavour deteriorates.
- **Pecorino** – a strong ewes' milk cheese, sometimes studded with peppercorns. Used for strongly flavoured dishes, it can be grated or thinly sliced.
- **Ricotta** – creamy-white in colour and made from the discarded whey of other cheeses, ricotta is widely used in fillings for pasta such as cannelloni and ravioli, and for sauces.
- **Mozzarella** – traditionally made from the milk of the water buffalo, mozzarella is pure white and creamy, with a mild but distinctive flavour, and usually round or pear-shaped. It will keep for only a few days in a container half-filled with milk and water.
- **Gorgonzola or dolcelatte** – these are both distinctive blue cheeses that can be used in sauces.

Equipment for preparing pasta dishes

The following equipment is used in pasta making:

- Pasta machine – used for rolling out the pasta to the correct thickness and size.
- Pastry brushes – used to brush the pasta with oil and to brush the excess semolina from the pasta after rolling.
- Fluted cutting roller – used to cut and shape and divide the pasta.
- Palette knife – used to lift the pasta sheets and shapes.
- Ravioli tray – use to mould and shape the ravioli.

▲ A pasta machine

Preparing and cooking pasta

Mixing

Always mix in a large bowl or saucepan, to enable the ingredients to be well distributed throughout the pasta. This is done with a large spoon, or if cold, the pasta can be mixed by hand.

Health and safety !

Make sure hands have been thoroughly washed before handling pasta; alternatively wear food gloves.

Cooking dried pasta

When using dried pasta, a rule of thumb for portion weights is 80–100 g per portion as a starter course. If larger portions are required, increase accordingly.

Most types of dried pasta will cook perfectly well in less than 10 minutes. Spaghetti that has been stored for too long and is over-dry may take longer than this, and you might not want to eat the result.

To cook dried pasta:

1 Bring plenty of water (at least 3.8 litres for every 585 g of dry pasta) to a rolling boil.
2 Add about 1 tablespoon of salt per 4 litres of water, if desired.
3 Add the pasta in small quantities to maintain the rolling boil.
4 Stir frequently to prevent sticking. Do not cover the pan.
5 Follow package directions for cooking time. Do not overcook. Pasta should be 'al dente'; it should be slightly resistant to the bite, but cooked through.
6 Drain to stop the cooking action. Do not rinse unless the recipe says to do so. For salads, drain and rinse pasta with cold water.

Professional tip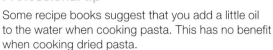

Some recipe books suggest that you add a little oil to the water when cooking pasta. This has no benefit when cooking dried pasta.

Professional tip

The water should always be at a rolling boil – the more water in proportion to pasta, the quicker it will return to the boil after the pasta is added. This means fast cooking and better-textured pasta.

Fresh egg pasta dough can also be made using a food processor (see recipe 9).

If using a pasta rolling machine, divide the dough into three or four pieces. Pass each section by hand through the machine, turning the rollers with the other hand. Repeat five or six times, adjusting the rollers each time to make the pasta thinner.

Professional tip

When cooking fresh pasta, add a little oil to the water to prevent the pieces sticking together.

Straining

Always strain pasta carefully as it is a delicate product. Use a colander or a spider.

Blanching and refreshing

Pasta can be cooked for a few minutes and then refreshed under cold water to speed up the service when finished to order in the restaurant. Always make sure you refresh the pasta in plenty of water, so that the pasta is free flowing and does not stick together.

Other cooking methods for pasta

- **Baking** – this technique is used for dishes such as cannelloni and pasta bakes. These dishes have usually been previously cooked and require baking to finish the product. This technique requires the dish to cook evenly and have a well distributed colour.

- **Deep frying** – some pasta dishes are first boiled, then coated and deep fried. For example, stuffed ravioli can be dipped in eggwash or butter milk, coated in breadcrumbs and deep fried.

Health and safety !

When cooked, the core temperature of pasta must be 75 °C. Always check the internal temperature using a temperature probe.

Step by step: making fresh egg pasta dough

To make 500 g of dough, use 400 g strong flour, 4 medium eggs (beaten), approximately 1 tbsp of olive oil (as required) and salt.

1 Sift the flour and salt.

2 Make a well in the flour. Pour the beaten eggs into the well.

3 Gradually incorporate the flour.

4 Mix until a dough is formed. Only add oil to adjust to required consistency. The amount of oil will vary according to the type of flour and the size of the eggs.

5 Pull and knead the dough until is of a smooth elastic consistency and then cover and allow to rest in a cool place for 30 minutes.

6 After resting, knead the dough again.
7 Roll out the dough on a well-floured surface to the thickness of 0.5 mm.
8 Trim the sides and cut as required using a large knife.

Step by step: making stuffed pasta (tortellini)

1 Place the filling in the centre of a piece of pasta. Lightly brush the pasta with beaten egg.

2 Fold the pasta over the filling, creating a semi-circle, and press down around the filling to seal.

3 Trim the excess pasta with a pastry cutter.

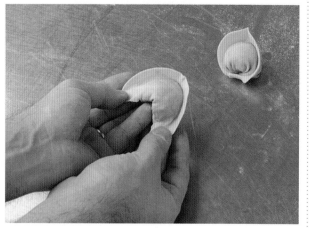

4 Bring the two ends of the long edge together, eggwash the seam and firmly press the ends together to seal.

Holding and storing pasta

Dry pasta

Dry pasta can be stored almost indefinitely if kept in a tightly sealed, airtight package or a covered container in a cool, dry place. The container should be labelled and dated.

When holding dried pasta which has been blanched for service, sprinkle with oil and mix to prevent sticking.

Fresh pasta

Store fresh pasta in the refrigerator below 5 °C. Shaped raw pasta is best stored in large containers sprinkled with semolina, layered with sheets of greaseproof or silicone paper or sheets of plastic in an airtight container.

Cooked pasta

If cooked pasta is not to be used immediately, drain and rinse thoroughly with cold water. If it is left to sit in water, it will continue to absorb water and become mushy. When the pasta is cool, drain and toss lightly with salad oil to prevent it from sticking and drying out. Cover tightly and refrigerate or freeze. Stuffed fresh pasta should be blanched, drained, frozen or chilled in small amounts which allows for easy separation.

- Cooked pasta may be stored in plastic bags in the refrigerator, labelled and dated. Refrigerate the pasta and sauce separately or the pasta will become soggy.
- Frozen pasta will keep for up to three months, but it is recommended that it is used within one month.

To reheat, put pasta in a colander and immerse in rapidly boiling water just long enough to heat through. Do not allow it to continue to cook. Pasta may also be reheated in a microwave.

It is advisable to serve pasta immediately after it is reheated and the dish is finished. If pasta is to be held on a buffet (for example, a tray of lasagne) then it must be kept at the required temperature of **65 °C and served within two hours**.

Activity

1 Which type of flour is used for pasta dough?
2 Name four different pasta shapes.
3 What does 'al dente' mean?
4 What equipment might you need when making fresh pasta?
5 How should cooked pasta be stored?

Grains

Cereals are the most important crops and are the oldest farmed agricultural products. A cereal is the edible fruit of any grass which is used as food. Cereals are used in a range of dishes and food products, including breads, soups, stews, pilaffs and risotto.

Grain is the name given to the edible fruit of cereals. In many countries grains are the main staple food as they are inexpensive and readily available.

The whole grain is made up of three parts of the grain kernel: the bran, endosperm and the germ.

- The **bran** is the outer layers of the cereal. Bran contains a high amount of dietary fibre, some of the B vitamins (for example, thiamine and niacin) and the minerals zinc, copper and iron. It also contains protein and other chemicals.
- The **endosperm** is the middle layer and is the largest section of the grain. It is the main energy supply of the plant and is rich in carbohydrates, protein and Vitamin B.
- The **germ** is the smallest part of the grain. It is rich in nutrients, containing B vitamins, minerals, vitamin E and other chemicals.

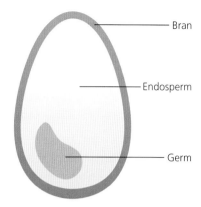

▲ The structure of a grain

Key terms	**Cereal**: the edible fruit of any grass used for food.
	Grain: edible fruit of cereals.
	Bran: outer layers of the cereal.
	Endosperm: the middle layer of the grain.
	Germ: the smallest part of the grain.

Types of grain and their uses

Barley

Barley grows in a wider variety of climatic conditions than any other cereal. It is usually found in the shops as whole or pot barley (or polished pearl barley), but you can also buy barley flakes or kernels. It can be cooked on its own (one part grain to three parts water for 45–60 minutes) and used as an alternative to rice, pasta or potatoes, or added to stews. Malt extract is made from sprouted barley grains.

Barley must have its fibrous hull (outer shell) removed before it is eaten (hulled barley). Hulled barley still has its bran and germ and is considered a whole grain, making it a popular health food. Pearl barley is hulled barley that has been processed further to remove the bran.

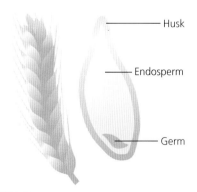

▲ A grain of barley

Corn/maize

Fresh corn – available in the form of sweetcorn and corn on the cob – is eaten as a vegetable. The dried grain is most often eaten as cornflakes or popcorn. Tortillas are made from maize meal, as are quite a lot of snack foods.

The flour made from corn (cornmeal or maize meal) is used to make **polenta** and can be added to soups, pancakes and muffins. When cooking polenta (one part grain to three parts water, for 15–20 minutes), stir carefully to avoid lumps. Use it like mashed potato. Polenta is quite bland, so try stirring in tasty ingredients like gorgonzola, parmesan and fresh herbs, or press it when cold, cut into slices, brush with garlicky olive oil and grill. You can also get ready made polenta.

Do not confuse cornmeal with refined corn starch/flour, which is used for thickening. Corn is gluten free.

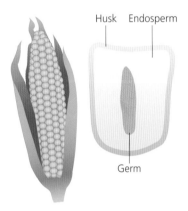

▲ A grain of maize

Wheat

This is the most familiar cereal in the UK. It is used for bread, cakes, biscuits, pastry, breakfast cereals and pasta. Wheat grains can be eaten whole (cook one part grain to three parts water for 40–60 minutes) and have a satisfying, chewy texture. Different types of wheat are described below.

- **Cracked or kibbled wheat** is the dried whole grains cut by steel blades.
- **Bulgar wheat** is parboiled before cracking, has a light texture and only needs rehydrating by soaking in boiling water or stock.
- **Semolina** is a grainy yellow flour ground from durum or hard wheat and is the main ingredient of dried Italian pasta.

- **Couscous** is made from semolina grains that have been rolled, dampened and coated with finer wheat flour. Soak couscous in two parts of water or stock to rehydrate; traditionally, it is steamed after soaking.

Strong wheat flour (with a high gluten content) is required for yeasted bread-making. Plain flour is used for general cooking, including cakes and shortcrust pastry. Wheat flakes are used for porridge, muesli and flapjacks.

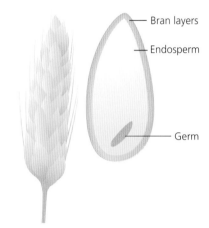

▲ A grain of wheat

Buckwheat

When roasted, the seeds of buckwheat are dark reddish-brown. It can be cooked (one part grain to two parts water for 6 minutes; leave to stand for 6 minutes) and served like rice, or it can be added to stews and casseroles. Buckwheat flour can be added to cakes, muffins and pancakes, where it gives a distinctive flavour. Soba noodles, made from buckwheat, are an essential ingredient in Japanese cooking. Buckwheat is gluten free.

▲ Buckwheat

Millet

The millets are a group of small-seeded cereal crops or grains widely grown around the world for food. The main millet varieties are:

- pearl millet
- foxtail millet
- proso millet (also known as common millet, broom corn millet, hog millet or white millet)
- finger millet.

▲ Millet

As none of the millets is closely related to wheat, they can be eaten by those with **coeliac disease** or other forms of allergies/intolerances to wheat. Coeliac patients can replace certain cereal grains in their diets with millets in various forms, including breakfast cereals. Millet can also often be used in place of buckwheat, rice or quinoa.

> **Key term**
>
> **Coeliac disease**: a disease in which a person is unable to digest the protein gluten (found in wheat and other cereals). Gluten causes the person's immune system to attack its own tissues, specifically the lining of the small intestine. Symptoms include diarrhoea, bloating, abdominal pain, weight loss and malnutrition.

In western India, millet flour (called 'bajari' in Marathi) has been commonly used with 'jowar' (sorghum) flour for hundreds of years to make the local staple flat bread, 'bhakri'.

The protein content in millet is very close to that of wheat; both provide about 11 per cent protein by weight. Millets are rich in B vitamins (especially niacin, B6 and folacin), calcium, iron, potassium, magnesium and zinc. Millets contain no gluten, so they cannot rise for bread. However, when combined with wheat or xanthan gum (for those who have coeliac disease), they can be used to make raised bread. Alone, they are suited to flatbread.

Millet can be used as an alternative to rice, but the tiny grains need to be cracked before they will absorb water easily. Before boiling, sauté with a little vegetable oil for 2–3 minutes until some crack, then add water carefully (one part grain to three parts water). Bring to the boil and simmer for 15–20 minutes until fluffy. Millet flakes can be made into porridge or added to muesli. Millet flour is also available and is sometimes made into pasta.

Oats

There are various grades of oatmeal, rolled oats or jumbo oat flakes. All forms can be used to make porridge, combined with groundnuts to make a nut roast or added to stews. Oatmeal is low in gluten so cannot be used to make a loaf, but can be mixed with wheat flour to add flavour and texture to bread, muffins and pancakes. Oatmeal contains some oils and can become rancid, so keep an eye on the best before date.

Oatmeal is created by grinding oats into coarse powder; various grades are available depending on thoroughness of grinding (including coarse, pinhead and fine). The main uses of oats are:

- as an ingredient in baking
- in the manufacture of bannocks or oatcakes
- as a stuffing for poultry
- as a coating for some cheeses
- as an ingredient of black pudding
- for making traditional porridge (or 'porage').

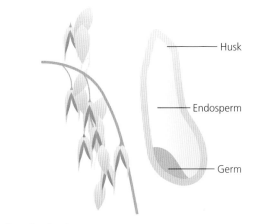

▲ A grain of oats

Rye

Rye is one of the few cereals (along with wheat and barley) that has enough gluten to make a yeasted loaf. However, with less gluten than wheat, rye flour makes a denser, richer-flavoured bread. It is more usual to mix rye flour with wheat flour. Rye grains should be cooked using one part grain to three parts water for 45–60 minutes. Kibbled (cracked) rye is often added to granary-type loaves. Rye grains can be added to stews and rye flakes are good in muesli.

Spelt

Originating in the Middle East, spelt is closely related to common wheat and has been popular for decades in Eastern Europe. It has an intense nutty, wheaty flavour. The flour is excellent for bread-making and spelt pasta is becoming more widely available.

Quinoa

Quinoa is an ancient crop that fed the South American Aztec Indians for thousands of years and has recently been cultivated in the UK. It is a seed that is high in protein, making it useful for vegetarians.

The small, round grains look similar to millet, but are pale brown in colour. The taste is mild and the texture firm and slightly chewy. It can be cooked like millet and absorbs twice its volume in liquid.

Cook for 15 minutes (one part grain to three parts water); it is ready when all the grains have turned from white to transparent and the spiral-like germ has separated. It can be used in place of more common cereals, pasta or rice (risottos, pilaff), and is served in salads and some stuffings.

Quality points

Grains should always look and smell faintly sweet or have no aroma at all. If you detect a musty or oily scent, the grains have passed their peak and should not be used.

Professional tip

Buy grains that are well packaged and sealed tightly. Check the sell-by date.

Preparing and cooking grains

Grains should first be washed under cold water in a colander to remove any dust or foreign bodies. Look for any unusual infestation such as insects. The dry grain does not need to be soaked.

Grains can vary in cooking time, depending on the age of the grain. Whole grains take longer to cook than grains which have been processed.

Cooking methods

Grains are usually boiled or steamed, but may be braised or stewed. Grains are starch based and as the grain is heated, it absorbs the water, swells and bursts, cooking at between 60 °C and 70 °C.

Grains such as couscous, bulgar wheat and millet only usually require boiling water to be poured onto them, stirred and cooled.

Porridge oats and oat flakes, polenta and cornmeal are also often soaked or par boiled, poured into a lined baking sheet (usually on a silpat mat) and baked in the oven. As the grains are baked, the water will cook the product, evaporate and the result is a dry baked grain.

Grains may be cooked in water or soaked in wine or fruit juice.

Storing grains

Whole grains must be stored more carefully than refined grains, since the healthy oils found largely in the germ of the whole grain can be negatively affected by heat, light and moisture. Because each grain has a different fat content, their shelf life varies. All whole grains should be stored in airtight containers with tight-fitting lids or closures.

- **Whole intact grains** – the shelf life of whole intact grains is generally longer than flours. If stored properly in airtight containers, intact grains will keep for up to 6 months in a cool, dry store, or up to one year in a freezer.
- **Whole grain flours and meals** – these spoil more quickly than intact grains because their protective bran layer has been broken up and oxygen can reach all parts of the grain, causing oxidation. If stored properly in airtight containers, most grain flours and meals will keep for 1 to 3 months in a cool, dry store or up to 2 to 6 months in a freezer.

It is advisable to serve grains immediately they are cooked or reheated. If they are to be held on a hot buffet the temperature must be retained at 63 °C for no longer than two hours. After such time they must be thrown away.

Activity

1 Name three different types of grain used in culinary work.
2 State three uses of wheat.
3 Describe how you would prepare and cook quinoa.
4 What is the nutritional value of grains in a menu?
5 Design a dish using a basic grain ingredient.

Eggs

Eggs are used widely in all sorts of cooking, both savoury and sweet. They are an important ingredient in many recipes, used for binding, enriching, colouring, emulsifying and aerating.

- The outer shell of an egg is mainly calcium carbonate lined with membranes and has a number of pores for gas exchange.
- These pores are covered by a wax-like layer, known as the cuticle. This cuticle partly protects the egg against microbial invasion and controls water loss.
- The egg white is divided into a thick layer around the yolk and a thinner layer next to the shell. The thick layer anchors the yolk, together with the chalazae, in the middle of the egg. The egg white has an important function as it possesses special antibacterial properties, which prevent the growth and multiplication of micro-organisms.
- The yolk is rich in nutrients.

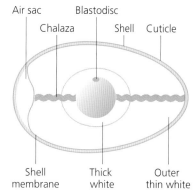

▲ The structure of an egg

Types of egg and their uses

Hens' eggs are almost exclusively used for cookery, but eggs from turkeys, geese, ducks, guinea fowl, quail and gulls are also edible.

Quails' eggs are used in a variety of ways, for example, as a garnish to many hot and cold dishes, as a starter or main course, such as a salad of assorted leaves with hot wild mushrooms and poached quail eggs, or tartlet of quail eggs on chopped mushrooms coated with hollandaise sauce.

▲ Quiche Lorraine is made using eggs

- Fresh eggs are used extensively in hors d'oeuvres, meat and poultry dishes, soup, pasta, egg dishes, salads, fish dishes, sweets and pastries, sauces and savouries.
- Most egg products are available in liquid, frozen or spray-dried form.
- Whole egg is used primarily for cake production, where its foaming and coagulation properties are required.
- Egg whites are used for meringues and light sponges where their foaming property is crucial.

- Eggs are useful as a main dish as they provide the energy, fat, minerals and vitamins needed for growth and repair of the body. The fat in the egg yolk is high in saturated fat. The egg white is made up of protein and water.

Free-range eggs

These are produced from birds that are allowed to roam freely outdoors in a farm yard or in a shed or chicken coop.

Barn yard eggs

Barn yard eggs are laid by chickens that are kept inside large barns with straw or sawdust to walk around on. These birds have the opportunity to walk around a large area and interact with each other, while still being protected from the weather and predators.

Battery eggs

Battery eggs are produced by chickens kept in cages. The birds cannot move around, stretch, rest or perform other behaviours like preening or scratching properly.

Organic eggs

Organic eggs are produced from chickens reared in a free-range environment. The environment focuses on sustainability issues, including soil health and biodiversity.

All boxes of whole eggs sold in this country must state the method of production clearly, so you can check whether the eggs have come from hens kept in cages or whether they have come from higher welfare alternative systems such as barn, free range or organic. Each egg is also stamped with a code for the method of production, country of origin and the originating farm:

- O = Organic
- 1 = Free range
- 2 = Barn
- 3 = Caged

Sizes

Hens' eggs are graded in four sizes: small, medium, large and very large, as shown in Table 11.2.

Table 11.2 Hens' egg sizes

Very large	73 g	Size 0
		Size 1
Large	63–73 g	Size 1
		Size 2
		Size 3
Medium	53–63 g	Size 3
		Size 4
		Size 5
Small	53 g and under	Size 5
		Size 6
		Size 7

Quality points for eggs

- The eggshell should be clean, well-shaped, strong and slightly rough.
- When eggs are broken there should be a high proportion of thick white to thin white. If an egg is kept, the thick white gradually changes into thin white, and water passes from the white into the yolk.
- The yolk should be firm, round (not flattened) and of a good even colour. Over time, as eggs are kept, the yolk loses strength and begins to flatten, water evaporates from the egg and is replaced by air.

Grading

The size of the eggs does not affect their quality, but it does affect their price. Eggs are tested for quality, then weighed and graded.

- Grade A – naturally clean, fresh eggs, internally perfect with intact shells and an air cell not exceeding 6 mm in depth.
- Grade B – eggs that have been downgraded because they have been cleaned or preserved or because they are internally imperfect, cracked or have an air cell exceeding 6 mm but not more than 9 mm in depth. Grade B eggs are broken out and pasteurised.
- Grade C – eggs that are fit for breaking for manufacturing purposes but cannot be sold in their shells to the public.

British Lion Quality Code of Practice

The 'Lion' quality mark on eggs and egg boxes means that the eggs have been produced to the highest standards of food safety in the world, including a programme of vaccination against **salmonella**.

The Code of Practice covers breeding flocks and hatcheries, pullet rearing, laying birds, including both hygiene and animal welfare requirements, farm handling of eggs, distribution of eggs from farm, feed, hen disposal, packing centre, procedures, advice to retailers, consumers and caterers and environmental policy and enforcement.

To guarantee traceability, all breeding farms, hatcheries, rearing and laying farms, feed mills and packing centres involved in the production of Lion Quality eggs must be approved. All Lion Quality hen flocks must be accompanied by a passport certificate and all Lion Quality egg movement has to be fully traceable.

Health and safety

Hens can pass salmonella bacteria into their eggs and therefore cause food poisoning. To reduce this risk, pasteurised eggs may be used where appropriate (e.g. in omelettes, scrambled eggs).

Preparation and cooking

Eggs are very versatile. Fried, scrambled, poached and boiled eggs and omelettes are mainly served at breakfast. A variety of dishes may be served for lunch, high tea, supper and snacks (this may include scotch eggs, which are deep fried). They are also used widely in baking and in desserts.

Health and safety

Hands should be washed before and after handling eggs.

Preparation surfaces, utensils and containers should be cleaned regularly and always cleaned between preparation of different dishes.

Sauces and additions

Eggs are very versatile and can be served in a variety of ways with different garnishes and sauces. Sauces can be hot (for example, tomato, cream sauce, curry sauce, cheese sauce) or cold (for example, mayonnaise and green sauce).

There are many different types of fillings for omelettes, such as mushrooms, ham, cheese, mixed herbs and smoked fish. Omelettes may also be coated with a sauce, for example, cheese sauce, cream sauce or tomato sauce.

Scrambled eggs may be garnished with smoked salmon, smoked eel or smoked mackerel. The egg mixture may be flavoured with mixed herbs and chilli.

Holding, serving and storing eggs

- Store eggs in a cool but not too dry place – 0 °C to 5 °C is ideal – where the humidity of the air and the amount of carbon dioxide present are controlled. Eggs will keep for up to nine months under these conditions, but always follow the advice on packaging.
- Because eggshells are porous, eggs will absorb any strong odours, so they should not be stored near strong-smelling foods such as onions, fish and cheese.
- Eggs should be stored away from possible contaminants such as raw meat.
- Stocks should be rotated: first in, first out.
- Pasteurised eggs are washed, sanitised and then broken into sterilised containers. After combining the yolks and whites, they are strained, pasteurised – heated to 63 °C for 1 minute – then rapidly cooled.
- Egg dishes should be consumed as soon as possible after preparation or, if not for immediate use, refrigerated.

- It is advisable to serve eggs immediately they are cooked. It is not advisable to hold cooked eggs such as fried, scrambled or poached for too long on a buffet.
- Poached eggs may be cooked in advance, chilled in ice water and reheated in a water bath when required.

Activity

1 How is the quality of hens' eggs determined?
2 Name the food poisoning bacteria associated with hens' eggs.
3 Name four basic egg dishes.
4 Give an example of a garnish that could be used with scrambled eggs.
5 Describe how eggs should be stored.

Test yourself

1 State the difference between wholegrain and basmati rice.
2 How much liquid to rice would you use when cooking risotto?
3 State **three** sauces that could be served with pasta.
4 State **three** pieces of equipment you would use when preparing fresh pasta.
5 What is the minimum legal temperature for holding cooked lasagne hot for service?
6 State **one** use of each of the following grains:
   a) wheat
   b) oats
   c) millet
7 What is an appropriate cooking method for rye?
8 State **four** quality points to look for when buying fresh eggs.
9 Describe the process for cooking a poached egg.
10 How can quail's eggs be used?

1 Braised or pilaff rice (*riz pilaff*)

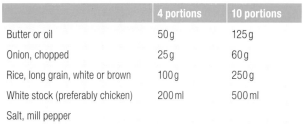

	4 portions	10 portions
Butter or oil	50 g	125 g
Onion, chopped	25 g	60 g
Rice, long grain, white or brown	100 g	250 g
White stock (preferably chicken)	200 ml	500 ml
Salt, mill pepper		

Energy	Cals	Fat	Sat fat	Carb	Sugar	Protein	Fibre *
774 KJ	184 kcal	10.4 g	4.5 g	22.1 g	0.3 g	1.9 g	0.6 g

* Using white rice and hard margarine. Using brown rice and hard margarine, 1 portion provides: 769 kJ/183 kcal energy; 10.9 g fat; 4.6 g sat fat; 20.7 g carb; 0.7 g sugar; 1.9 g protein; 1.0 g fibre

1 Place half the butter or oil into a small sautéuse. Add the onion.

2 Cook gently without colouring for 2–3 minutes. Add the rice.

3 Cook gently without colouring for 2–3 minutes.

4 Add twice the amount of stock to rice.

5 Season, cover with buttered paper, bring to the boil.

6 Place in a hot oven (230–250 °C) for approximately 15 minutes, until cooked.

7 Remove immediately into a cool sautéuse.

8 Carefully mix in the remaining butter or oil with a two-pronged fork.

9 Correct the seasoning and serve.

Note

It is usual to use long-grain rice for pilaff because the grains are firm and there is less likelihood of them breaking up and becoming mushy. During cooking, the long-grain rice absorbs more liquid, loses less starch and retains its shape as it swells; short or medium grains may split at the ends and become less distinct in outline.

Variation

Add wild mushrooms – about 50–100 g for 4 portions.

Pilaff may also be infused with herbs and spices such as cardamom.

Professional tip

Cook the rice for the exact time specified in the recipe. If it cooks for longer, it will be overcooked and the grains will not separate.

Healthy eating tips

● Use an unsaturated oil (sunflower or olive). Lightly oil the pan and drain off any excess after the frying is complete.
● Keep the added salt to a minimum.

1 Cook the rice gently without colouring

2 Add the stock

3 Cover with buttered paper, with a small hole at the centre

2 Steamed rice

	4 portions
Rice (dry weight)	100g

Energy	Cals	Fat	Sat fat	Carb	Sugar	Protein	Fibre
1277KJ	305kcal	1.4g	0.0g	63.7g	0.0g	7.1g	0.0g

1 Place the washed rice into a saucepan and add water until the water level is 2.5cm above the rice.

2 Bring to the boil over a fierce heat until most of the water has evaporated.

3 Turn the heat down as low as possible, cover the pan with a lid and allow the rice to complete cooking in the steam.

4 Once cooked, the rice should be allowed to stand in the covered steamer for 10 minutes.

3 Plain boiled rice

	4 portions
Rice (dry weight)	100g

Energy	Cals	Fat	Sat fat	Carb	Sugar	Protein	Fibre
37kJ	90kcal	0.1g	0.0g	20.0g	0.0g	1.9g	0.0g

1 Pick and wash the long-grain rice. Add to plenty of boiling salted water.

2 Stir to the boil and simmer gently until tender (approximately 12–15 minutes).

3 Pour into a sieve and rinse well under cold running water, then boiling water. Drain and leave in a sieve, placed over a bowl and covered with a cloth.

4 Place on a tray in the hotplate and keep hot.

5 Serve separately in a vegetable dish.

4 Stir-fried rice

2 Place a wok or thick-bottomed pan over fierce heat, add some oil and heat until smoking.

3 Add the cold rice and stir-fry for about 1 minute.

4 Add the other ingredients and continue to stir-fry over fierce heat for 4–5 minutes.

5 Add the beaten egg and continue cooking for a further 1–2 minutes.

6 Correct the seasoning and serve immediately.

Note

Stir-fried rice dishes consist of a combination of cold pre-cooked rice and ingredients such as cooked meat or poultry, fish, vegetables or egg.

Energy	Cals	Fat	Sat fat	Carb	Sugar	Protein	Fibre	*
1423kJ	338kcal	10.2g	1.9g	30.6g	0.6g	32.7g	0.6g	

* Using 125g chicken (average dark and light meat) and 25g mung beans per portion

1 Prepare and cook meat or poultry in fine shreds; dice and lightly cook any vegetables. Add bean sprouts just before the egg.

Healthy eating tips
- Use an unsaturated oil (sunflower or olive) to lightly oil the pan.
- Soy sauce adds sodium, so no added salt is needed.

5 Paella (savoury rice with chicken, fish, vegetables and spices)

Energy	Cals	Fat	Sat fat	Carb	Sugar	Protein	Fibre	*
3383kJ	804kcal	31.0g	6.2g	48.8g	3.8g	85.7g	1.3g	

* Using edible chicken meat

	4 portions	10 portions
Lobster, cooked	400g	1kg
Squid	200g	500g
Gambas (Mediterranean prawns), cooked	400g	1kg
Mussels	400g	1kg
White stock	1 litre	2.5 litres
Pinch of saffron		
Onion, finely chopped	50g	125g
Clove of garlic, finely chopped	1	2–3
Red pepper, diced	50g	125g
Green pepper, diced	50g	125g
Roasting chicken, cut for sauté	1.5kg	3.75kg
Olive oil	60ml	150ml
Short-grain rice	200g	500g
Thyme, bay leaf, seasoning	200g	500g
Tomatoes, skinned, deseeded, diced		
Lemon wedges, to finish		

1 Prepare the lobster: cut it in half, remove the claws and legs, discard the sac and trail. Remove the meat from the claws and cut the tail into 3–4 pieces, leaving the meat in the shell.

2 Clean the squid: pull the body and head apart. Extract the transparent 'pen' from the body. Rinse well, pulling off the thin purple membrane on the outside. Remove the ink sac. Cut the body into rings and the tentacles into 1 cm lengths.

3 Prepare the gambas by shelling the body.

4 Boil the mussels in water or white stock until the shells open. Shell the mussels and retain the cooking liquid.

5 Boil the white stock and mussel liquor together, infused with saffron. Simmer for 5–10 minutes.

6 Sweat the finely chopped onion in a suitable pan, without colour. Add the garlic and the peppers.

7 Sauté the chicken in olive oil until cooked and golden brown, then drain.

8 Add the rice to the onions and garlic and sweat for 2 minutes.

9 Add about 200 ml white stock and mussel liquor.

10 Add the thyme, bay leaf and seasoning. Bring to the boil, then cover with a lightly oiled greaseproof paper and lid. Cook for 5–8 minutes, in a moderately hot oven at 180 °C.

11 Add the squid and cook for another 5 minutes.

12 Add the tomatoes, chicken and lobster pieces, mussels and gambas. Stir gently, cover with a lid and reheat the rice in the oven.

13 Correct the consistency of the rice if necessary by adding more stock, so that it looks sufficiently moist without being too wet. Correct the seasoning.

14 When all is reheated and cooked, place in a suitable serving dish, decorate with 4 (10) gambas and 4 (10) mussels halved and shelled. Finish with wedges of lemon.

Note

For a traditional paella, a raw lobster may be used, which should be prepared as follows. Remove the legs and claws and crack the claws. Cut the lobster in half crosswise, between the tail and the carapace. Cut the carapace in two lengthwise. Discard the sac. Cut across the tail in thick slices through the shell. Remove the trail, wash the lobster pieces and cook with the rice.

Healthy eating tips
- To reduce the fat, skin the chicken and use a little unsaturated oil to sweat the onions and fry the chicken.
- No added salt is necessary.
- Serve with a large green salad.

ASSESSMENT

6 Risotto of Jerusalem artichoke and truffle

	4 portions	10 portions
Shallots, diced	50 g	125 g
Vegetable oil	10 g	25 g
Risotto rice (Carnaroli)	150 g	375 g
White wine	75 ml	180 ml
Vegetable stock	1 litre	2.5 litres
Artichoke purée	10 g	25 g
Butter	50 g	125 g
Seasoning		
Parmesan Reggiano, grated	2 tsps	5 tsps
Truffle oil		
Chives, chopped	5 g	12 g
Chervil, freshly picked		
Truffle, chopped (optional)	25 g	62 g

Energy	Cals	Fat	Sat fat	Carb	Sugar	Protein	Fibre	Sodium
1360 kJ	325 kcal	16.2 g	8.9 g	34	3.6 g	8.7 g	1.9 g	0.222 g

1 Sweat the shallots in the oil, without colour, for 5 minutes.

2 Add the rice and sweat for a further minute.

3 Add the wine and cook out until completely reduced.

4 Add the stock ladle by ladle until the rice is 95 per cent cooked. (You may not need all the stock.)

5 Add the purée and butter and reduce until emulsified.

6 Season the risotto, then add the Parmesan, truffle and chives.

Note

To serve, place the risotto in a bowl and garnish with some picked chervil and freshly sliced truffle (optional).

Professional tip

Add the stock slowly, stirring well, to create a pudding-like consistency.

ASSESSMENT

7 Risotto with Parmesan (risotto con Parmigiano)

	4 portions	10 portions
Chicken stock	1.2 litres	3 litres
Butter	80 g	200 g
Onion, peeled and finely chopped	½	1
Arborio rice	240 g	600 g
Parmesan, freshly grated	75 g	180 g
Salt, pepper		

Energy	Cals	Fat	Sat fat	Carb	Sugar	Protein	Fibre
2598 kJ	621 kcal	36.2 g	14.1 g	49.9 g	4.2 g	23.0 g	0.3 g

1 Bring the stock to a simmer, next to where you will cook the risotto. Take a wide, heavy-bottomed pan or casserole, put half the butter in over a medium heat and melt.

2 Add the onion and sweat until it softens and becomes slightly translucent.

3 Add the rice and stir with a heat-resistant spatula until it is thoroughly coated in butter (about 2 minutes). Then take a soup ladle of hot stock and pour it into the rice.

4 Continue to cook and stir until this liquid addition is completely absorbed (about 3 minutes).

5 Repeat this procedure several times until the rice has swollen and is nearly tender. The rice should not be soft but neither should it be chalky. Taste and wait: if it is undercooked, it will leave a gritty, chalky residue in your mouth.

6 Normally the rice is ready about 20 minutes after the first addition of stock.

7 Add the other half of the butter and half the Parmesan off the heat. Stir these in, season and cover. Leave to rest and swell a little more for 3 minutes. Serve immediately after this in soup plates, with more Parmesan offered separately.

Healthy eating tips
● Use an unsaturated oil (sunflower or olive), instead of butter, to sweat the onion. Lightly oil the pan and drain off any excess after the frying is complete.
● Additional salt is not necessary.
● Serve with a large salad and tomato bread.

Professional tip

Add the stock slowly, to give the rice time to absorb the liquid. Stir regularly during cooking.

Variation

Risotto variations include:
● **saffron or Milanese-style** – soak ¼ teaspoon saffron in a little hot stock and mix into the risotto near the end of the cooking time.
● **seafood** – add any one or a mixture of cooked mussels, shrimp, prawns, etc., just before the rice is cooked; also use half fish stock, half chicken stock.
● **mushrooms**.

8 Risotto with asparagus for amuse bouche

See risotto recipe (recipe 7)

Garnish the risotto with fresh cooked asparagus heads.

Note

Many other recipes are suitable for an amuse bouche, such as different risottos, ravioli with different fillings, different types of soups with a range of combinations and flavours, various fritters, vegetable, meat, fish and poultry. A common amuse bouche which is simple and quick is deep fried king prawns with a chilli sauce.

Remember: Amuse bouche are bite-sized appetizers.

Video: Risotto
http://bit.ly/
1vGih2Q

9 Fresh egg pasta dough

Ingredient	4 portions	10 portions
Pasta flour	175 g	350 g
Whole eggs	1	2
Egg yolks	3	6

Energy	Cals	Fat	Sat fat	Carb	Sugar	Protein	Fibre
1672 kJ	400 kcal	17.2 g	9.4 g	50.0 g	10.2 g	11.8 g	4.0 g

Method A:

1 Place all the ingredients into a food processor and mix quickly until a wet crumb mix appears; this should take no more than 30–45 seconds.

2 Tip the mix out on to a clean surface; this is where the working of the pasta begins.

3 The pasta dough may feel wet at this stage, however the working of the gluten will take the moisture back in to the dry mass, leaving a velvety-smooth finish that is malleable and easy to work; most of this process should be carried out using a pasta machine.

4 Rest the dough for 30 minutes and then it is ready to use.

5 For a classical noodle shape, roll out to a thin rectangle 45 × 15 cm. Cut into 0.5 cm strips. Leave to dry.

Fresh egg pasta dough: method A

1 Combine the ingredients into a wet crumb mix

2 Work and roll out the pasta using a pasta machine

3 A pasta machine with an attachment can be used to cut noodles

Fresh egg pasta dough: method B

1 Sieve the flour and salt, shape into a well. Pour the beaten eggs into the well.

2 Gradually incorporate the flour and only add oil to adjust to required consistency. The amount of oil will vary according to the type of flour and the size of the eggs.

3 Pull and knead the dough until it is of a smooth elastic consistency. Cover the dough with a dampened cloth and allow to rest in a cool place for 30 minutes.

4 After resting, knead the dough again.

5 Roll out the dough on a well-floured surface to a thickness of ½ mm or use a pasta rolling machine.

6 Trim the side and cut the dough as required using a large knife.

Professional tip

Do not knead the dough too much, or it will become tough.

Let it rest before rolling it out.

The best way to roll out pasta dough at the correct thickness is to use a pasta machine.

Video: Making fresh pasta http://bit.ly/ 1MxDxCK

10 Lasagne

	4 portions	10 portions
Lasagne	200 g	500 g
Oil	1 tbsp	3 tbsp
Streaky bacon, thin strips of	50 g	125 g
Onion, chopped	100 g	250 g
Carrot, chopped	50 g	125 g
Celery, chopped	50 g	125 g
Minced beef	200 g	500 g
Tomato purée	1 tbsp	2 ½ tbsp
Jus lié or demi-glace	375 ml	1 litre
Clove of garlic	1	1 ½
Salt, pepper		
Marjoram	½ tsp	1 ½ tsp
Mushrooms, sliced	100 g	250 g
Béchamel sauce	250 ml	600 ml
Parmesan or Cheddar cheese, grated	25 g	125 g

Energy	Cals	Fat	Sat fat	Carb	Sugar	Protein	Fibre
2416 kJ	575 kcal	28.7 g	11.4 g	56.1 g	10.0 g	26.7 g	5.8 g

Note

This recipe can be made using 200 g of ready-bought lasagne or it can be prepared fresh using 200 g flour noodle paste. Wholemeal lasagne can be made using noodle paste made with 100 g wholemeal flour and 100 g strong flour.

1 Prepare the fresh egg pasta dough and roll out to 1 mm thick.

2 Cut into 6 cm squares.

3 Allow to rest in a cool place and dry slightly on a cloth dusted with flour.

4 Whether using fresh or ready-bought lasagne, cook in gently simmering salted water for approximately 10 minutes (3 minutes for fresh pasta).

5 Refresh in cold water, then drain on a cloth.

6 Gently heat the oil in a thick-bottomed pan, add the bacon and cook for 2–3 minutes.

7 Add the onion, carrot and celery, cover the pan with a lid and cook for 5 minutes.

8 Add the minced beef, increase the heat and stir until lightly brown.

9 Remove from the heat and mix in the tomato purée.

10 Return to the heat, mix in the jus lié or demi-glace, stir to boil.

11 Add the garlic, salt, pepper and marjoram, and simmer for 15 minutes. Remove the garlic.

12 Mix in the mushrooms, reboil for 2 minutes, then remove from the heat.

13 Butter an ovenproof dish and cover the bottom with a layer of the meat sauce.

14 Add a layer of lasagne and cover with meat sauce.

15 Add another layer of lasagne and cover with the remainder of the meat sauce.

16 Cover with the béchamel.

17 Sprinkle with cheese, cover with a lid and place in a moderately hot oven at 190 °C for approximately 20 minutes.

18 Remove the lid, cook for a further 15 minutes and serve in the cleaned ovenproof dish.

1 Brown the minced beef in a thick-bottomed pan

2 Place a layer of lasagne over a layer of meat sauce

3 Cover the final layer with béchamel

Variations

Traditionally, pasta dishes are substantial in quantity but because they are so popular they are also sometimes requested as lighter dishes. Obviously the portion size can be reduced but other variations can also be considered.

For example, freshly made pasta cut into 8–10 cm rounds or squares, rectangles or diamonds, lightly poached or steamed, well drained and placed on a light tasty mixture (e.g. a tablespoon of mousse of chicken or fish or shellfish, well-cooked dried spinach flavoured with toasted pine nuts and grated nutmeg or a duxelle mixture) using just the one piece of pasta on top or a piece top and bottom. A light sauce should be used (e.g. a measure of well-reduced chicken stock with a little skimmed milk, blitzed to a froth just before serving, pesto sauce, a drizzle of good-quality olive oil, or a light tomato sauce. The dish can be finished with a suitable garnish (e.g. lightly fried wild or cultivated sliced mushrooms).

Fillings for lasagne can be varied in many ways. Tomato sauce may be used instead of jus lié.

Healthy eating tips

- Use an unsaturated oil (sunflower or olive). Lightly oil the pan and drain off any excess after the frying is complete. Skim the fat from the finished meat sauce.
- Season with the minimum amount of salt.
- The fat content can be proportionally reduced by increasing the ratio of pasta to sauce and thinning the béchamel.

11 Pumpkin tortellini with brown butter balsamic vinaigrette

	4 portions	10 portions
Small pumpkin	1	2½
Olive oil	1 tbsp	2½ tbsp
Ground cinnamon	½ tsp	1¼ tsp
Ground nutmeg	¼ tsp	¾ tsp
Caster sugar	1 tsp	1½ tsp
Seasoning		
Ravioli paste (recipe 12)		
Egg	1	2
Butter	50g	125g
Shallots, finely chopped	25g	62g
Balsamic vinegar	2 tbsp	5 tbsp
Spinach leaves	100g	250g
Sage, chopped	1 tbsp	2½ tbsp

Energy	Cals	Fat	Sat fat	Carb	Sugar	Protein	Fibre
1744kJ	417kcal	24.6g	9.0g	43.2g	4.1g	8.2g	3.0g

1 First prepare the pumpkin filling. Cut in half and scoop out the seeds.

2 Place in a roasting tray. Sprinkle with olive oil, cinnamon and nutmeg. Add a little water to the pan. Roast the pumpkin at 350 °C for approximately 45 minutes, until tender.

3 Remove from the oven, allow to cool, scrape out the flesh. Purée the flesh with the sugar in a food processor until smooth, then season.

4 To make the tortellini, roll out the ravioli paste into 2 mm thick sheets. Cut the pasta sheets into 8 cm squares.

5 Place 1 teaspoon of the pumpkin filling in the centre of each square. Lightly brush two sides of the pasta with beaten egg and fold the pasta in half, creating a triangle. Join the two ends of the long side of the triangle to form the tortellini, eggwash the seam and firmly press the ends together to seal.

6 Cook the tortellini in boiling salted water for 3–4 minutes until al dente.

7 To prepare the vinaigrette, cook the butter until nut brown, remove from the heat, add the shallots and balsamic vinegar, then season.

8 Place the washed spinach leaves in a pan with one-third of the vinaigrette and quickly wilt the spinach. Season.

9 To serve, place the wilted spinach in the centre of the plates. Arrange the well-drained tortellini on the spinach. Spoon the vinaigrette around the plates. Finish with a sprinkling of fresh sage or flat parsley.

Healthy eating tips
- Lightly brush the pumpkin with olive oil when roasting.
- Keep the amount of added salt to a minimum throughout.

12 Ravioli

Energy	Cals	Fat	Sat fat	Carb	Sugar	Protein	Fibre
1027 kJ	249 kcal	9.4 g	1.4 g	38.9 g	0.8 g	4.8 g	1.6 g

To make the dough and form the ravioli:

1 Sieve the flour and salt. Make a well. Add the liquid.

2 Knead to a smooth dough. Rest for at least 30 minutes in a cool place.

3 Roll out to a very thin oblong: 30 cm × 45 cm.

4 Cut in half and eggwash.

5 Place the stuffing in a piping bag with a large plain tube.

6 Pipe out the filling in small pieces, each about the size of a cherry, approximately 4 cm apart, on to one half of the paste.

7 Carefully cover with the other half of the paste and seal, taking care to avoid air pockets.

8 Mark each with the back of a plain cutter.

9 Cut in between each line of filling, down and across with a serrated pastry wheel.

10 Separate on a well-floured tray.

11 Poach in gently boiling salted water for approximately 10 minutes. Drain well.

12 Place in an earthenware serving dish.

13 Cover with 250 ml jus lié, demi-glace or tomato sauce.

14 Sprinkle with 50 g grated cheese.

15 Brown under the salamander and serve.

	4 portions	10 portions
Flour	200 g	500 g
Salt		
Olive oil	35 ml	150 ml
Water	105 ml	250 ml

Note

Fresh egg pasta dough (recipes 1 or 2) can also be used. If you have prepared the dough, start this recipe at step 3.

Possible fillings

Here are some examples of stuffing for ravioli, tortellini and other pastas. Each recipe provides enough stuffing to use with 400 g pasta. The photo shows ravioli that has been stuffed with spinach and ricotta cheese, poached and served with slices of parmesan. The ravioli has been drizzled with olive oil and garnished with micro herbs.

Chicken	
Chicken, cooked, minced	200 g
Ham, minced	100 g
Butter	25 g
2 yolks or 1 egg	
Cheese, grated	25 g
Nutmeg, grated	pinch
Salt and pepper	
Fresh white breadcrumbs	25 g

Spinach and ricotta	
Dry spinach, cooked, puréed	200 g
Ricotta cheese	200 g
Butter	25 g
Nutmeg	
Salt and pepper	

Pork and veal	
Lean pork mince, cooked	200 g
Lean veal mince, cooked	200 g
Butter	25 g
Cheese, grated	25 g
2 yolks or 1 egg	
Fresh white breadcrumbs	25 g
Salt and pepper	

Beef	
Beef or pork mince, cooked	200 g
Spinach, cooked	100 g
Onion, chopped, cooked	50 g
Oregano	
Salt and pepper	

Ricotta and parmesan	
Marjoram, chopped	Pinch
Ricotta cheese	150 g
Parmesan, grated	75 g
Egg	1
Nutmeg	
Salt and pepper	

Fish	
Fish, chopped, cooked	200 g
Mushrooms, chopped, cooked	100 g
Parsley, chopped	
Anchovy paste	

13 Cannelloni

Use the same ingredients as for ravioli dough (recipe 12).

1 Roll out the paste as for ravioli.

2 Cut into squares approximately 6 cm × 6 cm.

3 Cook in gently boiling salted water for approximately 10 minutes. Refresh in cold water.

4 Drain well and lay out singly on the table. Pipe out the required filling across each.

5 Roll up like sausage rolls. Place in a greased earthenware dish.

6 Add 250 ml demi-glace, jus lié or tomato sauce.

7 Sprinkle with 25–50 g grated cheese.

8 Brown slowly under the salamander or in the oven, then serve.

Note

A wide variety of fillings may be used, such as those given in recipe 11.

	4 portions	10 portions
Flour	200 g	500 g
Salt		
Olive oil	35 ml	150 ml
Water	105 ml	250 ml
Fresh egg pasta (recipe 17) can also be used		

Energy	Cals	Fat	Sat fat	Carb	Sugar	Protein	Fibre *
1823 kJ	435 kcal	20.3 g	5.6 g	44.2 g	4.3 g	21.6 g	4.1 g

* 1 portion with beef

14 Spaghetti with tomato sauce (*spaghetti alla pomodoro*)

1 Plunge the spaghetti into a saucepan containing boiling salted water. Allow to boil gently.

2 Stir occasionally with a wooden spoon. Cook for approximately 12–15 minutes, until *al dente*.

3 Drain well in a colander. Return to a clean, dry pan.

4 Mix in the butter and add the tomato sauce. Correct the seasoning.

5 Add the tomato concassé and 4–5 leaves of fresh basil torn into pieces with your fingers or flat parsley, and serve with grated cheese.

Professional tip

Cook pasta to an *al dente* texture.

	4 portions	10 portions
Spaghetti	100 g	250 g
Butter (optional) or olive oil	25 g	60 g
Tomato sauce (page 145)	250 ml	625 ml
Salt, mill pepper		
Fresh basil, to serve		
Grated cheese, to serve		
Tomato concassée, to serve		

Healthy eating tips
- Use very little or no salt as there is already plenty from the cheese.
- Reduce or omit the butter and serve with a large green salad.

* Using hard margarine instead of butter

Energy	Cals	Fat	Sat fat	Carb	Sugar	Protein	Fibre	*
1672 kJ	400 kcal	17.2 g	9.4 g	50.0 g	10.2 g	11.8 g	4.0 g	

1 Place the spaghetti into boiling water

2 Drain the cooked pasta

3 Add the sauce to the pasta

15 Spaghetti Bolognaise (*spaghetti alla bolognese*)

1 Place half the butter or oil in a sautéuse.
2 Add the chopped onion and garlic, and cook for 4–5 minutes without colour.
3 Add the beef and cook, colouring lightly.
4 Add the jus lié, the tomato purée and the herbs.
5 Simmer until tender.
6 Add the mushrooms and simmer for 5 minutes. Correct the seasoning.
7 Meanwhile, cook the spaghetti in plenty of boiling salted water.
8 Allow to boil gently, stirring occasionally with a wooden spoon.
9 Cook for approximately 12–15 minutes. Drain well in a colander.
10 Return to a clean pan containing the rest of the butter or oil (optional).
11 Correct the seasoning.
12 Serve with the sauce in centre of the spaghetti.
13 Serve grated cheese separately.

	4 portions	10 portions
Butter or oil	20 g	50 g
Onion, chopped	50 g	125 g
Clove of garlic, chopped	1	2
Lean minced beef or tail end fillet (see note), cut into 3 mm dice	400 g	1 kg
Jus lié	125 ml	300 ml
Tomato purée	1 tbsp	2 ½ tbsp
Marjoram or oregano	Pinch	½ tsp
Mushrooms, diced	100 g	250 g
Salt, mill pepper		
Spaghetti	100 g	250 g
Grated cheese, to serve		

Energy	Cals	Fat	Sat fat	Carb	Sugar	Protein	Fibre	Sodium *
1741 kJ	416 kcal	22.7 g	12 g	21.7	2.7 g	32.5 g	2 g	0.403 g

* Using butter

Note

There are many variations on Bolognaise sauce, e.g. substitute lean beef with pork mince or use a combination of both; add 50 g each of chopped carrot and celery; add 100 g chopped pancetta or bacon.

Healthy eating tips
● Use an unsaturated oil (sunflower or olive). Lightly oil the pan and drain off any excess after the frying is complete. Skim the fat from the finished dish.
● Season with the minimum amount of salt.
● Try using more pasta and extending the sauce with tomatoes.
● Serve with a large green salad.

Alternative recipe for bolognaise sauce:

	4 portions	10 portions
Olive oil	1 tbsp	2 ½ tbsp
Beef mince and pork mince	270 g	700 g
Onion, chopped	½	1
Mushrooms, sliced	100 g	250 g
Carrots, peeled and cut as for paysanne	1	2
Red wine	75 ml	180 ml
Beef stock or meat stock, reduced	100 ml	250 ml
Tomato purée	1 tbsp	2 tbsp
Tabasco sauce (optional)	½ tsp	1 tsp
Salt and freshly ground black pepper, to taste		
Fresh parsley, chopped	2 tbsp	5 tbsp
Fresh chives, chopped, to garnish		

1 Heat the olive oil in a frying pan, over a medium heat.

2 Add the beef and pork mince and the chopped onion and pan-fry for 4–6 minutes, stirring well, until the mince has browned and the onion has softened.

3 Add the mushrooms and carrots and cook for a further minute before adding the red wine, beef stock and tomato purée.

4 Add the Tabasco sauce and season to taste (optional).

5 Add the chopped parsley and cook for 2–4 minutes more to allow the wine and stock to reduce a little.

6 When mixing the pasta into the sauce, first drain the water thoroughly from the pasta then place into the bolognaise sauce.

7 Toss well, to evenly coat, then spoon into a serving bowl.

8 Garnish with the chopped chives, to serve (optional).

16 Macaroni cheese

	4 portions	10 portions
Macaroni	100 g	250 g
Butter or oil, optional	25 g	60 g
Grated cheese	100 g	250 g
Thin béchamel	500 ml	1.25 litres
Diluted English or continental mustard	¼ tsp	1 tsp
Salt, mill pepper		

Energy	Cals	Fat	Sat fat	Carb	Sugar	Protein	Fibre	*
7596 kJ	1808 kcal	116.6 g	64.2 g	136.6 g	26.6 g	60.0 g	6.8 g	

* For 4 portions

1 Plunge the macaroni into a saucepan containing plenty of boiling salted water.

2 Allow to boil gently and stir occasionally with a wooden spoon.

3 Cook for approximately 15 minutes and drain well in a colander.

4 Return to a clean pan containing the butter.

5 Mix with half the cheese and add the béchamel and mustard. Season.

6 Place in an earthenware dish and sprinkle with the remainder of the cheese.

7 Brown lightly under the salamander and serve.

Note

Browning the macaroni well gives it a good flavour, texture and presentation.

Healthy eating tips
● Half the grated cheese could be replaced with a small amount of Parmesan (more flavour and less fat).
● Use semi-skimmed milk for the béchamel. No added salt is necessary.

Variation

Variations include the addition of cooked, sliced mushrooms, diced ham, sweetcorn, tomato, and so on. Macaroni may also be prepared and served as for any of the spaghetti dishes.

17 Noodles with butter

	4 portions	10 portions
Noodles	400g	1kg
Salt, mill pepper		
A little grated nutmeg		
Butter or sesame oil	50g	125g

1 Cook the noodles in plenty of gently boiling salted water.

2 Drain well in a colander and return to the pan.

3 Add the seasoning and butter and toss carefully until mixed.

4 Correct the seasoning and serve.

Energy	Cals	Fat	Sat fat	Carb	Sugar	Protein	Fibre *
796kJ	191kcal	12.3g	7.1g	18.0g	0.6g	3.1g	0.7g

* Using margarine

Healthy eating tip
● Keep the added salt to a minimum.

Note

Noodles may also be used as a garnish with meat and poultry dishes (e.g. braised beef).

18 Tagliatelle carbonara

	4 portions	10 portions
Tagliatelle	300g	750g
Olive oil	1 tbsp	2½ tbsp
Cloves of garlic, peeled and crushed	2	5
Smoked bacon, diced	200g	500g
Eggs	4	10
Double or single cream	4 tbsp	150ml
Parmesan cheese	4 tbsp	150ml

Energy	Cals	Fat	Sat fat	Carb	Sugar	Protein	Fibre	Sodium
2911kJ	698kcal	44.8g	20.8g	43.0g	1.9g	33.4g	0.2g	1.0g

1 Cook the tagliatelle in boiling salted water until *al dente*. Refresh and drain.

2 Heat the oil in a suitable pan. Fry the crushed and chopped garlic. Add the diced, smoked bacon.

3 Mix together the beaten eggs, cream and Parmesan. Season with black pepper.

4 Add the tagliatelle to the garlic and bacon. Add the eggs and cream, stirring until the eggs cook in the heat. Serve immediately.

19 Crisp polenta and roasted Mediterranean vegetables

	4 portions	10 portions
Polenta		
Water	200 ml	500 ml
Butter	30 g	75 g
Polenta flour	65 g	160 g
Parmesan, grated	25 g	60 g
Egg yolks	1	2
Crème fraiche	110 g	275 g
Seasoning		
Roasted vegetables		
Red peppers	2	5
Yellow peppers	2	5
Courgettes	2	5
Red onions	2	5
Vegetable oil	200 ml	500 ml
Seasoning		
Clove of garlic	1	3
Thyme, sprigs	2	5

Energy	Cals	Fat	Sat fat	Carb	Sugar	Protein	Fibre	Sodium
3267 kJ	790 kcal	71.4 g	18.9 g	28.6 g	14.0 g	10.1 g	6.6 g	0.1 g

Polenta:

1 Bring the water and the butter to the boil.

2 Season the water well and whisk in the polenta flour.

3 Continue to whisk until very thick.

4 Remove from the heat and add the Parmesan, egg yolk and crème fraiche.

5 Whisk until all incorporated; check the seasoning.

6 Set in a lined tray.

7 Once set, cut using a round cutter or cut into squares.

8 Reserve until required.

Roasted vegetables:

1 Roughly chop the vegetables into large chunks. Ensure the seeds are removed from the peppers.

2 Toss the cut vegetables in the oil and season well.

3 Place the vegetables in an oven with the aromats for 30 minutes at 180 °C.

4 Remove from the oven and drain. Reserve until required.

To serve:

1 To serve the dish, shallow-fry the polenta in a non-stick pan until golden on both sides.

2 Warm the roasted vegetables and place them in the middle of the plate. Place the polenta on top.

Note

Serve with rocket salad and balsamic dressing.

Professional tip

Line the tray with cling film and silicone paper before pouring in the polenta – this will stop it from sticking to the tray when it sets.

20 Couscous with chorizo sausage and chicken

1 Prepare the couscous in a suitable bowl and gently pour over 300 ml of boiling water (750 ml for 10 portions).

2 Stir well, cover and leave to stand for 5 minutes.

3 Heat the olive oil in a suitable frying pan, add the chopped garlic, then sauté for 1 minute.

4 Add the chorizo sausage (sliced 1 cm thick) and the chicken cut into fine strips. Cook for 5–6 minutes.

5 Add the couscous, sunblush tomatoes (skinned or diced) and parsley, mix thoroughly and heat for a further 2–3 minutes.

6 Drizzle with olive oil, serve as a warm salad.

7 Garnish with mixed leaves and flat parsley.

Healthy eating tips
- Use an unsaturated oil (sunflower or olive) to lightly oil the pan to sauté the garlic.
- Drain off any excess fat after cooking the sausage and chicken.
- Serve with mixed leaves.

	4 portions	10 portions
Couscous	250 g	625 g
Olive oil	1 tbsp	1 ½ tbsp
Garlic cloves, finely chopped	2	3
Chorizo sausage	150 g	400 g
Suprêmes of chicken, skinned	3	7
Sunblush tomatoes	75 g	200 g
Fresh parsley	¼ tsp	½ tsp

Energy	Cals	Fat	Sat fat	Carb	Sugar	Protein	Fibre
1590 kJ	380 kcal	13.1 g	4.3 g	34.1 g	1.7 g	33.1 g	0.3 g

21 Gnocchi parisienne

	4 portions	10 portions
Water	125 ml	300 ml
Margarine or butter	50 g	125 g
Salt		
Flour, white or wholemeal	60 g	150 g
Eggs	2	5
Cheese, grated	50 g	125 g
Béchamel (thin) (see page 130)	250 ml	625 ml
Salt, pepper, to season		

Energy	Cals	Fat	Sat fat	Carb	Sugar	Protein	Fibre	Sodium *
1385 kJ	334 kcal	24.5 g	12.6 g	18.4	3.4 g	10.8 g	0.8 g	0.497 g

* Made with butter

1 Boil the water, margarine or butter, and salt in a saucepan. Remove from the heat.

2 Mix in the flour with a kitchen spoon. Return to a gentle heat.

3 Stir continuously until the mixture leaves the sides of the pan.

4 Cool slightly. Gradually add the eggs, beating well. Add half the cheese.

5 Place in a piping bag with ½ cm plain tube.

6 Pipe out in 1 cm lengths into a shallow pan of gently simmering salted water. Do not allow to boil.

7 Cook for approximately 10 minutes. Drain well in a colander.

8 Combine carefully with the béchamel. Correct the seasoning.

9 Pour into an earthenware dish.

10 Sprinkle with the remainder of the cheese.

11 Brown lightly under the salamander and serve. Gnocchi may be used to garnish goulash or navarin in place of potatoes.

Professional tip

Mix the eggs into the paste carefully and slowly, but make sure they are well mixed in. If there is too much egg, the mixture will be slack.

Healthy eating tip
● No added salt is necessary because of the presence of the cheese.

1 Pipe the choux paste into the simmering water; a string tied across the pan can be used to form the lengths of paste

2 Allow the gnocchi to simmer

3 Remove the gnocchi from the water and drain them well

22 Couscous fritters with feta for amuse bouche

Ingredient	4 portions	10 portions
Couscous	80 g	200 g
Vegetable stock	100 mls	250 mls
Beaten egg	½	1
Natural yoghurt	1 tbsp	2 ½ tbsp
Feta cheese cut into 1 cm dice	40 g	100 g
Tomatoes, skinned, deseeded, cut into small dice	25 g	60 g
Spring onions, finely chopped	2	5
Vegetable oil	1 tbsp	2 ½ tbsp

Energy	Cals	Fat	Sat fat	Carb	Sugar	Protein	Fibre	Sodium
533 kJ	128 kcal	6.9 g	2.3 g	11.8	1.5 g	5.2 g	0.3 g	0.174 g

1 Place the couscous in a suitable bowl; pour in the boiling stock, stir. Allow to stand until the couscous absorbs the stock

2 Add the egg and yogurt, mix well, season, fold in the feta cheese, tomatoes and spring onions

3 Divide the mixture into the number of portions, shape into small cakes

4 Shallow fry the fritters in vegetable oil on both sides, until golden brown

5 Serve as an amuse bouche on a fresh tomato sauce seasoned with chilli, in each fritter garnish with a suitable chutney, red onion, beetroot or fig.

23 Gnocchi romaine (semolina)

	4 portions	10 portions
Milk	500 ml	1.5 litre
Semolina	100 g	250 g
Salt, pepper		
Grated nutmeg		
Egg yolk	1	3
Cheese, grated	25 g	60 g
Butter or margarine	25 g	60 g
Tomato sauce (see page 145)	250 ml	625 ml

Energy	Cals	Fat	Sat fat	Carb	Sugar	Protein	Fibre	*
1066 kJ	254 kcal	12.5 g	6.9 g	27.5 g	7.0 g	9.8 g	0.8 g	

* Using semi-skimmed milk

1 Boil the milk in a thick-bottomed pan.

2 Sprinkle in the semolina, stirring continuously. Stir to the boil.

3 Season and simmer until cooked (approximately 5–10 minutes). Remove from heat.

4 Mix in the egg yolk, cheese and butter.

5 Pour into a buttered tray 1 cm deep.

6 When cold, cut into rounds with a 5 cm round cutter.

7 Place the debris in a buttered earthenware dish.

8 Neatly arrange the rounds on top.

9 Sprinkle with melted butter and cheese.

10 Lightly brown in the oven or under a salamander.

Note

Serve with a border of tomato sauce round the gnocchi.

Professional tip

Make sure the mixture has chilled until it is completely set, before cutting it into shape – it is much easier to handle once it has set

Healthy eating tip

● No added salt is necessary because of the presence of the cheese.

1 Stir the semolina into the milk

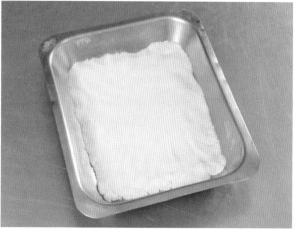

2 Pour the mixture into a greased tray and leave to cool

3 Cut the gnocchi into shape

4 Sprinkle grated cheese over the dish

24 Scrambled eggs (basic recipe) *(oeufs brouillés)*

	4 portions	10 portions
Eggs	6–8	15–20
Milk (optional)	2 tbsp	5 tbsp
Salt, pepper		
Butter or oil	50g	125g

Energy	Cals	Fat	Sat fat	Carb	Sugar	Protein	Fibre *
1105kJ	263kcal	22.9g	8.7g	0.5g	0.5g	13.9g	0.0g

* Using hard margarine instead of butter

The photo to the left shows scrambled eggs with smoked salmon.

1 Break the eggs in a basin, add milk (if using), lightly season with salt and pepper and thoroughly mix with a whisk.

2 Melt half the butter in a thick-bottomed pan, add the eggs and cook over a gentle heat, stirring continuously until the eggs are lightly cooked.

3 Remove from the heat, correct the seasoning and mix in the remaining butter. (A tablespoon of cream may also be added at this point.)

Serve in individual egg dishes or on a slice of freshly butter toast with the crust removed.

Variation

Scrambled eggs may be served with smoked salmon.

Note

If scrambled eggs are cooked too quickly or for too long the protein will toughen, the eggs will discolour because of the iron and sulphur compounds being released, and syneresis (separation of water from the eggs) will occur. This means that they will be unpleasant to eat. The heat from the pan will continue to cook the eggs after it has been removed from the stove; therefore, the pan should be removed from the heat just before the eggs are cooked.

Healthy eating tips
- Try to keep the butter used in cooking to a minimum and serve with unbuttered toast.
- Garnish with a grilled tomato.

25 Soft-boiled eggs in the shell *(oeufs à la coque)*

Allow 1 or 2 eggs per portion.

Method 1 (soft):

1 Place the eggs in cold water and bring to the boil.

2 Simmer for 2–2½ minutes, then remove from the water.

3 Serve at once in an egg cup.

Method 2 (medium soft):

1 Plunge the eggs in boiling water, then reboil.

2 Simmer for 4–5 minutes.

3 Serve at once in an egg cup.

Energy	Cals	Fat	Sat fat	Carb	Sugar	Protein	Fibre *
340KJ	81kcal	6.0g	1.9g	0.0g	0.0g	6.8g	0.0g

* Using 1 egg per portion

26 Hard-boiled eggs with cheese and tomato sauce (oeufs aurore)

	4 portions	10 portions
Hard-boiled eggs	4	10
Duxelle		
Shallots, chopped	10 g	25 g
Butter, margarine or oil	10 g	25 g
Mushrooms	100 g	250 g
Parsley or other fresh herbs, chopped		
Salt, pepper		
Béchamel sauce (see page 130)	250 ml	625 ml
Tomato sauce or purée		
Parmesan cheese, grated		

1 Cut the eggs in halves lengthwise.
2 Remove the yolks and pass them through a sieve.
3 Place the whites in an earthenware serving dish.
4 Prepare the duxelle by cooking the chopped shallot in the butter without colouring, add the well-washed and finely chopped mushroom or mushroom trimmings, cook for 3–4 minutes.
5 Mix the yolks with the duxelle and parsley and correct the seasoning.
6 Spoon or pipe the mixture into the egg white halves.
7 Add a little tomato sauce or tomato purée to the béchamel sauce to give it a pinkish colour.
8 Mask the eggs with the sauce and sprinkle with grated cheese.
9 Gratinate under the salamander.

Healthy eating tips
● Serve with French bread or toast and a green salad.
● There is plenty of salt in the cheese, so additional salt is not necessary.

Energy	Cals	Fat	Sat fat	Carb	Sugar	Protein	Fibre	Sodium
1293 kJ	311 kcal	22.4 g	10.4 g	7.8	4.1 g	19.8 g	0.8 g	0.561 g

27 French-fried eggs (deep-fried eggs)

1 Half cover a shallow pan with vegetable oil.
2 Heat gently until a slight haze is seen.
3 Break a fresh egg into the oil.
4 Carefully flick the white over the yolk, using a heatproof plastic spoon, until it cooks to a golden brown colour.
5 When cooked, serve immediately.

Energy	Cals	Fat	Sat fat	Carb	Sugar	Protein	Fibre	Sodium [*]
595 kJ	143 kcal	12.3 g	2.9 g	0	0 g	8.2 g	0 g	0.096 g

[*] One egg

Professional tip

The eggs must be fried quickly. It is important to flick the white over the yolk during the cooking.

28 Fried eggs (*oeufs frits*)

Allow 1 or 2 eggs per portion.

1 Melt a little fat in a frying pan. Add the eggs.

2 Cook gently until lightly set. Serve on a plate or flat dish.

Professional tip

To prepare an excellent fried egg, it is essential to use a fresh high-quality egg, to maintain a controlled low heat and to use a high-quality fat (butter or oil, such as sunflower oil).

Health and safety

Lightly cooked eggs do not reach high enough temperatures to kill all bacteria that may be present. Do not serve lightly cooked eggs to people in high-risk groups: very young children, elderly people, pregnant women or people who are ill.

Energy	Cals	Fat	Sat fat	Carb	Sugar	Protein	Fibre	*
536kJ	128kcal	31.0g	9.8g	0.0g	0.0g	7.6g	0.0g	

* Fried in sunflower oil

29 Poached eggs with cheese sauce (*oeufs pochés mornay*)

	4 portions	10 portions
Eggs	4	10
Short paste tartlets	4	10
or		
Half slices of buttered toast	4	10
Mornay sauce (see page 131)	250 ml	625 ml

Energy	Cals	Fat	Sat fat	Carb	Sugar	Protein	Fibre	Salt
1177kJ	280kcal	19.1g	8.7g	15.2g	3.4g	12.8g	0.8g	

1 Carefully break the eggs one by one into a pan of vinegar water (approximately 15 per cent acidulation) and make sure the water is at a gentle simmer

2 Cook just below simmer until lightly set, for approximately 3–3 ½ minutes.

3 Remove carefully with a perforated spoon into a bowl of ice water.

4 Trim the white if necessary.

5 Reheat, when required, by placing into hot salted water for approximately ½–1 minute.

6 Remove carefully from the water using a perforated spoon. Drain on a cloth.

7 Place tartlets or toast in an earthenware dish (the slices of toast may be halved, cut in rounds with a cutter, crust removed).

8 Add the hot, well-drained eggs.

9 Completely cover with the sauce, sprinkle with grated Parmesan cheese, brown under the salamander and serve.

Variation

Florentine – poached eggs on a bed of leaf spinach and finished as for mornay.

Washington – on a bed of sweetcorn coated with sûpreme sauce (page 135) or cream.

30 Omelette (*omelette nature*)

	1 portion
Eggs	2–3
Salt, pepper	
Butter or oil	10 g

Energy	Cals	Fat	Sat fat	Carb	Sugar	Protein	Fibre *
990 kJ	236 kcal	20.2 g	9.1 g	0.0 g	0.0 g	13.6 g	0.0 g

* Using 2 eggs per portion. Using 3 eggs per portion, 1 portion provides: 1330 kJ/317 kcal energy; 26.2 g fat; 11.0 g sat fat; 0.0 g carb; 0.0 g sugar; 20.3 g protein; 0.0 g fibre.

Video: Making an omelette http://bit.ly/ 1MxDy9I

1 Break the eggs into a basin, season lightly with salt and pepper.

2 Beat well with a fork, or whisk until the yolks and whites are thoroughly combined and no streaks of white can be seen.

3 Heat the omelette pan; wipe thoroughly clean with a dry cloth.

4 Add the butter; heat until foaming but not brown.

5 Add the eggs and cook quickly, moving the mixture continuously with a fork until lightly set; remove from the heat.

6 Half fold the mixture over at right angles to the handle.

7 Tap the bottom of the pan to bring up the edge of the omelette.

8 With care, tilt the pan completely over so as to allow the omelette to fall into the centre of the dish or plate.

9 Neaten the shape if necessary and serve immediately.

Healthy eating tip
● Use salt sparingly and serve with plenty of starchy carbohydrate and vegetables or salad.

1 Whisk the eggs until the yolks and whites are combined

2 Move the mixture continuously while it cooks

3 Carefully tip the omelette out of the pan

Variation

Variations to omelettes can easily be made by adding the ingredient that the guest or dish may require. For example:

- fine herbs (chopped parsley, chervil and chives)
- mushroom (cooked, sliced, wild or cultivated)
- cheese (25 g grated cheese added before folding)
- tomato (incision made down centre of cooked omelette, filled with hot tomato concassé; served with tomato sauce)
- bacon (grill and then julienne into small strips and fold in at the end).

31 Egg white omelette

Being prepared and cooked without the egg yolks means that this is almost fat free. The whites are three-quarter whipped, lightly seasoned and then cooked as for any other omelette, folded or flat, garnished or served plain.

Energy	Cals	Fat	Sat fat	Carb	Sugar	Protein	Fibre	*
453 kJ	109 kcal	8.2 g	5.2 g	0.1	0.1 g	8.7 g	0 g	

* Using butter and 3 eggs

32 Spanish omelette

	1 portion
Eggs	2–3
Salt, pepper	
Butter, or oil	10 g
Tomato concassé	50 g
Onions, cooked	100 g
Red pepper, diced	100 g
Parsley, chopped	

1 Make up an omelette following recipe 30, steps 1–6, but including the tomato, onion, red pepper and parsley with the eggs.

2 Sharply tap the pan on the stove to loosen the omelette and toss it over as for a pancake.

Note

This omelette is cooked and served flat. Many other flat omelettes can be served with a variety of ingredients.

Energy	Cals	Fat	Sat fat	Carb	Sugar	Protein	Fibre	Sodium
1726kJ	416kcal	30.9g	11.2g	10.9g	8.2g	24.6g	2.5g	0.8g

When the butter is foaming, add the egg mixture

The omelette is tipped out flat

33 Feta, mint, lentil and pistachio omelette

Energy	Cals	Fat	Sat fat	Carb	Sugar	Protein	Fibre	Sodium
2007 kJ	481 kcal	32.8 g	8.1 g	17.5	0.8 g	30.3 g	5.4 g	0.416 g

	4 portions	10 portions
Vegetable oil	4 tbsp	10 tbsp
Cooked brown lentils	400 g	1 kg
Feta cheese	50 g	125 g
Sorrel	20 leaves approximately	50 leaves
Fresh mint chopped	2 tbsp	5 tbsp
Toasted pistachio nuts	2 tbsp	5 tbsp
Seasoning		
Eggs	2	5

Filling:

1 Heat the oil in a pan. Add the lentils and the sorrel, season with salt and pepper. Stir until the sorrel is wilted.

2 Remove from the heat; add the crumbled feta cheese, chopped mint and pistachio nuts.

Note

Serve on plates garnished with mint leaves and wedges of lemon or lime.

Omelette:

1 Beat the eggs well, add a teaspoon of water or cream to every three eggs.

2 Heat sufficient oil or butter in an omelette pan and proceed to make the omelettes.

3 When nearly cooked through, tilt the omelette pan and start to fold the omelette.

4 Add the filling and continue to finish folding the omelette.

34 Scotch eggs

Energy	Cals	Fat	Sat fat	Carb	Sugar	Protein	Fibre	Sodium
2906 kJ	692 kcal	30.9 g	8.5 g	80.2	4.7 g	28.2 g	2 g	1.167 g

	4 portions	10 portions
Eggs	4	10
Pork sausage meat	275 g	700 g
Fresh thyme leaves	1 tsp	2 tsp
Fresh parsley, chopped	1 tsp	2 tsp
Spring onion, very finely chopped	1	3
Plain flour, seasoned	125 g	300 g
Egg, beaten	1	2
Breadcrumbs	250 g	625 g
Salt and freshly ground black pepper		
Vegetable oil for deep-frying		

1 Place the eggs, still in their shells, in a pan of water.

2 Place over a high heat and bring to the boil, then reduce the heat to simmer for approximately 9 minutes.

3 Drain and refresh the eggs under cold running water, then peel.

4 Mix the sausage meat with the thyme, parsley and spring onion in a bowl, season well with salt and freshly ground black pepper.

5 Divide the sausage meat mixture into four and flatten each out on a clean surface into ovals about 12 cm long and 8 cm at the widest point.

6 Roll the boiled egg in the seasoned flour.

7 Place each egg onto a sausage meat oval, then wrap the sausage meat around the egg, making sure the coating is smooth and completely covers the egg.

8 Dip each meat-coated egg in the beaten egg, covering the entire surface area.

9 Roll in the breadcrumbs to coat completely.

10 Heat the oil in a deep heavy-bottomed pan, to 180 °C.

11 Carefully place each Scotch egg into the hot oil and deep-fry for 6–8 minutes, until golden and crisp and the sausage meat is completely cooked.

12 Carefully remove from the oil with a slotted spoon and drain on kitchen paper.

Note

To serve, cut the egg in half and season slightly with rock salt. The Scotch eggs can be served hot, warm or cold.

1 Flatten out an oval of the sausage meat mixture

2 Flour the egg and wrap the meat around it until it is completely covered

3 Dip in flour, then beaten egg

4 Roll the egg in the breadcrumbs

5 The egg should be completely coated in breadcrumbs, ready for frying

Variation

For a **vegetarian** version of the traditional pork Scotch egg, follow the same method as above, replacing the sausage meat with 350 g of dry mashed potato.

A **fish** version can be made. Follow the same method as above, using 300 g fish mousse (this works best using salmon) instead of sausage meat.

35 Eggs in cocotte (oeufs en cocotte)

1 Butter the appropriate number of egg cocottes.
2 Break an egg carefully into each and season.
3 Place the cocottes in a sauté pan containing 1 cm water.
4 Cover with a tight-fitting lid, place on a fierce heat so that the water boils rapidly.
5 Cook for 2–3 minutes until the eggs are lightly set, then serve.

Variation

Half a minute before the cooking is completed, add 1 tsp of cream to each egg and complete the cooking

When cooked, add 1 tsp of jus lié to each egg

Place diced cooked chicken, mixed with cream, in the bottom of the cocottes; break the eggs on top of the chicken and cook

As above, using tomato concassé in place of chicken.

	4 portions	10 portions
Butter	25g	60g
Eggs	4	10
Salt, pepper		

Energy	Cals	Fat	Sat fat	Carb	Sugar	Protein	Fibre
534KJ	127kcal	11.2g	5.2g	0.0g	0.0g	6.8g	0.0g

36 Eggs sur le plat

Allow 1 or 2 eggs per portion.

1 Take a china *sur le plat* dish. Add a teaspoon of olive oil or butter. Heat it on the side of the stove, until it is moderately hot.
2 Break in 1 or 2 eggs. Allow them to set on the stove.
3 Transfer to the oven for 2–4 minutes to finish cooking.

Energy	Cals	Fat	Sat fat	Carb	Sugar	Protein	Fibre	Sodium [*]
875kJ	211kcal	16.9g	6.3g	0	0g	14.8g	0g	0.196g

[*] 2 eggs per portion

Note

A *sur le plat* dish is a shallow porcelain dish used for cooking and serving eggs.

12 Produce hot and cold desserts and puddings

This chapter will help you to:

1 prepare, cook and finish hot and cold desserts and puddings, including:
   – working safely and hygienically
   – using the correct equipment
   – applying quality points
   – evaluating the finished dish.
2 know how to:
   – identify different hot and cold desserts and hot puddings

– understand the quality points of ingredients and how to adjust the quantity
– describe preparation and cooking methods
– finish and decorate dishes
– identify sauces, creams, coulis and accompaniments
– apply portion control
– hold and store finished dishes safely
– identify ingredients that may cause allergic reactions.

Recipes in this chapter

Ingredients used in the pastry kitchen

The following information about ingredients and commodities is relevant to several units of your course: Produce hot and cold desserts and puddings; Produce paste products; Produce biscuit, cake and sponge products; and Produce fermented dough products.

The principal building blocks of pastry dishes are flour, fat, sugar, raising agents, eggs and cream.

Flour

Flour is probably the most common commodity in daily use. It forms the foundation of bread, pastry and cakes and is also used in soups, sauces, batters and other foods. It is one of the most important ingredients in patisserie, if not *the* most important.

There are a great variety of high-quality flours made from cereals, nuts or legumes, such as chestnut flour and cornflour. They have been used in patisserie, baking, dessert cuisine and savoury cuisine in all countries throughout history. The most significant of which is wheat flour.

▲ Flour is used in a variety of recipes

Wheat flour

Wheat flour is composed of starch, gluten, sugar, fats, water and minerals.

- Starch is the main component, but gluten is also a significant element. Gluten is elastic and **impermeable** and therefore makes wheat flour the most common flour used in bread making.
- The quantity of sugar in wheat is very small but it plays a very important role in **fermentation**.

- Wheat contains a maximum of only 16 per cent water, but its presence is important.
- The mineral matter (ash), which is found mainly in the husk of the wheat grain and not in the kernel, determines the purity and quality of the flour.

Production of flour

From the ear to the final product, flour, wheat goes through several distinct processes. These are carried out in modern industrial plants, where wheat is subjected to the various treatments and phases necessary for the production of different types of flour. These arrive in perfect condition at our workplaces and are made into preparations like sponge cakes, yeast dough, puff pastries, biscuits, pastries and much more.

White flour is made up almost entirely of the part of the wheat grain known as the **endosperm**, which contains starch and protein. When flour is mixed with water it is converted into a sticky dough. This characteristic is due to the gluten, which becomes sticky when moistened. The relative proportion of starch and gluten varies in different wheats, and those with a low percentage of gluten (soft flour) are not suitable for bread making. For this reason, wheat is blended.

In milling, the whole grain is broken up, the parts separated, sifted, blended and ground into flour. Some of the outer coating of bran is removed, as is the **wheatgerm**, which contains oil and is therefore likely to become rancid and spoil the flour. For this reason wholemeal flour should not be stored for more than 14 days.

Types of flour

- White flour contains 72–85 per cent of the whole grain (the endosperm only).
- Wholemeal flour contains 100 per cent of the whole grain.
- Wheatmeal flour contains 85–95 per cent of the whole grain.
- High-ratio or patent flour contains 40 per cent of the whole grain.
- Self-raising flour is white flour with baking powder added to it.
- Semolina is granulated hard flour prepared from the central part of the wheat grain. White or wholemeal semolina is available.

Storing flour

Flour is a particularly delicate living material and it must be used and stored with special care. It must always be in the best condition, which is why storing large quantities is not recommended. It must be kept in a suitable environment: a clean, organised, disinfected and aerated storeroom. Warm and humid places must be avoided.

Fats

Pastry goods may be made from various types of fat, either a single named fat or a combination. Examples of fats are butter, margarine, shortening and lard.

Butter and other fats

Butter brings smoothness, rich aromas and impeccable textures to patisserie products.

▲ Butter is a key ingredieant in patisserie products

Butter is an **emulsion** – the perfect interaction of water and fat. It is composed of a minimum of 82 per cent fat, a maximum of 16 per cent water and 2 per cent dry extracts.

- Butter is the most complete fat in terms of what contributes to patisserie products.
- It is a very delicate ingredient that can quickly spoil if a series of basic rules are not followed in its use.
- It absorbs odours very easily, so it should be kept well covered and should always be stored far from anything that produces strong odours.
- When kept at 15 °C, butter is stable and retains all its properties: finesse, aroma and creaminess.
- It should not be kept too long: it is always better to work with fresh butter.
- Good butter has a stable texture, pleasing taste, fresh odour, homogenous (even) colour and, most important, it must melt perfectly in the mouth.
- It softens preparations like cookies and petit fours, and keeps products like sponge cakes soft and moist.
- Butter enhances flavour – as in brioches, for example.
- The melting point of butter is between 30 °C and 35 °C.

Margarine

Margarine is often made from a blend of oils that have been hardened or **hydrogenated** (had hydrogen gas added). Margarine may contain up to 10 per cent butterfat.

Cake margarine is again a blend of oils, hydrogenated, to which is added an emulsifying agent that helps combine water and fat. Cake margarine may contain up to 10 per cent butterfat.

Pastry margarine is used for puff pastry. It is a hard plastic or waxy fat that is suitable for layering.

Shortening

Shortening is another name for fat used in pastry making. It is made from oils and is 100 per cent fat, such as hydrogenated lard; another type of shortening is rendered pork fat.

Key terms

Emulsion: a mixture of two or more liquids that are normally immiscible (non-mixable or un-blendable).

Hydrogenated: a substance that has had hydrogen gas added to it. This is used to harden oils in margarine.

Shortening: fat used in pastry making; it is made from oils and is 100 per cent fat.

Sugar

Sugar (or sucrose) is extracted from sugar beet or sugar cane. The juice is crystallised by a complicated manufacturing process. It is then refined and sieved into several grades, such as granulated, caster or icing sugars.

Syrup and treacle are produced as a bi-product during the production of refined sugar. Simple sugar syrups are produced by dissolving sugar with water and heating to invert the sugar. The density and viscosity required to produce different products, such as sorbets and ice-creams, is based on the ratio or percentage of sugar to water. The higher the percentage of sugar, the more dense and viscous the syrup will be. The density and sweetness of sugar syrups can be measured using equipment/instruments such as a **refractometer**, which measures the level of sweetness on the Brix (°Bx) scale and **hydrometer**, which measures density using the Baumé scale. For example, a fruit sorbet mixture will typically measure around 17–18°Baumé/30–31°Brix.

Loaf or cube sugar is obtained by pressing the crystals together while they are slightly wet, drying them in blocks, and then cutting the blocks into squares.

Fondant is a cooked mixture of sugar and glucose which, when heated, is coloured and flavoured, and used for decorating cakes, buns, gateaux and petits fours. Fondant is generally bought ready made.

Inverted sugar

When sucrose is broken down with water in a chemical process called **hydrolysis**, it separates into its two constituent parts: fructose and glucose. Sugar that has been treated in this way is called inverted sugar and is, after sucrose, one of the most commonly used sugars in the catering profession, thanks to its sweetening properties. Inverted sugar comes in liquid and syrup forms:

- **Liquid inverted sugar** is a yellowish liquid with no less than 62 per cent dry matter. It contains more than 3 per cent inverted sugar, but less than 50 per cent. It is used mainly in the commercial food industry.
- **Inverted sugar syrup** is a white, sticky paste and has no less than 62 per cent dry matter and more than 50 per cent inverted sugar. It is the form in which inverted sugar is most commonly used. With equal proportions of dry matter and sucrose, its sweetening capacity is 25–30 per cent greater than sucrose.

Inverted sugar:

- improves the aroma of products
- improves the texture of doughs
- prevents the dehydration of frozen products
- reduces or stops crystallisation
- is essential in ice cream making – it greatly improves its quality and lowers its freezing point.

> **Key terms**
>
> **Refractometer**: equipment used to measure sweetness on the Brix scale.
>
> **Hydrometer**: equipment used to measure density on the Baumé scale.
>
> **Hydrolysis**: a chemical reaction in which a compound – like sugar – breaks down by reacting with water.

Glucose

Glucose is available in various forms:

- the characteristics of a viscous syrup, called crystal glucose
- its natural state, in fruit and honey
- a dehydrated white paste (used mainly in the commercial food industry, but also used in catering)
- 'dehydrated glucose' (atomised glucose) – a glucose syrup from which the water is evaporated; this is used in patisserie, but mainly in the commercial food industry.

Glucose syrup is a transparent, viscous paste. It:

- prevents the crystallisation of boiled sugars, jams and preserves
- delays the drying of a product
- adds plasticity and creaminess to ice cream and the fillings of chocolate bonbons
- prevents the crystallisation of ice cream.

Honey

Honey, a sweet syrup that bees make with the nectar extracted from flowers, is the oldest known sugar. A golden-brown thick paste, it is 30 per cent sweeter than sucrose.

Honey lowers the freezing point of ice cream. It can also be used like inverted sugar, but unlike inverted sugar, will give flavour to the preparation. Also, it is inadequate for preparations that require long storage, since honey re-crystallises after time.

Isomalt

Isomalt sugar is a sweetener that is less well known in the patisserie world, but it has been used for some time. It has different properties from those of the sweeteners already mentioned. It is produced through the hydrolysis of sugar, followed by hydrogenation (the addition of hydrogen).

Produced through these industrial processes, this sugar has been used for many years in industry in confectionery and chewing gum production and is now earning a place in the culinary kitchen.

One of its most notable characteristics is that it can melt without the addition of water or another liquid. This is a very interesting property for making artistic decorations in caramel. Its appearance is like that of confectioners' sugar: a glossy powder. Its sweetening strength is half that of sucrose and it is much less soluble than sugar, which means that it melts less easily in the mouth.

Over the past few years isomalt has been used as a replacement for normal sugar or sucrose when making sugar decorations, blown sugar, pulled sugar or spun sugar. Isomalt is not affected by air humidity, so sugar pieces will keep for longer.

Raising agents

A **raising agent** is a substance added to a cake or bread mixture to give lightness to the product. A raising agent produces gases – air, carbon dioxide or water vapour – which expand when heated. These gases are introduced before baking or are produced by substances added to the mixture before baking. When the product is cooked, the gases expand and are trapped in the gluten of the wheat flour. On further heating and cooking, the pressure of the gluten causes the product to rise and set.

Baking powder

Chemical raising agents cause a reaction between certain acidic and alkaline compounds, which produce carbon dioxide. The alkaline component is almost always sodium bicarbonate or sodium acid carbonate, commonly known as baking soda. It is ideal because it is cheap to produce, easily purified, non-toxic and naturally tasteless. Potassium bicarbonate is available for those on low-sodium diets, but this compound tends to absorb moisture and react prematurely, giving off a bitter flavour.

Baking powder may be used without the addition of acid if the dough or batter is already acidic enough to react with it to produce carbon dioxide. Yoghurt and sour milk contain lactic acid and often are used in place of water or milk in such products; sour milk can also be added along with the baking soda as a separate 'natural' component of the **leavening**.

Baking powder contains baking soda and an acid in the form of salt crystals that dissolve in water. Ground dry starch is also added to prevent premature reactions in humid air by absorbing moisture and to dilute the powder.

Most baking powders are 'double acting' – that is, they produce an initial set of gas bubbles when the powder is mixed into the batter and then a second set during the baking process. The first and smaller reaction is necessary to form many small gas bubbles in the batter or dough; the second is necessary to expand these bubbles to form the final light texture. This second reaction must happen late enough in the baking for the surrounding materials to have set, preventing the bubbles from escaping and the product from collapsing.

Baking powder is made from alkali (bicarbonate of soda) plus acid (cream of tartar – potassium hydrogen tartrate). Commercial baking powders differ mainly in their proportions of the acid salts. Cream of tartar is not normally used due to its high cost, so calcium phosphate and gluconodelta-lactose are now commonly used in its place. Sodium aluminium sulphate is an acid that is active only at higher oven temperatures and has an advantage over other powders, which tend to produce gas too early.

Use of water vapour

Water vapour is produced during the baking process from the liquid content used in the mixing. Water vapour has approximately 1,600 times the original volume of the water. The raising power is slower than that of a gas. This method is used in the production of choux pastry, puff pastry, rough puff, flaky and batter products.

> **Key terms**
>
> **Raising agent:** a substance added to a cake or bread mixture produces gases that give lightness to the product. Baking powder is an example of a raising agent.
>
> **Leavening:** the process where a substance, such as yeast or baking powder, is used to produce fermentation in a dough or batter

Points to remember

- Always buy a reliable brand of baking powder.
- Store in a dry place in an airtight tin.
- Do not store for long periods of time, as baking powder loses some of its residual carbon dioxide over time and therefore will not be as effective.
- Check the recipe carefully, making sure that the correct preparation for the type of mixture is used; otherwise, under- or over-rising may result.
- Sieve the raising agent with the flour and/or dry ingredients to give an even mix and therefore an even reaction.
- Distribute moisture evenly into the mixture to ensure even action of the raising agent.
- If a large proportion of raising agent has been added to a mixture and is not to be cooked immediately, keep the mixture in a cool place to avoid too much reaction before baking.

What happens if too much raising agent is used?

Too much raising agent causes:

- over-risen product that may collapse, giving a sunken effect
- coarse texture
- poor colour and flavour
- fruit sinking to the bottom of the cake
- a bitter taste.

What happens if not enough raising agent is used?

Insufficient raising agent causes:

- lack of volume
- insufficient lift
- close texture
- shrinkage.

Salt

Salt (chemical name 'sodium chloride') is one of the most important ingredients. It is well known that salt is a necessary part of the human diet, present in small or large proportions in many natural foods. Salt considerably enhances many products, sweet or savoury.

We generally associate salt with seasoning foods to improve their flavour, but it is also necessary in the making of many sweet dishes. It is a good idea to add a pinch of salt to all sweet preparations, nougats, chocolate bonbons and cakes to intensify flavours. Salt also softens sugar and butter, activates the taste buds and enhances all aromas.

Salt gives us the possibility of many combinations. At times, these may seem normal, for example, a terrine of *foie gras* and coarse salt, while others are surprising, for example, praline with coarse salt.

The addition of salt enhances the flavour of foods when its quantity is well adjusted; but if we add it in greater quantity than we are used to, it produces a very interesting, completely unknown result. It certainly is not adequate in all preparations, so it is important to check results consistently.

Excessive salt can cause high blood pressure, which can lead to strokes or heart attacks, so it should be used in moderation.

Eggs

The egg is one of the principal ingredients of the culinary world. Its great versatility and extraordinary properties as a thickener, emulsifier and stabiliser make its presence important in various creations in patisserie including sauces, creams, sponge cakes, custards and ice creams. Although it is not often the main ingredient, it plays specific and determining roles in terms of texture, taste and aroma. The egg is fundamental in preparations such as brioche, crème anglaise, sponge cake and crème pâtissière. A good custard cannot be made without eggs, as they cause the required **coagulation** and give it the desired consistency and finesse. Eggs are also an important ingredient in ice cream, where the yolk acts as an emulsifier. The extent to which eggs are used (or not) makes an enormous difference to the quality of the product.

▲ Eggs are a key ingredient in quiche

Egg yolk is high in saturated fat. The yolk is a good source of protein and also contains vitamins and iron. The egg white is made up of protein (albumen) and water. The egg yolk also contains lecithin, which acts as an **emulsifier** in dishes such as mayonnaise – it helps to keep the ingredients mixed, so that the oils and water do not separate.

Hens' eggs are graded in four sizes: small, medium, large and very large. For the dessert, paste and cake recipes in this book, use medium-sized eggs (approximately 50 g).

> **Key term**
>
> **Coagulation:** to change consistency from a fluid into a thickened mass.
>
> **Emulsifier:** emulsifiers are made up of molecules with one water-loving (hydrophilic) and one oil-loving (hydrophobic) end. They make it possible for liquids that are normally immiscible to become finely dispersed in each other, creating a stable, homogenous, smooth emulsion.

What you need to know about eggs

- Eggs act as a texture agent in, for example, patisseries and ice creams.
- They intensify the aroma of pastries like brioche.
- They enhance flavours.
- They give volume to whisked sponges and batters.
- They strengthen the structure of preparations such as sponge cakes.
- They act as a thickening agent, e.g. in crème anglaise.
- They act as an emulsifier in preparations such as mayonnaise and ice cream.
- A fresh egg should have a small, shallow air pocket inside it.
- The yolk of a fresh egg should be bulbous, firm and bright.
- The fresher the egg, the more viscous the egg white.
- Eggs should be stored away from strong odours as, despite their shells, odours are easily absorbed.
- In a whole 60 g egg, the yolk weighs about 20 g, the white 30 g and the shell 10 g.
- Eggs contain protein and fat.

Egg whites

- To avoid the danger of salmonella, if the egg white is not going to be cooked or will not reach a temperature of 70 °C, use pasteurised egg whites. Egg white is available chilled, frozen or dried.
- Equipment must be thoroughly clean and free from any traces of fat, as this prevents the whites from whipping; fat or grease prevents the albumen strands from bonding and trapping the air bubbles.
- Take care that there are no traces of yolk in the white, as yolk contains fat.
- A little acid (cream of tartar or lemon juice) strengthens the egg white, extends the foam and produces more meringue. The acid also has the effect of stabilising the meringue.
- If the foam is over-whipped, the albumen strands, which hold the water molecules with the sugar suspended on the outside of the bubble, are overstretched. The water and sugar make contact and the sugar dissolves, making the meringue heavy and wet. This can sometimes be rescued by further whisking until it foams up, but very often you will find that you may have to discard the mixture and start again. Beaten egg white forms a foam that is used for aerating sweets and many other desserts, including meringues (see page 472).

Milk

Milk is a basic and fundamental element of our diet throughout our lives. It is composed of water, sugar and fat (with a minimum fat content of 3.5 per cent). It is essential to numerous preparations, from cream, ice cream, yeast dough, mousse and custard to certain types of ganache, cookies, tuiles and muffins. A yeast dough will change considerably in texture, taste and colour if made with milk instead of water.

Milk has a slightly sweet taste and little odour. Two distinct processes are used to conserve it:

1 **Pasteurisation** – the milk is heated to between 73 °C and 85 ° for a few seconds, then cooled quickly to 4 °C.
2 **Sterilisation (UHT)** – the milk is heated to between 140 °C and 150 °C for 2 seconds, then cooled quickly.

Milk is **homogenised** to disperse the fat evenly, since the fat has a tendency to rise to the surface (see 'Cream', below).

Useful facts

- Pasteurised milk has a better taste and aroma than UHT milk.
- Milk is useful for developing flavour in sauces and creams, due to its **lactic fermentation**.
- Milk is an agent of colour, texture and aroma in dough.
- Because of its lactic ferments, it helps in the maturation of dough and cream.
- There are other types of milk, such as sheep's milk, that can be interesting to use in desserts.
- Milk is much more fragile than cream. In recipes, adding it in certain proportions is advisable for a much more subtle and delicate final product.

Cream

Cream is used in many recipes because of its high fat content and great versatility. Cream is the concentrated milk fat that is skimmed off the top of the milk when it has been left to sit. A film forms on the surface because of the difference in density between fat and liquid. This process is speeded up mechanically in large industries by heating and using **centrifuges**.

Cream should contain at least 18 per cent butter fat. Cream for whipping must contain more than 30 per cent butter fat. Commercially frozen cream is available in 2 kg and 10 kg slabs. Types, packaging, storage and uses of cream are listed in Table 12.1.

Table 12.1 Types of cream

Type of cream	Legal minimum fat (%)	Process and packaging	Storage	Characteristics and uses
Half cream	12	Homogenised and may be pasteurised or ultra-heat treated.	2–3 days	Does not whip; used for pouring; suitable for low-fat diets.
Cream or single cream	18	Homogenised and pasteurised by heating to about 79.5 °C for 15 seconds and then cooled to 4.5 °C. Automatically filled into bottles and cartons after processing. Sealed with foil caps. Bulk quantities according to local suppliers.	2–3 days in summer; 3–4 days in winter under refrigeration	A pouring cream suitable for coffee, cereals, soup or fruit. A valuable addition to cooked dishes. Makes delicious sauces. Does not whip.
Whipping cream	35	Not homogenised, but pasteurised and packaged as above.	2–3 days in summer; 3–4 days in winter under refrigeration	The ideal whipping cream. Suitable for piping, cake and dessert decoration, ice-cream, cake and pastry fillings.
Double cream	48	Slightly homogenised, and pasteurised and packaged as above.	2–3 days in summer; 3–4 days in winter under refrigeration	A rich pouring cream which will also whip. The cream will float on coffee or soup.
Double cream 'thick'	48	Heavily homogenised, then pasteurised and packaged. Usually only available in domestic quantities.	2–3 days in summer; 3–4 days in winter under refrigeration	A rich spoonable cream that will not whip.
Clotted cream	55	Heated to 82 °C and cooled for about 4½ hours. The cream crust is then skimmed off. Usually packed in cartons by hand. Bulk quantities according to local suppliers.	2–3 days in summer; 3–4 days in winter under refrigeration	A very thick cream with its own special flavour and colour. Delicious with scones, fruit and fruit pies.
Ultra-heat treated (UHT) cream	12, 18, 35	Half (12%), single (18%) or whipping cream (35%) is homogenised and heated to 132 °C for one second and cooled immediately. Aseptically packed in polythene and foil-lined containers. Available in bigger packs for catering purposes.	6 weeks if unopened. Needs no refrigeration. Usually date stamped.	A pouring cream.

Whipping and double cream may be whipped to make them lighter and to increase volume. Cream will whip more easily if it is kept at refrigeration temperature. All cream products must be kept in the refrigerator for health and safety reasons. They should be handled with care and, because they will absorb odour, they should never be stored near onions or other strong-smelling foods.

As with milk, there are two main methods for conserving cream:

1 **Pasteurisation** – the cream is heated to between 85 °C and 90 °C for a few seconds and then cooled quickly; this cream retains all its flavour properties
2 **Sterilisation (UHT)** – this consists of heating the cream to between 140 °C and 150 °C for 2 seconds; cream treated this way loses some of its flavour properties, but it keeps for longer.

Always use pasteurised cream when possible, for example, in the restaurant when desserts are made for immediate consumption.

Key terms

Pasteurisation: a process where heat is applied to products such as milk and cream for a short period of time before being cooled quickly. This helps to kill harmful bacteria and extend shelf-life whilst maintaining flavour properties.

Sterilisation: another process where heat is applied but at much higher temperatures. This increases shelf-life further than pasteurisation but products treated this way tend to lose some of their flavour properties.

Homogenise: a process in the production of milk in which the fats are emulsified so that the cream does not separate.

Lactic fermentation: a biological process in which sugars (e.g. sucrose or lactose) are converted into cellular energy

Centrifuge: a piece of laboratory equipment, driven by a motor, which spins liquid samples at high speed. Centrifuges work by the sedimentation principle to separate substances of greater and lesser density.

Useful facts

- Cream whips with the addition of air, thanks to its fat content. This retains air bubbles formed during beating.
- Cream adds texture.

- All cream, once boiled and cooled, can be whipped again.
- Once cream is boiled and mixed or infused with other ingredients to add flavour, it will whip again if first left to cool completely.
- To whip cream well, it must be cold (around 4 °C).
- Cream can be infused with other flavours when it is hot or cold. If cold, it requires sufficient infusion time to absorb the flavours.

Convenience products

Convenience mixes, such as short pastry, sponge mixes and choux pastry mixes, are now becoming increasingly used in a variety of establishments. These products have improved enormously over the last few years. Using such products gives the chef the opportunity to save on time and labour, and with skill, imagination and creativity, the quality of the finished products is not reduced.

Large food manufacturers produce frozen puff pastry and many caterers, including some luxury establishments, use this regularly. It is available in 30 cm squares, ready rolled, therefore avoiding the possibility of uneven thickness and the waste that can occur when rolling out yourself. Manufactured puff pastry is available in three types, defined often by their fat content. The cheapest is made with white hydrogenated fat, which gives the product a pale colour and a waxy taste. Puff pastry made with bakery margarine has a better colour and, often, a better flavour. The best-quality puff pastry is made with butter, giving a richer texture, colour and flavour.

Pastry bought in blocks is cheaper than pre-rolled separate sheets, but has to be rolled evenly to give an even bake. The sizes of sheets do vary with manufacturers; all are interleaved with greaseproof paper.

Filo pastry is another example of a convenient pastry product; it is available in frozen sheets of various sizes. No rolling out is required and once thawed, it can be used as required and moulded if necessary.

As well as convenience pastry mixes, there is also a whole range of frozen products suitable to serve as sweets and afternoon tea pastries. These include fruit pies, flans, gateaux and charlottes. The vast majority are

ready to serve once defrosted, but very often they do require a little more decorative finish. The availability of such products gives the caterer the advantage of further labour cost reductions, while allowing the chef to concentrate on other areas of the menu.

Points to remember

- Check all weighing scales for accuracy.
- Follow the recipe carefully.
- Check all storage temperatures are correct.
- Fat is better to work with if it is 'plastic' (i.e. at room temperature). This will make it easier to cream.
- Always cream the fat and sugar well, before adding the liquid.
- Always work in a clean, tidy and organised way; clean all equipment after use.
- Handle all equipment carefully to avoid cross-contamination.
- Always store ingredients correctly: eggs should be stored in a refrigerator; flour in a bin with a tight-fitting lid; sugar and other dry ingredients in air-tight storage containers.
- Ensure all cooked products are cooled before finishing.
- Understand how to use fresh cream; remember that it is easily over-whipped.
- Always plan your time carefully.
- Use silicone paper for baking in preference to greaseproof.
- Keep all small moulds clean and dry to prevent rusting.

Healthy eating and puddings and desserts

Desserts and puddings remain popular with the consumer, but there is now a demand for products with reduced fat and sugar content, as many people are keen to eat healthily. Chefs will continue to respond to this demand by modifying recipes to reduce the fat and sugar content; they may also use alternative ingredients, such as low-calorie sweeteners where possible and unsaturated fats. Although salt is an essential part of our diet, too much of it can be unhealthy (see page 66) and this should be taken into consideration.

Allergies

Although it is essential to clearly list all potential allergens used to make products, the allergens that are most likely to be used in the production of hot and cold desserts include:

- gluten – flours and any products made from wheat, rye, barley and oats
- nuts – such as hazelnuts, walnuts, Brazil nuts and almonds. These can form part of desserts or be used to make components, such as praline.
- peanuts
- eggs – used in many ways, for example, in sponge bases, mousses, meringues, sauces
- lactose – in milk and milk products such as yoghurt and cheese
- sesame seeds – regularly used in Greek and Eastern European desserts such as Baklava
- sulphites – commonly found in wine which may form part of a jelly or sauce as a component of a dessert.

From December 2014 new legislation requires restaurants to identify to the customer any of the listed allergens which the food may contain. To the list above, the following are included: soybeans, milk, celery, mustards, lupin, fish, seafood (including molluscs).

Types of desserts and puddings

Egg custard-based desserts

Egg custard mixture provides the chef with a versatile basic set of ingredients for a wide range of sweets. Often the mixture is referred to as **crème renversée**. Egg custard uses eggs, milk (full cream, semi-skimmed or skimmed) and cream (which is often added to egg custard desserts to enrich them and to improve the feel in the mouth (mouth-feel) of the final product). (For more information on these ingredients, see above.)

Some examples of sweets produced using this mixture are:

- crème caramel
- bread and butter pudding
- diplomat pudding
- cabinet pudding
- queen of puddings
- baked egg custard.

▲ Crème caramel

Savoury egg custard is used to make:

- quiches
- tartlets
- flans.

When a starch such as flour is added to the ingredients for an egg custard mix, it changes the characteristic of the end product.

Basic egg custard sets by coagulation of the egg protein. Egg white coagulates at approximately 60 °C and egg yolk at 70 °C. Whites and yolks mixed together will coagulate at 66 °C. If the egg protein is overheated or overcooked, it will shrink and water will be lost from the mixture, causing undesirable bubbles in the custard. This loss of water is called **syneresis**.

> **Key terms**
>
> **Crème renversée**: egg custard mixture made using eggs, milk and cream.
>
> **Syneresis**: loss of water from a mixture.

Traditional custard made from custard powder

Custard powder is used to make custard sauce. It is made from vanilla-flavoured cornflour with yellow colouring added, and is a substitute for eggs. Sweetness is adjusted by adding sugar before mixing with milk and heating. The fat content can be reduced by making it with semi-skimmed milk rather than full-fat milk.

Points to remember

- Always work in a clean and tidy way, complying with food hygiene regulations.
- Prevent cross-contamination by not allowing any potentially harmful substances to come into contact with the mixture.
- Always heat the egg yolks or eggs to 70 °C or use pasteurised egg yolks or eggs.
- Follow the recipe carefully.
- Ensure that all heating and cooling temperatures are followed.
- Always store the end product carefully at the right temperature.
- Check all weighing scales.
- Check all raw materials for correct use-by dates.
- Always wash your hands when handling fresh eggs or dairy products and other pastry ingredients.
- Never use cream to decorate a product that is still warm.
- Always remember to follow the Food Safety and Hygiene (England) Regulations 2013.
- Check the temperature of refrigerators and freezers to ensure that they comply with the current regulations.

Ice cream

Traditional ice cream is made from a basic egg custard sauce. The sauce is cooled and mixed with fresh cream. It is then frozen by a rotating machine where the water content forms ice crystals.

Ice cream should be removed from the freezer a few minutes before serving. Long-term storage should be at between –18 °C and –20 °C.

The traditional method of making ice cream uses only egg yolks and sugar and the traditional anglaise base. The more modern approach to making ice cream uses **stabilisers** and different sugars, as well as egg whites.

> **Key term**
>
> **Stabiliser**: a substance added to foods to help to preserve its structure.

Food Standards (Ice Cream) Regulations 1959 and 1963

The Food Standards (Ice Cream) Regulations 1959 and 1963 require ice cream to be pasteurised by heating to:

- 65 °C for 30 minutes or
- 71 °C for 10 minutes or
- 80 °C for 15 seconds or
- 149 °C for 2 seconds (sterilised).

After heat treatment, the mixture is reduced to 7.1 °C within 1 ½ hours and kept at this temperature until the freezing process begins. Ice cream needs this treatment in order to kill harmful bacteria. Freezing without the correct heat treatment does not kill bacteria – it allows them to remain dormant. The storage temperature for ice cream should not exceed –20 °C.

Any ice cream sold must comply with the following standards.

- It must contain not less than 5 per cent fat and not less than 2.5 per cent milk protein (not necessary in natural proportions).
- It must conform to the Dairy Product Regulations 1995.

For further information contact the Ice Cream Alliance (see www.ice-cream.org).

Ice cream making process

1 **Weighing** – ingredients should be weighed precisely in order to ensure the best results and regularity and consistency.
2 **Pasteurisation** – this is a vital stage in making ice cream. Its primary function is to minimise bacterial contamination by heating the mixture of ingredients to 85 °C, then quickly cooling it to 4 °C.
3 **Homogenisation** – high pressure is applied to cause the explosion of fats, which makes ice cream more homogenous, creamier, smoother and much lighter. It is not usually done for homemade ice cream.
4 **Ripening** – this basic but optional stage refines flavour, further develops aromas and improves texture. This occurs during a rest period (4–24 hours), which gives the stabilisers and proteins time to act, improving the overall structure of the ice cream. This has the same effect on a crème anglaise, which is much better the day after it is made than it is on the same day.
5 **Churning** – here, the mixture is frozen while at the same time air is incorporated. The ice cream is removed from the machine at about 10 °C.

Main components of ice cream

- **Sucrose** (common sugar) not only sweetens ice cream, but also gives it body. An ice cream that contains only sucrose (not recommended) has a higher freezing point.
- The optimum sugar percentage of ice cream is between 15 and 20 per cent.
- Ice cream that contains **dextrose** (another type of sugar) has a lower freezing point and better taste and texture. The quantity of dextrose used should be between 6 and 25 per cent of the substituted sucrose (by weight).
- As much as 50 per cent of the sucrose can be substituted with other sweeteners, but the recommended amount is 25 per cent.
- **Glucose** (another type of sugar) improves smoothness and prevents the crystallisation of sucrose. The quantity of glucose used should be between 25 and 30 per cent of the sucrose by weight.
- **Atomised glucose** (glucose powder) is more water absorbent, so helps to reduce the formation of ice crystals.
- **Inverted sugar** is a paste or liquid obtained from heating sucrose with water and an acid (e.g. lemon juice). Using inverted sugar in ice cream lowers the freezing point. Inverted sugar also improves the texture of ice cream and delays crystallisation. The quantity of inverted sugar used should be a maximum of 33 per cent of the sucrose by weight. It is very efficient at sweetening and gives the ice cream a low freezing point.
- **Honey** has similar properties to inverted sugar.
- The purpose of **cream** in ice cream is to improve creaminess and taste.
- **Egg yolks** act as stabilisers for ice cream due to the lecithin they contain; they help to prevent the fats and water in the ice cream from separating. Egg yolks improve the texture and viscosity of ice cream.
- The purpose of stabilisers (e.g. gum Arabic, gelatine, pectin) is to prevent crystal formation by absorbing the water contained in ice cream and making a stable gel. The quantity of stabilisers in ice cream should be between 3 g and 5 g per kg of mix, with a maximum of 10 g. Stabilisers promote air absorption, making products lighter to eat and also less costly to produce, as air makes the product go further.

What you need to know about ice cream

- Hygienic conditions are essential while making ice cream – personal hygiene and high levels of cleanliness in the equipment and the kitchen environment must be maintained.
- An excess of stabilisers in ice cream will make it sticky.
- Stabilisers should always be mixed with sugar before adding, to avoid lumps.
- Stabilisers should be added at 45 °C, which is when they begin to act.
- Cold stabilisers have no effect on the mixture, so the temperature must be raised to 85 °C.
- Ice cream should be allowed to 'ripen' for 4–24 hours. This helps to improve its properties.
- Ice cream should be cooled quickly to 4 °C, because micro-organisms reproduce rapidly between 20 °C and 55 °C.

Activity

1 Create your own dessert using ice cream, meringue and fresh fruit using a plate presentation.
2 Cost your dish and calculate a 70% gross profit.

Sorbets

Sorbets belong to the ice cream family; they are a mixture of water, sucrose, atomised glucose, stabiliser, fruit juice, fruit pulp and, sometimes, liqueurs.

What you need to know about sorbet

- Sorbet is generally more refreshing and easier to digest than ice cream.
- Fruit for sorbets must always be of a high quality and perfectly ripe.
- The percentage of fruit used in sorbet varies according to the type of fruit, its acidity and the quality desired.
- The percentage of sugar will depend on the type of fruit used.
- The minimum sugar content in sorbet is about 13 per cent.

- As far as ripening is concerned, the syrup should be left to rest for 4–24 hours and never mixed with the fruit because its acidity would damage the stabiliser.
- Stabiliser is added in the same way as for ice cream.
- Sorbets are not to be confused with granitas, which are semi-solid.

Stabilisers

Gelling substances, thickeners and emulsifiers are all stabilisers. These products are used regularly and each has its own specific function, but their main purpose is to retain water to make a gel. In ice-cream they are used to prevent ice crystal formation. They are also used to stabilise the emulsion, increase the viscosity of the mix and give a smoother product that is more resistant to melting. There are many stabilising substances, both natural and artificial, as follows.

- **Edible gelatine** is extracted from animals' bones (pork and veal) and, more recently, fish skin. Sold in sheets of 2 g, it is easy to precisely control the amount used and to manipulate it. Gelatine sheets should be soaked in cold water to soften and then drained before use. Gelatine sheets melt at 40 °C and should be melted in a little of the liquid from the recipe before adding it to the base preparation.
- **Pectin** is another commonly used gelling substance because of its great absorption capacity. It comes from citrus peel (orange, lemon, etc.), though all fruits contain some pectin in their peel. It is a good idea to mix pectin with sugar before adding it to the rest of the ingredients.
- **Agar-agar** is a gelatinous marine algae found in Asia. It is sold in whole or powdered form and has a great absorption capacity. It dissolves very easily and, in addition to gelling, adds elasticity and resists heat (this is classified as a non-reversible gel).

Other stabilisers:

- **Carob gum** – this comes from the seeds of the carob tree, makes sorbets creamier and improves heat resistance.
- **Guar gum** and **carrageen** – like agar-agar, these are extracted from marine algae and are some of the many existing gelling substances available, but they are used less often.

Fruit-based desserts

Fruit is used as an ingredient in many desserts. It can be the main feature of a dessert, as in the case of a baked apple (bonne-femme), peach melba or pear belle Hélène, or in conjunction with other dessert bases and ingredients. Fruit can also form the main component of batter-based desserts, such as fritters and clafoutis, for example.

Fruit is used to contribute to sponge-based desserts, such as baked Alaska, as a platform to support fruit mousses and/or bavarois, or as a component in steamed-sponge puddings. Fruit is also regularly used in a variety of pastry-based desserts, such as tarte tatin, fruit tarts and barquettes.

Other dessert mediums include meringue (vacherins), egg custards (crème renversée) and purées (to flavour ice-creams and sorbets). These are just a few examples of the versatility of fruit and how it can be used alongside other dessert mediums to produce an endless variety of desserts.

▲ Apple Charlotte (recipe available on Dynamic Learning)

Meringue-based desserts

Meringue is a whipped mixture of sugar and egg whites which is used to aerate soufflés, mousses and cake mixtures. It is also used to make pie toppings, such as lemon meringue pie, and to cover desserts such as Baked Alaska. Meringue mixtures can also be piped and baked until the surface is crisp to produce shells and other shapes, as in vacherins, for example. There are three types of meringue, used for different purposes.

- **French meringue** – this uncooked meringue is probably the most common. Caster sugar is gradually whisked into the egg whites once they have reached soft peaks until the mixture reaches

firm peaks. This type of meringue is the least stable but the lightest, which makes it perfect for aerating desserts such as soufflés.

- **Italian meringue** – this is the most stable form of meringue. It is made with sugar syrup that has been heated to the soft-ball stage (121 °C). The hot syrup is gradually beaten into the egg whites after soft peaks have formed and then whipped to firm glossy peaks. Its stability and smooth texture make it great for parfaits and mousses, particularly if the product is not going to be cooked or baked beyond the addition of the meringue. An uncooked meringue, particularly if made with unpasteurised eggs, would not be suitable due to this reason.

- **Swiss meringue** – this produces a firmer and slightly denser result than the other types of meringue. Swiss meringue is produced by whisking caster sugar and egg whites together over a pot of simmering water. The early addition of the sugar prevents the egg whites from increasing as much in volume as they do in the other meringues, but adds to its fine texture. Swiss meringue is often used in buttercreams or baked to produce meringue shells.

▲ Italian meringue is used to cover baked Alaska

Mousses

Dessert mousses are generally made from a base of vanilla, fruit or chocolate. The base is usually mixed with whipped egg whites (meringue) to aerate and/or whipped cream and usually served chilled with an appropriate accompanying sauce. A gelling agent such as gelatine or agar-agar can also be added during the mixing stage to help the mousse set once it is chilled. Mousses can be served in a mould or de-moulded.

Rice desserts

Rice desserts are one of the classics, although they are not seen as often in restaurants in current times. Rice desserts are usually produced using a plump, short-grained (pudding) rice from which the starch is released into the cooking liquor to produce a sauce-like bind. Rice desserts can be served hot or cold and can also be set to produce a combination similar to that of a mousse. Often the rice pudding will be flavoured with vanilla, cinnamon or nutmeg, for example.

Batter-based desserts

Batters are used in the production of fritters. They are often used to coat fruits before frying, as in apple fritters, for example. Batters can also be baked to produce desserts such as clafoutis. Batters are general made from a flour base utilising a liquid such as water, milk or even beer, as well as a raising/lightening agent such as egg-white, baking powder or yeast.

Soufflés

Soufflés form part of the world's classic dessert repertoire and there are many different types. The classic 'dessert' soufflé is baked and served in a ramekin. The base of dessert soufflés is usually flavoured with vanilla, fruit or chocolate and then aerated with whisked egg whites. This causes the mix to rise beyond the rim of the ramekin or dish to give that classic soufflé appearance and lightness. However, this type of soufflé is not the most stable and the dish needs to be consumed quickly after baking as the soufflé will start to collapse and shrink after a short period of time.

Other types of soufflé include the 'pudding' soufflé which is usually baked in dariole moulds in a bain-marie and served de-moulded on a plate with an appropriate sauce. There are also cold and iced soufflés, which are mousse- and parfait-based desserts, set in lined moulds to provide the appearance of a classic soufflé, but served chilled or frozen, as appropriate. Finally, there are omelette soufflés, which is a classic dessert soufflé mix, baked inside a folded omelette.

Sponge-based desserts

Sponges usually form a component of desserts: the base for a mousse, for example, or sometimes as a lining for a mould before it is filled. Some desserts, such as steamed puddings and baked puddings such as 'sticky toffee pudding', have sponge-like characteristics and mouth-feel but sponges in their true sense are rarely served as a dessert on their own.

Milk puddings

Milk is used as a major ingredient in many desserts and regularly forms a component of desserts. For example, milk is used to make egg-custards and is a key commodity in the production of a classic rice pudding. Milk-based puddings are not as commonly seen today as much as they were in the past. Semolina pudding, where semolina is cooked in milk with the possible inclusion of cream alongside other flavours and sweeteners is an example of a milk pudding.

Cereal

As per rice and milk puddings, cereal-based puddings are not seen as regularly as they were in the past, although cereals may be used to add a dimension to other desserts, for example, oats used as part of a crumble mix.

Suet-paste based desserts

Suet is traditionally associated with the production of steamed desserts such as jam roly-poly and spotted dick. As suet is an animal fat, taken from the fat surrounding the kidneys of cattle and sheep, it is often considered unhealthy or neglected by customers. However, vegetable suet can be used to replace the animal suet, thereby resolving this issue and allowing these traditional puddings to be made without the use of animal fats.

Crêpes

Crêpes are a traditional pancake dessert belonging to France. In their simplest form, crêpes are served with a sprinkling of sugar and a splash of fresh lemon juice. They can also be taken further to produce flamed (flambé) dishes such as the classic Crêpe Suzette. Crêpes are fine pancakes and should not be mistaken for Scotch pancakes or American pancakes, which are much thicker and spongier.

Finishing desserts and puddings

Sauces, creams and coulis

Desserts are often complemented by the addition of a sauce. Some of the most commonly used sauces include:

- **Crème anglaise** – the classic dessert sauce made from egg yolks and sugar, mixed with vanilla-infused milk and cooked gently to produce a delicious custard-style sauce. Crème anglaise can be served hot or cold, depending on the type of dessert.
- **Fruit coulis** – fruit coulis are strained purées of fruit that are sometimes sweetened with sugar or sugar syrup. The consistency of the desired coulis has to be taken into consideration and adjusted to meet the requirements of the sauce. This can be achieved through the density of the syrup or through adjustment by reduction, the use of a starch or a stabilising agent such as ultratex.
- **Cooked fruit sauces** – depending on the ripeness of the fruit in question, it may be necessary that the fruit is cooked before it is blended or passed to make into a sauce. Additional sugar may be required to balance sweetness with any tart or bitter elements from the fruit in question.
- **Chocolate** – chocolate sauce is usually made by melting chocolate and combining it with a liquid such as cream. Depending on the type of sauce required, additional ingredients such as butter (for richness) or sugar (for sweetness) may be added to the sauce alongside any potential additional flavouring.
- **Flavoured syrups** – simple syrups are made by inverting (dissolving) sugar with water. The higher the percentage of sugar, the more dense and viscous the syrup will become. Additional flavours can be incorporated from fruits such as lemon or orange or spices such as vanilla, star anise or cinnamon.

Finishing and decorating techniques

Piping

- Piping can be used to enhance desserts – a swirl of cream or buttercream, for example, or a fine chocolate motif.
- Piping fresh cream is a skill and like all other skills it takes practice to become proficient. The finished item should look attractive, simple, clean and tidy, with neat piping.
- All piping bags should be sterilised after each use, as these may be a source of contamination; alternatively use a disposable piping bag.
- Make sure that all the equipment you need for piping is hygienically cleaned before and after use to avoid cross-contamination.

> **Health and safety** ⚠
> All piping bags must be sterilised after each use.

Filling

Some dessert products are finished by being filled, such as profiteroles and crêpes. Other desserts might include a chocolate cup filled with a mousse or cream

Saucing

The primary use of sauces is to complement the dessert and to make the eating experience more pleasurable and digestible for the customer. The way sauces are presented can also add to the presentation of the dessert. The use of sauce bottles can help apply sauces in artistic ways – swirls, line and dots, for example. Consistency and viscosity are important considerations for the stability of the sauce.

Glazing

Some desserts are finished by being glazed or gratinated, such as crème brûlée or as sometimes used to finish bread and butter pudding. This is usually achieved by lightly coating the surface of the dessert with sugar (icing, caster, Demerara, etc.) and then caramelising it with the use of a blow-torch or under a hot grill.

Dusting

Dusting is the simple process of lightly sieving a delicate coating of products such as icing sugar/neige décor and cocoa powder to create a light dust-like finish. A fine sieve is best to create this affect.

Additions

Desserts can often have additional ingredients added to enhance the eating quality of the dish. Current menus often use terms such as 'textures of' commodities such as fruits. In this case the chef may add a variety of ways in which the fruit can be presented – dried, puréed, as a jelly, as a crisp, for example.

Motifs/run-outs

A motif or run-out refers to chocolate that has been tempered and piped finely into a design or shape, usually onto greaseproof or silicone paper. Once the chocolate has set, it can be lifted from the paper and used to garnish a dessert. Motifs vary from being simple shapes to quite elaborate pieces and may even be three dimensional.

Cigarettes

Cigarettes are produced by spreading tempered couverture/chocolate finely over a flat surface such as granite. Once the chocolate is almost set, use a scraper at an angle in short, sharp motions to force the chocolate into fine rolls, approximately the length of a cigarette. Chocolate cigarettes are often used to provide dimension to desserts by being placed gently, perhaps at an angle, into a quenelle of cream, sorbet or ice-cream, for example.

Moulding

The use of moulds creates a neat, uniform finish to desserts. They also produce portions of consistent sizes. Moulds are made in many shapes and sizes, offering chefs the opportunity to create interesting presentations. Moulds can also be used to set items such as chocolate rings and tears before they are filled.

Chocolate transfer sheets

Chocolate transfer sheets are produced by lining sheets of acetate with designs printed using coloured cocoa butter. When tempered couverture/chocolate is spread over the sheet and left to set, the design will be transferred to the chocolate. As well as the various designs, it is now possible to have signatures and logos professionally printed in this method, giving chefs a simple way of producing high quality personalised chocolate products.

Portioning

Many desserts are produced in multiple portions, a raspberry délice or a chocolate tart, for example. It is important that when dividing multiple portion desserts that this is done equally to produce portions of the same size. It is also important to use clean, hygienic equipment at all times. This will obviously help to maintain food safety but will also help to produce cleanly cut and neat portions to enhance their presentation when served.

Holding and storing desserts and puddings

- Store all goods according to the Food Safety and Hygiene Regulations 2013 and the Food Safety Temperature Control Regulation 1995.
- Always store the end product carefully at the right temperature.
- Take special care when using cream, and ensure that products containing cream are stored under refrigerated conditions.
- Always make sure that storage containers are kept clean and returned ready for re-use. On their return they should be hygienically washed and stored.
- Ice cream should be removed from the freezer a few minutes before serving. Long-term storage should be at between $-18\,°C$ and $-20\,°C$.

Test yourself

1   Name **three** types of setting agent.

2   Describe what would happen to a crème caramel if it was cooked at 180 °C.

3   Name the **three** main types of meringues and describe their production and use.

4   Describe the conditions that promote the foam of egg-whites when making meringues.

5   Name **two** desserts that are finished with a glaze.

6   What is the difference between a cabinet and diplomat pudding?

7   Name **five** fruits suitable for stewing.

8   Describe the differences between the production of a 'pudding soufflé' and a 'fruit soufflé'.

9   Name **four** types of sugar and give an example of their use in a dessert.

10 Describe why salt is sometimes used in the production of desserts.

11 Describe **three** ways in which chocolate can be used as a decorating medium.

12 Name the **two** pieces of equipment used to measure the density and sweetness of sugar syrups.

13 Describe the quality points to look for in the following desserts:

   a) ice-cream

   b) crème brulée

   c) strawberry mousse

14 Name **four** desserts produced from milk, eggs and sugar.

15 At what temperature should an individual vanilla soufflé be baked, and for how long?

1 Chantilly cream

	500 ml
Whipping cream	500 ml
Caster sugar	100 g
Vanilla essence/fresh vanilla pod	A few drops to taste/seeds from 1 vanilla pod

1 Place all ingredients in a bowl. Whisk over ice until the mixture forms soft peaks. If using a mechanical mixer, stand and watch until the mixture is ready – do not leave it unattended as the mix will over-whip quickly, curdling the cream.

2 Cover and place in the fridge immediately.

ASSESSMENT

2 Pastry cream (*crème pâtissière*)

Left to right: pastry cream, crème diplomat and crème chiboust

	Approximately 750 ml
Milk	500 ml
Vanilla pod	1
Egg yolks	4
Caster sugar	125 g
Soft flour	75 g
Custard powder	10 g

1 Heat the milk with the cut vanilla pod and leave to infuse.

2 Beat the sugar and egg yolks together until creamy white. Add the flour and custard powder.

3 Strain the hot milk, gradually blending it into the egg mixture.

4 Strain into a clean pan and bring back to the boil, stirring constantly.

5 When the mixture has boiled and thickened, pour into a plastic bowl, sprinkle with caster sugar and cover with cling film.

6 Chill over ice and refrigerate as soon as possible. Ideally, blast chill.

7 When required, knock back on a mixing machine with a little kirsch.

Professional tip

At Step 4, the microwave may be used effectively. Pour the mixture into a plastic bowl and cook in the microwave for 30-second periods, stirring in between, until the mixture boils and thickens.

Variations

Additional flavourings can also be added to crème pâtissière, crème diplomat or crème chiboust.

● **Crème mousseline**: beat in 100 g of soft butter (a pomade). The butter content is usually about 20 per cent of the volume but this can be raised to 50 per cent depending on its intended use.

● **Crème diplomate**: when the pastry cream is chilled, fold in an equal quantity of whipped double cream.

● **Crème chiboust**: when the pastry cream mixture has cooled slightly, fold in an equal quantity of Italian meringue (see page 742).

3 Buttercream

	350 g
Icing sugar	150 g
Butter	200 g

1 Sieve the icing sugar.
2 Cream the butter and icing sugar until light and creamy.
3 Flavour and colour as required.

Variations

Rum buttercream – add rum to flavour and blend in.

Chocolate buttercream – add melted chocolate, sweetened or unsweetened according to taste.

4 Boiled buttercream

1 Beat the eggs and icing sugar until at ribbon stage (sponge).
2 Boil the granulated or cube sugar with water and glucose to 118 °C.
3 Gradually add the sugar at 118 °C to the eggs and icing sugar at ribbon stage, whisk continuously and allow to cool to 26 °C.
4 Gradually add the unsalted butter while continuing to whisk until a smooth cream is obtained.

Variations

Buttercream may be flavoured with numerous flavours and combinations of flavours, for example:
- chocolate and rum
- whisky and orange
- strawberry and vanilla
- lemon and lime
- apricot and passionfruit
- brandy and praline
- coffee and hazelnut.

	750 ml
Eggs	2
Icing sugar	50 g
Granulated sugar or cube sugar	300 g
Water	100 g
Glucose	50 g
Unsalted butter	400 g

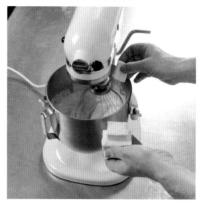

1 Whisk the eggs   **2** Add the boiling sugar and water   **3** Add the butter

5 Ganache

Version 1 (for decoration):	750 g
Double cream	300 ml
Couverture, cut into small pieces	350 g
Unsalted butter	85 g
Spirit or liqueur	20 ml
Version 2 (for a filling):	1 kg
Double cream	300 ml
Vanilla pod	½
Couverture, cut into small pieces	600 g
Unsalted butter	120 g

1 Boil the cream (and the vanilla for Version 2) in a heavy saucepan.

2 Pour the cream over the couverture. Whisk with a fine whisk until the chocolate has melted.

3 Whisk in the butter (and the liqueur for Version 1).

4 Stir over ice until the mixture has the required consistency.

Note

The two versions have different textures. Version 1 is ideal for truffles; version 2 for tortes or fillings.

6 Italian meringue

	Makes 250 g	Makes 625 g
Granulated or cube sugar	200 g	500 g
Water	60 ml	140 g
Cream of tartar	Pinch	Large pinch
Egg whites	4	10

1 Boil the sugar, water and cream of tartar to hard-ball stage of 121 °C. (So that the sugar is not heated beyond this point, remove from the heat at 115 °C. The sugar will continue to rise in temperature, giving time to ensure the egg whites are whipped to the correct point.)

2 While the sugar is cooking, beat the egg whites to full peak and, while stiff, beating slowly, pour on the boiling sugar.

1 Boil the sugar.

2 Combine with the beaten egg whites.

3 The mixture will stand up in stiff peaks when it is ready.

7 Swiss meringue

Ingredient	10 portions	15 portions
Egg whites, pasteurised	190 ml	300 ml
Caster sugar	230 ml	340 ml

1 Whisk the pasteurised egg whites and sugar over a bain-marie of simmering water until a light and aerated meringue is achieved.

8 Frangipane (almond cream)

	8 portions
Butter	100 g
Caster sugar	100 g
Eggs	2
Ground almonds	100 g
Flour	10 g

1 Cream the butter and sugar until aerated.

2 Gradually beat in the eggs.

3 Mix in the almonds and flour (mix lightly).

4 Use as required.

Variation

Try adding lemon zest or vanilla seeds to the recipe.

1 Cut the butter into small pieces and add to the sugar.

2 Cream the butter and sugar together.

3 Beat in the eggs before adding to the ground almonds and flour.

9 Fruit coulis

	1.4 litres
Fruit purée	1 litre
Caster sugar	500 g
Lemon juice	10 g

1 Warm the purée.

2 Boil the sugar with a little water to soft-ball stage (121 °C).

3 Pour the soft-ball sugar into the warm fruit purée while whisking vigorously. Add the lemon juice. Bring back to the boil.

4 This will then be ready to store.

> **Professional tip**
>
> The reason the soft-ball stage needs to be achieved when the sugar is mixed with the purée is that this stabilises the fruit and prevents separation once the coulis is presented on the plate.
>
> Adding lemon juice brings out the flavour of the fruit.

10 Apple purée (*marmalade de pomme*)

	400 g	1 kg
Cooking apples	400 g	1 kg
Butter or margarine	10 g	25 g
Sugar	50 g	125 g

1 Peel, core and slice the apples.

2 Place the butter or margarine in a thick-bottomed pan; heat until melted.

3 Add the apples and sugar, cover with a lid and cook gently until soft.

4 Drain off any excess liquid and pass through a sieve or liquidise.

11 Apricot glaze

	150 ml
Apricot jam	100 g
Stock syrup (see page 477) or water	50 ml

1 Boil the apricot jam with a little syrup or water.

2 Pass through a strainer. The glaze should be used hot.

Professional tip

A flan jelly (commercial pectin glaze) may be used as an alternative to apricot glaze. This is usually a clear glaze to which food colour may be added.

12 Fresh egg custard sauce (*sauce à l'anglaise*)

1 Mix the yolks, sugar and vanilla in a bowl.

2 Whisk in the boiled milk and return to a thick-bottomed pan.

3 Place on a low heat and stir with a wooden spoon until it coats the back of the spoon. Do not allow the mix to boil or the egg will scramble. A probe can be used to ensure the temperature does not go any higher than 85 °C.

4 Put through a fine sieve into a clean bowl. Set on ice to seize the cooking process and to chill rapidly.

Variation

Other flavours may be used in place of vanilla, for example, coffee, curaçao, chocolate, Cointreau, rum, Tia Maria, brandy, whisky, star anise, cardamom seeds, kirsch, orange flower water.

	300 ml	700 ml
Egg yolks, pasteurised	40 ml	100 ml
Caster or unrefined sugar	25 g	60 g
Vanilla extract or vanilla pod (seeds)	2–3 drops/ ½ pod	5–7 drops/ 1 pod
Milk, whole or skimmed, boiled	250 ml	625 ml

13 Custard sauce

Ingredient	Makes 250 ml
Custard powder	10 g
Milk, whole or semi-skimmed	250 ml
Caster or unrefined sugar	25 g

Energy	Cals	Fat	Sat fat	Carb	Sugar	Protein	Fibre *
1,245 kJ	296 kcal	9.6 g	6.0 g	47.2 g	38.0 g	8.3 g	0.3 g

* Using whole milk.

1 Dilute the custard powder with a little of the milk.
2 Boil the remainder of the milk.
3 Pour a little of the boiled milk on to the diluted custard powder.
4 Return to the saucepan.
5 Stir to the boil and mix in the sugar.

14 Chocolate sauce (*sauce au chocolat*)

	300 ml	750 ml
Method 1		
Double cream	150 ml	375 ml
Butter	25 g	60 g
Milk or plain couverture callets	180 g	420 g
Method 2		
Caster sugar	40 g	100 g
Water	120 ml	300 ml
Dark chocolate couverture (75 per cent cocoa solids)	160 g	400 g
Unsalted butter	25 g	65 g
Single cream	80 ml	200 ml

Method 2:

1 Dissolve the sugar in the water over a low heat.
2 Remove from the heat. Stir in the chocolate and butter.
3 When everything has melted, stir in the cream and gently bring to the boil.

Energy	Cals	Fat	Sat fat	Carb	Sugar	Protein	Fibre	Sodium
1012 kJ	244 kcal	18.7 g	11.5 g	13.9 g	13 g	2.9 g	2.6 g	0.02 g

Method 1:

1 Place the cream and butter in a saucepan and gently bring to a simmer.
2 Add the chocolate and stir well until the chocolate has melted and the sauce is smooth.

Energy	Cals	Fat	Sat fat	Carb	Sugar	Protein	Fibre	Sodium *
1287 kJ	310 kcal	26 g	16 g	17.5 g	17.5 g	2.7 g	0.2 g	0.09 g

* Analysed using standard milk chocolate

15 Stock syrup

	750 ml	1.5 litres
Water	500 ml	1.25 litres
Granulated sugar	250 g	625 g
Glucose	50 g	125 g

1 Boil the water, sugar and glucose together.
2 Strain and cool.

Professional tip
The glucose helps to prevent crystallising.

16 Caramel sauce

	750 ml
Caster sugar	100 g
Water	80 ml
Double cream	500 ml
Egg yolks, lightly beaten (optional)	2

1 In a large saucepan, dissolve the sugar with the water over a low heat and bring to boiling point.
2 Wash down the inside of the pan with a pastry brush dipped in cold water to prevent crystals from forming.
3 Cook until the sugar turns to a deep amber colour. Immediately turn off the heat and whisk in the cream.
4 Set the pan back over a high heat and stir the sauce with the whisk. Let it bubble for 2 minutes, then turn off the heat.
5 You can now strain the sauce and use it when cooled or, for a richer, smoother sauce, pour a little caramel onto the egg yolks, then return the mixture to the pan and heat to 80 °C, taking care that it does not boil.
6 Pass the sauce through a conical strainer and keep in a cool place, stirring occasionally to prevent a skin from forming.

Energy	Cals	Fat	Sat fat	Carb	Sugar	Protein	Fibre	Sodium
883 kJ	213 kcal	19.9 g	12.1 g	8.1 g	8.1 g	1 g	0 g	0.01 g

17 Butterscotch sauce

	300 ml	750 ml
Double cream	250 ml	625 ml
Butter	62 g	155 g
Demerara sugar	100 g	250 g

1 Boil the cream, then whisk in the butter and sugar.

2 Simmer for 3 minutes.

Energy	Cals	Fat	Sat fat	Carb	Sugar	Protein	Fibre	Sodium
883kJ	213kcal	19.9g	12.1g	8.1g	8.1g	1g	0g	0.01g

18 Bramley apple spotted dick

	10 puddings
Soft flour	350 g
Salt	Pinch
Baking powder	20 g
Suet	150 g
Light brown sugar	100 g
Currants	150 g
Lemon zest	1
Bramley apples	2 medium sized
Milk	250 ml

Energy	Cals	Fat	Sat fat	Carb	Sugar	Protein	Fibre	Sodium *
1456kJ	346kcal	14.5g	8.2g	53	23.8g	4.6g	2.4g	0.273g

* Using whole milk

1 Sieve the flour, salt and baking powder into a bowl.

2 Stir in the suet, sugar, currants and grated lemon zest.

3 Peel and dice the apple into small cubes and add to the ingredients above.

4 Stir in the milk to form a sticky dough.

5 Divide the mixture between buttered dariole moulds (or similar).

6 Cover and seal the tops with foil and steam for 1 ½ hours.

Note

Serve with crème anglaise or custard sauce.

Professional tip

Vegetarian suet can be used in this recipe.

Alternatively, this recipe can be cooked in the oven in a bain-marie.

Variation

Serve with an apple and vanilla compote:

Vanilla pod	1
Sugar	300g
Water	75ml
Apples	4–5
Sultanas	50g
White wine	50ml

1 Split the vanilla pod and bring to the boil with the sugar and water.
2 Prepare the apples as for the spotted dick above.
3 Add the apples, sultanas and wine to the boiling syrup, remove from the heat and leave to stand before serving.

19 Sticky toffee pudding

1 Remove stones and chop the dates, place in the water and simmer for about 5 minutes until soft, set aside to cool.
2 Butter and sugar individual dariole moulds.
3 Cream the butter and sugar until light in colour and aerated.
4 Gradually add the beaten eggs, beating continuously.
5 Sieve the flour and baking powder twice and fold in.
6 Finally add the dates and water and vanilla compound.
7 Fill the moulds three-quarters full and bake at 180°C for 30–35 minutes.

Sticky toffee sauce:

1 Make a dry caramel by carefully melting the sugar until a deep golden colour is achieved.
2 Cut the butter into small cubes, add to the cream and heat.
3 Gradually add the hot cream and butter to the caramel a little at a time.
4 Finally stir in the brandy.

	10 puddings
Dates	375g
Water	625g
Butter	125g
Caster sugar	375g
Eggs	5
Soft flour	375g
Baking powder	10g
Vanilla compound	1 tsp
Sticky toffee sauce:	
Granulated sugar	600g
Unsalted butter	300g
Double cream	450g
Brandy	30ml

Note

To serve, coat the pudding with the sauce and serve with vanilla or milk ice cream.

Professional tip

Sticky toffee pudding can be steamed instead of baked. If steaming, remember to cover with a disc of silicone paper and seal with a pleated square of foil, as for steamed puddings (Recipe 19).

Energy	Cals	Fat	Sat fat	Carb	Sugar	Protein	Fibre
4103kJ	980kcal	60.4g	36.7g	106.7g	78.9g	9.1g	1.8g

20 Golden syrup pudding

	6 portions	12 portions
Flour	150 g	300 g
Salt	Pinch	Large pinch
Baking powder	10 g	20 g
or		
Self-raising flour	150 g	300 g
Suet, chopped	75 g	150 g
Caster or unrefined sugar	50 g	100 g
Lemon, zest of	1	2
Egg, beaten	1	2
Milk, whole or skimmed	125 ml	250 ml
Golden syrup	125 ml	250 ml

Energy	Cals	Fat	Sat fat	Carb	Sugar	Protein	Fibre
1315 kJ	313 kcal	13.0 g	5.9 g	47.8 g	26.6 g	4.3 g	0.9 g

1 Sieve the flour, salt and baking powder (or replace the flour and baking powder with self-raising flour) into a bowl.
2 Mix the suet, sugar and zest.
3 Add the beaten egg and milk and mix to a medium dough.
4 Pour the syrup in a well-greased basin or individual moulds (1 hour cooking time). Place the pudding mixture on top.
5 Cover securely; steam for 1 ½ –2 hours.

Note

Serve with a sauceboat of warm syrup containing the lemon juice, or with sauce anglaise or ice cream.

Variation

To make a treacle pudding, use a light treacle in place of the golden syrup. Vegetarian suet is available.

21 Eve's pudding with gooseberries

	10 portions
Gooseberries, washed, topped and tailed	500 g
Caster sugar	150 g plus a little for the fruit
Butter	150 g
Vanilla essence	
Eggs, beaten	150 g
Self-raising flour	240 g
Milk	60 g

Energy	Cals	Fat	Sat fat	Carb	Sugar	Protein	Fibre	Sodium *
1234 kJ	294 kcal	14.7 g	8.5 g	37.9	20 g	4.9 g	2.6 g	0.182 g

* Using whole milk

1 Arrange the gooseberries in the bottom of a buttered dish or individual ramekins. Sprinkle with caster sugar.

2 Cream the sugar, butter and vanilla essence together until white.

3 Gradually add the eggs to the butter mixture.

4 Sieve the flour twice, then fold it in to the eggs and butter. Adjust the consistency with milk.

5 Spread the mixture over the fruit, to a thickness of about 2 cm. This will form the sponge.

6 Bake for 30–40 minutes in a pre-heated oven at 180 °C.

7 Rest for 5 minutes before removing from the dish. Brush with boiling apricot glaze.

Note

Serve with custard or crème anglais.

22 Chocolate fondant

	10 portions
Unsalted butter	260 g
Dark couverture	260 g
Eggs, pasteurised	120 g
Egg yolks, pasteurised	40 g
Caster sugar	150 g
Instant coffee	5 g
Plain flour	110 g
Baking powder	5 g
Cocoa powder	75 g
Salt	Pinch

Energy	Cals	Fat	Sat fat	Carb	Sugar	Protein	Fibre
2830 kJ	675 kcal	46.8 g	29.6 g	55.9 g	40.9 g	11.0 g	0.6 g

1 Melt the butter and couverture together.

2 Warm the eggs, egg yolks, sugar and coffee and whisk to the ribbon stage.

3 Sieve all the dry ingredients twice.

4 Fold the chocolate and butter into the eggs.

5 Fold in the dry ingredients.

6 Pipe into individual stainless steel rings lined with silicone paper and placed on a silicone paper-lined baking sheet.

7 Bake at 190 °C for 5 minutes.

8 Carefully slide off the rings and serve with vanilla ice cream.

Professional tip

These fondants can be kept in the refrigerator and cooked to order. If they are chilled, then extend the cooking time by 2 minutes.

Chocolate fondant should have a liquid centre with a rich, buttery, chocolate taste. Because of the liquid centre, they are very delicate; if piped inside a ring, they are much easier and quicker to serve, rather than trying to turn them out of a mould.

Precise timing is essential or the centre of the fondant will not be liquid.

Like most recipes, the quality of the finished product relies on the quality of the ingredients. Always use good quality chocolate (couverture) which contains a high percentage of cocoa butter and solids.

Variation

Try adding salted caramel to the centre by making and freezing it in ice cube trays.

Serve with malt ice cream (just add malt powder instead of vanilla and mix in some crushed chocolates) or replace the cream with crème fraiche to give a less rich ice cream.

Prepare fondants in moulds lined with melted butter and roasted sesame seeds.

1 Melt the chocolate and butter in small pieces.

2 Fold the melted chocolate into the egg mixture.

3 Add the dry ingredients.

4 To make a contrasting centre, add white chocolate pieces on a base of the chocolate mixture.

5 Pipe in more of the chocolate mixture until the mould is full.

23 Pancakes with apple (*crêpes normande*)

	4 portions	10 portions
Cooked apple		
Flour, white or wholemeal	100 g	250 g
Salt	Pinch	Large pinch
Egg	1	2–3
Milk, whole, semi-skimmed or skimmed	250 ml	625 ml
Melted butter, margarine or oil	10 g	25 g
Oil for frying		
Caster sugar to serve		

1 Place a little cooked apple in a pan, add the pancake mixture and cook on both sides.

2 Turn out, sprinkle with caster sugar and roll up.

Energy	Cals	Fat	Sat fat	Carb	Sugar	Protein	Fibre	*
1178 kJ	280 kcal	8.2 g	2.9 g	47.7 g	28.7 g	6.6 g	2.8 g	

*Using hard margarine

24 Crêpes Suzette

1 Make the crêpes.

2 Melt the butter. Add the sugar, zest, juice and Grand Marnier. Bring to the boil rapidly and reduce.

3 Dip each crêpe into the sauce, then fold and arrange on the plate. Keep hot.

4 Add the Cognac to the sauce and flambé.

5 Add the orange segments to the sauce and pour over the crêpes.

For the crêpes	
Eggs	2
Salt	Pinch
Caster sugar	112 g
Milk	575 ml
Strong flour	225 g
Melted butter	30 g
For the Suzette mixture	
Unsalted butter	60 g
Zest and juice of orange	1
Caster sugar	60 g
Grand Marnier	30 ml
Cognac	30 ml
Orange, peeled and divided into segments	2

Energy	Cals	Fat	Sat fat	Carb	Sugar	Protein	Fibre	Sodium	*
1258 kJ	299 kcal	11.3 g	6.5 g	42.3	25.7 g	6.4 g	1.7 g	0.099 g	

* Using whole milk

25 Apple fritters (*beignets aux pommes*)

Left to right: apple, fig and banana fritters

	4 portions	10 portions
Cooking apples	400 g	1 kg
Flour, as needed		
Frying batter	150 g	375 g
Apricot sauce	125 ml	300 ml

Energy	Cals	Fat	Sat fat	Carb	Sugar	Protein	Fibre *
1034 kJ	246 kcal	10.2 g	1.9 g	38.9 g	25.0 g	2.1 g	3.0 g

* Fried in peanut oil

1 Peel and core the apples and cut into ½ cm rings.
2 Pass through flour, shake off the surplus.
3 Dip into the frying batter (see page 376).
4 Lift out with the fingers, into fairly hot deep fat: 185 °C.
5 Cook for about 5 minutes on each side.
6 Drain well on kitchen paper, dust with icing sugar and glaze under the salamander.

Note

Serve with hot apricot sauce.

26 Bread and butter pudding

	10 portions
Washed sultanas	100 g
Thin slices of white bread	Approximately 5
Melted butter	200 g
Custard	
Vanilla pod	1
Milk	300 ml
Cream	300 ml
Eggs	5
Caster sugar	100 g
Nutmeg	
Apricot jam	100 g

Energy	Cals	Fat	Sat fat	Carb	Sugar	Protein	Fibre
1093 kJ	260 kcal	11.6 g	5.9 g	30.4 g	23.4 g	10.6 g	1.0 g

1 Butter an earthenware or other suitable dish and sprinkle with the sultanas.

2 Cut the crusts off the bread, dip in melted butter on both sides and cut in half diagonally.

3 Arrange overlapping bread slices neatly in the dish.

4 Sprinkle with more sultanas and cover with another layer of bread.

5 To make the custard, split the vanilla pod, add to the milk and cream and slowly bring to the boil.

6 Whisk the eggs and sugar together and add the boiling liquid, leave to infuse for 5 minutes before passing through a conical strainer.

7 Pour the custard over the bread and grate on some fresh nutmeg.

8 Place in a bain-marie and place in a moderate oven at 160 °C, pour hot water into the bain-marie until it comes half way up the dish.

9 Bake for around 45 minutes until the custard is just set.

10 Once removed from the oven, sprinkle with sugar and place under the salamander to crisp up and colour the top.

11 Finally, brush with boiled apricot glaze and serve with pouring cream or crème fraiche.

Professional tip

Add the custard in two or three lots, allowing it to soak in before adding the next. This will prevent the bread floating to the top.

Healthy eating tips
● Reduce the sugar content and add more dried fruit, apricots or cranberries.
● Try using milk only, semi-skimmed or skimmed.
● Dip the bread in the butter on just one side to reduce the fat content.

Variations

This pudding can be made in individual dishes or baked in a tray and cut and plated.

Try using alternatives to bread such as fruit loaf, brioche, baguette slices or panettone.

Soak the sultanas in rum the day before.

Try adding a layer of caramelised apple slices.

A chocolate version can be made by adding couverture (good-quality chocolate) to the custard.

27 Cabinet pudding (*pouding cabinet*)

	4 portions	10 portions
Plain sponge cake	100 g	250 g
Zest of unwaxed lemons, grated		
Currants and sultanas	25 g	60 g
Milk, whole or skimmed	0.5 litres	1.25 litres
Eggs	3–4	8–10
Caster or unrefined sugar	50 g	125 g
Vanilla essence or a vanilla pod	2–3 drops (1 pod)	7 drops (2 pods)

Energy	Cals	Fat	Sat fat	Carb	Sugar	Protein	Fibre
1427 kJ	340 kcal	15.8 g	7.2 g	40.9 g	35.5 g	11.0 g	0.7 g

* Using whole milk and 3 eggs. Using whole milk and 4 eggs: 1512 kJ/360 kcal; 17.3 g fat; 7.7 g sat fat; 40.9 g carb; 35.5 g sugar; 12.7 g protein; 0.7 g fibre

Note

Serve a fresh egg custard (page 475) or hot apricot sauce separately.

Variation

Diplomat pudding is made as for cabinet pudding, but served cold with either redcurrant, raspberry, apricot or vanilla sauce.

1 Cut the cake into 0.5 cm dice.
2 Mix with the lemon zest and fruits (which can be soaked in rum).
3 Place in a greased, sugared charlotte mould or 4 dariole moulds. Do not fill more than halfway.
4 Warm the milk and whisk on to the eggs, sugar and essence (or vanilla pod).
5 Strain on to the mould.
6 Place in a roasting tin, half full of water; allow to stand for 5–10 minutes.
7 Cook in a moderate oven at 150–160 °C for 30–45 minutes.
8 Leave to set for a few minutes before turning out.

Activity

1 What is the purpose of a bain-marie?
2 Why is steaming the preferred method when cooking puddings made with suet?
3 Describe the correct procedure when scaling up (increasing) or scaling down (decreasing) a recipe.
4 List the differences between a soufflé and a pudding soufflé.

28 Rice pudding

1 Rinse a heavy pan with cold water and add the milk.

2 Split the vanilla pod, scrape out the seeds and add along with the pod.

3 Slowly bring to the boil.

4 Wash the rice and sprinkle into the boiling milk, stir, cover with a lid and allow to simmer until the rice is tender.

5 In a bowl whisk the eggs and sugar and drop in the butter.

6 Ladle a quarter of the boiling milk and rice onto the liaison, mix well and return all to the pan, carefully cook out until the mixture thickens, before removing from the heat (it must not be allowed to boil).

7 Place into suitable individual or large (usually china) dishes.

8 Grate with nutmeg and glaze under the salamander.

Note

Serve with a warm seasonal fruit compote.

Variations

Serve with apple compote (see page 499).

Place some good-quality jam in the base of the dish.

Place in a serving dish before piping meringue on top and baking in a hot oven until coloured.

Leftover rice pudding can be used as an alternative to crème pâtissière or frangipane as a filling for a baked flan.

	10 portions
Milk	650 ml
Vanilla pod	1
Short grain rice	60 g
Liaison	
Pasteurised egg	60 g
Caster sugar	60 g
Butter (diced)	30 g

Energy	Cals	Fat	Sat fat	Carb	Sugar	Protein	Fibre
644 kJ	153 kcal	2.7 g	1.7 g	28.6 g	18.7 g	5.2 g	0.0 g

Professional tip

Rinsing out the saucepan with cold water and adding the milk to the wet pan will help prevent the milk from catching on the bottom.

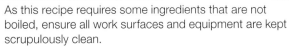

Health and safety

As this recipe requires some ingredients that are not boiled, ensure all work surfaces and equipment are kept scrupulously clean.

It is recommended that pasteurised eggs are used.

Rice pudding can be held over service at a temperature of no less than 75 °C for 2 hours.

Any leftover rice pudding must be cooled to below 5 °C within 20 minutes, labelled and stored in a refrigerator.

29 Soufflé pudding (*pouding soufflé*)

1 Boil the milk in a sautéuse.

2 Combine the flour, butter and sugar.

3 Whisk into the milk and reboil.

4 Remove from heat, add the egg yolks one at a time, whisking continuously.

5 Stiffly beat the whites and carefully fold into the mixture.

6 Three-quarters fill buttered and sugared dariole moulds.

7 Place in a roasting tin, half full of water.

8 Bring to the boil and place in a hot oven at 230–250 °C for 12–15 minutes.

9 Turn out on to a flat dish.

	6 portions	10 portions
Milk, whole or skimmed	185 ml	375 ml
Flour, white or wholemeal	25 g	50 g
Butter or margarine	25 g	50 g
Caster or unrefined sugar	25 g	50 g
Eggs, separated	3	6

Energy	Cals	Fat	Sat fat	Carb	Sugar	Protein	Fibre	*
510 kJ	122 kcal	7.6 g	3.2 g	5.9 g	4.8 g	0.2 g	0.0 g	

* Using white flour and hard margarine

Note

Serve with a suitable hot sauce, such as custard or sabayon sauce.

Variation

Orange or lemon soufflé pudding is made by flavouring the basic mixture with the grated zest of an orange or lemon and a little appropriate sauce. Use the juice in the accompanying sauce.

30 Christmas pudding

	2 × 1 kg puddings
Currants	175 g
Sultanas	175 g
Raisins	350 g
Guinness	500 ml
Cognac	50 ml
Strong flour	175 g
Mixed spice	1 tsp
Nutmeg	¼ tsp
Cinnamon	1 tsp
Breadcrumbs	175 g
Suet	350 g
Mixed peel	80 g
Ground almonds	80 g
Eggs	4
Soft dark brown sugar	175 g
Lemon juice and zest	1

Energy	Cals	Fat	Sat fat	Carb	Sugar	Protein	Fibre	Sodium
2077 kJ	495 kcal	24 g	12 g	65 g	46 g	6 g	3.5 g	0.17 g

1 Place all the dried fruit in a bowl, pour over the Guinness and cognac and leave to soak overnight.

2 Sieve the flour with the mixed spice, grate over the nutmeg and cinnamon and place in a large bowl.

3 Add the breadcrumbs, suet, peel and ground almonds and mix well.

4 Make a well in the centre.

5 Whisk the eggs, sugar and salt, add the lemon juice and zest.

6 Pour the wet ingredients into the well and add the soaked fruit.

7 Mix well.

8 Place mixture into two buttered pudding basins, cover with a disc of silicone paper and seal with foil, crimping around the edges.

9 Steam for 7 hours, cool and store in the fridge.

10 Re-heat in the steamer for a couple of hours.

Note

Serve with brandy or rum sauce and/or brandy butter.

Professional tip

Like a Christmas fruit cake, Christmas pudding is best made in September and allowed to mature.

31 Baked Alaska (*omelette soufflé surprise*)

1 Sit the ice cream or parfait on a base of sponge.

2 Cut more sponge to fit and completely cover.

3 Brush all over with the syrup.

4 Set on squares of silicone paper, coat with the meringue and decorate by piping on a design with a small plain tube.

5 Dust with icing sugar and place in a very hot oven at 230 °C for 2–3 minutes until the meringue is coloured.

Note

Serve immediately with crème anglaise or a fruit coulis.

Professional tip

Baked Alaska is best made in advance and held in the freezer, then flashed through the oven just before serving. It is now common practice to colour the meringue with a blowtorch, but the meringue will have a much better texture and more even colouring if it is finished in the oven.

If making individual baked Alaskas, as in the photographs, take care not to upset the balance between filling and meringue – when scaled down it is easy to pipe on too much meringue.

	10 portions
Vanilla ice cream or parfait	10 × 5 cm diameter rings (500 g approx)
Roulade sponge (see page 555)	1 sheet
Stock syrup flavoured with rum or kirsch	50 ml
Italian meringue	500 g

Energy	Cals	Fat	Sat fat	Carb	Sugar	Protein	Fibre
290 kJ	521 kcals	16.4 g	7.3 g	91.3 g	81.2 g	7.7 g	0.6 g

1 Brush the sponge with syrup

2 Coat with meringue to cover

3 Pipe swirls of meringue to decorate

Variation

Classic variations are omelette soufflé milady, which contains poached sliced peaches with vanilla or raspberry ice cream, and omelette soufflé milord, which contains poached sliced pear with vanilla ice cream.

Health and safety

Under no circumstances should this dessert be re-frozen once it has been removed from the freezer and baked. Ice cream is highly susceptible to contamination by bacteria which can cause food poisoning.

32 Tatin of apple (*tarte tatin*)

1 Make a dry caramel by placing the granulated sugar in a hot heavy-based saucepan. When the sugar reaches a deep amber colour, pour it out onto a silicone mat and leave to cool completely.

2 When cold, crush the caramel into small pieces.

3 Take a medium-sized sauteuse and spread the butter thickly around the base and sides. Sprinkle over the caster sugar and then sprinkle over the caramel. (Any spare caramel can be stored in an airtight container for later use.)

4 Peel, core and halve the apples (if large, cut into quarters) and pack into the sauteuse core-side up and with the cores running horizontally, not facing outside.

5 Roll out the pastry 2 mm thick and leave to rest.

6 Place the pan on a medium heat for 10–12 minutes to allow the caramel to melt and infuse.

7 Quickly lay over the pastry and trim, tucking the edges down the side of the pan.

8 Bake at 220 °C for 15 minutes until the pastry is crisp and the apples cooked through.

9 Invert onto a hot plate – please be aware this procedure can be tricky and requires two dry cloths and very careful handling.

10 Serve with cream, crème fraiche or ice cream.

Ingredient	10 portions
Soft butter	120g
Caster sugar	120g
Dessert apples	5
Caramel, crushed	120g
Puff paste	150g
For the caramel	
Granulated sugar	500g

Energy	Cals	Fat	Sat fat	Carb	Sugar	Protein	Fibre
1299kJ	308kcal	12.6g	7.2g	50.2g	43.6g	1.8g	5.2g

Note

This is the name given to an apple tart that is cooked under a lid of pastry, but then served with the pastry underneath the fruit. This is a delicious dessert in which the taste of caramel is combined with the flavour of the fruit and finished with a crisp pastry base.

It was the creation of the Tatin sisters, who ran a hotel-restaurant in Lamotte-Beuvron at the beginning of the last century. Having been made famous by the Tatin sisters the dish was first served at Maxim's in Paris as a house speciality. It is still served there to this day.

33 Apple crumble tartlets

	10 tarts
Sweet paste	500 g
Dessert apples	5
Filling	
Soured cream	500 ml
Caster sugar	70 g
Plain flour	75 g
Egg	1
Vanilla extract	
Crumble	
Plain flour	80 g
Walnuts, chopped	60 g
Brown sugar	65 g
Ground cinnamon	Pinch
Salt	Pinch
Unsalted butter, melted	65 g
Icing sugar, to garnish	

Energy	Cals	Fat	Sat fat	Carb	Sugar	Protein	Fibre	Sodium
2200 kJ	541 kcal	36 g	19.3 g	51 g	20 g	7.3 g	2.6 g	0.33 g

1 Line individual tartlet moulds with the sweet paste.
2 Peel, core and finely slice the apples and divide between the tartlets.
3 Whisk together the soured cream, sugar, flour, egg and a few drops of vanilla, and pass through a conical strainer.
4 Pour over the apples and bake at 190 °C for 10 minutes.
5 Combine the dry crumble ingredients and mix with the melted butter.
6 Divide the crumble mixture between the tartlets and bake for a further 10 minutes.
7 Allow to cool slightly before unmoulding. Dust with icing sugar and serve with *sauce à l'anglaise*.

Variation

This dish could be made with pears or plums instead of apples.

34 Steamed fruit pudding

	10 individual fruit puddings or 1 large pudding
Suet paste (see page 522)	300 g
Fruit	1 kg
Sugar	200 g
Water	60 ml

Energy	Cals	Fat	Sat fat	Carb	Sugar	Protein	Fibre	Sodium
975 kJ	231 kcal	6.3 g	3.1 g	44 g	33 g	1.8 g	2.6 g	0.14 g

1 Grease a basin or individual moulds.

2 Line the moulds, using three-quarters of the paste.

3 Add the prepared and washed fruit and the sugar. (Add between one and two cloves in an apple pudding.)

5 Add water. Moisten the edge of the paste.

6 Cover with the remaining quarter of the pastry and seal firmly.

7 Cover with greased greaseproof paper, a pudding cloth or foil.

8 Steam for about 1 ½ hours (large basin) or 40 minutes (individual moulds).

9 Serve with custard.

Note

Suet paste is used for steamed fruit puddings, steamed jam rolls, steamed meat puddings and dumplings. Vegetarian suet is also available to enable products to be meat free. Here is an example of its use in the pastry kitchen to produce a steamed fruit pudding using apple.

Variation

Steamed fruit puddings can be made with apple, apple and blackberry, rhubarb, rhubarb and apple and so on.

35 Fruit mousse

	10 portions
Egg yolks	4
Sugar	50 g
Fruit purée	250 g
Gelatine	4 leaves
Lemon juice	
Lightly whipped cream	250 g
Italian meringue	
Sugar	112 g
Egg whites	2
Cream of tartar	pinch
Glaze topping	
Stock syrup	150 ml
Fruit purée	150 ml
Gelatine	3 leaves, soaked in cold water

Energy	Cals	Fat	Sat fat	Carb	Sugar	Protein	Fibre	Sodium
950 kJ	227 kcal	12.4 g	7 g	26 g	26 g	4 g	2 g	0.03 g

1 Mix the egg yolks and sugar together and slowly add the boiled fruit purée which has been flavoured with a squeeze of lemon juice.

2 Return to the stove and cook to 80 °C until slightly thickened. Do not boil.

3 Add the previously softened gelatine to the warm purée and mix until fully dissolved. Chill down.

4 Prepare the Italian meringue by placing the sugar in a pan and saturating in water.

5 Boil the sugar to 115 °C, then whisk the egg whites with a pinch of cream of tartar.

6 Once the egg whites are at full peak, gradually add the boiled sugar which now should have reached the temperature of 121 °C. Whisk until cold.

7 Once the purée is cold, but not set, incorporate the Italian meringue and whipped cream.

8 Place into piping bag and pipe into the desired ring mould, normally lined with a suitable sponge such as a jaconde.

9 Level the surface using a palette knife and refrigerate.

10 Once set, glace the surface, refrigerate.

11 To remove from the mould, warm the outside of the mould with a blow torch and remove the ring mould.

Glaze:

1 Warm the syrup. Add the gelatine and stir until dissolved, then add the desired fruit purée.

2 Apply to the surface of the chilled mousse whilst in a liquid state, but not hot.

36 Chocolate mousse

Ingredient	8 portions	16 portions
Stock syrup at 30° Baumé (equal quantities of sugar and water will give 30° Baume)	125 ml	250 ml
Pasteurised egg yolks	80 ml	160 ml
Bitter couverture, melted	250 g	500 g
Gelatine	2 leaves	4 leaves
Whipping cream, whipped	500 ml	1 litre

Energy	Cals	Fat	Sat fat	Carb	Sugar	Protein	Fibre	Sodium
1760 kJ	419 kcal	37 g	22 g	13.7 g	12.8 g	5.1 g	2.6 g	0.03 g

1 Boil the syrup.

2 Place the yolks into the bowl of a food mixer. Pour over the boiling syrup and whisk until thick. Remove from the mixer.

3 Add all the melted couverture at once and fold it in quickly.

4 Drain the gelatine, melt it in the microwave and fold it into the chocolate sabayon mixture.

5 Add all the whipped cream at once and fold it in carefully.

6 Place the mixture into prepared moulds. Refrigerate or freeze immediately.

Faults

Possible causes of a heavy texture in chocolate mousse:

● The pâte à bombe is under-aerated.
● The cream is insufficiently whipped.
● The mix has been over-worked when folding in the cream and Italian meringue.

37 Bavarois: basic recipe and a range of flavours

What happens if too much	6–8 portions
Gelatine	10g
Eggs, pasteurised, separated	2
Caster sugar	50g
Milk, whole, semi-skimmed or skimmed	250ml
Whipping or double cream or non-dairy cream	125ml

Energy	Cals	Fat	Sat fat	Carb	Sugar	Protein	Fibre
970kJ	231kcal	18.2g	10.9g	11.8g	11.8g	5.8g	0.0g

Variation

Raspberry or strawberry bavarois: when the custard is almost cool, add 200g of picked, washed and sieved raspberries or strawberries. Decorate with whole fruit and whipped cream.

Chocolate bavarois: dissolve 50g chocolate couverture in the milk. Decorate with whipped cream and grated chocolate.

Coffee bavarois: proceed as for a basic bavarois, with the addition of coffee essence to taste.

Orange bavarois: add grated zest and juice of 2 oranges and 1 or 2 drops orange colour to the mixture, and increase the gelatine by 2 leaves. Decorate with blanched, fine julienne of orange zest, orange segments and whipped cream.

Lemon or lime bavarois: as orange bavarois, using lemons or limes in place of oranges.

Vanilla bavarois: add a vanilla pod or a few drops of vanilla essence to the milk. Decorate with vanilla-flavoured sweetened cream (crème Chantilly).

1 If using leaf gelatine, soak in cold water.

2 Cream the yolks and sugar in a bowl until almost white.

3 Whisk in the milk, which has been brought to the boil, mix well.

4 Clean the milk saucepan, which should be a thick-based one, and return the mixture to it.

5 Return to a low heat and stir continuously with a wooden spoon until the mixture coats the back of the spoon. The mixture must not boil.

6 Remove from the heat; add the gelatine and stir until dissolved.

7 Pass through a fine strainer into a clean bowl, leave in a cool place, stirring occasionally until almost at setting point.

8 Fold in the lightly beaten cream.

9 Fold in the stiffly beaten whites.

10 Pour the mixture into a mould or individual moulds (which may be very lightly greased with almond oil).

11 Allow to set in the refrigerator.

12 Shake and turn out on to a flat dish or plates.

Note

Bavarois may be decorated with sweetened, flavoured whipped cream (crème Chantilly). It is advisable to use pasteurised egg yolks and whites.

38 Lime soufflé frappe

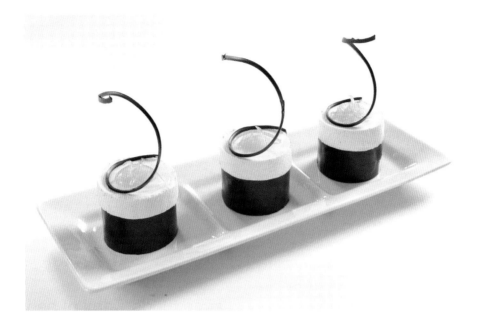

patisseries and ice cream	10 portions	15 portions
Couverture	150 g	200 g
Sponge, thin slices, cut into rounds	10	15
Lime syrup	100 ml	150 ml
Swiss meringue		
Egg whites, pasteurised	190 ml	300 ml
Caster sugar	230 ml	340 ml
Sabayon		
Whipping cream	600 ml	900 ml
Lime zest, finely grated and blanched, and juice	8	12
Egg yolks	10	15
Caster sugar	170 g	250 g
Leaf gelatine, soaked in iced water	9½	14
To decorate		
Confit of lime segments		
Moulded chocolate		

Energy	Cals	Fat	Sat fat	Carb	Sugar	Protein	Fibre	Sodium
2734 kJ	655 kcal	40.8 g	20.7 g	66.9 g	61.2 g	9.2 g	0.8 g	0.2 g

1 Use individual stainless steel ring moulds. Cut a strip of acetate, 8 cm wide, to fit inside each ring. Cut a 6 cm strip to fit inside the first, spread it with tempered couverture and place inside the first strip, in the mould.

2 Place a round of sponge in the base of each mould and moisten with lime syrup.

3 Make a Swiss meringue by whisking the pasteurised egg whites and sugar over a bain-marie of simmering water until a light and aerated meringue is achieved.

4 Whisk the cream until it is three-quarters whipped, then chill.

5 Whisk together the egg yolks, sugar and blanched lime zest. Boil the juice and pour it over the mixture to make the sabayon. Whisk over a bain-marie until it reaches 75 °C, then continue whisking away from the heat until it is cold.

6 Drain and melt the gelatine. Fold it into the sabayon.

7 Fold in the Swiss meringue, and then the chilled whipped cream.

8 Fill the prepared moulds. Level the tops and chill until set.

9 To serve, carefully remove the mould, peel away the acetate, plate and decorate.

39 Vanilla panna cotta served on a fruit compote

	6 portions
Milk	125 ml
Double cream	375 ml
Aniseeds	2
Vanilla pod	½
Gelatine (soaked)	2 leaves
Caster sugar	50 g
Fruit compote	
Apricot purée	75 g
Vanilla pod	½
Peach	1
Kiwi fruit	1
Strawberries	75 g
Blueberries	75 g
Raspberries	50 g

Energy	Cals	Fat	Sat fat	Carb	Sugar	Protein	Fibre
1565kJ	378kcal	34.0g	21.1g	16.1g	16.1g	2.9g	1.5g

1 Prepare the fruit compote by boiling the apricot purée and infusing with vanilla pod. Remove pod, allow purée to cool.

2 Finely dice the peach and the kiwi and quarter the strawberries. Mix, then add blueberries and raspberries.

3 Bind the fruit with the apricot purée. A little stock syrup (see page 477) may be required to keep the fruit free flowing.

4 For the panna cotta, boil the milk and cream, add aniseeds, infuse with the vanilla pod and remove after infusion.

5 Heat again and add the soaked gelatine and caster sugar. Strain through a fine strainer.

6 Place in a bowl set over ice and stir until it thickens slightly; this will allow the vanilla seeds to suspend throughout the mix instead of sinking to the bottom.

7 Fill individual dariole moulds.

8 Place the fruit compote with individual fruit plates, turn out the panna cotta, place on top of the compote and finish with a tuile biscuit.

40 Poached fruits or fruit compote (compote de fruits)

	4 portions	10 portions
Stock syrup (see page 477)	250 ml	625 ml
Fruit	400 g	1 kg
Sugar	100 g	250 g
Lemon, juice of	½	1

Energy	Cals	Fat	Sat fat	Carb	Sugar	Protein	Fibre *
531 kJ	126 kcal	0.0 g	0.0 g	33.5 g	33.5 g	0.2 g	2.2 g

* Using pears

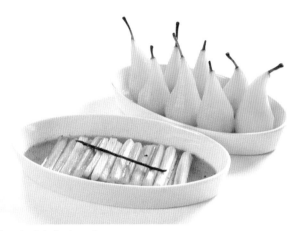

Poached rhubarb and pear

Apples, pears:

1 Boil the water and sugar.

2 Quarter the fruit, remove the core and peel.

3 Place in a shallow pan in sugar syrup.

4 Add a few drops of lemon juice.

5 Cover with greaseproof paper.

6 Allow to simmer slowly, preferably in the oven, cool and serve.

Soft fruits (raspberries, strawberries):

1 Pick and wash the fruit. Place in a glass bowl.

2 Pour on the hot syrup. Allow to cool and serve.

Stone fruits (plums, damsons, greengages, cherries):

1 Wash the fruit, barely cover with sugar syrup and cover with greaseproof paper or a lid.

2 Cook gently in a moderate oven until tender.

Rhubarb:

1 Trim off the stalk and leaf and wash.

2 Cut into 5 cm lengths and cook as above, adding extra sugar if necessary. A little ground ginger may also be added.

Gooseberries, blackcurrants, redcurrants:

1 Top and tail the gooseberries, wash and cook as for stone fruit, adding extra sugar if necessary.

2 The currants should be carefully removed from the stalks, washed and cooked as for stone fruits.

Dried fruits (prunes, apricots, apples, pears):

1 Dried fruits should be washed and soaked in cold water overnight.

2 Gently cook in the liquor with sufficient sugar to taste.

Variations

A piece of cinnamon stick and a few slices of lemon may be added to the prunes or pears, one or two cloves to the dried or fresh apples.

Any compote may be flavoured with lavender and/or mint.

Healthy eating tips
● Use fruit juice instead of stock syrup.
● If dried fruits are used, no added sugar is needed.

41 Lime and mascarpone cheesecake

	1 cheesecake
Packet of ginger biscuits	200 g approx
Butter, melted	200 g
Egg yolks, pasteurised	125 g
Caster sugar	75 g
Cream cheese	250 g
Mascarpone	250 g
Gelatine, softened in cold water	15 g
Limes, juice and grated zest of	2
Semi-whipped cream	275 ml
White chocolate, melted	225 g

Energy	Cals	Fat	Sat fat	Carb	Sugar	Protein	Fibre	Sodium
2064 kJ	633 kcal	54.0 g	32.3 g	31.5 g	24.3 g	7.1 g	0.0 g	0.3 g

1 Blitz the biscuits in a food processor. Mix in the melted butter. Line the cake ring with this mixture and chill until required.

2 Make a sabayon by whisking the egg yolks and sugar together over a pan of simmering water.

3 Stir the cream cheese and mascarpone into the sabayon until soft.

4 Meanwhile, warm the gelatine in the lime juice, and pass through a fine chinois. Whip the cream.

5 Pour the gelatine and melted white chocolate into the cheese mixture.

6 Remove from the food mixer and fold in the whipped cream with a spatula. Finally, whisk in the lime zest.

7 Pour over the prepared base. Chill for 4 hours.

42 Baked blueberry cheesecake

	8–12 portions
Base	
Digestive biscuits	150 g
Butter, melted	50 g
Filling	
Full-fat cream cheese	350 g
Caster sugar	150 g
Eggs	4
Lemon, zest and juice of	1
Vanilla essence	5 ml
Blueberries	125
Soured cream	350 ml

Energy	Cals	Fat	Sat fat	Carb	Sugar	Protein	Fibre
1791 kJ	431 kcal	33.5 g	19.5 g	28.0 g	19.7 g	6.4 g	0.4 g

1 Blitz the biscuits in a food processor. Stir in the melted butter. Press the mixture into the bottom of a lightly greased cake tin with a removable collar.

2 Whisk together the cheese, sugar, eggs, vanilla and lemon zest and juice until smooth.

3 Stir in the blueberries, then pour the mixture over the biscuit base.

4 Bake at 160 °C for approximately 30 minutes.

5 Remove from the oven and leave to cool slightly for 10–15 minutes.

6 Spread soured cream over the top and return to the oven for 10 minutes.

7 Remove and allow to cool and set. Chill.

43 Trifle

	6–8 portions
Sponge (made with 3 eggs)	1
Jam	25 g
Tinned fruit (pears, peaches, pineapple)	1
Sherry (optional)	
Custard	
Custard powder	35 g
Milk, whole or skimmed	375 ml
Caster sugar	50 g
Cream (¾ whipped) or non-dairy cream	125 ml
Whipped sweetened cream or non-dairy cream	250 ml
Angelica	25 g
Glacé cherries	25 g

Energy	Cals	Fat	Sat fat	Carb	Sugar	Protein	Fibre
2280 kJ	543 kcal	29.1 g	17.1 g	66.2 g	51.3 g	8.2 g	1.9 g

1 Cut the sponge in half, sideways, and spread with jam.

2 Place in a glass bowl or individual dishes and soak with fruit syrup drained from the tinned fruit; a few drops of sherry may be added.

3 Cut the fruit into small pieces and add to the sponge.

4 Dilute the custard powder in a basin with some of the milk and add the sugar.

5 Boil the remainder of the milk, pour a little on the custard powder, mix well, return to the saucepan and over a low heat and stir to the boil. Allow to cool, stirring occasionally to prevent a skin forming; fold in the three-quarters whipped cream.

6 Pour on to the sponge. Leave to cool.

7 Decorate with the whipped cream, angelica and cherries.

Variation

Other flavourings or liqueurs may be used in place of sherry (such as whisky, rum, brandy, Tia Maria).
For raspberry or strawberry trifle use fully ripe fresh fruit in place of tinned and decorate with fresh fruit in place of angelica and glacé cherries.

A fresh egg custard may be used with fresh egg yolks (see page 475).

44 *Crème brûlée* (Burned, caramelised or browned cream)

	4 portions	10 portions
Milk	125 ml	300 ml
Double cream	125 ml	300 ml
Natural vanilla essence or pod	3–4 drops	7–10 drops
Eggs	2	5
Egg yolk	1	2–3
Caster sugar	25 g	60 g
Demerara sugar		

Energy	Cals	Fat	Sat fat	Carb	Sugar	Protein	Fibre
1154 kJ	278 kcal	21.9 g	12.1 g	14.8 g	14.8 g	6.2 g	0.0 g

1 Warm the milk, cream and vanilla essence in a pan.

2 Mix the eggs, egg yolk and caster sugar in a basin and add the warm milk. Stir well and pass through a fine strainer.

3 Pour the cream into individual dishes and place them into a tray half-filled with warm water.

4 Place in the oven at approximately 160 °C for about 30–40 minutes, until set.

5 Sprinkle the tops with Demerara sugar and glaze under the salamander or by blowtorch to a golden brown.

6 Clean the dishes and serve.

Video: Crème brulée
http://bit.ly/1vWYRwH

Use a blowtorch carefully to glaze the top

Variation

Sliced strawberries, raspberries or other fruits (e.g. peaches, apricots) may be placed in the bottom of the dish before adding the cream mixture, or placed on top after the creams are caramelised.

45 Cream caramel (*crème caramel*)

1 Prepare the caramel by placing three-quarters of the water in a thick-based pan, adding the sugar and allowing to boil gently, without shaking or stirring the pan.

2 When the sugar has cooked to a golden-brown caramel colour, add the remaining quarter of the water, reboil until the sugar and water mix, then pour into the bottom of dariole moulds.

3 Prepare the cream by warming the milk and whisking on to the beaten eggs, sugar and essence (or vanilla pod).

4 Strain and pour into the prepared moulds.

5 Place in a roasting tin half full of water.

6 Cook in a moderate oven at 150–160 °C for 30–40 minutes.

7 When thoroughly cold, loosen the edges of the cream caramel with the fingers, shake firmly to loosen and turn out on to a flat dish or plates.

8 Pour any caramel remaining in the mould around the creams.

Note

Cream caramels may be served with whipped cream or a fruit sauce such as passion fruit, and accompanied by a sweet biscuit (e.g. shortbread, palmiers).

Professional tip

Adding a squeeze of lemon juice to the caramel will invert the sugar, thus preventing recrystallisation.

	4–6 portions	10–12 portions
Caramel		
Sugar, granulated or cube	100 g	200 g
Water	125 ml	250 ml
Cream		
Milk, whole or skimmed	0.5 litres	1 litre
Eggs	4	8
Sugar, caster or unrefined	50 g	100 g
Vanilla essence or a vanilla pod	3–4 drops	6–8 drops

Energy	Cals	Fat	Sat fat	Carb	Sugar	Protein	Fibre	*
868 kJ	207 kcal	7.2 g	3.3 g	30.2 g	30.2 g	7.3 g	0.0 g	

* Using whole milk

46 Meringue

	4 portions	10 portions
Lemon juice or cream of tartar		
Egg whites, pasteurised	4	10
Caster sugar	200 g	500 g

Energy	Cals	Fat	Sat fat	Carb	Sugar	Protein	Fibre	Sodium
913 kJ	214 kcal	0.1 g	0 g	52 g	52 g	4 g	0 g	0.07 g

1 Whip the egg whites stiffly with a squeeze of lemon juice or cream of tartar.

2 Sprinkle on the sugar and carefully mix in.

3 Place in a piping bag with a large plain tube and pipe onto silicone paper on a baking sheet.

4 Bake in the slowest oven possible or in a hot plate (110 °C). The aim is to dry out the meringues without any colour whatsoever.

Whipping egg whites

The reason egg whites increase in volume when whipped is because they contain so much protein (11 per cent). The protein forms tiny filaments, which stretch on beating, incorporate air in minute bubbles then set to form a fairly stable puffed-up structure expanding to seven times its bulk. To gain maximum efficiency when whipping egg whites, the following points should be observed.

Because of possible weakness in the egg-white protein, it is advisable to strengthen it by adding a pinch of cream of tartar and a pinch of dried egg-white powder. If all dried egg-white powder is used no additions are necessary.

Other points to note:
- Eggs should be fresh.
- When separating yolks from whites, no speck of egg yolk must be allowed to remain in the white; egg yolk contains fat, the presence of which can prevent the white being correctly whipped.
- The bowl and whisk must be scrupulously clean, dry and free from any grease.
- When egg whites are whipped, the addition of a little sugar (15 g to 4 egg whites) will assist efficient beating and reduce the chances of over-beating.

47 Vacherin with strawberries and cream (*vacherin aux fraises*)

	4 portions	10 portions
Egg whites	4	10
Caster sugar	200 g	500 g
Cream (whipped and sweetened) or non-dairy cream	125 ml	300 ml
Strawberries, picked and washed)	100–300 g	250–750 g

Energy	Cals	Fat	Sat fat	Carb	Sugar	Protein	Fibre
1436 kJ	341 kcal	12.6 g	7.9 g	56.3 g	56.3 g	3.9 g	0.6 g

1 Stiffly whip the egg whites. (Refer to the notes in Recipe 44 for more guidance.)

2 Carefully fold in the sugar.

3 Place the mixture into a piping bag with a 1 cm plain tube.

4 Pipe on to silicone paper on a baking sheet.

5 Start from the centre and pipe round in a circular fashion to form a base of 16 cm then pipe around the edge 2–3 cm high.

6 Bake in a cool oven at 100 °C until the meringue case is completely dry. Do not allow to colour.

7 Allow the meringue case to cool then remove from the paper.

8 Spread a thin layer of cream on the base. Add the strawberries.

9 Decorate with the remainder of the cream.

Note

A vacherin is a round meringue shell piped into a suitable shape so that the centre may be filled with sufficient fruit (such as strawberries, stoned cherries, peaches and apricots) and whipped cream to form a rich sweet. The vacherin may be prepared in one-, two- or four-portion sizes, or larger.

Variation

Melba sauce (see page 511) may be used to coat the strawberries before decorating with cream.

Raspberries can be used instead of strawberries.

Healthy eating tip

● Try 'diluting' the fat in the cream with some low-fat fromage frais.

48 Vanilla ice cream *(glace vanille)*

	8–10 portions
Egg yolks	4
Caster or unrefined sugar	100 g
Milk, whole or skimmed	375 ml
Vanilla pod or essence	
Cream or non-dairy cream	125 ml

Energy	Cals	Fat	Sat fat	Carb	Sugar	Protein	Fibre *
616 kJ	147 kcal	8.1 g	4.2 g	15.8 g	15.8 g	3.5 g	0.0 g

* Using whole milk and single cream

1 Whisk the yolks and sugar in a bowl until almost white.

2 Boil the milk with the vanilla pod or essence in a thick-based pan.

3 Whisk on to the eggs and sugar; mix well.

4 Return to the cleaned saucepan, place on a low heat.

5 Stir continuously with a wooden spoon until the mixture coats the back of the spoon.

6 Pass through a fine strainer into a cold bowl.

7 Freeze in an ice cream machine, gradually adding the cream.

Variations

Coffee ice cream: add coffee essence, to taste, to the custard after it is cooked.

Chocolate ice cream: add 50–100 g of chopped couverture to the milk before boiling.

Strawberry ice cream: add 125 ml of strawberry pulp in place of 125 ml of milk. The pulp is added after the custard is cooked.

Rum and raisin ice cream: soak 50 g raisins in 2 tbsp rum for 3–4 hours. Add to mixture before freezing.

1 Whisk boiling milk into the egg yolks and sugar

2 Return the mixture to the hot pan used for the milk

3 Test the consistency on the back of a spoon

4 Pass through a fine strainer into a cold pot

5 The mixture will cool down; if it was left in the hot pan it would continue to cook

6 Gradually add cream to the mixture in the ice cream machine

49 Lemon curd ice cream

	6–8 portions
Lemon curd	250 g
Crème fraiche	125 g
Greek yoghurt	250 g

Energy	Cals	Fat	Sat fat	Carbs	Sugar	Protein	Fibre
774 kJ	185 kcal	8.9 g	5.2 g	24.8 g	16.7 g	2.8 g	0.0 g

1 Mix all ingredients together.

2 Churn in the ice-cream machine.

50 Caramel ice cream

Energy	Cals	Fat	Sat fat	Carb	Sugar	Protein	Fibre
862 kJ	206 kcal	12.0 g	6.4 g	21.7 g	20.6 g	4.2 g	3.4 g

	8 portions
Crème anglaise	
Milk	500 ml
Egg yolks	5
Caster sugar	25 g
Whipping cream	100 ml
Inverted sugar (Trimoline)	25 g
Caramel	
Glucose	20 g
Caster sugar	100 g
Butter	10 g
Water, boiling	40 ml

1 Make the crème anglaise in the normal manner, then add the inverted sugar.

2 To make the caramel, melt the glucose in a thick-bottomed pan.

3 Add half the sugar to the melted glucose and heat until a caramel colour starts to appear.

4 Gradually add the remaining sugar and continue to cook until a golden caramel is obtained.

5 Add the butter and the boiling water to arrest the cooking of the sugar and dilute the caramel.

6 Add the caramel to the crème anglaise and freeze down in the sorbetière (sorbet machine).

Health and safety !

Remember that caramel is extremely hot; be very careful when pouring onto the crème anglaise.

Professional tip

Always have a frozen metal container in the deep freezer to transfer the ice cream into. This will prevent the base of the ice cream melting.

51 Apple sorbet

	8–10 portions
Granny Smith apples, washed and cored	4
Lemon, juice of	1
Water	400 ml
Sugar	200 g
Glucose	50 g

Energy	Cals	Fat	Sat fat	Carb	Sugar	Protein	Fibre
673 kJ	158 kcal	0.1 g	0.0 g	41.5 g	38.7 g	0.4 g	2.4 g

1 Cut the apples into 1 cm pieces and place into lemon juice.

2 Bring the water, sugar and glucose to the boil, then allow to cool.

3 Pour the water over the apples. Freeze overnight. Blitz in a food processor.

4 Pass through a conical strainer, then churn in an ice-cream machine.

Professional tip

For best results, after freezing, process in a Pacojet.

Variation

Fruits of the forest sorbet: use a mixture of forest fruits instead of apples.

52 Chocolate sorbet

	8 portions
Water	400 ml
Skimmed milk	100 ml
Sugar	150 g
Ice-cream stabiliser	40 g
Cocoa powder	30 g
Dark couverture	60 g

1 Combine the water, milk, sugar, stabiliser and cocoa powder. Bring to the boil slowly. Simmer for 5 minutes.

2 Add the couverture and allow to cool.

3 Pass and churn.

Energy	Cals	Fat	Sat fat	Carb	Sugar	Protein	Fibre
544 kJ	129 kcal	3.0 g	1.8 g	25.4 g	24.9 g	1.6 g	6.3 g

53 Orange brandy granita

Orange juice	500 ml
Brandy	40 ml
Stock syrup at 30° Baumé (equal quantities of sugar and water will give 30° Baumé)	100 ml
Water	175 ml

Energy	Cals	Fat	Sat fat	Carb	Sugar	Protein	Fibre	Sodium
2130 kJ	503 kcal	0.5 g	0 g	106.3	106.3 g	2.5 g	0.7 g	0.055 g

1 Mix all the ingredients together.

2 Pour into a gastronorm tray and place in the freezer.

3 Fork up to produce crystals.

54 Peach Melba (pêche Melba)

1 Poach the peaches. Allow to cool, then peel, halve and remove the stones.

2 Dress the fruit on a ball of the ice cream in an ice-cream coupe or in a tuile basket.

3 Finish with the sauce.

The traditional presentation is to coat the peach in Melba sauce or coulis and decorate with whipped cream.

Professional tip

If using fresh peaches, dip them in boiling water for a few seconds, cool them by placing into cold water, then peel and halve.

Variation

Fruit Melba can also be made using pear or banana instead of peach. Fresh pears should be peeled, halved and poached. Bananas should be peeled at the last moment.

	4 portions	10 portions
Peaches	2	5
Vanilla ice cream	125 ml	300 ml
Melba sauce or raspberry coulis	125 ml	300 ml

Energy	Cals	Fat	Sat fat	Carb	Sugar	Protein	Fibre
607 kJ	145 kcal	2.6g	1.3g	30.5g	30.2g	1.6g	1.3g

55 Pear belle Hélène (poire belle Hélène)

1 Serve a poached pear with a ball of vanilla ice cream on a plate or, traditionally, in a coupe.

2 Decorate with whipped cream. Serve with a sauceboat of hot chocolate sauce.

Energy	Cals	Fat	Sat fat	Carb	Sugar	Protein	Fibre
673 kJ	158 kcal	0.1g	0.0g	41.5g	38.7g	0.4g	2.4g

13

Produce paste products

This chapter will help you to:

1 prepare, cook and finish paste products, including:
   - using tools and equipment correctly, in a safe and hygienic way
   - producing short, sweet, puff and choux paste products
   - checking that the finished product meets requirements.

2 know how to:
   - identify different paste products, their uses and preparation and cooking methods
   - understand the quality points of ingredients and how to adjust the quantity to give correct portions
   - identify fillings, glazes, creams and icings, and finishing and decorating techniques
   - store finished products safely
   - identify ingredients that may cause allergic reactions.

The key ingredients for pastry work, such as flour, eggs and sugar, are described in Chapter 12. Make sure you read and understand this section.

Recipes in this chapter

Types of paste and their uses

Short paste

The shortness of a paste refers to the crisp, light and sometimes crumbly texture of the finished paste. The term 'shortening' describes the effect of the fat when rubbed gently into the flour, breaking down the gluten strands in the flour and producing the short texture qualities. Short pastry is typically used as a lining for savoury and sweet pies, tarts and flans.

Sweet paste

Sweet paste is a short paste that has been sweetened with the addition of sugar and often enriched by the addition of egg. The type of sugar used is normally caster sugar or icing sugar. This helps to achieve a fine, smooth paste. Sweet paste is commonly used to line sweet tarts, tartlets and flans.

Puff paste

Puff paste is a laminated paste. The term '**lamination**' refers to the layers that are produced when making puff paste. To make puff paste, a dough is produced using a strong flour as the dough needs to be elastic and robust enough to incorporate layers of butter without splitting or oozing. The butter is added to the paste in a layer which is multiplied hundreds of times through the process known as '**turning**'. Each turn multiplies the layers of paste and butter until the desired amount is reached, usually four 'double' or 'book' turns. When the paste is baked, the layers of fat produce steam resulting in a rising between the layers of dough. This is what causes the rising of puff paste and the development of hundreds of fine, delicate layers in the finished, baked product. Puff paste is used to make sweet and savoury products such as turnovers, pastry cases (bouchées, vol-au-vents), pies, palmiers, fruit bands and mille-feuilles.

Choux paste

Choux paste is made by melting butter in water, binding this mixture by cooking to a paste with flour before beating in eggs to produce a fairly thick but slack paste of a 'dropping consistency'. It is then piped into the desired shapes and baked. During the baking process the moisture from the water content helps to produce an air bubble around which the paste bakes to form a light batter-like product. Choux paste is used to produce products such as profiteroles, éclairs, gâteaux Paris-Brest and the famous French dessert Croquembouche. It can also be used to produce savoury products – small choux buns filled with a savoury mousse, for example.

Techniques

Adding fat to flour

Fats act as a **shortening agent**. The fat has the effect of shortening the gluten strands, producing a pastry, which are easily broken when eaten, making the texture of the product more crumbly. The development of gluten in puff pastry is very important as long strands are needed to trap the expanding gases, and this is what makes the paste rise.

Fat can be added to flour by:
- rubbing in by hand: short pastry.
- rubbing in by machine: short pastry.
- creaming method by machine or by hand: sweet pastry.
- lamination: puff pastry.
- boiling: choux pastry.

Other techniques

Folding: an example is folding puff pastry to create its layers.

Kneading: using your hands to work dough or puff pastry in the first stage of making.

Blending: mixing all the ingredients carefully by weight.

Relaxing: keeping pastry covered with a damp cloth, cling film or plastic to prevent a skin forming on the surface. Relaxing allows the pastry to lose some of its resistance to rolling.

Cutting:
- Always cut with a sharp, clean, damp knife.
- When using cutters, always flour them before use by dipping in flour. This will give a sharp, neat cut.
- When using a lattice cutter, use only on firm pastry; if the pastry is too soft, you will have difficulty lifting the lattice.

Rolling:

- Roll the pastry on a lightly floured surface; turn the pastry to prevent it sticking. Keep the rolling pin lightly floured and free from the pastry.
- Always roll with care, treating the pastry lightly – never apply too much pressure.
- Always apply even pressure when using a rolling pin.

Shaping: this refers to producing flans, tartlets, barquettes and other such goods with pastry. Shaping also refers to crimping with the back of a small knife using the thumb technique.

Docking: this is piercing raw pastry with small holes to prevent it from rising during baking, as when cooking tartlets blind.

Key terms

Shortening agent: a fat used to help prevent the development of gluten strands when making pastry. This helps to make the texture of the product more crumbly.

Rubbing in: a technique where flour is rubbed into a fat to make products such as short pastry and crumbles. Using the fingertips, flour and butter are rubbed gently together until the mixture resembles fine breadcrumbs.

Creaming: the initial mixing of sugar and cream together using a wooden spoon or electric mixer until a smooth mixture is formed. This is often used in the production of sweet/sugar pastry.

Lamination: the term for the process of alternating layers of dough and butter when making puff pastry, croissants or Danish pastries.

Boiling: this method is unique to the production of choux paste, where the butter is initially melted in boiling water before being made into a paste with the addition of flour and then eggs.

Turning: the term used to describe the process of producing the layers in laminated pastry. Each time the paste is rolled and folded, it is referred to as a turn.

Glazing

A glaze is something that gives a product a smooth, shiny surface. Examples of glazes used for pastry dishes are as follows:

- A hot clear gel produced from a pectin source obtainable commercially for finishing flans and tartlets; always use while still hot. A cold gel is exactly the same except that it is used cold. The gel keeps a sheen on the goods and keeps out all oxygen, which might otherwise cause discoloration.
- Apricot glaze, produced from apricot jam, acts in the same way as gels.
- Eggwash, applied prior to baking, produces a rich glaze during the cooking process.
- Icing sugar dusted on the surface of the product caramelises in the oven or under the grill.
- Fondant gives a rich sugar glaze, which may be flavoured and/or coloured.
- Water icing gives a transparent glaze, which may also be flavoured and/or coloured.

Finishing and presentation

It is essential that all products are finished according to the recipe requirements. Finishing and presentation is often a key stage in the process, as failure at this point can affect sales. The way goods are presented is an important part of the sales technique. Each product of the same type must be of the same shape, size, colour and finish. The decoration should be attractive, delicate and in keeping with the product range. All piping should be neat, clean and tidy.

Fillings, glazes, cream and icings

Many different fillings are used in pastry products, including include crème pâtissière, frangipane and fresh fruit. Cream and butter cream, preserves and jam can also be used.

Finishing and decorating techniques

Some methods of finishing and presentation are as follows.

- **Dusting** – sprinkling icing sugar on a product using a fine sugar dredger or sieve.
- **Piping** – using fresh cream, chocolate or fondant.
- **Filling** – with fruit, cream, pastry cream, etc. Avoid overfilling as this can give the product a clumsy appearance.
- **Icing**: Some paste products, such as a Bakewell tart, are glazed using an icing, such as water icing in this example.

Storage

- Store all goods according to the Food Safety and Hygiene Regulations 2013/Food Safety Temperature Control Regulation 1995 and General Food Regulations (2004).
- Always make sure that storage containers are kept clean and returned ready for re-use. On their return they should be hygienically washed and stored.
- Freshly made, raw paste should be wrapped tightly in secure film or placed in an air-tight, sealed bag. It should then be clearly labelled and dated before storing in a refrigerator or freezer.
- Finished paste products can be refrigerated to maintain food safety. However, pastry does not tend to maintain its quality in refrigerated conditions. The moist atmosphere leads to pastes softening, losing their crisp and short properties. Any additional ingredients also have to be considered. Creams can lose their viscosity and can retract from the pastry lining and prepared fruits can weep, losing their structure.
- Some cooked pastry products are suitable for freezing. For example, unfilled, blind-baked pastry cases freeze well for use at a later stage. Other completed products need to be analysed as to their suitability for freezing, based on the additional ingredients used and their suitability.

Allergies

Although it is essential to clearly list all potential allergens when making paste products, the allergens that are most like to be used in their production include:

- gluten – flours and any products made from wheat, rye, barley and oats.
- nuts – such as ground hazelnuts, and almonds. These can be added to flavour pastes such as sablé.
- eggs – used in the production of sweet and choux paste.

Beyond the basic preparation of pastes, attention is also required with regard to the additional ingredients that are used to complete pastry products. Tarts are often filled with creams, produced with milk and/or cream (lactose). Other fillings may include nuts, such as frangipane, so it is vitally important to assess any of the other potential allergens that are incorporated into pastry products as well as the paste itself.

Test yourself

1. What is the ratio of fat to flour for:
   a) short pastry
   b) puff pastry
   c) sugar pastry?
2. How is the fat added to the flour in the production of choux pastry?
3. What type of fat is required for the production of suet paste?
4. What is meant by the term 'lamination'?
5. What is the filling for a classical gâteau Pithiviers?
6. Provide **five** examples of products that can be produced using puff pastry.
7. Name **one** pastry product, eaten as a dessert, which would be unsuitable for a vegetarian customer.
8. Describe **three** fillings that can be used in the production of sweet tarts.
9. Other than éclairs and profiteroles, name **three** products that are made using choux paste.
10. What quality points indicate a well-produced lemon tart?
11. Describe the finishing stages when producing mille-feuilles.
12. Describe **three** considerations when refrigerating a freshly baked strawberry tart, filled with crème patissière.

1 Sugar (or sweet) paste (*pâte à sucre*)

Sugar pastry is used for products such as flans, fruit tarts and tartlets.

	400 g	1 kg
Sugar	50 g	125 g
Butter or block/cake margarine	125 g	300 g
Eggs	1	2–3
Flour (soft)	200 g	500 g
Salt	Pinch	Large pinch

Method 1 – sweet lining paste (rubbing in).

1 Sieve the flour and salt. Lightly rub in the margarine or butter to achieve a sandy texture.

2 Mix the sugar and egg until dissolved.

3 Make a well in the centre of the flour. Add the sugar and beaten egg.

4 Gradually incorporate the flour and margarine or butter and lightly mix to a smooth paste. Allow to rest before using.

Method 2 – traditional French sugar paste (creaming).

1 Taking care not to over-soften, cream the butter and sugar.

2 Add the beaten egg gradually and mix for a few seconds.

3 Gradually incorporate the sieved flour and salt. Mix lightly until smooth.

4 Allow to rest in a cool place before using.

1 Measure out the sugar and cut the butter into small chunks.

2 Cream the butter and sugar together.

3 Add the beaten egg in stages, thoroughly mixing each time.

4 Incorporate the flour and salt.

5 Press into a tray and leave to chill.

6 The paste will need to be rolled out before use in any recipe.

From left to right: short paste (recipe 2), rough puff paste (recipe 3) and sugar paste (recipe 1)

2 Short paste (*pâte à foncer*)

Short pastry is used in fruit pies, Cornish pasties, etc.

	400 g	850 g
Flour (soft)	250 g	500 g
Salt	Pinch	Large pinch
Butter or block/cake margarine	125 g	250 g
Water	40–50 ml	80–100 ml

1 Sieve the flour and salt.
2 Rub in the fat to achieve a sandy texture.
3 Make a well in the centre.
4 Add sufficient water to make a fairly firm paste.
5 Handle as little and as lightly as possible. Refrigerate until firm before rolling.

Variations

For wholemeal short pastry, use wholemeal flour in place of half to three-quarters of the white flour.

Short pastry for sweet dishes such as baked jam roll may be made with self-raising flour.

Lard can be used in place of some or all of the fat (the butter or cake margarine). Lard has excellent shortening properties and would lend itself, in terms of flavour, to savoury products, particularly meat-based ones. However, many people view lard as an unhealthy product as it is very high in saturated fat. It is also unsuitable for anyone following a vegan or vegetarian diet as it is an animal product.

Professional tip

The amount of water used varies according to:
● the type of flour (a very fine soft flour is more absorbent)
● the degree of heat (for example, prolonged contact with hot hands, or warm weather conditions).

Different fats have different shortening properties. For example, paste made with a high ratio of butter to other fat will be harder to handle.

Faults

Possible reasons for faults in short pastry are detailed below.

Hard:
- too much water
- too little fat
- fat rubbed in insufficiently
- too much handling and rolling
- over-baking.

Soft–crumbly:
- too little water
- too much fat.

Blistered:
- too little water
- water added unevenly
- fat not rubbed in evenly.

Soggy:
- too much water
- too cool an oven
- baked for insufficient time.

Shrunken:
- too much handling and rolling
- pastry stretched while handling.

▲ From left to right: correct, blistered and shrunken short paste

3 Rough puff paste

	475 g	1.2 kg
Flour (strong)	200 g	500 g
Salt	1 large pinch	2 large pinches
Butter or block/cake margarine (lightly chilled)	150 g	375 g
Water, ice-cold	125 ml	300 ml
Lemon juice, ascorbic or tartaric acid	10 ml	25 ml

1 Sieve the flour and salt.
2 Cut the fat into small pieces and lightly mix them into the flour without rubbing in.
3 Make a well in the centre.
4 Add the liquid and mix to a dough. The dough should be fairly tight at this stage.
5 Turn on to a floured table and roll into an oblong strip, about 30 × 10 cm, keeping the sides square.
6 Give one double turn (as for puff pastry).
7 Allow to rest in a cool place, covered with cloth or plastic for 30 minutes.
8 Give three more double turns, resting between each. (Alternatively, give six single turns.) Allow to rest before using.

Professional tip

Each time you leave the paste to rest, gently make finger indentations, one for each turn you have made.

1 Make a well in the centre of the flour and butter and add the liquid

2 Mix to a fairly stiff dough

3 Roll out and fold the ends to the middle

4 Keep rolling, folding and turning

5 The finished paste, ready to rest and then use

4 Choux paste (*pâte à choux*)

Choux paste is used to make products such as éclairs, profiteroles and gâteau Paris-Brest.

	750 g	1.5 kg
Water	250 ml	500 ml
Sugar	Pinch	Large pinch
Salt	Pinch	Large pinch
Butter or block/cake margarine	100 g	200 g
Flour (strong)	150 g	300 g
Eggs	4–5	8–10

1 Bring the water, sugar, salt and fat to the boil in a saucepan. Remove from the heat.

2 Add the sieved flour and mix in with a wooden spoon.

3 Return to a moderate heat and stir continuously until the mixture leaves the sides of the pan. (This is known as a panada.)

4 Remove from the heat and allow to cool.

5 Gradually add the beaten eggs, beating well. Do not add all the eggs at once – check the consistency as you go. The mixture should just flow back when moved in one direction (it may not take all the egg).

Variation

50 per cent, 70 per cent or 100 per cent wholemeal flour may be used to make choux paste.

1 Cut the butter into cubes and then melt them in the water

2 Add the flour

3 When the panada is ready, it will start to come away from the sides

4 Add egg until the mixture is the right consistency – it should drop from a spoon under its own weight

5 Pipe the paste into the shape required – these rings could be used for Paris-Brest (Recipe 22)

6 A selection of shapes in raw choux paste

Faults

Greasy and heavy paste:
- the basic mixture was over-cooked.

Soft paste, not aerated:
- flour insufficiently cooked
- eggs insufficiently beaten in the mixture
- oven too cool
- under-baked.

Split or separated mixture:
- egg added too quickly.

▲ The choux buns on the left are light and well risen; those on the right are poorly aerated.

Video: Choux paste
http://bit.ly/1Ldujdh

5 Suet paste

Suet paste is used for steamed fruit puddings, steamed jam rolls, steamed meat puddings and dumplings.

1 Sieve the flour, baking powder and salt.

2 Mix in the suet. Make a well. Add the water.

3 Mix lightly to a fairly stiff paste.

Professional tip

Self-raising flour already contains baking powder so this element could be reduced in the recipe if using self-raising flour.

Vegetarian suet is also available to enable products to be meat-free.

	400 g	1 kg
Flour (soft) or self-raising flour	200 g	500 g
Baking powder	10 g	25 g
Salt	Pinch	Large pinch
Prepared beef or vegetarian suet	100 g	250 g
Water	125 ml	300 ml

Faults

Heavy and soggy paste:
● cooking temperature may have been too low.

Tough paste:
● handled too much or over-cooked.

6 Quiche Lorraine (cheese and ham savoury flan)

	4 portions	10 portions
Short paste	100 g	250 g
Ham, chopped	75 g	150 g
Cheese, grated	50 g	125 g
Egg	1	2
Milk	125 ml	300 ml
Cayenne	1–2 g	3 g
Sea-salt (e.g. Maldon)	2 g	5 g

Energy	Cals	Fat	Sat fat	Carb	Sugar	Protein	Fibre
2955 kJ	704 kcal	48.4 g	22.6 g	38.1 g	6.5 g	31.6 g	1.8 g

Variation

The filling can be varied by using lightly fried lardons of bacon (in place of the ham), chopped cooked onions and chopped parsley.

A variety of savoury flans can be made by using imagination and experimenting with different combinations (for example, stilton and onion; salmon and dill; sliced sausage and tomato).

1 Lightly grease an appropriately sized flan ring or barquette, or tartlet moulds if making individual portions. Line thinly with pastry.

2 Prick the bottom of the paste two or three times with a fork to dock.

3 Cook in a hot oven at 200 °C for 3–4 minutes or until the pastry is lightly set. Reduce the oven temperature to 160 °C.

4 Remove from the oven; press the pastry down if it has tended to rise.

5 Add the chopped ham and grated cheese.

6 Mix the egg, milk, salt and cayenne thoroughly. Strain over the ham and cheese.

7 Return to the oven at 160 °C and bake gently for approximately 20 minutes or until nicely browned and the egg custard mix has set.

7 Flan case

1 Allow 25 g flour per portion and prepare sugar pastry as per recipe 1.

2 Grease the flan ring and baking sheet.

3 Roll out the pastry 2 cm larger than the flan ring. The pastry may be rolled between greaseproof or silicone paper.

4 Place the flan ring on the baking sheet.

5 Carefully place the pastry on the flan ring, by rolling it loosely over the rolling pin, picking up and unrolling it over the flan ring.

6 Press the pastry into shape without stretching it, being careful to exclude any air.

7 Allow a ½ cm ridge of pastry on top of the flan ring.

8 Cut off the surplus paste by rolling the rolling pin firmly across the top of the flan ring.

9 Mould the edge with thumb and forefinger. Decorate (a) with pastry tweezers or (b) with thumbs and forefingers, squeezing the pastry neatly to form a corrugated pattern.

 Video: Lining a flan http://bit.ly/17grHMP

8 French apple flan (*flan aux pommes*)

	4 portions	10 portions
Sweet paste	100 g	250 g
Pastry cream (crème pâtissière) (see page 469)	250 ml	625 ml
Cooking apples	400 g	1 kg
Sugar	50 g	125 g
Apricot glaze	2 tbsp	6 tbsp

Energy	Cals	Fat	Sat fat	Carb	Sugar	Protein	Fibre
1428 kJ	340 kcal	13.8 g	5.8 g	53.8 g	36 g	3.5 g	2.9 g

1 Line a flan ring with sugar paste. Pierce the bottom several times with a fork.

2 Pipe a layer of pastry cream into the bottom of the flan.

3 Peel, quarter and wash the selected apple.

4 Cut into neat thin slices and lay carefully on the pastry cream, overlapping each slice. Ensure that each slice points to the centre of the flan then no

difficulty should be encountered in joining up the pattern neatly.

5 Sprinkle a little sugar on the apple slices and bake the flan at 200–220 °C for 30–40 minutes.

6 When the flan is almost cooked, remove the flan ring carefully, return to the oven to complete the cooking. Mask with hot apricot glaze or flan jelly.

1 Pipe the filling neatly into the flan case

2 Slice the apple very thinly for decoration

3 Arrange the apple slices on top of the flan

ASSESSMENT

9 Pear and almond tart

	8 portions
Sweet paste	200 g
Apricot jam	25 g
Almond cream	350 g
Poached pears	4
Apricot glaze	
Flaked almonds	
Icing sugar	

Energy	Cals	Fat	Sat fat	Carb	Sugar	Protein	Fibre	Sodium
1500 kJ	359 kcal	23 g	10.3 g	34 g	24 g	5.7 g	3.6 g	0.28 g

1 Line a buttered 20 cm flan ring with sweet paste. Trim and dock.

2 Using the back of a spoon, spread a little apricot jam over the base.

3 Pipe in almond cream until the flan case is two-thirds full.

4 Dry the poached pears. Cut them in half and remove the cores and string.

5 Score across the pears and arrange on top of the flan.

6 Bake in the oven at 200 °C for 25–30 minutes.

7 Allow to cool, then brush with apricot glaze.

8 Sprinkle flaked almonds around the edge and dust with icing sugar.

10 Treacle tart

	4 portions	10 portions
Short paste	125 g	300 g
Treacle	100 g	250 g
Water	1 tbsp	2 ½ tbsp
Lemon juice	3–4 drops	8–10 drops
Fresh white bread or cake crumbs	15 g	50 g

Energy	Cals	Fat	Sat fat	Carb	Sugar	Protein	Fibre
1100 kJ	262 kcal	10.7 g	5.8 g	41.1 g	20.3 g	2.8 g	0.8 g

1 Lightly grease an appropriately sized flan ring, or barquette or tartlet moulds if making individual portions.

2 Line with pastry.

3 Warm the treacle, water and lemon juice; add the crumbs.

4 Place into the pastry ring and bake at 170 °C for about 20 minutes.

Variation

This tart can also be made in a shallow flan ring. Any pastry debris can be rolled and cut into ½ cm strips and used to decorate the top of the tart before baking.

Try sprinkling with vanilla salt as a garnish.

11 Egg custard tart

	8 portions
Sweet paste	250 g
Egg yolks	9
Caster sugar	75 g
Whipping cream, gently warmed and infused with 2 sticks of cinnamon	500 ml
Nutmeg, freshly grated	

Energy	Cals	Fat	Sat fat	Carb	Sugar	Protein	Fibre	Sodium
1998 kJ	482 kcal	39 g	22 g	27 g	15.8 g	6.4 g	0.6 g	0.17 g

1 Roll out the pastry on a lightly floured surface, to 2 mm thickness. Use it to line a 20 cm flan ring, placed on a baking sheet.

2 Line the pastry with food-safe cling film or greaseproof paper and fill with baking beans. Bake blind in a preheated oven at 190 °C for about 10 minutes or until the pastry is turning golden brown. Remove the paper and beans, and allow to cool. Turn the oven down to 130 °C.

3 To make the custard filling, whisk together the egg yolks and sugar. Add the cream and mix well.

4 Pass the mixture through a fine sieve into a saucepan. Heat to 37 °C.

5 Fill the pastry case with the custard to ½ cm below the top. Place it carefully into the middle of the oven and bake for 30–40 minutes or until the custard appears to be set but not too firm.

6 Remove from the oven and dust with icing sugar and a little grated nutmeg. Allow to cool to room temperature.

12 Bakewell tart

	8 portions
Sugar paste	200 g
Raspberry jam	50 g
Eggwash	1 egg
Apricot glaze	50 g
Icing sugar	35 g
Frangipane (almond cream)	250 g

Energy	Cals	Fat	Sat fat	Carb	Sugar	Protein	Fibre	Sodium
1308 kJ	313 kcal	18.5 g	8.6 g	34 g	24 g	5 g	1308 g	313 g

1 Line a 20 cm flan ring using three-quarters of the paste, 2 mm thick.

2 Pierce the bottom with a fork.

3 Spread with jam and the frangipane.

4 Roll the remaining paste, cut into neat 0.5 cm strips and arrange neatly criss-crossed (lattice) on the frangipane; trim off surplus paste. Brush with eggwash.

5 Bake in a moderately hot oven at 200–210 °C for 30–40 minutes. Brush with hot apricot glaze.

6 When cooled, brush over with very thin water icing. Sprinkle with flaked almonds

13 Lemon tart (*tarte au citron*)

	8 portions
Sweet paste	200 g
Lemons	Juice of 3, zest from 4
Eggs	8
Caster sugar	300 g
Double cream	250 ml

Energy	Cals	Fat	Sat fat	Carb	Sugar	Protein	Fibre	Sodium
1907 kJ	456 kcal	25 g	13.4 g	53 g	44 g	8.5 g	0.5 g	0.2 g

1 Prepare 200 g of sweet paste, adding the zest of one lemon to the sugar.

2 Line a 20 cm flan ring with the paste.

3 Bake blind at 190 °C for approximately 15 minutes.

4 Prepare the filling: mix the eggs and sugar together until smooth, add the cream, lemon juice and zest. Whisk well.

5 Seal the pastry, so that the filling will not leak out. Pour the filling into the flan case and bake for 30–40 minutes at 150 °C until just set. (Take care when almost cooked as overcooking will cause the filling to rise and possibly crack.)

6 Remove from the oven and allow to cool.

7 Dust with icing sugar and glaze under the grill or with a blowtorch. Portion and serve.

Variation

Limes may be used in place of lemons. If so, use the zest and juice of 5 limes or use a mixture of lemons and limes.

Professional tip

If possible, make the filling one day in advance. The flavour will develop as the mixture matures.

Note

The mixture will fill one 16 × 4 cm or two 16 × 2 cm flan rings. If using two flan rings, double the amount of pastry and reduce the baking time when the filling is added.

14 Baked chocolate tart

	8 portions
Sweet paste	200 g
Filling	
Eggs	3
Egg yolks	3
Caster sugar	60 g
Butter	200 g
Chocolate pistoles (55% cocoa, unsweetened)	300 g

Energy	Cals	Fat	Sat fat	Carb	Sugar	Protein	Fibre	Sodium
2414 kJ	580 kcal	42.4 g	24.8 g	44.9	35 g	7.4 g	1.8 g	0.240 g

1 Roll out the sweet paste and line a 20 cm flan ring. Bake the flan case blind.

2 For the filling, whisk the eggs, yolks and sugar together to make a sabayon.

3 Bring the butter to the boil, remove and mix in the chocolate pistoles until they are all melted.

4 Once the sabayon is light and fluffy, fold in the chocolate and butter mixture, mixing very carefully so as not to beat out the air.

5 Pour into the cooked flan case and place in the oven at 150 °C until the edge crusts (approximately 5 minutes). Chill to set.

6 Once set, remove from fridge and then serve at room temperature.

Note

Pistoles or pellets are one form in which chocolate is sold. They are very versatile and easy to use for melting purposes due to their uniform size.

Add chocolate pistols to the melted butter

Fold in the chocolate

Pour the mixture into the flan case

15 Lemon meringue pie

	2 × 20 cm flan rings (16 portions)
Sweet paste flan cases	2
Granulated sugar	450 g
Lemons, grated zest	2
Fresh lemon juice	240 ml
Eggs, large	8
Large egg yolks	2
Unsalted butter, cut into small pieces	350 g
Meringue:	
Egg whites	6
Caster sugar	600 g

Energy	Cals	Fat	Sat fat	Carb	Sugar	Protein	Fibre
12138 kJ	2895 kcal	147.7 g	84.8 g	379.4 g	305.0 g	36.4 g	4.2 g

1 Place the sugar into a bowl and grate the zest of lemon into it, rubbing together.
2 Strain the lemon juice into a non-reactive pan. Add the eggs, egg yolks, butter and zested sugar. Whisk to combine.
3 Place over a medium heat and whisk continuously for 3–5 minutes, until the mixture begins to thicken.
4 At the first sign of boiling, remove from the heat. Strain into a bowl and cool before filling the pastry cases.
5 Make the meringue (see page 472). Pipe it on top of the filled pie.
6 Colour in a hot oven at 220 °C.

16 Mince pies

	12 small pies
Sweet paste	200 g
Mincemeat (see below)	200 g
Eggwash	1 egg
Icing sugar	

Energy	Cals	Fat	Sat fat	Carb	Sugar	Protein	Fibre	Sodium
2009 kJ	479 kcal	23.4 g	0.0 g	66.6 g	32.0 g	4.6 g	2.8 g	0.3 g

1 Roll out the pastry 3 mm thick.
2 Cut half the pastry into fluted rounds 6 cm in diameter.
3 Place on a greased, dampened baking sheet.
4 Moisten the edges. Place a little mincemeat in the centre of each.
5 Cut the remainder of the pastry into fluted rounds, 8 cm in diameter.
6 Cover the mincemeat with pastry and seal the edges. Brush with eggwash.
7 Bake at 210 °C for approximately 20 minutes.
8 Sprinkle with icing sugar and serve warm.

Note

Accompany with a suitable sauce, such as custard, brandy sauce or brandy cream. Tartlette moulds may also be used.

Mincemeat:

Suet, chopped	100 g
Mixed peel, chopped	100 g
Currants	100 g
Sultanas	100 g
Raisins	100 g
Apples, chopped	100 g
Barbados sugar	100 g
Mixed spice	5 g
Lemon, grated zest and juice of	1
Orange, grated zest and juice of	1
Rum	60 ml
Brandy	60 ml

1 Mix the ingredients together.

2 Seal in jars and use as required.

Variation

Short or puff pastry may also be used. Various toppings can also be added, such as crumble mixture or flaked almonds and an apricot glaze.

17 Banana flan (*flan aux bananes*)

	4 portions	10 portions
Sweet paste	100 g	250 g
Pastry cream (see page 469) or thick custard	125 ml	250 ml
Bananas	2	5
Apricot glaze	2 tbsp	5 tbsp

1 Line a flan ring with sugar paste. Cook blind and allow to cool.

2 Make pastry cream (see page 469) or custard; pour while hot into the flan case.

3 Allow to set. Peel and slice the bananas neatly.

4 Arrange overlapping layers on the pastry cream. Coat with glaze.

Energy	Cals	Fat	Sat fat	Carb	Sugar	Protein	Fibre
1549 kJ	369 kcal	16.0 g	6.9 g	53.7 g	30.3 g	6.0 g	2.9 g

18 Fruit tart, tartlets and barquettes

	4 portions
Sweet paste	250g
Fruit (e.g. strawberries, raspberries, grapes, blueberries)	500g
Pastry cream	
Glaze	5 tbsp

Energy	Cals	Fat	Sat fat	Carb	Sugar	Protein	Fibre	Sodium
1907 kJ	454 kcal	18.7g	10.7g	68g	39g	6.8g	3.6g	0.32g

Fruit tart:

1 Line a flan ring with paste and cook blind at 190°C. Allow to cool.

2 Pick and wash the fruit, then drain well. Wash and slice/segment, etc. any larger fruit being used.

3 Pipe pastry cream into the flan case, filling it to the rim. Dress the fruit neatly over the top.

4 Coat with the glaze. Use a glaze suitable for the fruit chosen, for example, with a strawberry tart, use a red glaze.

Note

Certain fruits (such as strawberries and raspberries) are sometimes served in boat-shaped moulds (barquettes). The preparation is the same as for tartlets. Tartlets and barquettes should be glazed and served allowing one large or two small per portion.

Tartlets:

1 Roll out pastry 3 mm thick.

2 Cut out rounds with a fluted cutter and place them neatly in greased tartlet moulds. If soft fruit (such as strawberries or raspberries) is being used, the pastry should be cooked blind first.

3 After baking and filling (or filling and baking) with pastry cream, dress neatly with fruit and glaze the top.

Professional tip

Brush the inside of the pastry case with melted couverture before filling. This forms a barrier between the pastry and the moisture in the filling.

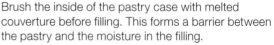

Faults

Although this strawberry tart may appear to be fine at first glance, the husks of the strawberries are visible. It would be better to present the strawberries with their tops pointing upwards or sliced and overlapping.

There is also quite a wide gap between the rows of strawberries, showing the crème pâtissière underneath. This should be avoided.

The second photo shows the importance of ensuring that fillings are prepared and/or cooked properly. In this case, the crème pâtissière has not been cooked sufficiently or prepared accurately as the filling is not structured sufficiently to support the fruit once the tart has been cut.

19 Fruit slice (*bande aux fruits*)

1 Roll out the pastry 2 mm thick in a strip 12 cm wide.

2 Place on a greased, dampened baking sheet.

3 Moisten two edges with eggwash; lay two 1.5 cm-wide strips along each edge.

4 Seal firmly and mark with the back of a knife. Prick the bottom of the slice.

5 Depending on the fruit used, either put the fruit (such as apple) on the slice and cook together, or cook the slice blind and afterwards place the pastry cream and fruit (such as tinned peaches) on the pastry. Glaze and serve as for flans.

Note

Fruit slices may be prepared from any fruit suitable for flans/tarts.

Energy	Cals	Fat	Sat fat	Carb	Sugar	Protein	Fibre	Sodium
847 kJ	202 kcal	10.3 g	3.5 g	26 g	14.3 g	3.2 g	1.6 g	200 mg

	8–10 portions
Puff pastry	250 g
Fruit (see note)	400 g
Pastry cream	250 ml (approximately)
Apricot glaze	2 tbsp

Variation

Alternative methods are to use:
- short or sweet pastry for the base and puff pastry for the two side strips
- sweet pastry in a slice mould.

20 Chocolate éclairs (*éclairs au chocolat*)

	12 portions
Choux paste	200 ml
Whipped cream/Chantilly cream	250 ml
Fondant	100 g
Chocolate couverture	25 g

Variations

For coffee éclairs (éclairs au café) add a few drops of coffee extract to the fondant instead of chocolate; coffee éclairs may also be filled with pastry cream (see page 469) flavoured with coffee.

Energy	Cals	Fat	Sat fat	Carb	Sugar	Protein	Fibre
516 kJ	123 kcal	9.5 g	5.7 g	8.8 g	7.3 g	1.1 g	0.1 g

1 Place the choux paste into a piping bag with a 1 cm plain tube.

2 Pipe into 8 cm lengths onto a lightly greased, dampened baking sheet.

3 Bake at 200–220 °C for about 30 minutes.

4 Allow to cool. Slit down one side, with a sharp knife.

5 Fill with Chantilly cream (or whipped cream) using a piping bag and small tube. The continental fashion is to fill with pastry cream.

6 Warm the fondant, add the finely cut chocolate, allow to melt slowly, adjusting the consistency with a little sugar and water syrup if necessary. Do not overheat or the fondant will lose its shine.

7 Glaze the éclairs by dipping them in the fondant; remove the surplus with the finger. Allow to set.

Note

Traditionally, chocolate éclairs were filled with chocolate pastry cream.

1 Pierce the éclair

2 Pipe in the filling

3 Dip the éclair in fondant; wipe the edges to give a neat finish

21 Profiteroles and chocolate sauce (*profiteroles au chocolat*)

	10 portions
Choux paste	200 ml
Chocolate sauce (see page 476)	250 ml
Chantilly cream	250 ml
Icing sugar, to serve	

Energy	Cals	Fat	Sat fat	Carb	Sugar	Protein	Fibre
919 kJ	219 kcal	16.2 g	9.7 g	16.4 g	12.8 g	2.9 g	0.2 g

Variations

Coffee sauce may be served and the profiteroles filled with non-dairy cream. Profiteroles may also be filled with chocolate-, coffee- or rum-flavoured pastry cream.

1 Spoon the choux paste into a piping bag with a plain nozzle (approx. 1.5 cm diameter).

2 Pipe walnut-sized balls of paste onto the greased baking sheet, spaced well apart. Level the peaked tops with the tip of a wet finger.

3 Bake for 18–20 minutes at 200 °C, until well risen and golden brown. Remove from the oven, transfer to a wire rack and allow to cool completely.

4 Make a hole in each and fill with Chantilly cream.

5 Dredge with icing sugar and serve with a sauceboat of cold chocolate sauce or coat the profiteroles with the sauce.

22 Gâteau Paris-Brest

	8 portions
Choux paste	200 ml
Crème diplomat or pastry cream (see page 469)	400 ml
For the praline	
Flaked almonds, hazelnuts and pecans (any combination)	200 g
Granulated sugar	250 g

Energy	Cals	Fat	Sat fat	Carb	Sugar	Protein	Fibre
2089 kJ	501 kcal	32.1 g	10.8 g	47.5 g	39.8 g	8.2 g	0.4 g

Praline:

1 Place the nuts on a baking sheet and toast until evenly coloured. Sprinkle with flaked almonds before baking.

2 Place the sugar in a large, heavy, stainless steel saucepan. Set the pan over a low heat and allow the sugar to caramelise. Do not over-stir, but do not allow the sugar to burn.

3 When the sugar is lightly caramelised and reaches a temperature of 170 °C, remove from the heat and stir in the nuts.

4 Immediately deposit the mixture on a silpat mat. Place another mat over the top and roll as thin as possible.

5 Allow to cool completely. Break up and store in an airtight container.

Paris-Brest:

1 Pipe choux paste (recipe 4) into rings and bake at 200 °C for 30 minutes.

2 Slice each ring in half. Fill with a mixture of crème diplomat or pastry cream and praline.

23 Eccles cakes

	12 cakes
Puff pastry or rough puff pastry	300 g
Egg white, to brush	
Caster sugar, to coat	
Filling	
Butter	50 g
Raisins	50 g
Demerara sugar	50
Currants	200
Mixed spice (optional)	Pinch

Energy	Cals	Fat	Sat fat	Carb	Sugar	Protein	Fibre
691 kJ	164 kcal	8.6 g	3.7 g	22.1 g	17.3 g	1.1 g	1.4 g

1 Roll out the pastry 2 mm thick.

2 Cut into rounds 10–12 cm diameter. Damp the edges.

3 Mix together all the ingredients for the filling and place 1 tbsp of the mixture in the centre of each round.

4 Fold the edges over to the centre and completely seal in the mixture.

5 Brush the top with egg white and dip into caster sugar.

6 Place on a greased baking sheet.

7 Cut two or three incisions with a knife so as to show the filling.

8 Bake at 220 °C for 15–20 minutes.

24 Pear jalousie

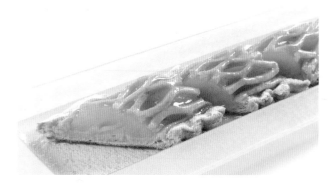

Energy	Cals	Fat	Sat fat	Carb	Sugar	Protein	Fibre
1178kJ	282kcal	17.8g	5.1g	27.2g	17.5g	3.8g	0.8g

	8–10 portions
Puff pastry	200g
Frangipane	200g
Pears, poached or tinned (cored and cut in half lengthways)	5

1 Roll out two-thirds of the pastry 3mm thick into a strip 25 × 10cm and place on a greased, dampened baking sheet.

2 Pierce with a docker. Moisten the edges.

3 Pipe on the frangipane, leaving 2cm free all the way round. Place the pears on top.

4 Roll out the remaining one-third of the pastry to the same size. Chill before cutting.

5 Cut the dough with a trellis cutter to make a lattice.

6 Carefully open out this strip and neatly place onto the first strip.

7 Trim off any excess. Neaten and decorate the edge. Brush with eggwash.

8 Bake at 220°C for 25–30 minutes.

9 Glaze with apricot glaze. Dust the edges with icing sugar and return to a very hot oven to glaze.

25 Cheese straws (*paillettes au fromage*)

	8–10 portions	16–20 portions
Puff paste or rough puff paste	100g	250g
Cheese, grated	50g	125g
Cayenne pepper		

Energy	Cals	Fat	Sat fat	Carb	Sugar	Protein	Fibre
2562kJ	610kcal	48.1g	24.1g	28.7g	0.6g	17.4g	1.4g

1 Roll out the pastry to 60 × 15cm, 3mm thick.

2 Sprinkle with the cheese and cayenne pepper.

3 Roll out lightly to embed the cheese.

4 Cut the paste into thin strips by length.

5 Twist each strip to form rolls in the strip.

6 Place on a silicone mat.

7 Bake in a hot oven at 230–250°C for 10 minutes or until a golden brown. Cut into lengths as required.

26 Mille-feuilles (puff pastry slices)

	10 portions
Puff pastry trimmings	600 g
Pastry cream	400 ml
Apricot glaze	
Fondant	350 g
Chocolate	100 g

Energy	Cals	Fat	Sat fat	Carb	Sugar	Protein	Fibre
1158 kJ	369 kcal	10.9 g	1.3 g	67.7 g	52.3 g	4.9 g	0.1 g

1 Roll out the pastry 2 mm thick into an even-sided square.

2 Roll up carefully on a rolling pin and unroll onto a greased, dampened baking sheet.

3 Dock well.

4 Bake in a hot oven at 220 °C for 15–20 minutes; turn over after 10 minutes. Allow to cool.

5 Using a large knife, cut into three even-sized rectangles.

6 Keeping the best strip for the top, pipe the pastry cream on one strip.

7 Place the second strip on top and pipe with pastry cream.

8 Place the last strip on top, flat side up. Press gently. Brush with boiling apricot glaze to form a key.

Decorate by feather icing:

1 Warm the fondant to 37 °C (warm to the touch) and correct the consistency with sugar syrup if necessary.

2 Pour the fondant over the mille-feuilles in an even coat.

3 Immediately pipe the melted chocolate over the fondant in strips, ½ cm apart.

4 With the back of a small knife, wiping after each stroke, mark down the slice at 2 cm intervals.

5 Quickly turn the slice around and repeat in the same direction with strokes in between the previous ones.

6 Allow to set and trim the edges neatly.

7 Cut into even portions with a sharp, thin-bladed knife; dip into hot water and wipe clean after each cut.

8 For a traditional finish, crush the pastry trimmings and use them to coat the sides.

Variation

Whipped fresh cream may be used as an alternative to pastry cream.

The pastry cream or whipped cream may also be flavoured with a liqueur if so desired, such as curaçao, Grand Marnier or Cointreau.

1 Pipe cream between layers of pastry

2 Ice the top with fondant

3 Decorate with chocolate

27 Gâteau Pithiviers

	2 × 22 cm gâteaux
Puff pastry	1 kg
Pastry cream	60 g
Frangipane	600 g
Eggwash (yolks only)	
Granulated sugar	

Energy	Cals	Fat	Sat fat	Carb	Sugar	Protein	Fibre	Sodium
1452.8kJ	349.2kcal	25.8g	9.4g	25.6g	10.4g	5.3g	1.7g	0.4g

1 Divide the paste into four equal pieces. Roll out each piece in a circle with a 22 cm diameter, 4 mm thick.

2 Rest in the fridge between sheets of cling film, preferably overnight.

3 Lightly butter two baking trays and splash with water. Lay one circle of paste onto each tray and dock them.

4 Mark a 16 cm diameter circle in the centre of each.

5 Beat the pastry cream, if desired, and mix it with the frangipane.

6 Using a plain nozzle, pipe the cream over the inner circles, making them slightly domed.

7 Eggwash the outer edges of the paste. Lay one of the remaining pieces over the top of each one, smooth over and press down hard.

8 Mark the edges with a round cutter. Cut out a scallop pattern with a knife or use a cut piping nozzle as shown in the photo sequence.

9 Eggwash twice. Mark the top of both with a spiral pattern.

10 Bake at 220 °C for 10 minutes. Remove from the oven and sprinkle with granulated sugar. Turn the oven down to 190 °C and bake for a further 20 to 25 minutes.

11 Glaze under a salamander.

1 Adding the filling to the rolled base　**2** Trimming the edge　**3** Marking the top

28 Palmiers

	20–30 (depending on thickness and size)
Puff pastry (see page 519)	200 g
Caster sugar	50 g
Eggwash	50 ml

Note

Palmiers are usually made from leftover or off-cuts of puff pastry. As a more biscuit-like property is sought, previously rolled pastry can be utilised because the rise required is not as much as in products such as bouchées and vol-au-vents.

1　Roll out puff pastry (see page 519) 3 mm thick, into a square.

2　Sprinkle liberally with caster sugar on both sides and roll into the pastry.

3　Fold into three from each end so as to meet in the middle; brush with eggwash and fold in two.

4　Cut into strips approximately 2 cm thick; dip one side in caster sugar.

5　Place on a greased baking sheet, sugared side down, leaving a space of at least 2 cm between each.

6　Bake in a very hot oven for about 10 minutes.

7　Turn with a palette knife, cook on the other side until brown and the sugar is caramelised.

Variation

Puff pastry trimmings are suitable for this recipe. Palmiers may be made in a wide variety of sizes. Two joined together with a little whipped cream may be served as a pastry or small ones for petits fours. They may be sandwiched together with soft fruit, whipped cream and/or ice cream and served as a sweet.

29 Baklava (filo pastry with nuts and sugar)

	4 portions	10 portions
Filo pastry, sheets of	12 (200 g)	30 (500 g)
Clarified butter or ghee	200 g	500 g
Hazelnuts, flaked	100 g	250 g
Almonds, nibbed	100 g	250 g
Caster sugar	100 g	250 g
Cinnamon	10 g	25 g
Grated nutmeg		
Syrup		
Unrefined sugar or caster sugar	200 g	500 g
Lemons, grated zest and juice of	2	5
Water	60 ml	150 ml
Orange, grated zest and juice of	1	2
Cinnamon stick	1	2
Rose water	2–3 drops	4–6 drops

Energy	Cals	Fat	Sat fat	Carb	Sugar	Protein	Fibre	*
5488 kJ	1314 kcal	83.5 g	35.8 g	132.6 g	85.2 g	16.6 g	6.1 g	

* Using recipe of filo pastry, and ghee

1 Prepare a shallow tray slightly smaller than the sheets of filo pastry by brushing with melted clarified butter or ghee.

2 Place the sheets of filo pastry on the tray, brushing each with the fat.

3 Prepare the filling by mixing the nuts, sugar and spices together; place into the prepared tray, layered alternately with the filo pastry. Brush each layer with the clarified fat so that there are at least 2–3 layers of filling separated by filo pastry.

4 Cover completely with filo pastry and brush with the clarified fat.

5 Mark the pastry into diamonds, sprinkle with water and bake in a moderately hot oven at 190 °C for approximately 40 minutes.

6 Meanwhile make the syrup: place all the ingredients, except the rose water, in a saucepan and bring to the boil. Simmer for 5 minutes, pass through a fine strainer and finish with the drops of rose water.

7 When the baklavas are baked, cut into diamonds, place on a suitable serving dish and mask with the syrup.

Healthy eating tips
● Use oil to brush the sheets of filo pastry.
● Less sugar can be used in the filling as it should be sweet enough with the syrup used for masking.

30 Sweet samosas

See page 296 for the basic samosa recipe.

Filling 1: pears and ginger:

	8 portions
Du Comice or conference pears	4
Lemon syrup	250 ml
Stem ginger, cut into brunoise	50 g
Mascarpone cheese	250 g

1 Poach the pears in a 75 per cent lemon syrup until they are just tender. Drain.

2 Place a small quenelle of mascarpone into each samosa, and the fruit on top.

Filling 2: apricot and almond:

	8 portions
Frangipane (see page 473)	250 g
Dried apricots, diced	100 g

1 Pipe a little frangipane into each samosa.

2 Top with dried apricots.

This chapter will help you to:

1 prepare, cook and finish biscuit, cake and sponge products, including:
   - working safely and hygienically, using the correct tools and equipment
   - preparing and cooking mixtures for baking
   - finishing, presenting and evaluating products.

2 know how to:
   - identify different products, their uses and preparation and cooking methods
   - understand the quality points of ingredients and how to adjust the quantity
   - identify fillings, glazes, creams and icings, and finishing and decorating techniques
   - store finished products safely
   - identify ingredients that may cause allergic reactions.

The key ingredients for biscuits, cakes and sponges, such as flour, eggs, sugar and raising agents are described in Chapter 12. Make sure you read and understand this section.

Recipes in this chapter

Biscuits, cakes and sponges come in a variety of forms. They are produced in different ways to achieve a range of qualities and characteristics.

Biscuits

Some biscuits are short, in that they are crisp and crumbly, such as a shortbread, whereas other biscuits vary in texture from sponge-like to open-textured cookies. Depending on the type of biscuit being produced, the method of production differs to produce a variety of desired textures such as the dense-sponge/biscuit cross-texture of chocolate brownies or the biscuit discs used in the production of dobos torte. This is described below in further detail, with examples of biscuits suited to each method provided.

Preparation methods

Biscuits and cookies may be produced by the following methods.

Rubbing in

This is probably the best-known method and is used to produce some of the most famous types of biscuits, such as shortbread. The method is exactly the same as that for producing short pastry.

- Rub the fat into the flour, by hand or by machine, adding the liquid and the sugar and mixing in the flour to produce a smooth biscuit paste.
- Do not overwork the paste otherwise it will not combine and as a consequence you will not be able to roll it out.

Foaming

This is where a foam is produced from egg whites, egg yolks or both. Sponge fingers are an example of a two-foam mixture. Meringue is an example of a single-foam mixture using egg whites. Great care must be taken not to over-mix the product.

Sugar batter method

Fat and sugar are mixed together to produce a light and fluffy cream. Beaten egg is added gradually. The dry ingredients are then carefully folded in. Cats' tongues and sablé biscuits use this method.

Flour batter method

Half the sieved flour is creamed with the fat. The eggs and sugar are beaten together before they are added to the fat and flour mixture. Finally, the remainder of the flour is folded in, together with any other dry ingredients. Cookies use the flour batter method.

Blending method

In several biscuit recipes, the method requires the chef only to blend all the ingredients together to produce a smooth paste. Almond biscuits (using basic almond commercial mixture) use the blending method.

Cakes

There are various methods used to make cakes as described below. However, the sugar batter/creaming method is the most popular and practical method of making a cake. Cakes are produced in many different shapes and sizes. They vary from single portion-sized cakes, as in cupcakes, to large, multi-portioned products such as wedding cakes, intended to serve hundreds of guests. The production of cakes can vary slightly to incorporate flavourings and additional ingredients such as mashed bananas in banana cake, red wine for red wine cake, lemon syrup for lemon drizzle cake and dried fruits and spices when making a rich fruit cake. However, cakes share similar quality points in that they should be aerated, slightly domed with a consistent, moist crumb. They should also deliver good clean flavours and a consistent spread of any additional ingredients, such as fruit, throughout the mix.

Preparation methods

There are three basic methods of making cake mixtures, also known as cake batters. The working temperature of cake batter should be 21 °C.

Sugar batter method

1 Soften the butter

2 Cream the sugar and butter thoroughly to ensure a good, light crumb

3 Slowly add the egg, a little at a time

4 Once all the egg is incorporated, add the flour

5 Fold in the flour

Sugar batter/creaming method

For this method, the fat (cake margarine, butter or shortening) is blended in a machine with caster sugar. This is the basic or principal stage; usually the other ingredients are then added in the order shown in the steps on the previous page.

Flour batter method

For this method the eggs and sugar are whisked to a half sponge; this is the basic or principal stage, which aims to foam the two ingredients together until half the maximum volume is achieved. Other ingredients are added as shown in the diagram.

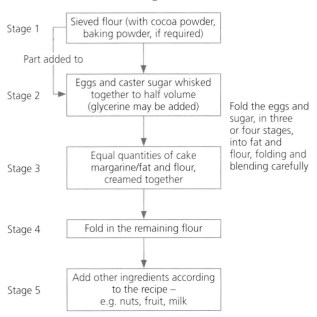

A type of product called a **humectant**, which helps the product to stay moist, may be added (e.g. glycerine or honey); if so, add this at stage 2.

Blending method

This is used for high-ratio cake mixtures. It uses high-ratio flour specially produced so that it will absorb more liquid. It also uses a high-ratio fat, made from oil to which a quantity of emulsifying agent has been added, enabling the fat to take up a greater quantity of liquid.

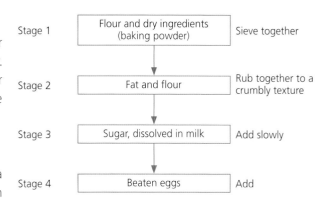

All-in-one method

The all-in-one method is a more user-friendly modern variation. This is perhaps one example of where a method is suited to making a specific type of cake, and other methods would not be suitable.

The all-in-one method is often used for cakes which contain oil or little or no fat – a tea loaf or banana cake, for example. For this reason, the all-in-one is the most relevant method after the sugar batter/creaming method.

High-ratio cakes contain more liquid and sugar, resulting in a fine stable crumb, extended shelf life, good eating and excellent freezing qualities.

The principal or basic stage is the mixing of the fat and flour to a crumbling texture. It is essential that each stage of the batter is blended into the next to produce a smooth batter, free from lumps.

When using mixing machines, it is important to remember to:
● blend on a slow speed
● beat on a medium speed, using a paddle attachment.

When blending, always clear the mix from the bottom of the bowl to ensure that any first- or second-stage batter does not remain in the bowl.

Baking powder

Baking powder may be made from one part sodium bicarbonate to two parts cream of tartar. In commercial baking the powdered cream of tartar may be replaced by another acid product, such as acidulated calcium phosphate.

When used under the right conditions, with the addition of liquid and heat, it produces carbon dioxide gas. As the acid has a delayed action, only a small amount of gas is given off when the liquid is added, and the majority is released when the mixture is heated. Therefore, when cakes are mixed they do not lose the property of the baking powder if they are not cooked right away.

Possible reasons for faults in cakes

Uneven texture:

- fat insufficiently rubbed in
- too little liquid
- too much liquid.

Close texture:

- too much fat
- hands too hot when rubbing in
- fat to flour ratio incorrect.

Dry:

- too little liquid
- oven too hot.

Poor shape:

- too much liquid
- oven too cool
- too much baking powder.

Fruit sunk:

- fruit wet
- too much liquid
- oven too cool.

Cracked:

- too little liquid
- too much baking powder.

> **Key terms**
>
> **Humectant**: a hygroscopic (helps to retain water) substance used to keep products moist. Honey is an example used in this way.
>
> **High-ratio cakes**: prepared with a relatively high proportion of sugar and eggs compared to flour.

Batters and whisked sponges

Sponges are generally a lot lighter and more aerated than cakes. Their production normally follows the whisking of warmed eggs and sugar until they reach what is referred to as the 'ribbon stage' or a 'sabayon' before folding in sieved, soft flour and melted butter, if this is required to enrich the sponge. In the production of a chocolate sponge, a percentage of the flour is replaced with cocoa powder, which is sieved together with the flour to ensure an even distribution. Sponges are very versatile. They are used as the primary component in the production of gâteaux, where a genoese sponge is often used, for example. Alternatively, when multiple layers are a requirement, sponges are sliced into discs or baked in thin sheets. The classic gâteau 'Opera' provides a good example, or when making a roulade or Swiss roll.

Batters and sponges allow us to make a large assortment of desserts and cakes. Basically, they are a mix of eggs, sugar, flour and the air incorporated when these are beaten. Certain other raw materials can be combined – for example, almonds, hazelnuts, walnuts, chocolate, butter, fruit, ginger, anise, coffee and vanilla.

Sponge mixtures are produced from a foam of eggs and sugar. The eggs may be whole eggs or separated. Examples of sponge products are gâteaux, sponge fingers and sponge cakes.

The egg white traps the air bubbles. When eggs and sugar are whisked together, they thicken until maximum volume is reached; then flour is carefully folded in by a method known as **cutting in**. This is the most difficult operation, as the flour must not be allowed to sink to the bottom of the bowl, otherwise it becomes lumpy and difficult to clear. However, the mixture must not be stirred as this will disturb the aeration and cause the air to escape, resulting in a much heavier sponge. If butter, margarine or oil is added, it is important that this is added at about 36 °C, otherwise overheating will cause the fat or oil to act on the flour and create lumps, which are difficult, often impossible, to get rid of.

Stabilisers are often added to sponges to prevent them from collapsing. The most common are ethylmethyl cellulose and glycerol monostearate; these are added to the eggs and sugar at the beginning of the mixing.

> **Key words**
>
> **Cutting in**: the method used to describe the way in which flour is carefully folded in to sponge batters.
>
> **Stabiliser**: a product added to sponges to help prevent them from collapsing.

What you need to know about sponge cakes

- Never add flour or ground dry ingredients to a batter until the end because they prevent the air absorption in the first beating stage.
- When making sponge cakes, always sift the dry ingredients (flour, cocoa powder, ground nuts, etc.) to avoid clumping.
- Mix in the flour as quickly and delicately as possible, because a rough addition of dry ingredients acts like a weight on the primary batter and can remove part of the air already absorbed.
- Flours used in sponge cakes are low in gluten content. In certain sponge cakes, a portion of the flour can be left out and substituted with cornstarch. This yields a softer and more aerated batter.
- The eggs used in sponge cake batters should be fresh and at room temperature so that they take in air faster.
- Adding separately beaten egg whites produces a lighter and fluffier sponge cake.
- Once sponge cake batters are beaten and poured into moulds or baking trays, they should be baked as soon as possible, otherwise, the batter loses volume.

Methods of making sponges

- **Foaming method** – whisking eggs and sugar together to ribbon stage; folding in/cutting flour.
- **Melting method** – as with foaming, but adding melted butter, margarine or oil to the mixture. The fat content enriches the sponge, improves the flavour, texture and crumb structure, and will extend shelf life.
- **Boiling method** – sponges made by this method have a stable crumb texture that is easier to handle and crumbles less when cut than the standard basic sponge containing fat (known as Genoese sponge). This method will produce a sponge that is suitable for dipping in fondant. The stages are shown in the diagram below.
- **Blending method** – this is used for high-ratio sponges, which follow the same principles as high-ratio cakes. As with cakes, high-ratio goods produce a fine, stable crumb, an even texture, excellent shelf life and good freezing qualities.

- **Creaming method** – this is the traditional method and is still used today for Victoria sandwiches and light fruit cakes. The fat and sugar are creamed together, then beaten egg is added and, finally, the sieved flour is added with the other dry ingredients as desired. Despite its title, a Victoria sponge sandwich really falls into the category of a cake rather than a sponge.
- **Separate yolk and white method** – this method is used for sponge fingers (recipe 14). Sponge fingers fall into the category of biscuits.

Preparing and lining moulds

All equipment should be prepared and ready for use before any mixing begins. Line moulds evenly, ensuring a light, even distribution. The fat used to line a mould should be soft rather than melted. A melted fat will tend to run to the bottom of the mould and collect in a puddle where the base meets the side.

For extra security and protection from sticking, collars and circles of greaseproof or silicone paper are often used to line moulds. This allows the product to be slipped from the mould in the paper, which is then gently removed once the product has cooled slightly.

Many modern moulds have improved non-stick properties, which help to prevent sticking and the damage this causes to cakes and sponges when they stick to their moulds.

Baking: the introduction of steam or moisture

Because they become too dry while baking (due to the oven temperature producing a dry atmosphere), some cakes require the injection of steam. Combination ovens are ideally suited for this purpose. The steam delays the formation of the crust until the cake batter has become fully aerated and the proteins have set. Alternatively, add a tray of water to the oven while baking. If the oven is too hot, the cake crust will form early and the cake batter will rise into a peak.

Possible reasons for faults in sponges

Close texture:
- under-beating
- too much flour
- oven too cool or too hot.

'Holey' texture:
- flour insufficiently folded in
- tin unevenly filled.

Cracked crust:
- oven too hot.

Sunken:
- oven too hot
- tin removed during cooking.

White spots on surface:
- insufficient beating.

Possible reasons for faults in Genoese sponges

Close texture:
- eggs and sugar overheated
- eggs and sugar under-beaten
- too much flour
- flour insufficiently folded in
- oven too hot.

Sunken:
- too much sugar
- oven too hot
- tin removed during cooking.

Heavy:
- butter too hot
- butter insufficiently mixed in
- flour over-mixed.

Points to remember

- Check all ingredients carefully.
- Make sure scales are accurate; weigh all ingredients carefully.
- Check ovens are at the right temperature and that the shelves are in the correct position.
- Check that all work surfaces and equipment are clean.
- Check that all other equipment required, such as cooling wires, is within easy reach.

- Always sieve flour to remove lumps and any foreign material.
- Make sure that eggs and fats are at room temperature.
- Check dried fruits carefully; wash, drain and dry if necessary.
- Always follow the recipe carefully.
- Always scrape down the sides of the mixing bowl when creaming mixtures.
- Always seek help if you are unsure or lack understanding.
- Try to fill the oven space when baking by planning production carefully; this saves time, labour and money.
- Never guess quantities. Time and temperature are important factors; they too should not be guessed.
- The shape and size of goods will determine the cooking time and temperature: the wider the cake, the longer and more slowly it will need to cook.
- Where cakes contain a high proportion of sugar in the recipe, this will caramelise the surface quickly before the centre is cooked. Therefore cover the cake with sheets of silicone or dampened greaseproof paper and continue to cook.
- When cake tops are sprinkled with almonds or sugar, the baking temperature needs to be lowered slightly to prevent over-colouring of the cake crust.
- When glycerine, glucose and invert sugar, honey or treacle is added to cake mixtures, the oven temperature should be lowered as these colour at a lower temperature than sugar.
- Always work in a clean and hygienic way; remember the hygiene and safety rules, in particular the Food Safety Act 1990, and the Food Safety and Hygiene Regulations 2013.
- All cakes and sponges benefit from being allowed to cool in their tins as this makes handling easier. If sponges need to be cooled quickly, place a wire rack over the top of the tin and invert, then remove the lining paper and cool on a wire rack.

Convenience cake, biscuit and sponge mixes

There is now a vast range of prepared mixes and frozen goods available on the market. Premixes enable the caterer to calculate costs more effectively, reduce labour costs (with less demand for highly skilled labour) and limit the range of stock items to be held.

Every year, more and more convenience products are introduced to the market by food manufacturers. The caterer should be encouraged to investigate these products, and to experiment in order to assess their quality and assess their value and contribution to the business.

Decorating and finishing for presentation

Finishing and decorating techniques

Filling

Cakes, sponges and biscuits may be filled or sandwiched together with a variety of different types of filling, including:

- creams – buttercream (plain, flavoured and/or coloured), pastry cream (flavoured and/or coloured), whipped cream or clotted cream
- fruit – fresh fruit purée, jams, fruit pastries, fruit mousses, preserves and fruit gels
- pastes and spreads – chocolate, praline, nuts and curds.

Spreading and coating

This is where smaller cakes and gâteaux are covered top and sides with any of the following:

- fresh whipped cream
- fondant
- chocolate
- royal icing
- buttercream
- water icing
- meringue (ordinary, Italian or Swiss)
- commercial preparations.

Piping

Piping is a skill that takes practice. There are many different (plain or fluted) types and sizes of piping tube available. The following may be used for piping:

- royal icing
- meringue
- chocolate
- boiled sugar
- fondant
- fresh cream.

Dusting, dredging, sprinkling

These techniques are used to give the product a final design or glaze during cooking, using sugar:

- dusting – a light dusting, giving an even finish
- dredging – heavier dusting with sugar
- sprinkling – a very light sprinkle of sugar.

The sugar used may be icing, caster or granulated white, Demerara, Barbados or dark brown sugar.

The product may be returned to the oven for glazing or glazed under the salamander.

Other decorative media

Remember that decorating is an art form and there is a range of equipment and materials available to assist you in this work. Some examples of decorative media are as follows.

- Glacé and crystallised fruits – cherries, lemons, oranges, pineapple, figs.
- Crystallised flowers – rose petals, violets, mimosa, lilac.
- Crystallised stems – angelica.
- Nuts – almonds (nibbed, flaked), coconut (fresh slices, desiccated), hazelnuts, brazil nuts, pistachio.
- Chocolate – rolls, vermicelli, flakes, piping chocolate, chips.

Biscuit pastes

Piped biscuits can be used for decoration. For example:

- cats' tongues (recipe 16)
- piped sable pasté (recipe 17)
- almond biscuits.

Storage

- Store all goods according to the Food Safety and Hygiene Regulations 2013/Food Safety Temperature Control Regulation 1995 and General Food Regulations (2004).
- Handle all equipment carefully to avoid cross-contamination.
- Always make sure that storage containers are kept clean and returned ready for re-use. On their return they should be hygienically washed and stored.
- Freshly baked cakes and sponges should be wrapped tightly in secure film or placed in an air-tight, sealed bag. They should then be clearly labelled and dated before storing in a refrigerator or freezer.

- Finished cakes and sponges can be refrigerated to maintain food safety. However, attention to quality must be observed in refrigerated conditions. The moist atmosphere leads to sponges losing moisture and hardening in texture. Any additional ingredients also have to be considered. Creams can lose their viscosity and piped cream can retract, losing its fresh appearance. Prepared fruits, such as sliced strawberries, will weep, losing their structure and staining other elements of the product such as the sponge or cream.
- Some baked products are suitable for freezing. Sponge bases, for example, freeze well for use at a later stage. Other completed products need to be analysed as to their suitability for freezing, based on the additional ingredients used and their suitability and composition.
- Biscuits are best stored in airtight containers. If left in open-air for too long, biscuits will lose their crispness and short qualities.

Allergies

Although it is essential to clearly list all potential allergens when making cakes, sponges and biscuits, the allergens that are most like to be used in their production include:

- gluten – flours and any products made from wheat, rye, barley and oats
- nuts – such as ground hazelnuts and almonds; these can also be added to flavour pastes such as sable
- eggs – widely used in the production of cakes, sponges and biscuits
- lactose – found in milk and milk products (used in some cake recipes)
- sesame seeds – may be incorporated into biscuits – biscuits served with cheese is a common example.

Also refer to page 69 for the 14 listed allergens under the legislation.

Beyond the basic preparation of the cake, sponge or biscuit base, attention is also required with regard to the additional ingredients that are used to complete this range of products. Cakes and gâteaux are often filled with creams, produced with milk and/or cream (lactose). Other fillings and decorations may include nuts, such as frangipane or sugared hazelnuts, so it is vitally important to assess any of the other potential allergens that are incorporated into products as well as the base product itself.

Test yourself

1. How much flour is required to produce a four-egg Genoese sponge?
2. Describe what is meant by the 'creaming' method.
3. Describe the production of biscuit à la cuillere.
4. What is the ratio of fat to flour for shortbread biscuits?
5. Describe tuiles biscuits and what they are used for.
6. Describe the preparation and baking of the following:
   a) Madeleines
   b) Sable à la poche.
7. List the ingredients and method for a traditional Victoria sandwich.
8. List the various shapes that can be produced from a brandy snap mixture.
9. Describe three faults that are common when producing cakes and sponges, giving the reasons why the fault may have occurred.
10. Describe the quality points to look for in a fresh cream fruit gateau.

1 Genoese sponge (*génoise*)

	Single sponge	Double sponge
Eggs	4	10
Caster sugar	100 g	250 g
Flour (soft)	100 g	250 g
Butter, margarine or oil	50 g	125 g

1 Whisk the eggs and sugar with a balloon whisk in a bowl over a pan of hot water.

2 Continue until the mixture is light and creamy and has doubled in bulk.

3 Remove from the heat and whisk until cold and thick (ribbon stage). Fold in the flour very gently.

4 Take a small amount of the mixture and combine it with the melted butter. Then return this to the rest of the mixture and fold through.

5 Place in a greased, floured Genoese mould.

6 Bake in a moderately hot oven, at 200–220 °C, for about 30 minutes.

Energy	Cals	Fat	Sat fat	Carb	Sugar	Protein	Fibre	*
5978 kJ	1423 kcal	65.8 g	25.6 g	182.8 g	106.6 g	36.5 g	3.6 g	

* Using hard margarine (4 portions)

1 Ingredients for Genoese sponge and boiling water ready for use

2 Add the sugar to the eggs

3 Whisk them together over boiling water

4 Carry on whisking as the mixture warms up

5 When the mixture is ready, it will form ribbons and you can draw a figure eight with it

6 Fold in the flour

7 Add part of the flour mixture to the butter

8 Place the mixture into greased cake tins

9 After baking, turn the sponges out to cool on a rack

Video: Making a Genoese
http://bit.ly/1znWjDj

---

2 Chocolate Genoese sponge (*génoise au chocolat*)

	2 × 16 cm sponges
Eggs	8
Caster sugar	225 g
Flour	175 g
Cocoa powder	50 g
Butter, melted	65 g

Energy	Cals	Fat	Sat fat	Carb	Sugar	Protein	Fibre	Sodium *
1428 kJ	340 kcal	13.9 g	6.6 g	47 g	30 g	9.5 g	1.6 g	0.24 g

* ¼ of a single 16 cm sponge

1 Whisk the eggs and sugar together to form a sabayon.

2 Slowly fold in the flour and cocoa powder.

3 Take a small amount of the mixture and combine it with the melted butter. Then return this to the rest of the mixture and fold through.

4 Place in a lined mould and bake at 180 °C for 15–20 minutes.

Make sure you have prepared all the equipment before you start.

Variation

For a lighter sponge use 100 g of soft flour and 75 g of corn flour.

3 Fresh cream and strawberry gâteau

	8 portions
Genoese sponge made with vanilla	1
Stock syrup (see page 477)	100 ml
Raspberry jam	50 g
Whipping or double cream	500 ml
Icing sugar	75 g
Strawberries, sliced	1 punnet

Energy	Cals	Fat	Sat fat	Carb	Sugar	Protein	Fibre
1975 kJ	473 kcal	28.4 g	11.1 g	530 g	39.7 g	4.5 g	0.9 g

1 Carefully slice the sponge cake into three equal discs. Brush each with syrup.

2 Slowly whip the cream with the icing sugar to achieve the correct consistency.

3 Place the first piece of sponge on a cake board. Soak with syrup. Spread with a layer of jam, then a layer of cream. Scatter sliced strawberries on top.

4 Place the next piece of sponge on top. Repeat the layers of syrup, cream and strawberries. Top with additional cream.

5 Place the final piece of sponge on top.

6 Coat the top and sides with cream. Chill.

7 Comb scrape the sides of the gâteau. Pipe 12 rosettes on top. Decorate with strawberries and raspberries and add rounds of white chocolate to the sides.

4 Chocolate gateau

	Single gâteau	Double gâteau
Chocolate Genoese sponge (page 552)		
Eggs	4	10
Chocolate vermicelli or flakes	50 g	125 g
Stock syrup (see page 477), as required		
Buttercream		
Unsalted butter	200 g	500 g
Icing sugar	150 g	375 g
Block chocolate (melted in a basin in a bain-marie)	50 g	125 g

Energy	Cals	Fat	Sat fat	Carb	Sugar	Protein	Fibre	*
20113 kJ	4789 kcal	260.9 g	148.7 g	606.0 g	533.2 g	41.6 g	4.8 g	

* Using hard margarine and butter (4 portions)

1 Cut the Genoese into three slices crosswise.

2 Prepare the buttercream and mix in the melted chocolate.

3 Lightly moisten each slice of Genoese with stock syrup, which may be flavoured with kirsch, rum, etc.

4 Lightly spread each slice of Genoese with buttercream and sandwich together.

5 Lightly coat the top and sides with a chocolate glaze. Decorate the top and sides with chocolate pieces/shapes as desired.

6 Neatly smooth the top using a little more buttercream if necessary.

Note

Chocolate glaze may be purchased as a commercial product.

5 Coffee gâteau

	1 × 16 cm gâteau
Plain Genoese sponge (recipe 1)	1 × 16 cm
Stock syrup flavoured with rum	50 ml
Coffee buttercream	750 g
Coffee marzipan	100 g
Fondant	500 g
Crystallised violets	
Chocolate squares	

Energy	Cals	Fat	Sat fat	Carb	Sugar	Protein	Fibre	Sodium
7881 kJ	1873 kcal	75 g	41 g	303 g	282 g	12 g	1.8 g	0.63 g

1 Carefully split the sponge into three and line up the three pieces

2 Place the sponge base on a cake card and moisten with rum syrup.

3 Pipe on an even layer of buttercream, no thicker than that of the sponge.

4 Place on the next layer of sponge, moisten with the syrup and repeat to give three layers of sponge and two of buttercream. Moisten the top with syrup.

5 Put in the fridge for 1–2 hours to firm up.

6 Work some coffee essence into the marzipan, roll out to 2 mm thick and lay over the gâteau, working the sides to prevent any creases.

7 Warm the fondant to blood heat, flavour with coffee essence and then adjust consistency with syrup.

8 Place the gâteau on a wire rack with a tray underneath to catch the fondant.

9 Starting in the centre and moving outwards, pour over the fondant to completely cover. Draw a palette knife across the top to remove the excess.

10 Add some melted chocolate to some of the fondant, adjust the consistency and squeeze through muslin. Decorate the gâteau by piping on a fine line design.

11 Finish the sides with squares of chocolate and the top with crystallised violets.

Professional tip

Mark the sponge by cutting a 'v' on the side before splitting horizontally; when re-assembling, line up the marks so it goes back together exactly as it came apart.

Turn the sponge upside down before splitting so the base becomes the top; this is the flattest surface and will give the best finish.

It is best practice to use a Genoese that was made the day before – fresh sponges do not cut well and are susceptible to falling apart.

Fondant should never be heated above 30 °C, as the shine will be lost.

A good-quality coffee gâteau should have a moist sponge and a good balance between sponge and filling (as a guide, the thickness of the sponge and the depth of the buttercream should be equal). The coffee flavour should not be in question, and the decoration should reflect and complement the coffee theme. (It is sometimes easy to get carried away, so it is good to remember when decorating, 'less is definitely more'.)

Variation

Instead of enrobing with fondant, the top and sides can be covered with buttercream, the sides can be either comb-scraped or masked with toasted nibbed/flaked almonds or grated chocolate. The top can be piped with buttercream and/or decorated with coffee marzipan cut-out shapes.

To add another texture, place a disc of meringue or dacquoise on the bottom layer. Dacquoise is an Italian meringue with the addition of toasted ground hazelnuts, spread or piped onto a silicone mat and baked at 180 °C for 15–20 minutes. Cut out the desired shape half way through cooking.

ASSESSMENT

6 Roulade sponge

You should be able to bend a roulade sponge

	2 sheets	4 sheets
Eggs	8	16
Egg yolk	2	4
Caster sugar	260 g	520 g
Soft flour	170 g	340 g

1 Make sure the mixing bowl is clean, dry and free from grease.
2 Line the baking sheets with silicone paper cut to fit.
3 Set the oven at 230 °C.
4 Place the eggs and sugar in a mixing bowl, and stir over hot water until warm.
5 Whisk to the 'ribbon' stage and sieve the flour onto greaseproof paper.
6 Carefully fold in the flour.
7 Divide equally between the baking sheets and spread evenly with a drop blade palette knife. Place immediately in the oven for between 5 and 7 minutes.
8 As soon as the sponge is cooked, turn it out onto sugared paper, place a damp, clean cloth over it and lay the hot baking sheet back on top, then leave to cool. (This will help keep the sponge moist and flexible as it cools.)

Faults

There are two reasons why a roulade sponge might become hard and crisp, instead of being pliable:
- baked at too low a temperature for too long
- mixture spread too thin.

Variation

A chocolate version can be made by substituting 30–40 per cent of the flour for cocoa powder. For a coffee sponge, add coffee extract to the eggs after whisking.

A roulade sponge may also be made using a 'split-egg' method, separating the eggs.

7 Rich fruit cake

Energy	Cals	Fat	Sat fat	Carb	Sugar	Protein	Fibre	Sodium
2367 kJ	563 kcal	24.8 g	11.3 g	81.9 g	69.4 g	8.8 g	2.8 g	0.6 g

Variation

If using square cake tins, increase the quantities by a quarter.

This cake can be made less rich by cutting down on the fruit and spices – these are all 'carried' ingredients and will not affect the cake as long as the basic ingredients (butter, sugar, eggs, flour) are not tampered with.

	16 cm diameter, 8 cm deep	21 cm diameter, 8 cm deep	26 cm diameter, 8 cm deep
Butter	150 g	200 g	300 g
Soft brown sugar	150 g	200 g	300 g
Eggs	4	6	8
Black treacle	2 tsp	3 tsp	1 tbsp
Soft flour	125 g	175 g	275 g
Salt	6 g	8 g	10 g
Nutmeg	3 g	4 g	5 g
Mixed spice	3 g	4 g	5 g
Ground cinnamon	3 g	4 g	5 g
Ground almonds	75 g	100 g	125 g
Currants	150 g	200 g	300 g
Sultanas	150 g	200 g	300 g
Raisins	125 g	150 g	225 g
Mixed peel	75 g	100 g	125 g
Glacé cherries	75 g	100 g	125 g
Grated zest of lemon	½	¾	1
Oven temperatures			
	150 °C	140 °C	130 °C
Approximate cooking times			
	2 hours	3 hours	4 ½ hours

1 Cream the butter and sugar until soft and light.

2 Break up the eggs and beat in gradually.

3 Add the black treacle.

4 Sieve all the dry ingredients together and fold in.

5 Finally fold in the dried fruit and lemon zest.

6 Deposit into buttered cake tins lined with silicone paper.

7 Level the mix and make a well in the centre.

8 Check the cakes during baking, turn to make sure they are being cooked evenly.

9 Test to see if cooked with a metal skewer or needle.

10 Allow to cool completely before wrapping and storing in an airtight container.

Note

In the UK, fruit cakes are traditionally used as a base for celebration cakes such as Simnel and Christmas cakes and for weddings.

Professional tip

This is a dense mixture. To prevent the outside becoming overcooked, insulate the cake tins by standing on newspaper and tying several layers of newspaper around the sides.

The dried fruit can be pre-soaked in brandy or rum the day before or, as the cake matures, it can be given a 'drink' every so often.

Take a spoon and make a well in the centre of the mixture, this will help stop the cake doming as it bakes.

Unless filling the oven with cakes, it is advisable to place a tray of water in the oven when baking. This will create steam and allow the cake to expand before the crust sets.

To test, insert a needle in the centre, when the cake is cooked the needle should come out clean and hot.

After cooling, wrap in paper or foil and place in an airtight container and leave to mature for 3–4 weeks before covering with marzipan and decorating with icing.

Faults

A   B

C   D

Cake A is domed ('cauliflower top'). This occurs if:
- the flour used is too strong
- the oven is too hot and/or too dry
- there is not enough fat
- the ingredients are over-mixed after adding flour.

Cake B has a sunken top ('M' fault). This is caused by adding too much baking powder and/or too much sugar.

Cake C has a sunken top and sides ('X' fault). This occurs if the mixture is too wet.

Cake D has a low volume. This occurs if:
- too much fat is added
- the mixture is too dry
- there is not enough aeration.

A good-quality fruit cake will:
- have straight sides, a flat top and good height
- have an even distribution of fruit
- be moist and dark.

8 Banana bread

	3 cakes
Ripe bananas	460 g
Vegetable oil	110 ml
Melted butter	140 g
Caster sugar	460 g
Eggs	4
Soft flour	460 g
Baking powder	20 g
Salt	½ tsp

Energy	Cals	Fat	Sat fat	Carb	Sugar	Protein	Fibre	Sodium
1421 kJ	338 kcal	13.6 g	2.4 g	52.7 g	36.3 g	4.4 g	2.0 g	0.1 g

1 Beat the bananas, oil and butter together at a medium speed with the paddle attachment in a food mixer.

2 Add sugar and eggs and mix until smooth.

3 Add the dry ingredients and mix well.

4 Place mixture into three well-greased or silicon-lined tins (7.5 cm × 17.5 cm long × 10 cm wide).

5 Bake at 170 °C in a medium fan oven for 35 minutes and then check if cooked by inserting a skewer into the cake mixture. If the skewer comes out clean, the banana bread is done.

6 Allow to cool.

9 Lemon drizzle cake

Energy	Cals	Fat	Sat fat	Carb	Sugar	Protein	Fibre	Sodium
1437 kJ	342 kcal	14.6 g	8.6 g	51.7 g	33.5 g	4 g	0.9 g	0.3 g

	2 × 16 cm cakes
Butter	250 g
Caster sugar	400 g
Grated zest of lemons	3
Soft flour	380 g
Baking powder	10 g
Eggs	4
Vanilla extract	½ tsp
Milk	25 ml
Syrup	
Lemons, juice of	3
Caster sugar	100 g

1 Cream the butter, sugar and zest until soft and light.

2 Sieve the flour and baking powder twice.

3 Mix together the eggs and vanilla extract.

4 Beat the eggs into the butter and sugar mixture.

5 Fold in the flour.

6 Add milk to achieve a dropping consistency.

7 Deposit into buttered and floured cake tins.

8 Bake at 165 °C for approximately 45 minutes.

9 Boil the lemon juice and sugar.

10 When the cake is cooked, stab with a skewer and pour over the syrup.

11 Leave to cool in the tin.

This cake can be finished with lemon icing and decorated with strips of crystallised lemon peel.

10 Victoria sandwich

	2 × 18cm cakes
Butter	250 g
Caster sugar	250 g
Soft flour	250 g
Baking powder	10 g
Eggs	5
Vanilla extract	½ tsp
Jam to fill	

Energy	Cals	Fat	Sat fat	Carb	Sugar	Protein	Fibre
6866 kJ	1635 kcal	94.3 g	39.3 g	184.7 g	106.6 g	23.3 g	3.6 g

1 Cream the butter, sugar until soft and light.

2 Sieve the flour and baking powder twice.

3 Mix together the eggs and vanilla extract.

4 Beat the eggs gradually into the butter and sugar mixture.

5 Fold in the flour.

6 Deposit into buttered and floured cake tins and level.

7 Bake at 180 °C for approximately 15–20 minutes.

8 Turn out onto a wire rack to cool.

9 Spread the bottom half with softened jam.

10 Place on the top sponge and dust with icing sugar.

Variations

In addition to jam, the sponge can be filled with either butter icing or Chantilly cream.

The official Women's Institute version specifies the cake is filled with jam only and dusted with caster not icing sugar.

Note

This is a classic afternoon tea cake named after Queen Victoria. Although traditionally made in two halves, a slimmer version can be made by using a single sponge and splitting it.

1 Beat the sugar and butter together

2 Place the mixture into buttered cake tins

3 Flatten the top before baking

11 Swiss roll

	4 portions	10 portions
Eggs	4	10
Caster sugar	100 g	250 g
Self-raising flour	100 g	250 g
Jam, as required		

Energy	Cals	Fat	Sat fat	Carb	Sugar	Protein	Fibre
4445 kJ	1058 kcal	25.3 g	8.0 g	182.7 g	106.5 g	36.5 g	3.6 g

1 Whisk the eggs and sugar with a balloon whisk in a bowl over a pan of hot water.

2 Continue until the mixture is light, creamy and double in bulk.

3 Remove from the heat and whisk until cold and thick (ribbon stage).

4 Fold in the flour very gently.

5 Grease a Swiss roll tin and line with greased greaseproof or silicone paper.

6 Pour in the mixture and bake at 220 °C for about 6 minutes.

7 Turn out on to a sheet of paper sprinkled with additional caster sugar.

8 Remove the paper from the Swiss roll, spread with warm jam.

9 Immediately roll up as tight as possible and leave to cool completely.

12 Scones

	16 scones
Plain flour	450g
Baking powder	25g
Salt	Pinch
Butter	225g
Caster sugar	170g
Sour cream	300ml

Energy	Cals	Fat	Sat fat	Carb	Sugar	Protein	Fibre
678kJ	162kcal	5.8g	2.5g	26.3g	7.5g	2.7g	1.0g

1 Sieve the flour, baking powder and salt.

2 Cut the butter into small pieces and rub into the flour to achieve a sandy texture.

3 Dissolve the sugar in the cream.

4 Add the liquid to the dry ingredients and cut in with a plastic scraper, mix lightly and do not overwork. Wrap in cling film and chill for 1 hour.

5 Set the oven at 180°C and line a baking sheet with silicone paper.

6 Roll out 2cm thick on a floured surface, cut out with a plain or fluted cutter.

7 Brush with milk or eggwash and bake at 180°C for approximately 15–20 minutes.

8 After 15 minutes, pull one apart to test if they are cooked.

9 Allow to cool and dust with icing sugar before serving.

Scones are traditionally served at afternoon tea with jam and butter or clotted cream, and are best served on the day they are made.

Variation

For fruit scones, add 50g sultanas to the basic mix, or try adding dried cranberries or apricots as alternatives.

Professional tip

After cutting out the scones, turn upside down on the baking sheet – this will help them rise with straight sides.

13 Cupcakes

	20 portions
Flour (soft) or self-raising	200 g
Baking powder (if using plain flour)	1 level tsp
Salt (optional)	Pinch
Margarine or butter	125 g
Caster sugar	125 g
Eggs	2–3

Energy	Cals	Fat	Sat fat	Carb	Sugar	Protein	Fibre *
947 kJ	225 kcal	11.6 g	4.8 g	28.8 g	13.4 g	3.3 g	0.7 g

* Using hard margarine

Method 1: rubbing in

1 Sieve the flour, baking powder and salt (if using).

2 Rub in the butter or margarine to achieve a sandy texture. Add the sugar.

3 Gradually add the well-beaten eggs and mix as lightly as possible until combined.

Method 2: creaming

1 Cream the margarine and sugar in a bowl until soft and fluffy.

2 Slowly add the well-beaten eggs, mixing continuously and beating really well between each addition.

3 Lightly mix in the sieved flour, baking powder and salt (if using).

Note

In both cases, the consistency should be a light dropping one and, if necessary, it may be adjusted with the addition of a few drops of milk.

This is a great base for a cupcake.

Variations

Cherry cakes: Add 50 g glacé cherries cut in quarters and 3–4 drops vanilla essence to the basic mixture (method 2) and divide into 8–12 lightly greased cake tins or paper cases. Bake in a hot oven at 220 °C for 15–20 minutes.

Coconut cakes: In place of 50 g flour, use 50 g desiccated coconut and 3–4 drops vanilla essence to the basic mixture (method 2) and cook as for cherry cakes.

Raspberry buns: Divide basic mixture (method 1) into 8 pieces. Roll into balls, flatten slightly, dip tops into milk then caster sugar. Place on a greased baking sheet, make a hole in the centre of each and add a little raspberry jam. Bake in a hot oven at 200 °C for 15–20 minutes.

Queen cakes: To the basic mixture (method 2) add 100 g washed and dried mixed fruit and cook as for cherry cakes.

14 Sponge fingers (*biscuits à la cuillère*)

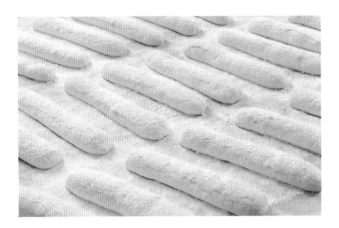

	Approximately 60 × 8 cm fingers
Egg yolks	180 g
Caster sugar	125 g
Vanilla essence	Few drops
Soft flour	125 g
Cornflour	125 g
Egg whites	270 g
Caster sugar	125 g

Energy	Cals	Fat	Sat fat	Carb	Sugar	Protein	Fibre	Sodium
372 kJ	88 kcal	2 g	0.6 g	16 g	8.8 g	1.3 g	0.2 g	0.02 g

1 Prepare a baking sheet by lining with silicone paper cut to fit and set the oven at 160 °C. Have ready a piping bag fitted with a medium plain tube. Scald two mixing bowls to ensure they are clean and free of grease.

2 Whisk the yolks, sugar and vanilla over a bain-marie until warm, then continue whisking off the heat until a thick, sabayon-like consistency is reached.

3 Sieve the flours onto paper.

4 In a second mixing bowl, whisk the whites with the sugar to a soft meringue.

5 Add the whisked yolks to the meringue and start folding in. Add the flour in 2 or 3 portions, working quickly but taking care not to overwork the mixture.

6 Using a plain piping tube, immediately pipe onto the prepared baking sheet in neat rows.

7 Dust evenly with icing sugar and immediately place in the oven for approximately 25 minutes.

8 When cooked, slide the paper (and biscuits) onto a cooling rack.

9 When cool, remove from the paper and store in an airtight container at room temperature, or leave on the paper and store in a dry cabinet.

Professional tip

It is easier to pipe the fingers all the same length if a template marked with parallel lines is placed under the silicone paper.

A common problem with this recipe is over-mixing and/or not working fast enough or being disorganised, which results in biscuits that collapse.

Sponge fingers should be pale in colour, very light in texture, be dusted with icing sugar and have a rounded shape. They should also be identical in length and width.

Note

The literal translation of this is 'spoon biscuits', which comes from a time when the mixture would have been shaped between two spoons instead of being piped. They are traditionally used to line the mould for a Charlotte Russe, although the 'spooned' version would not lend itself to that.

Variations

For a chocolate version, instead of 125 g each of soft flour and cornflour, use 120 g soft flour, 60 g cornflour and 70 g cocoa powder.

Othellos: Use the above recipe to make small, domed sponges. Hollow them out and fill with crème mousseline. Sandwich pairs together and coat with coloured fondant.

15 Shortbread biscuits

Energy	Cals	Fat	Sat fat	Carb	Sugar	Protein	Fibre	*
507 kJ	121 kcal	7.0 g	4.4 g	14.1 g	4.6 g	1.2 g	0.5 g	

* Using butter

Method 1:

	12 portions
Flour (soft)	150 g
Salt	pinch
Butter or margarine	100 g
Caster sugar	50 g

1 Sift the flour and salt.

2 Mix in the butter or margarine and sugar with the flour.

3 Combine all the ingredients to a smooth paste.

4 Roll carefully on a floured table or board to the shape of a rectangle or round, ½ cm thick. Place on a lightly greased baking sheet.

5 Mark into the desired size and shape. Prick with a fork.

6 Bake in a moderate oven at 180–200 °C for 15–20 minutes.

Method 2:

	12 portions
Flour (soft), white or wholemeal	100 g
Rice flour	100 g
Butter or margarine	100 g
Caster or unrefined sugar	100 g
Egg, beaten	1

1 Sieve the flour and rice flour into a basin.

2 Rub in the butter until the texture of fine breadcrumbs. Mix in the sugar.

3 Bind the mixture to a stiff paste using the beaten egg.

4 Roll out to 3 mm using caster sugar, prick well with a fork and cut into fancy shapes. Place the biscuits on a lightly greased baking sheet.

5 Bake in a moderate oven at 180–200 °C for 15 minutes or until golden brown.

6 Remove with a palette knife on to a cooling rack.

Method 3:

	12 portions
Butter or margarine	100 g
Icing sugar	100 g
Egg	1
Flour (soft)	150 g

1 Cream the butter or margarine and sugar thoroughly.

2 Add the egg and mix in. Mix in the flour.

3 Pipe onto lightly greased and floured baking sheets using a large star tube.

4 Bake at 200–220 °C, for approximately 15 minutes.

16 Cats' tongues *(langues de chat)*

Pipe cats' tongues into their distinctive shape, thicker at the ends

	Approximately 40
Icing sugar	125 g
Butter	100 g
Vanilla essence	3–4 drops
Egg whites	3–4
Flour (soft)	100 g

Energy	Cals	Fat	Sat fat	Carb	Sugar	Protein	Fibre	Sodium
676 kJ	161 kcal	8.3 g	5.2 g	20.7 g	13.2 g	2.1 g	0.4 g	0.1 g

1 Lightly cream the sugar and butter, add the vanilla essence.

2 Add the egg whites one by one, continually mixing and being careful not to allow the mixture to curdle.

3 Gently fold in the sifted flour and mix lightly.

4 Pipe onto a lightly greased baking sheet using a 3 mm plain tube, 2½ cm apart.

5 Bake at 230–250 °C, for a few minutes.

6 The outside edges should be light brown and the centres yellow.

7 When cooked, remove onto a cooling rack using a palette knife.

17 Piped biscuits (*sablés à la poche*)

	20–30 biscuits
Caster or unrefined sugar	75 g
Butter or margarine	150 g
Egg	1
Vanilla essence	3–4 drops
or	
Grated zest of one lemon	
Soft flour, white or wholemeal	200 g
Ground almonds	35 g

Energy	Cals	Fat	Sat fat	Carb	Sugar	Protein	Fibre	Sodium
993 kJ	237 kcal	15.2 g	8.2 g	23.3 g	8.4 g	3.4 g	0.8 g	0.2 g

1 Cream the sugar and butter until light in colour and texture.

2 Add the egg gradually, beating continuously, add the vanilla essence or lemon zest.

3 Gently fold in the sifted flour and almonds, mix well until suitable for piping. If too stiff, add a little beaten egg.

4 Pipe onto a lightly greased and floured baking sheet using a medium-sized star tube (a variety of shapes can be used).

5 Some biscuits can be left plain, some decorated with half almonds or neatly cut pieces of angelica and glacé cherries or whole almonds.

6 Bake in a moderate oven at 190 °C for about 10 minutes.

7 When cooked, remove onto a cooling rack using a palette knife.

18 Tuiles

	15–20 portions
Butter	100 g
Icing sugar	100 g
Flour	100 g
Egg whites	2

1 Mix all ingredients; allow to rest for 1 hour.

2 Spread to the required shape and size.

3 Bake at approximately 200–210 °C.

4 While hot, mould the biscuits to the required shape and leave to cool.

Energy	Cals	Fat	Sat fat	Carb	Sugar	Protein	Fibre	Sodium
417 kJ	100 kcal	5.5 g	3.4 g	12.1 g	7 g	1.1 g	0.3 g	0.1 g

19 Brandy snaps

1 Combine the flour and ginger in a bowl on the scales. Make a well.
2 Pour in golden syrup until the correct weight is reached.
3 Cut the butter into small pieces. Add the butter and sugar.
4 Mix together at a slow speed.
5 Divide into 4 even pieces. Roll into sausage shapes, wrap each in cling film and chill, preferably overnight.
6 Slice each roll into rounds. Place on a baking tray, spaced well apart.
7 Flatten each round using a fork dipped in cold water, keeping a round shape.
8 Bake in a pre-heated oven at 200 °C until evenly coloured and bubbly.
9 Remove from oven. Allow to cool slightly, then lift off and shape over a dariole mould.
10 Stack the snaps, no more than 4 together, on a stainless steel tray and store.

	Approximately 20
Strong flour	225 g
Ground ginger	10 g
Golden syrup	225 g
Butter	250 g
Caster sugar	450 g

Energy	Cals	Fat	Sat fat	Carb	Sugar	Protein	Fibre	Sodium [*]
2146 kJ	510 kcal	21 g	13.1 g	82 g	66 g	1.5 g	1 g	0.39 g

[*] Per 2 snaps

20 Madeleines

	Makes 45
Caster sugar	125 g
Eggs	3
Vanilla pod, seeds from	1
Flour	150 g
Baking powder	1 tsp
Beurre noisette	125 g

Energy	Cals	Fat	Sat fat	Carb	Sugar	Protein	Fibre	Sodium [*]
392 kJ	94 kcal	5.2 g	3 g	10.8 g	5.8 g	0.7 g	0.2 g	0.1 g

[*] Per 2 madeleines

1 Whisk the sugar, eggs and vanilla seeds to a hot sabayon.
2 Fold in the flour and the baking powder.
3 Fold in the beurre noisette and chill for up to two hours.

4 Pipe into well-buttered madeleine moulds and bake in a moderate oven.
5 Turn out and allow to cool.

21 Cigarette paste cornets

	Approximately 30
Icing sugar	125g
Butter, melted	100g
Vanilla essence	3–4 drops
Egg whites	3–4
Soft flour	100g

Energy	Cals	Fat	Sat fat	Carb	Sugar	Protein	Fibre	Sodium *
444kJ	106kcal	5.6g	3.6g	14g	8.8g	0.3g	0.2g	0.09g

* Per 2 cornets

1 Proceed as for Steps 1–3 of recipe 16 (cats' tongues).

2 Using a plain tube, pipe out the mixture onto a lightly greased baking sheet into bulbs, spaced well apart. Place a template over each bulb and spread it with a palette knife.

3 Bake at 150°C, until evenly coloured.

4 Remove the tray from the oven. Turn the cornets over but keep them on the hot tray.

5 Work quickly while the cornets are hot and twist them into a cornet shape using the point of a cream horn mould. (For a tight cornet shape it is best to set the pieces tightly inside the cream horn moulds and leave them until set.) If the cornets set hard before you have shaped them all, warm them in the oven until they become flexible.

6 The same paste may also be used for cigarettes russes, coupeaux and other shapes.

This chapter will help you to:

1 prepare, cook and finish fermented dough products, including:
  – using tools and equipment correctly, in a safe and hygienic way
  – preparing products for baking
  – checking that the finished product meets requirements.

2 know how to:
  – identify different products, their uses and preparation and cooking methods
  – store raw dough and finished products safely
  – understand the quality points of ingredients and how to adjust the quantity
  – identify fillings, glazes, creams and icings, and finishing and decorating techniques
  – identify ingredients that may cause allergic reactions.

Recipes included in this chapter

Preparing and cooking dough products

Bread and dough products contain wheat flour and yeast. Bread and bread products form the basis of our diet and are staple products in our society. We eat bread at breakfast, lunch and dinner, as sandwiches, bread rolls, croissants, French sticks, etc. Bread is also used as an ingredient for many other dishes, either as slices or as breadcrumbs.

Flour-based products provide us with variety, energy, vitamins and minerals. Wholemeal bread products also provide roughage, an essential part of a healthy diet.

Preparation methods

Kneading and proving

Dough consists of strong flour, water, salt and yeast, which are kneaded together to the required consistency at a suitable temperature. It is then allowed to **prove** (to rise and increase in size), when the yeast produces carbon dioxide and water, which aerates the dough. When baked it produces a light digestible product with flavour and colour. Proving allows the dough to ferment; the second prove is essential for giving dough products the necessary volume and a good flavour.

Video: Principles of breadmaking http://bit.ly/ 17grKYK

Knead the dough

Before and after proving: the same amount of dough is twice the size after it has been left to prove

Salted dough is much more manageable than unsalted dough. Salt is usually added a few moments before the end of the kneading, since its function is to help expand the dough's volume.

! Health and safety

Always remember the health and safety rules when using machinery. When using machines such as planetary mixers, check that they are in safe working order.

Knocking back

Remember to **knock the dough back** (re-knead it) carefully once proved, as this will expel the gas and allow the yeast to be dispersed properly, coming back into direct contact with the dough.

Fermentation

For dough to become **leavened** bread (bread that has risen, rather than flat bread) it must go through a **fermentation** process. This is brought about by the action of yeast, a living microorganism rich in protein and vitamin B. The yeast reacts with enzymes in the dough, which convert sugar into alcohol, producing the characteristic flavour of bread. The action also produces carbon dioxide, which makes the bread rise.

Yeast requires ideal conditions for growth. These are:

- warmth – a good temperature for dough production is 22–30 °C

- moisture – the liquid should be added at approximately 37 °C
- food – this is obtained from the starch in the flour
- time – this is needed to allow the yeast to grow.

Dried yeast has been dehydrated and must be creamed with a little water before use. It will keep for several months in its dry state. Some types of dried yeast can be used straight from the packet.

Yeast will not survive in a high concentration of sugar or salt, and its growth will slow down in a very rich dough with a high fat and egg content.

When mixing yeast in water or milk, make sure that the liquid is at the correct temperature (37 °C) and disperse the yeast in the liquid. (As a living organism cannot be dissolved, the word 'disperse' is used.)

Yeast should be removed from the refrigerator and used at room temperature.

Key terms

Leavened: bread that has risen.

Fermentation: this occurs when yeast and/or bacteria convert carbohydrates to carbon dioxide, causing gas bubbles to form. This has a leavening effect on products such as dough when making bread.

Prove: process of allowing dough to rise and increase in size.

Knocking back: re-kneading the dough once proved.

The process of dough fermentation is extraordinary, but because we see it so frequently in our profession, we do not pay much attention to how it happens. It is very interesting to know why doughs ferment and what the effects are on the end product. In order to understand why yeast dough rises, we must note that the main ingredients of natural leavening are water, air and, most importantly, sugar, which is transformed into carbon dioxide and alcohol and causes the leavening. This carbon dioxide forms bubbles inside the dough and makes it rise. Fermentation is a transformation undergone by organic matter (sugars).

Weighing, measuring and portion control

- Check that all ingredients are weighed carefully.
- Divide the dough with a dough divider, hard scraper or hydraulic cutting machine.
- Check the divided dough pieces for weight. When weighing, remember that doughs lose up to 12.5 per cent of their water during baking.

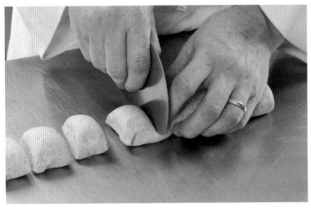

▲ Dividing dough into evenly sized pieces

Other points to remember

- Work in a clean and tidy manner to avoid cross-contamination.
- Check all temperatures carefully.
- Wholemeal doughs absorb more water than white doughs. The volume of water absorbed by flour also varies according to its strength (protein and bran content).
- Keep the flour, bowl and liquid warm.
- Time and temperature are crucial when cooking dough products.

Cooking methods

Not all dough products are baked. Doughnuts, for example, are deep-fried. In Chinese cookery, dough buns are steamed and filled with fillings, pork being the most common (pork buns). Steam is injected into the oven during the baking process; the steam helps to keep the outside surface of loaves moist and supple so that the bread can 'spring' for as long as possible. Once the outside of the loaf begins to dry out it hardens, preventing further spring and the crust begins to form.

Dough products come in a variety of forms and styles. The variety of flour alongside the additional ingredients incorporated, and whether the dough is leavened or unleavened, provide dough products with their own uniqueness. The majority of doughs have some sort of leavening agent, commonly yeast or a from a starter, from which the natural yeast in flour is developed slowly over a long period of time and replaced with fresh flour and water as the required amount of the starter is used to produce the bread in question.

Some dough products do not require yeast as a raising agent. Soda bread, for example, uses bicarbonate of soda, an alkali which reacts with the acidic components within doughs and batters to release carbon dioxide. The carbon dioxide raises the product and helps with the development of texture. Other dough products, such as pitta bread and flatbreads, do not use a raising agent and are referred to as unleavened breads.

Doughs are divided into different categories, which are dependent on the way they are produced and the ingredients they contain:

- A **simple dough** contains flour, salt, yeast, water and sometimes fat.
- **Enriched doughs** contain the same base ingredients, but are enriched with additional ingredients such as eggs, sugar, butter, milk in place of water and often include dried fruits and spices. Chelsea buns with dried fruit and spices and brioche, a rich yeast dough with a high fat and butter content, are good examples.
- **Laminated doughs** are simple doughs that are laminated with layers of fat, traditionally butter for its rich flavour. Croissants and Danish pastries are enriched with fat in layers referred to as lamination.

This makes them softer to eat because the fat in the dough insulates the water molecules, keeping the moisture level higher during baking. The raising agent is a combination of the fermentation of yeast and the steam produced from the lamination of the butter. Danish pastries may be filled with fruit, frangipane, apple, custard, cherries, crème pâtissière and many other ingredients

- The final type of dough is referred to as a **batter**. A batter is looser in structure than other types of dough. This is due to the wet consistency of the dough. Therefore, batters are shaped and baked using moulds. Rum babas and savarins provide good examples.

Speciality doughs

Speciality doughs from around the world include:

- blinis – a type of savoury pancake traditionally made from buckwheat flour
- naan bread – a leavened Indian bread traditionally cooked in a tandoor (oven)
- pitta bread – Middle Eastern and Greek unleavened bread
- chapatti – Indian unleavened bread made from a fine ground wholemeal flour, known as 'atta'
- pizza dough – a dough of Italian origin traditionally made using 00 flour. This is a fine flour produced from the central part of the wheatgrain which produces light, crisp doughs. Pizza dough is often enriched with the addition of olive oil to provide moisture and flavour.

> **Key term**
>
> **Lamination**: dough that is produced by building layers of paste and fat.

Bread

It is customary today for restaurants to offer a range of different flavoured breads. Internationally there is a wide variety available; different nations and regions have their own speciality breads. Bread plays an important part in many religious festivals, especially Christian and Jewish.

Bulk fermentation

The traditional breadmaking process is known as the **bulk fermentation** process. This was used by many bakers before the introduction of high-speed mixing and dough conditioners, which both eliminate the need for bulk fermentation time. However, this traditional method produces a fine flavour due to the fermentation and is evident in the final product.

Bulk fermentation time (BFT) is the term used to describe the length of time that the dough is allowed to ferment in bulk. BFT is measured from the end of the mixing method to the beginning of the scaling (weighing) process. The length of BFT can be from 1 to 6 hours and is related to the level of salt and yeast in the recipe, as well as the dough temperature.

It is important during the bulk fermentation process that ideal conditions are adhered to:

- the dough must be kept covered to prevent the surface of the dough developing a skin.
- the appropriate temperature must be maintained to control the rate of fermentation.

> **Key terms**
>
> **Bulk fermentation**: a proving/fermentation process in which a leavened dough will double in size.
>
> **Bulk fermentation time**: the time it takes for the dough to double in size.

▲ From left to right: overripe dough (proven too long), well-proven dough (good shape, structure and volume) and underripe dough.

Storage of dough

Raw dough can be stored for use at a later time. For long-term storage, dough should be wrapped securely, labelled and placed in a freezer. For short-term storage, or to **retard** a dough, it can be placed into a refrigerator. The dough should be covered to prevent a skin forming on the surface of the dough as well as following good food safety practices.

> **Key term**
>
> **Retarding dough**: reducing the fermentation process of a dough by placing it in chilled conditions

Convenience dough products

There are many different types of convenience dough product on the market.

- Fresh and frozen pre-proved dough products: rolls; croissants; Danish pastries; French breads.
- Bake-off products that are finished and ready for baking. These can be bought either frozen or fresh, or in modified-atmosphere packaged forms (this method replaces most of the oxygen around the product to slow down spoilage). These products have to be kept refrigerated. They include garlic bread, rolls and Danish pastries.

Health and safety

When using frozen dough products, always follow the manufacturer's instructions. Contamination can occur if doughs are defrosted incorrectly.

Faults

If your yeast dough has a close texture this may be because:
- it was insufficiently proved
- it was insufficiently kneaded
- it contains insufficient yeast
- the oven was too hot
- too much water was added
- too little water was added.

If your dough has an uneven texture this may be because:
- it was insufficiently kneaded
- it was over-proved
- the oven was too cool.

If your dough has a coarse texture this may be because:
- it was over-proved, uncovered
- it was insufficiently kneaded.

- too much water was added
- too much salt was added

If your dough is wrinkled this may be because:
- it was over-proved.

If your dough is sour this may be because:
- the yeast was stale
- too much yeast was used.

If the crust is broken this may be because:
- the dough was under-proved at the second stage.

If there are white spots on crust this may be because:
- the dough was not covered before second proving.

Finishing bread and dough products

Depending of the type of product being made, there are a number of different finishes that can be applied to dough products. Certain breads, such as baguettes, are scored before they are baked which helps to produce an appealing visual finish to the baked product.

Many breads are sprinkled with seeds such as poppy, sesame and fennel before they are baked. Others may have herbs added, such as the red onion and sage rolls that feature in this chapter, or sprinkled with cheese as seen with Parmesan rolls. A common but perhaps

the most simple of finishes applied to breads is a light dusting of the same flour used to produce the bread. This is sieved over the bread once it has cooled and applies to many of the examples shown in this chapter.

Many dough products including breads, bread rolls and laminated doughs such as croissant and pain-au-chocolat are brushed with egg-wash before they are baked. This produces a light, golden-brown glaze during the baking process. Other products are glazed after baking, such as Swiss buns with fondant and Danish pastries, which are often finished with a fruit glaze and water icing. Other enriched doughs such as Chelsea buns are soaked with bun syrup whilst still hot after baking and sprinkled with nibbed sugar.

Storage of dough products

Crusty rolls and bread are affected by changes in storage conditions; they are softened by a damp environment and humid conditions, so should be stored in a dry environment to keep them crusty.

Always store dough products in suitable containers at room temperature or in a freezer for longer storage. Do not store in a refrigerator unless you want the bread to stale quickly for use as breadcrumbs. Staling will also occur quickly in products that contain a lot of fat and milk. Many commercial dough products contain anti-staling agents.

Allergies

Gluten is the protein found in wheat, barley and rye, and to a lesser extent in yeast. An increasing number of people are intolerant to gluten, which results in damage to the lining of the small intestine. This is known as coeliac disease and people who are intolerant must avoid the consumption of wheat and flour-based products.

Although it is essential to clearly list all potential allergens when making fermented dough products, the allergens that are most likely to be used in their production include:

- gluten – flours and any products made from wheat, rye, barley and oats
- nuts – such as hazelnuts and nibbed almonds added to garnish Danish pastries, for example
- sesame seeds – often sprinkled on the surface of breads and rolls
- eggs – used in the production of enriched doughs
- lactose – for example, milk used in place of water in the production of dough; cheese used to glaze breads; yoghurt used in speciality doughs, such as naan.

Beyond the basic preparation of fermented doughs, attention is also required with regard to the additional ingredients that are used to complete the product. It is vitally important to assess any of the other potential allergens that are incorporated into fermented doughs, as well as the dough itself.

Test yourself

1   Give **two** examples, with descriptions, of dough products in the following categories:
   a) enriched doughs
   b) laminated doughs
   c) speciality doughs
2   List four products produced from a basic bun dough.
3   What is meant by fermentation?
4   What is the difference between strong and soft flour?
5   What is the difference between leavened and unleavened bread?
6   Why is temperature so important when making bread dough using yeast?
7   What is yeast and what is its use in the pastry kitchen?
8   What raising agent is used in the production of soda bread?
9   Name three seeds that are often sprinkled on bread rolls before baking.
10   What is the meaning of the term 'scaling'?

1 Sun-dried tomato bread

	2 × 450 g loaves
Sun-dried tomatoes, chopped	100 g
Water	300 ml
Bread flour	500 g
Salt	10 g
Skimmed milk powder	12.5 g
Shortening	12.5 g
Yeast (fresh)	20 g
Sugar	12.5 g

Energy	Cals	Fat	Sat fat	Carb	Sugar	Protein	Fibre	Sodium
10,192 kJ	2,414 kcal	70.8 g	12.8 g	401.8 g	29.6 g	67.4 g	20.7 g	5.0 g

1 Soak the sun-dried tomatoes in boiling water for 30 minutes.

2 Sieve the flour, salt and skimmed milk powder.

3 Add the shortening and rub through the dry ingredients.

4 Disperse the yeast into warm water, approximately 37 °C. Add and dissolve the sugar. Add to the above ingredients.

5 Mix until a smooth dough is formed. Check for any extremes in consistency and adjust as necessary until a smooth elastic dough is formed.

6 Cover the dough, keep warm and allow to prove.

7 After approximately 30–40 minutes, knock back the dough and mix in the chopped sun-dried tomatoes (well drained).

8 Mould and prove again for another 30 minutes (covered).

9 Divide the dough into two and mould round.

10 Rest for 10 minutes. Keep covered.

11 Re-mould into ball shape.

12 Place the dough pieces into 15 cm diameter hoops laid out on a baking tray. The hoops must be warm and lightly greased.

13 With the back of the hand flatten the dough pieces.

14 Prove at 38–40 °C in humid conditions, preferably in a prover.

15 Bake at 225 °C for 25–30 minutes.

16 After baking, remove the bread from the tins immediately and place on a cooling wire.

2 Wholemeal bread

	2 loaves
Unsalted butter or oil	60 g
Honey	3 tbsp
Water, lukewarm	500 ml
Fresh yeast	25 g
or	
Dried yeast	18 g
Salt	1 tbsp
Flour, unbleached strong white	125 g
Flour, stoneground wholemeal	625 g

Energy	Cals	Fat	Sat fat	Carb	Sugar	Protein	Fibre
6,893 kJ	1,628 kcal	32.5 g	16.7 g	302.3 g	62.6 g	50.5 g	40.0 g

1 Melt the butter in a saucepan.

2 Mix together 1 tbsp of honey and 4 tbsp of the water in a bowl.

3 Disperse the yeast into the honey mixture.

4 In a basin, place the melted butter, remaining honey and water, the yeast mixture and salt.

5 Add the white flour and half the wholemeal flour. Mix well.

6 Add the remaining wholemeal flour gradually, mixing well between each addition.

7 The dough should pull away from the sides of the bowl and form a ball. The resulting dough should be soft and slightly sticky.

8 Turn out onto a floured work surface. Sprinkle with white flour, knead well.

9 Brush a clean bowl with melted butter or oil. Place the dough in the bowl, cover with a damp cloth and allow to prove in a warm place. This will take approximately 1–1 ½ hours.

10 Knock back and further knead the dough. Cover again and rest for 10–15 minutes.

11 Divide the dough into two equal pieces.

12 Form each piece of dough into a cottage loaf or place in a suitable loaf tin.

13 Allow to prove in a warm place for approximately 45 minutes.

14 Place in a pre-heated oven, 220 °C and bake until well browned (approximately 40–45 minutes).

15 When baked, the bread should sound hollow and the sides should feel crisp when pressed.

16 Cool on a wire rack.

Variation

Alternatively, the bread may be divided into 50 g rolls, brushed with eggwash and baked at 200 °C for approximately 10 minutes.

Healthy eating tip

● Only a little salt is necessary to 'control' the yeast. Many customers will prefer less salty bread.

3 Rye bread

	1 loaf
Fresh yeast (or dried yeast may be used)	15 g
Water	60 ml
Black treacle	1 tbsp
Vegetable oil	1 tbsp
Caraway seeds (optional)	15 g
Salt	15 g
Lager	250 ml
Rye flour	250 g
Unbleached bread flour	175 g
Polenta	
Eggwash	

Energy	Cals	Fat	Sat fat	Carb	Sugar	Protein	Fibre	Sodium
7,174 kJ	1,690 kcal	24.7 g	2.9 g	331.8 g	12.5 g	46.7 g	46.2 g	6.0 g

1 Disperse the yeast in the warm water (at approximately 37 °C)

2 In a basin mix the black treacle, oil, two-thirds of the caraway seeds (if required) and the salt. Add the lager. Add the yeast and mix in the sieved rye flour. Mix well.

3 Gradually add the bread flour. Continue to add the flour until the dough is formed and it is soft and slightly sticky.

4 Turn the dough onto a lightly floured surface and knead well.

5 Knead the dough until it is smooth and elastic.

6 Place the kneaded dough into a suitable bowl that has been brushed with oil.

7 Cover with a damp cloth and allow the dough to prove in a warm place until it is double in size. This will take about 1 ½–2 hours.

8 Turn the dough onto a lightly floured work surface, knock back the dough to original size. Cover and allow to rest for approximately 5–10 minutes.

9 Shape the dough into an oval approximately 25 cm long.

10 Place onto a baking sheet lightly sprinkled with polenta.

11 Allow the dough to prove in a warm place, preferably in a prover, until double in size (approximately 45 minutes to 1 hour).

12 Lightly brush the loaf with eggwash, sprinkle with the remaining caraway seeds (if required).

13 Using a small, sharp knife, make three diagonal slashes, approximately 5 mm deep into the top of the loaf.

14 Place in a pre-heated oven at 190 °C and bake for approximately 50–55 minutes.

15 When cooked, turn out. The bread should sound hollow when tapped and the sides should feel crisp.

16 Allow to cool.

Healthy eating tip
● Only a little salt is necessary to 'control' the yeast. Many customers will prefer less salty bread.

4 Soda bread

	2 loaves
Flour, wholemeal	250 g
Flour (strong)	250 g
Bicarbonate of soda	1 tsp
Salt	1 tsp
Buttermilk	200 g
Water, warm	60 ml
Butter, melted	25 g

Energy	Cals	Fat	Sat fat	Carb	Sugar	Protein	Fibre	Sodium
8,341 kJ	1,970kcal	39.8g	20.9g	357.8g	18.5g	67.9g	20.9g	3.6g

1 Sift the flours, salt and bicarbonate of soda into a bowl.

2 Make a well and add the buttermilk, warm water and melted butter.

3 Work the dough for about 5 minutes.

4 Mould into 2 round loaves and mark the top with a cross.

5 Bake at 200 °C for about 25 minutes. When the bread is ready, it should make a hollow sound when tapped.

5 Olive bread

Energy	Cals	Fat	Sat fat	Carb	Sugar	Protein	Fibre	Sodium
5,174 kJ	1,229kcal	44.2g	6.5g	188.3g	3.5g	30.9g	15.9g	5.2g

	4 loaves
Starter	
Yeast	40 g
Water at 37 °C	180 ml
Strong flour	225 g
Sugar	5 g
Dough	
Strong flour	855 g
Sugar	40 g
Salt	20 g
Water at 37 °C	450 ml
Olive oil	160 ml
Green olives, cut into quarters	100 g

1 For the starter, dissolve the yeast in the water, add the flour and sugar, mix well, cover and leave to ferment for 30 minutes.

2 For the dough, sieve the flour, sugar and salt into a mixing bowl, add the water followed by the starter and start mixing slowly.

3 Gradually add the oil and continue mixing to achieve a smooth dough.

4 Cover with cling film and prove for 1 hour or until double in size.

5 Knock back, add the olives and divide the dough into four.

6 Roll into long shapes and place on a baking sheet sprinkled with rice cones, return to the prover and leave until double in size.

7 Brush with olive oil and bake at 220 °C for 20–25 minutes.

8 When cooked, the bread should sound hollow when tapped on the base.

9 Leave to cool on a wire rack.

1 Make up the starter

2 Starter ready for use after proving

3 Start mixing in the ingredients for the main dough, tearing up the starter

4 Continue mixing in the ingredients and working the dough

5 Shape the dough

6 Divide and roll into loaves

6 Bun dough and varieties of bun

	12 buns	24 buns
Strong flour	500 g	1 kg
Yeast	25 g	50 g
Milk (scalded and cooled to 40 °C)	250 ml	500 ml
Butter	60 g	120 g
Eggs	2	4
Sugar	60 g	120 g
Bun wash		
Milk	250 ml	
Caster sugar	100 g	

Method: sponge and dough

1 Sieve the flour.

2 Dissolve the yeast in half the milk and add enough of the flour to make a thick batter, cover with cling film and place in the prover to ferment.

3 Rub the butter into the rest of the flour.

4 Beat the eggs and add the salt and sugar.

5 When the batter has fermented, add to the flour, together with the liquid.

6 Mix slowly for 5 minutes to form a soft dough.

7 Place in a lightly oiled bowl, cover with cling film and prove for 1 hour at 26 °C.

8 Knock back the dough and knead on the table, rest for 10 minutes before processing.

Bun wash:

1 Bring both ingredients to the boil and brush over liberally as soon the buns are removed from the oven. The heat from the buns will set the glaze and prevent it from soaking in, giving a characteristic sticky coat.

1 Sift the flour.

2 Rub in the fat.

3 Make a well in the flour and pour in the beaten egg.

4 Pour in the liquid.

5 Fold the ingredients together.

6 Knead the dough.

7 Before and after proving: the same amount of dough is twice the size after it has been left to prove.

7 Bath buns

	12–14 buns
Basic bun dough (recipe 6)	1 kg
Bun spice	20 ml
Sultanas	200 g
Sugar nibs	360 g
Egg yolks	8

Energy	Cals	Fat	Sat fat	Carb	Sugar	Protein	Fibre	Sodium
827 kJ	196 kcal	6.5 g	3.6 g	31.9 g	13.4 g	4.5 g	1.4 g	0.1 g

1 Mix the bun spice into the basic dough and knead.

2 Add the sultanas, two-thirds of the sugar nibs and all the egg yolks.

3 Using a plastic scraper, cut in the ingredients (it is usual for the ingredients not to be fully mixed in).

4 Scale into 60 g pieces.

5 Place on a paper-lined baking sheet in rough shapes.

6 Sprinkle liberally with the rest of the nibbed sugar.

7 Allow to prove until double in size.

8 Bake at 200 °C for 15–20 minutes.

9 Brush with bun wash as soon as they come out of the oven.

8 Hot cross buns

	12–14 buns	24 buns
Basic bun dough (recipe 6)	1 kg	2 kg
Currants	75 g	150 g
Sultanas	75 g	150 g
Mixed spice	5 g	10 g
Crossing paste		
Strong flour	125 g	250 g
Water	250 ml	500 ml
Oil	25 ml	50 ml

Energy	Cals	Fat	Sat fat	Carb	Sugar	Protein	Fibre	Sodium
744 kJ	177 kcal	6.7 g	3.6 g	26.8 g	8.3 g	4.6 g	1.2 g	0.1 g

1 Add the dried fruit and spice to the basic dough, mix well.

2 Scale into 60 g pieces and roll.

3 Place on a baking sheet lined with silicone paper in neat rows opposite each other and eggwash.

4 Mix together the ingredients for the crossing paste. Pipe it in continuous lines across the buns.

5 Allow to prove.

6 Bake at 220 °C for 15–20 minutes.

7 Brush with bun wash as soon as they come out of the oven.

Variation

To make fruit buns, proceed as for hot cross buns without the crosses.

9 Swiss buns

Energy	Cals	Fat	Sat fat	Carb	Sugar	Protein	Fibre	Sodium
697 kJ	165 kcal	5.6 g	3.4 g	27.0 g	8.4 g	3.4 g	1.0 g	0.0 g

	12–14 buns
Basic bun dough (recipe 6)	1 kg
Fondant	500 g
Lemon oil	5 ml

1 Scale the dough into 60 g pieces.
2 Roll into balls then elongate to form oval shapes.
3 Place on a baking sheet lined with silicone paper, eggwash.
4 Allow to prove.
5 Bake at 220 °C for 15–20 minutes.
6 Allow to cool then dip each bun in lemon-flavoured fondant or plain white fondant.

ASSESSMENT

10 Doughnuts

	12 doughnuts
Basic bun dough (recipe 6)	1 kg
Caster sugar	500 g
Raspberry jam	250 g

Energy	Cals	Fat	Sat fat	Carb	Sugar	Protein	Fibre
918 kJ	218 kcal	13.3 g	4.0 g	22.6 g	4.0 g	3.6 g	1.2 g

1 Scale the dough into 60 g pieces.
2 Roll into balls and make a hole in the dough using a rolling pin.
3 Prove on an oiled paper-lined tray.

4 When proved, carefully place in a deep fat fryer at 180 °C.
5 Turn over when coloured on one side and fully cook.
6 Drain well on absorbent paper.
7 Toss in caster sugar.
8 Make a small hole in one side and pipe in the jam.

Variation

The caster sugar can be mixed with ground cinnamon.

Health and safety

As a fryer is not a regular piece of equipment found in a patisserie, a portable fryer is often used. Always make sure it is on a very secure surface in a suitable position. Never attempt to move it until it has completely cooled down. In addition, extreme care must be taken to avoid serious burns.

- Only use a deep fat fryer after proper training.
- Make sure the oil is clean and the fryer is filled to the correct level.
- Pre-heat before using but never leave unattended.
- Always carefully place the products into the fryer – never drop them in. Use a basket if appropriate.
- Never place wet products into the fryer.

11 Seeded bread rolls

	30 rolls
Strong flour	1 kg
Yeast	30 g
Water at 37 °C	600 ml
Salt	20 g
Caster sugar	10 g
Milk powder	20 g
Sunflower oil	50 g
Eggwash	
Poppy seeds	
Sesame seeds	

Energy	Cals	Fat	Sat fat	Carb	Sugar	Protein	Fibre	Sodium
633 kJ	150 kcal	3.4 g	0.5 g	26 g	1.2 g	5.3 g	1.4 g	0.27 g

Professional tip

Instead of weighing out each 50 g piece of dough, weigh out 100 g pieces and then halve them.

Placing bread rolls in staggered rows means they are less likely to 'prove' into each other. The spacing allows them to cook more evenly and more will fit on the baking sheet.

Method: straight dough

1 Sieve the flour onto paper.
2 Dissolve the yeast in half the water.
3 Dissolve the salt, sugar and milk powder in the other half.
4 Add both liquids and the oil to the flour at once and mix on speed 1 for 5 minutes or knead by hand for 10 minutes.
5 Cover with cling film and leave to prove for 1 hour at 26 °C.
6 'Knock back' the dough and scale into 50 g pieces.
7 Shape and place in staggered rows on a silicone paper-covered baking sheet.
8 Prove until the rolls almost double in size.
9 Eggwash carefully and sprinkle with seeds.
10 Bake immediately at 230 °C with steam for 10–12 minutes.
11 Break one open to test if cooked.
12 Allow to cool on a wire rack.

Variation

Try using other types of seed such as sunflower, linseed or pumpkin.

For a beer glaze mix, together 150 ml beer with 100 g rye flour and brush on before baking.

12 Parmesan rolls

1 Follow method for seeded rolls (recipe 11) up to Step 5.
2 Lightly flour work surface and roll the dough into a rectangle until 3 cm thick.
3 Make sure the dough is not stuck to the surface.
4 Brush with water and cover with Parmesan.
5 Using a large knife, cut into squares 6 × 6 cm.
6 Place on a silicone paper-covered baking sheet and leave to prove until almost double in size.
7 Bake at 230 °C for 10–12 minutes with steam.
8 Cool on a wire rack.

	30 rolls
Grated Parmesan cheese	200 g (approximately)

Energy	Cals	Fat	Sat fat	Carb	Sugar	Protein	Fibre	Sodium
2,169 kJ	512 kcal	9.9 g	2.2 g	94.3 g	1.8 g	17.5 g	5.2 g	1.0 g

Professional tip

When making bread that requires rolling out as opposed to being individually shaped, it is helpful to decrease the liquid content by 10 per cent so it will be easier to process.

To ensure the squares are all the same size, mark a grid using the back of the knife before cutting.

13 Red onion and sage rolls

	Serves 8	Serves 10
Red onion	½	1
Dried sage	¼ tsp	½ tsp
Bread roll dough (see recipe 11 but omit the seeds)		
Oil	1 tbsp	2 tbsp

Energy	Cals	Fat	Sat fat	Carb	Sugar	Protein	Fibre	Sodium
2,169 kJ	512 kcal	9.9 g	2.2 g	94.3 g	1.8 g	17.5 g	5.2 g	1.0 g

1 Finely dice the red onion. Sweat it, then leave to cool.
2 Chop the sage and add it to the onion.
3 Pin out bread dough in a rectangle. Spread the onion and sage mixture over seven-eighths of the dough. Eggwash the exposed edge.
4 Roll the dough as you would for a Swiss roll, and seal the edge.
5 Cut into 50 g slices.
6 Place the slices on a prepared baking sheet and eggwash. Bake in a pre-heated oven at 220 °C for approximately 10 minutes. Cool on a wire rack.

14 Bagels

	10–12 bagels
Strong flour	450 g
Yeast	15 g
Warm water	150 ml
Salt	10 g
Caster sugar	25 g
Oil	45 ml
Egg yolk	20 g
Milk	150 ml
Poppy seeds	

Energy	Cals	Fat	Sat fat	Carb	Sugar	Protein	Fibre	Sodium
670 kJ	158 kcal	2.1 g	0.5 g	32.7 g	5.0 g	6.2 g	1.6 g	0.8 g

1 Sieve the flour, place in a mixing bowl.

2 Make a well and add the yeast which has been dissolved in the water.

3 Mix a little of the flour into the yeast to form a batter, sprinkle over some of the flour from the sides and leave to ferment.

4 Mix together the salt, sugar, oil, egg yolk and milk.

5 When the batter has fermented, add the rest of the ingredients and mix to achieve a smooth dough.

6 Cover and prove for 1 hour (BFT).

7 Knock back and scale at 50 g pieces, shape into rolls and make a hole in the centre using a small rolling pin.

8 Place on a floured board and prove for 10 minutes.

9 Carefully drop into boiling water and simmer until they rise to the surface.

10 Lift out and place on a silicone-covered baking sheet, eggwash, sprinkle or dip in poppy seeds and bake at 210 °C for 30 minutes.

1 Use a rolling pin to make a hole in the centre of each bagel

2 Poach the bagels in water

3 Eggwash the bagels and sprinkle with seeds before baking

15 Focaccia

	1 loaf
Active dry yeast	2 packets
Sugar	1 tsp
Lukewarm water (about blood temperature)	230 ml
Extra virgin olive oil, plus extra to drizzle on the bread	70 g
Salt	1 ½ tsp
Flour, unbleached all-purpose	725 g
Coarse salt	
Picked rosemary	

Energy	Cals	Fat	Sat fat	Carb	Sugar	Protein	Fibre	Sodium
12,915 kJ	3,052 kcal	78.7 g	11.5 g	553.6 g	14.7 g	66.7 g	30.0 g	5.6 g

1 Dissolve the yeast and sugar in half of the lukewarm water in a bowl; let sit until foamy. In another bowl, add the remaining water, the olive oil and the salt.

2 Pour in the yeast mixture.

3 Blend in the flour, a quarter at a time, until the dough comes together. Knead on a floured board for 10 minutes, adding flour as needed to make it smooth and elastic. Put the dough in an oiled bowl, turn to coat well, and cover with a towel.

4 Let rise in a warm, draught-free place for 1 hour, until doubled in size.

5 Knock back the dough, knead it for a further 5 minutes, and gently roll it out into a large disc or sheet to approximately 2 cm thick.

6 Let rise for 15 minutes, covered. Oil your fingers and make impressions with them in the dough, 3 cm apart. Let prove for 1 hour.

7 Preheat the oven to 210 °C. Drizzle the dough with olive oil and sprinkle with coarse salt and picked rosemary.

8 Bake for 15–20 minutes in a very hot oven at 200 °C, until golden brown. Sprinkle with additional oil if desired. Cut into squares and serve warm.

16 Pizza

	2 × 18 cm
Flour, strong white	200 g
Pinch of salt	
Margarine	12 g
Yeast	5 g
Water or milk at 24 °C	125 ml
Caster sugar	5 g
Onions, finely chopped	100 g
Cloves of garlic, crushed	2
Sunflower oil	60 ml
Plum tomatoes, canned	200 g
Tomato purée	100 g
Oregano	3 g
Basil	3 g
Sugar	10 g
Cornflour	10 g
Mozzarella cheese	100 g

Energy	Cals	Fat	Sat fat	Carb	Sugar	Protein	Fibre *
3956 kJ	941 kcal	46.3 g	13 g	114.4 g	20.1 g	23.6 g	8.4 g

* Using 100 per cent strong white flour

1 Sieve the flour and the salt. Rub in the margarine.

2 Disperse the yeast in the warm milk or water; add the caster sugar. Add this mixture to the flour.

3 Mix well, knead to a smooth dough, place in a basin covered with a damp cloth and allow to prove until doubled in size.

4 Knock back, divide into two and roll out into two 18 cm discs. Place on a lightly greased baking sheet.

5 Sweat the finely chopped onions and garlic in the oil until cooked.

6 Add the roughly chopped tomatoes, tomato purée, oregano, basil and sugar. Bring to the boil and simmer for 5 minutes.

7 Dilute the cornflour in a little water, stir into the tomato mixture and bring back to the boil.

8 Take the discs of pizza dough and spread 125 g of filling on each one.

9 Sprinkle with grated mozzarella cheese or lay the slices of cheese on top.

10 Bake in a moderately hot oven at 180 °C, for about 10 minutes.

The pizza dough may also be made into rectangles so that it can be sliced into fingers for buffet work.

Note

Pizza is a traditional dish originating from southern Italy. In simple terms it is a flat bread dough that can be topped with a wide variety of ingredients and baked quickly. The only rule is not to add wet ingredients, such as tomatoes, which are too juicy, otherwise the pizza will become soggy. Traditionally, pizzas are baked in a wood-fired brick oven, but they can be baked in any type of hot oven for 8–15 minutes depending on the ingredients. The recipe given here is a typical one.

Variation

Oregano is sprinkled on most pizzas before baking. This is a basic recipe and many variations exist. Some have the addition of olives, artichoke hearts, prawns, mortadella sausage, garlic sausage or anchovy fillets; other combinations include:

● mozzarella cheese, anchovies, capers and garlic
● mozzarella cheese, tomato and oregano
● ham, mushrooms, egg and parmesan cheese
● prawns, tuna, capers and garlic
● ham, mushrooms and olives.

17 Cholla bread

	2 loaves
Butter or margarine	56 g
Flour (strong)	500 g
Caster sugar	18 g
Salt	1 tsp
Egg	1
Yeast	25 g

Energy	Cals	Fat	Sat fat	Carb	Sugar	Protein	Fibre	Sodium
4,876 kJ	1,154 kcal	30.1 g	16.1 g	198.1 g	13.1 g	35.0 g	10.3 g	1.2 g

1 Rub the butter or margarine into the sieved flour in a suitable basin.

2 Mix the sugar, salt and egg together.

3 Disperse the yeast in the water.

4 Add all these ingredients to the sieved flour and mix well to develop the dough. Cover with a damp cloth or plastic and allow to ferment for about 45 minutes.

5 Divide into 125–150 g strands and begin to plait as follows:

4–strand plait	5–strand plait
2 over 3	2 over 3
4 over 2	5 over 2
1 over 3	1 over 3

6 After moulding, place on a lightly greased baking sheet and eggwash lightly.

7 Prove in a little steam until double in size. Eggwash again lightly and decorate with maw seeds (poppy seeds).

8 Bake in a hot oven, at 220 °C for 25–30 minutes.

18 Savarin dough and derivatives

	35 items
Basic dough	
Strong flour	450 g
Yeast	1 g
Water at 40 °C	125 ml
Eggs	5
Caster sugar	60 g
Salt	Pinch
Melted butter	150 g

Method: ferment and dough

1 Sieve the flour and place in a bowl. Make a well.

2 Make a ferment by dissolving the yeast in the water and pour into the well.

3 Gradually mix the flour into the liquid, forming a thin batter. Sprinkle over a little of the flour to cover, then leave to ferment.

4 Whisk the eggs, sugar and salt.

5 When the ferment has erupted through the flour, add the eggs and mix to a smooth batter. Cover and leave to prove until double in size.

6 Add the melted butter and beat in.

7 Pipe the batter into prepared (buttered and floured) moulds one-third full.

8 Prove until the mixture reaches the top of the mould and bake at 220 °C for 12–20 minutes, depending on the size of the mould.

9 Unmould and leave to cool.

1 Cream the yeast in milk to make a ferment

2 Add the dissolved yeast to the flour and sprinkle a little flour over it

3 The mixture after fermentation

4 Add beaten eggs, sugar and salt

5 The dough after proving

6 Add the butter

7 After proving, pipe into moulds

8 After proving for the final time

Professional tip

Savarin and savarin-based products are never served without first soaking in a flavoured syrup. They are literally dry sponges and should be:

- golden brown in colour with an even surface
- smooth, with no cracks, breaks or tears
- evenly soaked without any hard or dry areas
- sealed by brushing with apricot glaze after soaking.

Cooked products can be stored in the fridge overnight, but if left for too long they will dry out and cracks will appear. They are best wrapped in cling film, labelled and stored in the freezer.

Savarin syrup:

	3 litres
Oranges	2
Lemons	2
Water	2 litres
Sugar	1 kg
Bay leaf	2
Cloves	2
Cinnamon sticks	2

1 Peel the oranges and lemons and squeeze the juice.

2 Add all the ingredients into a large pan and bring to the boil, simmer for 2–3 minutes and pass through a conical strainer.

3 Allow to cool and measure the density (it should read 22° Baumé). Adjust if necessary. (More liquid will lower the density, more sugar will increase it.)

4 Re-boil then dip the savarins into the hot syrup until they swell slightly. Check they are properly soaked before carefully removing and placing onto a wire rack with a tray underneath to drain.

5 When cooled, brush with boiling apricot glaze.

Note

It is important that savarin syrup is at the correct density. It should measure 22° Baumé on the saccharometer. If the syrup is too thin, the products are likely to disintegrate. If it is too dense, it will not fully penetrate the product and leave a dry centre.

19 Savarin with fruit

A savarin is baked in a ring mould, either large or individual.
Before glazing, sprinkle with kirsch and fill the centre with prepared fruit. Serve with a crème anglaise or raspberry coulis.

Energy	Cals	Fat	Sat fat	Carb	Sugar	Protein	Fibre	Sodium
1021 kJ	241 kcal	4.6 g	2.5 g	49 g	40 g	2.7 g	0.7 g	0.08 g

20 Blueberry baba

For a baba, currants are usually added to the basic savarin dough before baking.

As for marignans, split the glazed baba and fill with crème diplomate and blueberries or Chantilly cream.

Energy	Cals	Fat	Sat fat	Carb	Sugar	Protein	Fibre	Sodium
1415 kJ	337 kcal	14.4 g	8.7 g	52 g	42 g	3 g	0.9 g	0.09 g

21 Marignans Chantilly

A marignan is baked in an individual boat-shaped mould or barquette.

Split the glazed marignans and fill with Chantilly cream. Once split and before filling, they can be sprinkled with rum or Grand Marnier.

Energy	Cals	Fat	Sat fat	Carb	Sugar	Protein	Fibre	Sodium
1407 kJ	335 kcal	14.4 g	8.7 g	51 g	41 g	2.9 g	0.5 g	0.09 g

Professional tip

Savarin paste is notorious for sticking in the mould. Always butter moulds carefully and flour. After use, do not wash the moulds but wipe clean with kitchen paper.

Glossary

Aerated To introduce air into. An 'aerated storeroom' is one that air is allowed to circulate through

Al denté Cooked until firm, crisp and with a bite

Allergenic A reaction by the immune system to certain foods or ingredients

Allergy When the immune system reacts to or rejects certain foods or ingredients

Amino acid The structural units of protein

Anaphylactic shock Anaphylaxis is a severe, potentially life-threatening allergic reaction that can develop rapidly

Aromats Herbs such as parsley, chervil and basil used as a flavour base; may also include vegetables such as onions and celery

Balanced diet A diet which includes all the nutrients necessary for good health (from all the food groups), without too much or too little of any of the nutrients an individual needs

Basting Moistening meat periodically, especially while cooking, using a liquid such as melted butter, or a sauce

Best before date Date coding appearing on packaged foods that are stored at room temperature and are an indication of quality. Use of the food within the date is not legally binding but it is bad practice to use foods that have exceeded this date

Binary fission The process by which bacteria divide in half and multiply

Biological contamination Contamination by living organisms

Bivalves Molluscs with a single spiral shell; for example, winkles or whelks

Blanch Plunging food into boiling water for a brief time before plunging into cold water to halt the cooking process. The purpose of blanching is to soften and/or partly cook the food without colouring it

Boiling This method is unique to the production of choux paste, where the butter is initially melted in boiling water before being made into a paste with the addition of flour and then eggs

Bran Outer layers of the cereal

Broth A soup consisting of a stock or water in which meat or fish and/or vegetables have been simmered

Brown rice Any rice that has had the outer covering removed, retaining its bran

Brown stock Stock produced by browning vegetables and bones before covering in water, boiling and simmering

Bulk fermentation time A proving/fermentation process in which a leavened dough will double in size

Bullying Threatening and oppressive behaviour towards an individual or group of individuals over a period of time

Catering The provision of facilities, including food and drinks

Centrifuge A piece of laboratory equipment, driven by a motor, which spins liquid samples at high speed. Centrifuges work by the sedimentation principle to separate substances of greater and lesser density

Cephalopods Molluscs with a soft body and an internal shell; for example squid and octopus

Cereal The edible fruit of any grass used for food

Chef de partie In charge of a specific section within the kitchen

Chemical contamination Contamination by chemical compounds used for a variety of purposes such as cleaning and disinfection

Clean in place Cleaning items where they are rather than moving them to a sink. This is used for large equipment such as mixing machines

Cleaning schedule Planned and recorded cleaning of all areas and equipment

Cleaning The removal of dirt and grease, usually with the assistance of hot water and detergent

Coagulate The transformation of liquids or moisture in meat to a solid form

Coagulation To change consistency from a fluid into a thickened mass

Coarse cut Cuts from the neck legs and forequarters; these are tougher cuts and therefore often cooked using slower methods such as braising and stewing

Coeliac disease A disease in which a person is unable to digest the protein gluten (found in wheat and other cereals). Gluten causes the person's immune system to attack its own tissues, specifically the lining of the small intestine. Symptoms include diarrhoea, bloating, abdominal pain, weight loss and malnutrition

Collagen White protein found in connective tissue

Commercial sector Businesses such as hotels, restaurants, cafés, pubs and clubs that operate to make a profit

Commis chef A junior chef working under the supervision of the sous chef

Connective tissue animal tissue that binds together the fibres of meat

Consommé A completely clear broth

Contact dermatitis A skin reaction suffered by people who are allergic to certain food items, chemicals, plastics or cleaning materials

Control measure Measures put in place to minimise risk

Convalescent carrier Someone recovering from a salmonella-related illness who still carries the organism

Cook/chill meals Pre-cooked foods that are rapidly chilled and packaged then held at chiller temperatures before being reheated for use.

Corrosive Something which can eat away or destroy solid materials

COSHH Regulations Legal requirement for employers to control substances that are hazardous to health to prevent any possible injury to those using the substances

Cost sector/secondary service sector Businesses working in the public sector (which was traditionally non-profit making) but who aim to make a profit

Creaming Creaming refers to the initial mixing of sugar and cream together using a wooden spoon or electric mixer until a smooth mixture is formed. This is often used in the production of sweet/sugar pastry

Crème renversée Egg custard mixture made using eggs, milk and cream

Critical control point (CCP) A point in a procedure or process where a hazard could occur if controls were not in place

Cross-contamination Contaminants such as pathogenic bacteria transferred from one place to another. This is frequently from raw food to cooked/high risk food

Crustaceans Shellfish with tough outer shells and flexible joints to allow quick movement; for example, crab and lobster

Danger zone The temperature range at which bacteria are most likely to multiply. Danger zone temperature range is between 5°C and 63°C with most rapid activity around 37°C

Deglaze To add wine stock or water to the pan in which the fish was cooked to use the sediments and flavours left in the pan

Demersal fish Live in deep water and feed from the bottom of the sea; they are almost always white fleshed fish and can be round or flat

Descaler A substance to remove the hard deposit formed by chemicals in some water supplies. A descaler is often used on kettles, coffee machine pipes and water boilers

Detergent A substance that is soluble in water and breaks down grease and holds dirty particles in suspension

Diabetes A disease in which the body produces no insulin (Type 1) or insufficient insulin (Type 2) and is therefore unable to regulate the amount of sugar in the blood. If left untreated, it causes thirst, frequent urination, tiredness and other symptoms. There are different kinds of diabetes, not all of which need to be treated with insulin. Type 1 diabetes tends to occur in people under 40 and in children; Type 2 diabetes is more common in overweight and older people and can sometimes be controlled by diet alone

Disinfectant Destroys pathogenic bacteria, bringing it to a safe level

Disinfection Action to bring micro-organisms to a safe level. This can be done with chemical disinfectants or heat

Double sink method Items are washed in one sink with detergent and hot water; they are then placed in racks and rinsed in very hot water in a second sink and allowed to air dry

Due diligence Written and recorded proof that a business took all reasonable precautions to avoid food safety problems and food poisoning

Elastin Yellow protein found in connective tissue. This needs to be removed

Emulsifier Emulsifiers are made up of molecules with one water-loving (hydrophilic) and one oil-loving (hydrophobic) end. They make it possible for liquids that are normally immiscible to become finely dispersed in each other, creating a stable, homogenous, smooth emulsion

Emulsion An emulsion is a mixture of two or more liquids that are normally immiscible (non-mixable or un-blendable)

Endosperm Part of the wheat grain containing starch and protein and used to make flour

Environmental cause Accidents due to a person's surroundings or location

Environmental health officer (EHO) A person employed by the local authority to advise upon, inspect and enforce food safety legislation in their area. An EHO is now sometimes called an environmental health practitioner (EHP)

Enzyme Proteins that speed up the rate of a chemical reaction, causing food to ripen, deteriorate and spoil

Fermentation Fermentation occurs when yeast and/or bacteria convert carbohydrates to carbon dioxide causing gas bubbles to form. This has a leavening (raising) effect on products such as dough when making bread

Fixed costs Regular charges, such as labour and overheads, that do not vary according to the volume of business

Flat fish Have a flatter profile and always have white flesh because the oils are stored in the liver. They include sole, plaice, dabs, turbot, brill, bream, flounder and halibut

Food intolerance Does not involve the immune system, but it does cause a reaction to some foods

Food poisoning A range of illnesses of the digestive system, usually caused by consuming food and drinks that have become contaminated with pathogenic bacteria (bacteria that causes bacterial infection), viruses, chemicals or toxins

Food spoilage Foods spoiled by the action of bacteria, moulds yeasts or enzymes. The food may smell or taste unpleasant, be sticky, slimy, dry, wrinkled or discoloured. Food spoilage is usually detectable by sight, smell or touch

Forequarter The front section of the side of meat

Franchise When a company grants permission for someone to open and run a branch of their company and sell their products

Gelatine A nearly transparent, glutinous substance, obtained by boiling the bones, ligaments, etc., of animals, and used in making jellies

Germ The smallest part of the grain

Glaze A reduced stock with a concentrated flavour. Often used to enhance the flavour of soups and sauces

Global Worldwide or universal, applying to the whole world. For example we talk about the global economy, to signify the economy of the whole world

Grain Edible fruit of cereals

Gross profit The difference between the cost of an item and the price at which it is sold

Harassment One or more serious incidents that create an intimidating, hostile or offensive environment. This can take many forms and happen for many reasons. It may be related to a person's age, sex, race, disability, religion, sexuality or any other personal characteristic of an individual

Hazard Analysis Critical Control Point (HACCP) A system for identifying the food safety hazards within a business or procedure and putting suitable controls in place to make them safe. Details of the system must be recorded and available for inspection. All food businesses must now have a food safety system based on HACCP

Hazard Something that can cause harm

Head chef Has overall responsibility for the organisation and management of the kitchen

Health and Safety Executive (HSE) The national independent authority for work-related health, safety and illness. It acts to reduce work-related death and serious injury across Great Britain's workplaces

Healthy carrier Someone carrying salmonella in their intestine without showing any signs of illness

High-ratio cakes A high ratio cake is prepared with a relatively high proportion of sugar and eggs compared to flour

Hindquarter The back part of the side of meat

Hogget A sheep over a year old

Homogenise A process in the production of milk in which the fats are emulsified so that the cream does not separate

Hospitality The friendly and generous treatment of guests

Human carrier Someone carrying bacteria (usually salmonella) in their intestines but not showing any signs of illness. They may pass on the salmonella bacteria to food they work with and this could then cause food poisoning in others

Human cause Accidents due to your own or another person's actions

Human Resources (HR) Department within an organisation that manages employee and employer relations. Responsible for recruitment and dismissal of staff and usually handle employee complaints or disputes. HR is sometimes needed to act as a moderator between employer and employee, or between two employees

Humectant A humectant is a hygroscopic (helps to retain water) substance used to keep products moist. Honey is an example used in this way

Hydrogenated A substance that has had hydrogen gas added to it. This is used to harden oils in margarine

Hydrolysis a chemical reaction in which a compound – like sugar – breaks down by reacting with water

Hydrometer Equipment used to measure density on the Baumé scale

Immune system A system of structures and processes in the human body which defend against harmful substances and maintain good health. Occasionally the immune system in some people recognises ordinary food as harmful and a reaction occurs

Impermeable Something that liquid cannot pass through

Improvement notice A business is given a set amount of time to improve health and safety issues highlighted by an enforcement officer

Insecticide A chemical substance that is used to kill insects

International When two or more countries are involved in an industry or business.

Knocking back Re-keading the dough once proved

Lactic fermentation Lactic fermentation is a biological process in which sugars (e.g. sucrose or lactose) are converted into cellular energy

Lamb a sheep under a year old

Lamination Lamination is the term for the process of alternating layers of dough and butter when making puff pastry, croissants or Danish pastries

Leavened Bread that has risen

Leavening The process where a substance, such as yeast or baking powder, is used to produce fermentation in a dough or batter

Liaison A mixture of egg yolks and cream that is used to thicken a sauce

Limited liability company A business in which the amount the owners will have to pay to cover the business's debts if it fails or if it is sued is limited to the value of the shares each shareholder (owner) owns

Linear workflow A flow of work that allows the processing of food to be moved smoothly in one direction through the premises from the point of delivery to the point of sale or service

Liquefied Petroleum Gas (LPG) Also referred to as propane or butane; it is used to fuel some cooking appliances

Local Specific to a local area such as a small family-run restaurant or local cheeses

Long-grain rice A narrow, pointed grain that has had the full bran and most of the germ removed. Used for plain boiling and in savoury dishes

Maillard reaction The chemical reaction that occurs when heat is applied to meat, causing browning

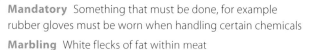

Mandatory Something that must be done, for example rubber gloves must be worn when handling certain chemicals

Marbling White flecks of fat within meat

Metamyoglobin Created when myoglobin is oxidised (reacts with oxygen in the air). This changes the colour of meat to dark red or brown

Mirepoix Approximately 1 cm diced carrot, onion and celery cooked in fat or oil and used as a flavour base for soups

Mise-en-place A French term meaning 'preparation prior to service'

Modified atmosphere packaging Food is placed in a package then surrounded with a gas mixture that helps to slow down its deterioration (often the oxygen has been removed). The package is sealed to keep the food in its own atmosphere. This method is used for a variety of foods including salads, prepared fruit and meat

Molluscs Shellfish with either a hinged double shell, such as mussels, or a spiral shell, such as winkles

Multinational A term to describe a company that operates in several countries.

Muscle Wastage when muscles wither away

Mutton Meat from a mature sheep

Myoglobin Pigment in the tissues which gives meat its bright red colour

National Available in one country, for example a chain of fish and chip restaurants only operating in the UK

Net profit The difference between the selling price of an item and the total cost of the product (this includes food, labour and overheads)

Occupational cause Accidents that are work- or activity-related

Oily fish Are always round and, because the fish oils are dispersed through the flesh (rather than stored in the liver as in white fish), the flesh is darker. These include mackerel, salmon, sardines, trout, herrings and tuna

Osteoporosis A disease in which the density or thickness of the bones breaks down, putting them at greater risk of fracture. Exercise and good nutrition can reduce the risk of developing osteoporosis

Overheads Expenses associated with operating the business, such as rent, rates, heating, lighting, electricity, gas, maintenance and equipment

Pané Coating the fish with a light coating of seasoned flour, beaten egg then breadcrumbs

Papin An enzyme that is sometimes injected into animals before slaughter to speed up the softening of fibres and muscles

Partie system A food production system devised by French chef, August Escoffier, in which different sections of the kitchen are delegated to carry out specific jobs

Partnership Consists of two or more people working together as the owners of a business; the partners take all the risks, stand any losses and keep any profits

Passed A thin soup such as a consommé, served by passing through a fine muslin cloth to remove the solid particles

Pasteurisation Pasteurisation is a process where heat is applied to products such as milk and cream for a short period of time before being cooled quickly. This helps to kill harmful bacteria and extend shelf-life whilst maintaining flavour properties

PAT testing Portable appliance testing of electrical appliances and equipment by a qualified electrician to make sure they are safe to use. A record is kept of this and a label or sticker is placed on the appliance to show that it has been tested

Pathogenic bacteria Pacteria that can cause illness either by infection or by the toxins they may produce

Pelagic fish Live in more shallow or mid-depth waters and are usually round, oily fish such as mackerel, herrings and sardines

Personal development plan A statement outlining a person's career aspirations and work-related goals, and a description of the steps to be taken to ensure the plan is achieved

Physical contamination By an object which can be of any shape, size or type

Potage A thick soup

Primary service sector Hospitality in banks, law firms and other large corporate businesses

Prime cut The leanest and most tender cuts of meat; these come from the hindquarters

Prohibition notice A business or business procedure is deemed to be unsafe by an enforcement officer and the activity must stop immediately

Prohibition Something that is not allowed and must not be done, for example smoking in certain outside areas

Prove Process of allowing dough to rise and increase in size

Provenance: Where food comes from, for example, where it is grown, reared, produced or finished

Public (service) sector Establishments such as schools, hospitals, care homes, armed services and prisons

Public limited company (PLC) A company that can sell shares to the public.

Purée A soup with a vegetable base that has been puréed

Raising agent A substance added to a cake or bread mixture while produces gases that give lightness to the product. Baking powder is an example of a raising agent

Refractometer Equipment used to measure sweetness on the Brix scale

Regional Applies to a specific region or area, for example small hotel businesses operating only in Wales or the Lake District

Retarding dough Reducing the fermentation process of a dough by placing it in chilled conditions

Rickets A disease of the bones

RIDDOR Reporting Injuries, Diseases and Dangerous Occurrences Act 1996. All injuries, diseases and dangerous occurrences happening in the workplace or because of work carried out on behalf of the employer must be reported to the Health and Safety Executive. This is a legal requirement and it is the employer's responsibility to make any such reports

Risk assessment The process of identifying and evaluating hazards and risks and putting measures in place to control them. This process should be recorded and reviewed

Risk The chance of somebody being harmed by a hazard

Rodenticide A chemical substance that is used to kill rodents such as rats and mice

Round fish Can vary greatly in size from small sardines to very large tuna. They can either have white flesh, such as bass, grouper, mullet, haddock and cod, or darker, oily flesh such as tuna, mackerel, herring, trout and salmon

Roux A soup thickened with a traditional roux of fat and flour

Rubbing in Rubbing in is a technique where flour is rubbed into a fat to make products such as short pastry and crumbles. Using the fingertips, flour and butter are rubbed gently together until the mixture resembles fine breadcrumbs

Sanitiser A chemical with detergent and disinfecting properties; it breaks down dirt and grease and controls bacteria

Sanitiser Cleans and disinfects and usually comes in spray form

Scurvy A disease that can cause bleeding gums and other symptoms

Self-assisted service Someone is on duty to help the customer choose; in some cases there will be a section on a buffet where a chef will be cooking fresh items such as stir fry, omelettes, waffles and pancakes. Here the guest is helped to choose and will take the finished item to their table. This is also known as 'theatre cookery'

Self-service Customers serve themselves from a self-service counter or buffet

Septic A cut or other wound that has become infected with bacteria. It is often wet with a white or yellow appearance

Septicaemia Blood poisoning. It occurs when an infection in the bloodstream causes the body's immune system to begin attacking the body itself

Shortening Fat used in pastry making; it is made from oils and is 100 per cent fat

Shortening agent A fat used to help prevent the development of gluten strands when making pastry. This helps to make the texture of the product more crumbly

Short-grain rice A short, rounded grain with a soft texture. Suitable for sweet dishes and risotto

Small- to medium-sized enterprise (SME) Businesses with up to 250 employees

Socio-cultural The customs, beliefs, values and language which may shape a person's identity, lifestyle and expectations

Sole trader The simplest form of a business; the sole trader owns the business, takes all the risks, is liable for any losses and keeps any profits

Solvent A liquid that is able to dissolve other substances

Sous chef Takes overall responsibility for the kitchen when the head chef is absent; may have a specific area of responsibility

Spoilage bacteria Cause food to change and spoil, for example, develop a bad smell or go slimy

Spore A resistant, resting phase for some bacteria when they form protection around the essential part of the cell that can then survive, boiling, freezing and disinfection

Stabiliser A stabiliser is a substance added to foods to help to preserve its structure

Sterilisation Sterilisation is a process where heat is applied but at much higher temperatures. This increases shelf-life further than pasteurisation but products treated this way tend to lose some of their flavour properties

Steriliser Can be chemical or through the action of extreme heat. It will kill all living micro-organisms

Stock rotation Managing stock by using older items before newer items, provided the older items are in sound condition and are still within use by or best before dates

Syneresis Loss of water from a mixture.

Toxin A poison produced by some bacteria as they multiply in food or as they die in the human body

Traceability Use of records to track food from its source through production and distribution to help control hazards

Turning A turn is the term used to describe the process of producing the layers in laminated pastry. Each time the paste is rolled and folded, it is referred to as a turn

Univalves Molluscs with an external hinged double shell; for example, scallops and mussels

Unpassed A thin soup such as a broth which is served along with all the ingredients used

Use-by date Date coding appearing on packaged perishable foods that need to be stored in the refrigerator. Use of the food within this date is a legal requirement

Variable costs Costs that vary according to the volume of business; includes food and materials costs

Vegan A vegetarian who also does not eat eggs or milk, or anything containing eggs or milk

Virus Micro-organism even smaller than bacteria. It does not multiply in food but can enter the body via food where it then invades living cells

Water retention When the body does not get rid of enough water

Wheatgerm Part of the wheat grain containing oil which is removed in the milling process

White stock A stock produced by blanching but not browning vegetables and bones, to give a clear stock

Index of recipes

This index lists every recipe in the book, grouped by major commodity and by type of dish.
There is a full topic index at the pack of the book.

Index